110653800

Schott's
Almanac

2007

Everyone spoke of information overload,
but what there was, in fact, was a non-information overload.
— RICHARD SAUL WURMAN, *What-If, Could-Be*, 1976

Schott's Almanac 2007 ™ · Schott's Almanac ™
Schott's Annual Astrometer ™ © 2007

Published by Bloomsbury Publishing Plc.
36 Soho Square, London, W1D 3QY, UK

www.schottsalmanac.com · www.benschott.com

1 2 3 4 5 6 7 8 9 10

NOTE · Information included within is believed to be correct at
the time of going to press. Neither the author nor the publisher
can accept any responsibility for any error or subsequent changes.

ISBN 978 0 7475 8470 4
A CIP catalogue record for this book is available from the British Library.

Designed & typeset by BEN SCHOTT
Printed in Great Britain by CLAYS Ltd., ST IVES Plc.

Also by BEN SCHOTT
Schott's Original Miscellany
Schott's Food & Drink Miscellany
Schott's Sporting, Gaming, & Idling Miscellany
Schott's Miscellany Diary (with Smythson of Bond St.)

American and German editions of *Schott's Almanac 2007* are also available

Schott's Almanac

2007

LIBER PRAETERITORUM ET POSTERITATIS CARMEN

· *The book of things past and the song of the future* ·

Conceived, edited, and designed by

BEN SCHOTT

assistant editor

Claire Cock-Starkey

BLOOMSBURY

Preface

A calendar, a calendar! look in the almanack;
find out moonshine, find out moonshine.
— A Midsummer Night's Dream, III i

Completely revised and updated, *Schott's Almanac 2007* picks up from where the 2006 edition left off, to create a seamless biography of the year. ❧ The journalist and Hollywood screen writer Ben Hecht (1894–1964) once observed that 'trying to determine what is going on in the world by reading newspapers is like trying to tell the time by watching the second hand of a clock'. *Schott's Almanac* aspires to follow the minute hand of the clock of world events – stepping back from the barrage of rolling news, to offer an informative, selective, and entertaining analysis of the year. ❧ The C21st almanac is necessarily different from some of its distinguished predecessors [see p.6], which were published in times when the year was defined by matters astronomical, ecclesiastical, or aristocratic. By exploring high art and pop culture, geopolitics and gossip, scientific discovery and sporting achievement, *Schott's Almanac* endeavours to describe the year as it is lived, in all its complexity.

— *Schott's* is an almanac written to be read.

THE ALMANAC'S YEAR

In order to be as inclusive as possible, the *Schott's Almanac* year runs until mid-September.

Data cited in *Schott's Almanac* are taken from the latest sources available at the time of writing.

ERRORS & OMISSIONS

Every effort has been taken to ensure that the information contained within *Schott's Almanac* is both accurate and up-to-date, and grateful acknowledgement is made to the various sources used. However, as Goethe once said: 'error is to truth as sleep is to waking'. Consequently, the author would be pleased to be informed of any errors, inaccuracies, or omissions that might help improve future editions.

Please send all comments or suggestions to the author, care of:

Bloomsbury Publishing Plc, 36 Soho Square, London, W1D 3QY
or email *editor@schottsalmanac.com*

The author is grateful to the many readers who sent in comments on the 2006 edition. Notable corrections have been included in the Errata section on p.352.

Contents

EARLY ALMANACS OF NOTE

Solomon Jarchi	*c.*1150	Regiomontanus (at Nuremberg)	1474
Peter de Dacia	*c.*1300	Zainer (at Ulm)	1478
Walter de Elvendene	1327	Richard Pynson	1497
John Somers (Oxford)	1380	Stoffler (in Venice)	1499
Nicholas de Lynna	1386	Poor Robin's Almanack	1652
Purbach	1150–1461	Francis Moore's Almanack	1698–1713
After the invention of printing		Almanach de Gotha	1764
Gutenberg (at Mainz)	1457	Whitaker's Almanack	1868

ALMANAC vs ALMANACK

The spelling and etymology of 'almanac' are the subject of some dispute. The *Oxford English Dictionary* notes the very early use of 'almanac' by Roger Bacon in 1267, though Chaucer used 'almenak' in *c.*1391; and Shakespeare, 'almanack' in 1590. Variations include almanach(e), amminick, almanacke, almanack, &c. A number of etymologies for *almanac* have been suggested: that it comes from the Arabic *al* [the] *mana(h)* [reckoning or diary]; that it comes from the Anglo-Saxon *al-moan-heed* 'to wit, the regard or observations of all the moons', or from the Anglo-Saxon *al-monath* [all the months]; or that it is linked to the Latin for sundial, *manachus*. In 1838, *Murphy's Almanac* made the bold prediction that 20 January that year would be 'Fair, prob. lowest deg. of winter temp'. When, on the day, this actually turned out to be true, *Murphy's Almanac* became a best seller.

SYMBOLS & ABBREVIATIONS

>	greater than	km	kilometre
≥	greater than or equal to	m	metre
<	less than	mi	mile
≤	less than or equal to	'/"	feet/inches
♂	male/men	C	Century (e.g. C20th)
♀	female/women	ONS	Office of National Statistics
c.	*circa*, meaning around or roughly	Crown ©	Crown Copyright

Throughout the *Almanac*, some figures may not add to totals because of rounding.

'AVERAGES'

With the following list of values: 10, 10, 20, 30, 30, 30, 40, 50, 70, 100 = 390

MEAN or AVERAGE	the sum divided by the number of values	39
MODE	the most popular value	30
MEDIAN	the 'middle' value of a range, here: (30+30)/2	30
RANGE	the difference between the highest & lowest values	90

Chronicle

Days and months are itinerants on an eternal journey;
the years that pass by are also travellers. — MATUSO BASHŌ (1644–94)

──────── SOME AWARDS OF NOTE ────────

TIME Magazine Persons of the Year [2005]
BONO and BILL & MELINDA GATES
'For being shrewd about doing good, for rewiring politics
and re-engineering justice, for making mercy smarter and hope
strategic and then daring the rest of us to follow …'

Tipperary international peace prize . . . . .Rafik Hariri
Woodrow Wilson award for public service . . .Edward P. Roski Jr [CEO Majestic Realty]
Robert Burns humanitarian award . . . . Marla Ruzicka
Australian of the year . . . . .Professor Ian Frazer [immunologist]
BP portrait award . . . . .Andrew Tift, for *Kitty*
Car of the year [*What Car?*] . . . . .BMW 320d ES
Prison officer of the year [HM Prison Service] . . . . Linda Horsfield [HMP Styal]
International engine of the year . . . . BMW 5-litre V10 (M5, M6)
Cmsn. for Racial Equality's media personality . . . . Sir Trevor McDonald
International Wine Challenge · champion red . . . . . . Viñas del Jaro Chafardin 2003
– champion white . . . . .Wine & Soul 2004
Charity of the year [Charity Awards] . . . . .P3 [a social inclusion charity]
GQ woman of the year . . . . .Billie Piper
RNID ear of the year [sexiest celebrity ears] . . . . Charlotte Church; David Tennant
AA Insurance best British car park . . . . St James Street, King's Lynn
Annual Ernest Hemingway look-alike award . . . . .Chris Storm, USA
Women's World Awards, World Social Award . . . . Sarah Fergusson
Slimmer of the year . . . . Karen Heppleston-Baines [lost 63kg · 10st 2lb]
Pet slimmers of the year . . . . .Scrappy the dog [lost 29kg]; Benji the cat [lost 3·5kg]
Rears of the year . . . . Javine Hylton; Ian Wright
Sexiest pensioner [Virgin Money Pensions] . . . . Sean Connery
Celebrity mum of the year . . . . Sharon Osbourne
Best British cuppa [UK Tea Council] . . . . . .Hazelmere Café & Bakery, Grange-over-Sands

──────── PLAIN ENGLISH CAMPAIGN · 2005 ────────

Rhodri Morgan won the PEC's 'Foot in Mouth Award' (for the second time) with:

'The only thing which isn't up for grabs is no change and
I think it's fair to say it's all to play for, except for no change'

——————— MISC. LISTS OF 2006 ——————— —2007 WORDS—

INSPIRATIONAL HERO
(*AOL poll*)

1 .... Winston Churchill
2 .... Nelson Mandela
3 Martin Luther King Jr
4 .... Muhammad Ali
5 .... Mother Theresa
6 .... Elvis Presley
7 .... Gandhi
8 .... Margaret Thatcher
9 ...... (Princess) Diana
10 ..... Ellen MacArthur

IMPORTANT TOOLS
*Forbes.com's list of
the tools that have
'most impacted human
civilization'*

the knife · the abacus
the compass · the pencil
the harness · the scythe
the rifle · the sword
eyeglasses · the saw
the watch · the lathe
the needle · the candle
the scale · the pot
the telescope · the level
the fish hook · the chisel

MADAME TUSSAUDS
*New waxworks for 2006
in the London museum*

José Mourinho
Davina McCall
(in *Big Brother* 'diary room')
Prince Harry
Shayne Ward
(first ever reality TV
participant to be in wax)
Wayne Rooney
Johnny Depp
Orlando Bloom
Keira Knightley

TIME TRAVEL POLL
*Doctor Who Adventures
magazine asked which
period of time 24–45s
would like to visit*

1 ...... Swinging Sixties
2 .... right now/2006
3 .... Victorian times
4 ..... 1966 World Cup
5 .... 1800s/C19th
6 .... 1950s
7 .... 2nd World War
8 .. 1970s NY Disco Era
9 .... 1920s Jazz Age
10 .... 1900s

WORST BRITONS
(*BBC History Magazine*)

c20th .... Oswald Mosley
c19th .... Jack the Ripper
c18th . D of Cumberland
c17th .... Titus Oates
c16th ... Sir Richard Rich
c15th .. Thomas Arundel
c14th .. Hugh Despenser
c13th .... King John
c12th .. Thomas à Becket
c11th ..... Eadric Streona

HAPPIEST COUNTRIES
IN WHICH TO LIVE
*According to 2006
analysis by the New
Economics Foundation*

Vanuatu · Colombia
Costa Rica · Dominica
Panama · Cuba
Honduras · Guatemala
El Salvador · St Lucia
Vietnam · Bhutan
W. Samoa · Sri Lanka
Antigua & Barbuda
Philippines · Nicaragua

—2007 WORDS—

The following words
celebrate anniversaries
in 2007, based upon the
earliest cited use traced
by the venerable *Oxford
English Dictionary*:

{1507} *banishment*
(expelling from a state)
{1607} *archaeology* (the
study of ancient history)
· *glossographer* (a
writer of commentaries) ·
morological (relating to
foolish words) ·
nightcapped (wearing said
bed-wear) · *thimbleful* (as
much as a thimble will hold)
{1707} *bourgeoisie*
(the freemen of a French
town) · *dustman* (one
who disposes of refuse) ·
vivisection (cutting part of
a living organism) · {1807}
mispunctuation (faulty
punctuation) · *whimsy-
whamsy* (fanciful nonsense)
{1907} *anorexic*
(characterised by a lack of
appetite) · *chemotherapy*
(treatment of disease with
chemicals) · *unk* (colloquial
abbreviation of uncle) ·
{1957} *bleep* (to make a
high-pitched bleeping sound)
· *sputnik* (unmanned
[Russian] artificial earth
satellite) · *transsexual*
(pertaining to transsexualism)
{1997} *blamestorming*
(investigating or
apportioning blame) ·
Muggle (in J.K. Rowling's
work, one with no magical
powers, and by extension,
anyone lacking in skill)

————————SOME SURVEY RESULTS OF 2005–06————————

%	result (of British adults, unless stated)	source & month
82	consider domestic water wastage 'nothing' compared to pipe leakage	[Populus; Jun]
81	of Londoners opposed the scrapping of Routemaster buses	[Populus/*Eve. Standard*; Jun]
80	of children 8–14 oppose the Iraq war	[*First News*; Sep]
79	consider reading to be an 'important activity'	[BBC/World Book Day; Mar]
76	want Blair to focus more on domestic than international issues	[Populus; Jun]
76	favour an annual limit on immigration	[YouGov; Migrationwatch UK; Apr]
75	of all religions say the UK should 'retain Christian values'	[BBC; Nov 05]
73	consider inheritance tax to be an unfair way to raise revenue	[Populus/BBC; Jul]
72	favour the monarchy	[MORI/*The Sun*; Apr]
69	think 'history is cool'	[MORI; Jul]
65	think Britain should have a nuclear deterrent whatever the cost	[Populus; Jun]
64	think the Queen should never retire	[MORI/*The Sun*; Apr]
64	of businessmen think Liverpudlian accents sound unsuccessful	[Aziz Corp; Dec 05]
63	oppose an official aeroplane for use by the Prime Minister	[Populus; Jun]
63	of Londoners oppose the clocks going back in winter	[Mayor of London; Oct 05]
62	think Saddam Hussein is getting a fair trial	[MORI; Mar]
62	of UK residents speak no other language than English	[Eurobarometer; Feb]
56	of men (16–24) think 'protecting family' defines 'a real man'	[British Army; Mar]
55	of 15–24s always use a condom with a new sexual partner	[National Aids Trust; May]
54	favour more nuclear power to cut global warming	[MORI; Jan]
45	consider they do not get enough sleep	[Legal & General; Mar]
41	of women 'constantly' watch what they eat	[*Grazia*; Apr]
39	consider that Prince Charles does more good than harm	[YouGov; Feb]
38	of Blacks and Asians fear police will not take their complaints seriously	[BBC; Feb]
37	feel too ignorant to negotiate with tradesmen	[MyVoice; Jul]
32	of children have a personal computer in their bedroom	[Lloyds TSB; Feb]
29	of London schoolchildren admit to carrying a knife	[Peace Alliance; Sep 05]
29	of women cut the 'size labels' from their clothes	[*Grazia*; Apr]
28	of married couples have experienced a 'financial crisis'	[IFA Promotion; Jan]
28	feel that their daily routine causes them stress	[Legal & General; Mar]
28	of parents spend less time in London with children post 7/7	[MORI/BBC; Oct 05]
23	of state school pupils admit to playing truant	[Smart Technologies; Feb]
20	consider it acceptable to burp at the dinner table	[Arthur Price; Nov 05]
19	thought England would win the World Cup [see p.294]	[*The Times*/Populus; Jun]
18	consider looking at pornography 'always morally wrong'	[*Spectator*/YouGov; Feb]
17	of private school pupils admit to playing truant	[Smart Technologies; Feb]
16	of 18–29s do not give blood because it 'takes too long'	[easyMoney.com; Mar]
11	of people say that they shout when worried	[Bupa; Feb]
11	claim to regularly attend a church on Sundays	[YouGov; Jun]
10	admit to wearing the same item of underwear for 3 days in a row	[Surcare; Mar]
8	of British Asians (16–34) think 'honour killings' can be justified	[ICM/BBC; Sep]
8	consider there is not enough sex on television and in film	[*Spectator*/YouGov; Feb]
4	of house-sellers remove the house number when they leave	[Halifax; May]
4	of 11–15s took Class A drugs in 2005	[Info Centre Health & Soc Care; Mar]
2	worry about catching a sexually transmitted disease	[Legal & General; Mar]

— WORDS OF THE YEAR —

YO BLAIR · Bush's friendly/belittling (depending on your viewpoint) private greeting for Blair, caught by the press when a microphone was left live at the Moscow G8 conference. Discussing the Israel–Lebanon crisis, Bush was overheard telling Blair, 'What they need to do is to get Syria to get Hezbollah to stop doing this SHIT and it's over'.

BROWNSPLOITATION · nickname for the profusion of products cashing in on the success of Dan Brown's books.

IED · Improvised Explosive Devices, like roadside bombs, that have proved so devastating to Allied forces in Iraq. To check for IEDs, US soldiers perform '5s AND 25s' when leaving their vehicles: walking 5 metres, and visually scanning a 25 metre perimeter. *Also* VBED · Vehicle-Born (Improvised) Explosive Device.

SLOWRINO · comment on the leisurely pace of the Torino Winter Olympics.

CASSEURS · French for 'smashers', used to describe the rioters who infiltrated the Paris labour law demonstrations.

CIVIL WAR · controversial description of the state of post-invasion Iraq.

HANNIBAL DIRECTIVE · *Nohal Hannibal* · rumoured to be the unofficial Israeli order for soldiers to open fire on those kidnapping a comrade, even at the cost of his life, on the basis that a dead soldier is better than one whose life can be bartered for political gain.

TRASH · Annie Proulx's mischievous reference to *Crash* – the film that beat (her story) *Brokeback Mountain* to the Best Picture Oscar [see p.150].

BIG BLU · a 30,000lb bunker-busting bomb (ready for use in 2007), that some claim will be the weapon of choice for a US attack on Iranian nuclear facilities.

COLLECTIVE PUNISHMENT · controversial description of Israel's attack on Gaza and Lebanon [see p.30–31]. Such punishments are banned by Article 33 of the 4th Geneva Convention, 1949.

NAHR · Arabic word for the slaughter of sheep, used by 'Islamic' extremists as a euphemism for beheading victims.

JAMES BLAND · disparaging nickname for Daniel Craig's James Bond.

WARLORDISTAN · nickname for post-2001 Afghanistan. *Also* HAMASTAN · nickname for Hamas-run Palestine.

BINNERS · British Ministry of Defence nickname for Osama bin Laden. *Also* KSM · nickname for alleged Al-Qaeda chief Khalid Sheikh Mohammed. In Spain, €500 notes are known as 'bin Ladens', because they are the highest value euro notes, thought to be used in crime, and no one ever sees them.

ANOMALY · Tony Blair's description of Guantánamo Bay.

ANTI-ANTI-AMERICANS · the people against the people against America.

PHARM ANIMAL · GM animals bred to make transgenic drugs for humans.

MUFFIN TOP · a roll of abdominal fat that spills from the top of tight jeans.

AROUND-SOURCING · where work (in developing nations) is outsourced from cities to nearby villages.

———————————— WORDS OF THE YEAR cont. ————————————

LETHAL AMBIGUITY · where military 'rules of engagement' are deliberately left unclear, to provide soldiers a degree of protection from prosecution.

HOTSPUR · codename for the US/UK 'war game' mock invasion of Iran, held at Fort Belvoir, VA, in July 2004.

THE POODLE PROBLEM · Whitehall slang for the perception that Tony Blair is merely a cipher for George Bush.

SIDESTABBER · one who warns a potential victim that a backstabber is about to strike but, by swearing the victim to secrecy, protects both themselves and the backstabber. *Also* FRENEMY · one who pretends to be your friend, but is really your enemy.

GREY-MAIL · legal tactic of deliberately seeking classified evidence (that will not be released) in order to claim that an adequate defence cannot be mounted · *Also* term for suspected spam.

THE LONG WAR · Pentagon's replacement for the abstract 'War on Terror'.

FRATIRE · male equivalent of chick lit, emphasising sex, drinking, sport, &c; part of the MENAISSANCE rejection of metrosexuality and gender ambiguity.

KATYUSHA ('little Katherine') ROCKETS · Soviet-era design un-guided rockets deployed in July and August against targets in N. Israel by Hezbollah, and alleged to be supplied by Iran.

GURGITATOR · one who participates in eating competitions.

LEONARDOS · marketing term for 30-somethings who like arts and sciences.

HOUSE FLUFFING · titivating a house to entice prospective buyers.

HAJJI · honorific title for one who has made the Hajj [see p.290]. Used by US soldiers as a generic term of abuse for Iraqis (as they called the Vietcong 'gooks'). *Also* HAJJINET · small-scale informal internet services set up by US soldiers in Iraq, to provide internet access for their colleagues. *Also* MUJ · nickname for the Mujahideen.

COCKTAIL No. 4 · a mixture of urine, faecal matter, semen, and spit that, it has been claimed, some Guantánamo Bay inmates throw at their guards.

ISLAMIC FASCISM · comparison of certain 'Islamic' extremists (like Al-Qaeda) with the Nazis, both for their violent methods and their anti-Semitism.

QUAILGATE · nickname for Dick Cheney's accidental shooting of Harry Whittington in the face while quail hunting, and the subsequent fallout.

PIMPFANTS · children dressed up like pimps [see p.157]. *Also* GRUPS · adult kids. *Also* CHILEBRITIES · kids of celebs.

LOCATIONSHIP · a relationship based on geographical proximity rather than true attraction (e.g. dating a roomate).

BILLANTHROPHY · spectacular form of philanthropy practised by Bill Gates, Warren Buffett, and the like.

PUSH PRESENTS · gifts given to (and increasingly expected by) women who have just given birth.

SMIRTING · flirting between those who have been banished outside to smoke.

———————— WORDS OF THE YEAR cont. ————————

ELBOW BUMP · the pandemic-friendly greeting to replace the handshake.

HEZBOLLYWOOD · allegation that some of the Western media accept without question Hezbollah 'spin'.

HELICOPTER PARENTS · those who hover over their offspring.

LO SCROCCONE (*the scrounger*) · the nickname given to Tony Blair by the Italian media, because of his fondness for supposedly 'freebie' holidays.

BOOZE BUS or ASBO AMBULANCE · non-emergency ambulance used to 'treat' drunken revellers. *Also* BUTT BUS · vehicle parked outside non-smoking premises to allow customers to circumvent smoking bans.

POTTING · when prisoners hurl the contents of slop buckets over guards.

BLAIRITE OUTRIDERS · 'independent' politicians, like Alan Milburn and Stephen Byers, who are considered to be speaking for the PM – usually to the annoyance of Gordon's BROWNIES.

BUNCH · to send or receive flowers. (At PMQs, David Cameron said he had been 'bunched' by both Nos 10 and 11 Downing Street when his wife gave birth.)

FAUXHUNT · a hunt that follows (or claims to follow) a scent [legal] rather than a fox [illegal].

CAMEROONIANS · David Cameron's supporters. *Also* NOTTING HILL SET.

LIST 99 · the register of those barred from working with children by the Department for Education and Skills.

RATE TART · one who moves savings or debts to get the best interest rates.

TOFF ROADER · a posh off-road 4x4. *Also* PROLE'S ROYCE · nickname for stretched limousines that are filled with drunken teenage girls.

WAGs · Wives and Girlfriends (of the England football squad).

NOT FIT FOR PURPOSE · John Reid's description of the immigration service when he became Home Secretary.

CROSS DRESSING · Blair's description of post-tribal politics, where traditional left/right policy divisions are outdated.

VERTICAL DRINKING · bars designed with few or no seats that encourage people to drink more, faster.

MINI-MOTOS · small, noisy, 'pocket' motorbikes often ridden without due care, attention, or consideration.

GUILTY PLEASURES · unfashionable yet seemingly irresistible music.

PHONE SCREWING · Fleet Street slang for the illegal interception of (mobile) phone conversations or voicemails.

STABLE AND ORDERLY TRANSITION · 'spin' term for the process of Tony Blair's eventual retirement.

16/8 · shorthand for the possible date of an alleged plot to bring down planes over the Atlantic on 16 August [see p.28].

TRAVELLING WHILE ASIAN · term to describe the concern that PASSENGER PROFILING at airports might create a presumption of guilt against Asians.

——OBJECT OF THE YEAR: THE FLAG OF ST GEORGE——

It was estimated that by the end of World Cup 2006 well over 1½ million St George's flags had been bought: sold mainly by petrol stations and supermarkets, adorned mainly on cars and vans, and made mainly in China and Eastern Europe. ❦ The use of the flag of St George by English sports fans is relatively novel. When England won the World Cup in 1966, streets and stadia were awash with the red, white, and blue of the Union Jack. The adoption of the flag of St George seems to have come about during Euro '96, when England played Scotland in the shadow of likely devolution. From then on, the English flag has increasingly been flown for English teams in a range of sports. ❦ Inevitably, the profusion of St George's flags in 2006 prompted a flurry of news items: Tyne & Wear Fire Brigade suggested flags in pubs might be hazardous; the Chief Inspector of Prisons banned St George's tie-pins; the Deputy Chief Constable of N. Wales warned that 'incessant' flag waving might cause violence; Nike courted controversy with an advert that showed a bare-chested Rooney 'crucified' with red paint; and a host of companies tried to prevent their staff from flying the flag. Outraged by such 'madness', the *Sun* went 'into battle to defend the right of all English men and women to fly our national flag'. ❦ Little is known about St George (?C3–4th), the patron saint of soldiers (and syphilitics). It seems likely that the red cross of St George was first adopted for English soldiers by Richard I, and was further popularised by Edward III, who made St George the Patron of the Knights of the Garter in 1348, and later proclaimed him to be Patron Saint of England. ❦

In recent years, the flag of St George has been associated with racial violence, football hooliganism, and the darker side of right-wing English nationalism. Prior to the World Cup, concerns about the flag were heightened by the relative success of the British National Party (BNP) in the 2006 local elections [see p.256]. (Actually, the BNP worries that the flag of St George is part of a plan to divide the nation. Instead, the BNP advocates the flying of the 'White Dragon of Wessex' as the flag of the 'ethnic-English community within England'.) ❦ World Cup 2006 helped to rehabilitate the flag of St George politically. Tony Blair ordered it to be flown above No. 10 for England games, the Minister for Culture attached it to her car, and Tory leader David Cameron flew it from his bike. Such political gestures were reinforced by a barrage of St George-related advertising by Official England sponsors. Interestingly, the World Cup had a similar effect on the national flag of Germany, where *'das Car Flag'* proved almost as popular as in England. The black, red, and gold of Germany's *Bundesflagge* had been associated with democracy since its adoption in 1848, and for that reason was never used by the Nazis. Yet a post-War reticence towards patriotism meant that the *Bundesflagge* was flown only modestly at sporting encounters. Its popularity in 2006 signalled for Germany a confident step away from its past. Echoing what some said about the flag of St George, German President Horst Köhler called the revival of the *Bundesflagge* 'a sign that the country is increasingly returning to normal, that one can show uninhibited pride in your national flag and drape yourself in it'.

──────────────SIGNIFICA · 2006──────────────

Some (in)significa(nt) footnotes to the year ❦ If all the Lego in the world were evenly divided, we would each receive 30 pieces [*Prospect*] ❦ William Shatner sold a kidney stone to raise $25,000 for a housing charity [BBC] ❦ Bangladeshi authorities ordered mobile phone providers to halt free calls after midnight, after parents complained that children were using the service to form premarital romantic attachments [BBC] ❦ In New Delhi, microchips were inserted into the stomachs

of cows so that, if lost, they could be traced and returned to their owners [*Wall St Journal*] ❦ 'Sonic fibre', a textile woven from cassette tape, was invented by artist Alyce Santoro; when tape heads are run over the material, the clothes will play [*Guardian*] ❦ Pope Benedict XVI had his library of 20,000 books photographed shelf-by-shelf, so they could be re-assembled in the Vatican precisely as they were in his apartment [*NYT*] ❦ The President of Turkmenistan (His Excellency Saparmurat Niyazov 'Turkmenbashi') declared that those who read his

President Niyazov

book of moral and spiritual guidance (the *Rukhnama*) three times ('at home, at sunset, and at dawn') will go to heaven [*Guardian*] ❦ The world's smallest vertebrate was discovered in Sumatra; *Paedocypris progenetica*, a member of the carp family, grows to a maximum length of 1cm [*New Scientist*] ❦ Former Italian PM Silvio Berlusconi took a vow of sexual abstinence for the 10 weeks leading up to the general election [BBC] ❦ Uzbekistan banned fur-lined underwear, deeming it likely to cause 'unbridled fantasies' [*Telegraph*] ❦ 40 Austrian songbirds thought to have died of avian flu were actually drunk; having gorged on fermented berries, they flew into windows [*NYT*] ❦ Taiwanese drunk-drivers were given the option of playing Mah Jong with the elderly instead of paying a fine [*Guardian*] ❦ Mattel unveiled a makeover for Barbie's companion, Ken; in addition to facial resculpting, Ken was given torn jeans and board shorts to reflect the time he spent 'exploring the world and himself' [BBC] ❦ Willie Nelson released a song about gay cowboys, to coincide with *Brokeback Mountain* – 'Cowboys Are Secretly, Frequently (Fond of Each Other)' [BBC] ❦ Supreme Court Justices upheld the use of the hallucinogenic *hoasca* tea in a four-hour, twice-monthly church service in New Mexico [MSNBC] ❦ The US military funded a computer game to teach troops how to decipher Iraqi body language; other games in development include Tactical Pashto (Afghanistan) and Tactical Levantine (Lebanon) [BBC] ❦ In Baghdad's Al Hakimiya prison, a 'price list' of bribes was reported, including: $30,000 to be released; $200 to make a mobile phone call; and $13 for an hour of sunlight. Victims of torture rich enough could buy painkillers from their guards [*Newsweek*] ❦ 42,578 MySpace.com users declared themselves a 'friend' of Madonna [*Guardian*] ❦ Romanian soccer team *Regal Hornia* bought defender Marius Cioara for 15 kilos of pork sausages [*Seattle Times*] ❦ The Chinese government announced it would introduce a 5% chopstick tax to preserve its forests [BBC] ❦ Tory peer Lord Inglewood suggested that British children be encouraged to eat grey squirrels in school dinners to preserve the red variety [BBC] ❦ Emergency services in Las Vegas invested in a fleet of 'bariatric ambulances' (equipped with a winch) to deal with increasing numbers of obese patients; in just 6 months, medics had collected 75 patients over 497lb [*USA Today*] ❦ It was alleged that Dick Cheney requires TVs in his

SIGNIFICA · 2006 cont.

hotel rooms to be pre-tuned to Fox News [*thesmokinggun.com*] ❦ After complaints of rude behaviour, it was announced that Russian police would be taught table manners and an appreciation of poetry, literature, art, music, and dance [ananova.com] ❦ The venture capital arm of the CIA is named 'In-Q-Tel' in honour of 'Q', the inventor and tinkerer in the James Bond films [*Washington Post*] ❦ A Californian good Samaritan returned a bag containing a Cartier watch, diamond and ruby rings, pearl earrings, diamond necklaces, and hundreds of dollars in cash, worth >$1m, to a woman whose husband had lost the bag while they were sightseeing [ABC] ❦ Pope Benedict XVI blessed a fleet of 45 Ferraris in St Peter's Square [Catholic News Agency] ❦ A judge in Manila was removed from the bench after it emerged he was consulting three imaginary mystical dwarves – Armand, Luis, and Angel [Reuters] ❦ Rains in Penglai City, China, created a rare mirage in which a whole section of the city, including buildings and crowds of people, appeared to float above the shore [chinadaily.com] ❦ The 888-foot retired aircraft carrier USS *Oriskany* was sunk to the bottom of the Gulf of Mexico to create the world's largest artificial reef [CNN] ❦ Because of a visit by Pope Benedict XVI, the Polish town of Wadowice restricted the sale of alcohol and ice cream, and halted TV ads for contraceptives and tampons [BBC] ❦ FIFA forced Dutch football fans at the World Cup to remove their bright orange trousers (*leeuwenhose*) before entering a Stuttgart stadium, since they bore the name of a Bavarian brewery, a rival of tournament sponsor Budweiser [*Guardian*] ❦ A British insurance agency withdrew a £1m policy that covered three Scottish nuns in the event that they immaculately conceived the Second Coming [*Times*] ❦ In the week before Valentine's Day, people were more likely to search online for the key words 'love poems' than for 'flowers' or 'lingerie' [*New York Times*] ❦ The perm, invented in 1906 by German émigré Karl Nessler, celebrated its 100th anniversary [*Guardian*] ❦ David Beckham revealed that he had spent months battling obsessive-compulsive disorder; he disclosed that he has to have his belongings arranged in straight lines, and buys exactly 20 packets of 'super noodles' every time he visits the supermarket [*Independent*] ❦ After a survey predicted the last fluent Sissenton-Wahpeton speaker would die in 2025, the Dakota Sioux set up an interschool Scrabble tournament to prolong the use of its language [MSNBC] ❦ While playing James Bond, Sean Connery wrote a ballet called *Black Lake*, according to his ex-wife's autobiography [*Guardian*] ❦ A host of celebrities (including writer Stephen King) urged J.K. Rowling not to 'kill off' Harry Potter in the last (planned) book of the series [BBC] ❦ Concerned about the promotion of 'feudalism and feudal beliefs', Chinese authorities banned the sale of voodoo dolls from Beijing shops [*Newsweek*] ❦ Zimbabwe introduced a $100,000 bill, worth US$1 at official exchange rates [BBC] ❦ Residents of Hell (pop. 72), MI, celebrated

J.K. Rowling

6·6·06 with '666' branded T-shirts and mugs, and sold deeds to 1 sq. inch of Hell for $6·66 [MSNBC] ❦ Osama bin Laden's satellite-phone number was (or is?) 00 873 682 505 331 [*Guardian*] ❦ The Turkmenbashi [see p.14] had a melon named in his honour during Turkmenistan's national and annual Melon Day [AFP] ❦ In August, Iranian President Mahmoud Ahmadinejad [see p.32] launched his own blog – ahmadinejad.ir – which is translated into Persian, Arabic, English, and French.

2005 PAKISTAN/KASHMIR EARTHQUAKE

DATE: Saturday, 8 October 2005 · TIME: 08:50:40 at epicentre
QUAKE MAGNITUDE: 7·6 Richter Scale [see p.75] · DEPTH: 26km (16·2 miles)
LOCATION: Pakistan, 34·493°N, 73·629°E · [Source: US Geological Survey]
105km NNE of Islamabad, Pakistan · 115km ESE of Mingaora, Pakistan
125km WNW of Srinagar, Kashmir · 165km SSW of Gilgit, Kashmir

The earthquake that struck Pakistan-adminstered Kashmir killed >86,000, wiped out entire villages, and devastated the local infrastructure. The immediate problem facing the Pakistani government was that of galvanising a co-ordinated response to the tragedy. The quake struck a remote mountainous region and destroyed many of the access roads, making rescue and recovery difficult and hazardous. As temperatures dropped and the delivery of aid stalled, increasing numbers of desperate refugees fled their homes to gather in camps in the Kashmiri valleys. A harsh winter loomed, and with *c.*3m thought to be homeless, provision of shelter and food became urgent. ❦ The delicate relationship between India and Pakistan, who both lay claim to the entire Kashmir region, was further tested by the disaster. Pakistan's President Musharraf suggested the earthquake might be an opportunity to resolve the long-running dispute; in a gesture that further raised hopes of a reconciliation, India pledged £14m of aid to Pakistan. ❦ Aid agencies feared that the inter-national response to earlier disasters (southeast Asia's tsunami, Darfur, &c.) had depleted national annual aid budgets. And, a month after the quake, it emerged that just 30% of the UN's aid target had been pledged – a response derided by UN Secretary-General Kofi Annan as 'weak' and 'tardy'. Stung into action, the international community promised $5·4bn to Pakistan (exceeding the $5·2bn requested) – with Muslim nations accounting for the majority of the donations. The British government pledged £58m in short-term aid, and £70m for long-term reconstruction. An estimated 1·5m Britons knew someone affected by the quake and, as after the 2004 tsunami, the British public reacted to the tragedy more quickly than the government, donating £40m. ❦ It is feared that the widespread desertion of the mountainous communities in Kashmir could severely affect the reconstruction of the area, leaving a region of ghost towns with thousands permanently displaced. Current estimates from Pakistan suggest that recovery might take as long as a decade.

—————————— AVIAN FLU ——————————

As of 14·9·2006, the World Health Organisation [WHO] had confirmed 246 human cases of Avian Influenza A(H5N1) – 144 of which had been fatal (a mortality rate of *c*.58%) [see chart]. Although some of the most dire predictions of a human pandemic have failed yet to materialise, governments around the world continue to stockpile drug treatment [see p.181]. And while most human cases have been caused by direct contact with diseased animals, international organisations continue to monitor the emergence of disease 'clusters' that might give an early warning of human-to-human transmission. ❦ The H5N1 strain was initially identified amongst birds in 1961, and the first human infections were in Hong Kong in 1997; of the 18 people infected, 6 died, and only the swift destruction of Hong Kong's entire poultry population (*c*.1½m birds) averted a possible pandemic. The latest H5N1 outbreak is thought to have begun with a number of undetected and unreported cases in Asia in mid-2003. By January 2004, Korea, Vietnam, Japan, Thailand, Cambodia, and Laos had all reported H5N1 in poultry, and the first human cases had been confirmed. Throughout Asia, tens of millions of birds have died from the disease and in mass culls to prevent its spread. However, avian migration (and possibly the international poultry trade) has spread H5N1 around the globe. ❦ On April 5, 2006, the UK declared its first case of H5N1, when an infected swan was found dead in Cellardyke, near St Andrews. DNA tests showed that the bird was a whooper swan (a species not native to Britain) and it was suggested that the bird may have been washed ashore having died elsewhere. On April 26, a farm in Norwich tested positive for the (slightly less deadly) H7 strain of avian flu, leading to a cull of 35,000 chickens. ❦ July 2006 data from the World Organisation for Animal Health [OIE] show H5N1 in >50 countries. As the virus spreads and more animals are infected, the risk that H5N1 will mutate to cause human-to-human infections grows. ❦ According to the WHO, seasonal flu epidemics hit 5–15% of the world population every year, killing between ¼–½ million, mostly the sick and elderly. However, flu *pandemics* typically occur every 10–50 years, with much more devastating results. The C20th saw 3 flu pandemics: the 1918 Spanish Flu (*c*·40m deaths); the 1957 Asian Flu (>2m deaths); and the 1968 Hong Kong Flu (*c*.1m deaths). For obvious reasons, many organisations are reluctant to estimate potential death tolls for a hypothetical H5N1 pandemic. Yet the WHO states that modelling of the current population suggests that 'at a minimum' 2–7·4 million might die in the next pandemic, a statistic that does not take into account non-fatal morbidity, nor the potentially catastrophic socio-economic toll of a pandemic.

Human Cases of H5N1

at 14·9·06	cases	deaths
Azerbaijan	8	5
Cambodia	6	6
China	21	14
Djibouti	1	0
Egypt	14	6
Indonesia	65	49
Iraq	2	2
Thailand	24	16
Turkey	12	4
Vietnam	93	42
Total	246	144

World Health Organisation

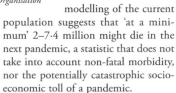

ENRON, SKILLING, & LAY

Another chapter of the Enron scandal closed in May 2006, when founder Kenneth Lay and former CEO Jeffrey Skilling were convicted on multiple charges of fraud and conspiracy. Six weeks later, Lay died suddenly from heart disease. ❦ Prior to bankruptcy in 2001, Enron was America's 7th-largest company, employing *c*.21,000 in >40 countries, and declaring revenues of $100bn (2000). For six consecutive years *Fortune* declared Enron to be *America's Most Innovative Company*; at its peak, Enron stock traded at *c*.$90. Although it began as a gas pipeline company, Enron took advantage of market de-regulations to trade in myriad fields, from natural resources and energy to broadband internet capacity and fluctuations in the weather. Yet, as Enron grew, exactly what it did and how it made such massive profits were unclear. A *Fortune* article in March 2001 is credited with exposing chinks in the company's armour. Under the prescient headline '*Is Enron Overpriced?*', journalist Bethany McLean called the firm's operations 'mind-numbingly complex', and quoted one financial analyst who described Enron as 'a big black box'. ❦

With Enron's collapse came a rapid unravelling of the convoluted and arcane techniques to maximise the appearance of profits, while shifting debts and losses 'off balance-sheet'. ❦ Six years later, the consequences of Enron are still being assessed. A number of high-profile financial collapses followed in the wake of Enron, as did the Sarbanes-Oxley Act 2002, which tightened the US law on corporate governance. Enron may also have led to a harsher treatment of white-collar criminals, now denied the privilege of a discreet arrest and paraded in handcuffs on the 'perp walk'. ❦ At the time of writing, Skilling had not been sentenced and planned to appeal, and the consequences of Lay's death were still being assessed. Yet the Enron trial (and those that followed) served notice on corporate America that prosecutors were willing to take on the wealthy and well-connected in highly complex cases, and focus their charges in a way that juries could understand. It was in this way that Enron's arrogant and criminally corrupt culture was distilled to the personal liability of those who led what the London *Financial Times* called 'a virtual company with virtual profits'.

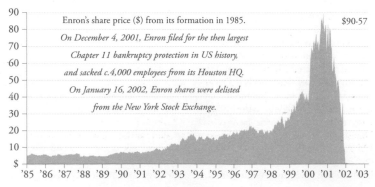

Enron's share price ($) from its formation in 1985. $90·57

On December 4, 2001, Enron filed for the then largest

Chapter 11 bankruptcy protection in US history,

and sacked c.4,000 employees from its Houston HQ.

On January 16, 2002, Enron shares were delisted

from the New York Stock Exchange.

'85 '86 '87 '88 '89 '90 '91 '92 '93 '94 '95 '96 '97 '98 '99 '00 '01 '02 '03

MUHAMMAD CARTOON CRISIS

On 30 September, 2005, the Danish national newspaper *Jyllands-Posten* printed twelve cartoons on the subject of Muhammad – many of which contravened strict Islamic tradition by actually portraying images of the Prophet. The cartoons were commissioned to explore why a Danish author had struggled to find artists willing to illustrate his children's book about the Prophet. Under the headline 'The Face of Muhammad', the paper's culture editor wrote: '*The modern, secular society is rejected by some Muslims. They demand a special position, insisting on special consideration of their own religious feelings. It is incompatible with contemporary democracy and freedom of speech, where you must be ready to put up with insults, mockery and ridicule*'.

The cartoons represented Muhammad in a variety of ways, including one of the Prophet refusing suicide bombers entry into heaven, claiming they had run out of virgins. Yet, the most iconic and controversial image was that by artist Kurt Westergaard, who depicted Muhammad as a terrorist, wearing not a turban but a bomb with a lit fuse, inscribed in Arabic with the Muslim declaration of faith. ❦ A fortnight after publication, a peaceful protest was held in Copenhagen, but quickly the controversy proved another example of political 'chaos theory', where local incidents can rapidly have global repercussions. By early 2006, demonstrations of increasing violence had erupted in Europe and across the Islamic world, from Afghanistan, Libya, and Iran to Somalia, Nigeria, and Pakistan. In a professed show of solidarity for press freedom, newspapers in dozens of countries reprinted the cartoons. Each new publication sparked further protest, and several editors were sacked. Danish embassies were attacked, Danes were advised to leave Indonesia and warned against travelling to the Middle East, and a Muslim-wide boycott of Danish goods was attempted. Danish PM Anders Fogh Rasmussen declared the incident to be Denmark's worst international crisis since World War II.

❦ At the heart of the crisis was the clash of two 'self-evident' and 'inalienable' rights: the right to free expression and the right to religious respect. Though much of the hurt expressed by Muslims was genuine, some suggested the crisis had been deliberately fomented. It was claimed that certain Islamic states found it useful to attach themselves to a popular cause (an Iranian newspaper solicited cartoons satirizing the Holocaust), while radical Islamists used the crisis as an aid to recruitment (Osama bin Laden called for the cartoonists to be tried by Al-Qaeda and executed). However, the February 2006 jailing of David Irving for Holocaust denial [see p.63] led many to question whether liberal Europe had a double standard: Islam could be 'defamed' with impunity whereas Judaism had legal protection. ❦ Although the direct attribution of casualties to the cartoons is complex, it is thought that *c.*823 were injured and *c.*139 killed by the time the protests had faded in April–May. Speaking at the World Editor's Forum in Moscow in June 2006, *Jyllands-Posten* editor-in-chief Joern Mikkelsen reflected on his decision to print the cartoons: 'Would we do it again? I have been asked time and time again. It is very hard to tell. I have said that we wouldn't do it if we had known the consequences'.

— THE LANGUAGE OF DETENTION & INTERROGATION —

Since the 2003 invasion of Iraq, controversy has surrounded the US techniques of detention and interrogation – catalysed by reports and images of abuse in Abu Ghraib, Guantánamo Bay [Gitmo], and elsewhere. The early classification of terror suspects as 'Illegal Enemy Combatants' has allowed the US to justify abrogations from conventions (including Geneva, 1949) that proscribe cruel and degrading treatment. America's use of 'enhanced interrogation techniques' has been defended by President Bush, who argues that a 'new paradigm' is required to crack 'the worst of the worst'. (According to a US official, Guantánamo Bay was designed to be the 'legal equivalent of outer space'.) ❦ It is beyond the remit of *Schott's Almanac* to detail the ongoing allegations, investigations, and prosecutions of mistreatment – some of which go well beyond 'torture lite' into severe physical, sexual, and psychological abuse. Yet, one of the novel features of this reappraisal of detention and interrogation is the vocabulary of its practitioners. For example, when three Gitmo inmates committed suicide in June 2006, the camp commander called it an 'act of *asymmetrical warfare* waged against us'. Another spokesman described the deaths as 'a *good PR move*'. Below are some other terms that have recently emerged:

HOODING · covering prisoners' heads to render them docile and deprive them of sensory input. The wearing of gloves, goggles, and headphones can produce hallucinations within 48 hours.

FUTILITY MUSIC · violent, aggressive, repetitive, and 'culturally insensitive' music played at high volume for hours on end, often combined with strobe lights. Various reports have listed the musicians inflicted on suspects, including: Eminem, Bruce Springsteen, Limp Bizkit, Christina Aguilera, Metallica, Britney Spears, and, bizarrely, Barney the Dinosaur. Other sounds employed include 'Halloween noises', cats meowing, and babies crying inconsolably.

THE BLACK ROOM · 'a windowless jet-black garage-size room' (formerly a Saddam torture chamber) in Camp Nama, Baghdad, where US troops 'beat prisoners with rifle butts, yelled and spit in their faces and, in a nearby area, used detainees for target practice in a game of JAILER PAINTBALL', where, according to a printed sign, the rule was 'NO BLOOD, NO FOUL' [*NY Times*].

SLEEP ADJUSTMENT · manipulating and repeatedly interrupting the sleep of prisoners, while theoretically allowing them adequate overall hours of sleep. In Gitmo, the technique of moving detainees from cell to cell every few hours to disrupt their sleep was known as the FREQUENT FLYER PROGRAMME.

INTERNAL NUTRITION · US military euphemism for force-feeding.

WATER-BOARDING · where prisoners are strapped to an inclined board and made to feel they will drown – either by submerging them in water or by wrapping their faces with plastic and pouring water over them. Senator John McCain said, 'I believe that [water-boarding] is torture, very exquisite torture', and, according to ABC News, CIA operatives who underwent this technique lasted just 14 seconds. *Also* THE WATER CURE · where prisoners are strapped down with a rag in their mouths onto which water is poured. *Also* WATER PIT · a void filled with water in which prisoners have to stand on tiptoe to avoid drowning.

————————THE LANGUAGE OF DETENTION cont.————————

TICKING TIME BOMB · a justification for torture, premised on the scenario of a prisoner who has vital information on an *imminent* explosion that can only be extracted by the use of torture.

ATTENTION GRAB · where an interrogator forcefully grabs the clothes of a prisoner and shakes him. *Also* ATTENTION SLAP · an open-handed slap to cause pain and trigger fear. *Also* BELLY SLAP · a hard, open-handed slap to the stomach, to cause pain, but not internal injury. *Also* SISSY SLAP · where prisoners are touched with an inflated latex glove labelled 'sissy slap glove'.

MOCK BURIAL · where prisoners are made to think they will be buried alive. *Also* FAKE EXECUTION · convincing prisoners they are about to be killed.

DIETARY MANIPULATION · where a prisoner's rations are changed (e.g. cold instead of hot food), not as deprivation but to upset routine. *Also* ENVIRONMENTAL MANIPULATION · where the prisoners' cells are made uncomfortable (e.g. with noxious smells, excrement, temperature changes, sounds, &c.).

EXTRAORDINARY RENDITION (aka RUMSFELD PROCESSING) · moving suspects from countries where torture is banned to those where it is not. George W. Bush has admitted that the US OUTSOURCES detention to countries like Syria, and operates an archipelago of secret prisons (BLACK SITES) in eastern Europe, Thailand, Afghanistan, &c. It has been claimed that the CIA owns a number of private jets to fly GHOST PRISONERS around the world. *Also* REVERSE RENDITION · when foreign powers arrest suspects in non-combat areas and hand them over to the US.

FORCED GROOMING · shaving off body hair – especially effective against Muslims, for whom hair is sacred.

PRIDE AND EGO DOWN · employing humiliation to crush a prisoner's sense of pride and self (e.g. abusing copies of the Koran or wrapping prisoners in the Stars and Stripes). Recent allegations against US forces include the 'invasion of space by a female' – e.g. enforced nudity in front of female soldiers, lap-dancing, making prisoners wear female underwear, and daubing prisoners with perfume and fake menstrual blood.

STRESS POSITIONS · forcing prisoners into discomfort for hours on end, or keeping them in confined spaces where they can neither sit nor stand. *Also* SHORT SHACKLE · where prisoners' wrists and ankles are fixed to eyebolts in the floor, forcing them to crouch. *Also* LONG-TIME STANDING · making prisoners stand and denying them sleep. *Also* COLD CELL · keeping prisoners naked in 50°F cells and dousing them in water. *Also* FORCED EXERCISE · gratuitous physical training. *Also* CLAUSTROPHOBIC TECHNIQUES · tying prisoners into sleeping bags or cramming them into metal lockers.

REMOVAL OF COMFORT ITEMS · denial of items that, though not essential, give prisoners a sense of self or comfort (e.g. cigarettes); recently, the removal of prayer rugs and Korans from Muslims.

EXPLOIT PHOBIAS · using factors that play on a prisoner's fears (e.g. directing dogs to growl, bark, and show teeth).

[Sources: *New York Times*; *Guardian*; Amnesty Int.; ACLU; MSNBC; *New Yorker*; BBC; HRW; ABC; US Dept of Defense; &c.]

──────────── UK THREAT LEVELS ────────────

In August 2006, the British government made public for the first time a simplified system of 'threat levels' that had been used covertly for some years†. According to MI5, they were released to give the public a 'broad indication of the likelihood of a terrorist attack'. To avoid the accusations of political manipulation that dog the US Homeland Security threat condition, the UK levels are set by the purportedly apolitical Joint Terrorism Analysis Centre (JTAC), which analyses international terrorism, and MI5, which analyses domestic and Irish terrorism. These two groups assess a range of indicators, including: available intelligence (what is known about an attack), terrorist capability (the scale of an attack), terrorist intentions (the aim and targets of an attack), and time-scale (how long an attack takes to plan, and when it might be launched). The Home Office states that the threat levels 'do not require specific responses from the public', since 'they are a tool for security practitioners working across different sectors of … the Critical National Infrastructure'. Indeed, though the national threat level is made public, separate threat levels are issued privately for specific areas, buildings, organisations, and individuals. Below are the (un-colour-coded) threat levels, and their associated response levels:

Response Level	Threat Level	Description
Normal	LOW attack is unlikely ───────── MODERATE attack possible, but not likely	Routine and appropriate protective security measures
Heightened	SUBSTANTIAL attack is a strong possibility ───────── SEVERE attack is highly likely	Additional and sustainable protective security measures
Exceptional	CRITICAL attack is expected imminently	Maximum protective security measures

On 1 August 2006, the UK's threat level was initially assessed to be Severe – but, on 10 August, it was raised to Critical in response to the disruption of an alleged transatlantic 'terror plot' [see p.28]. The level was reduced to Severe on 14 August, though the Home Secretary, Dr John Reid, warned, 'I want to stress … that the change in the threat level does not mean that the threat has gone away. There is still a very serious threat of an attack. The threat level is at Severe, indicating the high likelihood of an attempted terrorist attack at some stage, and I urge the public to remain vigilant.' ❦ A senior Whitehall source told the BBC's security correspondent, Gordon Corera, 'if [the level] moves to Critical, you should worry'.

† The old system was: *Negligible, Low, Moderate, Substantial, Severe General, Severe Defined, Critical.*

RATING BLAIR & BUSH, POST-9/11

2006 · 2005 · 2004 · 2003 · 2002 · 2001

J F M A M J J A S O N D

Significant news events

Alleged plot to bomb planes foiled
Israel and Lebanon in escalated attacks
Shalit kidnapped; Israel attacked Gaza
Immigration protests across America
Iran announced uranium enrichment
Slobodan Milosevic died at The Hague
Dick Cheney shot Harry Whittington
Hamas won Palestinian elections
WTO conference in Hong Kong
Michael Bloomberg won 2nd term
Bali bombs · Kashmir earthquake
Hurricane Rita
Hurricane Katrina
7/7 London bombs · G8 Conference
Michael Jackson found not guilty
Tony Blair won a historic 3rd term
Pope John Paul II died
Terri Schiavo died
Kyoto Protocol came into force
Parliamentary elections in Iraq
Southeast Asian tsunami
George W. Bush defeated John Kerry
Trial of Saddam Hussein began
Beslan school siege, Russia
Athens Olympic Games began
Groundbreaking of Freedom Tower
Iyad Allawi became Iraqi PM
Massachusetts legalized gay marriage
Abu Ghraib abuse became public
Madrid, Spain, train bombings
CIA 'no imminent Iraq WMD threat'
Hutton Report published in Britain
US forces captured Saddam Hussein
Bush made a state visit to Britain
Red Cross criticized Guantánamo Bay
Kim Jong-il 're-elected', North Korea
NATO peacekeepers to Afghanistan
WHO declared SARS contained
G8 Summit in Evian, France
Bush: end to major combat in Iraq
Allied forces took Baghdad
Invasion of Iraq began
Space shuttle *Columbia* disintegrated
Dept of Homeland Security started
Iraq report denied WMD
Midterm elections
Bali bombs
Bush called for Iraq 'regime change'
Severe flooding in Europe
WorldCom filed for bankruptcy
Brazil beat Germany in the World Cup
US-Russia arms reduction agreement
Israel occupied West Bank
US Op. Anaconda in Afghanistan
Salt Lake City Winter Olympics
George W. Bush choked on a pretzel
Enron collapsed
AA Flight 587 crashed in NYC
US attacks on Afghanistan
September 11 attacks
Macedonia peace agreement
Genoa G8 Conference
Tony Blair won 2nd election
Israel bombed the West Bank
US spy plane crash-landed in China
UK Foot & Mouth epidemic
Ariel Sharon elected Israeli PM
Inauguration of George W. Bush

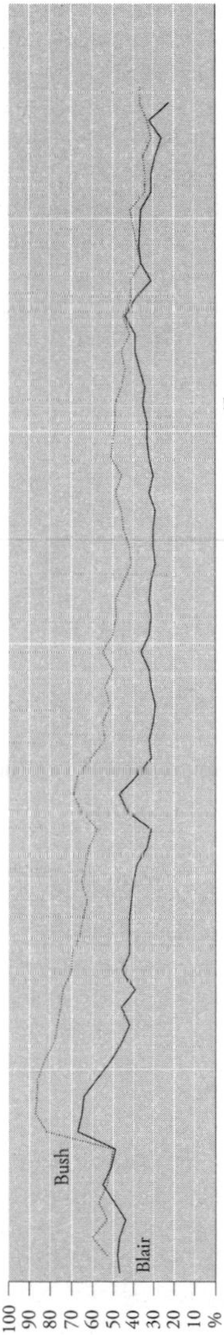
Bush
Blair
100
90
80
70
60
50
40
30
20
10
%

Approval ratings of Tony Blair & George W. Bush

[CBS/*New York Times*; Mori Political Tracker]

Significant news events continued

Escalation of Blair/Brown tension
Pluto stripped of planetary status
Zidane sent off during World Cup final
Lord Levy arrested
Labour local election losses & reshuffle
Labour's 'triple whammy Wednesday'
Menzies Campbell Lib Dem leader
IAEA voted to report Iran to Security Council
Muhammad cartoon controversy [see p.19]
David Cameron became Tory leader
David Blunkett resigned for the 2nd time
British fuel protests
England won the Ashes
Robin Cook died
London win 2012 Olympics · IRA cease-fire
John Sentamu appointed Archbishop of York
France voted against a new EU referendum
New Pope elected: Benedict XVI
Indonesian earthquake
Prince Charles & Camilla Parker Bowles engaged
Ban on hunting with dogs
David Blunkett resigned for the 1st time
Parliament Act invoked for hunting ban
Blair: 'I will not stand for a 4th term'
Pro-fox-hunting group stormed Parliament
Kelly Holmes won 2 Golds
Butler Report published
Labour suffer local election losses
EU admitted 10 new member states
Darfur cease-fire signed
Vladimir Putin re-elected with 70%
Hajj stampede killed 251 [see p.290]
Dr Harold Shipman found hanged
Ian Huntley found guilty of Soham murders
Michael Howard became Tory leader
Iain Duncan Smith resigned
Final submissions in the Hutton Enquiry
Blair became the longest serving Labour PM
Dr David Kelly found dead
Alan Milburn resigned
Clare Short resigned
Human genome project completed
Robin Cook resigned
Worldwide protests against invasion of Iraq
'Shoebomber' Richard Reid jailed for life
Lord of the Rings: The Two Towers released
Hans Blix & weapons inspectors arrived in Iraq
Estelle Morris resigned
Mass 'Countryside March'
Soham murders
C of E permitted divorcees to marry
Queen celebrated 50 years on the throne
Stephen Byers resigned · Cabinet reshuffle
The Queen Mother's funeral
The Queen Mother died
Milosevic's Hague trail began
Start of the euro
Taleban surrendered Kandahar
Michael Bloomberg elected NY Mayor
Apple launched the iPod
Iain Duncan Smith Tory Leader
Milosevic charged with genocide
Race riots in Bradford
Race riots in Burnley
John Prescott punched a man in a brawl
UK census conducted
MIR Space-station fell into the Pacific
Selby rail crash
Peter Mandelson resigned for 2nd time

──────── IRAQ · CIVILIAN & MILITARY FATALITIES ────────

The lack of official data on civilian deaths in Iraq became increasingly controversial during 2006, as the violence of the insurgency intensified and the country's descent into 'civil war' was debated. The civilian fatality data below come from the respected Iraq Body Count (IBC), which cautions, 'there is no such thing (and will probably never be such a thing) as a "wholly accurate" figure, which could be accepted as historical truth by all parties'. Below are the IBC's maximum and minimum figures for civilian deaths in Iraq, from the allied attack in March 2003 until July 2006:

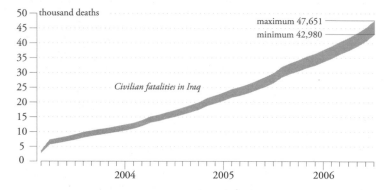

According to the Brookings Institution, as of September 2006 there were *c.*7,200 UK military personnel in Iraq, compared to *c.*133,000 US troops. Below are the latest figures of coalition military fatalities, by month, up to 25 September 2006.

	US deaths	UK deaths	other states	total			US deaths	UK deaths	other states	total			US deaths	UK deaths	other states	total
						Apr	135	0	5	140		Aug	85	0	0	85
						May	80	0	4	84		Sep	49	3	0	52
						Jun	42	1	7	50		Oct	96	2	1	99
Mar '03	65	27	0	92		Jul	54	1	3	58		Nov	84	1	1	86
Apr	74	6	0	80		Aug	66	4	5	75		Dec	68	0	0	68
May	37	4	0	41		Sep	80	3	4	87		Jan '06	62	2	0	64
Jun	30	6	0	36		Oct	63	2	2	67		Feb	55	3	0	58
Jul	48	1	0	49		Nov	137	4	0	141		Mar	31	0	2	33
Aug	35	6	2	43		Dec	72	1	3	76		Apr	76	1	5	82
Sep	31	1	1	33		Jan '05	107	10	10	127		May	69	9	1	79
Oct	44	1	2	47		Feb	58	0	2	60		Jun	61	0	2	63
Nov	82	1	27	110		Mar	35	1	3	39		Jul	43	1	2	46
Dec	40	0	8	48		Apr	52	0	0	52		Aug	65	1	0	66
Jan '04	47	5	0	52		May	80	2	6	88		Sep	61	3	2	66
Feb	20	1	2	23		Jun	78	1	4	83		*Total*	2703	118	117	2938
Mar	52	0	0	52		Jul	54	3	1	58		[Iraq Coalition Casualty Count]				

Increasing violence in Afghanistan during 2006 led to calls for the NATO forces to be strengthened. As of 8 September, 40 UK troops had been killed while on operations in Afghanistan since 2001 – 21 of whom died from accidents, illness, or non-combat injuries. [Source: BBC, MoD]

—INTERNATIONAL AFFAIRS · BAROMETER OF OPINION—

OPINION OF AMERICA & AMERICANS

The shift between 2000–06 in those with a favourable opinion of the US

% favourable	2000	2006
China	—	47
Egypt	—	30
France	62	39
GB	83	56
Germany	78	37
India	—	56
Indonesia	75	30
Japan	77	63
Jordan	—	15
Nigeria	46	62
Pakistan	23	27
Russia	37	43
Spain	50	23
Turkey	52	12

The difference between those with a favourable opinion of America vs Americans

(2006) % favourable	America	Americans
China	47	49
Egypt	30	36
France	39	65
GB	56	69
Germany	37	66
India	56	67
Indonesia	30	36
Japan	63	82
Jordan	15	38
Nigeria	62	56
Pakistan	27	27
Russia	43	57
Spain	23	37
Turkey	12	17

[Pew Global Attitudes Project 15-nation study · June 2006]

THE 'SPECIAL RELATIONSHIP'

63% of the British said T. Blair had tied Britain too closely to the White House; 30% called the relationship 'just right'.

[*Guardian*/ICM July 2006]

GUANTÁNMO, RENDITION, & HUMAN RIGHTS

The % that said the US policies of detention at Guantánamo Bay are not legal

Germany	85
United Kingdom	65
Poland	50
India	34

The % that said the US should not be allowed to use their airspace for rendition [see p.20]

United Kingdom	66
Germany	55
Poland	48
India	42

The % that said the US does a bad job of advancing human rights abroad

Germany	78
Russia	66
United Kingdom	56
Poland	33
India	19

[WorldPublicOpinion.org/ Knowledge Networks · July 2006]

VIEW OF GB's WORLD INFLUENCE

The % that said GB has a mainly negative influence on the world and world events

Iran	66
Iraq	57
Argentina	51
Turkey	41
Mexico	36
Germany	33
Philippines	33
France	32
Saudi Arabia	30
Brazil	29
Indonesia	29
Congo	28
Australia	26
China	26
Finland	26
Italy	26
Spain	26
Afghanistan	21
Canada	19
Zimbabwe	19
South Korea	18
Senegal	16
Tanzania	16
India	15
South Africa	14
United States	14
Kenya	13
Russia	13
Nigeria	11
Sri Lanka	11
Ghana	10
Poland	5

When asked, 26% of the British thought that GB had a mainly negative influence.

[BBC World Service/Globescan/ PIPA · January 2006]

THE WORLD CUP FINAL

9 July 2006 · Olympiastadion, Berlin · Attendance: 69,000
ITALY 1–1 FRANCE (AET) · ITALY WON 5–3 ON PENALTIES

Few predicted a France–Italy final to a World Cup in which no country excelled. Italy, dogged by domestic match-fixing accusations, managed to shrug off the uncertainty surrounding many of their players (who faced relegation to the lower echelons of Italian football [see p.299]), to produce a strong team performance. The ageing French team was captained by Zinedine Zidane (who came out of retirement to help France qualify) – yet his reputation as the finest player of the modern game was tarnished during the final when he was sent off for headbutting Materazzi[†].

ITALY (left to right): Buffon; Cannavaro (c), Zambrotta, Materazzi, Grosso; Pirlo, Gattuso, Camoranesi (Del Piero 86), Perrotta (Iaquinta 61), Totti (De Rossi 61); Toni

FRANCE (right to left): Malouda, Zidane (c) (Trezeguet 100), Ribery, Vieira (Diarra 56), Makelele, Henry (Wiltord 107), Abidal, Gallas, Thuram, Sagnol, Barthez

ITALY	FRANCE
5 shots 13	
3 shots on goal 5	
17 fouls 24	
5 corners 7	
0 penalty kicks 1	
4 offsides 2	
51% possession 49%	
39' actual playing time 32'	
37 tackles 25	
81·1 tackles success 76	
1 yellow cards 3	
0 red cards 1	

Minute	key moment
3'	Henry dazed by bang on head
7'	Materazzi clipped Malouda in the box
7'	penalty to France – Zidane's chipped spot kick hit the bar, but bounced in
19'	Materazzi scored from Pirlo's corner
35'	Toni hit the crossbar
53'	Malouda brought down in box
53'	referee refused calls for 2nd penalty
56'	Vieira hobbled off injured
62'	Toni 'goal' ruled offside
109'	Zidane headbutted Materazzi[†]
110'	Zidane sent off

† Zidane apologised for his assault (witnessed by the 4th official and millions of viewers) but refused to express regret, claiming that Materazzi had verbally abused his family. Materazzi later admitted to insulting Zidane's sister. In July 2006, FIFA fined Materazzi £2,170 and banned him for 2 games; Zidane was fined £3,260 and banned for 3 games, a token punishment given his earlier retirement.

The penalty shoot-out	I–F		
Pirlo slotted one down the middle	1–0	De Rossi powered one home	3–1
Wiltord scored easily	1–1	Abidal scored	3–2
Materazzi netted a low shot	2–1	Del Piero blasted one in	4–2
Trezeguet hit the bar	2–1	Sagnol held his nerve and scored	4–3
		Grosso scored, Italy won	5–3

—————————OTHER MAJOR STORIES IN BRIEF—————————

'Quailgate' · *Whittington & Cheney*

On 11 February 2006, Vice President Dick Cheney accidentally shot his 78-year-old lawyer friend Harry Whittington in the face, neck, and chest with an Italian 28-gauge Perazzi shotgun, while hunting quail in Texas. Whittington was rushed to hospital in Corpus Christi, where, a few days later, he suffered a mild heart attack caused by a pellet lodged in his heart. The controversy surrounding the incident was exacerbated by allegations of Cheney's obfuscatory delay in informing the police, the President, and the media. As he left the hospital a week after the shooting, Whittington noted 'accidents do and will happen', and he apologised 'for all that Vice President Cheney and his family have had to go through'.

ETA Cease-fire

At midnight on 24 March 2006, the Basque separatists ETA (Euskadi Ta Askatasuna, 'Basque Homeland & Freedom') began a 'permanent cease-fire'. The group promised to 'promote a democratic process in the Basque country', a pledge greeted with caution – since earlier ETA cease-fires had ended within months. Spain, the US, and the EU classify ETA as a terrorist organisation, and the group is held responsible for >800 deaths since it was founded in 1959. Although ETA's campaign had been in decline, it seems likely that this latest cease-fire was catalysed by the arrest of a swathe of members, and by a shift in Spanish public opinion after the 2004 Madrid train bombings.

French Labour Law Demonstrations

In March 2006, French PM Dominique de Villepin pushed through a controversial new labour law in an attempt to revive the country's stagnant economy and reduce high rates of youth unemployment (>22% of French 18–25s are unemployed). The law created a 2-year trial contract for those under 26 (*Contrat Première Embauche,* CPE) that employers could terminate without explanation and with minimum notice. This attempt to create a more flexible youth workforce was immediately rejected by unions and students, who feared the CPE would be exploited by large employers. During March and April, mass protests and strikes swept across France – and violent rioting saw shops damaged and cars burned. Despite a tough initial stance, de Villepin and President Chirac were shocked by the vehemence of the public's rejection of the contracts and, on 10 April, the CPEs were withdrawn. It is thought that this embarrassing *volte-face* may have seriously damaged de Villepin's chance of succeeding Chirac in the 2007 French presidential elections.

'Cash for Peerages'

In March 2006, Scotland Yard announced that it was examining complaints that the major political parties may have broken laws, dating from 1925 and 1889, prohibiting the 'sale' of honours. All three major political parties admitted that they had accepted 'secret loans' from wealthy supporters – possibly to circumvent the 2000 rules that require donations above £5000, and those from abroad, to be declared. It has been insinuated that a link may exist between those loaning money to political parties, and the award of peerages. During the summer, a number of high-profile politicians were questioned by the police, and a number of arrests were made. At the time of writing, enquiries by the police and the Electoral Commission were ongoing, all those

──────── OTHER MAJOR STORIES IN BRIEF cont. ────────

involved had denied wrongdoing, and no charges had been brought. Whatever the outcome of the investigations, it seems likely that the rules on funding of political parties will be tightened further, possibly with the introduction of state (i.e. taxpayer) funding.

Java Earthquakes

On 26 May 2006, at 22:53:58 UTC, a 6·3 Richter earthquake occurred under the Indian Ocean, 10 miles SSE of Yogyakarta, on the S. side of Java. The worst-affected area, Bantul, was densely populated, and the latest estimate was of $c.5,782$ deaths, $c.36,299$ injuries, and $c.600,000$ homeless. The international aid response was hindered by poor local coordination. ❦ On 17 July, at 08:19:28 UTC, a 7·7 Richter earthquake caused a 6½-ft tsunami to hit a 125-mile stretch of Java's S. shore near Pangandaran. >500 are thought to have died in the tsunami – a death toll exacerbated by the Indonesian government's apparent unwillingness and inability to pass on the early warning it had received.

Alleged Transatlantic Terror Plot

On 10 August 2006, British police announced that an alleged plot to blow up $c.9$ aircraft in mid-air between Britain and America had been foiled. $c.21$ were arrested in raids across Britain, and 7 were detained in Pakistan. ❦ It emerged that the plan involved the use of liquid explosives. In response, Britain raised its security state to *Critical* [see p.22], and airports adopted unprecedented security measures – refusing all hand luggage, save for a few small items, and prohibiting any liquids or gels on board. The US Homeland Security threat was raised to *Severe* (red) for UK flights bound for the US, and *High* (orange) for flights in or destined

for the US. ❦ The disclosure that all of those arrested were followers of, or recent converts to, Islam added to concerns about the radicalization of sections of the Muslim community. ❦ At the time of writing, a number of suspects had been charged in Britain (others remained in custody), and airport security had been relaxed only slightly.

Darfur Crisis

The conflict in the Darfur region of Sudan, waged since 2003, has killed >200,000 and created >2m refugees. Rebels in the south claim that the Sudanese government is actively oppressing black Africans in the area, in favour of the Arab population. It is further alleged that the Sudanese state supports the Janjaweed militia, who have been accused of grotesque violations of human rights in an attempt to 'ethnically cleanse' black African areas. Sudan's President Omar al-Bashir has denied links to the Janjaweed, but admits to creating militias to defend against rebel attacks. ❦ In May 2006, the Sudanese government signed a peace deal with some of the southern rebels, promising the possibility of a regional government. Additionally, rebel fighters in the south were to be incorporated into the army, in return for the Janjaweeed's disbandment. Within months, however, this fragile peace was overwhelmed by a return to violence. ❦ A number of organisations (including the US Congress) have described the slaughter in Darfur as 'genocide', though the UN has been notably reticent to use this term and, at the time of writing, states only that 'war crimes' have been committed. ❦ At the time of writing, the Sudanese government was under intense international pressure to accept a UN peacekeeping force of 20,000

─────── OTHER MAJOR STORIES IN BRIEF cont. ───────

troops to replace the ineffective African Union monitoring force of 7,000. ❦ On 17 September, hundreds of thousands demonstrated in an international day of protest against the genocide in Darfur – a protest supported by a myriad of politicians, religious leaders, musicians, and celebrities. One of the most vocal campaigners, Hollywood actor George Clooney, addressed the UN Security Council: 'it is the first genocide of the C21st and if it continues unchecked, it will not be the last'.

The TB–GBs

Speculation about when Tony Blair would retire has been intense since late 2004, when the PM announced that he would serve a full 3rd-term, but not stand for a 4th. However, the speculation reached fever pitch in August–September 2006. In an interview with the *Times*, Blair refused to specify when he would step down, prompting a barrage of thinly veiled attacks from Blair's critics and supporters of Gordon Brown. Days of internecine skirmishes across the media culminated in a series of letters calling on Blair to resign, and a number of junior resignations from government. ❦ In an attempt to end the infighting, which was embarrassingly juxtaposed with the Israel–Hezbollah crisis, Blair publicly apologised on behalf of his party: 'the last week, which, with everything that's been going on back here and in the world, has not been our finest hour, to be frank'. ❦ Brown's somewhat clumsy handling of the crisis was widely perceived to have damaged his hopes for a seamless and triumphant accession to Prime Minister. (He was even forced to explain a photograph of him smiling in his car as he left a supposedly difficult meeting in Downing Street.) ❦ Although, at the

time of writing, Brown's ascendancy appeared reasonably probable, a leadership challenge, possibly by John Reid or Alan Johnson, was being debated.

Pope Benedict XVI & Islam

On 12 September 2006, Benedict XVI gave an address to the University of Regensburg, Germany, entitled 'Faith, Reason and the University: Memories and Reflections'. The speech itself was somewhat academic and inaccessible, for example, 'this modern concept of reason is based, to put it briefly, on a synthesis between Platonism (Cartesianism) and empiricism, a synthesis confirmed by the success of technology'. However, in commenting on the subject of holy war, the Pope quoted the C14th Byzantine Emperor Manuel II Paleologus, who claimed that Muhammad had brought the world 'things only evil and inhumane'. In a reaction that had echoes of the Danish cartoon crisis [see p.19], Benedict XVI's words were condemned across much of the Muslim world. A number of governments (including Pakistan, Turkey, and Afghanistan) demanded the Pope retract his comments, and sporadic demonstrations broke out in Gaza, the West Bank, Iran, India, and elsewhere. Clearly surprised at the intensity of anger, the Vatican was forced to issue a clarification of the Pope's position. Yet, this statement did little to mollify the Pope's critics and, five days after making his speech, Benedict XVI apologised in person from the balcony of Castel Gandolfo: 'I wish also to add that I am deeply sorry for the reactions in some countries to a few passages of my address …'. However, as he apologised not for the words he quoted, but for the reaction to them of others, not all in the Muslim world were placated.

—————————————— ISRAEL, GAZA, & LEBANON ——————————————

In summer 2006, a long history of skirmishes along Israel's borders with Gaza and Lebanon escalated into a major conflict, after 3 Israeli soldiers were kidnapped in two separate raids that also left 10 Israeli soldiers dead. ❦ On June 25, Corporal Gilad Shalit was seized by Palestinian militants who tunnelled into Israel under the S. Gaza border. Rejecting as 'extortion' the kidnappers' demands for a prisoner swap, Israeli PM Ehud Olmert ordered attacks on Gaza and the arrest of dozens of Hamas politicians. On July 12, Hezbollah fighters in S. Lebanon launched a cross-border raid and kidnapped Israeli soldiers Ehud Goldwasser and Eldad Regev. Olmert declared this an 'act of war', and said that the Lebanese government (of which Hezbollah is a part) was 'responsible for the consequences'. His cabinet ordered 'severe and harsh' retaliation that would, in the words of one Israeli colonel, 'turn Lebanon's clock back 20 years'. In response, Hezbollah's leader, Hassan Nasrallah, promised 'open war' on Israel. ❦ Israel enforced an air and sea blockade of Lebanon, and for 34 days Israeli forces conducted thousands of air and ground attacks, hitting any targets they suspected of harbouring or helping Hezbollah. In retaliation, Hezbollah conducted guerila attacks, and indiscriminately fired thousands of rockets into densely populated northern Israeli cities. ❦ While the West denounced Hezbollah's provocation and defended Israel's right to self-defence, the scale of the Israeli response quickly drew condemnation – especially after bridges, roads, TV and phone antennas, water treatment centres, and powerplants were destroyed. Israel justified its attacks, claiming that Hezbollah was 'mixing in' with the general population and firing rockets from civilian locations. Israel insisted that, unlike Hezbollah, it did not deliberately target civilians, and even dropped leaflets warning of raids. But Israel's standing was not helped by attacks like that on the S. Lebanese village of Qana on July 30, when *c*.28 Lebanese civilians, including *c*.16 children, were killed; or by the negligent killing of 4 unarmed UN observers on July 25. Some described the magnitude of Israel's attacks (where *c*.10 Lebanese died for every Israeli) as 'disproportionate', and even as a 'collective punishment' – significantly, the Geneva Convention defines the latter as a war crime. ❦ As the fighting intensified, the international community moved slowly into action. A UN-led summit in Rome on July 26 failed to demand an immediate cease-fire, a decision that Israel claimed authorised their offensive. An 'immediate' cease-fire was supported by the UN, France, Germany, Italy, Spain, Greece, Jordan, Russia, Saudi Arabia, Canada, Egypt, and Cyprus; it was rejected by the US and Britain, who instead called for a 'sustainable' cease-fire. This crucial semantic difference effectively granted Israel 3 further weeks of attacks. In Britain, Blair again faced accusations of slavishly following US foreign policy; opponents of Bush condemned what they saw as his uncritical support of Israel. Some suggested that America viewed the conflict as a proxy war against Tehran and Damascus; Bush himself said 'responsibility for the suffering of the Lebanese people also lies with Hezbollah's state sponsors, Iran and Syria'. Writing in the *New Yorker*, Seymour Hersh claimed that the US 'was closely involved in the planning of Israel's retaliatory attacks'. ❦ On August 11, after intense negotiation, the UN Security Council approved Resolution 1701, which called for the 'full cessation of hostilities' and a 15,000-strong UN force to replace Israeli troops south of the River Litani. The resolution received a guarded welcome from Israel, Lebanon, and Hezbollah, and the cease-fire came into effect at 0500 GMT

——————— ISRAEL, GAZA, & LEBANON cont. ———————

on August 14. ❦ As *c.*600,000 refugees poured back into Lebanon, and tensions eased in Israel's northern towns, all sides claimed victory. Hezbollah, Syria, and Iran argued that Israel had been fought to a standstill, and Nasrallah mocked its 'failure and impotency'. Conversely, Bush boldly declared, 'Hezbollah started the crisis, and Hezbollah suffered a defeat in this crisis'. Olmert's reaction was muted by continuing insecurity in Gaza, a sharp swing in Israeli public opinion against his handling of the war, and surprise and anger at the shortcomings of Israel's army and intelligence. Olmert claimed that the 'strategic balance' in the region had shifted against Hezbollah, but he could not dodge his failure to achieve his stated war aims: to return the Israeli hostages, to disarm Hezbollah, and to secure S. Lebanon. ❦ At the time of writing, the fragile cease-fire was holding, despite skirmishes on both sides. However, the formation of the UN's peacekeeping mission was beset by delays and disputes as to the composition of the force and its precise mandate.

As of 24·8·06, Israel claimed that 43 Israeli civilians had died and c.1,340 had been wounded; 119 Israeli soldiers had died and c.400 had been wounded. Hezbollah reported that 74 of its soldiers had been killed; however Israel claimed >500. The Lebanese government claimed that c.1,130 civilians had been killed, and c.3,800 injured. According to the BBC, at the time of the cease-fire on August 14, Israel had hit c.7,000 targets in air strikes, and c.3,700 Hezbollah rockets had landed in Israel.

Hezbollah kidnappings

Approximate range of most Hezbollah rockets

≈ deepest Hezbollah rocket attack in Israel

Shalit kidnapped

Tripoli

LEBANON

Baalbek

Beirut

River Litani

Sayda

Damascus

Tyre

Qana

Golan Heights

SYRIA

Haifa

Sea of Galilee

Hadera

Tel Aviv

W. BANK

Amman

Jerusalem

JORDAN

Gaza

GAZA

Dead Sea

Rafah

ISRAEL

EGYPT

0 miles   30

——————— PROFILE: MAHMOUD AHMADINEJAD ———————

Since becoming President of Iran in August 2005, Mahmoud Ahmadinejad has adopted a provocative stance. He has questioned the Nazi Holocaust, demanded the elimination of Israel and the resettlement of all Israelis, insinuated a US conspiracy over 9/11, fomented the crisis between Israel and Hezbollah, insisted that Iran has the right to a peaceful programme for nuclear power, and threatened that this programme may not remain peaceful if Iran is attacked. Yet, his speeches and interviews (and his personal letter to George W. Bush) are embellished with exhortations to harmony, peace, justice, spirituality, equality, compassion, and tranquility. In 2006, this (calculatedly?) mercurial mix of firebrand and philosopher fortified his position on the world stage. ❧ Ahmadinejad was born in 1956, in a small village near Garmsar, the fourth son of a blacksmith and one of seven children. He moved with his family to Tehran, where he attended school. In 1975 he was admitted to study civil engineering at Tehran's Science and Technology University (where he obtained a PhD in traffic and transportation in 1997). Uncertainty surrounds Ahmadinejad's activities during the 1979 Revolution and the 1980–88 Iran-Iraq War. His official biography states he engaged in 'political activities' and 'was actively present as a member of the [Revolutionary Guard] in different parts and divisions of the battlefronts'. Other accounts allege involvement in covert operations in Iraq, assassinations of dissidents, and executions in Tehran's bloody Evin prison. (The US claims he led the seizing of the American embassy in Tehran in 1979.) After serving regional governorships in the 1980s, Ahmadinejad was appointed Mayor of Tehran in 2003, where he reversed many earlier reforms, closing fast-food restaurants, requiring women to use separate elevators, ordering male city employees to wear beards, &c. (In 2005, Ahmadinejad was a finalist in the World Mayor contest, alongside London's Mayor Ken Livingstone.) ❧ Ahmadinejad's deliberately modest 2005 Presidential bid focused on Islam, social justice, poverty, and corruption. But he also used the campaign to attack the US and challenge the UN, which he said was 'stacked against the Islamic world'. To the surprise of many, he beat ex-President Rafsanjani, 62% to 36%. At his inauguration, Ahmadinejad demonstrated his loyalty (and subjugation?) to Iran's Supreme Leader by kissing Ayatollah Khamenei's hand – an unusual public gesture of respect. ❧ Ahmadinejad's domestic policy has combined reaction (banning Western music) with reform (allowing women to watch sports), and he continues to struggle with Iran's economic inequalities and poverty. But it is internationally that Ahmadinejad has made his mark, strengthening relations with Islamic neighbours, fixing deals with China and Russia, and challenging the West by pursuing a nuclear fuel cycle. Time will tell whether Ahmadinejad's defiance of the IAEA is designed to extract concessions and credibility from the West, or to give Iran time to weaponise its research. If the latter, the US commitment to neutralise the threat may be circumscribed by overstretch in Afghanistan and Iraq, and by the ability of a weakened President to persuade the world that *this* time WMD exist. Israel, however, will be unlikely to feel any such constraints.

—SCHEMATIC · SOME WORLD EVENTS OF NOTE · 2006—

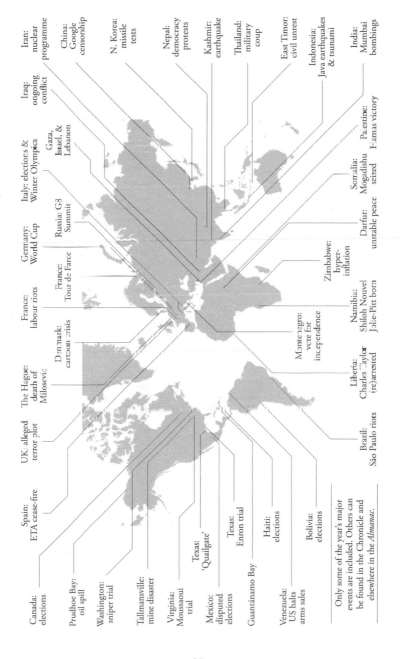

Iran: nuclear programme

China: Google censorship

N. Korea: missile tests

Nepal: democracy protests

Kashmir: earthquake

Thailand: military coup

East Timor: civil unrest

Indonesia: Java earthquakes & tsunami

India: Mumbai bombings

Iraq: ongoing conflict

Gaza, Israel, & Lebanon

Palestine: Hamas victory

Italy: elections & Winter Olympics

Somalia: Mogadishu seized

Russia: G8 Summit

Darfur: unstable peace

Germany: World Cup

Zimbabwe: hyperinflation

France: Tour de Farce

Namibia: Shiloh Nouvel Jolie-Pitt born

France: labour riots

Denmark: cartoon crisis

Montenegro: vote for independence

The Hague: death of Milosevic

Liberia: Charles Taylor (re)arrested

UK: alleged terror plot

Brazil: São Paulo riots

Spain: ETA cease-fire

Canada: elections

Prudhoe Bay: oil spill

Washington: sniper trial

Tallmansville: mine disaster

Virginia: Moussaoui trial

Texas: 'Quailgate'

Texas: Enron trial

Haiti: elections

Bolivia: elections

Mexico: disputed elections

Guantánamo Bay

Venezuela: US halts arms sales

Only some of the year's major events are included. Others can be found in the Chronicle and elsewhere in the *Almanac*.

IN BRIEF · SEPTEMBER – OCTOBER 2005

The daily chronicle below picks up from the 2006 edition of Schott's Almanac.

SEPTEMBER · {19} British forces in Basra stormed a police station to rescue 2 British soldiers held by militia. ❦ After an inconclusive German general election, the main parties began manoeuvring to form a ruling coalition; both Merkel and Schroeder claimed the position of Chancellor. {20} CCTV pictures released to the public showed the 7/7 bombers making a 'dummy run' weeks before their attacks. ❦ RIP @ 96 Simon Wiesenthal. {21} As Hurricane Rita advanced, Mayor of Houston, Bill White, announced an evacuation. ❦ Met Police Cmsr Sir Ian Blair backed an investigation into Kate Moss' alleged cocaine abuse. {22} Hussain Osman was extradited from Italy, and charged with taking part in the failed 21/7 bomb attack on London. ❦ Cars hit grid-lock fleeing Hurricane Rita. {23} The widow of Germaine Lindsay, one of the 7/7 bombers, told the *Sun* she strongly condemned the attacks, and claimed her husband had been brainwashed by extremists. {24} Hurricane Rita hit the Gulf Coast; it had dropped to a Category 1 storm, but still caused extensive damage. ❦ Israel launched air strikes against Gaza, its first such attack since withdrawing; >2 members of Hamas were reported to have been killed. {26} The head of the arms decommissioning body in N. Ireland, General John de Chastelain, announced he was satisfied that the IRA had decommissioned all its weapons. ❦ At the Labour Party conference, members of

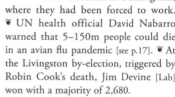

Kate Moss

the Cabinet indicated their approval for Gordon Brown to replace Tony Blair. {27} Al-Qaeda's alleged second in command in Iraq, Abu Azzam, was killed a US-Iraqi attack. ❦ US soldier Private Lynndie England was jailed for 3 years for her part in the Abu Ghraib prison abuse. {29} David Cameron and David Davis both launched bids for the leadership of the Conservative party. ❦ The Soham murderer, Ian Huntley, was sentenced to 40 years in prison after changes in the setting of tariffs delayed his sentencing. {30} 19 Eastern European women were rescued from a brothel in Birmingham, where they had been forced to work. ❦ UN health official David Nabarro warned that 5–150m people could die in an avian flu pandemic [see p.17]. ❦ At the Livingston by-election, triggered by Robin Cook's death, Jim Devine [Lab] won with a majority of 2,680.

OCTOBER · {1} 3 bombs hit restaurants in Bali, killing >19 and injuring many more. ❦ Aid agencies warned that up to half the population of Malawi faced starvation after maize crops failed. {2} The Bali attacks were blamed on suicide bombers, possibly from Jemaah Islamiah, targeting Western tourists. {3} The EU opened membership talks with Turkey after attempts by Austria to block full membership failed. ❦ The chemist Boots announced a merger with rival Alliance UniChem; the deal was worth £7bn, and would result in *c*.1,000 job losses. ❦ RIP @ 76 Ronnie Barker [see p.56]. {5} >3,000 were sacked by the City of New Orleans after Katrina devastated the local economy. ❦ Loyalist leader Jim

The consequences [of a bird flu pandemic] *in terms of human life ... are going to be extraordinary.* – DAVID NABARRO

——— IN BRIEF · OCTOBER 2005 ———

Gray was murdered on his Belfast doorstep. {6} >1,000 died in Guatemala after hurricane Stan; mudslides turned villages into mass graves. {8} A 7·6 earthquake shook India, Pakistan, and Afghanistan; initial reports suggested >3,000 deaths [see p.16]. {9} Pakistan's President Musharraf called for international aid, after the death toll from the earthquake was estimated at *c*.19,000. {11} Romanian officials culled thousands of farmyard birds after fears of bird flu. ❦ Aid arrived in the Kashmir region amidst criticisms of delays. ❦ After weeks of wrangling, Gerhard Schroeder agreed to stand down as Germany's Chancellor, effectively handing the position to Angela Merkel. {12} Tony Blair pledged £12m in aid for the areas of India and Pakistan affected by the earthquake; the British public raised £2m. {13} Tests showed the presence of avian flu virus H5 in Romanian ducks, the first outbreak in Europe; as a precaution, the EU banned all bird products from Romania. {15} The Pakistani government raised the earthquake death toll to *c*.38,000. {17} Joanne Lees gave evidence to an Australian court about the death of her boyfriend Peter Falconio; Bradley Murdoch was accused of abducting Lees and murdering Falconio, whose body was never found. ❦ Bird flu was found in a turkey in Greece. {18} Ken Clarke was knocked out of the Tory leadership race [see p.252]. {19} Saddam Hussein defiantly pleaded not guilty at his trial in Iraq. {20} Liam Fox was eliminated from the Tory party leadership, leaving Cameron and Davis. {21} Hurricane Wilma hit Mexico at Category 4. {22} A parrot that died in quarantine was confirmed as Britain's first case of avian flu [see p.17]. {23} Riots between Afro-Caribbean and Asian communities in Birmingham, sparked by the alleged rape of an asylum seeker by a Pakistani shop owner, left one man dead. ❦ A plane crash in Nigeria killed all 117 on board.

Angela Merkel

{24} Hurricane Wilma hit Florida at Category 3, having killed 17 across the Caribbean. {25} RIP @ 92 Rosa Parks, American civil rights activist. {26} An Iraqi referendum approved a draft constitution. ❦ The death toll of US soldiers killed in Iraq exceeded 2,000 [see p.24] ❦ China announced another outbreak of bird flu after 545 birds died in a village in Hunan Province. {27} George Best was reported to be close to death in a London hospital. ❦ Harriet Miers, the Texan lawyer nominated to the US Supreme Court by George W. Bush, stepped down after criticism from Republicans and Democrats over her lack of judicial experience. ❦ Youths in Paris rioted after the deaths of two teenagers were blamed on the police. {28} Lewis Libby, a top aide to US Vice President Dick Cheney, resigned after being accused of perjury over his part in naming a CIA agent. {29} >50 killed and many injured after bombs exploded in 2 Delhi markets.

I am deeply saddened that some people had to wait days before aid reached them. – PRESIDENT MUSHARRAF

{30} The Conservative party called for an inquiry into David Blunkett's conduct, after it emerged he had taken on the directorship of a DNA company after resigning from the Home Office, without consulting an independent advisory committee. {31} A group calling themselves Inqilabi claimed responsibility for the bomb attacks in Delhi, and said they were designed to force India to end its involvement in Kashmir.

─── IN BRIEF · NOVEMBER 2005 ───

NOVEMBER · {1} A memorial service for those killed on 7/7 was held at St Paul's. ❦ Blunkett faced continued pressure over his failure to report his jobs outside the Cabinet; he denied wrongdoing and refused to resign. ❦ Charles and Camilla began an official visit to America. ❦ Champion horse Best Mate died suddenly during a race at Haldon Gold Cup, Exeter. {2} David Blunkett resigned as Work & Pensions Secretary. ❦ After >5 nights of violence, the rioting in Parisian suburbs became more widespread. ❦ The 3rd trial of Sion

David Blunkett

Jenkins for the murder of Billie-Jo Jenkins began. {3} The trial of 7 British soldiers facing court martial over the death of an Iraqi boy in their custody collapsed due to insufficient evidence. ❦ The editor of the *Sun,* Rebekah Wade, was arrested after allegedly assaulting her husband, Ross Kemp. {4} Rioting in Paris spread to other parts of France. ❦ >45 Muslim graves were damaged after an attack on a Birmingham cemetery. {5} 11 were injured after a firework hit a crowd in Northamptonshire. ❦ RIP @ 79 author John Fowles. {6} >21 died when a tornado hit Indiana, US, and destroyed a trailer park. {8} Australian police claimed to have foiled a major terrorist plot after 16 were arrested in Sydney and Melbourne. ❦ The French government approved curfews to halt 12 days of rioting across France. {9} >57 died in 3 simultaneous bomb attacks on hotels in Amman, Jordan. ❦ Blair suffered his first Commons defeat, over controversial plans to introduce 90-day detention for suspected terrorists. ❦ The Republicans suffered losses in the US state and local elections; in NY, Republican mayor Michael Bloomberg was returned with a large majority. {10} Al-Qaeda claimed responsibility for the Jordanian bombings. ❦ >30 died in a suicide attack on a Baghdad restaurant. {11} RIP @ 66 Lord Lichfield. {13} The Queen led tributes at the Cenotaph Remembrance Day service. ❦ Iraqi President Jalal Talabani predicted that British troops could be out of Iraq by the end of 2006. {15} The Conservatives failed to halt legislation allowing pubs to extend their opening hours. {16} America admitted it had used white phosphorus (a chemical that can cause burning of the flesh) against Iraqi insurgents. ❦ The Americans called for an investigation, after 170 prisoners held by Iraqi forces showed signs of malnourishment and torture. {18} French police announced a return to normality after 3 weeks of rioting, in which >9,000 cars were torched and 2,921 people were arrested. ❦ Newspaper tycoon Conrad Black was accused of a number of counts of fraud, including diverting $84m from Hollinger International; Black denied all charges. ❦ The extent of Iranian president Ahmadinejad's purge of government officials and institutions became apparent, after some Iranian sources branded his actions a *coup d'état* [see p.32]. ❦ A policewoman was shot dead and another injured after responding to an armed robbery in Bradford. ❦ Martin Newland resigned as editor of the *Daily Telegraph.* {19} >50 killed in a wave of bomb attacks by insurgents across Iraq. ❦ Gary Glitter was arrested in Vietnam in connection with alleged sex offences against children. {20} The murdered Bradford policewoman

> *There is not one Iraqi that wants that forever the troops remain in the country* [sic]. – JALAL TALABANI

—— IN BRIEF · NOVEMBER – DECEMBER 2005 ——

was named as mother of 3, Sharon Beshenivsky; 5 were arrested in London in connection with her killing. ❦ George Best was re-admitted to intensive care. {21} Ariel Sharon announced he was leaving Israel's governing party, Likud, to form a new party ahead of elections. ❦ It was announced that the number of people estimated to be living with HIV worldwide had risen to a record 40·3m. {22} Christian Democrat leader, Angela Merkel, was sworn in as Germany's first female Chancellor. ❦ The British government obtained injunctions to prevent publication of a leaked memo which alleged Blair dissuaded Bush from bombing the Arabic TV station Aljazeera. ❦ The CPS announced that the prime suspect in the stabbing of Abigail Witchalls, Richard Cazaly, would have faced prosecution had he not killed himself days after the attack. {23} New licensing laws came into force which allowed pubs and clubs to extend their opening hours. {24} The water supply in the Chinese city of Harbin was shut off, after an explosion at a chemical factory caused a nearby river to become contaminated. ❦ A rape case collapsed after the 21-year-old victim admitted being too drunk to remember whether she had consented to sex; the judge declared that drunken consent was still consent. ❦ A Foreign Office report admitted mistakes were made in the aftermath of the Asian tsunami, with phone lines overwhelmed and help slow to arrive. ❦ RIP @ 73 Noriyuki 'Pat' Morita, Mr Miyagi in *The Karate Kid*. {25} Snow fell across the UK: 8cm in parts of Scotland, 5cm in Swansea. ❦ RIP @ 59 George Best. ❦ Gary Glitter was jailed in

There are significant problems in our pensions system.
— TURNER REPORT

George Best

Vietnam for 4 months while child abuse allegations were investigated. {26} A 5·7 earthquake killed >15 in China's Jiangxi province. {27} A British aid worker, Prof. Norman Kember, two Canadians, and an American were kidnapped in Iraq. ❦ The *News of the World* published images that appeared to show British Marines involved in an initiation ceremony in which soldiers fought each other naked. {28} The trial of Saddam Hussein resumed in Baghdad. ❦ 2 British pilgrims were killed near Baghdad. {30} The much anticipated Turner Report on pensions was published; it proposed a gradual rise in the state pension age to 68. ❦ A video showing Norman Kember and his fellow hostages was released; his captors claimed Kember was a spy. ❦ A 19-year-old man was charged with the murder of WPC Beshenivsky. ❦ Surgeons in France carried out the first human face transplant.

DECEMBER · {1} Shimon Peres quit Israel's Labour party to support Ariel Sharon in his re-election bid. ❦ The cousins found guilty of the racially motivated murder of Anthony Walker were sentenced: Paul Taylor to 23 years, Michael Barton to 17. {2} America carried out its 1,000th execution since re-introducing capital punishment in 1976. {3} George Best's funeral was held at Stormont, Belfast. {5} Gordon Brown announced in his pre-budget speech that his estimate of growth in 2005 was too generous; he halved it to 1·75%. ❦ The first witness in Saddam Hussein's trial described torture and murder in his Shia village of Dujail. ❦ A mass inquest into

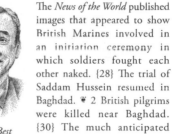

─────── IN BRIEF · DECEMBER 2005 ───────

the UK victims of the 2005 Tsunami opened in London. ❦ Simon Starling won the Turner Prize [see p.165]. {6} An Iranian military plane crashed, killing >90. ❦ Dame Kelly Holmes announced her retirement. ❦ David Cameron won the Conservative leadership [see p.252]. {7} Saddam refused to return to the courtroom for the continuation of his trial. {7} Law Lords ruled that evidence gained through torture was not admissible in British courts. ❦ Al-Qaeda leader, Abu Qatada, held in a British jail on terrorism charges, made a video plea to Norman Kember's captors requesting his release. ❦ The 25th anniversary of John Lennon's death was marked. {9} Nearly all Routemaster buses were withdrawn from service in London. ❦ England were drawn against Paraguay, Trinidad & Tobago, and Sweden in the football World Cup. {10} At a climate-control summit in Montreal, signatories to the Kyoto Protocol agreed to set new targets for greenhouse gas emissions once the treaty ends in 2012. America conceded to non-binding talks on climate change. ❦ RIP @ 65 Richard Pryor [see p.56]. {11} The Buncefield oil depot in Hemel Hempstead exploded, injuring *c.*43, and causing extensive damage; thick smoke billowed across the southeast. {12} Fire crews in Hemel Hempstead continued to fight the Buncefield blaze. ❦ Rioting erupted between White and Middle-Eastern youths in the beach suburb of Cronulla in Sydney, Australia. {13} Fire crews at Buncefield extinguished all but 3 of the 20 burning oil tanks. ❦ After pleas for clemency failed, Stanley 'Tookie' Williams (founder of the Crips gang) was executed

David Cameron

If he is not found quickly he will die, as he relies on his parents for food.
– KATHERINE BRIGHT on Toga

by lethal injection in California. ❦ After a second night of rioting in Sydney, police were given new powers to control the situation. ❦ World Trade Organisation (WTO) talks began in Hong Kong amidst anti-globalisation protests. ❦ Australian Bradley Murdoch was found guilty of murdering British backpacker Peter Falconio and abducting his girlfriend, Joanne Lees. He was sentenced to life. {14} The British government was widely criticised for refusing to hold an inquiry into 7/7. {15} Iraqis went to the polls to elect their first full-time government. {16} Denis Donaldson was expelled from Sinn Féin after admitting to have been a British spy for >20 years. ❦ President Bush was accused of allowing National Security agents to wire-tap US citizens. {17} A 2·1 tonnes bronze Henry Moore sculpture, worth £3m, was stolen from a museum in Hertfordshire. ❦ Blair was criticised for giving up £1bn of the UK's rebate in EU budget talks. {18} A modest WTO deal was reached in Hong Kong; Europe agreed to end farm export subsidies by 2013. ❦ Ariel Sharon suffered a small stroke. {19} A N. Irish couple, Shannon Sickles and Grainne Close, became the first people in the UK to enter into a same-sex civil partnership [see p.97]. ❦ Evo Morales won the Bolivian presidential election, becoming the first indigenous Indian to lead the country since the end of Spanish rule. {20} Binyamin Netanyahu, former Israeli PM, became leader of the right-wing Likud party. ❦ A baby penguin named Toga was stolen from an Isle of Wight zoo; his parents were reported to be pining. {21} Elton John and David Furnish married in Windsor on the first

——— IN BRIEF · DECEMBER 2005 - JANUARY 2006 ———

day same-sex civil partnerships became legal in England. {22} Tony Blair made a surprise Christmas visit to British troops in Basra. ❦ New fishing quotas were agreed after 3 days of EU talks; cod fishing was cut by 5% to protect stocks. {25} The Queen made her Christmas Day broadcast [see p.277]. {26} The first anniversary of the Asian tsunami was marked around the world. {27} RIP @ 68 media magnate Kerry Packer. {28} British aid worker Kate Burton and her parents were kidnapped in Gaza. ❦ A 6-year-old girl was found naked in the street after being abducted from her bath in Tyneside. {29} A Serbian soldier, Slobodan Davidovic, was jailed for 15 years for his part in the 1995 massacre of Muslims in Srebrenica. {30} Kate Burton and her parents were released by their captors in Palestine. {31} Tube strikes in London disrupted New Year's Eve travel. ❦ Ashes cricketers and emergency workers from 7/7 were recognised in the New Year's Honours list [see p.279].

George Galloway

J ANUARY 2006 · {1} Russia halted gas supplies to Ukraine, after Ukraine refused to pay a fourfold price increase. {2} 21-year-old student Katherine Horton was found murdered on the Thai island of Koh Samui. ❦ 13 men were trapped underground after an explosion at a mine in West Virginia, US. {3} Senior Lib Dem Lord McNally criticised Charles Kennedy amidst ongoing debate over his leadership. {4} Celebrations in West Virginia were cut short when it transpired that an early report was wrong, and 12 out of the 13 miners had died, rather than survived. ❦ Russia and Ukraine reached a

I've been coming to terms with and seeking to cope with a drink problem.
– CHARLES KENNEDY

deal, alleviating the gas crisis. ❦ RIP @ 62 Sheikh Maktoum, ruler of Dubai. ❦ >200 died after landslides engulfed villages in E. Java. ❦ The US Congress came under scrutiny after lobbyist Jack Abramoff pleaded guilty to fraud, conspiracy, and tax evasion. Under the terms of his plea bargain, Abramoff agreed to help prosecutors uncover corrupt lawmakers. {5} 2 teenagers in Turkey died of bird flu – the first human fatalities outside SE Asia. ❦ Sharon's condition was described as 'severe' after he suffered a major stroke. ❦ >50 died in a suicide bombing in Karbala, Iraq. ❦ Charles Kennedy admitted to struggling with alcoholism, and called a leadership election to re-establish his position. ❦ MP George Galloway entered the Celebrity Big Brother house. {6} Gary Glitter was charged with committing obscene acts with two young Vietnamese girls; a charge of rape was dropped due to lack of evidence. {7} Kennedy resigned as Lib Dem leader after failing to secure support from his MPs; deputy leader Sir Menzies Campbell announced he would stand [see p.253]. {8} RIP @ 62 Tony Banks, former Labour sports minister. {9} 5 further human cases of bird flu were identified in Turkey. ❦ 2 Thai men were arrested after DNA evidence linked them to the rape and murder of British backpacker Katherine Horton. ❦ Crisp company Golden Wonder went into administration [see p.203]. {10} Mark Oaten announced that he would stand for the Lib Dem leadership. {11} Blair warned that Iran could be referred to the UN Security Council for resuming nuclear activity. ❦ The trial of Muslim cleric Abu Hamza opened at the Old

IN BRIEF · JANUARY 2006

Bailey. {12} Education Sec. Ruth Kelly faced questions in the Commons, after it was claimed she had allowed a registered sex offender to work in a school. {13} >350 pilgrims were killed in a stampede at the Hajj [see p.290]. {14} A US airstrike on a Pakistani village, intended to target an Al-Qaeda leader, killed 18 innocent locals. {15} A *News of the World* 'fake Sheikh' sting targeted Sven-Göran Eriksson, encouraging him to consider job offers and comment on players. {16} Ellen Johnson-Sirleaf was sworn in as Africa's first female president, after beating former footballer George Weah in the Liberian elections. ❧ Michelle Bachelet became Chile's first female President. {17} Gordon Brown announced that his wife Sarah was pregnant. {18} 2 Thai fisherman were sentenced to death for the rape and murder of British backpacker Katherine Horton. ❧ A plot to kidnap Blair's youngest son was uncovered by the police; a radical wing of the group Fathers for Justice was implicated. ❧ Japan's stock exchange closed early, for the first time in its history, in an attempt to stem heavy selling. {19} Ruth Kelly announced that anyone cautioned or charged with sexual offences would be banned from working in schools. ❧ A report into the shooting of Jean Charles de Menezes was given to the CPS, pending a decision on whether any police officers would be charged in relation to his death. ❧ Mark Oaten withdrew from the Lib Dem leadership contest, citing a lack of support. ❧ Aljazeera aired an audio-tape in which Osama bin Laden threatened further attacks on America, while offering the possibility of a truce. {20} A 17ft bottle-nosed whale was spotted in the

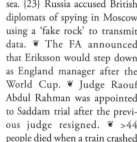

Chantelle

Thames. ❧ RIP @ 64 Wilson Pickett [see p.56]. {21} Mark Oaten stood down as Lib Dem home affairs spokesman [see p.253]. ❧ Crowds lined the Thames to watch an attempt to save the stranded whale; it died before it could be released into the sea. {23} Russia accused British diplomats of spying in Moscow using a 'fake rock' to transmit data. ❧ The FA announced that Eriksson would step down as England manager after the World Cup. ❧ Judge Raouf Abdul Rahman was appointed to Saddam trial after the previous judge resigned. ❧ >44 people died when a train crashed into a ravine in Serbia-Montenegro. {25} Palestinians went to the polls. ❧ A postmortem on the Thames whale revealed it died from dehydration and muscle damage. ❧ George Galloway was evicted from the Big Brother house to a chorus of boos. ❧ RIP @ 43 Chris Penn, Hollywood actor. {26} Hamas won a majority in the Palestinian elections; PM Ahmed Qurei resigned, leaving Hamas to form a new government. ❧ Lib Dem leadership candidate Simon Hughes admitted to gay relationships in his past. ❧ Saudi Arabia recalled its ambassador to Denmark over the Muhammad cartoon row [see p.19]. {27} Israel rejected diplomatic relations with Hamas. ❧ Celebrity Big Brother took a post-modern turn, when the only non-famous person in the house, Chantelle Houghton, won. {28} In a new video of hostage Norman Kember, his captors demanded the release of Iraqi prisoners. {29} The roof of an exhibition centre in Poland collapsed under the weight of snow; 66 died. {31} The EU, US, China, and Russia agreed that Iran should be referred to the UN

> *Peace is not the problem.*
> *The problem is the Israeli occupation.*
> – ISMAIL HANIYA, Hamas official

————— IN BRIEF · JANUARY – FEBRUARY 2006 —————

Security Council for its nuclear activity [see p.32]. ❦ A British soldier was killed in a roadside attack in Umm Qas, the 100th British death since the Iraq conflict began. ❦ Kofi Annan said that UN aid to the Palestinian Authority was dependant on Hamas recognising Israel and committing to peace. ❦ The Government suffered two defeats in the Commons on a controversial 'race hate' bill. ❦ A number of Muslim countries imposed sanctions against Denmark [see p.19]. ❦ RIP @ 78 Coretta King, widow of Martin Luther King Jr.

Abu Hamza

that Omar Khayam was a convicted drug dealer who had been released early from jail; police deemed that he had broken the terms of his licence, and he was returned to jail. ❦ >12 died in bomb blast in Kandahar, Afghanistan. ❦ Scientists announced the discovery of a virtually untouched area of jungle in Indonesian Papua; many new species had been discovered, including 20 frogs and 4 butterflies. ❦ Muslim cleric Abu Hamza was found guilty on 11 charges of inciting murder and race hate; he was sentenced to 7 years. {9} Bird flu was discovered in Nigeria; Africa's first case. ❦ Sion Jenkins was formally acquitted of the murder of his foster daughter Billie-Jo, after a third trial. ❦ RIP @ 84 ex-England manager Ron Greenwood. ❦ George W. Bush revealed details of a foiled 2002 plot to fly planes into LA's tallest building. {10} Labour suffered a shock defeat in the Dunfermline and West Fife by-election, Lib Dem Willie Rennie secured a 1,800 majority. ❦ RIP @ 83 Sir Freddie Laker. ❦ The Winter Olympics opened in Turin [see p.296]. {12} Bird flu was found in wild migratory swans in Italy. ❦ The *News of The World* published images that appeared to show British troops assaulting 4 young Iraqis after a riot in 2004. {13} US Vice President Dick Cheney accidentally shot his friend Harry Whittington in the face, while quail hunting. {14} A female police officer was shot and injured during a robbery in Nottingham. {15} MPs voted for a total ban on smoking in all pubs and clubs. ❦ Protests over the Muhammad cartoons continued across the Muslim world: 3 died in Pakistan. ❦ New images of American

F EBRUARY · {1} In his State of the Union address, Bush warned that America was 'addicted' to oil and should seek alternative energy sources. {2} Shell reported record profits of £13·12b. ❦ The editor of *France Soir* was sacked after reprinting cartoons of Muhammad. ❦ BNP leader Nick Griffin and his colleague Mark Collett were cleared of race hate charges, pending a retrial on 4 further charges. {3} An Egyptian ferry carrying 1,400 passengers sank in the Red Sea; >300 were rescued. ❦ Damien Hanson was jailed for 36 years for murdering the banker John Monckton and injuring his wife during a burglary at their Chelsea home. ❦ At a demo in London against the Danish cartoons, protesters waved placards glorifying the 7/7 attacks, and one dressed as a suicide bomber. {4} The IAEA [see p.62] voted to report Iran to the UN Security Council. {6} 2 were killed during cartoon protests in Afghanistan. ❦ The British Muslim, Omar Khayam, who dressed as a suicide bomber at a London protest, apologised for his actions. {7} It was revealed

America is addicted to oil, which is often imported from unstable parts of the world. – GEORGE W. BUSH

──────── IN BRIEF · FEBRUARY – MARCH 2006 ────────

abuse in Abu Ghraib prison were broadcast on Australian TV. {17} A mudslide hit the Philippine village of Guinsaugon; hundreds were feared dead, and >1,500 were missing. ❦ Cabinet minister Peter Hain called for Guantánamo Bay to be shut, after a UN report that said many of the its practices were tantamount to torture [see p.20]. ❦ British Gas announced it was raising prices by 22%, in response to a 70% rise in wholesale energy costs. {19} Bird flu was discovered in France. ❦ Israel announced it would withhold tax payments to the Palestinian Authority, in response to the *Menzies Campbell* election of Hamas. ❦ 16 died in Nigerian riots over the Danish cartoons. ❦ Tessa Jowell's husband, David Mills, denied taking a bribe to give a false testimony for Italian PM Silvio Berlusconi. {20} British historian David Irving was jailed for 3 years in Austria for Holocaust denial [see p.63]. ❦ Andy Murray won his first ATP title, beating Leyton Hewitt in the final of the SAP San Jose Open. ❦ The average price of a home in England and Wales rose above £200,000 for the first time. {21} The FA announced that Wembley Stadium would not be ready in time for the FA Cup final, which would instead move to Cardiff. ❦ Tower of London ravens were taken indoors to protect them from bird flu. ❦ Mark Bolland, Prince Charles' former secretary, claimed in a witness statement given in connection with the Prince's case against the *Daily Mail*, that Prince Charles saw himself as a dissident working against the prevailing political consensus. {22} A bomb attack by insurgents in Samarra, Iraq, damaged one of the most holy Shia shrines, sparking widespread unrest between Sunnis and Shias. {23} In Britain's largest bank robbery, thieves stole *c*.£50m from a Securitas depot in Tonbridge, Kent. {24} Concerns were raised that Iraq was descending into civil war, after >130 were killed in sectarian attacks on Sunnis. ❦ 3 were arrested in connection with the Tonbridge raid. ❦ The Philippine government declared a state of emergency, after it was revealed it had foiled an attempted coup. ❦ Ken Livingstone was suspended as London Mayor for 4 weeks by adjudicators, after allegedly comparing a journalist to a concentration camp guard. The suspension was frozen by a High Court judge pending the Mayor's appeal against the adjudication panel's decision. {25} Hundreds marched in favour of building a new animal testing biomedical research centre in Oxford [see p.88]. {27} The High Court heard the initial submissions in *The Da Vinci Code* trial [see p.163]. ❦ In France, *c*.1m free-range ducks and geese were vaccinated against the H5N1 virus. ❦ The trial of Serbia for genocide against the people of Bosnia-Hercegovina opened at the International Court of Justice. {28} 2 British soldiers died in a roadside attack in Iraq. ❦ RIP @ 48 much-loved comedienne Linda Smith.

Safe pair of hands yes, but ready to take risks, ready to challenge orthodoxy.
– MENZIES CAMPBELL

MARCH · {2} Sir Menzies Campbell won the Lib Dem leadership [see p.253]. ❦ Blair cleared Tessa Jowell of breaching the Ministerial Code, after she denied knowledge of a £344,000 gift her husband had received. {3} Gary Glitter was imprisoned for 3 years by a Vietnamese court for abusing 2 girls. ❦

─── IN BRIEF · MARCH 2006 ───

Millions of pounds were found in a garage in SE London, after a raid in connection with the Tonbridge robbery. ❦ In an interview with Michael Parkinson, Blair said that he prayed to God for guidance over the decision to send troops into Iraq. {4} Tessa Jowell separated from her husband, David Mills. {6} The trial of 9/11 conspirator Zacarias Moussaoui opened in Virginia. ❦ 3 British climbers died in the Spanish Sierra Nevada mountains. {7} A further tape of hostage Norman Kember was aired on Aljazeera, raising hopes for his release. {8} The 10-year ban on exporting British beef to Europe was lifted. ❦ The Parliamentary Standards watchdog cleared Tessa Jowell over her failure to declare shares owned by her estranged husband. ❦ The IAEA referred its report on Iran's nuclear ambitions to the UN Security Council. {10} RIP @ 91 John Profumo. ❦ Michael Jackson was ordered to close his Neverland ranch after he failed to pay his staff. ❦ >250 doctors from 7 nations signed a letter condemning the US force-feeding of prisoners on hunger strike at Guantánamo Bay. ❦ Tom Fox, the US hostage held with Norman Kember, was found shot dead. {11} Former Yugoslav president Slobodan Milosevic was found dead in his cell in the Hague. {12} An Australian shepherd dog won Crufts [see p.226]. ❦ RIP @ 61, Celtic and Scotland legend, Jimmy Johnstone. {13} Thames Water announced a hosepipe and sprinkler ban to its 8m customers. ❦ Preliminary autopsy results concluded that Slobodan Milosevic died from a heart attack. ❦ Families of victims marked the 10th anniversary of the Dunblane massacre. ❦ John Reid

Slobodan Milosevic

We hope Iran will co-operate closely with the IAEA. – LI ZHAOXING
Chinese Foreign Minister

announced that 800 British troops would withdraw from Iraq. ❦ Work began on the tribute to the victims of 9/11 at 'Ground Zero'. {14} Israeli soldiers stormed a Palestinian prison and seized a prisoner accused of murdering an Israeli minister. Violence erupted across the region, mainly against interests of Britain and America which were condemned for withdrawing their monitors from the prison just prior to the attack. {15} 6 men were admitted to hospital after taking part in a clinical drugs trial in London. ❦ The 18th Commonwealth Games opened in Melbourne [see p.298]. {16} The drug company responsible for the London trial that went wrong apologised to the families of the victims. ❦ A Bill that would give schools greater control over admissions and budgets was voted through (458 to 115) – but only with Conservative support. ❦ The US launched an operation targeting insurgents in Samarra; it was reported to be the largest air operation since the invasion began in 2003. {17} Claims emerged that Labour accepted £14m of secret loans to fund its election campaign; the party pledged to name benefactors after accusations that donors had been rewarded with peerages [see p.27]. ❦ 5 men from S. London were found guilty of raping and murdering Mary-Ann Leneghan. ❦ 4 of those injured in the London drug trial regained consciousness; 2 remained in a critical condition. {19} Riots hit Paris after protests across France against new labour laws for young people. {20} Abdul Rahman was imprisoned in Afghanistan for converting to Christianity; under Sharia law, he faced death. ❦ The Lord Chancellor announced that secret loans

—————— IN BRIEF · MARCH – APRIL 2006 ——————

to political parties would be banned. ❦ RIP @ 18 Humphrey, the Downing St cat. ❦ The 3-year anniversary of the invasion of Iraq was marked. ❦ Alexander Lukashenko won the Belarussian election with 82% of the vote; the opposition claimed the vote was rigged. ❦ *The Da Vinci Code* trial ended, pending a ruling. ❦ Tropical cyclone Larry hit Australia's NW coast, making thousands homeless and severely damaging the banana crop. {21} It emerged that the killers of Mary-Ann Leneghan had been on probation at the time of her murder. ❦ Insurgents raided a prison near Baghdad, releasing all the prisoners and killing 17 police. ❦ 7 British men went on trial at the Old Bailey accused of plotting to bomb a target in the UK. {22} Gordon Brown delivered his 10th budget [see p.228]. ❦ Basque separatists ETA declared permanent cease-fire [see p.27]. ❦ The international community appealed to Afghanistan to spare the life of the Christian convert, Abdul Rahman. {23} British hostage Norman Kember and 2 Canadian fellow peace workers were rescued from their Iraqi captors by multinational forces. ❦ Prominent Labour donor Rod Aldridge stepped down as head of IT firm Capita, after claims that his £1m loan to Labour led to his firm winning lucrative contracts. {24} Capt Peter Norton, who lost a leg in a bomb attack, was awarded the George Cross for his service in Iraq. ❦ A Chinese man, Lin Liang Ren, was found guilty of the 2004 manslaughter of 21 cockle-pickers who drowned in Morecambe. {25} RIP @ 75 Lynne Perrie, *Coronation Street* actress. {26} The ban on smoking in public places came into effect

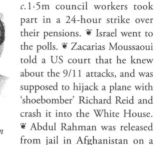

Gordon Brown

You go as a peace activist and are rescued by the SAS.
– NORMAN KEMBER

in Scotland. ❦ The closing ceremony of the Commonwealth Games was held in Melbourne. ❦ During an interview on Australian TV, Blair admitted it may have been a mistake to declare he would step down before the next election. {28} c.1·5m council workers took part in a 24-hour strike over their pensions. ❦ Israel went to the polls. ❦ Zacarias Moussaoui told a US court that he knew about the 9/11 attacks, and was supposed to hijack a plane with 'shoebomber' Richard Reid and crash it into the White House. ❦ Abdul Rahman was released from jail in Afghanistan on a technicality; he was offered asylum in Italy by the Pope. {29} Ariel Sharon's party, Kadima, won the Israeli election, despite Sharon remaining comatose; Ehud Olmert became acting PM. ❦ A report into the deaths of 4 recruits at the Deepcut army barracks concluded that they had all committed suicide and that a public inquiry was not needed; the families of the soldiers vowed to fight on. {30} A parliamentary report concluded that the security services were not at fault over the 7/7 London bombings. ❦ US reporter Jill Carrol was released after 11 weeks captivity in Iraq. {31} >57 died, including 13 Britons, after a pleasure boat capsized in Bahrain. ❦ >50 died and c.800 were injured after 6·0 earthquakes hit Iran. ❦ The FA announced that all football matches scheduled for Wembley in 2006 would be played elsewhere because of construction delays.

APRIL · {2} The Tories announced they would reveal privately to the Electoral Commission the names of those who had loaned them

─── IN BRIEF · APRIL 2006 ───

money. {3} 900 doctors wrote to the government, urging reforms to NHS funding. ❦ A 13-year-old boy became the first person to die from measles in the UK in 14 years. ❦ Hassan Jihad was cleared of the murder of Damilola Taylor. {4} The jury in the trial of Zacarias Moussaoui decided that he was eligible for the death penalty. ❦ 2 brothers were found not guilty of murdering Damilola Taylor, pending a retrial for manslaughter. ❦ Former senior Sinn Féin member Denis Donaldson was found murdered at his remote cottage in Ireland. {5} A swan found in Fife was confirmed to have died from H5N1 bird flu. ❦ RIP @ 65 Gene Pitney [see p.56]. {7} 17 birds in Scotland were taken to be tested for bird flu. ❦ The European Commission temporarily suspended aid to the Palestinian Authority, until the Hamas-led government recognised Israel and renounced violence. ❦ The High Court ruled that Dan Brown had not breached the copyright of another book for his novel *The Da Vinci Code* [see p.163]. {9} Italy went to the polls. {10} Jacques Chirac announced he would withdraw new labour laws that had caused protests across France. ❦ The US denied exploring options for nuclear strikes against Iran.
{11} Romano Prodi claimed victory in the Italian elections; he won 49·8% of the vote in the lower house. ❦ Israeli politicians voted to declare Ariel Sharon permanently incapacitated, formally ending his premiership. ❦ Spain charged 29 people over the 2004 Madrid bombings. {12} Iran announced that it had successfully enriched low-grade uranium. ❦ Prince Harry passed out from Sandhurst. {13} IAEA head Mohamed ElBaradei visited

Z. Moussaoui

We won and it is useless for Berlusconi to try to delay it. Berlusconi must go home. – ROMANO PRODI

Tehran in an attempt to halt Iran's nuclear ambitions. ❦ >7,000 NHS jobs were cut as NHS Trusts tried to control budget deficits. {15} >34 killed in violence across Iraq. ❦ RIP @ 88 Muriel Spark [see p.56]. {16} The Labour Party warned of growing support for the BNP, raising concerns that it might win seats in Barking [see p.256]. {17} A Palestinian suicide bomber killed 9 and injured >50 in an attack on Tel Aviv – the first such attack since Hamas came to power. {19} 2,300 jobs were lost in Coventry, after Peugeot announced a factory closure. {20} 2 died in Kathmandu during protests against the absolute power of the King. {21} The Queen celebrated her 80th birthday [see p.272]. ❦ Nigeria paid off its multi-billion dollar debt, becoming the first African nation so to do. {22} >150 were injured when 100,000 Nepalis marched in Kathmandu against the King. {23} Aljazeera broadcast a message from bin Laden, in which he stated that the conflicts in Sudan, Palestine, and Iraq proved the West was waging a 'Zionist-crusader war'. ❦ *c.*35,000 ran the London Marathon [see p.297]. {24} >23 died and many were injured in 3 bombs in the Egyptian resort of Dahab. ❦ Nepali King Gyanendra announced a return to democracy, ending weeks of protest against his absolute rule. ❦ Home Office figures revealed that >1,023 foreign prisoners were released from British jails after completing their sentences, instead of being considered for deportation. {26} Home Sec. Charles Clarke said that Blair had refused to accept his resignation over the prisoner releases. ❦ John Prescott admitted to a 2-year extramarital affair with one of his secretaries. ❦ Patricia

─────── IN BRIEF · APRIL – MAY 2006 ───────

Hewitt was slow hand-clapped by a group of nurses as she spoke about the future of the NHS. ❦ The 20th anniversary of the Chernobyl disaster was commemorated in Ukraine. {27} >35,000 chickens were slaughtered after a bird died of the H7 strain of avian flu in Norfolk.
❦ The FA offered the job of England manager to Luiz Felipe Scolari. {28} It was revealed that 20 of the most dangerous criminals released instead of being deported were not on the police national computer, thus hindering the search for them. ❦ Scolari turned down the England job, blaming media intrusion. {29} Chelsea clinched the Premiership title [see p.302]. ❦ Wayne Rooney injured his foot, putting his World Cup fitness in doubt.

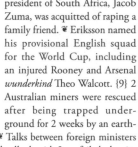

Wayne Rooney

MAY · {1} Rebels in Darfur rejected a proposed peace deal. {2} A Norwegian court found 3 guilty of the theft of Munch's *The Scream*. {3} 113 died after an Armenian aircraft crashed into the Black Sea. {4} Zacarias Moussaoui was sentenced to life in a maximum security prison for his role in 9/11. ❦ English local elections were held. {5} Labour lost >300 councillors at the local elections; the Tories had their best showing since 1992 [see p.256].
❦ Blair made a sweeping Cabinet reshuffle [see p.251]. ❦ Steve McClaren accepted the job of England manager. ❦ A peace deal between the Sudanese government and the largest group of rebels in Darfur was signed; the government agreed to disband the Janjaweed militia [see p.28]. {6} A British helicopter was shot down in Basra; the resulting civil unrest caused the deaths of 5 British soldiers and 5 Iraqis. {7} Pressure

America you lost ... I won.
– ZACARIAS MOUSSAOUI

mounted on Blair to set a date for his departure. {8} The MoD announced the names of the 5 British soldiers killed in the Basra helicopter crash; among them was Flt Lt Sarah-Jayne Mulvihill, the first female servicewoman to die on active service in Iraq. ❦ Former deputy president of South Africa, Jacob Zuma, was acquitted of raping a family friend. ❦ Eriksson named his provisional English squad for the World Cup, including an injured Rooney and Arsenal *wunderkind* Theo Walcott. {9} 2 Australian miners were rescued after being trapped underground for 2 weeks by an earthquake. ❦ Talks between foreign ministers on the deadlock with Iran failed, despite Ahmadinejad sending a personal letter to Bush in an effort to find 'new solutions' [see p.32]. {10} The EU, UN, US, and Russia agreed a deal to send aid directly to Palestinians, bypassing the Hamas-led Palestinian Authority. ❦ Middlesbrough were defeated by Sevilla 4–0 in the UEFA Cup final. {11} A Commons Intelligence and Security Cmte report into the 7/7 bombings concluded that the security services could not have prevented the attacks. {12} Blair and Brown agreed a new deal to link pensions to earnings from 2012. {13} Liverpool won the FA Cup on penalties [see p.303]. {14} >52 died in Brazil after a government crack-down on gangs; police stations were attacked and prisoners rioted. {15} N. Irish politicians took their seats at Stormont for the first time since 2002, in the first step to the revival of power-sharing. {16} The European Court of Justice ruled that the NHS should pay for patients to be treated abroad if they faced unreasonably long waiting times at home.

─── IN BRIEF · MAY – JUNE 2006 ───

❦ After 4 days of violence, the revolts in 70 prisons across Brazil were quelled; 81 people had died in the unrest. {17} Vauxhall confirmed that 900 jobs would be lost at Ellesmere Port. ❦ The WHO confirmed that 5 people died of bird flu in Indonesia. ❦ Arsenal lost to Barcelona in the Champions League final in Paris [see p.303]. {18} >40 died in S. Afghanistan during clashes between the Taleban and the police. {19} The UN Committee Against Torture released a report calling for Guantánamo Bay to be closed, since it contravened the UN Convention against torture.

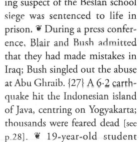

John Prescott

❦ Education Sec. Alan Johnson published nutrition guidelines for school meals, banning food too high in salt or fat. ❦ 15-year-old Kiyan Prince was stabbed to death after an argument outside his school in N. London. {20} Finnish 'troll rockers' *Lordi* won Eurovision [see p.140]. {21} >16 civilians and >60 Taleban fighters died in US airstrikes on a village in S. Iraq. {22} In a referendum, Montenegro voted for independence from Serbia. ❦ Blair arrived in Iraq for a meeting with the new Iraqi PM, Nouri Maliki. ❦ A 16-year-old boy appeared in court charged with the murder of Kiyan Prince. {23} A group of British doctors wrote to the NHS, urging a cut in funding for 'alternative' therapies. ❦ New Home Sec. John Reid harshly criticised the immigration service, declaring it 'not fit for purpose'. {24} 500 police officers took part in raids across Britain, targeting suspects said to be responsible for terrorism abroad. ❦ A new audio message from Osama bin Laden, posted on an 'Islamist' website, claimed that Moussaoui was not involved in 9/11. ❦ C4's Big Brother

My continued use of Dorneywood is getting in the way of doing my job in government. – JOHN PRESCOTT

claimed its first victim; Shabaz quit the show after threatening on air to kill himself [see p.116]. {25} Following increasing violence in Palestine, Fatah and Hamas met for crisis talks. {26} RIP @ 64 Desmond Dekker. ❦ The sole surviving suspect of the Beslan school siege was sentenced to life in prison. ❦ During a press conference, Blair and Bush admitted that they had made mistakes in Iraq; Bush singled out the abuse at Abu Ghraib. {27} A 6·2 earthquake hit the Indonesian island of Java, centring on Yogyakarta; thousands were feared dead [see p.28]. ❦ 19-year-old student Tom Grant was stabbed to death on a train after trying to stop an argument between a man and woman. {28} Pressure on John Prescott to resign intensified, with consternation that he kept his 'grace and favour' homes despite losing many of his ministerial responsibilities. {29} It was confirmed that >5,000 had died and >20,000 were injured in the Indonesian earthquake; aid began to arrive in the region. ❦ 2 British journalists working for CBS were killed in a roadside bomb attack in Iraq. {30} Vodafone announced losses of £14·9bn. ❦ The president of East Timor, Xanana Gusmao, took on emergency powers to stem mounting social unrest. {31} The government admitted that >£2bn in tax credits had been overpaid, for a second year.

JUNE · {1} John Prescott gave up his use of Dorneywood (one of his grace-and-favour residences), after he was photographed playing croquet on its lawns during office hours. {2} 250 police mounted an anti-terror raid on a house in Forest Gate, London;

IN BRIEF · JUNE 2006

a suspect was shot but not badly hurt. ❦ US, UK, France, Germany, Russia, and China agreed a package of incentives and penalties designed to halt Iran's nuclear programme. {3} The police claimed that the Forest Gate raid was prompted by intelligence reports of a 'suicide vest' laced with deadly chemicals. {4} A masked gunman shot a 13-year-old boy once, and a 15-year-old boy five times, as they played outside their home in Manchester. ❦ In a province N. of Baghdad, >20 people were pulled from their vehicles and shot dead. ❦ 17 people were charged with terrorism offences in Canada, in relation to an alleged bomb plot against Toronto. {5} A London Assembly committee report into the 7/7 bombings criticised poor communication between emergency workers in the aftermath of the attacks. {6} EU foreign policy chief, Javier Solana, presented to the Iranians proposals to halt Iran's nuclear development. {7} University lecturers accepted a pay deal and ended a boycott that had delayed the marking of exams. ❦ An activist for the Respect Party called on Muslims to stop co-operating with the police in response to the raid in Forest Gate. ❦ After a scan on his foot, Wayne Rooney was declared fit to join the England squad in Germany. {8} Abu Musab al-Zarqawi, a prominent

Al-Zarqawi

I apologise for the hurt that we may have caused [after the Forest Gate raid].
– Asst Cmsnr ANDY HAYMAN

Al-Qaeda leader, was killed in a US raid on Basra. {9} The World Cup kicked off [see p.295]. ❦ The National Institute for Health & Clinical Excellence (NICE) ruled that women with early stage breast cancer could receive the drug Herceptin. ❦ 7 people, including 3 children, were killed when Israeli airstrikes hit a family on a beach in Gaza. {11} England's World Cup campaign got off to a winning (if slow) start; they beat Paraguay 1–0 [see p.294]. ❦ The 2 men arrested during the Forest Gate raid were released without charge; the police were criticised for heavy-handedness and inaccurate intelligence. ❦ Hamas announced that, in response to the Israeli attack on a beach, rockets had been fired from Gaza into Israel, ending the 16-month truce. {12} 3 detainees at Guantánamo Bay killed themselves in what was believed to be a suicide pact; the camp Commander described the deaths as 'an act of asymmetrical warfare' [see p.20]. ❦ *c.*300 people protested outside Scotland Yard over the Forest Gate raid; the Independent Police Complaints Commission announced an investigation. {13} The Attorney General announced he would investigate the sentencing of paedophile Craig Sweeney; Home Sec. John Reid had criticised the leniency of a 'life' sentence, for which Sweeney could serve just 5 years because he pleaded guilty. ❦ RIP @ 80 former Irish PM Charles Haughey. {14} 40,000 US and Iraqi troops were posted onto the streets of Baghdad to maintain security after the death of Zarqawi. ❦ Police apologised for the hurt caused to the brothers wrongly arrested in Forest Gate. {15} >60 died in Sri Lanka after a bus hit a landmine. {17} 2 US soldiers were kidnapped in Iraq during an attack in which a third was killed. ❦ After a series of high profile child abuse cases, John Reid announced he would send a minister to the US to see whether Megan's Law should be applied in Britain. {18} >30 died after Taleban fighters attacked civilians in Afghanistan. ❦ After a 5-day International Whaling Commission

IN BRIEF · JUNE – JULY 2006

meeting, Japan secured a resolution backing an eventual return to commercial whaling. {20} Japan announced it would withdraw its troops from Iraq. ❦ The bodies of 2 US soldiers kidnapped in Iraq were found; it was claimed that the newly appointed leader of Al-Qaeda in Iraq, Abu Hamza al Muhajir, had personally executed them. ❦ Michael Owen was taken off injured during England's 2–2 draw with Sweden. {21} An EU–US summit began in Austria; the EU pushed for the closure of Guantánamo Bay. ❦ The BBC announced it would axe *Top of the Pops*. ❦ One of

Gilad Shalit

Saddam's defence lawyers was shot dead in Baghdad. ❦ Gordon Brown signalled his intention to replace Britain's Trident nuclear weapons, angering the anti-nuclear lobby. {22} 7 US marines were charged with murdering a disabled Iraqi civilian. {23} 7 men were arrested in Miami after an alleged plot to bomb Chicago's Sears Tower was uncovered. ❦ RIP @ 83 Aaron Spelling [see p.57]. {24} >150 England football supporters were arrested in Stuttgart after clashes with rival fans. {25} Palestinian fighters tunnelled into Israel, attacked a tank, killed 2 Israeli soldiers, and kidnapped a third – Corporal Gilad Shalit. ❦ A man was arrested in Morocco in connection with the Tonbridge robbery. {26} Warren Buffett

I am not an enthusiast of dynastic wealth.
– WARREN BUFFETT

announced he was donating the majority of his fortune (*c.*£20bn) to the Bill and Melinda Gates Foundation. ❦ Bruno, an Italian bear that had strayed into Germany, was shot dead by German authorities who considered him a threat. {27} In a series of interviews, former Home Sec. Charles Clarke criticised Blair for sacking him, and questioned the PM's authority. ❦ In response to Israeli demands for the release of Shalit, the Palestinians demanded Israel release all women and child prisoners. {28} Israeli soldiers moved into Gaza in an attempt to free Shalit; Israel's first incursion into Gaza since its withdrawal in 2005. {29} Israel launched punitive airstrikes on Gaza, hitting bridges and a power plant; Israel also captured 20 Palestinian MPs and 7 government ministers. {30} In by-elections, Labour failed to win back Blaenau Gwent (the seat went to Independent Dai Davies); the Tories held Bromley & Chislehurst, but their majority was slashed from 13,342 votes to 633 by the Lib Dems.

JULY · {1} England exited the World Cup competition after losing on penalties to Portugal [see p.294]. {2} David Beckham resigned as England captain but insisted he would still like to play internationals. ❦ Israel launched an air strike on the Palestinian PM's office, injuring 3. ❦ A UK heatwave warning was issued after temperatures reached 32ºC. {3} Palestinians gave Israel until 0300 GMT to free all Palestinian prisoners in return for Shalit. ❦ >30 died in a train crash in Valencia, Spain. {4} Muslim MP Sadiq Khan criticised the government's response to 7/7. ❦ Israeli soldier Shalit was reported to still be alive. ❦ Comedian David Walliams swam the Channel (in aid of Sport Relief); he achieved one of the 50th fastest-ever times. {5} The UN Security Council called an urgent meeting after N. Korea test-fired 6 nuclear missiles. ❦ Prescott denied allegations of sleaze, after it emerged that he had held

IN BRIEF · JULY 2006

meetings with US millionaire Philip Anschutz, who hopes to run Britain's first 'supercasino'. ❦ RIP @ 64 Kenneth Lay, former Enron chief executive [see p.18]. {6} Israeli tanks re-occupied parts of Gaza. ❦ Aljazeera aired a video of 7/7 suicide bomber Shehzad Tanweer blaming British foreign policy for his attack, and warning of many more. {7} The anniversary of the 7/7 London bombings was marked. {8} Amelie Mauresmo beat Justine Henin-Hardenne in the Wimbledon ladies' final [see p.312]. {9} >40 died in sectarian attacks on Sunnis in Baghdad; later, car bombs killed >25 Shia Muslims in what appeared to be revenge attacks. ❦ >122 people died after a plane crashed on a runway in Siberia. ❦ Federer beat Nadal to win his 4th Wimbledon [see p.312]. ❦ Italy beat France on penalties in the World Cup final; Zinedine Zidane was sent off for headbutting Marco Materazzi, after apparently being insulted by the Italian [see p.26]. ❦ The *Mail on Sunday* reported that Prescott was given a 'cowboy outfit' by Anschutz while staying at his ranch. {10} >45 died in plane crash in Pakistan. {11} 7 bombs exploded on rush hour trains in Mumbai, killing >160; initial suspicion fell on Kashmiri separatists. ❦ RIP @ 60 Syd Barrett [see p.57]. {12} The death toll from the Mumbai train bombs rose to 183, with 714 injured. ❦ Lebanese group Hezbollah seized 2 Israeli soldiers in fighting on the border; Israel threatened that anyone trying to test its resolve would 'pay a heavy price'. ❦ America announced that prisoners in Guantánamo Bay would be treated in line with the Geneva Conventions. ❦ Zidane appeared on French TV; he apologised for head-butt-

Sven-Göran Eriksson

I can't regret what I did because it would mean that he was right to say all that. – ZINEDINE ZIDANE

ing Materazzi but said he could not regret the incident, as it would mean Materazzi's insults to his family were true. ❦ Labour's chief fundraiser, Lord Levy, was arrested and bailed by police in connection with the 'cash-for-honours' enquiry. He denied any wrongdoing. ❦ MPs voted to adjourn the Commons early in a symbolical protest against the planned extradition to America of 3 ex-Natwest bankers. {13} Israel launched airstrikes against Lebanon and blocked Lebanese ports in an escalation of the crisis. ❦ The 'Natwest 3' were handed over to US marshals at Gatwick. A witness in the case was found dead in a London park, amid claims that he had been hounded by the FBI. {14} Govt ministers Lord Sainsbury and Ian McCartney were questioned by police in relation to 'cash for honours'. ❦ The UN Security Council held an emergency meeting as Israel intensified its attack on Lebanon. ❦ The police reported that 100,000 weapons were surrendered during a 5-week knife amnesty. {15} The UN Security Council unanimously voted to impose sanctions on North Korea in response to its recent nuclear tests. {16} At the G8 Summit in St Petersburg, Russia, the deepening crisis in the Middle East dominated proceedings. Consensus on a unified reaction could not be reached after America pledged its support for Israel. {17} Kofi Annan and Tony Blair called for an international force to be sent into Lebanon to halt the violence; the first Britons were evacuated from Beirut. ❦ >48 died in a bomb attack on a market town south of Baghdad. ❦ The CPS announced that no one would be charged in connection with the fatal shooting of Jean Charles

─IN BRIEF · JULY – AUGUST 2006─

de Menezes at Stockwell tube. ❦ >100 died when a tsunami hit the coast of the Indonesian island of Java after a 7·7 earthquake [see p.28]. ❦ *Discovery* landed safely in Florida after its 13-day mission [see p.189]. {18} The death toll in the Javan tsunami reached 339. ❦ >53 were killed by car bomb in the Iraqi city of Kufa. {19} The highest British temperature for July was recorded in Wisley, Surrey: 36·5°C. {20} Thousands of Britons were evacuated from Lebanon as the violence continued. {21} A US judge ruled that the 'Natwest 3' could not return to Britain while they awaited trial. ❦ Michael Burgess, the coroner due to hear the inquest into the death of Princess Diana, announced that he was quitting his post due to a heavy workload. ❦ The Commons Standards committee ruled that John Prescott had broken the rules by not declaring his stay at Philip Anschutz's ranch, but no action would be taken as the trip had subsequently been registered. {22} A 20 year-old Asian man, Shezan Umarji, was stabbed to death during a mass brawl in Preston; the attack was thought to have been racially motivated. {23} The UN's emergency relief chief, Jan Egeland, said that Israel's devastation of Beirut was a violation of humanitarian law. ❦ 2 died and 13 were injured after a huge inflatable art installation blew free from its moorings in Durham. ❦ Saddam was taken to hospital after spending 16 days on hunger strike. ❦ Tiger Woods secured his 3rd Open victory at Hoylake [see p.305]. {25} Condoleezza Rice held talks with Israeli PM Ehud Olmert in an effort to broker peace. ❦ The government announced it would axe the fail-

Saddam Hussein

ing Child Support Agency. {26} Despite repeated warnings as to their position, 4 UN observers were killed by Israeli bombs in S. Lebanon; Kofi Annan called for an investigation. ❦ Foreign Ministers from across the world met in Rome to discuss the crisis in the Middle East; Israel did not send a representative. ❦ The Independent Police Complaints Commission (IPCC) announced it would investigate allegations that police corruption had hampered the prosecution of the killers of Stephen Lawrence. {27} Talks in Rome failed to produce a cease-fire agreement; Israel and Hezbollah continued their attacks. ❦ Tour de France winner Floyd Landis tested positive for excessive levels of testosterone. The cycling champion denies cheating and, at the time of writing, is formally challenging the accuracy of the test results [see p.297]. {29} George W. Bush apologised to Tony Blair for using Prestwick Airport to refuel planes taking US bombs to Israel. ❦ The Sudanese peace agreement collapsed after government troops and Janjaweed militia attacked rebels. {30} Israel bombed the Lebanese town of Qana, killing *c.*28 civilians; Human Rights Watch accused Israel of war crimes. ❦ The last edition of *Top of the Pops* was broadcast by the BBC. {31} Ehud Olmert ruled out a cease-fire in Lebanon, despite widespread condemnation of Israel's attack on Qana.

> *What has happened in Qana shows this is a situation that simply cannot continue.* – TONY BLAIR

AUGUST · {1} The Israeli cabinet voted to extend the ground offensive into Lebanon. ❦ It was announced that the new Wembley stadium might not be ready for use until June 2007. ❦ 2 British soldiers were killed

─────────IN BRIEF · AUGUST 2006─────────

in an ambush by Taleban fighters in S. Afghanistan. ❦ After undergoing surgery, Cuban president Fidel Castro temporarily ceded power to his brother, Raul. {2} Israel announced it had captured a number of Hezbollah fighters after raids in Lebanon; Hezbollah claimed that the captives were ordinary civilians. {3} In a leaked memo to Tony Blair, outgoing ambassador to Baghdad, William Patey, warned that Iraq was heading towards civil war. {4} While the UN debated the wording of a cease-fire resolution, Israel renewed air strikes on Lebanon, ❦ Tony Blair delayed his summer holiday to continue working on the UN resolution for Lebanon. ❦ MSP Tommy Sheridan won a defamation case against the *News of the World*; the newspaper was ordered to pay Sheridan £200,000 in damages. {5} America and France agreed the text of a UN resolution to bring a halt to fighting in the Middle East. ❦ Israel arrested the Speaker of the Palestinian parliament, Aziz Dweik; Israel argued he was a legitimate target as he was a prominent member of Hamas. {6} >15 were killed by a Hezbollah rocket attack on N. Israel. ❦ Jenson Button secured his first Grand Prix victory in Hungary [see p.314]. {7} UN diplomats met to discuss Lebanese objections to the text of the proposed cease-fire agreement.

Fidel Castro

I told David I was looking to change things, looking to go in a different direction. – STEVE McCLAREN

❦ >200 died after floods in Ethiopia. {8} Charles Allen, ITV's chief executive, resigned in response to his channels' recent poor performance. ❦ A 43rd person died from bird flu in Indonesia. {9} 3 people were arrested, including the *News of the World*'s royal editor, over suspicions of their involvement in the tapping of Royal phone calls. ❦ Danny

and Rickie Preddie were found guilty of the manslaughter of Damilola Taylor. ❦ The Israeli cabinet backed a proposal to push troops further into Lebanon. {10} 21 people were arrested in raids across Britain, after police announced they had foiled an alleged plot to blow up a number of transatlantic planes [see p.28]. The UK threat level was raised to Critical; airports in Britain and many other countries restricted hand luggage; passengers around the world experienced cancellations and long delays. {11} The terror threat remained at Critical, and more flights were cancelled. ❦ German Nobel laureate and peace activist, Günter Grass admitted in an interview to having being a member of the Waffen SS. {12} The UN unanimously approved a new resolution calling for 'a full cessation of hostilities' between Lebanon and Israel. Israeli forces continued to bombard Lebanon; Ehud Olmert said that fighting would continue until his government formally approved the cease-fire. ❦ England manager Steve McClaren picked his first squad; in omitting David Beckham he signalled the possible end to the former captain's international career. {13} Olmert ordered Israeli troops to cease fighting at 23:00. {14} The UK terror threat was downgraded to Severe. ❦ Police continued to question 23 people over their possible involvement in the alleged plot to blow up planes. ❦ The truce between Israel and Hezbollah came into force; both sides claimed victory. ❦ 7 were killed in a car bomb in Colombo, Sri Lanka; the Tamil Tigers were blamed. The Sri Lankan government responded with an air strike that killed 19. {16} Despite sporadic violence,

——— IN BRIEF · AUGUST 2006 cont. ———

the truce in Lebanon held for a third day. ❦ An investigation was launched after it was revealed that a 12-year-old boy had boarded a Gatwick–Lisbon flight, despite having no passport, ticket, or boarding pass. {17} A-Level results were released; 24·1% achieved grade As, heralding the traditional debate about declining standards. ❦ A judge granted police the right to continue questioning the 23 people held on suspicion of terrorism offences. {18} Police announced they had found a suitcase containing bomb-making materials in a wood near High Wycombe. ❦ Pete

Ehud Olmert

Bennett won Big Brother 7 [see p.116]. {19} Kofi Annan expressed concern after an Israeli raid into Lebanon appeared to break the terms of the fragile truce. {20} >20 were killed and >300 injured after gunmen opened fire on a crowd of Shia pilgrims in Iraq. ❦ Pakistan forfeited the final Test against England [see p.307]. {21} >50 were killed and >130 injured when 2 commuter trains crashed in Egypt. ❦ The CPS announced that 11 of the 24 people held over the alleged aircraft bomb plot would be charged. {22} >170 were killed when a Russian plane crashed in Ukraine. {23} UN incentives for Iran to stop its nuclear programme by 31·08·06 were rejected by Tehran, which instead proposed 'serious talks'. ❦

I promised myself I would grow older, stronger and sturdier to be able to break free. – NATASCHA KAMPUSCH

Paramount ended a 14-year working relationship with Tom Cruise, citing his recent strange behaviour as 'unacceptable'. {24} Syria threatened to close its border with Lebanon if UN peace keepers were stationed there. ❦ The GCSE pass rate rose to 98·1%. ❦ At a meeting of the International Astronomical Union 2,500 astronomers voted that Pluto should no

longer be classified as a planet [see p.58]. ❦ Austrian Natascha Kampusch was reunited with her parents after escaping from the cellar in which she had been held captive, having been kidnapped 8 years earlier. {25} A report by the Department of Health predicted that, if no action was taken, 13m Britons would be obese by 2010. ❦ A Europe-wide study published in *Global Change Biology* warned that climate change was causing the seasons to shift, with spring arriving on average 6–8 days earlier than 30 years ago. {26} Ryanair announced it would sue the government over the £3·3m losses it incurred as a result of increased airport security. {27} Hassan Nasrallah, the leader of Hezbollah, said that he would not have ordered the kidnapping of 2 Israeli soldiers had he known the 'scale and magnitude' of Israel's attack [see p.31]. ❦ 49 died after a plane crashed in Kentucky; only the co-pilot survived. ❦ A British soldier was killed in the Helmand province of Afghanistan, bringing the number killed there since 2001 to 21. {28} >21 were injured when 3 bombs exploded in the Turkish resort of Marmaris, and 6 were injured after another attack in Istanbul; Kurdish militants claimed responsibility. ❦ 3 were killed and >20 injured after further attacks on the Turkish resort of Antalya. ❦ Kofi Annan requested that Hezbollah release the Israeli soldiers it held captive, and urged Israel to lift the blockade of Lebanese ports. {29} A new biography of Charles Kennedy alleged that he had been suffering from alcoholism since before becoming leader in 1999, and that senior party members, including Menzies Campbell, had known

──────── IN BRIEF · AUGUST – SEPTEMBER 2006 ────────

but kept silent for the sake of party unity. ❦ >34 were killed after a bomb attack in S. Iraq. {30} >24 died in a bomb attack in Baghdad, Iraq. ❦ The British Fertility Society recommended that women with a Body Mass Index >36 should be denied fertility treatment. {31} Mahmoud Ahmadinejad announced that 'Iran will not back down an inch' in response to the UN's 31 August deadline for Tehran to suspend uranium enrichment. ❦ RIP @ 90 actor Glenn Ford. ❦ Munch's paintings *The Scream* and *Madonna* were recovered, 2 years after they were stolen from a museum in Oslo.

Tony Blair

of the country, so that 'the public remember him as he should be'. ❦ Ian Huntley attempted suicide at Wakefield prison. {6} 6 junior members of government and a junior minister resigned after sending Blair a letter urging him to step down. ❦ Sean Gerard Hoey went on trial in Belfast for the 1998 Omagh bombing which killed 29. ❦ George W. Bush admitted that the CIA operated a network of secret prisons outside of America; detainees included Khalid Sheikh Mohammed, the man thought to have organised 9/11 attacks. {7} Natascha Kampusch appeared on Austrian television in her first interview; she described her 8 years of captivity and the mixed feelings she had towards her captor. {8} Aljazeera broadcast a video of Osama bin Laden meeting the 9/11 hijackers. {9} A 15-year-old boy, Jessie James, was shot dead in Moss Side, Manchester, in a supposed case of mistaken identity. {10} Blair announced that he hoped to focus on securing peace in the Middle East during his last few months in power; after meeting Blair, Palestinian president Mahmoud Abbas said he was ready to have unconditional talks with Ehud Olmert. ❦ In an interview with Andrew Marr, Gordon Brown said that he welcomed a challenge for the leadership of the Labour Party, and denied any involvement with a letter demanding Blair's resignation. ❦ RIP @ 88, King Taufa'ahau Tupou IV of Tonga. {11} The fifth anniversary of 9/11 was commemorated around the world. {12} 3 gunmen were killed when they tried to launch an attack on the American embassy in Syria. ❦ George W. Bush admitted that Saddam Hussein had nothing to do with

SEPTEMBER · {2} 14 British servicemen died after their Nimrod reconnaissance aircraft crashed in Afghanistan; the Taleban claimed to have shot down the plane, but the British blamed the crash on a technical fault. ❦ 14 men were arrested during anti-terror raids in London; an Islamic school in Tunbridge Wells was also searched during the operation. ❦ England beat Andorra 5–0 in an European qualifier [see p.304]. {3} Iraqi authorities announced that they had captured a man alleged to be Al-Qaeda's second in command in Iraq. ❦ >200 Taleban fighters were killed during NATO's Operation Medusa near Kandahar; 4 Canadian soldiers also died in the offensive. {4} RIP @ 44 'crocodile hunter' Steve Irwin [see p.57]. ❦ A British man was killed, and 5 foreign tourists were injured, when a gunman opened fire at a Roman amphitheatre in Jordan; the gunman was arrested by police. {5} A leaked memo suggested that Tony Blair might have been planning a farewell tour

I am not going to set a precise date now. I don't think that's right.
– TONY BLAIR

——— IN BRIEF · SEPTEMBER 2006 ———

the 9/11 attacks. {13} Police carried out a raid in Kent, uncovering a large stash of weapons thought to have been used in a number of shootings in N. London. ❦ Iraqi police reported that, during just one day in Baghdad, they found 60 bodies which had been bound and shot. ❦ Despite pleas from NATO commanders for *c.*2,500 extra troops for Afghanistan, no NATO state offered to send additional forces. {14} 1 person was killed and 19 were injured after a gunman indiscriminately opened fire in a college in Montreal, Canada. ❦ The IAEA protested to Washington over an American report into Iran's nuclear activity; the IAEA denounced the report as 'erroneous' and 'misleading'. {15} The Muslim community reacted with consternation to a speech by Pope Benedict XVI, in which he quoted the C14th Emperor Manuel II Paleologus who claimed that Muhammad had brought the world 'things only evil and inhumane' [see p.29]. {16} The Vatican apologised for the offence caused to Muslims by the Pope's speech; demonstrations against the Pope continued across the world. ❦ A major new offensive against Taleban forces in SE Afghanistan was initiated by NATO forces. {17} A Darfur Day of Action was held in 30 cities worldwide, to encourage an end to the ongoing violence in the region [see p.28]. ❦ The Pope made another apology relating to his speech [see p.29]. {18} Kofi Annan warned that Iraq was in danger of descending into 'full-scale civil war'. {19} Riots broke out across Hungary in response to a leaked tape, in which the PM Ferenc Gyurcsany admitted to lying about the state of his country's finances during the election. ❦

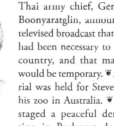

Benedict XVI

> *We lied morning, noon and night.*
> – FERENC GYURCSANY
> Prime Minister of Hungary

A bloodless military coup took place in Thailand while PM Thaksin Shinawatra was at a UN meeting in New York. ❦ BBC's *Panorama* made allegations of corruption in British football; the FA announced they would investigate. {20} Thai army chief, Gen. Sonthi Boonyaratglin, announced in a televised broadcast that the coup had been necessary to unite the country, and that martial law would be temporary. ❦ A memorial was held for Steve Irwin at his zoo in Australia. ❦ *c.*10,000 staged a peaceful demonstration in Budapest demanding the resignation of PM Ferenc Gyurcsany; later, some protestors clashed with police. ❦ At his court martial, British soldier Cpl Donald Payne admitted to inhumane treatment of Iraqi prisoners but denied manslaughter; the admission makes him the first British soldier to admit to a war crime. {21} Co-presenter of BBC's *Top Gear*, Richard Hammond, was seriously injured after crashing a car during an attempt at the land-speed record. ❦ A UN report declared torture in Iraq to be more common and severe than during Saddam Hussein's rule. ❦ Pakistan President Pervez Musharraf alleged that, in the days after 9/11, America threatened to bomb his country 'back to the stone age' unless it helped in the war against terror. ❦ US space shuttle *Atlantis* touched down after a successful 12-day mission to restart construction of the International Space Station. {22} The King of Thailand appeared to give his approval to the military coup.

————

The daily chronicle will continue in the 2008 edition of Schott's Almanac.

─────SOME GREAT LIVES IN BRIEF─────

RONNIE BARKER
25·9·1929–3·10·2005 (76)

One of the brightest stars in the firmament of British comedy, Barker's reputation for 'genius' is founded upon the vast quantity of material he wrote and performed – most notably with Ronnie Corbett in *The Two Ronnies*. His legacy will be secured by these sketches, and by two iconic (and much repeated) characterisations: wise old lag Norman Stanley Fletcher in *Porridge*, and the stuttering skinflint shopkeeper Albert Arkwright in *Open All Hours*.

GEORGE BEST
22·5·1946–25·11·2005 (59)

The legendary status of the Man. Utd. and N. Ireland footballer was captured in the elegant phrase, 'Maradona good, Pelé better, George Best'. Best once boasted that he had moved football from the sports pages to the front page. Sadly, more often than not, this was for the womanising and drinking that eventually outshone his versatile talent, and caused his premature retirement and death. As he famously remarked, 'I spent a lot of money on booze, birds and fast cars. The rest I just squandered'.

RICHARD PRYOR
1·12·1940–10·12·2005 (65)

Pryor's uncompromising and profane routines on sex, race, and poverty set the stage for a host of comics, and made him one of comedy's first superstars. Yet, his edgy stand-up was diluted by a string of mainstream movies, including *Superman III* – which earned him $4m, then a record fee for a black actor. Pryor's private life was not as successful. Married 6 times (to 5 wives), he struggled with alcohol, drugs, and the police. In 1980, he suffered 3rd degree burns while freebasing cocaine.

WILSON 'WICKED' PICKETT
18·3·1941–19·1·2006 (64)

A gospel singer lured by rhythm and blues, Pickett achieved fame with a string of soul classics, including *Land of 1,000 Dances*, *In the Midnight Hour*, *Mustang Sally*, *634–5789* and *Everybody Needs Somebody to Love*. Although his career dwindled, and he had a number of altercations with the law, he was, in the words of Aretha Franklin, 'one of the greatest soul singers of all time'.

JOHN PROFUMO
30·1·1915–9·3·2006 (91)

While Sec. of State for War under Macmillan, Profumo had an affair with the teenage 'model' Christine Keeler, who was also the mistress of the Soviet assistant naval attaché. The resulting scandal, one of the most notorious in British politics, rocked the security services and the government. Admitting he had lied to the Commons, Profumo resigned as an MP in 1963. He dedicated his next 40 years to charity work in London's East End, for which he was awarded the CBE in 1975.

GENE PITNEY
17·2·1941–5·4·2006 (65)

A tenor crooner whose quavering voice captured the pathos of teenage love, Pitney wrote and performed an array of songs and had 16 *Top 20* hits, 1961–8. Amongst his most famous songs were *That Girl Belongs to Yesterday*, *Town Without Pity*, *(The Man Who Shot) Liberty Valance*, and *24 Hours From Tulsa*.

DAME MURIEL SPARK
1·2·1918–13·4·2006 (88)

Best known for her semi-autobiographical novel *The Prime of Miss Jean Brodie*, Spark was a waspish, witty, and prolific Scottish writer. Her prose style (at once

—————————— SOME GREAT LIVES IN BRIEF cont. ——————————

crisp, elegant, sinister, and macabre) was heavily influenced by Roman Catholicism, to which she converted at 36.

GYÖRGY LIGETI
28·5·1923–12·6·2006 (83)

Ligeti achieved fame as a composer with complex, idiosyncratic, and anarchic works that defined one strand of post-War classical music. Some of his compositions attracted derision, including one that called for the smashing of a tea service, and a work for 100 metronomes. His popular fame derives from the pieces Stanley Kubrick used in his films – notably *2001: a Space Odyssey*.

AARON SPELLING
22·4·1923–23·6·2006 (83)

Spelling found early work acting in *Gunsmoke* and *Dragnet*. But he found fame and fortune behind the lens, producing glitzy dramas like *Dynasty, Charlie's Angels,* and *Beverly Hills, 90210* – an oeuvre of excess he called 'mind candy', but which gave him the world record for hours of TV produced.

HARRIET
c. 1830–23·6·2006 (≈175)

One of the world's oldest known living creatures, Harriet (a giant Galapagos tortoise) died of heart failure in an Australian zoo, aged c.175. At the time of her death, she weighed 23 stone and was 'roughly the size of a dinner table'. It has been suggested that Harriet might have been one of a number of tortoises studied by Charles Darwin and taken by him to Britain on the *Beagle*.

'FIERY' FRED TRUEMAN
6·2·1931–1·7·2006 (75)

Trueman was one of England's finest fast bowlers, one of sport's greatest characters, and one of Yorkshire's proudest sons. In 1964, he became the first bowler to take 300 Test wickets, and in the 67 Tests in which he played, he took 307 wickets at an average of 21·57. His best Test record was 8 for 31; his best first class record, 8 for 28.

ROGER 'SYD' BARRETT
6·1·1946–7·7·2006 (60)

Barrett was the creative force of early *Pink Floyd* (writing their first two hits); he was also responsible for the band's name (a fusion of the bluesmen Pink Anderson and Floyd Council). Yet Barrett found himself unable to handle the band's success or his drug addiction, and in 1968 he quit. After a short-lived solo career, Barrett entered a reclusive retirement that lasted thirty years.

MICKEY SPILLANE
9·3·1918–17·7·2006 (88)

A failed attempt to be a lawyer, a stint as a circus trampolinist, summer jobs as a lifeguard, time spent as a fighter pilot, and undercover work for the FBI, all gave Spillane the perfect crime-writer's training. Blasted by critics but loved by readers, Spillane's hard-boiled pulp fiction sold by the million to become, in his words, 'the chewing gum of American literature'.

STEVE IRWIN
22·2·1962–4·9·2006 (44)

Known around the world as 'the crocodile hunter', Irwin was a fearless showman of animal stunts and a tireless champion of conservation. In his trademark khaki clothes, with his trademark cry of 'crikey!', Irwin captured TV's fascination with venomous and dangerous animals. He died in a freak accident, after being stabbed in the heart by a stingray's barb, only the 4th such attack in Australian waters in a century.

The World

The world is large, when its weary leagues two loving hearts divide;
But the world is small, when your enemy is loose on the other side.
— JOHN BOYLE O'REILLY (1844–90)

THE CLASSICAL PLANETS

symbol	name	diameter	no. of moons	surface gravity	rings?	distance from Sun	mean temp	day length
		km		m/s²		x10⁶ km	°C	hours
☿	Mercury	4,878	0	3·7	N	57·9	167	4222·6
♀	Venus	12,102	0	8·9	N	108·2	462	2802·0
⊕	Earth	12,756	1	9·8	N	149·6	15	24·0
♂	Mars	6,794	2	3·7	N	227·9	–65	24·6
♃	Jupiter	142,800	63	23·1	Y	778·4	–110	9·9
♄	Saturn	120,536	47	9·0	Y	1,433·5	–148	10·7
♅	Uranus	51,118	27	8·4	Y	2,872·5	–195	17·2
♆	Neptune	49,492	13	10·7	Y	4,495·1	–200	16·1

CLASSICAL PLANETARY MNEMONIC

Many **V**ery **E**ducated **M**en **J**ustify **S**tealing **U**nique **N**inth
ercury enus arth ars upiter aturn ranus eptune

PLUTO & THE DWARF PLANETS

In August 2006, at a meeting of the International Astronomical Union (IAU) in Prague, 2,500 scientists voted to strip Pluto of the planetary status it had been granted in 1930, when Clyde Tombaugh wrongly estimated it to be larger than the Earth. As celestial knowledge developed, Pluto's classification as a planet became increasingly tenuous and when, in 2005, a new object larger than Pluto was identified (2003 UB313), the issue of planetary nomenclature was brought to the fore. Scientists agreed at the 2006 IAU conference that for a celestial body to qualify as a planet it must be in orbit around the Sun, it must be large enough that its gravity makes it nearly spherical, and, critically, it must clear its orbit of other objects. This ruling disqualified Pluto, which has an elliptical orbit that overlaps Neptune's. Astronomers now recognise 8 'classical planets' (Mercury, Venus, Earth, Mars, Jupiter, Saturn, Uranus, and Neptune), alongside a new 'dwarf planet' category that includes Pluto, 2003 UB313, and Ceres – the largest asteroid in the Solar System.

THE CONTINENTS

Continent	area km²	est. population	population density
Asia	45,036,492	3,776m	83·4
Africa	30,343,578	832m	27·4
North America	24,680,331	501m	20·3
South America	17,815,420	357m	20·0
Antarctica	12,093,000	(the odd scientist)	—
Europe	9,908,599	727m	73·3
Australia†	7,682,850	20m	2·6

† Australia is usually considered a continent because it is a continuous landmass, though this leaves Polynesia, New Zealand, and many other areas unclassified. Consequently, some prefer the usage of Oceania – a continental grouping that includes all the Pacific islands surrounding Australia. ❧ Geographically, there are six continents, but the Americas are generally split into two. ❧ c.225m years ago the only continent was Pangaea – a supercontinent surrounded by the Panthalassa ocean. c.180m years ago Pangaea split into two, Laurasia and Gondwanaland, before shifting plate tectonics created the still-evolving landmasses we have today.

THE OCEANS

Oceans are the largest bodies of water, making up more than 70% of the globe's surface. The structure of the continents demarcates the Pacific, Indian, and Atlantic oceans, to which maritime organisations added the Arctic. In 2000, the International Hydrographic Organization, the body responsible for charting the oceans, defined the Southern (or Antarctic) ocean, due to its unique eco-system.

Ocean	area km²	greatest known depth at	depth
Pacific	155,557,000	Mariana Trench	11,033m
Atlantic	76,763,000	Puerto Rico Trench	8,605m
Indian	68,556,000	Java Trench	7,258m
Southern	20,327,000	South Sandwich Trench	7,235m
Arctic	14,056,000	Fram Basin	4,665m

DESERTS

Deserts cover roughly 33% of Earth's landmass, and this is increasing. Deserts can be hot or cold; about one sixth of deserts are permanently covered in snow and ice. The characteristics common to all types of desert are: irregular rainfall of <250mm per year; low humidity; and very high evaporation rates. Some major deserts are:

Desert	location	area km²
Sahara	N. Africa	9,065,000
Gobi	Mongolia/China	1,295,000
Patagonian	Argentina	673,000
Rub al-Khali	Saudi Arabia	647,500
Kalahari	SW Africa	582,800
Chihuahuan	Mexico/USA	362,600
Taklimakan	N. China	362,600

—————— A WORLD OF SUPERLATIVES ——————

Highest city	La Paz, Bolivia	3,636m
Highest mountain	Everest, Nepal/Tibet	8,850m
Highest volcano	Ojos del Salado, Chile	6,908m
Highest dam	Rogan, Tajikistan	335m
Highest waterfall	Angel Falls, Venezuela	979m
Biggest waterfall (volume)	Inga, Dem. Rep. of Congo	43,000m³/s
Lowest point	Dead Sea, Israel/Jordan	400m
Deepest point	Challenger Deep, Mariana Trench	11,033m
Deepest ocean	Pacific	average depth 4,300m
Deepest freshwater lake	Baikal, Russia	1,741m
Largest lake	Caspian Sea	370,848km²
Largest desert	Sahara	9,065,000km²
Largest island	Greenland	2,174,760km²
Largest country	Russia	17,068,759km²
Largest population	China	1·3bn
Largest monolith	Uluru, Australia	345m high; 9·4km base
Largest landmass	Eurasia	54,745,500km²
Largest river (volume)	Amazon	28bn gall/min
Largest peninsula	Arabian	3,236,250km²
Largest rainforest	Amazon, South America	1·2bn acres
Largest forest	Northern Russia	1·87bn acres
Largest atoll	Kwajalein, Marshall Islands	16km²
Largest glacier	Vatnajökull, Iceland	8,100km²
Largest concrete banana	The Big Banana, Australia	13m x 5m
Largest archipelago	Indonesia	17,508 islands
Largest lake in a lake	Manitou, on an island in Lake Huron	155km²
Largest city by area	Mount Isa, Australia	40,977km²
Smallest country	Vatican City	0·44km²
Smallest population	Vatican City	932 people
Smallest republic	Republic of Nauru	21km²
Longest coastline	Canada	202,080km
Longest mountain range	Andes	8,500km
Longest suspension bridge	Akashi-Kaikyo, Japan	1,990m
Longest rail tunnel	Seikan, Japan	53km
Longest road tunnel	Laerdal, Norway	24·5km
Longest river	The Nile	6,677km
Tallest inhabited building	Taipei 101, Taiwan	508m
Tallest structure	KVLY-TV Mast, USA	629m
Most land borders	China & Russia	14 countries
Most populated urban area	Tokyo, Japan	35·2m
Most remote settlement	Tristan da Cunha	2,334km from neighbours
Least populous capital city	Torshavn, Faroe Islands	pop. 16,300
Warmest sea	Red Sea	Average temp. c.25ºC
Longest bay	Bay of Bengal	1,850km
Largest banknote	Brobdingnagian bills, Philippines	14" x 8½"

Unsurprisingly, a degree of uncertainty and debate surrounds some of these entries and their specifications.

—————————— WORLD BIRTH & DEATH RATES ——————————

Births	time unit	deaths	change
130,860,569	per YEAR	56,579,396	+74,281,173
10,905,047	per MONTH	4,714,950	+6,190,098
358,522	per DAY	155,012	+203,510
14,938	per HOUR	6,459	+8,480
249	per MINUTE	108	+141
4·1	per SECOND	1·8	+2·4

[Source: US Census Bureau, 2006 · Figures may not add to totals because of rounding]

—————————— AGEING POPULATION ——————————

In 2003, 65 countries had fertility rates that were below the 'replacement level' (the level required to replace the dying), which for most countries is 2·1 children per woman. The following UN figures (World Population Prospects) show the countries with the oldest and the youngest populations, by median age, over time:

1950		1975		2005	
oldest population		*oldest population*		*oldest population*	
rank	median age	rank	median age	rank	median age
1 .. Austria	35·8	1 .. Germany	35·4	1 .. Japan	42·9
2 .. Channel Is.	35·7	2 .. Sweden	35·3	2 .. Italy	42·3
3 .. Belgium	35·6	3 .. Latvia	34·8	3 .. Germany	42·1
youngest population		*youngest population*		*youngest population*	
1 .. St Vincent	15·4	1 .. Yemen	15·0	1 .. Uganda	14·8
2 .. Tonga	15·5	2 .. Kenya	15·1	2 .. Niger	15·5
3 .. Djibouti	16·5	3 .. Botswana	15·5	3 .. Mali	15·8

—————————— THE TOP TEN MOST POPULOUS COUNTRIES ——————————

rank	1950	2002	2050 (est.)	rank
1	China	China	India	1
2	India	India	China	2
3	United States	United States	United States	3
4	Russia	Indonesia	Indonesia	4
5	Japan	Brazil	Nigeria	5
6	Indonesia	Pakistan	Bangladesh	6
7	Germany	Russia	Pakistan	7
8	Brazil	Bangladesh	Brazil	8
9	United Kingdom	Nigeria	Congo	9
10	Italy	Japan	Mexico	10

[Source: US Census, Global Population Profile 2002]

—————————— NOBEL PEACE PRIZE ——————————

The 2005 Nobel Peace Prize was awarded to the INTERNATIONAL ATOMIC
ENERGY AGENCY, and its Director General DR MOHAMED ELBARADEI (1942–)

*for their efforts to prevent nuclear energy from being used for military purposes and
to ensure that nuclear energy for peaceful purposes is used in the safest possible way*

Mohamed ElBaradei was born in Egypt in 1942, and studied law in Cairo before joining the Egyptian Ministry of Foreign Affairs in 1964. He ascended the diplomatic ladder before taking a doctorate in International Law from New York University. ElBaradei joined the International Atomic Energy Agency (IAEA) in 1984, and succeeded Hans Blix as Director General in 1997. ❦ The IAEA was established in 1957, in Vienna, to promote the development of peaceful nuclear research and oversee controls governing the misuse of nuclear power for military ends. The IAEA employs *c.*2,200 from >90 countries, and has 139 state members. ❦ Since becoming Director General, ElBaradei has argued passionately for a stronger global stance on nuclear non-proliferation. At present, efforts towards worldwide nuclear disarmament have reached an impasse. But ElBaradei has been unafraid to attack the hypocrisy of those states who hold nuclear weapons whilst criticising other countries for pursuing their own nuclear ambitions. During his leadership, ElBaradei has had to guide the agency through difficult times, most notably the unsuccessful efforts to establish the presence of nuclear weap-

ElBaradei

ons in Iraq. Recently, the IAEA has been working to prevent Iran and North Korea from developing or procuring nuclear weapons [see p.71]. In 2005, ElBaradei was reappointed Director General for a third four-year term – despite reported efforts by the United States to have him replaced. Washington's impatience with ElBaradei stems from his unwillingness to denounce Iran's alleged nuclear arms programme until he has absolute proof of its existence. ❦ Over the years, the Nobel Committee has frequently rewarded those who have campaigned for the abolition of nuclear weapons and other weapons of mass destruction [see below]. Currently many thousands of nuclear warheads wait armed and ready – approximately as many as there were when the first Non-Proliferation Treaty was signed in 1970 [see p.71]. Many saw the Nobel Committee's 2005 decision particularly appropriate, since that year marked the 60th anniversary of the atom bomb attacks on Hiroshima and Nagasaki. ❦ On accepting his Laureate, Mohamed ElBaradei declared, 'the award gives me lots of pride and also lots of responsibility. It sends a very strong message: keep doing what you are doing'.

*Some Nobel Peace Laureates who
received the Prize for their work
towards nuclear disarmament:*
1962...................... Linus Pauling
1975.........Andrei Sakharov [see p.63]

1982...... Alva Myrdal; Garcia Robles
1985....*International Physicians for the
Prevention of Nuclear War*
1995..........Joseph Rotblat; *Pugwash
Conferences on Science & World Affairs*

HOLOCAUST DENIAL

Holocaust deniers question the Nazi's genocide of 6 million Jews, often asserting that a Jewish conspiracy has perpetuated a myth of the Holocaust for political and financial gain. Germany introduced a Holocaust denial law in 1985, making it a crime to deny the organised extermination of Jews. These laws were tightened in 1994, so that anyone who publicly endorses, denies, or denigrates the Holocaust can be jailed for up to five years. The law in Austria, introduced in 1946 to prevent the possible resurgence of a fascist regime, is the most stringent of all Holocaust denial laws. This 'forbidding law' prevents anyone from questioning the Holocaust or glorifying the Nazis by, for example, displaying the swastika. In 2004, the Austrian authorities charged 724 people under this law – those convicted face up to ten years in prison[†]. The following eleven countries have laws banning Holocaust denial:

Austria · Belgium · Czech Republic · France · Germany · Israel
Lithuania · Poland · Romania · Slovakia · Switzerland

[†] British academic David Irving was jailed by an Austrian court in February 2006 for a speech he made in 1989 questioning the existence of gas chambers in Auschwitz. Irving pleaded guilty, and was sentenced to three years in prison – a punishment that was hailed by some as a victory against Holocaust denial, and derided by others as a denial of the right to freedom of thought and speech.

TOP TEN RECIPIENTS OF UK AID

The 10 top UK aid beneficiaries, according to latest figures from the OECD:

India............$419m	Ghana $200m	Malawi..........$115m
Bangladesh......$267m	Zambia..........$174m	South Africa.....$112m
Tanzania.........$265m	Congo DR......$162m	
Iraq.............$228m	Afghanistan $161m	[Source: OECD, 2004]

SAKHAROV PRIZE

Awarded by the European Union since 1988, the Sakharov Prize for Freedom of Thought aims to reward individuals and organisations who challenge oppression and campaign for human rights. It is named in honour of the Soviet physicist Andrei Sakharov (1921–89) who helped to develop the hydrogen bomb, but later won the Nobel Peace Prize for his work campaigning against nuclear weapons. In 2005, the European Parliament's €50,000 prize was shared by the following three: Nigerian lawyer, HAUWA IBRAHIM, for defending women who face execution by stoning for committing adultery · REPORTERS WITHOUT BORDERS, a group that works to protect from persecution and censorship those working in the media [see p.132] · and the LADIES IN WHITE, the wives and families of 75 Cuban dissidents who were imprisoned in 2003. The Ladies in White hold weekly vigils and peaceful demonstrations in an attempt to free their relatives. Unsurprisingly, the Cuban state prohibited the Ladies in White from travelling to Europe to accept their award.

—————————— UN PEACE AMBASSADORS ——————————

United Nations Secretary-General Kofi Annan personally recruits 'Messengers of Peace' – individuals with widely recognised talents in art, literature, music, or sport who have agreed to help focus attention on United Nations' projects. In 2006, renowned cellist Yo Yo Ma joined their ranks. The other UN Messengers of Peace are:

Muhammad Ali · Vijay Amritraj · Anna Cataldi · Michael Douglas
Jane Goodall · Enrico Macias · Wynton Marsalis · Luciano Pavarotti · Elie Wiesel

—————————— MOST COSTLY FLOODS ——————————

Below are the most costly flooding-related insurance losses, from 1970–2005, according to Swiss Re (excluding events of a geological origin, such as the 2004 Asian tsunami):

Event	location	year	victims	insured loss
Hurricane Katrina	US, Gulf of Mexico	2005	1,193	$45,000m
Hurricane Rita	US, Cuba, Mexico	2005	34	$10,000m
Hurricane Wilma	US, Mexico, Carribean	2005	20	$8,000m

—————————— THE DEATH PENALTY ——————————

Amnesty International reported that >2,148 people were executed in 22 countries during 2005. (Mexico and Liberia recently abolished their death penalties.) Below is Amnesty's estimate of the countries that executed the greatest number in 2005:

China......>1,770 | Saudi Arabia.. >86 | Pakistan ....31 | Vietnam 21
Iran...........>94 | USA ....60 | Yemen ....24 | Jordan 11

—————————— WORLD'S TEN WORST DICTATORS ——————————

American magazine *Parade* annually publishes a list of the world's worst dictators, by analysing their record of human rights abuse. The top ten from 2006 follows:

No.	Dictator	age	country	years' reign	facial hair?
1	Omar al-Bashir	62	Sudan	17	goatee
2	Kim Jong-il	63	North Korea	12	none
3	Than Shwe	72	Burma	14	none
4	Robert Mugabe	81	Zimbabwe	26	Hitleresque
5	Islam Karimov	67	Uzbekistan	16	none
6	Hu Jintao	63	China	4	none
7	King Abdullah	82	Saudi Arabia	11	cavalier beard
8	Saparmurat Niyazov	65	Turkmenistan	16	none
9	Seyed Ali Khamanei	66	Iran	17	bushy beard
10	Teodoro Obiang Nguema	63	Equatorial Guinea	27	none

——————————— TSUNAMI AID ———————————

In response to the 2004 Asian tsunami, governments worldwide pledged vast sums of money in aid. However, figures released in March 2006 by the Organisation for Economic Co-operation and Development (OECD) revealed that many countries had paid out only a small proportion of the money they had initially promised:

Country	$m pledge	paid	%		Country	$m pledge	paid	%
Australia	193	117	60·6		Japan	601	539	89·7
Canada	176	131	74·4		Netherlands	156	82	52·6
France	243	109	44·9		New Zealand	37	37	100·0
Germany	313	82	26·2		Norway	139	132	95·0
Greece	33	33	100·0		Portugal	13	7	53·8
Ireland	26	23	88·5		Spain	114	17	14·9
Italy	94	42	44·7		UK	149	130	87·2
					USA	792	277	35·0

——————————— GLOBAL FREEDOM ———————————

The US pressure group Freedom House annually compiles a *Freedom in the World Survey*, classifying countries by the political rights and civil liberties their citizens enjoy. Countries are judged to be: FREE, PARTLY FREE, or NOT FREE. The survey showed 27 countries became more free in 2006, and only 9 regressed. The following countries have been classified by *www.freedomhouse.org* as still being NOT FREE:

Algeria · Angola · Azerbaijan · Belarus · Bhutan · Brunei · Burma · Cambodia Cameroon · Chad · China · Congo (Kinshasa) · Côte d'Ivoire · Cuba · Egypt Equatorial Guinea · Eritrea · Guinea · Haiti · Iran · Iraq · Kazakhstan · Laos Libya · Maldives · Nepal · North Korea · Oman · Pakistan · Qatar · Russia Rwanda · Saudi Arabia · Somalia · Sudan · Swaziland · Syria · Tajikistan · Togo Tunisia · Turkmenistan · UAE · Uzbekistan · Vietnam · Zimbabwe

——————— INTERNATIONAL DEVELOPMENT & AID ———————

Organisation for Economic Co-operation and Development (OECD) figures show that development aid rose from $69bn in 2003 to $79·5bn in 2004, the highest ever level. However, only 5 of the 22 major donors had managed to hit the UN target of giving 0·7% of their Gross National Income to Overseas Development Aid:

Country	ODA $m	% GNI		Country	ODA $m	% GNI
Australia	1,460	0·25		Luxembourg	236	0·83
Canada	2,599	0·27		Netherlands	4,204	0·73
Denmark	2,037	0·85		Norway	2,199	0·87
France	8,473	0·41		Spain	2,437	0·24
Germany	7,534	0·28		Sweden	2,722	0·78
Ireland	607	0·39		UK	7,883	0·36
Japan	8,906	0·19		US	19,705	0·17

[Latest released figures: 2004]

—COMMONWEALTH OF INDEPENDENT STATES (CIS)—

The CIS was formed in 1991 to aid co-operation between the former Soviet states:

Armenia · Azerbaijan · Belarus · Georgia · Kazakhstan · Kyrgyzstan
Moldova · Russia · Tajikistan · Turkmenistan · Ukraine · Uzbekistan

—————————————CAPITAL OF BURMA—————————

The Myanmar/Burmese government declared a sudden surprise switch of capital city on 6 November 2005, giving startled officials no choice but to pile on to buses and relocate from bustling Rangoon (pop. *c.*4m) to sleepy Pyinmana (pop. *c.*50,000) – a remote half-built city surrounded by mountains and jungle. Pyinmana was swiftly renamed Naypyidaw Myodaw ('The Royal Capital') – a curious decision since the country has no monarch. The first official event to be held in Naypyidaw Myodaw took place in March 2006, when General Than Shwe addressed 12,000 of his troops in celebration of Armed Forces' Day. It is thought that the abrupt change of capital was prompted by the junta's fear of revolt, a general paranoia, and the prognostications of fortune tellers, who wield great influence within government.

————————————LANDLOCKED COUNTRIES————————

Afghanistan · Andorra · Armenia · Austria · Azerbaijan · Belarus
Bhutan · Bolivia · Botswana · Burkina Faso · Burundi · Central African Rep.
Chad · Czech Republic · Ethiopia · Holy See (Vatican City) · Hungary
Kazakhstan · Kyrgyzstan · Laos · Lesotho · Liechtenstein[†] · Luxembourg
Malawi · Mali · Moldova · Mongolia · Nepal · Niger · Paraguay · Rwanda
San Marino · Slovakia · Swaziland · Switzerland · Tajikistan
The Former Yugoslav Republic of Macedonia · Turkmenistan
Uganda · Uzbekistan[†] · West Bank · Zambia · Zimbabwe
[† *'double landlocked' countries, being those surrounded by landlocked countries*]

————————————SYMBOL OF CYPRUS————————————

The Republic of Cyprus announced in February 2006 that the cyclamen (*Cyclamen cyprium*) had been chosen as the national plant, and the golden oak (*Quercus alnifolia*) the national tree. The choice was hampered by stipulations that the symbols be native to the island and not used by another country. Whereas the golden oak was an easy choice (the only other indigenous tree is the cedar, which is the symbol of Lebanon), Cypriot officials took 15 years to choose the cyclamen from a list of 140 native plants. Both will now be used to promote tourism and the environment.

In 2006, Venezuela's legislators acquiesced to President Chavez's proposals to change the national symbols. The galloping 'Imperial' horse on the coat of arms will now face left rather than right. Commentators have speculated that the change mimics the new political direction of the country.

THE FBI'S MOST WANTED

Fugitive [as at 20·9·06]	*allegation*	*reward*
Osama bin Laden	terrorism	$25,000,000†
Diego Leon Montoya Sanchez	drug running	$5,000,000
James J. Bulger	murder; racketeering	$1,000,000
Victor Manuel Gerena	armed robbery	$1,000,000
Ralph B. Phillips (recaptured 9·9·06)	prison escape	$100,000
Robert William Fisher	murder; arson	$100,000
Glen Stewart Godwin	murder; prison escape	$100,000
Richard Steve Goldberg	child abuse	$100,000
Jorge Alberto Lopez-Orozco	murder	$100,000
Donald Eugene Webb	murder	$100,000

† An extra $2m is offered by the Airline Pilots Association and Air Transport Association.
(Contact your local FBI office or the US Consulate with any information on the above.)

UNIVERSAL DECLARATION OF HUMAN RIGHTS
---

[1] Right to equality and dignity. [2] Freedom from discrimination. [3] Right to life, liberty, personal security. [4] Freedom from slavery. [5] Freedom from torture and degradation. [6] Right to recognition before the law. [7] Equality before the law. [8] Right of appeal by competent tribunal. [9] Freedom from arbitrary arrest or exile. [10] Right to fair public hearing. [11] Presumption of innocence; freedom from retrospective law. [12] Freedom from interference with privacy, family, and correspondence. [13] Right of free movement. [14] Right to asylum from persecution. [15] Right to a nationality and freedom to change it. [16] Right to free marriage and family. [17] Right to own property. [18] Freedom of thought, belief, conscience, and worship. [19] Freedom of opinion and expression. [20] Right of peaceful assembly and association. [21] Right to participate in government; free elections under universal suffrage. [22] Right to social security. [23] Right to choose employment; join trades union; equal pay. [24] Right to rest and holidays. [25] Right to adequate living standards; protection of children. [26] Right to free elementary education. [27] Right to participate in cultural and scientific life. [28] Right to a social order that assures these rights. [29] Rights may only be limited by law to secure protection for others or the community. [30] Freedom from state or other interference in the above rights.　　*Condensed from the 1948 UN Universal Declaration*

FOREIGNERS WITHIN POPULATIONS

Below are the proportions of foreigners within various countries [OECD 2003 data]

Foreign population %		
Luxembourg 38·6	New Zealand 19·5	France 5·6
Australia 22·8	Canada 18·2	UK 4·8
Switzerland 20·0	USA 12·1	Spain 3·9
	Germany 8·9	Japan 1·5

WORLD'S MOTHERS REPORT

The disparity between the health of mothers and their babies in the developing world and the western world is highlighted by Save the Children's annual Mothers' Index – which reveals that 4m newborn babies die each year. The latest report, released in May 2006, ranked the status of mothers and babies in 125 countries, based on 10 indicators relating to health and education. The best and worst countries were:

Best countries		Worst countries	
1 . . . . Sweden	4= . . . . Norway	125 . . . . Niger	120 . . . . Sierra Leone
2= . . . . . . Denmark	7= . . . . Australia	124 . . . Burkina Faso	119 . . . . . . Ethiopia
2= . . . . Finland	7= . . . . . Netherlands	123 . . . . Mali	118 . . . . Yemen
4= . . . . Austria	9 . . . . Canada	122 . . . . Chad	117 . . C African Rep
4= . . . . Germany	10= . . . . USA	121 . . Guinea-Bissau	115= . D Rep Congo
	10= . . . . UK		115= . . . . Liberia

Compared to a mother in the top 10 countries, a mother in the bottom 10 countries is 28 times more likely to lose her child in the first year of its life, and >750 times more likely to die during pregnancy or childbirth. In the bottom countries, only 1 in 4 women are literate and just 1 in 3 children attend school. In the top ten countries, nearly every woman is literate and most children go to school. Simple solutions (providing midwives, &c), could reduce deaths by 70%.

UN MILLENNIUM DEVELOPMENT GOALS

By the year 2015, all 191 member states of the United Nations have pledged to meet the following 8 Millennium Development Goals to help the world's poor:

Eradicate extreme poverty and hunger · Achieve universal primary education
Promote gender equality and empower women · Reduce child mortality
Improve maternal health · Combat HIV/AIDS, malaria, and other diseases
Ensure environmental sustainability · Develop a global partnership for development

ERADICATION OF POLIO

In February 2006 the World Health Organization (WHO) announced that the number of countries with indigenous polio had fallen to an all-time low, and that the indigenous polio virus had not circulated in Egypt or Niger for over 12 months. Therefore, only 4 countries are currently affected by polio: Afghanistan, India, Nigeria, and Pakistan. ❦ The Global Polio Eradication Program was launched in 1988 with 166 member states; its aim was to rid the world of the virus by the end of the year 2000. Despite failing to meet this initial target, the programme has reduced cases of polio by 99% over the last 15 years and, by implementing mass immunization with 'next-generation' vaccines, it hopes soon to achieve total eradication. ❦ Poliomyelitis is an acute infectious disease (that mainly affects children), caused by a virus that can attack the central nervous system. Symptoms include the following: sore throat, headache, vomiting, and stiffness of neck and back. Polio can result in muscle atrophy, paralysis and deformity, and can be fatal.

——————————— INTERNATIONAL SHARK ATTACKS ———————————

The International Shark Attack File (ISAF) is a record of all known worldwide shark attacks against humans; it is collated by the American Elasmobranch[†] Society and the Florida Museum of Natural History. The file contains 4,000 investigations into shark attacks from the 1500s to the present day. The ISAF reported that in 2004 there were 109 shark-related incidents worldwide – 61 of which were confirmed cases of unprovoked attacks. The majority of these incidents (27 attacks) took place in North American waters. Other locations that witnessed multiple attacks were: Australia (12), Brazil (5), South Africa (5), and Reunion Island (3). The following table shows the total number of shark attacks worldwide between 1990–2004:

Year	attacks	deaths						
2004	61	7	1998	51	6	1991	33	3
2003	57	4	1997	49	9	1990	35	2
2002	63	3	1996	43	3			
2001	68	4	1995	67	10	† Elasomobranch are		
2000	78	11	1994	57	7	cartilaginous fish. Members		
1999	56	4	1993	41	11	of this class include sharks,		
			1992	48	6	rays, and skates.		

Three Florida women died in alligator attacks between 9–14 May 2006. Such attacks were previously rare: the Florida Fish & Wildlife Conservation Commission reports only 17 alligator-related deaths since 1948. The 2006 deaths were attributed to warm weather, which makes alligators more peckish.

——————————— THE RED LIST · 2006 ———————————

The World Conservation Union (IUCN) publishes an annual 'Red List' of species that are under threat worldwide – classifying them from those considered to be at a minor risk of extinction ('Least Concern'), to those actually rendered extinct:

Least Concern → *Near Threatened* → *Vulnerable* → *Endangered* →
Critically Endangered → *Extinct in the Wild* → *Extinct*

In 2006, the number of known threatened species was 16,119 – 784 species were declared extinct. The status of 871 species on the Red List was re-assessed: 172 declined in status and 139 improved. Below are some recent successes and failures:

Species	previous status	current status 2006
Common hippopotamus	Least Concern (1996)	Vulnerable
White-tailed eagle	Near Threatened (2004)	Least Concern
Common skate	Endangered (2000)	Critically Endangered
Dama gazelle	Endangered (1996)	Critically Endangered
Thick-billed ground dove	Critically Endangered (2004)	Extinct
Abbott's booby	Critically Endangered (2004)	Endangered
Angel shark	Vulnerable (2000)	Critically Endangered
Polar bear	Low Risk [sic] (1996)	Vulnerable
Kirtland's warbler	Vulnerable (2004)	Near Threatened

———————————————ASYLUM FATIGUE———————————————

In April 2006, the United Nations refugee agency (UNHCR) reported that there were 9·2m refugees globally in 2005, the lowest figure for 25 years. It is thought that numbers have fallen because the resolution of some conflicts (such as in Afghanistan and Angola) has allowed refugees to return home. However, the UNHCR warned of a disturbing increase in 'asylum fatigue', where refugees are perceived as illegal immigrants, criminals, or potential terrorists, rather than victims of conflict and displacement. Although *c.*65% of the world's refugees are in the developing world, there is a growing confusion in the West about the difference between refugees and illegal immigrants, resulting in a lack of support and tolerance for those in genuine need. UNHCR data below show the states with the highest refugee populations:

2004 *refugees/1,000 inhabitants*	
Armenia . . . . 78·0	Tanzania . . . . 15·7
Chad . . . . 26·7	Iran . . . . 15·0
Serbia & Montenegro . . . . 26·3	Zambia . . . . 14·9
Djibouti . . . . 22·7	Guinea . . . . 14·8
Congo . . . . 17·1	Denmark . . . . 12·0
	(United Kingdom . . . . 4·8)

Additionally, *c.*7·5m are 'internally displaced' from the conflicts in DR Congo and Sudan alone.

——————— SIGNIFICANT ONGOING CONFLICTS ———————

Middle East   *began*
US global 'war on terror' & 'terrorists with global reach' 2001
Iraq interim government and allies & Iraqi and foreign resistance 2003
Israel & Hamas, Hezbollah, Islamic Jihad, &c. 1975
Asia
Afghanistan: Kabul government & Al-Qaeda, Taleban and warlords 1978
India & Assam and Manipur insurgents (ULFA & NDFB), &c. 1982; 1986
Nepal & Maoist insurgents 1996
Philippines & Abu Sayyaf 1999
Latin America
Colombia & National Liberation Army (ELN) 1978
Colombia & Revolutionary Armed Forces of Colombia (FARC) 1978
Europe
Russia & Chechnya 1994; 1996
Africa
Democratic Republic of Congo & indigenous insurgents 1997
Nigeria: communal violence 1970
Somalia: Somaliland, Puntland, and other factions 1978
Sudan & Sudan Liberation and Justice and Equality Movements 1983; 2003

[Source: Center for Defense Information, as at 1 January 2006 · Only conflicts classed as significant included, 22 low-level political violence or conflicts in suspension are not included. Since 2005, when 22 conflicts were classed as significant, the situation has improved in eight countries.]

─── NUCLEAR PROLIFERATION ───

The debate over nuclear proliferation intensified in 2006, as Iran maintained its defiance of the UN [see p.32], tensions increased with N. Korea, and Gordon Brown signalled his intention to replace Trident. Below are the *estimated* stockpiles of nuclear warheads held by the 9 declared, suspected, or professed nuclear states:

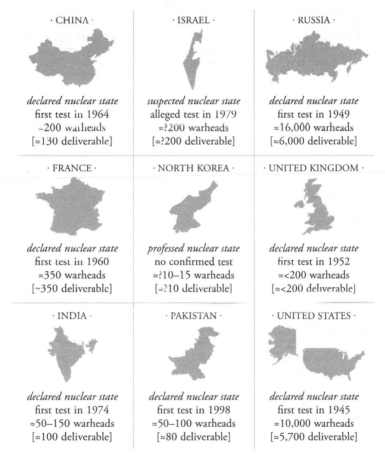

· CHINA ·

declared nuclear state
first test in 1964
~200 warheads
[≈130 deliverable]

· ISRAEL ·

suspected nuclear state
alleged test in 1979
≈?200 warheads
[≈?200 deliverable]

· RUSSIA ·

declared nuclear state
first test in 1949
≈16,000 warheads
[≈6,000 deliverable]

· FRANCE ·

declared nuclear state
first test in 1960
≈350 warheads
[~350 deliverable]

· NORTH KOREA ·

professed nuclear state
no confirmed test
≈?10–15 warheads
[≈?10 deliverable]

· UNITED KINGDOM ·

declared nuclear state
first test in 1952
≈<200 warheads
[≈<200 deliverable]

· INDIA ·

declared nuclear state
first test in 1974
≈50–150 warheads
[≈100 deliverable]

· PAKISTAN ·

declared nuclear state
first test in 1998
≈50–100 warheads
[≈80 deliverable]

· UNITED STATES ·

declared nuclear state
first test in 1945
≈10,000 warheads
[≈5,700 deliverable]

The respected *Bulletin of the Atomic Scientists* regularly charts the 'global level of nuclear danger and the state of international security' via its aptly-named 'doomsday clock'. In 1947, the clock was inaugurated at 7 minutes to midnight (–7), and has shifted with risk every few years since then. The clock hit –3 in 1949, when the Soviets exploded their first atomic bomb, and –2 in 1953, when US and Soviet tests occurred within nine months of each other. Over the decades, the clock has ticked closer to and further from doomsday – slipping back to –17 in 1991 with the US/Soviet Strategic Arms Reduction Treaty. The clock currently stands at –7. [Sources: Center for Nonproliferation Studies; US Congressional Research Service; globalsecurity.org; *Bulletin of the Atomic Scientists*]

VANISHING DELTAS

Research led by Jason Ericson at the Virginia Department of Conservation and Recreation, published in 2006 in the journal *Global and Planetary Change*, revealed the adverse effect that rising sea-levels may have on river deltas. Deltas are formed when river sediment settles in a large fan-like shape at the mouth of a river (they are so-named because the Nile delta resembles the Greek letter). Ericson sampled 40 deltas worldwide and, by extrapolating rising sea-level data, he suggested that by 2050, 28,000km^2 of land and 8·7m people could be at risk from rising seas, land sinkage, or storms. According to his data, the most vulnerable deltas worldwide are:

Delta	*people at risk by 2050*
Bengal delta, Bangladesh	3·4m
Mekong delta, Vietnam	1·9m
Nile delta, Egypt	1·3m
Yangtze delta, China	0·48m
Mississippi delta, USA	0·48m
Godavari delta, India	0·45m
	[Source: *New Scientist*]

DISAPPEARING FORESTS

A 2006 report by E. Katsigris et al., in the *International Forestry Review*, suggests that current rates of logging (in many cases driven by China's growing demand for imported wood) may deplete 'economically accessible mature natural forests' in the very near future. Of special concern are Cambodia (with *c.*4–9 years of logging left); Myanmar (with *c.*10–15 years); and Papua New Guinea (*c.*13–16 years).

ECOLOGICAL FOOTPRINT

Ecological footprints are a measure of the amount of land required sustainably to support a population. A country's footprint can be measured by comparing the total area required to grow the food it consumes, absorb the waste created from its energy consumption, and house its infrastructure. According to the World Wildlife Federation (WWF), the *global* ecological footprint in 2001 was 2·2 hectares per person. However, because mankind is using more of the world's resources than are being regenerated, the world's footprint exceeds its biocapacity by 21%. The following table shows a selection of national footprints and deficits (those with a minus deficit have a surplus of resources, and are thus living 'within their means'):

Footprint	*(global ha/person)*	*Deficit*
7·7	Australia	−11·5
2·2	Brazil	−8·0
6·4	Canada	−8·0
1·5	China	0·8
7·0	Finland	−5·4
5·8	France	2·8
1·7	Gabon	−18·4
4·8	Germany	2·9
0·8	India	0·4
4·3	Japan	3·6
4·4	Russia	−2·6
2·8	South Africa	0·8
9·9	UAE	8·9
5·4	UK	3·9
9·5	USA	4·7

(Therefore, the UK uses 3·9 hectares per person more than it can support.)

RECYCLING SYMBOLS

A bewildering array of recycling symbols exists across the world, and the general confusion they cause is exacerbated by a lack of international agreement. Below are some common everyday symbols and, underneath, some of those for plastics:

indicates recycling costs were paid	*recyclable glass*	*is recyclable or contains recycled material – often indicated by a percentage*		*recyclable aluminium*	*European Eco-labelling participant*

PETE	**HDPE**	**V**	**LDPE**	**PP**	**PS**	
polyethylene terephthalate	*high density polyethylene*	*PVC*	*low density polyethylene*	*polypropylene*	*polystyrene*	*other/hybrid materials*

THREATENED BY CLIMATE CHANGE

Environmental groups have alerted UNESCO, the body that oversees World Heritage [see p.218], that four sites are under threat from climate change (rising temperatures and the acidification of oceans are considered to be the cause). The sites at risk are:

Sagarmatha National Park in Nepal (the location of Mount Everest)
Belize Barrier Reef · Huascarán National Park, Peru
Waterton-Glacier International Peace Park, on the USA–Canada border

ENVIRONMENTAL PERFORMANCE

A team of environmental experts from Yale and Columbia Universities has ranked countries around the world on their environmental performance. The ranking, known as the Environmental Performance Index (EPI), scores 133 countries on 16 indicators, across 6 policy categories: environmental health; air quality; water resources; biodiversity; productive natural resources; and sustainable energy. The research was presented to the World Economic Forum in January 2006, in an effort to encourage policy-making on environmental issues. The following table shows the countries with the best and worst Environmental Performance Index scores:

The best		*The worst*	
1 ....New Zealand	6 ....Austria	133 .... Niger	128 ....Angola
2 ....Sweden	7 ....Denmark	132 .... Chad	127 ...... Pakistan
3 ....Finland	8 ....Canada	131 ... Mauritania	126 . Burkina Faso
4 ......Czech Rep.	9 ....Malaysia	130 .... Mali	125 ...Bangladesh
5 .... UK	10..........Ireland	129 ...... Ethiopia	124 ....Sudan

—— SAFFIR-SIMPSON HURRICANE INTENSITY SCALE ——

Category	wind (mph)	storm surge (ft)	description	example
1	74–95	3–5	Minimal	Gaston (2004)
2	96–110	6–8	Moderate	Frances (2004)
3	111–130	9–12	Extensive	Ivan (2004)
4	131–155	13–18	Extreme	Charley (2004)
5	>156	>18	Catastrophic	Katrina (2005)

With 27 named storms and 15 hurricanes, the 2005 Atlantic basin hurricane season (1 Jun–30 Nov) was the worst on record. Hurricanes are usually named from a pool of 21 names, which are recycled every 6 years. However, the freak conditions of 2005 forced the World Meteorological Organization (WMO) to call into service the letters of the Greek alphabet (e.g. Tropical Storm Alpha). ❧ Each year the names of particularly violent storms are permanently 'retired' – in 2006 the WMO declared that the names Dennis, Katrina, Rita, Stan, and Wilma would be replaced on the 2011 roster by Don, Katia, Rina, Sean, and Whitney. Since naming began in 1953, 67 names have been retired; 2005 had the most retired in a single season.

Atlantic basin hurricane names for 2007:	Dean	Jerry	Pablo
Andrea	Erin	Karen	Rebekah
Barry	Felix	Lorenzo	Sebastien
Chantal	Gabrielle	Melissa	Tanya
	Humberto	Noel	Van
	Ingrid	Olga	Wendy

—— VOLCANIC EXPLOSIVITY INDEX ——

Below is the Volcanic Explosivity Index (VEI) used to classify volcanic eruptions:

VEI	category	plume	frequency	classification
0	Non-explosive	<100m	daily	Hawaiian
1	Gentle	100m–1km	daily	Hawaiian/Strombolian
2	Explosive	1–5km	weekly	Strombolian/Vulcanian
3	Severe	3–15km	yearly	Vulcanian
4	Cataclysmic	10–25km	10s years	Vulcanian/Plinian
5	Paroxysmal	>25km	100s years	Plinian
6	Colossal	>25km	100s years	Plinian/Ultra-Plinian
7	Super-colossal	>25km	1,000s years	Ultra-Plinian
8	Mega-colossal	>25km	10,000s years	Ultra-Plinian

No VEI 8 volcano has exploded in recorded human history. The last VEI 8 event took place *c.*74,000 years ago when Toba erupted in Indonesia; it is speculated that this explosion may have pushed mankind to the very brink of extinction. Scientists continue to debate the risks posed by the supervolcano in Yellowstone National Park, USA, which has the potential to reach VEI 8. Explosions of that size take place every *c.*600,000 years, and one has not occurred at Yellowstone for 620,000 years. Were a VEI 8 event to hit Yellowstone, the global consequences would be dire.

─── BEAUFORT WIND SCALE ───

Beaufort Scale	sea height feet	wind knots	wind MPH	description
0	—	<1	<1	calm
1	¼	1–3	1–3	light air
2	½	4–6	4–7	light breeze
3	2	7–10	8–12	gentle breeze
4	3½	11–16	13–18	moderate breeze
5	6	17–21	19–24	fresh breeze
6	9½	22–27	25–31	strong breeze
7	13½	28–33	32–38	near gale
8	18	34–40	39–46	gale
9	23	41–47	47–54	strong gale
10	29	48–55	55–63	storm
11	37	56–63	64–72	violent storm
12	—	64	73	hurricane

─── EARTHQUAKE SCALES ───

RICHTER	MERCALLI SCALE & DESCRIPTION	SEVERITY
<4.3	i ..... barely noticeable; doors may swing ii .... detected by some; slight iii................... traffic-like vibration	Mild
4.3–4.8	iv................cars rock; pictures move v...........buildings tremble; trees shake	Moderate
4.8–6.2	vi.......... plaster cracks, hard to stand vii ....alarm; moderate building damage viii.......... fright; considerable damage	Intermediate
6.2–7.3	ix.......... panic; landslides, earth shifts x.......ground cracks; buildings collapse	Severe
>7.3	xi...... destruction; few buildings stand xii .. devastation; ground moves in waves	Catastrophic

[The relationship between Richter and Mercalli scales is approximate]

─── SIEBERG-AMBRASEYS SEAWAVE INTENSITY SCALE ───

1	Very Light	perceptible only on tide-gauge records
2	Light	noticed by those living along the shore
3	Rather Strong	generally noticed; flooding of sloping coasts; boats carried away
4	Strong	shore flooding; light scouring; solid structures on the coast damaged
5	Very Strong	shore flooding to some depth; solid structures damaged; light structures destroyed; severe scouring; people drowned; strong roar
6	Disastrous	partial or complete destruction of structures far from shore; coast flooding to great depths; big ships severely damaged; many casualties

WEATHER RECORDS

United Kingdom [Met Office]

Max. temperature	38·5°C	Brogdale nr. Faversham	10·08·2003
Lowest temperature	−27·2°C	Braemar, Grampian	11·02·1895
Max. rainfall 24 hrs	279mm	Martinstown, Dorset	18·07·1955
Max. rainfall 60 mins	92mm	Maidenhead, Berkshire	12·07·1901
Max. rainfall 5 mins	32mm	Preston, Lancashire	10·08·1893
Max. monthly sunshine	384 hrs	Eastbourne, Sussex	July 1911
Lowest monthly sunshine	0 hrs	Westminster, London	Dec 1890
Max. gust record	150 knots	Cairngorm, Grampian	20·03·1986

The World [NOAA]

Max. annual rainfall	13,299mm	Lloro, Colombia	average
Least annual rainfall	0·762mm	Arica, Chile	average
Max. temperature	57·7°C	Al Azizia, Libya	13·09·1922
Lowest temperature	−89·4°C	Vostok, Antarctica	21·07·1983

THE SUN INDEX

The Sun Index, designed to protect against UV radiation, categorises 4 skin types:

[1] *white skin that burns easily and tends not to tan*
[2] *white skin that tans easily* · [3] *brown skin* · [4] *black skin*

By estimating cloud cover, forecasters can then assess the risk for each skin type:

Skin type	Sun Index									
	1	2	3	4	5	6	7	8	9	10
1	risk: *low*	*medium*			*high*		*very high*			
2	risk: *low*				*medium*		*high*			
3	risk: *low*					*medium*				*high*
4	risk: *low*						*medium*			

Low risk: sun is harmless · *Medium risk*: sun not a danger but avoid spending >2 hours in direct sun · *High risk*: you could burn within 30 minutes; cover up, stay out of the sun, and wear sunscreen SPF 15 · *Very high risk*: you could burn severely in 20–30 minutes; cover up, stay out of sun, and wear sunscreen SPF 15.

SUN PROTECTION FACTOR

Sun Protection Factor (SPF) indicates the strength of a sunscreen lotion: the higher the SPF, the greater the protection. SPF is a measure of the time taken for skin to burn while wearing sunscreen compared to skin without protection. So, skin that would normally burn in 10 minutes, would be protected for *c.*20 minutes with a suncream SPF 2. In strong sun it is advisable to apply suncream of at least SPF 15.

--------------------- BIG CATS IN BRITAIN ---------------------

The British Big Cats Society (BBCS) reported in 2006 that sightings of big cats in Britain had increased, with 2,123 reports logged between April 2004 and July 2005. Although a proportion of sightings can be discounted as hoaxes, there is a growing body of evidence (including a recently discovered puma skull in Devon) that big cats are at large. 60% of the reports were of panther-like black cats; 32% were sandy-coloured, possibly pumas; and 6% resembled lynx. In the 1960s it was fashionable to keep big cats, and when the Dangerous Animals Act came into force in 1976, some owners chose to set them free rather than see them destroyed: the BBCS claims to have evidence of 23 such releases. The areas with the most sightings were:

Devon 132	Gloucestershire......104	Somerset..............91
Yorkshire 127	Sussex................103	Leicestershire........89
Scotland.............125	Cornwall 99	
Wales 123	Kent 92	[Source: BBCS, March 2006]

--------------- SPECIAL AREAS OF CONSERVATION---------------

The EU Habitats Directive (92/43/EEC) came into force in 1992, requiring member states to create *Natura 2000* – a network of Special Areas of Conservation (SACs) designed to afford protection to wild animals, habitats, and plants. The directive outlines 788 species and 189 'habitat types' across Europe that are in the greatest need of conservation. The UK has 76 of the described habitat types, and 43 of the listed animals are native to these shores. In 2000, the European Commission instigated legal action against the British government following their failure to create adequate SACs; since then, 608 SACs have been designated in these areas:

Region	SACs	area (ha)			
England	228	 808,976	Scotland............	235......	921,207
England/Scotland.....	3	 112,478	Wales	85......	589,890
England/Wales........	5	 5,552	UK Total	608....	2,504,016
Northern Ireland.....	52	65,913	[Source: Joint Nature Conservation Cmte]		

As part of the directive, the UK government should 'study the desirability of reintroducing species in Annex IV that are native to [its] territory'; this includes animals such as bears, wolves, and lynx.

--------------- CO_2 EMISSIONS BY AREA---------------

According to British Gas in 2006, a typical house in Reading uses 27% more gas in a year than the average, releasing the same CO_2 as a Boeing 747 flying 13,000 miles. The following towns have the greatest CO_2 emissions in kg *per* dwelling *per* year:

Reading........... 6,189	Sunderland....... 5,504	Leeds 5,333
Leicester.......... 5,565	Birmingham...... 5,424	Greater London.. 5,318
Bradford.......... 5,539	Nottingham...... 5,419	Sheffield.......... 5,247

WORLD WONDERS, & OTHER 7s

7 MODERN WONDERS
(American Society of Civil Engineers)
The Empire State Building
The Itaipu Dam · The CN Tower
The Panama Canal · Channel Tunnel
The North Sea Protection Works
The Golden Gate Bridge

7 CAUSES OF GREATNESS IN CITIES
The palace of a Prince
A navigable river
The residence of the nobility
The seat of justice
Public schools of good learning
Immunities from taxes
Opinion of sanctity

7 UNDERWATER WONDERS
Palau · The Belize Barrier Reef
The Galapagos Islands
The Northern Red Sea
Lake Baikal
The Great Barrier Reef
The Deep Sea Vents

7 PRE-MODERN WONDERS
Stonehenge · The Colosseum
The Catacombs of Kom el Shoqafa
The Great Wall of China
The Porcelain Tower of Nanjing
The Hagia Sophia
The Leaning Tower of Pisa

**7 WONDERS OF THE
ANCIENT WORLD**
The Pyramids of Egypt
The Colossus of Rhodes
The Hanging Gardens of Babylon
The Mausoleum of Halicarnassus
The Statue of Zeus at Olympia
The Temple of Artemis at Ephesus
The Pharos of Alexandria

7 NATURAL WONDERS
(according to CNN)
The Grand Canyon
The Harbour of Rio de Janeiro
The Northern Lights
The Great Barrier Reef
Victoria Falls
Mount Everest
Paricutin Volcano

7 WONDERS OF THE WEALD
Bedgebury National Pinetum
Lamberhurst Vineyard
The High Weald
Marie Place Gardens
Bayham Old Abbey
Scotney Castle Garden
Bewl Water

'No one can remember more than seven of anything.'— St Robert Bellarmine, on why his catechism omitted the eight beatitudes.

The New 7 Wonders Foundation is a privately funded organisation that is attempting to create a new list of world wonders. Since 2001, more than 19 million people worldwide have voted for their favourite landmarks. In January 2006, a short-list of 21 potential wonders was announced, to be voted on during the year. The new wonders will be revealed on 1 January 2007. The short-list comprised:

Acropolis, Greece	Eiffel Tower, France	Petra, Jordan
Alhambra, Spain	Great Wall, China	Pyramids of Giza, Egypt
Angkor, Cambodia	Hagia Sophia, Turkey	Statue of Liberty, USA
Chichen Itza, Mexico	Kyomizu Temple, Japan	Stonehenge, UK
Christ Redeemer, Brazil	Kremlin, Russia	Opera House, Australia
Colosseum, Italy	Machu Picchu, Peru	Taj Mahal, India
Easter Island Statues	Neuschwanstein, Ger.	Timbuktu, Mali

——EXPENSIVE CITIES——

The Economist Intelligence Unit annually charts the cost of living in cities around the world. The survey revealed that in 2005 Oslo usurped Tokyo as the world's most expensive city, after 14 years. Eight of the most expensive cities are in Europe, with the first US city, New York, ranks at 27. The ten most expensive cities were (2004 position in brackets):

1 (3)........Oslo	6(5) Copenhagen
2 (1)....... Tokyo	7 (7)..... London
3 (8)... Reykjavik	8 (6)...... Zurich
4= (2) ..... Osaka	9 (8)......Geneva
4= (4) ....Paris	10 (10) ..Helsinki

——— POLITE CITIES———

Reader's Digest sent reporters on to the streets in 2006, to explore which cities around the globe were the most polite. Researchers dropped papers in the street to see if anyone offered to help, counted how often doors were held open for them, and noted if shop assistants said thank you. Extensive investigation unmasked Mumbai as the rudest city. The most polite cities were:

1 ..... New York	4=........ Zagreb
2 .... Zurich	7=..... Auckland
3 ....'Toronto	7=....... Warsaw
4=........ Berlin	9 ... Mexico City
4=..... São Paulo	10.... Stockholm

————————— NOTES TO THE GAZETTEER —————————

The gazetteer on the following pages is designed to allow comparisons to be made between countries around the world. As might be expected, some of the data are tentative and open to debate. A range of sources has been consulted, including the CIA's *World Factbook*, Amnesty International, HM Revenue and Customs, &c.

Size km²	*sum of all land and water areas delimited by international boundaries and coastlines*
Population	*mainly July 2006 estimate; some vary*
Flying time	*approximate actual travelling time from London Heathrow to capital city;*
	will vary depending on route and connecting flight, as well as direction travelled, &c.
GMT	*based on capital city; varies across some countries; varies with daylight saving*
Life expectancy at birth	*in years; mainly 2006 estimate*
Infant mortality	*deaths of infants <1, per 1,000 live births, per year; mainly 2006 estimate*
Median age	*mainly 2006 estimate*
Birth & death rates	*average per 1,000 persons in the population at midyear; mainly 2006 estimate*
Fertility rate	*average theoretical number of children per woman; mainly 2006 estimate*
HIV rate	*percentage of adults (15–49) living with HIV/AIDS; mainly 2003 estimate*
Literacy rate	*definition (especially of target age) varies; mainly 2003 estimate*
Exchange rate	*spot rate at 6·30·06*
GDP per capita	*($) GDP on purchasing power parity basis/population; mainly 2005*
Inflation	*annual % change in consumer prices; years vary, generally from 2005*
Unemployment	*% of labour force without jobs; years vary, generally from 2005*
Voting age	*voting age; (U)niversal; (C)ompulsory for at least one election; *=entitlement varies*
Military service	*age, length of service, sex and/or religion required to serve vary*
Death penalty	*(N) no death penalty; (N*) death penalty not used in practice;*
	(Y) death penalty for common crimes; (Y) death penalty for exceptional crimes only*
National Day	*some countries have more than one; not all are universally recognised*

——— GAZETTEER · ALGERIA – SOUTH KOREA · [1/4] ———

Country	Size (km²)	Population (m)	Capital city	Phone access code	Phone country code	Flying time (h)	GMT
United Kingdom	244,820	60·6	London	00	44	—	n/a
United States	9,631,418	298·4	Washington, DC	011	1	7h50	−5
Algeria	2,381,740	32·9	Algiers	00	213	2h45	+1
Argentina	2,766,890	39·9	Buenos Aires	00	54	15h45	−3
Australia	7,686,850	20·3	Canberra	0011	61	25h	+9½
Austria	83,870	8·2	Vienna	00	43	2h20	+1
Belarus	207,600	10·3	Minsk	810	375	4h40	+2
Belgium	30,528	10·4	Brussels	00	32	1h	+1
Brazil	8,511,965	188·1	Brasilia	0014	55	16h	−3
Bulgaria	110,910	7·4	Sofia	00	359	3h	+2
Burma/Myanmar	678,500	47·4	[see p.66]	00	95	13h	+6½
Cambodia	181,040	13·9	Phnom Penh	001	855	14h	+7
Canada	9,984,670	33·1	Ottawa	011	1	7h45	−5
Chile	756,950	16·1	Santiago	00	56	17h	−4
China	9,596,960	1·3bn	Beijing	00	86	10h	+8
Colombia	1,138,910	43·6	Bogota	009	57	13h	−5
Cuba	110,860	11·4	Havana	119	53	12h	−5
Czech Republic	78,866	10·2	Prague	00	420	1h50	+1
Denmark	43,094	5·5	Copenhagen	00	45	1h50	+1
Egypt	1,001,450	78·9	Cairo	00	20	4h45	+2
Estonia	45,226	1·3	Tallinn	00	372	4h	+2
Finland	338,145	5·2	Helsinki	00	358	3h	+2
France	547,030	60·9	Paris	00	33	50m	+1
Germany	357,021	82·4	Berlin	00	49	1h40	+1
Greece	131,940	10·7	Athens	00	30	3h45m	+2
Haiti	27,750	8·3	Port-au-Prince	00	509	20h30	−5
Hong Kong	1,092	6·9	—	001	852	12h	+8
Hungary	93,030	10·0	Budapest	00	36	2h25	+1
India	3,287,590	1·1bn	New Delhi	00	91	8h30	+5½
Indonesia	1,919,440	245·5	Jakarta	001	62	16h	+8
Iran	1,648,000	68·7	Tehran	00	98	6h	+3½
Iraq	437,072	26·8	Baghdad	00	964	14h30	+3
Ireland	70,280	4·1	Dublin	00	353	1h	0
Israel	20,770	6·4	Jerusalem/Tel Aviv	00	972	5h	+2
Italy	301,230	58·1	Rome	00	39	2h20	+1
Japan	377,835	127·5	Tokyo	010	81	11h30	+9
Jordan	92,300	5·9	Amman	00	962	6h	+2
Kazakhstan	2,717,300	15·2	Astana	810	7	8h15	+4
Kenya	582,650	34·7	Nairobi	000	254	8h20	+3
Korea, North	120,540	23·1	Pyongyang	00	850	13h45	+9
Korea, South	98,480	48·8	Seoul	001	82	11h	+9

——————— GAZETTEER · KUWAIT – ZIMBABWE · [1/4] ———————

Country	Size (km²)	Population (m)	Capital city		Phone access code	Phone country code	Flying time (h)	GMT
United Kingdom	244,820	60·6	London		00	44	—	n/a
United States	9,631,418	298·4	Washington, DC	011	1	7h50	–5
Kuwait	17,820	2·4	Kuwait City		00	965	6h	+3
Latvia	64,589	2·3	Riga		00	371	2h45	+2
Lebanon	10,400	3·9	Beirut		00	961	4h45	+2
Liberia	111,370	3·0	Monrovia		00	231	12h	0
Lithuania	65,200	3·6	Vilnius		00	370	4h	+2
Malaysia	329,750	24·4	Kuala Lumpur		00	60	12h25	+8
Mexico	1,972,550	107·4	Mexico City		00	52	11h15	–7
Monaco	195	32·6k	Monaco		00	377	2h	+1
Morocco	446,300	33·2	Rabat		00	212	5h45	0
Netherlands	41,526	16·5	Amsterdam		00	31	1h15	+1
New Zealand	268,680	4·1	Wellington		00	64	28h	+12
Nigeria	923,768	131·9	Abuja		009	234	6h15	+1
Norway	324,220	4·6	Oslo		00	47	2h	+1
Pakistan	803,940	165·8	Islamabad		00	92	10h	+5
Peru	1,285,220	28·3	Lima		00	51	15h15	–5
Philippines	300,000	89·5	Manila		00	63	15h	+8
Poland	312,685	38·5	Warsaw		00	48	2h20	+1
Portugal	92,391	10·6	Lisbon		00	351	2h30	0
Romania	237,500	22·3	Bucharest		00	40	3h15	+2
Russia	17,075,200	142·9	Moscow		810	7	4h	+3
Rwanda	26,338	8·6	Kigali		00	250	11h20	+2
Saudi Arabia	1,960,582	27·0	Riyadh		00	966	6h15	+3
Singapore	692·7	4·5	Singapore		001	65	12h45	+8
Slovakia	48,845	5·4	Bratislava		00	421	3h30	+1
Slovenia	20,273	2·0	Ljubljana		00	386	3h30	+1
Somalia	637,657	8·9	Mogadishu		00	252	12h45	+3
South Africa	1,219,912	44·2	Pretoria/Tshwane	09	27	11h	+2
Spain	504,782	40·4	Madrid		00	34	2h20	+1
Sudan	2,505,810	41·2	Khartoum		00	249	12h	+3
Sweden	449,964	9·0	Stockholm		00	46	2h30	+1
Switzerland	41,290	7·5	Bern		00	41	2h	+1
Syria	185,180	18·9	Damascus		00	963	6h30	+2
Taiwan	35,980	23·0	Taipei		002	886	14h30	+8
Thailand	514,000	64·6	Bangkok		001	66	14h20	+7
Turkey	780,580	70·4	Ankara		00	90	5h15	+2
Ukraine	603,700	46·7	Kiev		810	380	3h25	+2
Venezuela	912,050	25·7	Caracas		00	58	11h30	–4
Vietnam	329,560	84·4	Hanoi		00	84	13h45	+7
Zimbabwe	390,580	12·2	Harare		00	263	12h50	+2

—— GAZETTEER · ALGERIA – SOUTH KOREA · [2/4] ——

Country	Male life expectancy	Female life expectancy	difference	Infant mortality	Median age	Birth rate	Death rate	Fertility rate	Adult HIV rate	Literacy
United Kingdom	76·1	81·1	−5·0	5·1	39·3	10·7	10·1	1·7	0·2	99
United States	75·0	80·8	−5·8	6·4	36·5	14·1	8·3	2·1	0·6	99
Algeria	71·7	74·9	−3·2	29·9	24·9	17·1	4·6	1·9	0·1	70
Argentina	72·4	80·1	−7·7	14·7	29·7	16·7	7·6	2·2	0·7	97
Australia	77·6	83·5	−5·9	4·6	36·9	12·1	7·5	1·8	0·1	99
Austria	76·2	82·1	−5·9	4·6	40·9	8·7	9·8	1·4	0·3	98
Belarus	63·5	75·0	−11·5	13·0	37·2	11·2	14·0	1·4	0·3	100
Belgium	75·6	82·1	−6·5	4·6	40·9	10·4	10·3	1·6	0·2	99
Brazil	68·0	76·1	−8·1	28·6	28·2	16·6	6·2	1·9	0·7	86
Bulgaria	68·7	76·1	−7·4	19·9	40·8	9·7	14·3	1·4	0·1	99
Burma/Myanmar	58·1	64·0	−5·9	61·9	27·0	17·9	9·8	2·0	1·2	85
Cambodia	57·4	61·3	−3·9	68·8	20·6	26·9	9·1	3·4	2·6	74
Canada	76·9	83·7	−6·8	4·7	38·9	10·8	7·8	1·6	0·3	99
Chile	73·5	80·2	−6·7	8·6	30·4	15·2	5·8	2·0	0·3	96
China	70·9	74·5	−3·6	23·1	32·7	13·3	7·0	1·7	0·1	91
Colombia	68·2	76·0	−7·8	20·4	26·3	20·5	5·6	2·5	0·7	93
Cuba	75·1	79·9	−4·8	6·2	35·9	11·9	7·2	1·7	0·1	97
Czech Republic	72·9	79·7	−6·8	3·9	39·3	9·0	10·6	1·2	0·1	99
Denmark	75·5	80·2	−4·7	4·5	39·8	11·1	10·4	1·7	0·2	99
Egypt	68·8	73·9	−5·1	31·3	24·0	22·9	5·2	2·8	0·1	58
Estonia	66·6	77·8	−11·2	7·7	39·3	10·0	13·3	1·4	1·1	100
Finland	75·0	82·2	−7·2	3·6	41·3	10·5	9·9	1·7	0·1	100
France	76·1	83·5	−7·4	4·2	39·1	12·0	9·1	1·8	0·4	99
Germany	75·8	82·0	−6·2	4·1	42·6	8·3	10·6	1·4	0·1	99
Greece	76·7	81·9	−5·2	5·4	40·8	9·7	10·2	1·3	0·2	98
Haiti	51·9	54·6	−2·7	71·7	18·2	36·4	12·2	4·9	5·6	53
Hong Kong	78·9	84·5	−5·6	3·0	40·7	7·3	6·3	1·0	0·1	94
Hungary	68·5	77·1	−8·6	8·4	38·7	9·7	13·1	1·3	0·1	99
India	63·9	65·6	−1·7	54·6	24·9	22·0	8·2	2·7	0·9	60
Indonesia	67·4	72·5	−5·1	34·4	26·8	20·3	6·3	2·4	0·1	88
Iran	68·9	71·7	−2·8	40·3	24·8	17·0	5·6	1·8	0·1	79
Iraq	67·8	70·3	−2·5	48·6	19·7	32·0	5·4	4·2	0·1	40
Ireland	75·1	80·5	−5·4	5·3	34·0	14·5	7·8	1·9	0·1	99
Israel	77·3	81·7	−4·4	6·9	29·6	18·0	6·2	2·4	0·1	95
Italy	76·9	82·9	−6·0	5·8	42·2	8·7	10·4	1·3	0·5	99
Japan	78·0	84·7	−6·7	3·2	42·9	9·4	9·2	1·4	0·1	99
Jordan	76·0	81·1	−5·1	16·8	23·0	21·3	2·7	2·6	0·1	91
Kazakhstan	61·6	72·5	−10·9	28·3	28·8	16·0	9·4	1·9	0·2	98
Kenya	49·8	48·1	1·7	59·3	18·2	39·7	14·0	4·9	6·7	85
Korea, North	68·9	74·5	−5·6	23·3	32·0	15·5	7·1	2·1	—	99
Korea, South	73·6	80·8	−7·2	6·2	35·2	10·0	5·9	1·3	0·1	98

────── GAZETTEER · KUWAIT – ZIMBABWE · [2/4] ──────

Country	Male life expectancy	Female life expectancy	difference	Infant mortality	Median age	Birth rate	Death rate	Fertility rate	Adult HIV rate	Literacy
United Kingdom	76·1	81·1	−5·0	5·1	39·3	10·7	10·1	1·7	0·2	99
United States	75·0	80·8	5·8	6·4	36·5	14·1	8·3	2·1	0·6	99
Kuwait	76·1	78·3	−2·2	9·7	25·9	21·9	2·4	2·9	0·1	84
Latvia	66·1	76·9	−10·8	9·4	39·4	9·2	13·7	1·3	0·6	100
Lebanon	70·4	75·5	−5·1	23·7	27·8	18·5	6·2	1·9	0·1	87
Liberia	38·0	41·4	−3·4	155·8	18·1	44·8	23·1	6·0	5·9	58
Lithuania	69·2	79·5	−10·3	6·8	38·2	8·8	11·0	1·2	0·1	100
Malaysia	69·8	75·4	−5·6	17·2	24·1	22·9	5·1	3·0	0·4	89
Mexico	72·6	78·3	−5·7	20·3	25·3	20·7	4·7	2·4	0·3	92
Monaco	75·9	83·7	−7·8	5·4	45·4	9·2	12·9	1·8	—	99
Morocco	68·6	73·4	−4·8	40·2	23·9	22·0	5·6	2·7	0·1	52
Netherlands	76·4	81·7	−5·3	5·0	39·4	10·9	8·7	1·7	0·2	99
New Zealand	75·8	81·9	−6·1	5·8	33·9	13·8	7·5	1·8	0·1	99
Nigeria	46·5	47·7	−1·2	97·1	18·7	40·4	16·9	5·5	5·4	68
Norway	76·9	82·3	−5·4	3·7	38·4	11·5	9·4	1·8	0·1	100
Pakistan	62·4	64·4	−2·0	70·5	19·8	29·7	8·2	4·0	0·1	49
Peru	68·1	71·7	−3·6	30·9	25·3	20·5	6·2	2·5	0·5	88
Philippines	67·3	73·2	−5·9	22·8	22·5	24·9	5·4	3·1	0·1	93
Poland	71·0	79·2	−8·2	7·2	37·0	9·9	10·0	1·3	0·1	100
Portugal	74·4	81·2	−6·8	5·0	38·5	10·7	9·9	1·5	0·4	93
Romania	68·1	75·3	−7·2	25·5	36·6	10·7	11·8	1·4	0·1	98
Russia	60·5	74·1	−13·6	15·1	38·4	10·0	14·7	1·3	1·1	100
Rwanda	46·3	48·4	−2·1	89·6	18·6	40·4	16·1	5·4	5·1	70
Saudi Arabia	73·7	77·8	−4·1	12·8	21·4	29·3	2·6	4·0	·01	79
Singapore	79·1	84·5	−5·4	2·3	37·3	9·3	4·3	1·1	0·2	93
Slovakia	70·8	78·9	−8·1	7·3	35·8	10·7	9·5	1·3	0·1	100
Slovenia	72·6	80·3	−7·7	4·4	40·6	9·0	10·3	1·3	0·1	100
Somalia	46·7	50·3	−3·6	114·9	17·6	45·1	16·6	6·8	1·0	38
South Africa	43·3	42·2	1·1	60·7	24·1	18·2	22·0	2·2	21·5	86
Spain	76·3	83·2	−6·9	4·4	39·9	10·1	9·7	1·3	0·7	98
Sudan	57·7	60·2	−2·5	61·1	18·3	34·5	9·0	4·7	2·3	61
Sweden	78·3	82·9	−4·6	2·8	40·9	10·3	10·3	1·7	0·1	99
Switzerland	77·7	83·5	−5·8	4·3	40·1	9·7	8·5	1·4	0·4	99
Syria	69·0	71·7	−2·7	28·6	20·7	27·8	4·8	3·4	0·1	77
Taiwan	74·7	80·5	−5·8	6·3	34·6	12·6	6·5	1·6	—	96
Thailand	70·0	74·7	−4·7	19·5	31·9	13·9	7·0	1·6	1·5	93
Turkey	70·2	75·2	−5·0	39·7	28·1	16·6	6·0	1·9	0·1	87
Ukraine	64·7	75·6	−10·9	9·9	39·2	8·8	14·4	1·2	1·4	100
Venezuela	71·5	77·8	−6·3	21·5	26·0	18·7	4·9	2·2	0·7	93
Vietnam	68·1	73·9	5·8	25·1	25·9	16·9	6·2	1·9	0·4	90
Zimbabwe	40·4	38·2	2·2	51·7	19·9	28·0	21·8	3·1	24·6	91

—— GAZETTEER · ALGERIA – SOUTH KOREA · [3/4] ——

Country	Currency	Currency code £1 =	GDP per capita $	Inflation %	Unemployment %	Fiscal year end
United Kingdom	Pound=100 Pence	GBP —	30,300	2·1	4·7	5 Apr
United States	Dollar=100 Cents	USD 1·8	41,800	3·2	5·1	30 Sep
Algeria	Dinar=100 Centimes	DZD 134·7	7,200	1·9	17·1	31 Dec
Argentina	Peso=10,000 Australes	ARS 5·7	13,100	9·6	11·6	31 Dec
Australia	Dollar=100 Cents	AUD 2·5	31,900	2·7	5·1	30 Jun
Austria	euro=100 cent	EUR 1·5	32,700	2·3	5·2	31 Dec
Belarus	Ruble=100 Kopecks	BYB 3932·9	6,900	10·3	1·6	31 Dec
Belgium	euro=100 cent	EUR 1·5	31,400	2·8	8·4	31 Dec
Brazil	Real=100 Centavos	BRL 4·0	8,400	6·9	9·8	31 Dec
Bulgaria	Lev=100 Stotinki	BGN 2·8	9,600	5·0	11·5	31 Dec
Burma/Myanmar	Kyat=100 Pyas	MMK 11·8	1,700	20·2	5·0	31 Mar
Cambodia	Riel=100 Sen	KHR 7429·1	2,200	5·8	2·5	31 Dec
Canada	Dollar=100 Cents	CAD 2·1	34,000	2·2	6·8	31 Mar
Chile	Peso=100 Centavos	CLP 999·4	11,300	3·1	8·1	31 Dec
China	Renminbi Yuan=100 Fen	CNY 14·7	6,800	1·8	c.9·0	31 Dec
Colombia	Peso=100 Centavos	COP 4663·0	7,900	5·0	11·8	31 Dec
Cuba	Peso=100 Centavos	CUP/C 1·8	3,500	7·0	1·9	31 Dec
Czech Republic	Koruna=100 Haléru	CZK 41·3	19,500	1·9	8·9	31 Dec
Denmark	Krone=100 Øre	DKK 10·9	34,600	1·8	5·7	31 Dec
Egypt	Pound=100 Piastres	EGP 10·5	3,900	4·9	9·5	30 Jun
Estonia	Kroon=100 sents	EEK 22·7	16,700	4·1	7·9	31 Dec
Finland	euro=100 cent	EUR 1·5	30,900	0·9	8·4	31 Dec
France	euro=100 cent	EUR 1·5	29,900	1·7	9·9	31 Dec
Germany	euro=100 cent	EUR 1·5	30,400	2·0	11·7	31 Dec
Greece	euro=100 cent	EUR 1·5	22,200	3·5	9·9	31 Dec
Haiti	Gourde=100 Centimes	HTG 71·6	1,700	15·7	c.65	30 Sep
Hong Kong	HK Dollar=100 Cents	HKD 14·3	32,900	0·9	5·5	31 Mar
Hungary	Forint=100 Fillér	HUF 407·8	16,300	3·6	7·2	31 Dec
India	Rupee=100 Paisa	INR 86·4	3,300	4·2	8·9	31 Mar
Indonesia	Rupiah=100 Sen	IDR 16830·2	3,600	10·5	11·8	31 Dec
Iran	Rial(=100 Dinars)	IRR 16814·6	8,300	13·5	11·2	20 Mar
Iraq	New Iraqi Dinar	NID 2706·8	3,400	33·0	c.27·5	31 Dec
Ireland	euro=100 cent	EUR 1·5	41,000	2·4	4·3	31 Dec
Israel	Shekel=100 Agora	ILS 8·2	24,600	1·3	9·0	31 Dec
Italy	euro=100 cent	EUR 1·5	29,200	2·0	7·7	31 Dec
Japan	Yen=100 Sen	JPY 215·4	31,500	−0·3	4·4	31 Mar
Jordan	Dinar=1,000 Fils	JOD 1·3	4,700	4·5	12·5	31 Dec
Kazakhstan	Tenge=100 Tiyn	KZT 217·1	8,200	7·6	8·1	31 Dec
Kenya	Shilling=100 Cents	KES 135·0	1,100	10·3	40·0	30 Jun
Korea, North	NK Won=100 Chon	KPW 248·1	1,700	—	—	31 Dec
Korea, South	SK Won=100 Chon	KRW 1762·2	20,400	2·8	3·7	31 Dec

Country	Currency	Currency code	£1 =	GDP per capita $	Inflation %	Unemployment %	Fiscal year end
United Kingdom	Pound=100 Pence	GBP	—	30,300	2·1	4·7	5 Apr
United States	Dollar=100 Cents	USD	1·8	41,800	3·2	5·1	30 Sep
Kuwait	Dinar=1,000 Fils	KWD	0·5	19,200	4·1	2·2	31 Mar
Latvia	Lats=100 Santims	LVL	1·0	13,200	6·7	7·5	31 Dec
Lebanon	Pound=100 Piastres	LBP	2773·5	6,200	2·4	18·0	31 Dec
Liberia	Dollar=100 Cents	LRD	1·8	1,000	15·0	85·0	31 Dec
Lithuania	Litas=100 Centas	LTL	5·0	13,700	2·7	4·8	31 Dec
Malaysia	Ringgit=100 Sen	MYR	6·8	12,100	3·0	3·6	31 Dec
Mexico	Peso=100 Centavos	MXN	20·0	10,000	4·0	3·6	31 Dec
Monaco	euro=100 cent	EUR	1·5	27,000	1·9	22·0	31 Dec
Morocco	Dirham=100 centimes	MAD	16·0	4,200	1·0	11·0	31 Dec
Netherlands	euro=100 cent	EUR	1·5	30,500	1·7	6·6	31 Dec
New Zealand	Dollar=100 Cents	NZD	3·0	25,200	3·0	3·7	30 Jun
Nigeria	Naira=100 Kobo	NGN	235·0	1,400	13·5	2·9	31 Dec
Norway	Krone=100 Øre	NOK	11·7	42,300	1·6	4·6	31 Dec
Pakistan	Rupee=100 Paisa	PKR	101·6	2,400	9·1	6·6	30 Jun
Peru	New Sol=100 Cénts	PEN	5·9	5,900	1·6	7·6	31 Dec
Philippines	Peso=100 Centavos	PHP	97·0	5,100	7·6	8·7	31 Dec
Poland	Zloty=100 Groszy	PLN	5·8	13,300	2·2	18·2	31 Dec
Portugal	euro=100 cent	EUR	1·5	19,300	2·3	7·6	31 Dec
Romania	New Leu=100 New Bani	ROL	5·2	8,200	9·0	5·9	31 Dec
Russia	Rouble=100 Kopecks	RUR	49·5	11,100	12·7	7·6	31 Dec
Rwanda	Franc=100 Centimes	RWF	1011·6	1,500	8·0	—	31 Dec
Saudi Arabia	Riyal=100 Halala	SAR	6·9	12,800	0·4	c.25	28 Feb
Singapore	Dollar=100 Cents	SGD	2·9	20,100	0·4	3·1	31 Mar
Slovakia	Koruna=100 Halierov	SKK	56·1	16,100	2·7	11·7	31 Dec
Slovenia	Tolar=100 Stotin	SIT	347·9	21,600	2·5	10·1	31 Dec
Somalia	Shilling=100 Cents	SOS	2458·0	600	—	—	31 Dec
South Africa	Rand=100 Cents	ZAR	13·1	12,000	4·0	26·6	31 Mar
Spain	euro=100 cent	EUR	1·5	25,500	3·4	9·2	31 Dec
Sudan	Dinar= 100 Piastres	SDD	398·3	2,100	9·0	18·7	31 Dec
Sweden	Krona=100 Øre	SEK	13·5	29,800	0·5	5·8	31 Dec
Switzerland	Franc=100 Centimes	CHF	2·3	32,300	1·2	3·8	31 Dec
Syria	Pound=100 Piastres	SYP	95·8	3,900	5·0	12·3	31 Dec
Taiwan	Dollar=100 Cents	TWD	60·5	27,600	2·3	4·1	31 Dec
Thailand	Baht=100 Satang	THB	70·2	8,300	4·5	1·8	30 Sep
Turkey	New Lira=100 New Kurus	TRL	2·9	8,200	8·2	10·2	31 Dec
Ukraine	Hryvena=100 Kopiykas	UAH	9·2	7,200	13·5	c.10	31 Dec
Venezuela	Bolívar=100 Centimos	VEB	4903·2	6,100	16·0	12·2	31 Dec
Vietnam	Dong=100 Xu	VND	29336·8	2,800	8·3	2·4	31 Dec
Zimbabwe	Dollar=100 Cents	ZWD	185628·0	2,300	266·8	80	31 Dec

—— GAZETTEER · ALGERIA – SOUTH KOREA · [4/4] ——

Country	Voting age	Driving side	UN vehicle code	Internet country code	Military service	Death penalty	National Day
United Kingdom	18 U	L	GB	.uk	N	N	—
United States	18 U	R	USA	.us	N	Y	4 Jul
Algeria	18 U	R	DZ	.dz	Y	N*	1 Nov
Argentina	18 UC	R	RA	.ar	N	Y*	25 May
Australia	18 UC	L	AUS	.au	N	N	26 Jan
Austria	18 UC*	R	A	.at	Y	N	26 Oct
Belarus	18 U	R	BY	.by	Y	Y	3 Jul
Belgium	18 UC	R	B	.be	N	N	21 Jul
Brazil	16 U*	R	BR	.br	Y	Y*	7 Sep
Bulgaria	18 U	R	BG	.bg	Y	N	3 Mar
Burma/Myanmar	18 U	R	BUR	.mm	N	N*	4 Jan
Cambodia	18 U	R	K	.kh	Y	N	9 Nov
Canada	18 U	R	CDN	.ca	N	N	1 Jul
Chile	18 UC	R	RCH	.cl	Y	Y*	18 Sep
China	18 U	R	RC	.cn	Y	Y	1 Oct
Colombia	18 U	R	CO	.co	Y	N	20 Jul
Cuba	16 U	R	CU	.cu	N	Y	10 Dec
Czech Republic	18 U	R	CZ	.cz	N	N	28 Oct
Denmark	18 U	R	DK	.dk	Y	N	5 Jun
Egypt	18 UC	R	ET	.eg	Y	Y	23 Jul
Estonia	18 U	R	EST	.ee	Y	N	24 Feb
Finland	18 U	R	FIN	.fi	Y	N	6 Dec
France	18 U	R	F	.fr	N	N	14 Jul
Germany	18 U	R	D	.de	Y	N	3 Oct
Greece	18 UC	R	GR	.gr	Y	N	25 Mar
Haiti	18 U	R	RH	.ht	N	N	1 Jan
Hong Kong	18 U*	L	CN/HK	.hk	N	N	1 Oct
Hungary	18 U	R	H	.hu	N	N	20 Aug
India	18 U	L	IND	.in	N	Y	26 Jan
Indonesia	17 U*	L	RI	.id	Y	Y	17 Aug
Iran	15 U	R	IR	.ir	Y	Y	1 Apr
Iraq	18 U	R	IRQ	.iq	N	Y	17 Jul
Ireland	18 U	L	IRL	.ie	N	N	17 Mar
Israel	18 U	R	IL	.il	Y	Y*	14 May
Italy	18 U*	R	I	.it	N	N	2 Jun
Japan	20 U	L	J	.jp	N	Y	23 Dec
Jordan	18 U	R	HKJ	.jo	N	Y	25 May
Kazakhstan	18 U	R	KZ	.kz	Y	Y	16 Dec
Kenya	18 U	L	EAK	.ke	N	N*	12 Dec
Korea, North	17 U	R	DVRK	.kp	N	Y	9 Sep
Korea, South	20 U	R	ROK	.kr	Y	Y	15 Aug

——————— GAZETTEER · KUWAIT – ZIMBABWE · [4/4] ———————

Country	Voting age	Driving side	UN vehicle code	Internet country code	Military service	Death penalty	National Day
United Kingdom	18 U	L	GB	.uk	N	N	—
United States	18 U	R	USA	.us	N	Y	4 Jul
Kuwait	21 C	R	KWT	.kw	Y	Y	25 Feb
Latvia	18 U	R	LV	.lv	Y	Y*	18 Nov
Lebanon	21 C*	R	RL	.lb	Y	Y	22 Nov
Liberia	18 U	R	LB	.lr	N	N	26 Jul
Lithuania	18 U	R	LT	.lt	Y	N	16 Feb
Malaysia	21 U	L	MAL	.my	N	Y	31 Aug
Mexico	18 UC	R	MEX	.mx	Y	N	16 Sep
Monaco	21 U	R	MC	.mc	N	N	19 Nov
Morocco	18 U	R	MA	.ma	Y	N	3 Mar
Netherlands	18 U	R	NL	.nl	N	N	30 Apr
New Zealand	18 U	L	NZ	.nz	N	N	6 Feb
Nigeria	18 U	R	WAN	.ng	N	Y	1 Oct
Norway	18 U	R	N	.no	Y	N	17 May
Pakistan	18 U	L	PK	.pk	N	Y	23 Mar
Peru	18 UC*	R	PE	.pe	Y	Y*	28 Jul
Philippines	18 U	R	RP	.ph	Y	N	12 Jun
Poland	18 U	R	PL	.pl	Y	N	3 May
Portugal	18 U	R	P	.pt	N	N	10 Jun
Romania	18 U	R	RO	.ro	Y	N	1 Dec
Russia	18 U	R	RU	.ru	Y	N*	12 Jun
Rwanda	18 U	R	RWA	.rw	N	Y	1 Jul
Saudi Arabia	21 C	R	SA	.sa	N	Y	23 Sep
Singapore	21 UC	L	SGP	.sg	Y	Y	9 Aug
Slovakia	18 U	R	SK	.sk	Y	N	1 Sep
Slovenia	18 U*	R	SLO	.si	N	N	25 Jun
Somalia	18 U	L	SO	.so	N	Y	1 Jul
South Africa	18 U	L	ZA	.za	N	N	27 Apr
Spain	18 U	R	E	.es	N	N	12 Oct
Sudan	17 U	R	SUD	.sd	Y	Y	1 Jan
Sweden	18 U	R	S	.se	Y	N	6 Jun
Switzerland	18 U	R	CH	.ch	Y	N	1 Aug
Syria	18 U	R	SYR	.sy	Y	Y	17 Apr
Taiwan	20 U	R	RC	.tw	Y	Y	10 Oct
Thailand	18 UC	L	T	.th	Y	Y	5 Dec
Turkey	18 U	R	TR	.tr	Y	N	29 Oct
Ukraine	18 U	R	UA	.ua	Y	N	24 Aug
Venezuela	18 U	R	YV	.ve	Y	N	5 Jul
Vietnam	18 U	R	VN	.vn	Y	Y	2 Sep
Zimbabwe	18 U	L	ZW	.zw	N	Y	18 Apr

Society & Health

Society is no comfort To one not sociable.
— WILLIAM SHAKESPEARE, *Cymbeline* IV:2

―――――――――― ANIMAL RIGHTS & 'EXTREMISM' ――――――――――

2006 marked the 30th anniversary of the Animal Liberation Front (ALF), an international group to which (vegans and vegetarians) engaging in direct action against 'animal abuse' may claim affiliation. Yet, 2006 seemed also to mark a shift in public opinion towards animal testing for medical research. ❦ The year started with the founding of the group 'Pro-Test' by 16-year-old Laurie Pycroft, with the aim 'to counter the irrational arguments of anti-vivisectionists by raising public awareness of the benefits of animal research'. ❦ In March, 6 men were admitted to intensive care in London after taking part in a trial for an anti-inflammatory drug that had already been tested on animals. ❦ On 9 May, GlaxoSmithKline obtained an injunction preventing protesters from threatening investors and revealing personal details of their shareholders. ❦ Days later, three animal rights activists were jailed for 12 years for a campaign of intimidation against a family guinea-pig breeding business. Their attacks culminated in the disinterment and theft of a human corpse. ❦ On 15 May, Tony Blair took the unusual step (for a PM) of signing the 'People's Petition' in support of animal testing. ❦ A fortnight later, the High Court tightened restrictions on protesters demonstrating at the construction of Oxford University's biomedical research centre.

❦ A 1999 *New Scientist* poll indicated that 64% opposed animal testing for medical research. In May 2006, a *Daily Telegraph* poll indicated that 70% now supported such research, and a *Newsnight* poll in July showed support at 57%. This apparent reverse might be explained by better communication by drug companies and medics, and a greater public acceptance that nearly all 'wonder-drugs' for HIV, asthma, diabetes, cancer, bird flu [see p.181], &c. derive from animal tests. Yet the most significant result of the *Telegraph*'s poll may be that 77% said that animal activists, like those jailed in May, were 'terrorists'. (The *Telegraph* called the ALF 'the most active terrorist organisation in Britain'.) It seems that post-9/11 (&c.) public opinion and political policy have a lower tolerance of 'direct action', regardless of its ideology. This has led to legislation (such as the Serious Organised Crime Act and the Proceeds of Crime Act) that allows police to target the activities and finances of 'extremists'. ❦ At present, it is unclear whether, if this change in public opinion is real, it represents a genuine acceptance of animal testing, or a rejection of those who seek to halt it with violence. The debate may intensify in the light of the latest Home Office figures that show a 1·4% increase in animal testing from 2004–5, and an 11% increase in testing on primates.

UK POPULATION FIGURES

(million)	1971	1981	1991	2001	2004	2011	2021
England	46·4	46·8	47·9	49·4	50·1	52·0	54·6
Wales	2·7	2·8	2·9	2·9	3·0	3·0	3·2
Scotland	5·2	5·2	5·1	5·1	5·1	5·1	5·1
N. Ireland	1·5	1·5	1·6	1·7	1·7	1·8	1·8
UK	55·9	56·4	57·4	59·1	59·8	61·9	64·7

[Mid-year estimates for 1971–2004; 2004-based projections for 2011 & 2021 · Source: ONS]

UK BIRTHS & DEATHS

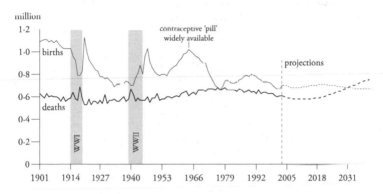

[Data for 1901–21 exclude Ireland. Data from 1981 exclude the non-residents of Northern Ireland. 2003-based projections for 2004–44. Source: Social Trends 35 · Crown ©]

AVERAGE AGE OF UK MOTHERS

The following ONS figures show the average age of mothers, by birth order:

Age	1st child	gap	2nd	gap	3rd	gap	4th	gap	≥5th	all births
1971	23·7	2·7	26·4	2·7	29·1	1·8	30·9	2·7	33·6	26·6
1981	24·8	2·5	27·3	1·9	29·2	1·7	30·9	2·9	33·8	27·0
1991	25·6	2·6	28·2	1·7	29·9	1·3	31·2	2·3	33·5	27·7
2001	26·6	2·6	29·2	1·5	30·7	0·8	31·5	2·9	34·4	28·6
2004	27·1	2·4	29·5	1·3	30·8	0·8	31·6	2·9	34·5	28·9

In July 2006, Dr Patricia Rashbrook gave birth to a baby boy at the age of 62, a feat achieved through IVF treatment in Russia. According to the Human Fertility and Embryology Authority, the number of older mothers in Britain is increasing: in 1992, just one baby was born to a woman over 50 after IVF; however, in 2002, 24 babies were born to women over 50. The NHS does not offer IVF to women over 39 years old, yet there is no legal age limit for private IVF treatment.

—————————— UK POPULATION BY AGE & SEX ——————————

Below is the breakdown of UK population (in 2003) by age and sex. It illustrates
the effects of the post-war boom in childbirth, and the subsequent boom when that
generation reached child-bearing age. It also shows how the population is ageing:

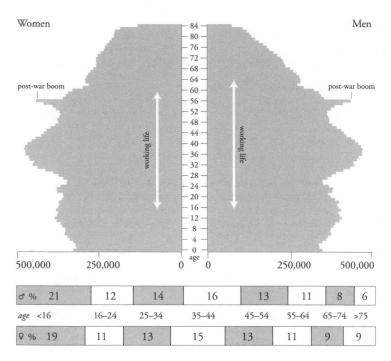

♂ %	21	12	14	16	13	11	8	6
age	<16	16–24	25–34	35–44	45–54	55–64	65–74	>75
♀ %	19	11	13	15	13	11	9	9

—————————— GB POPULATION BY ETHNIC GROUP ——————————

All White.....................91·9% {
- White British.....................88·2%
- White Irish.........................1·2%
- Other White.......................2·5%

All Asian or Asian British........4·1% {
- Indian ....1·8%
- Pakistani..........................1·3%
- Bangladeshi ....0·5%
- Other Asian.......................0·4%

All Black or Black British........2·0% {
- Black Caribbean ....1·0%
- Black African.....................0·9%
- Other Black.......................0·2%

Mixed.............................1·2%

Chinese...........................0·4%

Other ethnic groups ....0·4%

[Source: Social Trends 2005 · Crown ©
Data from 2001 Census]

—GROWTH OF ETHNIC MINORITY GROUPS · 1991–2001—

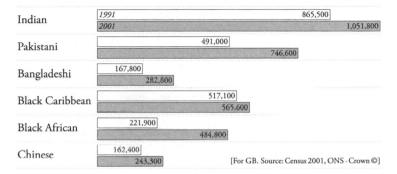

[For GB. Source: Census 2001, ONS · Crown ©]

—————— PERCEPTIONS OF RACIAL PREJUDICE——————

The following 2005 Home Office figures illustrate the percentage of people, by ethnicity, who considered there to be more racial prejudice in 2005 than in 2001:

%	Mixed race	White	Asian	Black	Chinese/other
2001	32	44	33	25	28
2005	33	50	35	22	32

The table below shows the percentage of people, grouped by ethnicity, who expect certain organisations to give them 'worse treatment' than other ethnic groups:

Organisation (%)	White	Asian	Black	Mixed	Chinese/other
Police	5	21	33	29	16
Prison service	2	15	22	22	10
Courts	6	9	20	14	7
Council housing dept	21	10	19	15	11
Local GP	1	2	5	2	3
Local school	2	4	11	7	7

[Source: Early Findings from the 2005 Home Office Citizenship Survey · Crown ©]

—————————— THE MEANING OF GAY——————————

In June 2006, the BBC ruled that DJ Chris Moyle's use of the word 'gay' on his radio show was acceptable, arguing that it was now common parlance for 'rubbish'. A listener complained that the use of the word was homophobic, after Moyles rejected a mobile ringtone from a fan, saying: 'I don't want that one, it's gay.' The BBC's Programme Complaints Cmte ruled that: 'the word "gay", in addition to being used to mean "homosexual" or "carefree", was often now used to mean "lame" or "rubbish". This is a widespread current usage of the word amongst young people'.

————————————— CITIZENSHIP TEST —————————————

As of November 2005, those aspiring to become British citizens are required to pass a 45-minute test on life in the UK (at a cost of £34). Potential citizens can take the test at one of 90 centres across the UK, and must achieve ≥75% in order to become eligible to participate in a formal citizenship ceremony. (If aspirant candidates do not have a good enough grasp of English [ESOL Entry 3], they may attend combined English and citizenship classes.) The test comprises 24 questions drawn from chapters 2, 3, and 4 of the handbook *Life in the United Kingdom: a Journey to Citizenship*. Below are a few example questions from the citizenship examination:

What are MPs? · What is the Church of England and who is its head?
Where are Geordie, Cockney, and Scouse dialects spoken?
What number do you have to dial in of case of emergency?
What is the date of St David's and St Andrew's days?

————————— APPLICATIONS FOR BRITISH CITIZENSHIP —————————

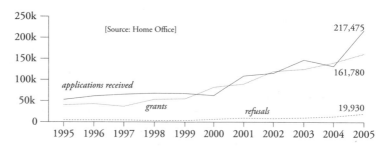

————————————— ENGLISH ICONS —————————————

In January 2006, the Department for Culture, Media, and Sport launched a new project – *Icons: a Portrait of England*. Its aim is to create an evolving list of symbols that reflect the character of England and the English. Members of the public are invited to nominate and vote for icons online (at icons.org.uk), and, every three months, twelve further icons will be added. For the launch of the project a panel of art experts and academics proposed the following twelve classic English icons:

Alice in Wonderland	The FA Cup	The Routemaster bus
The Angel of the North	*Henry VIII* by Holbein	Stonehenge
A cup of tea	*The King James Bible*	The Spitfire
SS Empire Windrush	Punch & Judy	Blake's *Jerusalem*

In response to the project, the *Sun* decided to list its own dozen icons of Englishness, they were: Jordan's boobs; chicken tikka masala; 12 pints of lager; the St George's cross [see p.13]; Burberry caps; *The Sun*; white vans; *Carry On* films; chips; wet weather; Blackpool Tower; & the Wembley Arch.

CHILDHOOD IMMUNISATION SCHEDULE

Age	vaccination	injections
2m	*diphtheria, tetanus, whooping cough, polio, Hib* [DTaP/IPV/Hib]	1
	pneumococcal conjugate vaccine [PCV]	1
3m	[DTaP/IPV/Hib] + *meningitis C* [MenC]	2
4m	[DTaP/IPV/Hib] + [MenC] + [PCV]	3
12m	[Hib/MenC]	1
13m	*measles, mumps, rubella* [MMR] + [PCV]	2
3y4m–5y	*diphtheria, tetanus, whooping cough, polio* [DTaP/IPV]	1
	measles, mumps, rubella [MMR]	1
13y–18y	*diphtheria, tetanus, polio* [Td/IPV]	1

This new schedule is due to come into effect across the country during 2006–07. (The above is only a guide and parents are advised to consult medical professionals.) Below are the notifications of measles, mumps, and rubella in the UK since 1991.

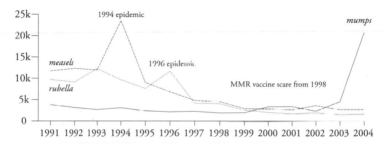

[Source: Social Trends 2006 · Crown © · NHS Immunisation Service]

MOST POPULAR NAMES · 2005

Below are the most popular names of 2005, from the Office of National Statistics:

Jack (–)	nickname for John	1	allegedly created by Shakespeare	(+2) Jessica
Joshua (–)	Jehova saves	2	from the Latin Aemilia	(–1) Emily
Thomas (–)	Greek form of Aramaic for 'twin'	3	French form of Sophia	(+1) Sophie
James (–)	English form of Jacomus and Jacob	4	? feminine version of Oliver	(+3) Olivia
Oliver (+2)	? from Latin for 'olive tree'	5	Greek for 'young green shoot'	(–) Chloe
Daniel (–1)	from Hebrew for 'God is my judge'	6	shortened form of Eleanor, &c.	(–4) Ellie
Samuel (–1)	from Hebrew for 'name of God'	7	from the Latin Gratia	(+4) Grace
William (–)	from German for 'protector'	8	from the Latin Lucia	(–2) Lucy
Harry (+2)	nickname for Henry	9	feminine form of Carlo/Charles	(–1) Charlotte
Joseph (–)	from Hebrew for 'God will add'	10	diminutive form of Kate	(–1) Katie

In 2005, the newly invented name Nevaeh stormed into the top-70 of the most popular American names. It rose to prominence after Christian rock-star Sonny Sandoval disclosed in an MTV interview (in 2000) that he chose the name for his daughter, since it is heaven spelled backwards.

EDUCATION KEY STAGES

The chart below illustrates the basic structure of the English education system:

Stage		*age*	*year*	*test or qualification*
FOUNDATION	{	3–4		
		4–5......	reception..................	*foundation stage profile*
KEY STAGE 1	{	5–6......	year 1	
		6–7......	year 2.....................	*tests in English & maths*
KEY STAGE 2	{	7–8......	year 3	
		8–9......	year 4	
		9–10......	year 5	
		10–11......	year 6...........	*tests in English, maths, & science*
KEY STAGE 3	{	11–12......	year 7	
		12–13......	year 8	
		13–14......	year 9...........	*tests in English, maths, & science*
KEY STAGE 4	{	14–15......	year 10........................	*some take* GCSEs
		15–16......	year 11..................	*most take* GCSEs *or other*
post compulsory	{	16–17......	year 12...................	AS *or* A LEVELS *or other*
education/training		17–18......	year 13........................	A LEVELS *or other*
		18–19		

FIGHTING IN SCHOOL

A World Health Organisation survey of 161,000 school children (aged 11–15) across 35 countries was published in January 2006 by the American Academy of Pediatrics. The research showed that a large percentage of children had been involved in fights in the preceding 12 months. The worst countries for fights were:

Rank	BOYS	*% fighting*	*Rank*	GIRLS	*% fighting*
1	Czech Republic	69	1	Hungary	32
2	Lithuania	67	2	Estonia	32
3	Russia	65	3	Lithuania	31
(10	Scotland	60)	(5	England	29)
(13	England	59)	(6	Scotland	29)
(26	Wales	53)	(12	Wales	25)

ROLE MODELS

10% of 16–19s would quit school if given a shot at fame[†], according to a Learning & Skills Council survey in 2006. Below are the most popular role models named:

1	Richard Branson	5	Tony Blair	9	Ms Dynamite
2	J.K. Rowling	6	David Attenborough	10	Alan Sugar
3	David Beckham	7	Frank Lampard	[† 16% believed they would
4	Andrew Flintoff	8	Stephen Hawking	become famous in the future.]

UNIVERSITIES

In 2003/04 there were 2·4m students in higher education in the UK (compared with 1·1m in 1990/1), served by 101 universities and 47 other institutions. The *Times Higher Education Supplement* ranked the top universities in 2005 thus:

Top UK universities	*Top universities worldwide*
Cambridge University	Harvard University, USA
Oxford University	Massachusetts Inst. of Tech, USA
London School of Economics	Cambridge University, UK
Imperial College London	Oxford University, UK
University College London	Stanford University, USA

UCAS figures show the popularity of courses in 2005 (by percentage of applications):

Most popular courses	*% applications*	*Least popular courses*	*% applications*
Business & admin. studies	11·4	Non-European languages	0·4
Creative arts & design	9·6	Technologies	0·5
Biological sciences	8·4	General, other combined	0·8
Social studies	8·1	Vet science and related	0·8
Subjects allied to medicine	8·1	European languages and related	1·1

According to UCAS, the most oversubscribed course in 2005 was medicine and dentistry. This can be explained in part by the high grades required, but also because few universities offer the course. As a result, only 10·3% of those applying in 2005 could expect a place. Other oversubscribed courses included: combined social science (15·5%), law (16·3%), and linguistics (16·4%). In contrast those wishing to study veterinary science have the best chance of getting a place (34·6%).

HESA figures show the level of degree attained by UK students in 2004/05:

Degree	1st	2:1	2:2	3rd	U[†]	Total
Students	25,755	110,685	71,785	14,370	15,145	237,735

† Unclassified · As might be expected, students have developed a rhyming slang for each result Geoff (Hurst), 1st; Attila (the Hun), 2:1; Desmond (Tutu), 2:2; and Douglas (Hurd), 3rd.

The DfES Student Income and Expenditure Survey 2004/5 revealed that 60% of full-time students felt that financial difficulties had affected their academic performance. The financial profile of the average full-time student in 2004/5 was:

Average annual total income	£8,333	Amount spent on housing	£2,280 p/a
Average annual expenditure	£10,270	– food	£1,490 p/a
Average student loan	£3,400	– entertainment	£1,200 p/a
Students undertaking paid work	56%	– books	£430 p/a

According to DfES figures on students loans, in 2005–06 the total amount lent to eligible UK students was £2,914·3m. 2·8m students had loans, of whom 1·7m were currently making repayments.

MARRIAGES & DIVORCES

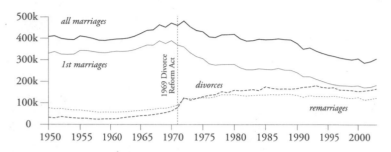

[1969 Act came into force in 1971 · Data for both partners · Divorce includes annulments. 1950–70 is for GB only. Remarriage is for one or both partners. Source: Social Trends 35 · Crown ©]

INTER-ETHNIC MARRIAGES

Ethnic group	same ethnic group marriage	inter-ethnic marriages
White	99%	
Indian	94%	6
Pakistani	96%	4
Bangladeshi	97%	3
Other Asian	82%	18
Black Caribbean	75%	25
Black African	84%	16
Other Black	59%	41
Chinese	78%	22
Mixed	22%	78
Other group	53%	47

Inter-ethnic marriages are those between people from different aggregate ethnic groups: e.g. a White person married to someone from a non-White ethnic group, or a Pakistani married to someone from a non-Asian ethnic group. [Source: Census 2001 · Crown © · data for England & Wales only]

PERFECT SAME-SEX PARTNER

A survey by the FX Channel, in January 2006, revealed that if straight men or women had to have a same-sex partner, they would choose the following people:

Men would choose	%	rank	%	women would choose
Ewan McGregor	32	1	27	Davina McCall
Brad Pitt	17	2	24	Jennifer Aniston
Tom Cruise	12	3	17	Kylie Minogue
Johnny Depp	10	4	12	Zoë Ball
Ben Affleck	9	5	9	Angelina Jolie

MARRIAGE SNAPSHOT · 2004

Number of marriages in England and Wales, 2004........................270,700
Rate of marriage ....10·2 per 1,000
Rate of marriage for men..27·5 per 1,000
Rate of marriage for women.......................................,....24·4 per 1,000
Average age of men at first marriage.......................................31·4 years
Average age of women at first marriage ....29·1 years
Average age of men at marriage ....35·8 years
Average age of women at marriage ....33·1 years
% of marriages that were first marriages for both parties.......................60%
% of marriages that were remarriages for both parties 18%
% of marriages with a religious ceremony .... 32·2%
% of marriages with a civil ceremony....................................... 67·8%
Number of men married in 2004 aged 16–19............................... 1,720
– number of those for whom it was a second marriage............................10
Number of women married in 2004 aged 16–19............................ 6,490
– number of those for whom it was second marriage............................ 40

[Source: ONS, figures relate to 2004 marriages] · A 2005 survey by Lloyds TSB revealed that the nation's favourite for a wedding first dance was *Everything I Do (I Do It For You)*, by Bryan Adams.

CIVIL PARTNERSHIP

The Civil Partnership Act 2004 came into force on 5 December 2005, allowing same-sex couples across the UK to gain legal recognition of their relationship. The Act created 'civil partners' – an entirely new legal status for same-sex couples, distinct from marriage. These partnerships afford same-sex couples the same rights, benefits, and responsibilities as married couples in a number of areas, including:

Tax, including inheritance tax
Most state benefits
Employment and income related benefits
A duty to provide maintenance for their
civil partner's children
Ability to apply for parental
responsibility for civil partner's children

Inheritance of tenancy agreement
Recognition under intestacy rules
Access to fatal accidents compensation
Protection from domestic violence
Recognition for immigration or
nationality purposes
Recognition as next-of-kin

There are a number of differences in the process of marriage and civil partnership. Whereas marriages are formed by the verbal and public exchange of vows, civil partnerships have no ceremonial requirement under the act, and may be established by signing the required documentation in private. However, civil partnership ceremonies may be held at any venue that is licensed for civil weddings. Like marriage, civil partnerships can only be ended by death, annulment, or dissolution (a court-based procedure similar to divorce). The first civil ceremonies took place in N. Ireland on 19 December 2005, in Scotland on the 20th, and in England and Wales on the 21st, due to different interpretations of the 15-day notice period.

—————————————— VIRGINITY ——————————————

Results of a 2006 Mori poll on the age at which British adults lost their virginity:

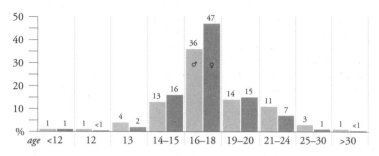

[Source: MORI, January 2006]

——————————— IMPORTANCE OF SEX ———————————

The *Global Study of Sexual Attitudes & Behaviours*, funded by Pfizer and released in 2006, shows the percentage of people who consider sex to be 'important' to them:

Korea..............89%	France.............77%	China..............55%
Italy................85%	USA...............73%	Japan..............53%
Australia...........78%	UK.................66%	Hong Kong........38%

——————— SEXUAL PARTNERS & MISCELLANY ———————

Durex conducts an annual survey into the sexual behaviour of adults worldwide. Below are the average reported number of sexual partners, by country (2005):

Turkey.............14·5	Japan...............10·2	Taiwan..............6·6
Australia...........13·3	UK...................9·8	Germany.............5·8
Italy................11·8	Austria...............9·7	Indonesia............5·1
Switzerland.........11·1	France................8·1	China................3·1
USA...............10·7	Singapore............7·2	India................3·0

[Global average=9 · men=10·2 · women=6·9 · © Durex 2005] The following facts were also revealed by the survey: Greek people reported having the most sex, on average 138 times a year ❦ 28% of Chileans claimed to have had sex at work ❦ 60% of Portuguese admitted to having sex in a lavatory, and 53% of Croatians confessed to having sex in their parents' bedroom. ❦ 47% of those questioned in Taiwan admitted to owning a vibrator ❦ 19% of Canadians liked using lubricants during sex as they 'taste nice', whereas 27% of Poles didn't know they existed. ❦ 58% of Turks admitted to extra-marital affairs ❦ 26% of Icelanders said that they had participated in a three-in-a-bed romp ❦ 13% of Chinese have sado-masochistic sex, although 17% claim not to have a high sex drive ❦ 70% of Norwegians had engaged in a one-night stand, compared to only 13% of Indians. ❦

JOB EQUALITY

Equal Opportunities Commission data from January 2006 show that, despite recent improvements, it will take 40 years for men and women to be equally represented at the director level of FTSE 100 companies. Below is a selection of women's representation in various positions of power and influence in 2005:

Sector	% ♀
Members of Welsh Assembly	50
Chief executives of voluntary orgs.	45
Members of Scottish Parliament	40
Chairs of national arts companies	33
Civil service top management	26
Directors of major museums	22
Members of Parliament	20
Editors of national papers	13
Directors of FTSE 100 companies	11
Senior police officers	10
Senior judiciary	9
Chief execs of national sports bodies	7
Senior ranks in the armed forces	1

GENDER PAY GAP

On average across Europe in 2004, men earned 15% more than women. The table below shows the percentage pay gap between women and men in a variety of European countries:

Country	pay gap (%)
Germany	23
UK	22
Netherlands	19
Sweden	17
Spain	15
France	12
Ireland	11
Greece	10
Italy	7
Belgium	6
Portugal	5

[Source: Eurostat, 2004]

JOBS & STRESS

Delegates at a 2006 conference of the British Psychological Society were presented with research that suggested librarians suffer greater stress at work than those working for the emergency services. The study, carried out by Saqib Saddiq, surveyed 300 people from five professions: firefighters, train drivers, police officers, teachers, and librarians. The research focused on nine key 'stressors', including: income, workload, and working environment. The research revealed that librarians were the most likely to be stressed, complaining that their work was unchallenging and repetitive, and gave them little scope for self-determination. The study concluded that police officers and firefighters were generally trained to deal with the types of work-related stress they may face, whereas no such support system existed for librarians.

MIGRANT WORKERS

Britain is one of only 3 EU countries that grants migrants from the 10 new member states of Europe full rights to work. Since Poland joined the EU in 2004, more than 300,000 Polish workers have formally settled in the UK. The table below shows the top ten nationalities whose members entered the UK in 2004/05 and were granted a National Insurance number.

Poland	62·6	Lithuania	15·6
India	32·7	France	13·3
Pakistan	20·3	China	12·6
S. Africa	19·3	Portugal	12·2
Australia	16·6	Slovakia	10·5

[Figures are in thousands and rounded to nearest hundred. Source: National Insurance Recording System as at June 2005]

——————————————— ON CLASS ———————————————

A May 2006 report by the Liverpool Victoria Friendly Society revealed that 43% of British people see themselves as middle class, and 53% as working class. (In 1966, just 30% described themselves as middle class.) Interestingly, the majority of both classes considered upbringing and employment the best definers of class, compared to income, education, or housing type or location. Below is a profile of each class:

Middle class	profile	working class
52·9%	with professional/managerial/technical jobs	31·4%
22·1%	with degree-level education or above	6·9%
84·4%	homeowners (including mortgagors)	75·0%
£25,485	average income (full-time only)	£20,553
£220,000	average value of home	£129,000
£7,878	average value of savings	£4,081
£7,672	average value of investments	£2,688
£3,267	average amount of debt	£2,770

The report also uncovered some anomalous groups that it defined as part of a new 'Muddle Class'. *Rich Ordinary Britons* – the 2·67m people who think of themselves as working class, despite ranking in the top fifth of the population for asset wealth. *High Earning Workers* – 534,000 people who earn >£100,000, but regard themselves as working class. And *Suburban Asset Lightweights* – 1·84m who say they are middle class, but are actually within the bottom fifth of the population for asset wealth.

The Office of National Statistics analyses UK social class by employing their 'Socio-Economic Classification' system. Below is their breakdown of class in 2003:

Social class	% ♂	% ♀	% all
Higher managerial and professional	14·8	6·0	10·5
Lower managerial and professional	20·5	23·5	21·9
Intermediate occupations	5·4	15·6	10·4
Small employers and own account workers	10·8	3·9	7·5
Lower supervisory and technical	12·5	5·4	9·1
Semi-routine occupations	9·6	16·7	13·0
Routine occupations	11·6	7·8	9·7
Never worked and long-term unemployed	14·8	21·1	17·9

Additional research by the Future Foundation in 2006 indicated the percentage of selected workers who described themselves as either middle or working class:

Middle class		working class		Middle class		working class	
79%	university lecturers	4%		44	civil servants	49	
75	clergy	19		35	hairdressers	50	
65	secondary school teachers	20		36	builders	55	
67	primary school teachers	27		28	cleaners	61	
50	farmers	29		23	lorry drivers	68	
57	accountants	43		16	firefighters	79	
45	nurses	45		12	painters/decorators	81	
				9	postal workers	91	

—————————————————— THE NHS ——————————————————

In 2005/06, the NHS reported:

Calls to NHS Direct .... 6·8m	No. of qualified nurses 404,160
Visits to NHS Direct online .... 13·5m	Total NHS workforce .... 1·4m
Visits to walk-in centres .... 2·5m	Wait in A&E <4 hours 97%
Visits to A&E .... 13·1m	Emergency calls .... 5·6m†
Average inpatient wait .... 7·3 weeks	Emergency incidents .... 4·5m
Average outpatient wait..... 6·13 weeks	Emergency patient journeys ...... 3·5m
No. of consultants 31,990	[† Emergency figures for 2004/5 · Source:
No. of GPs 32,740	2006 Chief Exec's Report to the NHS]

Prescriptions currently cost £6·65 per item. This does not reflect the cost of the item, but is considered a contribution towards NHS funds. In 2005, prescriptions cost the NHS £7·9bn.

—————————————— GP APPOINTMENTS ——————————————

The % of people able to get an appointment with their GP within 2 working days:

2002 .... 74·64% | 2004 .... 97·36% | 2006 .... 99·94%

[Source: Primary Care Access Survey] · In 2005 there were approximately 314m GP consultations.

—————————— HOSPITAL ADMISSIONS BY AGE ——————————

Patients' age	*admissions*	*%*			
0–4†	1,207,095	8·8	75–84 .... 2,039,267 ...... 14·9
5–14	512,381	3·7	>85 .... 898,009 .... 6·6
15–44	4,104,476	29·9	Unknown .... 28,110 .... 0·2
45–64	2,957,288	21·6	
65–74	1,960,139	14·3	† Includes babies born in hospital

[Source: HES · England · 2004/5]

————————— AVAILABILITY OF DENTISTS —————————

[September 2005]	*England*	*Wales*	*Scotland*	*N. Ireland*
Number of dentists	20,168	1,039	1,900	734
Average registrations per dentist	1,194	1,374	1,383	1,239
% of population with NHS dentist	48	49	52	53

[Source: ONS United Kingdom Health Statistics · 30·09·05] · According the British Dental Health Foundation (BDHF) survey, released in May 2006, the public is putting its teeth at risk by flossing with unsuitable and unwieldy implements. Over 60% admitted to flossing with whatever was close to hand, the most popular instruments being: screwdrivers, ear-rings, needles, keys, and paperclips. 23% confessed they generally just left food that got caught in their teeth. The BDHF recommends using dental floss at least once a day before brushing, and brushing twice a day with a fluoride toothpaste.

——————————— ORGAN DONATION & TRANSPLANT ———————————

As of 1·9·06, relatives lost the legal right to over-rule the wishes of a deceased next-of-kin who had given their consent to become an organ donor. The 2004 Human Tissue Act gave primacy to the wishes of those who consented to organ donation by joining the NHS Organ Donor Register[†], carrying a donor card, or giving their written or verbal consent. Prior to the Act, *c.*10% of organ donations were prevented because of family objections. Below are the transplant figures for 1·4·05–31·3·06:

Number of deceased who donated organs 765
Number of transplants resulting from those organs 2,196
Patients who received a kidney 1,799
Patients who received a pancreas 126
Patients who received a liver..586
Patients receiving a cardiothoracic (heart & lung) transplant...................262
Patients receiving a cornea... 2,503
Number of people waiting for transplant [as of April 2006] 6,700
Number of people on the Organ Donor Register [as of May 2006] ....13·2m

[† To enrol call 0845 60 60 400 or visit uktransplant.org.uk · Source: NHS UK Transplant]

——————————————— FIVE PORTIONS A DAY ———————————————

The World Health Organisation recommends that all adults consume at least five portions of fruit and vegetables a day (1 portion = 80g, which is roughly 3 heaped tablespoons). Below are the portions of fruit and veg we actually eat, by age group:

Portion	16–24	25–34	35–44	45–54	55–64	65–74	All ages
None	13%	10%	7%	6%	4%	4%	6%
<1	4	4	3	2	4	3	3
1–2	22	18	16	15	14	13	16
2–3	21	20	17	17	15	18	18
3–4	13	14	18	17	18	16	17
4–5	11	14	14	15	13	17	14
>5	17	22	25	28	33	29	26

[Source: Health Survey for England, Department of Health, 2004]

——————————— RECOMMENDED LEVELS OF EXERCISE ———————————

The government recommends moderately intense activity for at least 30 mins on 5 or more occasions a week. Below are the percentages of people meeting this target:

Age	%♂	%♀					
16–24	52	30	35–44	41	30	65–74	17	13
25–34	44	29	45–54	38	31	>75	8	3
			55–64	32	23	[Health Survey Eng., 2003]		

─────── SEXUALLY TRANSMITTED DISEASES ───────

Below are the new diagnoses of some sexually transmitted infections, in the UK:

Cases per 100,000	2000 ♂	2000 ♀	2002 ♂	2002 ♀	2004 ♂	2004 ♀
Syphilis	0·9	0·3	3·9	0·5	6·8	0·9
Herpes	23·7	36·5	24·9	40·2	24·6	38·6
Gonorrhoea	53·1	21·7	61·7	25·5	53·6	21·8
Chlamydia	103·9	127·6	133·5	161·1	165·1	182·7
Warts	131·2	111·6	137·7	115·6	145·3	121·5

[Source: Health Protection Agency, Communicable Disease Surveillance Centre]

─────── TRENDS IN HIV DIAGNOSIS & DEATHS ───────

According to a 2006 UN AIDS report, new cases of HIV in the UK have doubled since 2000, reaching *c*.7,700 in 2005. This increase is mainly attributed to hetero-sexual transmission, suggesting that the safe sex message is not reaching straight men and women [see table below]. Below are UK trends in HIV diagnosis and deaths:

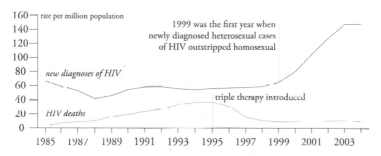

[Source: UK Health Statistics No. 2 2006, Crown ©]

─────── HIV: PROBABLE ROUTE OF INFECTION ───────

Probable route of infection %	England	Wales	Scotland	N. Ireland	UK
Homosexual contact	42·7	49·9	36·5	51·9	42·5
Injection drug use	2·4	2·8	19·1	2·1	3·2
Heterosexual contact	47·8	38·1	39·2	41·4	47·2
Blood/blood products	1·1	4·6	2·1	0·4	1·2
Mother to infant	3·6	3·0	0·5	3·3	3·5
Not known	2·4	1·6	2·7	0·8	2·5
Total number of individuals	38,799	677	1,917	239	42,092

[Source: Health Protection Agency, 2004]

——————— UK MOST COMMON CAUSE OF DEATH ———————

Male	cause of death	female
279·7	circulatory	177·3
226·3	cancers	159·8
94·8	respiratory	66·6

[2004 · Rates per 100,000 population · Source: UK Health Statistics 2006 · ONS · Crown ©]

——————— SOME CURIOUS ACCIDENTS OF NOTE ———————

The Department of Health's Hospital Episode Statistics (2004–5) reveal some of the myriad (and odd) causes behind the *c.*13m admissions to NHS hospitals each year:

Fall from ladder 5,705	*Contact with hot engine* 98
Fall: roller-skates, skis, &c 4,305	*Victim of volcanic eruption*...........86
Contact with non-powered tool ... 4,174	*Victim of lightning*....................81
Bitten or struck by dog............ 3,829	*Exposure to sunlight*...................38
Travel and motion 774	*Bitten by rat* 24
Contact with hot tap-water......... 738	*Explosion/rupture of a boiler*........... 8
Contact with sharp plants 221	*Contact with venomous spiders* 4

——————————— HEART DISEASE DEATHS ———————————

The following figures from British Heart Foundation show the coronary heart disease deaths by region from 2004, for those aged 35–74 (rates per 100,000):

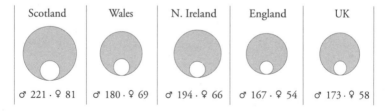

Scotland	Wales	N. Ireland	England	UK
♂ 221 · ♀ 81	♂ 180 · ♀ 69	♂ 194 · ♀ 66	♂ 167 · ♀ 54	♂ 173 · ♀ 58

——————— ENGLISH HEALTHIER THAN AMERICANS ———————

May 2006 research by the Rand Corporation and the Institute for Fiscal Studies at University College London suggested that middle-aged people in England are up to twice as healthy as their American counterparts. (This despite US medical spending per person being twice the amount spent in England.) Americans between 55–64 years old had a rate of diabetes over double that reported in England; rates of heart disease were 50% higher in America; and high blood-pressure was 10% more common in the US. The report suggested that these disparities might be due to lifestyle differences during childhood, and the shorter history of obesity in England.

PRO-ANA & PRO-MIA

Pro-Ana`and Pro-Mia [Pro-An^orexia; Pro-^Bulimia] are movements that seek to 'promote' anorexia and bulimia (respectively) as 'lifestyle choices', rather than psychological or medical disorders. A host of internet sites (like *anasblackrose.2ya.com*) offer 'thinspiration' to those desperate to lose weight. For example 'drink a glass of water every hour, it will make you feel full'. Not surprisingly, many in the medical community are concerned about the effects of such 'supportive advice'.

OBESITY

According to the Health Survey for England (2001), 21% of men and 23% of women are obese. Obesity is measured by the Body Mass Index (BMI), derived by dividing weight (Kg) by the square of height (m). A BMI >30 defines one as obese.

CLASS	underweight	normal	overweight	obese		
				class I 30–34·9	class II 35–39·9	class III >40
BMI	<18·5	18·5–24·9	25–29·9			
RISK	varies	average	increased	moderate	severe	very severe

Below are the percentages of adult populations around the world with a BMI >30:

Country (%)	1980	1990	2000	2001	2002	2003
United States	15·0	23·3	30·5	30·5	30·6	30·6
United Kingdom	7·0	14·0	21·0	22·0	22·0	23·0
France	—	5·8	9·0	9·0	9·4	9·4
Japan	2·0	2·3	2·9	3·2	3·6	3·2

[Source: OECD Health Data 2005] A survey by *Men's Fitness* magazine, in February 2006, listed the cities in the UK with the worst obesity problems. The results were based on incidence of heart disease; amount of junk food and alcohol consumed; and levels of gym membership. The fattest city was found to be Bradford, followed by Liverpool, Manchester, Newcastle, and Glasgow. On a more positive note, Southampton was named the fittest city.

PLASTIC SURGERY

Figures from the British Association of Aesthetic Plastic Surgeons (which uses the splendidly apt acronym, 'BAAPS') revealed a 35% increase in plastic surgery in Britain in 2005. The top-5 surgical procedures for men and women in 2005 were:

Women's procedures	*number*	*Men's procedures*	*number*
Breast augmentation	5,646	Rhinoplasty (nose job)	735
Blepharoplasty (eyelid lift)	2,868	Blepharoplasty (eyelid lift)	547
Breast reduction	2,593	Otoplasty (ear tweak)	526
Face/neck lift	2,135	Liposuction	220
Rhinoplasty (nose job)	1,533	Face/neck lift	144

————SOME HEALTH SCARES OF NOTE————

{SEP} · In a strongly worded report in the *BMJ*, doctors from Guy's and St Thomas' hospital warned that women who delay having children are defying nature, and urged them to conceive before they hit 35. {OCT} · A study conducted by São Paulo University, Brazil, suggested a link between high levels of air pollution and a reduction in the number of baby boys born. ❧ Research published in the *BMJ* indicated that those who retire early tended to die sooner. Those who stopped work at 55 had nearly double the death rate of those who work until 65. {NOV} ·

tea

A study by US National Institutes of Health suggested that drinking decaffeinated coffee may lead to a rise in cholesterol level. ❧ Research published in *Occupational & Environmental Medicine* linked stress at work to illness. The research involved over a quarter of a million workers worldwide, and proposed a connection between job dissatisfaction and depression. ❧ The Scientific Advisory Committee on Nutrition concluded that adding folic acid to flour could save hundreds of babies from birth defects. {DEC} · A Swedish study of 60,000 women suggested that those who drank two or more cups of tea a day had a *c.*50% lower risk of ovarian cancer than those who did not. ❧ An international team which analysed the evidence linking fibre consumption to protection from cancer, concluded that a high fibre diet makes little difference to the risk from cancer. {JAN 2006} · Scientists from Sense About Science criticised the detox industry, stating that water, fresh air, and sleep are all that are required for the body to recover from excesses at Christmas. ❧ Cedric Garland of the

University of San Diego conducted a review of studies examining the link between vitamin D and colorectal cancer. He concluded that taking 25 micrograms of the vitamin a day can halve the risk of contracting colorectal cancer. Vitamin D levels can also be improved by spending time in the sun, but experts are loath to recommend this, as spending too much time in the sun increases the risk of skin cancer. ❧ Over Christmas, GPs reported seeing a number of cases of 'glamrock shoulder', a strain injury caused when people who aren't used to gracing the dancefloor engage in energetic dance routines at yule-tide parties. ❧ Researchers suggested there may be a link between poor diet and the rise in mental illness. ❧ A study by INSERM, France's national institute for medical research, suggested that children who are exposed to household insecticides and head lice shampoos could double their risk of contracting leukaemia. ❧ Research published by the British section of a major 13-nation study into the link between mobile phones and brain tumours, indicated that mobile phones do not increase the risk of brain cancer. {FEB} · Three studies (part of the Women's Health Initiative study in America) into the health of 50,000 post-menopausal women, indicated that eating at least five portions of fruit and vegetables per day and reducing fat intake, did not reduce the risk of stroke, heart attack, breast or bowel cancer. ❧ A Canadian study showed that premature babies can achieve the same educational and employment levels as babies of normal birthweight. ❧ Advisers to the US Food and Drug Administration recommended

SOME HEALTH SCARES OF NOTE cont.

that drugs used to treat ADHD, like Ritalin, should display a prominent warning. The advice came after 25 people using such drugs suffered sudden death. {MAR} · Scientists at Leiden University suggested that low cabin pressure, cramped conditions, and lack of oxygen could add to the risk of deep vein thrombosis [DVT] on long-haul flights. ❧ Those who are genetically predisposed to be slow at breaking down caffeine are 64% more likely to suffer heart attacks, according to a study in Costa Rica. ❧ Research by the respected alternative medicine experts Prof. Edzard Ernst and Peter Canter concluded that there is no convincing evidence that chiropractors have a positive effect on health. ❧ Findings published in the *BMJ* cast doubt on the benefits of fish and linseed oils. An analysis of the top trials into fish oils concluded that there is little evidence to suggest they offer protection from heart disease, stroke, or cancer. {APR} · An American pharmacologist has suggested that one in four medicines may not work properly if used in conjunction with St John's Wort or Echinacea – as the herbal remedies may cause drugs to be quickly removed from the body. ❧ The Food Standards Agency warned cancer patients taking apricot kernels – which had been suggested by alternative practitioners as a potential cure – not to take more than one or two a day, as the kernels contain cyanide and, if taken in sufficient quantity, can cause death. {MAY} · A study following 128,000 people over 20 years concluded that drinking lots of filter coffee does not increase the risks of heart disease. ❧ Researchers from University College London suggested that working moth-

coffee

ers with happy relationships have the best health, while stay-at-home mothers were more likely to be obese. ❧ Children who are exposed to cats soon after birth have a greater risk of developing eczema, according to a team from the University of Arizona. ❧ A study of >50,000 people, published in the *BMJ*, indicated that men who drink alcohol every day have a lower risk of heart disease than those who do not – however drinking does not offer the same protection to women. {JUN} · A study of monkeys by researchers from North Carolina showed that trans fats (often used in processed foods to prolong shelf life) significantly increase the risk of developing a pot belly. ❧ A study conducted in California suggested that drinking coffee may provide some protection against liver damage in heavy alcohol drinkers. ❧ Research by the National Public Health Service for Wales indicated that 80% of head lice may now be now resistant to drugs. ❧ Evidence was presented that suggested exposure to unnatural light at night can increase the risk of cancer. Night workers, such as air stewardesses and nurses, may be *c.*60% more likely to develop breast cancer. {JUL} · According to hospital records, the number of people admitted with suspected anaphylactic shock – an extreme form of allergic reaction – has increased by 300% in the last decade. {AUG} · Drug regulators warned that fake copies of the statin Lipitor may have entered the NHS supply chain. ❧ Research published in *Neurology*, speculated that people who suffer severe allergies to pets, spores, and dust may be up to 3 times more likely to suffer from Parkinson's disease later in life.

——————————————— TEENS & DRUGS ———————————————

According to a 2006 report by the NHS Health & Social Care Information Centre, 1 in 4 secondary school children (11–15) says they drink alcohol; 1 in 10 smokes regularly; and 1 in 5 says they have tried drugs at least once in the past 12 months. Below are the percentages of children who had used drugs in the last year, by sex:

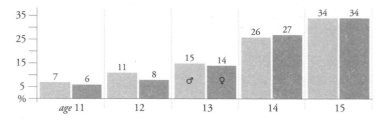

Below are the percentages of 11–15s who have been offered or use various drugs:

Drug	(%) offered	used
Cannabis	25	12
Cocaine	9	2
Crack	8	1
Ecstasy	8	1
Amphetamines	7	1
Poppers	12	4
LSD	5	1
Magic mushrooms	11	2
Ketamine	2	0
Heroin	6	1
Glue/solvents	18	7

Included within the pages of a Downing Street strategy unit report on drugs, commissioned by Tony Blair in 2003, was the following 'indicative pattern of drug use' amongst young people. The report stated that 'while light use of recreational drugs always precedes heavy use of heroin and/or crack, the key indicates for heavy use later are family background, criminal behaviour, and recreational drug use in early to mid teens'. Below is a schematic of this indicative pattern of drug use:

12 *years* . . . . . drink alcohol for first time
13 . . . . smoke first cigarette
14 . . . . try cannabis for the first time
15 . . . . drink & smoke heavily
        use cannabis occasionally

16 . . . . use cannabis frequently
17 . . . . try cocaine, amphetamines
           or ecstasy
18 . . . . use stimulants frequently
19 . . . . try heroin for the first time

Below are the average (2004) 'street' prices for various drugs, according to Druglink.

	Cannabis resin	Heroin	Cocaine	Crack	Ecstasy	Ketamine
	per ounce	per gram	per gram	per rock	per pill	per gram
London	£50	£40	£45	£7–15	£2	£15–40
Manchester	£50	£30–40	£40	£10–15	£3·30	£30–40
Birmingham	£35	£35–65	£40	£10	£3–6	£35
Glasgow	£40	£70	£40	–	£5	–
Belfast	£50	£100	£55	£30	£3	£25–30
Cardiff	£20	£40	£35–40	£20	80p–£2	£40–50

————————— ALCOHOL-RELATED DEATHS —————————

2004 figures from the Office of National Statistics illustrate the high number of alcohol-related deaths (per 100,000 of the population) by age, sex, and region:

	England		Wales		Scotland		N. Ireland	
Age	♂	♀	♂	♀	♂	♀	♂	♀
15–44	7·0	3·7	8·1	3·6	17·3	7·5	11·8	6·0
45–64	36·9	17·7	39·1	22·2	86·5	30·2	50·5	15·3
65–74	32·2	18·8	42·0	16·9	70·2	31·0	32·5	21·7
75–84	25·8	15·5	19·7	18·8	56·7	23·4	18·7	14·0
≥85	17·0	12·0	5·8	14·1	17·4	4·8	29·1	17·5
All ages	15·2	7·8	16·2	9·0	38·4	15·4	21·4	10·0

————————— DRINKING BY COUNTRY —————————

OECD data from 2005 show the average litres of alcohol consumed each year by the population (over the age of 15) of various different countries:

1980	country	2003
12·9*l*	Australia	9·8*l*
20·6	France	14·8
14·2	Germany	10·2
8·2	Hungary	13·4
9·6	Ireland	13·5
13·2	Italy	8·0
7·1	Japan	7·6
6·7	Sweden	7·0
9·4	UK	11·2
10·5	USA	8·3

————————— BINGE DRINKING —————————

A European Commission report by the Institute of Alcohol Studies, released in June 2006, showed that binge drinking[†] was rife across Europe. The table below shows the number of nights a year that adults reported binge drinking:

Finland	32	Germany	21
Ireland	32	France	20
UK[‡]	28	Netherlands	18
Belgium	27	Spain	14
Denmark	21	Greece	12

† Defined as 5 pints of beer, 1 bottle of wine, or 5 shots on one occasion. ‡ The average rate of UK binge drinking is about once every 13 days.

————————— GIVING UP SMOKING —————————

According to statistics released by the NHS Stop Smoking Service, over half a million people set a 'quit date' through the service during 2005, of whom 82% received Nicotine Replacement Therapy (NRT). Self-reported success rates follow:

Year	No. setting quit date	No. quit after 4 weeks	% success rate
2000/01	132,500	64,600	49
2001/02	227,300	119,800	53
2002/03	234,900	124,100	53
2003/04	361,200	204,900	57
2004/05	529,600	298,100	56
2005	598,600	328,900	55

PRISON POPULATION & STATISTICS

Prison population	*total*	♂	♀	*capacity*†
8 September 2006	79,066	74,500	4,566	79,988

† Useable operational capacity is the sum of all establishments' operational capacity, less 1,700 places for 'operating margin' caused by the need for separate accommodation for various classes of prisoner i.e. by sex, age, security category, conviction status, risk assessment, and geographical distribution.

Prison indicator	*2005–06*	
Overcrowding (average)	23·7%	Self-inflicted deaths.................68
Average cost/prisoner/year	£26,993	Minority ethnic prison staff.....5·7%
Escapes from escorts	6	Serious assaults by population.. 1·67%
Escapes from prisons	3	Serious assaults on fellow inmate . 827
Positive mandatory drug tests	10·3%	Serious sexual assaults 110
		Serious assaults on staff............ 155

[2005–6 figures for public sector England & Wales · Source: HMPS Annual Report · Crown ©]

Below are the Home Office statistics for the average prison population since 1980:

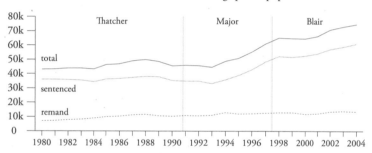

[For England & Wales · Includes non-criminal prisoners and those held in police cells · Crown ©]

Below are the 2004 Home Office figures for the punishment of offences, by offence and sentence

	discharge	fine	community service	fully suspended stnc	immediate custody	other
Theft and handling stolen goods	21%	17%	38%	–	21%	3%
Drug offences	18	36	23	1	20	2
Violence against the person	10	9	46	1	31	3
Burglary	4	2	48	–	45	1
Fraud and forgery	17	15	41	2	23	2
Criminal damage	20	14	48	–	11	7
Motoring	4	33	33	1	28	1
Robbery	1	–	31	–	67	1
Sexual offences	5	4	29	1	59	2
Other offences	9	39	21	1	19	11
All indictable offences	15	23	33	1	24	4

BRITISH CRIME SURVEY 2006

The annual British Crime Survey (BCS) measures crime in England and Wales by interviewing people about crimes they have experienced in the past year, and their fear of crime. The BCS is widely seen as a useful partner to the police's recorded crime figures since, for a number of reasons, certain crimes often go unreported.

% change in incidents of crime · British Crime Survey · 2004/5 – 2005/6

Vandalism	+7
Burglary	−3
All vehicle thefts	−8
Bicycle theft	+9
All BCS violence	0
Domestic violence	−11
All household crime	0
TOTAL BCS CRIME	+1

% change in police recorded crime · 2004/5 – 2005/6

Homicide	−12
Possession of weapons	−2
Violence against the person	+1
Sexual offences	0
Robbery	+8
Domestic burglary	−7
Other burglary	−4
Thefts of and from vehicles	3
Other thefts and handling	−2
Criminal damage	−1
TOTAL RECORDED CRIME	−1

THE POLICE SERVICE

As at 31 March 2005, there were 142,795 full-time police officers in England and Wales, serving in 43 forces – an increase of 2,209 (2%) since March 2004. Below are the number of officers serving in each rank, by sex and ethnic minority:

Rank	male	female	% female	% ethnic	Total
ACPO[†]	204	23	10	2·2	227
Chief Superintendent	502	40	7	1·7	542
Superintendent	930	99	10	2·3	1,029
Chief Inspector	1,765	203	10	2·5	1,968
Inspector	6,192	746	11	2·2	6,938
Sergeant	17,982	2,704	13	2·4	20,686
Constable	85,057	26,347	24	3·8	111,404
All ranks	112,633	30,162	21	3·5	142,795

[† Association of Chief Police Officers · Source: Home Office Statistical Bulletin]

────────YOUNG PEOPLE & VIOLENT CRIME────────

The 2004 *Offending Crime & Justice Survey* shows the percentage of young people in England & Wales that had committed a violent offence in the prior 12 months:

Age	♂%	♀%						
10–11	10	7	14–15	30	18	20–21	18	11
12–13	25	15	16–17	33	18	22–23	10	5
			18–19	21	11	24–25	12	3

Young offenders offered the following reasons for carrying out a violent offence:

Annoyed/upset by someone 47%	Friends encouraged/dare.............. 3
Self-defence 30	It was an accident..................... 2
Revenge 17	Under the influence of drugs......... 1
For the fun/buzz 12	They wanted what they stole 1
Was drunk............................ 9	Upset/frustrated...................... 1
Bored/nothing to do................. 6	Racially motivated ....<1

Below are the times of day when crimes are committed against those aged 10–25:

% of crimes by time (against 10–25s)	morning 0600–1200	afternoon 1200–1800	evening 1800–2200	night 2200–0600
Violent offences	10	36	23	20
Property offences	18	42	14	12

────────── ANTI-SOCIAL BEHAVIOUR ORDERS──────────

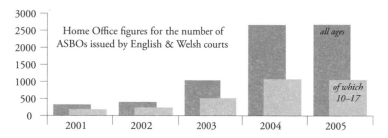

Home Office figures for the number of ASBOs issued by English & Welsh courts

all ages

of which 10–17

Research by security firm ADT, in May 2006, revealed the perceptions of the level of anti-social behaviour across Europe. The table below shows the percentage of those who consider anti-social behaviour to be a 'moderate' or 'big' problem:

Great Britain 76%	Germany 61%	Spain 51%
France 75%	Italy................52%	Netherlands 44%

Those in France and Italy perceived the location with the greatest risk of antisocial behaviour to be housing estates; Germans reported it to be transport termini; the Dutch said shopping areas; and the Spanish and English worried most in the neighbourhood of bars, pubs, and nightclubs.

———— THE SERIOUS ORGANISED CRIME AGENCY ————

The Serious Organised Crime Agency (SOCA), a new intelligence-gathering branch of the police force, was established on 1 April 2006. Given its remit of investigating organised and international crimes (such as drug trafficking, people smuggling, money laundering, and fraud), the agency has been likened to a British FBI. SOCA will act as a single agency with wide-ranging powers of search, seizure, arrest, and interrogation that were previously shared by police, customs, and immigration. Significantly, SOCA was also granted powers of Queen's Evidence which will allow the agency to strike 'deals' with suspects, offering immunity from prosecution or reduction in sentence in return for co-operation. When fully operational, SOCA will have *c*.4,000 officers and staff, and will work from 46 secret offices across Britain.

———————— WORST UK AREAS FOR CRIME ————————

Using 2005 data, the think-tank Reform ranked the UK areas worst hit by crime:

MURDER	RAPE	BURGLARY	GUN CRIME	ASSAULT
Nottingham	*Portsmouth*	*Stockport*	*Bradford*	*Leicester*
St Helens	*Peterbor'gh*	*Leeds*	*Leeds*	*Bradford*
Leeds	*Leeds*	*Nottingham*	*North'pton*	*Rotherham*
Rotherham	*Luton*	*Oldham*	*Nottingham*	*St Helens*
Newcastle	*Nottingham*	*Bradford*	*Stoke*	*Nottingham*

———————— RAPE CONVICTIONS ————————

2004 Home Office figures revealed the wide geographical differences across England and Wales in rates of conviction for rape. Only 4 out of the 42 police forces in England and Wales had rape conviction rates greater than 10%. Below are the complaint and conviction rates for rape, from a selection of police force regions:

Police force	reports	prosecutions	convictions	& rate (%)
Cambridgeshire	228	27	4	1·75
Cumbria	86	18	11	12·79
Essex	344	54	12	3·49
Gloucestershire	116	21	1	0·86
Greater Manchester	904	199	36	3·98
Metropolitan Police	2,481	516	121	4·88
North Wales	170	31	8	4·71
Northamptonshire	116	20	16	13·79
South Wales	197	90	24	12·18
South Yorkshire	242	66	26	10·74

Figures released by the Home Office in April 2006, revealed that in 2004, 40 sex offenders were given a caution after admitting rape. The Home Office said cautions were only used in 'exceptional circumstances', and re-iterated their commitment to increasing the conviction rate for rapists.

Media & Celebrity

I would much rather have men ask why I have no statue, than why I have one.
— CATO THE ELDER (234–149BC)

————HELLO! vs OK! COVER STARS————

Date	Hello!	OK!
04·01·06	Rod Stewart & Penny Lancaster	Jordan & Peter Andre
11·01·06	Shane Ritchie	Jane Danson's wedding
18·01·06	David & Victoria Beckham	Jordan
25·01·06	Angelina Jolie	Victoria Beckham
01·02·06	Eminem & wife Kim	Jordan & son Harvey
07·02·06	Amanda Holden & baby	Chantelle (winner of *Celebrity Big Brother*)
14·02·06	Preston (*Celebrity Big Brother*)	Jordan
21·02·06	Prince William & Kate Middleton	Chantelle
28·02·06	Madonna & Guy Ritchie	Victoria Beckham
07·03·06	Lisa Marie Presley	Jordan & son Junior
14·03·06	Geri Halliwell	Kerry Katona
21·03·06	Keira Knightley	Chantelle
28·03·06	Kate Middleton	Jordan & Peter
04·04·06	Elizabeth Hurley	Kate Garraway and baby
11·04·06	Charles & Camilla	Victoria Beckham
18·04·06	Victoria Beckham	Jennifer Aniston
25·04·06	Prince Harry	Kerry Katona
02·05·06	Brad & Angelina	Jordan
09·05·06	Kylie Minogue	Victoria Beckham
18·05·06	Laura Parker Bowles' wedding	Julia Haworth's wedding
23·05·06	Shane Ritchie, fiancée & new baby	Chantelle & Preston
30·05·06	Geri Halliwell & new baby	Jordan & her kids
06·06·06	Victoria Beckham	Steven Gerrard, Alex Curran & new baby
13·06·06	Brad Pitt, Angelina Jolie & baby Shiloh	Victoria Beckham
20·06·06	Tamzin Outwaithe's wedding	Victoria Beckham & other WAGs
27·06·06	Vic Reeves, Nancy & new twins	Nadine Coyle & Jesse Metcalfe
04·07·06	Nicole Kidman marries Keith Urban	David & Victoria Beckham
18·07·06	Wedding of Jasmine Guinness	Jordan & son Junior
25·07·06	Amanda de Cadenet	Cheryl Tweedy & Ashley Cole's wedding
01·08·06	Wayne Rooney & Coleen	Cheryl & Ashley Cole
08·08·06	David & Victoria Beckham	David & Victoria Beckham
15·08·06	Kate Middleton & Chelsy Davy	Pamela Anderson & Kid Rock
22·08·06	Paul McCartney & Heather Mills McCartney	Kerry Katona
29·08·06	Kate Moss & Pete Doherty	*Big Brother* winner Pete Bennett
05·09·06	Kate Middleton	Chantelle & Preston's wedding

Jan–Sep 2006, Jordan graced the cover of *OK!* 9 times, compared to 11 in the same period in 2005

——— SOME HATCHED, MATCHED, & DISPATCHED ———

HATCHED

Violet [♀] *to* ....Jennifer Garner & Ben Affleck
Alistair Wallace [♂] *to*................................Penny Lancaster & Rod Stewart
Matilda [♀] *to* ....Heath Ledger & Michelle Williams
Moses [♂] *to*.................................... Gwyneth Paltrow & Chris Martin
Suri [♀] (aka TomKItten) *to*................. Tom Cruise & Katie Holmes (aka TomKat)
Bluebell Madonna [♀] *to*.. Geri Halliwell
Shiloh Nouvel [♀] *to* ....Angelina Jolie & Brad Pitt (aka Brangelina)
Kingston James McGregor [♂] *to* .... Gwen Stefani & Gavin Rossdale
Henry Chance [♂] *to*............................Rachel Weisz & Darren Aronofsky
Sutton Pierce (unconfirmed) [♂] *to* ....Britney Spears & Kevin Federline
Chester [♂] *to* .... Davina McCall & Matthew Robertson

MATCHED

Christina Aguilera & Jordan Bratman................... *at* Napa Valley, California
Marilyn Manson & Dita Von Teese........................Castle Gurteen, Ireland
Matt Damon & Luciana Barroso ....Manhattan, New York
Pink & Carey Hart................................ Four Seasons resort, Costa Rica
Eminem & Kimberly Mathers................................ Rochester, Michigan
Avril Lavigne & Deryck Whibley..........................Montecito, Los Angeles
Nicole Kidman & Keith Urban...............................Sydney, Australia
Ant McPartlin & Lisa Armstrong....................... Taplow, Buckinghamshire
Pamela Anderson & Kid Rock......................................St Tropez, France

DISPATCHED

Jessica Simpson & Nick Lachey (*married for* 3 years)...................... divorced
Hilary Swank & Chad Lowe (8 years)............................. filed for divorce
David Hasselhoff & Pamela Bach (16 years) .... divorced
Heather Locklear & Richie Sambora (11 years).................... filed for divorce
Matt LeBlanc & Melissa McKnight (3 years) .... filed for divorce
Eminem & Kimberly Mathers (81 days) .... filed for divorce
Paul McCartney & Heather Mills (4 years) ....separated
Kate Hudson & Chris Robinson (6 years) ....separated
Whitney Houston & Bobby Brown (14 years).................... filed for divorce

———————CELEBRITY AUTOGRAPHS———————

In May 2006, American magazine *Autograph Collector* published a list of the best and worst celebrities to approach in hope of an autograph. The results were:

the most approachable signers	*the least approachable signers*
Johnny Depp · George Clooney	Cameron Diaz · Bruce Willis
Matt Damon · Al Pacino	Demi Moore · Tobey Maguire
Tom Cruise · Angelina Jolie	Alan Alda · Halle Berry
Elijah Wood · Brittany Murphy	Winona Ryder · Teri Hatcher

——— IACGMOOH ———

The fifth series of *I'm a Celebrity ... Get Me Out of Here* was unusually heartening, with the contestants displaying impressive camaraderie. Rank outsider Carol Thatcher surprised the bookies to be crowned *Queen of the Jungle*. The 'celebrities' left in the following order:

12th	Elaine Lordan (illness)
11th	Tommy Cannon
10th	Kimberley Davies (injury)
9th	Jilly Goolden
8th	David Dickinson
7th	Jenny Frost
6th	Antony Costa
5th	Bobby Ball
4th	Jimmy Osmond
3rd	Sid Owen
2nd	Sheree Murphy
WINNER	CAROL THATCHER

QUOTES OF NOTE
ELAINE LORDAN · I don't think I'm what you'd call a natural camper. ❦ ANTONY COSTA · *(when faced with a bushtucker trial)* I can't die can I? ❦ SHEREE MURPHY · *(of footballer husband, Harry Kewell)* He's got the smoothest, peachiest bum ever. ❦ DAVID DICKINSON · It just goes to show you how dangerous this place is – it's not a studio, it's the bloody jungle! ❦ JILLY GOOLDEN · I've got to get rid of the taste of [kangaroo's] penis. ❦

——— BIG BROTHER 7 ———

Tourette's sufferer Pete Bennett was the favourite to win BB7 from the start, but interest was sustained with a secret house next door, and the chance to become a housemate by finding a golden ticket in a KitKat. 1,700 viewers complained when producers allowed an evicted housemate to be voted back in.

Eviction order			
21.	Shahbaz (quit)	10 =	Spiral
20.	Dawn (ejected)	10 =	Michael
19.	Bonnie	9	Nikki
18.	George (quit)	8 =	Mikey
17.	Sezer	8 =	Suzie
16.	Sam	7	Imogen
15.	Grace	6	Jennie
14.	Lisa	5	Nikki
13.	Jonathan	4	Richard
12.	Lea	3	Aisleyne
11.	Jayne	2	Glyn
		WINNER	Pete

QUOTES OF NOTE
GRACE (*to Nikki*) · Please don't think I look down on you babes, I don't look down on anyone. ❦ NIKKI · Who is she? Who is she? I hate her! Who does she think she is? ❦ AISLEYNE · You better know yourself little girl. ❦ GLYN · Big Brother, not having any food to eat is making me hungry. ❦ NIKKI · I've never cried happy tears before. PETE · Really? I have. When I was 12 and I got a Sega-Mega drive. ❦

——— HOLLYWOOD'S WORST-DRESSED WOMEN ———

Each year, the fashion guru and former designer mysteriously known only as Mr Blackwell produces a list of Tinseltown's worst style offenders. His 2006 top 10:

1	Britney Spears	6	Paris Hilton
2	Mary Kate Olsen	7	Anna Nicole Smith
3	Jessica Simpson	8	Shakira
4	Eva Longoria	9	Lindsay Lohan
5	Mariah Carey	10	Renée Zellweger

─────── VANITY FAIR'S HOLLYWOOD · 2006 ───────

The stars featured on the cover of the 2006 *Vanity Fair* 'Hollywood issue' were:

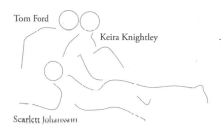

The cover of the 2006 Hollywood edition caused a degree of controversy, since it featured a very clothed Tom Ford alongside the very naked Knightley and Johansson. The girls' arms and legs were strategically placed to avoid embarrassment – though Johansson's bare buttocks were exposed on page 2 of the gatefold pullout cover. Ford claims he stepped in to the frame after Rachel McAdams decided she was not comfortable appearing unclad.

The '05 *Vanity Fair* Hollywood stars: Kate Winslet, Cate Blanchett, Uma Thurman, Rosario Dawson, Ziyi Zhang, Scarlett Johansson, Claire Danes, Kate Bosworth, Sienna Miller, & Kerry Washington.

─────── CELEBRITY SKIN ───────

A poll of the National Association of Screen Make-up Artists and Hairdressers revealed which celebrities had the most naturally flawless skin, and which needed a dab of concealer. Below are those named with the best and worst 'celebrity skin':

flawless, absolutely flawless	*not so flawless*
Scarlett Johansson · Orlando Bloom	Cameron Diaz · Michael Douglas
Kate Winslet · Jake Gyllenhaal	Keira Knightley · Bryan Adams
Catherine Zeta Jones · Johnny Depp	Joan Collins · Brad Pitt

[Source: NASMAH/Telewest, March 2006]

─────── SEXIEST MEN & WOMEN 2006 ───────

FHM's women		COMPANY's men
Keira Knightley	1	David Beckham
Keeley Hazel	2	Johnny Depp
Scarlett Johansson	3	Brad Pitt
Angelina Jolie	4	Orlando Bloom
Kelly Brook	5	Wentworth Miller
Cheryl Tweedy	6	Jake Gyllenhaal
Beyoncé Knowles	7	Robbie Williams
Evangeline Lily	8	Frank Lampard
Jessica Alba	9	Dermot O'Leary
Jessica Simpson	10	Steve Jones

Readers of American FHM voted Scarlett Johansson as the sexiest women of 2006. Angelina Jolie, Jessica Alba, Jessica Simpson, and Britain's very own Keira Knightley completed the FHM top five.

CELEBRITY IN QUOTES

DAVID BECKHAM · More men should take care of themselves. What gives us the right to start to look craggy when women don't? ❦ EDITH BOWMAN · My fear is that some lunatic will mix different flavoured crisps in a bowl at a party and I'll eat a cheese and minging by accident. ❦ BRIAN BLESSED · I hate catching myself in the flies. It takes ages to loosen yourself and it looks like you're masturbating. It happened to me when I was doing a voiceover for Rice Krispies – I was Crackle. ❦ LINDSAY LOHAN · I have fashion shows for myself every morning. My friends take pictures and we decide which outfit looks best on me. ❦ BEYONCÉ · Its frustrating for me because sometimes, when you are attractive people don't acknowledge that you are talented as well. That has been my toughest hurdle really. ❦ MADONNA · I hate people who hate woman. Actually, I hate people who hate. ❦ NOEL EDMONDS · I really ought to chill out more.

RUSSELL CROWE · I'd move to LA – if Australia and New Zealand were swallowed up by a huge tidal wave, if there was a bubonic plague in Europe, and if Africa disappeared from some Martian attack. ❦ JADE GOODY · I hate it when people say it's edited to make you look bad. I'd never say they edited it to make me look thick. I am silly and that's how I came across. ❦ SHARON STONE · I like to drive with my knees. Otherwise, how can I put on my lipstick and talk on the phone? ❦ GWEN STEFANI · Sometimes you have to sacrifice your performance for high heels. ❦ SIENNA MILLER · I've got this group of friends that are quite bohemian – we get drunk, get the poetry books out and read. It sounds so pretentious, but it's one of my favourite things. ❦ BRAD PITT · It's amazing what a midlife crisis will do for you. ❦ JENNIFER ANISTON · If you described me as an animal, I'd be a baboon.

UK'S MOST ELIGIBLE WOMEN

Men's magazine FHM produced a list of the UK's most eligible women in 2006:

1 .... Mischa Barton	5 .... Zara Phillips	9 .... Tamara Ecclestone
2 .... Naomi Watts	6 .... Elizabeth Jagger	10 ...... Mickey Sumner
3 .... Kate Moss	7 .... Keira Knightley	
4 .... Joss Stone	8 .... Rosamund Pike	(All were born in UK)

CELEBRITY SELLING POWER

American entertainment agency Davie-Brown Talent launched a celebrity index in 2006 that promised to reveal to advertisers and corporate clients (for the modest sum of $20,000) which celebrities had the greatest consumer appeal. The index employs a research panel of 1½m people to evaluate 1,500 celebrities in these categories: *appeal, trust, notice, trendsetting, influence, endorsement, awareness,* and *aspiration*. Keeping their cards close to their chest, Davie-Brown Talent revealed only the top two from their exclusive celebrity index: Tom Hanks and Oprah Winfrey.

—————CELEBRITY INTRIGUE—————

{SEP} · Kate Moss was dropped as the face of Burberry and Chanel after she was pictured in a Sunday paper allegedly taking cocaine. Moss released a statement in which she said, 'I take full responsibility for my actions. I also accept that there are various personal issues that I need to address and have started taking the difficult, yet necessary, steps to resolve them'. {OCT} · Gossip columns were filled with allegations that Tom Cruise had asked his pregnant fiancée Katie Holmes to give birth in silence, as is allegedly required of followers of Scientology. {NOV} · The editor of the *Sun*, Rebekah Wade, was arrested, but not charged, after she reportedly split the lip of her husband, *Eastenders*' hardman Ross Kemp. In a bizarre coincidence, Ross Kemp's on-screen brother, Steve McFadden, was allegedly assaulted by his ex-girlfriend on the same day. {DEC} · Colin Farrell went into rehab to treat exhaustion and an addiction to prescription drugs. {JAN 2006} · Lindsay Lohan claimed that her words had been 'misused and misconstrued' after *Vanity Fair* reported that she had admitted during an interview to suffering from bulimia and dabbling with drugs. {FEB} · Britney Spears was pictured driving her 4x4 with her baby son on her lap; Spears issued a statement claiming the paparrazzi had been harassing her, stating 'I love my child and would do anything to protect him'. ❦ George Michael was found slumped over the wheel of his car in London's West End. He was arrested on suspicion of possessing

Lindsay Lohan

I said things that I do not believe to be true and which are despicable.
— MEL GIBSON

Class C drugs, and later accepted a caution. {MAR} · A Scottish masseuse recounted to an employment tribunal that an un-named married Hollywood actor asked for a 'sweet' massage and then proceeded to indulge in a sex act. The masseuse claimed that the incident had induced post-traumatic stress. The tribunal judge ruled that the celebrity about whom the allegations were made could be named; it was Kevin Costner. He vehemently denies the masseuse's claims. ❦ Naomi Campbell was arrested in New York and charged with assault after allegedly throwing a telephone at her housekeeper's head. {APR} · Snoop Dog and five of his entourage were arrested during a fracas at Heathrow airport. {JUL} · Mel Gibson was alleged to have made anti-Semitic comments after being arrested in California for drink driving. He issued a statement apologising for his behaviour: 'I acted like a person completely out of control when I was arrested, and said things that I do not believe to be true and which are despicable'. Gibson later admitted to a long-running battle with alcoholism, and asked to meet Jewish leaders for 'a one-on-one discussion to discern the appropriate path for healing'. ❦ Following absences from the set of her latest film, *Georgia Rule*, Lindsay Lohan was criticised for her 'all-night heavy partying' in a letter from James G. Robinson, CEO of Morgan Creek Productions, and the executive behind the film. Robinson alleged that Lohan was acting like a 'spoiled child', and was 'discourteous, irresponsible and unprofessional'.

CELEBRITY BLOGS OF NOTE

Pearls of wisdom taken from a selection of celebrity websites and blogs in 2006:

PINK (April) · There is absolutely nothing wrong with being sexy, feeling sexy, or dressing sexy. My point is only this: 'SMART' and 'SEXY' are not oil and water. They can actually work together. You don't need to dumb yourself down in order to be cute.

MOBY (April) · i just had waffles and vegan sausage and it/they was/were excellent. they should prescribe waffles to people suffering from depression. waffles and puppies. how could anyone [be] depressed while eating waffles and playing with puppies? just imagine: a plate of waffles and maple syrup and a little box with jack russell puppies leaping around?

BRITNEY SPEARS (July) · In some ways, people are a lot like animals. We all hunger for the same things. Love, lust, danger, warmth and adventure. Like people, animals all have their own rhythm to life. I'm mesmerized by tigers.

GENE SIMMONS (May) · Some of you get sick and tired of seeing GENE SIMMONS in front of every project. Not my problem. I like it. I like me. And, I am unabashed and unapologetic of being in the Gene Simmons Business. If there can be Geffen Records and Bloomberg TV and Walt Disney Pictures ... there can be GENE SIMMONS EVERYTHING. Those guys did it right. And, I certainly intend to do the same.

IAN MCKELLAN (May) · Sometimes it seems as if actors in upcoming movies are trapped in a vice betwixt the publicity department, eager to prove their worth to the Studio, and the otherwise empty guest chairs on late night television. Does anyone go and see a film because of chats on late night television?

JODIE MARSH (June) · Everything I wear I get slated for (even though I LOVE my clothes, otherwise I wouldn't wear them!) therefore I can't be arsed with even letting anyone take my picture.

REALITY SHOW WINNERS · 2005/06

Channel & show	winner (prize)
BBC1....*Strictly Come Dancing*...............	Darren Gough (raised £1·5m for charity)
ITV1 ....*X-Factor*.................................	Shayne Ward (£1m recording contract)
C4.......*Celebrity Big Brother*.........................	Chantelle Houghton (£25,000)
ITV1 ....*Celebrity Fit Club*.....................................	Mick Quinn (lost 64lb)
ITV1 ....*Soapstar Superstar*.............	Richard Fleeshman (raised £100,000 for charity)
C4.......*The Games*	♀ Javine ♂ Jade Jones (raised money for charity)
BBC2....*The Apprentice*	Michelle Dewberry (£100k job with Sir Alan Sugar)
BBC1...*Just the Two of Us*........	Sian Reeves & Russell Watson (£20,000 for charity)
BBC1...*Strictly Dance Fever*.........	Hollie Robertson & Darrien Wright (£50,000)
ITV1 ....*Dancing on Ice*.......................................	Gaynor Faye (a trophy)
Sky1 ....*Project Catwalk*..........................	Kirsty Doyle (£20,000, spread in *Elle*)
ITV......*Celebrity X-Factor*....................	Lucy Benjamin (raised money for charity)
ITV .....*Love Island*............	Bianca Gascoigne & Callum Best (£100,000 to share)

——AD EXPENDITURE——

Greatest expenditure on UK adverts:

UK advertiser	2005 UK spend (£m)
Unilever	213·6
Procter & Gamble	180·3
COI Communications	166·3
L'Oréal Golden	102·8
BSkyB	98·3
DFS	83·3
Masterfoods	78·1
Orange	75·5
BT	73
Nestlé	68·5

[Source: Nielsen Media Research]

————AD COST————

Below are tabulated the costs of 30-second advertising slots during selected programmes (estimated using average 2006 national rates):

Programme (channel)	cost (£)
Champ. League Final (ITV1)	115,000
Coronation Street (ITV1)	57,000
Big Brother Final (C4)	41,000
The Simpsons (C4)	19,000
Prison Break (Five)	6,000
The Simpsons (Sky One)	5,000
Sky News (Sky News)	100

[Source: PHD · *The Guardian*]

——— MOST COMPLAINED-ABOUT ADVERTS ———

The Advertising Standards Authority (ASA) 2005 annual report detailed the most complained about broadcast adverts, the top eight of which were as follows:

KFC · An advert showing call-centre workers singing about KFC with their mouths full, prompted complaints that the ad might encourage bad manners.
1,671 complaints · Not upheld

LIVING TV · Complaints about suggestive posters for the lesbian TV show 'The L Word' which some claimed were degrading to women.
650 complaints · Not upheld

POT NOODLE · Concerns about the sexual innuendo of an advert where a man tries to conceal a large brass horn in his pocket, using the tagline 'Have you got the Pot Noodle horn?'
620 complaints · Not upheld

MAZDA · Complaints about an advert in which a man drives female mannequins around a city in a car that causes their nipples to become erect.
425 complaints · Not upheld

RYANAIR · Just days after 7 July attacks on London, Ryanair ran press adverts with the slogan 'London Fights Back', which some complained exploited the terrorist attacks for commercial gain.
319 complaints · Not upheld

CRAZY FROG · Misleading ads for mobile ringtones which drew people unwittingly into a commitment to subscribe.
298 complaints · Upheld

BARCLAYS · An ad in which a man is stung on the mouth by a bee and then lurches from disaster to disaster, was said to offend those suffering from allergies.
293 complaints · Upheld

DAMART · Complaints about promotional letters posted to customers which implied they were in debt.
273 complaints · Upheld

[Source: www.asa.org.uk]

—————————— OWNERSHIP OF TVs & RADIOs ——————————

Television sets	no. per household			*radios*
	0			1%
30%	1		25%	
34%	2		28%	
21%	3			20%
11%	4			13%
3%	≥5			13%

[Source: Ofcom, 2006 · figures are rounded]

————— THE INTERNET'S IMPACT ON OTHER MEDIA —————

To assess the impact of the internet on 'traditional' media, in 2006 Ofcom asked
a range of age groups, 'since using the internet for the first time, which if any of
the following activities do you believe you undertake less?' The results are below:

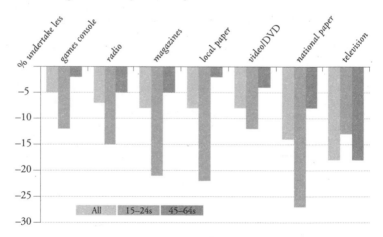

————— WEEKLY UK COMMUNICATION CONSUMPTION —————

Usage per week (hr:min)	*2001*	*2005*	*Change* (minutes or texts)
TV viewing	25:23	25:34	+11
Radio listening	20:30	20:06	−24
Landline phone	1:11	1:10	−1
Mobile phone	0:20	0:22	+2
Internet browsing	2:10	2:29	+19
SMS texts sent (number)	5½	11	+5½

[Source: Ofcom/operators/RAJAR/BARB/TGI-BMRB, 2006]

--------OFFENSIVE RADIO--------

2006 Ofcom data indicate the percentage of people who are offended by radio:

75%	16%	8%	2%
Never	*Rarely*	*Sometimes*	*Frequently*

Ofcom found that 35% of those who did take offence still believed the offensive material *should* have been aired. Below are the actions taken as a result of offence:

Action taken as a result of offence	%		
Switched off	43	Discussed it with others	15
Continued to listen/no action	21	Complained to broadcaster	3
Switched over	20	Complained to regulator	0
		Other	6

--------CHILDREN & MEDIA CONSUMPTION--------

In May 2006, Ofcom released a report on children's media consumption. The research surveyed 5,000 British children (8–15) to understand their views on, and usage of, television, radio, the internet, and mobile phones. The data below show the percentage of kids with ownership of, or access to, various types of media:

Ownership or access	% aged 8–15	% 8–11	% 12–15
Digital TV	72	73	72
Digital radio	47	48	46
Internet	64	61	67
Mobile phone	65	49	82

The chart below shows the time spent by children on different media each week:

Media (hr:min/week)	aged 8–11 all	♂	♀	aged 12–15 all	♂	♀
Television	13:2	13:6	12:9	14:7	14:3	15:1
DVDs or videos	4:5	4:5	4:5	4:8	6:0	3:8
Radio	3:7	3:3	4:1	6:4	6:5	6:4
Internet use (home)	2:1	2:2	2:1	4:9	4:6	5:2
Internet use (school)	1:6	1:5	1:6	2:1	2:1	2:1
Mobile calls (no./week)	5·8	4·9	6·7	9·2	9·9	8·6
Texts sent (no./week)	15·9	9·6	21·6	30·9	34·8	27·6

8–11s who say they mostly watch TV on their own ... 35%
12–15s who say they mostly watch TV on their own ... 49%
12–15s who say news programmes are always true ... 35%
12–15s who say reality TV programmes are always true ... 12%
12–15s who are solely responsible for paying their mobile bill ... 42%
Parents of 8–11s that use blocking software on their computer ... 56%
8–11s who own a games console ... 50%

————BRITAIN'S MOST WATCHED TV BY DECADE————

Show	channel	date	millions
2000s			
Only Fools and Horses	BBC1	25·12·01	21·34
Euro '04: England vs Portugal	BBC1	24·06·04	20·66
EastEnders	BBC1	05·04·01	20·05
Coronation Street	ITV	24·02·03	19·40
Tonight with Trevor McDonald†	ITV	21·04·03	16·10
Who Wants To Be a Millionaire?	ITV	19·01·00	15·90
1990s			
The Funeral of Princess Diana	BBC1 & ITV	06·09·97	32·10
Only Fools and Horses	BBC1	29·12·96	24·35
EastEnders	BBC1	02·01·92	24·30
Torvill & Dean – Winter Olympics	BBC1	21·02·94	23·95
World Cup '98: England vs Argentina	ITV	30·06·98	23·78
Panorama Special: Princess Diana	BBC1	20·11·95	22·78
1980s			
EastEnders	BBC1	25·12·86	30·15
Wedding of Charles & Diana	BBC1 & ITV	29·07·81	28·40
Coronation Street	ITV	19·03·89	26·93
Dallas	BBC1	22·11·80	21·60
To the Manor Born	BBC1	09·11·80	21·55
Neighbours	BBC1	04·04·89	20·92
1970s			
Apollo 13 Splashdown	BBC1 & ITV	17·04·70	28·60
FA Cup final replay: Chelsea vs Leeds	BBC1 & ITV	29·04·70	28·49
Princess Anne's Wedding	BBC1 & ITV	14·11·73	27·60
To the Manor Born	BBC1	11·11·79	23·95
Miss World	BBC1	20·11·70	23·76
Royal Variety Performance	BBC1	16·11·75	22·66
1960s			
The World Cup final	BBC1	30·07·66	32·30
The Royal Family	BBC1 & ITV	21·06·69*	30·69
Royal Variety Performance	ITV	14·11·65	24·20
News – JFK assassinated	BBC1 & ITV	22·11·63	24·15
Miss World	BBC1	19·11·67	23·76
Apollo 8 Splashdown	BBC1 & ITV	27·12·68	22·55
1950s			
Wagon Train	ITV	30·11·59	13·63
Take Your Pick	ITV	11·12·59	13·16
Sunday Palladium	ITV	06·12·59	13·08
Armchair Theatre: Suspicious Mind	ITV	22·11·59	12·74
The Army Game	ITV	11·12·59	12·60
Double Your Money	ITV	05·11·59	12·34

† The episode in question was 'Millionaire: A Major Fraud' regarding alleged cheating by Major Ingram on ITV's *Who Wants to be a Millionaire?*. * Shown on different days on different channels.

[Source: BFI, BARB, AGB, BBC, TAM, AC Nielsen]

DIGITAL TV SWITCHOVER

The switch from analogue to digital TV will begin in 2008; currently 63% of UK households have digital receivers. The Department of Culture, Media and Sport announced that the process will unfold by ITV region, in the following order:

2008	Border	2010 (cont.)	Scottish Television
2009	West Country, HTV Wales, Granada	2011	Yorkshire, Anglia, Central
2010	HTV West, Grampian,	2012	Meridian, Carlton/LWT, Tyne Tees, Ulster

According to Ofcom, the worldwide switch to digital TV will be complete by:

2009	USA	2011	Japan
2010	Germany, France, Australia	2012	UK

THE LICENCE FEE

The BBC licence fee is currently £131·50 a year for colour, and £44 for black and white. The figures below show how the licence is spent by the BBC, each month:

BBC One	34·9%	Local radio	6·3
BBC Two	15·0	bbc.co.uk	3·2
Radios 1, 2, 3, 4 and Five Live	10·2	Digital radio stations	0·83
Digital television channels	10·1		
Transmission & collection costs	10·1		
Nations & English regions TV	9·3		

[Source: TVL annual review · 2003/04 figures when the licence cost £121, or £9·67 a month]

BBC SALARIES LEAK

In April 2006, alleged salary details of BBC radio stars were leaked to the tabloids, causing heated debate about how the licence fee is spent. The BBC had previously declined to release this kind of commercially sensitive information despite frequent requests made through the Freedom of Information Act. BBC Director General Mark Thompson (who earns £459,000) defended these large salaries by stating:

The overall story is that [BBC] pay has run at a lower rate than the media sector as a whole ... what's happening is that other broadcasters are coming in and offering people working for us far, far higher rates than they are currently getting.

Selected reported BBC salaries			
Terry Wogan	£800,000	Jonathan Ross	£530,000
Chris Moyles	£630,000	Steve Wright	£440,000
Chris Evans	£540,000	Jo Whiley	£250,000
		Michael Parkinson	£115,000

In May '06 the 'mole' was unmasked as BBC temp Sam Walton, who earned £1,000 for the scoop.

THE TV BAFTAS · 2006

Award	winner
Best actor	Mark Rylance · *The Government Inspector* [C4]
Best actress	Anna Maxwell Martin · *Bleak House* [BBC1]
Entertainment performance	Jonathan Ross · *Friday Night With* ... [BBC1]
Comedy performance	Chris Langham · *The Thick Of It* [BBC4]
Single drama	*The Government Inspector* [C4]
Drama series	*Doctor Who* [BBC1]
Drama serial	*Bleak House* [BBC1]
Continuing drama	*EastEnders* [BBC1]
Feature	*The Apprentice* [BBC2]
Factual series or strand	*Jamie's School Dinners* [C4]
Huw Wheldon award for specialist factual	*Holocaust, A Music Memorial* [BBC2]
Flaherty award for single documentary	*Make Me Normal* [C4]
Sport	*The Ashes: England* vs *Australia* [C4]
News	BBC *Ten O'Clock News: 7 July 2005, London bombs* [BBC1]
Current affairs	*Dispatches: Beslan* [C4]
Lew Grade award for entertainment	*The X Factor* [ITV1]
Sitcom	*The Thick Of It* [BBC4]
Comedy programme or series	*Help* [BBC2]
Pioneer audience award	*Doctor Who* [BBC1]
Special award	*Sunset+Vine* for its innovative cricket production on C4
Richard Dimbleby award	Jamie Oliver
Alan Clarke award	Adam Curtis
Dennis Potter award	Russell T. Davies, writer *Doctor Who*
Fellowship	Ken Loach

BAFTA IN QUOTES

❦ ANNA MAXWELL MARTIN · I never expected to win. I've just felt very sweaty for the last hour and I desperately needed the loo. ❦ JONATHAN ROSS · I'm surprised, but not as surprised as Noel [Edmonds] who has had the most surprising comeback since the BNP. ❦ RUSSELL T. DAVIES · We were told that bringing it back would be impossible, that we would never capture this generation of children. But we did it. ❦

AWARDS SHOW RATINGS SLUMP

Viewing figures for awards shows have declined, possibly due to lengthy ceremonies and dull acceptance speeches. In February 2006, the Baftas attracted just 3m viewers – a record Bafta low. Below are the top televised awards shows between 2005–06:

Televised show	channel	viewers			
British Soap Awards	ITV1	7·8m	Brit Awards	ITV1	4·5m
National TV Awards	ITV1	7·1m	Bafta TV Awards	BBC1	4·5m
Pride of Britain	ITV1	5·5m	Bafta Film Awards	BBC1	3·0m
Comedy Awards	ITV1	5·4m	Political Awards	C4	0·6m
Sports Personality	BBC1	4·9m	Teaching Awards	BBC2	0·5m

[Source: *The Times*]

TV TALENT LIST

Broadcast magazine polled a host of television industry executives in November 2005 to create a list of the best of the UK's TV 'talent'. The top 10 were as follows:

1 .... David Tennant	5 .... Ant & Dec	9 ..... David Mitchell &
2 ....:.. Jamie Oliver	6 ....Paul O'Grady	Robert Webb
3 ....Catherine Tate	7 .... Julia Davis	10.Hardeep Singh Kohli
4 .... Bill Oddie	8 ... Richard Hammond	[Source: *Broadcast*]

OTHER TV AWARDS OF NOTE · 2006

Awards	category	winner
	Most popular actor	Christopher Eccleston · *Dr Who*
	Most popular actress	Billie Piper · *Dr Who*
National TV Awards [2005]	Most popular factual	*Jamie's School Dinners*
	Most popular drama	*Doctor Who*
	Most popular serial drama	*EastEnders*
TV Quick Awards	Best soap actress	Ursula Holden-Gill · *Emmerdale*
	Best soap actor	Bradley Walsh · *Coronation St*
	Best actor	Ross Kemp · *EastEnders*
British Soap Awards	Best actress	Lacey Turner · *EastEnders*
	Best soap	*EastEnders*
	Best villain	Billy Murray · *EastEnders*
	Actress in drama	Mariska Hargitay · *Law & Order*
	Actress in mini-series	Helen Mirren · *Elizabeth I*
Primetime Emmys	Actor in drama	Kiefer Sutherland · *24*
	Actor in mini-series	Andre Braugher · *Thief*
	Outstanding drama	*24*
	Outstanding comedy	*The Office*
	Sitcom and comedy drama	*The Thick of It*
	Entertainment	*The Catherine Tate Show*
Royal Television Society	Soap	*Emmerdale*
	Drama series	*Bodies*
	Drama serial	*Bleak House*

THE WORLD'S MOST POPULAR TV

In July 2006, the *Radio Times* published research by Informa Telecoms & Media that used TV ratings from 20 countries to rank the world's most popular shows:

1 ....*CSI: Miami*	6 ....*CSI: Crime Scene Investigation*
2 .... *Lost*	7 ....*Without a Trace*
3 ....*Desperate Housewives*	8 ....*Inocente de Ti*
4 .... *Te Voy a Ensenar a Querer*	9 .... *Anita, No Te Rajes!*
5 ....*The Simpsons*	10.... *The Adventures of Jimmy Neutron*

————————————— BBC WORLD SERVICE ———————————————

BBC World Service radio is now available in 150 out of 190 capital cities and, in 2006, it attracted a record 163m weekly listeners. The World Service is funded through a Grant-in-Aid from the Foreign Office to provide foreign language radio news programming across the globe. In 2006/07, the World Service grant will be £245m. But, after restructuring in March 2006, 10 language services were closed: Bulgarian, Croatian, Czech, Greek, Hungarian, Kazakh, Polish, Slovak, Slovene and Thai. Below are the 33 languages in which the World Service still broadcasts:

Albanian · Arabic · Azeri · Bengali · Burmese
Caribbean-English · Cantonese · English · French for Africa
Hausa · Hindi · Indonesian · Kinyarwanda/Kirundi · Kyrgyz
Macedonian · Mandarin · Nepali · Pashto · Persian · Portuguese for Brazil
Romanian · Russian · Serbian · Sinhala · Somali · Spanish · Swahili
Tamil · Turkish · Ukrainian · Urdu · Uzbek · Vietnamese

——————————— THE US MILITARY & THE MEDIA ————————————

Below are some selected excerpts from *Meeting the Media* – a manual for US military personnel, produced in 2003 by the Air Force Public Affairs Center of Excellence:

As many organizations have discovered, the days of ducking the media have vanished. ❧ Because the very existence of the Air Force depends on the 'consent of the governed', we have a duty to keep the citizenry informed. ❧ The news media are neither our friend nor our enemy. They are a conduit, albeit filtered, to the American public. ❧ Bad news does not improve with age. ❧ In this technologically advanced era, reality is not what actually exists, but what is perceived to exist. ❧ If you wear it, operate it, eat it, promote it, or shoot it, you can generally talk about it. ❧ Prepare for [the media] by identifying and organizing predetermined, positive messages. No matter what the interviewer asks, you should feel free to steer your response to the related message. ❧ Let the media know your plans in as much detail as practical. ❧ Treat the media as you would want others to treat you. ❧ Make short, simple, and direct statements. ❧ Don't pretend to be perfect. ❧ Discuss only matters of which you have direct knowledge. ❧ When given a multiple-part question, answer the one segment that allows you to make a positive point. ❧ Prior planning is critical; don't 'wing it'. ❧ Speak conversationally, as you would to a non-military high school friend. ❧ Avoid repeating or using 'color words' that may have a negative connotation. Words such as 'massacre', 'scandal', 'deaths', 'corruption', etc., induce overly strong, emotional reactions and may be counterproductive to your objectives. ❧ People will remember their impression of you, not necessarily what you said. ❧ You aren't obligated to tell everything you know. ❧ Questioning techniques used by reporters are just ways to push sources' buttons, to persuade the source to help them frame, support, or add color to their stories. ❧ By assuming an assertive and positive attitude, you will not be victimised by events no matter how disastrous.

NOTABLE DESERT ISLAND DISCS · 2006

Castaway	luxury	favourite Desert Island Disc
Mario Testino	his own pillow	Fina Estampa (Caetano Veloso)
Boris Johnson	a large pot of French mustard	finale of Variations on a theme by Haydn (Brahms)
Sir David Frost	the Sunday papers	The Dam Busters March (Eric Coates)
Chris Evans	swimming goggles with prescription lenses	Here, There and Everywhere (The Beatles)
Colin Firth	his guitar	opening of the Kyrie from Mass in C Minor (Mozart)
Dame Kelly Holmes	a large supply of chocolate	If I Ain't Got You (Alicia Keys)
Richard Griffiths	Las Meninas by Velázquez	Träumerei (Robert Schumann)
Frankie Dettori	a lifetime supply of Pinot Grigio	Amazing Grace (John Newton)
Shirley Williams	a PC linked to the internet	How Beautiful Are the Feet of Them (Handel)
Jeremy Irons	Liquorice-flavoured Rizla tobacco rolling papers	One Step at a Time (Clifton Chenier)
Rachel Whiteread	ink, pen, paper, and correction fluid	The Köln Concert, Part 1 (Keith Jarrett)
Jack Higgins	a mobile phone	Let's Face the Music and Dance (Fred Astaire)
Terence Stamp	his own wheat-free loaf of bread	Impromptu No. 4 in C sharp minor (Chopin)
Ruby Wax	a huge bed	A Day in the Life (The Beatles)
Ronald Searle	the best possible champagne	Champagne Polka (Johann Strauss)
Daniel Barenboim	a piano with a mattress	he said he would take no records, only scores
Darcey Bussell	eyelash curler	Virtual Insanity (Jamiroquai)
Sir Digby Jones	video or picture book of '100 examples of excellence'	Wind Beneath My Wings (Bette Midler)
David Cameron	a case of Scotch whisky	Tangled Up In Blue (Bob Dylan)
Armando Iannucci	the taste of sherry trifle	Opening of the 9th Symphony (Mahler)
George Davies	a Cannondale bike	You'll Never Walk Alone (Gerry and the Pacemakers)
Sir Peter Mansfield	a helicopter	Vltava suite from Má Vlast (Smetana)
Monty Don	Hendrickje Bathing in a River by Rembrandt	A Hard Day's Night (The Beatles)
Ian Rankin	a traditional American pinball machine	Solid Air (John Martyn)

In June 2006, the BBC announced Kirsty Young would succeed Sue Lawley as the presenter of *Desert Island Discs*. Lawley retired after 18 years of shipwrecking celebrities.

UK RADIO HALL OF FAME

The Radio Academy, a body that 'exists to celebrate excellence in all aspects of UK radio', oversees the UK Radio Hall of Fame. In 2005, the following were inducted:

Ray Moore · Douglas Adams · Gerry Anderson · Paul Gambaccini
Henry Hall · Derek McCulloch · Norman Painting
Tommy Vance · Johnnie Walker · David Rodigan

THE SONY AWARDS · 2006

For over twenty years, the Sony Radio Academy Awards have rewarded excellence in British radio with bronze, silver, or gold awards. Some of the 2006 golds were:

Breakfast show	Nick Ferrari at Breakfast [LBC 97·3]
Music radio personality of the year	Chris Evans [BBC Radio 2]
Music broadcaster of the year	Zane Lowe [BBC Radio 1]
Entertainment award	Chris Moyles [BBC Radio 1]
Speech broadcaster	Eddie Mair [PM for BBC Radio 4]
News journalist	Angus Stickler [BBC Radio 4]
Digital station of the year	Planet Rock
Station of the year UK	BBC Radio 1

AUDIENCE SHARE OF NATIONAL RADIO STATIONS

BBC Radio 2..... 15·7%	Talksport............ 1·7	BBC 7................ 0·4
BBC Radio 4........10·7	BBC Radio 3......... 1·1	BBC 6 music......... 0·2
BBC Radio 1........10·3	Virgin (AM) .... 0·9	BBC 1Xtra........... 0·1
BBC Five Live .... 4·5	BBC World Service.. 0·7	
Classic FM .... 4·2	BBC Asian Network. 0·4	[Source: Rajar, Q2 2006]

TOP TEN PODCASTS

According to the iTunes chart, the most popular podcasts in August 2006 were:

1 ..... The Official Big Brother podcast	6 .... *Casino Royale* podcast
2 ..The Ricky Gervais podcast: Series 1	7 .... Best of Moyles: BBC Radio 1
3 .... Russell Brand: BBC 6 Music	8 ......Scott Mills Daily: BBC Radio 1
4 .... The Now Show: BBC Radio 4	9 ....Comedy Central: Stand-up
5 ...... Best of Chris Moyles Enhanced	10...... The Adam & Joe Xfm podcast

All of the above podcasts are free. In February 2006, Ricky Gervais introduced a 95p per episode charge to download the second series of his popular podcast. After the fee was introduced, iTunes recategorised Gervais' podcasts as audiobooks, removing them from the podcast chart and sending them to the top of the audiobook chart; it is unclear how the charge affected the show's popularity.

THE PULITZER PRIZE

In his 1904 will, Joseph Pulitzer made provision for the establishment of the Pulitzer Prizes to 'promote excellence'. The 2006 journalism prizes were awarded to:

PUBLIC SERVICE AWARD
The *Sun Herald* for its *'valorous and comprehensive coverage of Hurricane Katrina, providing a lifeline for devastated readers, in print and online, during their time of greatest need'*. And the *Times-Picayune* for its *'heroic, multi-faceted coverage of Hurricane Katrina and its aftermath, making exceptional use of the newspaper's resources to serve an inundated city even after evacuation of the newspaper plant'*.

BREAKING NEWS REPORTING
The *Times-Picayune* for its *'courageous and aggressive coverage of Hurricane Katrina, overcoming desperate conditions facing the city and the newspaper'*.

INVESTIGATIVE REPORTING
Susan Schmidt, James V. Grimaldi and R. Jeffrey Smith of the *Washington Post* for their *'indefatigable probe of Washington lobbyist Jack Abramoff that exposed congressional corruption and produced reform efforts'*.

INTERNATIONAL REPORTING
Joseph Kahn and Jim Yardley of the *New York Times* for their *'ambitious stories on ragged justice in China as the booming nation's legal system evolves'*.

BREAKING NEWS PHOTOGRAPHY
Dallas Morning News staff for their *'vivid photographs depicting the chaos and pain after Hurricane Katrina engulfed New Orleans'*.

BRITISH PRESS AWARDS 2006

National paper .... *The Guardian*
Political journalist .... Francis Elliott · *The Independent on Sunday*
Show business .... Victoria Newton · *The Sun*
Columnist .... Lucy Kellaway · *The Financial Times*
Feature writer .... Bryan Appleyard · *The Sunday Times*
Interviewer .... Rachel Cooke · *The Observer*
Sports journalist .... Oliver Holt · *The Daily Mirror*
Reporter .... Oliver Harvey · *The Sun*
Scoop .... 'Cocaine Kate' by Stephen Moyes · *The Daily Mirror*
Front page .... 'Harry the Nazi' · *The Sun*
Team .... 7/7 · *The Daily Mirror*

After the 2005 fiasco, when 11 editors withdrew after Bob Geldof condemned them for failing to support Africa, the future of the Awards was uncertain. However, in June 2005, Piers Morgan and Matthew Freud took over the *Press Gazette* (which runs the Awards), and newspaper editors met with the aim of putting the Awards back in the hands of the industry. The *Mail* and *Telegraph* groups took exception to the involvement of Freud (PR man and son-in-law to Rupert Murdoch), due to a perceived conflict of interest, and ex-*Mirror* editor Morgan. The majority of editors agreed the Awards should continue under auspices of the *Press Gazette* for another year, with the prizes voted for by industry peers. This compromise failed to placate the *Mail*, *Express*, and *Telegraph* groups who boycotted the event.

———————————— WORLD PRESS FREEDOM INDEX ————————————

Reporters Without Borders, a group working to protect freedom of the press, annually compiles an index of press freedom. The ranking is created by assessing the degree of freedom that journalists and news organizations experience in each country. The index for 2005 shows that Europe enjoys the greatest freedom (the top 10 countries are exclusively European) – the United Kingdom ranked 24th. The United States dropped over 20 places from 2004, to 44th – because of the imprisonment of *New York Times* reporter Judith Miller. The countries with the least press freedom are those where privately owned media are not permitted and freedom of expression does not exist. The ten most and least free countries are shown below:

Most free press	*Least free press*
Denmark† · Finland · Iceland · Ireland	North Korea · Eritrea · Turkmenistan
Netherlands · Norway · Switzerland	Iran · Burma · Libya
Slovakia · Czech Republic · Slovenia	Cuba · Nepal · China · Vietnam

[†Denmark's ranking is of special interest given the Muhammad cartoon crisis; see p.19]

———————————— JOURNALISTS AT RISK ————————————

The Committee to Protect Journalists (CPJ) is a group of US foreign correspondents working to promote freedom of the press worldwide. The CPJ highlights abuses of the press, publicises the plight of imprisoned journalists, and records how many reporters are killed in the line of duty. In January 2006, the CPJ stated that during the previous year, 47 journalists had been killed worldwide – the majority of whom were victims of murder. Iraq was by far the most dangerous location: 22 journalists were killed there in 2005. In the Philippines, 4 reporters died (a fall from 8 in 2004); Lebanon, Russia, Bangladesh, Pakistan, Sri Lanka, and Somalia all recorded 2 deaths. 'Gulf War II' and its aftermath have made Iraq the deadliest conflict for journalists since the CPJ was established 24 years ago.

Conflict	*date*	*total killed*			
Iraq	2003–	60	Colombia	1986–	52
Algeria	1993–96	58	Balkans	1991–95	36
			Philippines	1983–87	36

The CPJ also reports how many journalists are imprisoned worldwide: as of December 2005, the total was 125. The countries with most jailed journalists are:

China	32	Ethiopia	13	USA	5
Cuba	24	Uzbekistan	6	Algeria	3
Eritrea	15	Burma	5	The Maldives	3

In November 2005, the International Federation of Journalists (IFJ) and the International News Safety Institute (INSI) presented a draft UN resolution to Kofi Annan. The resolution proposed the pursuit of governments that fail to prosecute those responsible for killing reporters. The IFJ and INSI hope to gather enough support to put the resolution before the United Nations Security Council.

MAJOR BRITISH NEWSPAPERS

Title	editorial address	phone	editor	circulation	readership	cost	owner	founded
Sun	1 Virginia St, Wapping, London E98 1SN	020 7782 4000	Rebekah Wade	3,207,430	8,073,000	35p	N	1911
Daily Mail	Northcliffe Ho, 2 Derry St, London W8 5TT	020 7938 6000	Paul Dacre	2,389,236	5,427,000	45p	A	1896
Daily Mirror	1 Canada Sq, Canary Wharf, London E14 5AP	020 7293 3000	Richard Wallace	1,660,151	3,884,000	38p	T	1903
Daily Telegraph	1 Canada Sq, Canary Wharf, London E14 5DT	020 7538 5000	John Bryant	897,416	2,061,000	70p	H	1855
Daily Express	10 Lower Thames St, London EC3R 6EN	0871 434 1010	Peter Hill	833,145	1,784,000	40p	S	1900
Daily Star	10 Lower Thames St, London EC3R 6EN	0871 434 1010	Dawn Neesom	797,132	1,530,000	35p	S	1888
Times	1 Virginia St, London E98 1XY	020 7782 5000	Robert Thomson	667,496	1,809,000	65p	N	1785
Financial Times	1 Southwark Bridge London SE1 9HL	020 7873 3000	Lionel Barber	423,548	348,000	100p	P	1888
Evening Standard	Northcliffe Ho, 2 Derry St, London W8 5TT	020 7938 6000	Veronica Wadley	300,993	786,000	50p	A	1827
Guardian	119 Farringdon Rd, London EC1R 3ER	020 7278 2332	Alan Rusbridger	370,612	1,158,000	70p	G	1821
Independent	191 Marsh Wall, London E14 9RS	020 7005 2000	Simon Kelner	250,761	751,000	70p	I	1986
News of the World	1 Virginia St, Wapping, London E98 1SN	020 7782 4550	Andy Coulson	3,482,856	8,562,000	85p	N	1843
Mail on Sunday	Northcliffe Ho, 2 Derry St, London W8 5TT	020 7933 6000	Peter Wright	2,221,338	6,146,000	130p	A	1982
Sunday Mirror	1 Canada Sq, Canary Wharf, London E14 5AP	020 7293 3000	Tina Weaver	1,502,414	4,228,000	85p	T	1915
Sunday Times	1 Virginia St, London E98 1XY	020 7782 5000	John Witherow	1,308,604	3,478,000	180p	N	1821
Sunday People	1 Canada Sq, Canary Wharf, London E14 5AP	020 7293 3000	Mark Thomas	840,860	1,945,000	80p	T	1881
Sunday Express	10 Lower Thames St, London EC3R 6EN	0871 434 1010	Martin Townsend	796,956	2,099,000	120p	S	1918
Sunday Telegraph	1 Canada Sq, Canary Wharf, London E14 5DT	020 7538 5000	Patience Wheatcroft	656,055	1,947,000	140p	H	1961
Observer	119 Farringdon Rd, London EC1R 3ER	020 7278 2332	Roger Alton	457,806	1,378,000	160p	G	1791
Independent on Sun.	191 Marsh Wall, London E14 9RS	020 7005 2000	Tristan Davies	216,175	775,000	150p	I	1990
Sunday Star	10 Lower Thames St, London EC3R 6EN	0871 434 1010	Gareth Morgan	403,824	932,000	75p	S	2002
(Sunday) Business	292 Vauxhall Br. Rd, London SW1V 1SS	020 7961 0000	Ian Watson	127,655	N/A	100p	H	1996

Ownership: [N]ews Corporation · Northern & [S]hell Media · [P]earson Press [H]oldings Ltd · [A]ssociated Newspapers · [G]uardian Media Group
[I]ndependent News & Media · [T]rinity Mirror · Circulation: ABC [J]uly 2006] · Readership: NRS [March 2006] · Founded dates relate for the paper's earliest incarnation.

READERSHIP OF NATIONAL PAPERS BY SEX

Below are the percentages of men and women who read selected national papers:

Newspaper	%♂	%♀
Sun	20	14
Daily Mirror	13	11
Daily Mail	11	12
Daily Telegraph	5	4
Daily Express	5	4
Daily Star	6	2
Times	4	3
Guardian	3	2
Independent	2	1
Financial Times	1	1
Any national daily	70	54

[Source: National Readership Survey, July 2004–June 2005]

PRESS COMPLAINTS

The 2005 annual report of the Press Complaints Commission (PCC) revealed the breakdown of complaints, by each clause of the Commission's Code of Practice:

Clause	% of complaints
1 ... *Accuracy*	67·4
2 ... *Opportunity to reply*	2·3
3 ... *Privacy*	12·5
4 ... *Harassment*	2·9
5 ... *Intrusion into grief/shock*	5·2
6 ... *Children*	3·4
7 ... *Children in sex cases*	0·1
8 ... *Hospitals*	0·0
9 ... *Reporting of crime*	1·3
10 .. *Clandestine devices/subterfuge*	0·9
11 .. *Victims of sexual assault*	0·0
12 .. *Discrimination*	2·7
13 .. *Financial journalism*	0·4
14 .. *Confidential sources*	0·4
15 .. *Witness payments*	0·0
16 .. *Payment to criminals*	0·5

The 16-clause Code of Practice was ratified by the PCC on 13 June 2005.

MOST MEMORABLE FRONT PAGES

To coincide with a May 2006 exhibition of famous newspaper front pages at the British Library, BBC's *Newsnight* held a vote to discover the most memorable British front page. The winner was the *Telegraph*'s post-9/11 'War on America'.

Headline	newspaper	date
Mrs Pankhurst arrested	Daily Mirror	May 1914
Dunkirk defence defies 300,000	Daily Sketch	June 1940
Games rocked by black power	Evening News	October 1968
The first footstep	Evening Standard	July 1969
Gotcha	Sun	May 1982
Freddie Starr ate my hamster	Sun	March 1986
Up yours Delors	Sun	November 1990
Murderers	Daily Mail	February 1997
He lied and lied and lied	Guardian	June 1997
War on America [winner]	Telegraph	September 2001
War is over, says IRA	Independent	July 2005

—————————————— LADS' MAG COVERS ——————————————

In March 2006, the National Federation of Retail Newsagents [NFRN] published voluntary guidelines for its 19,000 members on the display of so-called 'lads' mags'. Magazines like *Nuts* and *Zoo*, though not 'top-shelf' items, do rather relish featuring scantily clad lovelies on their covers, which can cause offence. To minimise complaints from customers, without diminishing sales, the NFRN recommends:

Do not display lads' mags at children's eye-level or below, to ensure that they are not in the direct sight and reach of children · Do not display them adjacent to the display of children's titles and comics · Where display space restraints preclude the above, ensure that titles with front covers that may cause concern are part-overlapped with other titles so as to minimise the potential offence

In April 2006, Sainsburys announced that it would conceal all lads' mags behind 'modesty covers' after customer complaints. These covers allow the title of the magazine to show but conceal potentially offensive pictures. The covers will apply to all editions of *Loaded, Maxim, FHM, Nuts,* and *Zoo.*

————————— TOP TEN 'ACTIVELY PURCHASED' MAGAZINES —————————

Title	circulation				
What's on TV	1,509,519	*Reader's Digest*	685,227	*Saga*	544,489
TV Choice	1,287,773	*Closer*	590,211		
Take a Break	1,082,051	*Glamour*	584,503	[Source: ABC	
Radio Times	1,058,972	*Heat*	579,883	January–June 2006 ·	
		Chat	554,375	Not including group titles]	

————————— CURIOUS MAGAZINE TITLES OF NOTE —————————

Animal Action
Classic Plant & Machinery
Country Walking · Cross Stitcher
Earthmovers · European Boatbuilder
Flypast · Metal Hammer
Practical Caravan

Practical Poultry
Period Living & Traditional Homes
Railway Modeller · Ships Monthly
Simply Knitting · Spirit & Destiny
Sporting Gun · Trucking
Waterways World · Your Dog

————————————— R.I.P. SMASH HITS —————————————

The last ever issue of the magazine *Smash Hits* went on sale on 13 February 2006, signalling the end of a (dubious) era. Launched in 1978, *Smash Hits* wholeheartedly embraced the world of pop – featuring posters, song lyrics, and cheeky interviews with whichever celebrity graced the top of the hit parade. At its peak in 1989, when Kylie and Jason were cover-stars, *Smash Hits* had one million readers – but, by 2006, its circulation had dropped to a mere 120,000. Overall sales of teen pop magazines have fallen by 30% over the past three years, a decline blamed on a migration to internet, television, and multimedia-based celebrity news and gossip.

Music & Cinema

*Why should people go out and pay money to see bad films when
they can stay at home and see bad television for nothing?*
— SAMUEL GOLDWYN (1882–1974)

UK NUMBER ONES · 2005–06

W/ending	weeks	artist	song
29·10·05	1	Arctic Monkeys	*I Bet You Look Good on the Dancefloor*
12·11·05	2	Westlife	*You Raise Me Up*
19·11·05	3	Madonna	*Hung Up*
10·12·05	2	Pussycat Dolls	*Stickwitu*
24·12·05	1	Nizlopi	*JCB Song*
31·12·05	4	Shayne Ward	*That's My Goal*
28·01·06	1	Arctic Monkeys [see below]	*When the Sun Goes Down*
04·02·06	2	Notorious BIG and friends	*Nasty Girl*
18·02·06	2	Meck featuring Leo Sayer	*Thunder in My Heart Again*
04·03·06	1	Madonna	*Sorry*
11·03·06	2	Chico	*It's Chico Time*
25·03·06	1	Orson	*No Tomorrow*
01·04·06	1	Ne-Yo	*So Sick*
07·04·06	9	Gnarls Barkley†	*Crazy*
10·06·06	1	Sandi Thom	*I Wish I Was a Punk Rocker*
17·06·06	3	Nelly Furtardo	*Maneater*
08·07·06	1	Shakira featuring Wyclef Jean	*Hips Don't Lie*
15·07·06	2	Lily Allen	*Smile*
29·07·06	1	McFly	*Please Please/Don't Stop Me Now*
05·08·06	4	Shakira featuring Wyclef Jean	*Hips Don't Lie*
02·09·06	1	Beyoncé feat. Jay-Z	*Déjà Vu*
09·09·06	1	Justin Timberlake	*Sexyback*

† *Crazy* by Gnarls Barkley was the first song to reach number one on download sales alone. ❦ In 2005, an artist needed to sell an average of 82,419 records a week to reach the British number one spot. They needed to sell 17,839 records to reach number 5; 10,553 for number 10; and 2,276 for number 40.

ARCTIC MONKEYS

In January 2006, Yorkshire guitar-band Arctic Monkeys released the fastest-selling début album in British history. *Whatever People Say I Am, That's What I'm Not* sold 363,735 copies in its first week of release – not including download sales. This figure easily eclipsed the success of previous record holders Hear'Say, whose album, *Popstars*, sold 306,631 copies in 2001 – shortly before the group disbanded.

—————— GLOBAL BEST-SELLING ALBUMS · 2005 ——————

Album	artist	publisher	global sales
X&Y	Coldplay	EMI	8·3m
The Emancipation of Mimi	Mariah Carey	Universal	7·7m
The Massacre	50 Cent	Universal	7·5m
Monkey Business	Black Eyed Peas	Universal	6·8m
American Idiot	Green Day	Warner	6·4m
Confessions on a Dance Floor	Madonna	Warner	6·3m
Breakaway	Kelly Clarkson	Sony BMG	6·1m
Curtain Call	Eminem	Universal	5·5m
Back to Bedlam	James Blunt	Warner	5·5m
Intensive Care	Robbie Williams	EMI	5·4m

[Sources: International Federation of the Phonographic Industry; BBC]

—————— SALES BY TYPE OF MUSIC ——————

The British Phonographic Industry (BPI) released figures in 2006 that revealed a rise in the number of new albums released – from 15,393 in 1996 to 31,291 in 2005. Successful albums from bands like Coldplay and Kaiser Chiefs have seen the rock genre grow in popularity, increasing its share of the market primarily at the expense of pop. Below are the album sales in Britain by genre, from 1998–2005:

	rock	pop	urban	MOR	dance	other
1998	24·5%	36·9	7·8	6·3	10·2	14·3
1999	22·4%	36·2	9·5	6·8	12·1	13·0
2000	25·9%	32·4	12·4	4·6	13·3	11·4
2001	27·9%	31·6	13·0	6·0	10·5	11·0
2002	31·0%	30·3	12·5	6·1	9·5	10·6
2003	29·2%	31·2	13·9	6·4	7·2	12·1
2004	29·8%	29·6	15·6	7·8	6·9	10·3
2005	36·2%	25·8	13·5	8·5	7·6	8·4

[Source: British Phonographic Industry/Official UK Charts Company]

—————— WORLDWIDE MUSIC SALES REVENUE BY FORMAT ——————

Format	2004 ($m)	2005 ($m)	% change
CD	18,109	17,019	−6%
DVD	1,610	1,540	−4%
Digital sales	397	1,143	188%
Singles	821	721	−12%
Tapes, LPs, VHS, &c.	531	372	−30%

[Source: International Federation of the Phonographic Industry]

―――――――――― THE BRIT AWARDS · 2006 ――――――――――

The 26th Brit Awards ceremony proved an unremarkable affair, with solid performances and a disappointing dearth of scandal. Chris Evans hosted for the second year with jokes that occasionally missed their mark[†]. And the 2006 winners were:

British male ....James Blunt
British female ....K.T. Tunstall
British group.. Kaiser Chiefs
British album ....Coldplay · *X & Y*
British single[1] ....Coldplay · *Speed of Sound*
British rock act[2]...Kaiser Chiefs
British urban act[3] ....Lemar
British live act[4].. Kaiser Chiefs
British breakthrough act[5]... Arctic Monkeys
Pop act[6] ....James Blunt
International male ....Kanye West
International female .... Madonna
International album...................................Green Day · *American Idiot*
International group..Green Day
International breakthrough artist .... Jack Johnson
Outstanding contribution to music...................Paul 'The Modfather' Weller

[1] Voted by commercial radio listeners. [2] Voted by Kerrang! TV viewers.
[3] Voted by MTV Base viewers. [4] Voted by Radio 2 listeners. [5] Voted by Radio 1 listeners.
[6] Voted by viewers of ITV1's CD:UK, readers of the *Sun*, and customers of O2 and Motorola.

THE BRIT AWARDS IN QUOTES

CHRIS MARTIN · It's hard for us sometimes because we are English and we do not like to admit that we think we are great, so tonight we would like to agree with you. ❦ JAMES BLUNT · I have been accused so many times of singing like a girl that it is amazing to be the best male. ❦ K.T. TUNSTALL · I'm delighted to be British and I'm even happier to be female, so to win this Brit is pretty cool. ❦ RICKY WILSON – KAISER CHIEFS · This is our first Brits. We weren't meant to win this one. This means the world. ❦ † CHRIS EVANS [to award presenter BOY GEORGE] · Did you really call the NYPD about a burglary when you had 10 bags of drugs under the bed? · BOY GEORGE · I think that might have been you, Chris. ❦

――――――――――――― NME COOL LIST ―――――――――――――

The coolest artists of 2005 – as judged by music magazine the *New Musical Express*:

1 ....Alex Turner (Arctic Monkeys)	6 ....Devendra Banhart
2 ....Liam Gallagher (Oasis)	7 ....Pete Doherty
3 ....Kanye West	8 .....Jemima Pearl (Be Your Own Pet)
4 ....Antony Hegarty	9 ....Bob Dylan
5 ....Brandon Flowers (The Killers)	10 ....Carl Barat (The Libertines)

UK MUSIC HALL OF FAME · 2005

Channel 4 launched their UK Music Hall of Fame in 2004. Five of the founding members were chosen by a panel of judges; the remaining inductees (one for each decade since the 1950s) were selected by public vote. The founding inductees were:

Founding members: Elvis Presley · The Beatles · Bob Marley · Madonna · U2
Public vote: Cliff Richard and the Shadows (1950s) · Rolling Stones (1960s)
Queen (1970s) · Michael Jackson (1980s) · Robbie Williams (1990s)

In 2005, the panel of music industry executives, artists, and journalists inducted:

Pink Floyd · The Who · Bob Dylan · The Kinks · New Order
Aretha Franklin · Jimi Hendrix · Eurythmics
Ozzy Osbourne and Black Sabbath · John Peel (honourary)

CHRISTMAS NUMBER ONE · 2005

X Factor winner Shayne Ward topped the 2005 yule-tide chart with his début single *That's My Goal*. Ward sold 742,180 copies in just 4 days, knocking Nizlopi's *JCB Song* to number 2. The Pogues made number 3 with *Fairytale of New York*.

ROCK & ROLL HALL OF FAME

The following were inducted into the American *Rock & Roll Hall of Fame* in 2006:

Black Sabbath (Geezer Butler, Tony Iommi, Ozzy Osbourne, Bill Ward)
Miles Davis · Blondie (Clem Burke, Jimmy Destri, Nigel Harrison,
Debbie Harry, Frank Infante, Chris Stein, Gary Valentine)
Sex Pistols (Paul Cook, Steve Jones, Glen Matlock, Johnny Rotten, Sid Vicious)
Lynyrd Skynyrd (Bob Burns, Allen Collins, Steve Gaines, Ed King, Billy Powell,
Artimus Pyle, Gary Rossington, Ronnie Van Zant, Leon Wilkeson)

Artists become eligible 25 years after their first record release. In February 2006, the Sex Pistols released a statement on their website: 'that hall of fame is a piss stain. Your museum. Urine in wine. We're not your monkey and so what? Fame at $25,000 if we paid for a table or $15,000 to squeak up in the gallery, goes to a non-profit organization selling us a load of old famous'.

GREATEST ALBUM OF ALL TIME

In June 2006, after questioning 40,000 music fans, the *Guinness Book of British Hit Singles & Albums* announced that *Definitely Maybe* by Oasis was the greatest album of all time. Controversially, the Oasis album nudged The Beatles' classic *Sgt Pepper* into second place by just 37 votes. *Revolver* by The Beatles, *OK Computer* by Radiohead, and *(What's the Story) Morning Glory?* by Oasis completed the top five.

─────── THE EUROVISION SONG CONTEST · 2006 ───────

The *Making Your Mind Up* final was held on 4 March 2006. The six acts that competed to represent Britain at the May Eurovision Song Contest final were:

Anthony Costa – *It's a Beautiful Thing* · City Chix – *All About You*
Daz Sampson – *Teenage Life* · Four Story – *Hand On My Heart*
Goran Kay – *Play Your Game* · Kym Marsh – *Whisper to Me*

The public voted for 32-year-old Daz Sampson's homage to his teenage years:

Ladbroke's odds for Eurovision winner
Romania 4/1 · Greece 7/2 · UK 10/1 · Russia 6/1 · Sweden 3/1 · Finland 9/1

THE FINAL · 20·05·06 · ATHENS, GREECE

The 51st Eurovision did not disappoint, entrancing the audience with a plethora of novelty acts, from Finland's be-masked 'troll rockers', to Germany's country and western offering. Europe seemed keen to embrace the alternative. The top 5 were:

Country	artist	song	score
Finland	Lordi	*Hard Rock Hallelujah*	292
Russia	Dima Bilan	*Never Let You Go*	248
Bos. & Herz.	Hari Mata Hari	*Layla*	229
Romania	Mihai Traistariu	*Tornero*	172
Sweden	Carola	*Invincible*	170

WOGANISMS OF NOTE

'White is the new black this year' ❧ 'We've got four dancers for whom modern dance stopped about 30 years ago' ❧ 'Last year was a kind of navel year. This year, the legs have it' ❧ 'It's the return of the Klingons and the Orcs ... some of the worst cases of broken veins I've ever seen' ❧ 'Spain lost the plot years ago' ❧ 'It's a shout-along; it's obviously much more fun to sing than to listen to' ❧ 'The first serious case of a short skirt and boots, and men in frocks' ❧ 'You'll see she's lumbered with what look to be trousers made from kitchen foil' ❧

SONG LYRICS OF MERIT

LITHUANIA · *We are the winners of Eurovision, We are, We are!* ❧ FINLAND · *Rock 'n' roll angels bring thine hard rock hallelujah, In God's creation supernatural high* ❧ RUSSIA · *Flesh of my flesh, bone of my bone, Love's carving it in the stone* ❧ GERMANY · *My love shines brighter than a twinkling star, baby no matter where you are* ❧ IRELAND · *Being strong, being tough, Never tender, always rough* ❧ CYPRUS · *Why do the angels cry? Innocent children die? When will it all ever end?* ❧ UK · *Now if you treat the kids fine, together they will shine, And if you give kids time, they won't do the crime* ❧

RECENT UK EUROVISION PLACINGS

Year	artist	song	points	position
2006	Daz Sampson	*Teenage Life*	25	19th
2005	Javine	*Touch My Fire*	18	22nd
2004	James Fox	*Hold On to Your Love*	29	16th

OTHER NOTABLE MUSIC AWARDS · 2006

Awards	prize	winner
	Best UK band	McFly
Smash Hits ['05]	*Most fanciable male*	Danny Jones · McFly
	Most fanciable female	Rachel Stevens
	Top pop mop	Dougie Poynter · McFly
	Best British band	Lost Prophets
Kerrang!	*Best band on the planet*	My Chemical Romance
	Best live band	Muse
NME	*Best British band*	Arctic Monkeys
	God-like genius award	Ian Brown
	Best video	Panic! At the Disco · *I Write Sins Not Tragedies*
MTV	*Best female video*	Kelly Clarkson · *Because of You*
	Best male video	James Blunt · *You're Beautiful*
	Best group video	All-American Rejects · *Move Along*
	Record of the year	Green Day · *Boulevard of Broken Dreams*
	Album of the year	U2 · *How to Dismantle an Atomic Bomb*
Grammys	*Song of the year*	U2 · *Sometimes You Can't Make It On Your Own*
	Best new age album	Paul Winter Consort · *Silver Solstice*
	Best song	K.T. Tunstall · *Suddenly I See*
Ivor Novello	*Songwriters of the year*	Damon Albarn & Jamie Hewlett
	Most performed work	James Blunt · *You're Beautiful*
	Best album	Kaiser Chiefs · *Employment*
	Best UK male	Lemar
MOBO	*Best UK female*	Corinne Bailey Rae
	Best R&B	Rihanna
	Best hip hop	Akala
Naomi	*Worst British male*	Lee Ryan
	Worst British female	Lisa Scott-Lee
	Icon award	Scott Walker
Mojo	*Hall of fame*	Sir Elton John
	Best new act	Corinne Bailey Rae

BRITISH ARTISTS IN THE BRITISH MARKET

According to the British Phonographic Industry (BPI), British acts are enjoying a resurgence in domestic sales. February 2006 figures showed that 49·4% of all non-compilation album sales in Britain in 2005 were by British artists. A record 62·4m albums were bought in 2005, the greatest number ever sold by UK musicians in a year. Below are the percentages of albums sold in Britain by nationality of artist:

Artist	1999	2000	2001	2002	2003	2004	2005
UK	47·0%	47·6	47·4	44·1	42·3	42·4	49·4
USA	32·3%	36·0	39·2	40·7	45·4	41·7	37·7
Other	20·7%	16·4	13·4	15·2	12·3	15·9	12·9

CELEBRITY PLAYLISTS

Apple's iTunes music store has canvassed personalised celebrity playlists from a wide range of musicians and film stars. Selections encompass everything from the dreary to the opportunistic (Beyoncé's list includes 8 tracks performed by relatives, former bandmates, or by the singer herself). The compilations are accompanied by comments explaining or justifying the choice of music. Below are some examples:

CRAIG DAVID
50 Cent · *Just a Lil' Bit*
'It rocks in my car and I'm all about hooking up my iPod into my car'

ROBBIE WILLIAMS
East 17 · *Deep*
'You can't argue with this'

KIEFER SUTHERLAND
Temple of the Dog · *Call Me a Dog*
'Do I really have to explain this one?'

GORILLAZ
Kaiser Chiefs · *I Predict a Riot*
'Singer looks a bit like that Damon Albarn bloke'

WILLIAM SHATNER
Ricky Lee Jones · *Horses*
'The song really captures the freedom I associate with riding'

BILL NIGHY
Isley Brothers
Take Some Time Out for Love
'Tough guys driven wild by love'

ALICE COOPER
Nirvana · *Smells Like Teen Spirit*
'One of those songs I kick myself for not writing'

RACHEL STEVENS
Rachel Stevens · *So Good*
'What can I say? Shameless plug!'

THE MERCURY MUSIC PRIZE · 2006

The 2006 Mercury Music Prize was awarded to the Arctic Monkeys for their hugely successful debut album, *Whatever People Say I Am, That's What I'm Not* [see p.136]. The prize is intended to reward musical quality rather than pure commercial success; in achieving both, the Monkeys established themselves as clear favourites. The judges said of the winning album: 'great songs, astonishingly performed. Essential.' The band announced that they would donate the £20,000 prize money to charity.

This award doesn't normally go to a band which has sold as many records as we have. But we are very pleased with it because it's really about cool tunes. That's what we try to do. — ALEX TURNER, Arctic Monkeys

The 2006 Mercury nominees:

Muse . . . . *Black Holes & Revelations*
Isobel Campbell & Mark Lanegan . . . . . *Ballad of the Broken Seas*
Zoe Rahman . . . . *Melting Pot*
Editors . . . . *The Back Room*
Lou Rhodes . . . . *Beloved One*
Scritti Politti . . *White Bread, Black Beer*
Richard Hawley . . . . *Coles Corner*
The Guillemots . . . . *Through the Windowpane*
Sway . . . . *This Is My Demo*
Hot Chip . . . . *The Warning*
Thom Yorke . . . . *The Eraser*

NOMS DE RAP

Listed below are the real names of some illustrious rappers and hip-hop artistes:

50 Cent.......	*Curtis James Jackson III*	Kano....................	*Kane Robinson*
Andre 3000	*Andre Benjamin*	LL Cool J............	*James Todd Smith*
Busta Rhymes.............	*Trevor Smith*	Ludacris	*Christopher Bridges*
Dizzee Rascal...............	*Dylan Mills*	Maggot	*Andrew Majors*
Ms Dynamite ...	*Niomi McLean-Daley*	Missy Elliott.............	*Melissa Elliott*
Eminem	*Marshall Mathers III*	Mos Def...................	*Dante Smith*
The Game................	*Jayceon Taylor*	Notorious B.I.G....	*Christopher Wallace*
Goldie.....................	*Clifford Price*	Roots Manuva...........	*Rodney Smith*
Grandmaster Flash......	*Joseph Saddler*	The Streets................	*Mike Skinner*
Ja Rule....................	*Jeffrey Atkins*	Sway.........................	*Derek Safo*
Jay-Z.....................	*Shawn Carter*	Vanilla Ice	*Robert Van Winkle*

FAVOURITE LYRICS

Below are the nation's favourite song lyrics, according to an April 2006 VH1 poll:

U2 · One – *One life, with each other, sisters, brothers.* ❦ The Smiths · How Soon Is Now – *So you go, and you stand on your own, and you leave on your own, and you go home, and you cry, and you want to die.* ❦ Nirvana · Smells Like Teen Spirit – *I feel stupid and contagious, here we are now, entertain us.* ❦ Bob Marley · Redemption Song – *Emancipate yourselves from mental slavery, none but ourselves can free our minds, have no fear for atomic energy, 'cos none of them can stop the time.* ❦ Coldplay · Yellow – *Look at the stars, look how they shine for you.* ❦ Eminem · Lose Yourself – *Look, if you had one shot or one opportunity, to seize everything you ever wanted, one moment, would you capture it or just let it slip?* ❦ Robbie Williams · Angels – *And through it all she offers me protection, a lot of love and affection, whether I'm right or wrong.*

WORST ALBUMS

Music magazine *Q* listed the worst albums ever. The abysmal top 10 are:

Duran Duran	*Thank You*
Spice Girls.....	any of their solo efforts
Various Artists.........	*Urban Renewal*
Lou Reed........	*Metal Machine Music*
Billy Idol	*Cyberpunk*
Naomi Campbell	*Baby Woman*
Kevin Rowland..............	*My Beauty*
Mick Jagger	*Primitive Cool*
Westlife...........	*Allow Us to Be Frank*
Tin Machine	*Tin Machine II*

POP'S TOP EARNERS

The highest earning musicians in 2006, according to *Rolling Stone* magazine:

U2.............................	$154·2m
Rolling Stones...................	92·5m
Eagles...........................	63·2m
Paul McCartney...................	56m
Elton John.......................	48·9m
Neil Diamond...................	44·7m
Jimmy Buffett....................	44m
Rod Stewart.....................	40·3m
Dave Matthews Band...........	39·6m
Celine Dion.....................	38·5m

THE CLASSICAL BRITS · 2006

Best album .... Katherine Jenkins · *Living a Dream*
Singer of the year .... Andreas Scholl · *Arias for Senesino*
Contemporary music award .... James MacMillan · *Symphony No. 3 'Silence'*
Young British classical performer .... Alison Balsom
Ensemble/orchestral album... Takács Quartet · *Beethoven, the Late String Quartets*
Soundtrack composer.......................... Dario Marinelli · *Pride & Prejudice*
Instrumentalist.......... Leif Ove Andsnes · *Rachmaninov Piano Concertos 1 & 2*
Critics' award ....Plácido Domingo & Antonio Pappano · *Tristan & Isolde*
Lifetime achievement... Plácido Domingo

MOZART'S BIRTHDAY

On 27 January 2006, the world celebrated Wolfgang Amadeus Mozart's 250th birthday (1756–91). Born in Salzburg, Austria, the composer was christened Johannes Chrysostomus Wolfgangus Theophilus Mozart, but he preferred to go by the more snappy Wolfgango Amadeo and, later in his life, just plain Wolfgang Amadé†.

Mozart Chocolates ('*Mozart Kugeln*'‡) produced annually 90m
Google search results for 'Mozart' [April '06]............................. 81,700,000
Annual visitors to Mozart's birthplace in Salzburg.......................... 500,000
Number of days Mozart spent travelling though Europe...................... 3,720
Number of cities on the 'European Mozart-Trail' 200
Germans who think Mozart more important than modern popstars........... 84%
Number of Mozart cities and towns worldwide 70
Of his 41 symphonies, the number that were in a minor key... 2 (G Minor; 25 & 40)

† In letters to his sister, however, he liked to write his name backward, thus signing with the silly 'Gnagflow Trazom'. ‡ The tasty rotund chocolates named after the composer are said to be an 1890 invention of Paul Fürst, an expert pastry cook from Salzburg. The core is pistachio-flavoured almond paste, wrapped in a layer of nougat, and enveloped in a sumptuous jacket of fine dark chocolate.

ROYAL PHILHARMONIC SOCIETY AWARDS · 2006

BBC Radio 3 listeners' award .... Marin Alsop
Chamber-scale composition.................... James Dillon · *String Quartet No. 4*
Concert series and festivals.............................. *Xenakis: Architect in Sound*
Conductor .... Mark Elder
Education .... Spitalfields Festival: On Spital Fields
Ensemble.. I Fagiolini
Instrumentalist.. Anthony Marwood
Large-scale composition .... Julian Anderson · *The Book of Hours*
Opera... Welsh National Opera · *Wozzeck*
Singer.. Joyce DiDonato
Young artist .... Andrew Kennedy

————————— CLASSIC FM HALL OF FAME · 2006 —————————

Each year the radio station *Classic FM* compiles a 'Hall of Fame', reflecting its listeners' 300 favourite classical pieces. With 24 entries in the 2006 chart, Mozart was again the most popular. Below are the top 10 pieces (2005 places in brackets):

1 ...Wolfgang Amadeus Mozart..........................*Clarinet Concerto in A*... [3]
2 ...Sergei Rachmaninov ....*Piano Concerto No. 2 in C minor*... [1]
3 ...Ralph Vaughan Williams ....*The Lark Ascending*... [2]
4 ...Ludwig Van Beethoven .... *Piano Concerto No. 5 in E flat (The Emperor)*... [4]
5 ...Max Bruch ....*Violin Concerto No. 1 in G minor*... [5]
6 ...Ludwig Van Beethoven ....*Symphony No. 6 (Pastoral)*... [6]
7 ...Edward Elgar..................................*Cello Concerto in E minor*... [7]
8 ...Ludwig Van Beethoven .... *Symphony No. 9 in D minor (The Choral)*.. [11]
9 ...Edward Elgar...*Enigma Variations*... [8]
10..Karl Jenkins ....*The Armed Man*... [9]

————————— QUEEN'S MEDAL FOR MUSIC —————————

On St Cecilia's Day[†] (22 November) 2005, Sir Charles Mackerras received the first Queen's Medal for Music, subsequently to be awarded annually to an individual of any nationality who has had a positive effect on British musical life. The nomination process for the recipient of the medal is overseen by a committee under the chairmanship of Sir Peter Maxwell Davies, Master of the Queen's Music. ❦ Mackerras, born in New York to Australian parents, moved to London in 1947 and, through a chance encounter in a café, won a scholarship to study in Prague. It was here that he discovered the scores of the Czech composer Leos Janáček (1854–1928), whose operas he resurrected, championed, and introduced to the British public. Mackerras has conducted extensively with the English National Opera, BBC Symphony Orchestra, Scottish Chamber Orchestra, and numerous European and American ensembles, amassing in the process a repertoire which the *Guardian* described as 'outrageously wide'. ❦ In addition to a wide range of musical honours, Sir Charles received a CBE in 1974, was knighted in 1979, and became a Companion of Honour in the 2003 Queen's Birthday Honours. Yet, music has always been his first passion, as he has said 'I always wanted to become a musician ... I was just crazy about it. It got to be that I was hardly interested in anything else'.

† Cecilia is the Patron Saint of music. 22 November is also Benjamin Britten's (1913–76) birthday.

————————— YOUNG MUSICIAN OF THE YEAR · 2006 —————————

17-year-old clarinettist Mark Simpson from West Derby was named BBC Young Musician of the Year in May 2006. His performance of Carl Neilsen's Clarinet Concerto won over the panel of judges, chaired by conductor Marin Alsop.

——————SOME CLASSICAL ANNIVERSARIES · 2007——————

2007 marks two major classical music anniversaries: the 150th anniversary of the birth of the self-taught composer EDWARD ELGAR[†] (2·6·1857); and the 75th anniversary of the death of the composer and conductor JOHN PHILIP SOUSA[‡] (6·3·1932). Other classical music anniversaries of note during 2007 are listed below:

b. 1567	Claudio Monteverdi	d. 1897	Johannes Brahms
d. 1757	Domenico Scarlatti	b. 1897	Alexandre Tansman
d. 1827	Ludwig Van Beethoven	d. 1937	George Gershwin
b. 1877	Ernst Von Dohnányi	d. 1957	Jean Sibelius
b. 1887	Ernst Toch	d. 1987	Dmitry Kabalevsky

[†] There are no fewer than 65 roads named after Elgar in the UK, including 6 in the counties of Herefordshire and Worcestershire. [‡] The esteemed musical instrument maker J.W. Pepper named his large bass tuba the 'Sousaphone', in gratitude for the composer's helpful suggestions during its design and construction in c.1893. In the same year, Sousa composed his jaunty *Liberty Bell March*, which was subsequently used as the theme tune for *Monty Python's Flying Circus* – first aired in 1969.

——————OPERA GRAND SLAM——————

For an opera singer to score a 'Grand Slam' they must perform at these four venues:

LA SCALA · Milan
opened 1778 · capacity: 2,400
Musical director: Stéphane Lissner
Notable premieres:
Verdi – *Otello* (1887)
Puccini – *Madama Butterfly* (1904)

STATE OPERA HOUSE · Vienna
opened 1869 · capacity: 2,282
Musical director: Seiji Ozawa
Notable premieres: Goldmark –
Königin von Saba (1875) · R Strauss –
Die Frau ohne Schatten (1919)

ROYAL OPERA HOUSE · London
opened 1732 · capacity: 2,267
Music director: Antonio Pappano
Notable premieres:
Birtwistle – *Gawain* (1991)
Maw – *Sophie's Choice* (2002)

METROPOLITAN OPERA · New York
opened 1883 · capacity: 2,065
Musical director: James Levine
Notable premieres: Barber – *Antony &
Cleopatra* (1966) · Puccini – *The Girl
of the Golden West* (1910)

——————OPERA COMPANIES OF NOTE——————

ENGLISH NATIONAL OPERA · London Coliseum, WC2 .... 0870 145 0200 · eno.org
ROYAL OPERA HOUSE · London, WC2............... 020 73044000 · royaloperahouse.org
GLYNDEBOURNE · Lewes, East Sussex................. 01273 813813 · glyndebourne.com
WELSH NATIONAL OPERA · Millennium Centre, Cardiff..... 070 040 2000 · wno.org.uk
OPERA NORTH · Grand Theatre, Leeds.................. 0870 125 1898 · operanorth.co.uk
SCOTTISH OPERA · Hope St., Glasgow.............. 0141 240 1133 · scottishopera.org.uk
GARSINGTON OPERA · Oxford .... 01865 361636 · garsingtonopera.org

———— WORLD'S SLOWEST RECITAL ————

In January 2006, a rare chord was sounded in the slowest recital in history, scheduled to last 639 years. The recital is the premiere of *Organ²/ASLSP* ('as slow as possible'), adapted from a piano composition by the American composer John Cage[†] (1912–92) by a group of philosophers and physicists; its length is intended to match the estimated lifespan of the organ itself. Every year, more than 10,000 devotees of experimental music flock to the small Saxony town of Halberstadt, Germany, to witness the phenomenon live. The concert began on 5 September 2001, when the composer would have turned 89, and there followed 1½ years of silence. Cage's piece cannot, for obvious reasons, be performed by an actual organist; a combination of sandbags and lead weights is used in the rare event that a new note requires articulation. The work has been divided into 9 sections, each lasting 71 years. The opening notes, and the dates on which they are played, are:

Date	pitch	Date	pitch
5 February 2003	G♯, B, G♯	5 August 2011	C, D♭
5 July 2004	E, E	5 October 2013	D♯, A♯, E
5 January 2006	A, C, F♯	5 September 2020	G♯, E
5 July 2008	C, A♭	5 February 2024	D
5 February 2009	D, E	5 August 2026	A
		5 April 2028	G

† Cage is perhaps best known to the public for his 1952 composition *4'33"*, which consists of 4 minutes and 33 seconds of silence. In 2002, the Cage Trust took Mike Batt, creator of *The Wombles*, to court for plagiarism, following the inclusion of the track *A Minute's Silence* on his album *Classical Graffiti*, recorded with rock band the Planets. The ensuing trial featured a simultaneous 'performance' of the two silences; Cage's publishers even hired a clarinettist for the purpose. Batt, though, was vehement: 'I certainly wasn't quoting his silence. I claim my silence is original silence'.

———— THE BBC'S UK THEME · R.I.P. ————

The *UK Theme*, a medley of tunes that presaged BBC Radio 4's service every morning for 33 years, was abandoned in January 2006. Arranged by the Austrian-born composer Fritz Spiegl[†], the *UK Theme* was broadcast at 0530 GMT to signal the handover from World Service to national programming. BBC Controller Mark Damazer's decision to replace it with a 'pacy news briefing' infuriated longtime listeners, who launched a website (savetheradio4theme.co.uk) to campaign for the medley's reinstatement[‡]. Ironically, the *UK Theme* aired for the last time on Sunday 23 April – St George's Day. The individual tunes that comprise Spiegl's theme are:

*Danny Boy · What Shall We Do With the Drunken Sailor? · Early One Morning
Scotland the Brave · Rule Britannia · Men of Harlech · Greensleeves · Londonderry Air*

† Spiegl (1926–2003) also composed the theme to *Z Cars*, adapted from the Liverpool sea shanty *Johnny Todd*. He once described The Beatles as 'the greatest confidence trick since the virgin birth'. ‡ The campaign also featured a Proms performance and a CD single release by the Royal Ballet Sinfonia, who embellished the medley with *Sailing By*, the theme to Radio 4's shipping forecast.

THE BBC PROMS · 2006

The 2006 Proms featured more concerts than ever before and, for the first time, TV broadcasts of performances could be downloaded from the BBC's website. Two major classical anniversaries (Mozart's 250th and Shostakovich's 100th) were celebrated with a range of events – including Mozart's 1st symphony, written in London when he was 9, and his only piece of incidental music for theatre, from *Thamos, King of Egypt*. A special concert to celebrate the 80th birthday of Queen Elizabeth II [see p.272] featured the world premieres of Elgar's *Pomp and Circumstance March No. 6* (by Anthony Payne), a new version of the *Blue Peter* theme, and a special commission by Sir Peter Maxwell Davies and Poet Laureate Andrew Motion.

PROM 73 · THE LAST NIGHT OF THE PROMS · 9·9·2006

Dmitri Shostakovich	*Festive Overture*
Aleksandr Borodin	*Prince Igor – aria 'No sleep, no rest'*
Giuseppe Verdi	*Ernani – recit and aria 'Gran dio! ... O de verd'anni miei'*
Anton Rubinstein	*Nero – Epithalamium*
Colin Matthews	*Vivo*
Sergey Prokofiev	*Violin Concerto No. 2 in G minor*
Richard Wagner	*Tannhäuser – Entry of the Guests*
Eric Coates	*March 'Calling All Workers'*
Georges Bizet	*Carmen – Toreador's Song*
Vasily Soloviev-Sedoy	*Moscow Nights*
Sonia Possetti (arr. Matthew Barley)	*Bullanguera*
Edward Elgar	*Pomp and Circumstance March No. 1*
Henry Wood (arr. Bob Chilcott)	*Fantasia on British Sea Songs*
Hubert Parry (orch. Edward Elgar)	*Jerusalem*
Traditional (arr. Henry Wood)	*The National Anthem*
Traditional	*Auld Lang Syne*

Mark Elder, conductor of the BBC Symphony Orchestra, used the Last Night concert to make a plea for the airport restrictions on hand luggage [see p.212] to be relaxed to allow musical instruments.

SOME ORCHESTRAS & PRINCIPAL CONDUCTORS

BBC Concert Orchestra	Barry Wordsworth
BBC National Orchestra of Wales	Richard Hickox
BBC Philharmonic	Gianandrea Noseda
BBC Scottish Symphony Orchestra	Ilan Volkov
BBC Symphony Orchestra	Jirí Belohlávek
Hallé	Mark Elder
London Philharmonic Orchestra	Kurt Masur
London Symphony Orchestra	Sir Colin Davis
Philharmonia Orchestra	Christoph Von Dohnányi
Royal Liverpool Philharmonic Orchestra	Vasily Petrenko
Royal Philharmonic Orchestra	Daniele Gatti
Royal Scottish National Orchestra	Stéphane Denève

UK TOP-GROSSING FILMS · 2005

Film	UK box office gross (£m)	Director
Harry Potter and the Goblet of Fire	48·6	Mike Newell
The Lion, the Witch & the Wardrobe	43·6	Andrew Adamson
Star Wars: Episode III: Revenge of the Sith	39·4	George Lucas
Charlie and the Chocolate Factory	37·5	Tim Burton
Wallace & Gromit: Curse of the Were-Rabbit	32·0	Steve Box & Nick Park
War of the Worlds	30·7	Steven Spielberg
King Kong	30·0	Peter Jackson
Meet the Fockers	28·9	Jay Roach
Madagascar	22·7	Eric Darnell & Tom McGrath
Hitch	17·4	Andy Tennant
Nanny McPhee	16·5	Kirk Jones
Batman Begins	16·4	Christopher Nolan
Pride and Prejudice	14·6	Joe Wright
Mr and Mrs Smith	13·6	Doug Liman

[Source: UK Film Council/Nielsen EDI · Box office gross as at 19 February 2006]

FILM MARKET SHARE BY COUNTRY OF ORIGIN

Below is a breakdown of the geographic origin of films shown in British cinemas:

Origin of film (%)	2002	2003	2004	2005
USA	73·4	81·6	73·2	63·1
UK	24·4	15·7	23·4	33·0
Europe	0·7	0·9	0·6	1·6
India	1·0	1·0	1·1	1·5
Rest of the world	0·5	0·8	1·8	0·8

[Source: Nielsen EDI/RSU analysis]

MALE AND FEMALE FILM PREFERENCES

Below are the films of 2005 with the greatest disparity in cinema attendance by sex:

> female audience share	♂%	♀%	> male audience share	♂%	♀%
Pride & Prejudice	29	71	*Kingdom of Heaven*	60	40
Nanny McPhee	30	70	*War of the Worlds*	61	39
Kinky Boots	31	69	*Fantastic Four*	61	39
The Wedding Date	31	69	*Hitchhiker's Guide*	62	38
Closer	34	66	*King Kong*	62	38
Charlie & Choc. Factory	41	59	*Batman Begins*	65	35

[Source: CAVIAR/BMRB/CAA, Quarterly Surveys 2005]

————— 78th ACADEMY AWARD WINNERS · 2006 —————

Presented by American satirist Jon Stewart, the 78th Oscars celebrated old school Hollywood glamour in an effort to entice the public back into cinemas. With no one film dominating, the surprise of the night came when *Crash* snatched Best Picture from the hotly tipped *Brokeback Mountain*. And the winners were...

Leading actor..................................... Philip Seymour Hoffman · *Capote*
Leading actress................................. Reese Witherspoon · *Walk the Line*
Supporting actor..George Clooney · *Syriana*
Supporting actress ....Rachel Weisz · *The Constant Gardener*
Best picture ....*Crash*
Directing... Ang Lee · *Brokeback Mountain*
Animated feature.... Park & Box · *Wallace & Gromit: the Curse of the Were-Rabbit*
Art direction .... John Myhre & Gretchen Rau · *Memoirs of a Geisha*
Cinematography................................Dion Beebe · *Memoirs of a Geisha*
Costume design.............................Colleen Atwood · *Memoirs of a Geisha*
Doc. feature............... Luc Jacquet & Yves Darondeau · *March of the Penguins*
Doc. short subject ......Corinne Marrinan & Eric Simonson · *A Note of Triumph*
Film editing... Hughes Winborne · *Crash*
Foreign language film... Gavin Hood · *Tsotsi*
Make-up...................... Howard Berger & Tami Lane · *Chronicles of Narnia*
Music (score)............................Gustavo Santaolalla · *Brokeback Mountain*
Music (song) .... *It's Hard Out Here for a Pimp* · *Hustle & Flow* [see p.157]
Short film (animated)....John Canemaker & Peggy Stern · *The Moon and the Son*
Short film (live)....................................Martin McDonagh · *Six Shooter*
Sound ....C. Boyes, M. Semanick, M. Hedges & H. Peek · *King Kong*
Sound editing.................. Mike Hopkins & Ethan Van der Ryn · *King Kong*
Visual effects ....J. Letteri, B. Van't Hul, C. Rivers & R. Taylor · *King Kong*
Screenplay (adapted).....Larry McMurtry & Diana Ossana · *Brokeback Mountain*
Screenplay (original)....................... Paul Haggis & Bobby Moresco · *Crash*
Honorary award .... Robert Altman

SOME OSCAR NIGHT QUOTES

❦ GEORGE CLOONEY · I guess this means I'm not going to win best director. ❦ PAUL HAGGIS · I just want to thank people who take big risks in their daily lives when there aren't cameras rolling. ❦ CHRISTOPHE LIOUD (Producer of *March of the Penguins*) · Looking at all the tuxedos tonight, it's like seeing the movie all over again. ❦ JON STEWART · Björk could not be here ... she was trying on her Oscar dress and Dick Cheney shot her. ❦ REESE WITHERSPOON · People used to ask June how she was doing, and she would say 'I'm just trying to matter.' I know what she means. ❦ RACHEL WEISZ · He [John le Carré] really paid tribute to the people who are willing to risk their own lives to fight injustice. And they're greater men and women than I. ❦ PHILIP SEYMOUR HOFFMAN · My mom's name is Marilyn O'Connor, and she's here tonight. And I'd like if you see her tonight to congratulate her. Because she brought up four kids alone, and she deserves congratulations for that ... be proud, mom, because I'm proud of you. ❦

OSCAR NIGHT FASHION · 2006

Star	*dress*	*designer*
Keira Knightley	*burgundy, single strap, fishtail*	Vera Wang
Uma Thurman	*cap-sleeved, slinky draped cream silk*	Versace
Jennifer Lopez	*olive green, toga-style, vintage, cinched waist*	Jean Dessès
Charlize Theron	*green/black silk, huge bow on shoulder*	Christian Dior
Michelle Williams	*saffron chiffon, deep v-neck*	Vera Wang
Dolly Parton	*candyfloss pink chiffon, criss-cross bodice*	Robert Behar
Reese Witherspoon	*long pale, vintage, tiered net*	Christian Dior
Nicole Kidman	*strapless, white, structured column dress*	Balenciaga
Naomi Watts	*nude, bunched tulle, single strap, net skirt*	Givenchy
Rachel Weisz	*simple black embroidered empire line*	Narcisco Rodriguez

ACCEPTANCE SPEECHES

Paul Payack of Global Language Monitor analysed Oscar acceptance speeches, from 1992–2004, employing the Flesch-Kincaid scale which is used to calculate the reading age of children's books. Below are the reading ages of some Oscar speeches:

Name	*Best ...*	*film*	*year*	*reading age*
Russell Crowe	actor	*Gladiator*	2000	14
Tom Hanks	actor	*Forrest Gump*	1994	13
Emma Thompson	actress	*Howard's End*	1992	12
Al Pacino	actor	*Scent of a Woman*	1992	10
Steven Spielberg	director	*Schindler's List*	1993	9
Halle Berry†	actress	*Monster's Ball*	2001	8
Jamie Foxx	actor	*Ray*	2004	7

† Halle Berry shoe-horned the word 'thank' into her acceptance speech an impressive 31 times.

CELEBRITY GIFT BASKETS

Burdening celebrities with gift baskets of 'swag' has become an integral part of Hollywood award shows. The total value of these baskets in 2006 was estimated to be: Grammys $54,000, Golden Globes $62,000, and Oscars $100,000. However, in April, the IRS reminded stars that 'merchants who participate in giving the gifts do not do so solely out of affection, respect or similar impulses. ... In general, the person has received taxable income equal to the fair market value of the bag and its contents'. Consequently, celebrities can expect to receive a tax demand for the swag they were given at 2006's Oscars, and the Academy has agreed to pay the tax on gift baskets from previous years. ❦ In 2006, the official Oscar haul of swag included: a 4-night stay in Honolulu, worth $25,000; a $600 Krups kitchen set; a 3-night stay for 2 (with 'personal surf-butler') at the St Regis Monarch Beach Resort & Spa in CA; a case of Shu Uemura cosmetics, including mink eyelashes; a year's supply of Vonage phone service; a dinner party at Morton's; &c. [Sources: *USA Today, NYT*, CBC]

—————————— THE BRITISH FILM INDUSTRY ——————————

The British film industry has begun to revive, in part due to the continued success of franchises such as *Harry Potter* [see below]. A snapshot of the industry follows:

TOP UK-MADE FILMS · 2005 · BOX OFFICE GROSS

Harry Potter: Goblet of Fire .... £48·6m	*Pride & Prejudice* .... 14·6
Charlie & the Chocolate Factory ... 37·5	*Hitchhiker's Guide to the Galaxy* ... 10·7
Wallace & G. – Were-Rabbit ...... 32·0	*Valiant* .... 8·5
Nanny McPhee .... 16·5	*Closer* .... 8·5
Batman Begins .... 16·4	*Kingdom of Heaven* .... 7·8

UK SCREEN ADMISSIONS

1998 .... 135·2m	2001 .... 155·9	2004 .... 171·3
1999 .... 139·1	2002 .... 175·9	2005 .... 164·7
2000 .... 142·5	2003 .... 167·3	[CAA/Nielsen EDI]

UK OSCAR NOMINATIONS 2006	
Judi Dench .... *actress*	Sharon Colman .... *short animated film*
Keira Knightley .... *actress*	Jeffrey Caine .... *adapted screenplay*
Rachel Weisz[†] .... *supporting actress*	Martin McDonagh[†] ..... *short live film*
Nick Park & Steve Box[†] .....*animation*	Peter Fudakowski[†] ... *foreign lang. film*
	[† indicates a winner, see p.150]

—————————— INTERNATIONAL BOX OFFICE ——————————

Figures released in February 2006 showed that the first three *Harry Potter* films already dominate all-time international box office sales. The chart below shows the 5 top-performing films of all time, outside American and Canadian markets:

Film box office ($)	
Titanic .... 1·2bn	*Harry Potter: Philosopher's Stone* . 657m
Lord of the Rings: Return of King . 752m	*Harry Potter: Chamber of Secrets* . 616m
	Harry Potter: Goblet of Fire 600m

—————— HASTY PUDDING MAN & WOMAN OF THE YEAR ——————

Harvard University's *Hasty Pudding*[†] *Theatricals*, America's oldest student drama troupe, each year presents a Pudding Award to actors who have made a 'lasting and impressive contribution to the world of entertainment'. In 2006 the Puddings were awarded to HALLE BERRY and RICHARD GERE. In acceptance of the prize, Halle Berry led a riotous parade through the streets of Cambridge, Massachusetts.

† Hasty pudding is an American version of porridge made with corn or maize. The Harvard troupe took its curious name from the pledge made when the society was created in 1795, that 'the members in alphabetical order shall provide a pot of hasty pudding for every meeting'.

MOVIE AWARDS OF NOTE

BAFTAs 2006 · *bafta.com*

Best film...*Brokeback Mountain*
Best British film...................*Wallace & Gromit: The Curse of the Were-Rabbit*
Best actor in a leading role......................Philip Seymour Hoffman · *Capote*
Best actress in a leading role...................Reese Witherspoon · *Walk the Line*
Best actor in a supporting role..............Jake Gyllenhaal · *Brokeback Mountain*
Best actress in a supporting role...........................Thandie Newton · *Crash*

MTV MOVIE AWARDS 2006 · *mtv.com*

Best performance...........................Jake Gyllenhaal · *Brokeback Mountain*
Best movie...*Wedding Crashers*
Best villain....................Hayden Christiansen · *Star Wars: Revenge of the Sith*
Best fight.........................Angelina Jolie & Brad Pitt · *Mr and Mrs Smith*
Best kiss..................Jake Gyllenhaal & Heath Ledger · *Brokeback Mountain*

GOLDEN GLOBES 2006 · *hfpa.org*

Best dramatic film..*Brokeback Mountain*
Best dramatic actress...............................Felicity Huffman · *Transamerica*
Best dramatic actor.............................Philip Seymour Hoffman · *Capote*
Best director..Ang Lee · *Brokeback Mountain*
Best actor in musical or comedy..................Joaquin Phoenix · *Walk the Line*
Best actress in musical or comedy.............Reese Witherspoon · *Walk the Line*

BRITISH INDEPENDENT FILM AWARDS 2005 · *bifa.org.uk*

Best British film..*The Constant Gardener*
Best actor...................................Ralph Fiennes · *The Constant Gardener*
Best actress...................................Rachel Weisz · *The Constant Gardener*
Richard Harris award for outstanding achievement.................Tilda Swinton

GOLDEN RASPBERRIES 2006 · *razzies.com*

Worst picture...*Dirty Love*
Worst actor........................Rob Schneider · *Deuce Bigalow: European Gigolo*
Worst actress...Jenny McCarthy · *Dirty Love*

EMPIRE AWARDS 2006 · *empireonline.co.uk*

Best actor..........................Johnny Depp · *Charlie & the Chocolate Factory*
Best actress...Thandie Newton · *Crash*
Best director........S. Box & Nick Park · *Wallace & Gromit: Curse of Were-Rabbit*
Best British film..*Pride & Prejudice*
Best film..*King Kong*

EVENING STANDARD BRITISH FILM AWARDS 2006

Best film...*The Constant Gardener*
Best actor...................................Ralph Fiennes · *The Constant Gardener*
Best actress...Natasha Richardson · *Asylum*
Most promising newcomer................................Saul Dibb · *Bullet Boy*

BRITISH FILM CLASSIFICATIONS

The British Board of Film Classification [BBFC] is an independent, non-governmental body responsible for viewing and classifying all films before they are released for public screening. Film classifications can be summarised thus:

Uc Particularly suitable for pre-school children.

U Universal, for audiences aged 4 and over. 'Films should be set within a positive moral framework and offer reassuring counterbalances to any violence, threat or horror.' Infrequent use of mild bad language, occasional natural nudity, and mild violence.

PG Parental Guidance; children of any age may watch. 'A PG film should not disturb a child aged 8 or older'. Mild bad language, infrequent implied sexual activity. Realistic weapons should not be glamourised. References to drugs should be innocuous and carry an anti-drugs message.

12A Not suitable for those under the age of 12. Mature themes acceptable but must be suitable for young teen viewers. Infrequent strong swearing, nudity shown only in context. Violence should not dwell on details. May be occasional gory moments.

15 Not suitable for those under the age of 15. 'No themes are prohibited, provided the treatment is appropriate to 15-year-olds.' Frequent use of strong language, nudity allowed in a sexual context but no overt detail. Violence may be strong but should not dwell on the infliction of pain. Strong threat and menace are allowed.

18 Not suitable for those under the age of 18. 'No constraints at this level on theme, language, nudity or horror. The Board may cut or reject detailed portrayal of violent or dangerous acts which are likely to promote the activity, or the more explicit images of sex.'

R18 To be supplied only in licensed sex shops or shown in specially licensed cinemas to adults over 18. The following themes are unacceptable: any breach of the Obscene Publications Act (1959), material likely to encourage sexual abuse, infliction of pain in a sexual context, sexual threats, or sexual humiliation.

[The signatures on the certification of films belong to Quentin Thomas and David Cooke.]

ADULT VIDEO NETWORK AWARDS · 2006

The Adult Video Network (AVN) awards are the highest accolades in pornography. The 2006 Best Feature went to *Pirates*, a high-budget (for porn) romp featuring a group of sailors searching for evil pirates and booty [of every kind]. Evan Stone, winner of Best Actor for his performance as the ship's captain, told the *New York Times* that the movie's authenticity was a crucial part of its success: 'take the sex out of this movie and it's Walt Disney'. Held on 8 January at the Venetian Hotel, Las Vegas, the AVN awards recognised 104 categories (some more 'specialist' than others).

——————————— HOLLYWOOD WALK OF FAME ———————————

In 1960, the Hollywood Chamber of Commerce created the *Hollywood Walk of Fame* by placing some 2,500 blank stars along (and around) Hollywood Boulevard. To date, approximately 2,317 of these stars have been occupied. Each year, the Hollywood Walk of Fame Committee considers the nominations for this honour. The stars are divided into five categories, each with its own symbol:

Symbol	*for*	
Record...........singers & songwriters	Television set............television stars	
Film camera.....film stars & directors	Microphone................. radio stars	
	Theatrical masks .....stage performers	

In 2006, the following celebrities were presented with a star – at a cost of $15,000:

Annette Bening · Matthew Broderick · Holly Hunter · Winnie the Pooh
William Hurt · Nathan Lane · Steve Martin · Charlize Theron
Judge Judy · Isaac Hayes · Mötley Crüe · Destiny's Child

————————————— COMAS IN MOVIES —————————————

Research by Dr Eelco Wijdicks on the depiction of comas in movies was published in *Neurology* in May 2006. Dr Wijdicks studied 30 films (made between 1970–2004) that portrayed actors in prolonged comas, and he concluded that only two films accurately depicted the state of a coma victim and the agony of waiting for a patient to awaken: *Reversal of Fortune* (1990) and *The Dreamlife of Angels* (1998). The remaining 28 were criticised for portraying miraculous awakenings with no lasting side effects; unrealistic depictions of treatments and equipment required; and comatose patients remaining tanned, muscular, and suspiciously well turned-out.

—————————— FILM CENSORSHIP IN BRITAIN ——————————

The table below shows the number of films classified and cut by the BBFC:

Year	*No. films*	*no. cut*	*% cut*				
2005	589	7	1·2	1965	868	179	20·6
2000	525	12	2·3	1955	1,200	292	24·3
1995	410	27	6·6	1945	1,030	92	8·9
1985	399	72	18·0	1935	1,267	140	11·0
1975	550	167	30·4	1925	18	2	11·1
				1915	36	1	2·8

Below is a breakdown of the number of films cut in 2005, by category of rating:

Category	*no. films*	*no. cut*	*% cut*				
U	63	0	0·0	15	218	1	0·5
PG	100	2	2·0	18	54	0	0·0
12A	153	4	2·6	R-18	1	0	0·0
				TOTAL	589	7	1·2

—————————— FILM FESTIVAL PRIZES · 2006 ——————————

Sundance · World Dramatic Grand Jury Prize [JAN].................. *Quinceanera*
W. Westmoreland & R. Glatzer
Berlin · Golden Bear [FEB] .... *Grbavica* · Jasmila Zbanic
Tribeca · Best Narrative Feature [APR] ...... *Iluminados por el Fuego* · Tristán Bauer
Cannes · Palme d'Or [MAY] .... *The Wind That Shakes the Barley* · Ken Loach
Moscow · Golden St George [JUN] .... *About Sara* · Karim Othman
Edinburgh · Audience Award [AUG] .... *Clerks II* · Kevin Smith
Montreal · International Film Critics Award [AUG] ...... *Nagai Sanpo* · Eiji Okuda
Venice · Golden Lion [SEP]................................. *Still Life* · Jia Zhang-Ke
Toronto · People's Choice Award [SEP] ...... *Bella* · Alejandro Gomez Monteverde
London · Sutherland Trophy [OCT '05].. *For the Living and the Dead* · K. Paljakka

—————————— EMPIRE'S GREATEST FILMS ——————————

Empire listed the 201 best films as chosen by 20,000 readers. The 2006 top 10 were:

1 .... *The Shawshank Redemption*	6 .... *Pulp Fiction*
2 .... *The Empire Strikes Back*	7 .... *The Return of the King*
3 .... *The Fellowship of the Ring*	8 .... *Fight Club*
4 .... *Star Wars*	9 .... *Goodfellas*
5 .... *The Godfather*	10.......................... *The Matrix*

—————————— SOME MOVIE TAGLINES OF NOTE ——————————

Captain Jack is back .... *Pirates of the Caribbean: Dead Man's Chest*
A story like mine has never been told........................... *Memoirs of a Geisha*
The eighth wonder of the world .... *King Kong*
Love is a burning thing... *Walk the Line*
Love. At any cost .... *The Constant Gardener*
Look up in the sky.. *Superman Returns*
Love is a force of nature....................................... *Brokeback Mountain*
Welcome to the suck .... *Jarhead*
In this world ... redemption just comes once...................... *Tsotsi*
Nick Naylor doesn't hide the truth ... he filters it .... *Thank You For Smoking*
At the end of the day, what will you hang on to? .... *Get Rich or Die Tryin'*
Passion, temptation, obsession .... *Match Point*
Something bunny is going on...... *Wallace & Gromit: the Curse of the Were-Rabbit*
Unlock the code .... *The Da Vinci Code*
Oh yes, there will be blood.. *Saw II*
He never thaw it coming...................................... *Ice Age: The Meltdown*
Take a stand.. *X-Men 3: The Last Stand*
Afraid of the dark? You will be....................................... *The Descent*
The lucky ones die first.. *The Hills Have Eyes*
The show must go on, but the clothes must come off ...... *Mrs Henderson Presents*

—————————— PIMP CHIC ——————————

The 2006 Academy Award for Best Song went to *It's Hard Out Here for a Pimp* from *Hustle & Flow* [see p.150] – it was only the second hip-hop song to win an Oscar (the first was Eminem's *Lose Yourself*, from *8 Mile*). Although most of the song's offensive lyrics were censored during the live performance (and 'bitches' was sung as 'witches'), the Academy Award legitimised 'pimp chic' and secured (at least for a time) its place in the cultural mainstream. ❦ From as early as the C17th, a pimp was a procurer – a man who controlled or pandered prostitutes and lived off their earnings – the word is found in the works of Pepys, Dryden, and Pope. Because pimping is both illegal and immoral, 'pimp' has long been considered an insult – so much so that even in the 1960s some US papers refused to print the word. However, in the 1970s, a modern, cool, and essentially African American pimp aesthetic was born, derived from blaxploitation films like *Shaft*, *Superfly*, *Hit Man*, *The Mack*, and *Black Caesar* – and their iconic soundtracks. The pimp style was one of cool, laid-back disdain, complemented by a strolling gait (the 'pimp roll'), and ostentatious street fashions of furs, fedoras, Cuban-heels, and jewellery. ❦ In recent years, the notion of the pimp has developed – 'to pimp' now also means any elaborate modification for show or effect where excess trumps taste. In the MTV series *Pimp My Ride* (first aired in the US in 2004), unfashionable cars are 'tricked out' with 'flames, wings, superchargers, chrome tailpipes, and more'. And, just as the phrase '__ is the new black' has entered the vernacular, so '*pimp my __*' has become a ubiquitous media cliché.

A brief search of recent news reveals a plethora of imprecations to pimp 'my husband', 'my librarian', 'my WMD', 'my Vespa', 'my life', and so on. In certain bars, 'pimp my drink' means either to use only the most expensive brands of liquor or to add a dash of champagne. By extension, a number of hip-hop artists have popularised 'pimp cups' – capacious, gaudy, bejewelled goblets with 'pimp', 'playa', or the bearer's name spelt out in (semi-) precious stones. ❦ Yet, some have noted that, even in its dilute pop form, pimp culture is rooted in misogyny, the (violent) exploitation of women, and the stereotyping of black men as criminal. The Body Shop founder Dame Anita Roddick criticised 'pimp and ho chic' for masking the 'dark' and 'evil' reality of the sex-trade; and director Spike Lee noted that 'no one gets upset any more that pimpdom gets elevated on a pedestal'. According to the British Crime Survey, in 2004/5 there were 117 recorded cases of 'exploitation of prostitution' (i.e. pimping); 21 cases of 'trafficking for sexual exploitation'; and 98 cases of 'abuse of children through prostitution and pornography'. ❦ Inevitably, high street fashion and mainstream advertising have seized on pimp chic. Volkswagen championed the supremacy of German engineering with the line 'unpimp the auto', Burger King ran a 'Pimp My Burger' competition, and Virgin Atlantic promoted a refurbished Upper Class clubhouse with the slogan 'pimp my lounge'. It seems possible that such campaigns could prove to be the high-water mark of 'pimp chic' – the corporate embrace finally suffocating a controversial and inherently ambiguous street culture.

Books & Arts

The secret of the arts is to correct nature.
— VOLTAIRE (François-Marie Arouet) (1694–1778)

─── NOBEL PRIZE IN LITERATURE ───

The 2005 Nobel Prize in Literature was awarded to HAROLD PINTER (1930–),

Who in his plays uncovers the precipice under everyday
prattle and forces entry into oppression's closed rooms

Illness prevented Pinter from receiving the award in person on 10 December, and it was accepted on his behalf by his publisher at Faber & Faber, Stephen Page. However, Pinter pre-recorded a pugnacious Nobel Lecture, broadcast by video to the Swedish Academy in Stockholm on 7 December. Speaking from his wheelchair (in a manner that provoked comparisons to Hamm in Beckett's *Endgame*), Pinter poured ironic scorn on America's postwar foreign policy, and George W. Bush's presidency in particular: 'I put it to you that the United States is without doubt the greatest show on the road. Brutal, indifferent, scornful, and ruthless it may be, but it is also very clever'. ❦ Pinter's work has long been concerned with the oppressiveness of authoritarian intervention. In *The Dumb Waiter* (1959), *The Birthday Party* (1958), and *The Hothouse* (1958), this oppression is manifest respectively in the power of state, family, and religion; in *One for the Road* (1984), *Mountain Language* (1988), and *Ashes to Ashes* (1996), it is stated more explicitly. It was perhaps *The Homecoming* (1964) and *The Caretaker* (1959) that made the strongest impression on critics; they prominently featured the relentless rhythms that became the hallmark of Pinter's style. The 'Pinteresque' entered the *Oxford English Dictionary* in 1989, and was defined as being 'characterised by implications of threat and strong feeling produced through colloquial language, apparent triviality, and long pauses'. ❦ Pinter was diagnosed with cancer of the oesophagus in January 2002, but in August of that year stated his intention to be 'even more of a pain in the arse' to the British government than before. Upon accepting the Nobel Laureateship, Pinter declared that he would be writing no further drama, and planned instead to devote all his time to poetry. ❦ Pinter's Nobel lecture was above all concerned with the themes central to his work: 'the dignity of man', and the 'crucial obligation which devolves upon us all' to 'define the truth of our lives and our societies'.

The 2004 winner was the Austrian writer Elfriede Jelinek (1946–), whose novels and plays *'with extraordinary linguistic zeal reveal the absurdity of society's clichés'*.

———— ODDEST BOOK TITLE OF THE YEAR · 2005 ————

The Diagram Group's *Oddest Book Title of the Year* has been contested annually since 1978. Previous winners have included: *Living with Crazy Buttocks*; *Proceedings of the Second International Workshop on Nude Mice*; *How to Avoid Huge Ships*; and *The Big Book of Lesbian Horse Stories*. 2005's winning title and runners-up were:

People Who Don't Know They Are Dead: How They Attach Themselves To Unsuspecting Bystanders and What To Do About It
Gary Leon Hill [WINNER]

Rhino Horn Stockpile Management: Minimum Standards and Best Practices from East and Southern Africa
Simon Milledge

Ancient Starch Research
Robin Torrence & Huw J. Barton

Soil Nailing: Best Practice Guidance
A. Phear, C. Dew, & B. Ozsoy

Bullying and Sexual Harassment: A Practical Handbook
T. Stephens & J. Hallas

Nessus, Snort & Ethereal Powertools
B. Caswell, G. Ramirez, J. Beale, & N. Rathaus

[The contest is run by *The Bookseller*, and voted on by the book trade.]

———— BULWER-LYTTON FICTION CONTEST ————

In 1982, the English Dept of San José State University created a literary contest in honour of E.G.E. Bulwer-Lytton (1803–73), who infamously opened his book *Paul Clifford* with 'It was a dark and stormy night.' The contest rewards the best 'bad' opening line to an imaginary novel. The 2006 prize went to Jim Guigli, for:

Detective Bart Lasiter was in his office studying the light from his one small window falling on his super burrito when the door swung open to reveal a woman whose body said you've had your last burrito for a while, whose face said angels did exist, and whose eyes said she could make you dig your own grave and lick the shovel clean.

———— TOP 10 BEST-SELLING UK BOOKS · 2005–06 ————

Dan Brown	*The Da Vinci Code*
Dan Brown	*Angels and Demons*
Jeremy Clarkson	*The World According to Clarkson*
Jamie Oliver	*Jamie's Italy*
Kate Mosse	*Labyrinth*
John Grisham	*The Broker*
Sharon Osbourne	*Extreme: My Autobiography*
Dan Brown	*Deception Point*
Dan Brown	*Digital Fortress*
Gloria Hunniford	*Next to You: Caron's Courage Remembered by Her Mother*

[Period: August 2005– August 2006 · Source: Nielsen BookScan TCM panel ©]

BAD SEX IN FICTION PRIZE · 2005

Each year the *Literary Review* awards its 'Bad Sex in Fiction' prize to a novel featuring the most 'inept, embarrassing and unnecessary' sex scene. The 2005 winner was the columnist and food critic GILES COREN, for his début *Winkler*:

And he came hard in her mouth and his dick jumped around and rattled on her teeth and he blacked out and she took his dick out of her mouth and lifted herself from his face and whipped the pillow away and he gasped and glugged at the air, and he came again so hard that his dick wrenched out of her hand and a shot of it hit him straight in the eye and stung like nothing he'd ever had in there, and he yelled with the pain, but the yell could have been anything, and as she grabbed at his dick, which was leaping around like a shower dropped in an empty bath, she scratched his back deeply with the nails of both hands and he shot three more times, in thick stripes on her chest. Like Zorro.

OTHER BOOK PRIZES OF NOTE · 2006

Carnegie Medal	Mal Peet · *Tamar*
Kate Greenaway Medal	Emily Gravett · *Wolves*
Commonwealth Writers' Prize	Kate Grenville · *The Secret River*
Forward Prize: best poetry collection [2005]	David Harsent · *Legion*
Guardian children's fiction [2005]	Kate Thompson · *The New Policeman*
First book award	Alexander Masters · *Stuart: A Life Backwards*
Orange prize	Zadie Smith · *On Beauty*
Samuel Johnson Prize for non-fiction	James Shapiro · *1599: A Year in the Life of William Shakespeare*
T.S. Eliot Prize for poetry	Carol Ann Duffy · *Rapture*
Whitbread (now Costa) First novel	Tash Aw · *The Harmony Silk Factory*
Children's prize	Kate Thompson · *The New Policeman*
Poetry	Christopher Logue · *Cold Calls*
Novel	Ali Smith · *The Accidental*
Overall Whitbread	Hilary Spurling · *Matisse the Master*
Nestlé (formerly Smarties) Prize [2005]: 5 & under	Oliver Jeffers · *Lost and Found*
6–8	Nick Butterworth · *The Whisperer*
9–11	Sally Gardner · *I, Coriander*
Pulitzer Prize: Fiction	Geraldine Brooks · *March*
Poetry	Claudia Emerson · *Late Wife*
British Book Awards: Author of the year	Alan Bennett
Book of the year	J.K. Rowling · *Harry Potter and the Half-Blood Prince*
Newcomer of the year	Marina Lewycka · *A Short History of Tractors in Ukrainian*
Sports book of the year	Andrew Flintoff · *Being Freddie*
Somerset Maugham Award	Chris Cleave · *Incendiary*
	Owen Sheers · *Skirrid Hill* & Zadie Smith · *On Beauty*
Impac	Colm Tóibín · *The Master*
Romantic Novel of the Year	Erica James · *Gardens of Delight*
James Tait Black Memorial Prize	Ian McEwan · *Saturday*

—————————— MAN BOOKER PRIZES ——————————

The 2005 (£50,000) Man Booker Prize for best novel was awarded to JOHN BANVILLE for *The Sea* (Picador). The shortlisted novels for the 2006 prize are:

Edward St Aubyn .... *Mother's Milk* .... Picador
Kiran Desai .... *The Inheritance of Loss* .... Hamish Hamilton
Kate Grenville........... *The Secret River* .... Canongate
M.J. Hyland.............. *Carry Me Down* .... Canongate
Hisham Matar .... *In the Country of Men* .... Viking
Sarah Waters .... *The Night Watch* .... Virago

> *Even if I'd lost I'd still think it was a good year for the Booker. It's been a good*
> *year for fiction. It's nice to see a work of art winning the Booker Prize*
> *— whether it's a good work of art or a bad one, it's what I intended it to be.*
> — JOHN BANVILLE

The inaugural International Man Booker was presented in June 2005 to Albanian dissident writer ISMAIL KADARÉ. The award will be presented every two years to a writer from any country, to reward that author's entire body of work.

—————————— INTERNET ABECEDARIAN ——————————

The alphabet of words most commonly looked up on dictionary.com in 2005:

Affect · Benevolent · Cynical · Definitely · Effect · Fallacious · Gregarious · Hyperbole
Irony · Jaded · Karma · Love · Metaphor · Naive · Oxymoron · Paradox · Quixotic
Rhetoric · Sex · Theme · Ubiquitous · Virtue · Whether · Xenophobia · Yield · Zeal

—————————— MOST VALUABLE BOOKS ——————————

In January 2006, *Book & Magazine Collector* magazine published a list of the most valuable C20th books. The results relate to first editions in 'very good' condition:

Title · author	published	value (£)
Ulysses · James Joyce	1922	100,000
The Hound of the Baskervilles · Arthur Conan Doyle	1902	80,000
Seven Pillars of Wisdom · T.E. Lawrence	1922	60,000
The Great Gatsby · F. Scott Fitzgerald	1925	50,000
The Tale of Peter Rabbit · Beatrix Potter	1901	50,000
Poems · W.H. Auden	1928	30,000
The Sun Also Rises · Ernest Hemingway	1926	30,000
Brighton Rock · Graham Greene	1938	25,000
The Maltese Falcon · Dashiell Hammett	1930	25,000
Night and Day · Virginia Woolf	1919	25,000
Three Stories & Ten Poems · Ernest Hemingway	1923	25,000

'CHAP-LIT'

Professor Lisa Jardine and Annie Watkins of Queen Mary College, London, interviewed 500 men about the novels that changed their lives. They found that men most treasured books involving solitary struggle and social angst (especially in hardback). Men's most life-changing books were:

The Outsider† .... Albert Camus
Heart of Darkness ...... Joseph Conrad
Crime and Punishment ....Dostoevsky
The Great Gatsby ....F. Scott Fitzgerald
Brighton Rock.......... Graham Greene
Catch 22..................Joseph Heller
High Fidelity..............Nick Hornby
Ulysses......................James Joyce
Metamorphosis............. Franz Kafka
The Book of Laughter and Forgetting ...
Milan Kundera
† Camus described his seminal novel thus: 'The study of an absurd man in an absurd world'.

TITLES THAT SELL

In 2005, literary website lulu.com undertook research into what makes a successful book title. By analysing 700 titles from the *New York Times* bestseller list over 50 years, Dr Atai Winkler, the project's statistician, claimed to have pinpointed the attributes common to popular books. According to his model, metaphorical titles are more successful than literal ones, and the length of title seems not to affect sales. The following books were judged to have the most commercially successful titles:

Sleeping Murder .... Agatha Christie
Something of Value.......Robert Ruark
Looking for Mr Goodbar.....J. Rossner
Presumed Innocent......... Scott Turow
Everything's Eventual .....Stephen King
Rising Sun .... Michael Crichton

AUTOBIOGRAPHIES

Below are the best-selling hardback autobiographies, since 1998:

Author · title	sales
Sharon Osbourne · *Extreme*	621,274
David Beckham · *My Side*	516,684
Paul Burrell · *A Royal Duty*	343,896
Katie Price · *Being Jordan*	334,881
Alan Bennett · *Untold Stories*	300,687

[Source: *The Bookseller*/Nielsen BookScan]

HAPPY ENDINGS

A World Book Day survey of the British reading public revealed that 41% said they were 'overwhelmingly in favour' of books with happy endings. Below are the public's top 5 favourite happy endings, and 5 unhappy endings that readers would dearly like to change.

FAVOURITE HAPPY ENDINGS
Pride and Prejudice · Jane Austen
To Kill A Mocking Bird
Harper Lee
Jane Eyre · Charlotte Brontë
The Curious Incident of the Dog in the Night-time · Mark Haddon
Rebecca · Daphne du Maurier

UNHAPPY ENDINGS
Tess of the D'Urbervilles · Hardy
Harry Potter and the Half Blood Prince
J.K. Rowling
Wuthering Heights · Emily Brontë
Gone With the Wind · M. Mitchell
Doctor Zhivago · Boris Pasternak

MEDAL FOR POETRY

Fleur Adcock received the Queen's Gold Medal for Poetry in April 2006 for her collection, *Poems 1960–2000*.

'THE DA VINCI CODE' RULING

In February 2006, Michael Baigent and Richard Leigh sued Random House in the British High Court, claiming that Dan Brown's (>40m) best-selling novel, *The Da Vinci Code* (DVC), had copied the central ideas of their 1982 non-fiction book, *The Holy Blood & The Holy Grail* (HBHG), also published by Random House. Baigent and Leigh argued that DVC appropriated 'the whole architecture' of their theory that Jesus and Mary Magdalene were married and that their blood line lasts to this day. Because copyright infringement is notoriously difficult to prove, many legal pundits

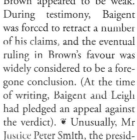

Dan Brown

were sceptical as to the plaintiffs' case. Intense media interest faded as the trial progressed and the evidence against Brown appeared to be weak. During testimony, Baigent was forced to retract a number of his claims, and the eventual ruling in Brown's favour was widely considered to be a foregone conclusion. (At the time of writing, Baigent and Leigh had pledged an appeal against the verdict). ❦ Unusually, Mr Justice Peter Smith, the presiding judge, entered into the spirit of the case – inserting into his 71-page formal judgment a set of seemingly random letters, singled out in bold italic type:

s, m, i, t, h, y, c, o, d, e, J, a, e, i, e, x, t, o, s, t, g, p, s, a, c, g, r, e, a, m, q, w, f, k, a, d, p, m, q, z, v, z

A London lawyer, Dan Tench, spotted these anomalies and soon, after hints from the judge to refer to his *Who's Who* entry and employ the Fibonacci sequence, journalists uncovered the disappointingly naval message '*Smithy Code Jackie Fisher who are you Dreadnought*'. It seems that this statement refers only to Justice Smith's passion for obscure Royal Navy history and not, as hoped, the meaning of life.

AMAZON'S TEXT STATS

By analysing the entire text of individual works, amazon.com created the *Text Stats* service that enables purchasers to compare the readability and complexity of books featured on their site. Below are the *Text Stats* for some selected recent works:

Benchmark	Zadie Smith *On Beauty*	Dan Brown *Da Vinci Code*	Levitt & Dubner *Freakonomics*	A. Hollinghurst *Line of Beauty*
Fog Index†	8·7	9·1	11·1	9·8
Complex words‡	9%	12%	14%	8%
Syllables per word	1·5	1·6	1·6	1·5
Words per sentence	13·0	11·1	14·1	16·1
Total characters	880,751	821,310	399,657	901,131
Total words	154,512	137,100	63,809	158,559
Total sentences	11,913	12,354	4,511	9,837

† The Fog Index measures readability by suggesting how many years of formal education would be required to comprehend the text. ‡ A word is classed as complex if it has 3 or more syllables.

LIBRARY LENDING

The Public Lending Right (PLR) pays authors 'royalties' when their books are borrowed from public libraries. Payments are calculated using an annually reviewed Rate per Loan which, in 2006, was 5·57p per loan (5·26p in 2005) – although the maximum that any one author can receive per year is £6,000. Below are the top ten 'most borrowed' authors from public libraries in 2004–5:

1 ...Jacqueline Wilson (1)
2 ......Josephine Cox (3)
3 ....Danielle Steel (2)
4 .....James Patterson (6)
5 ....Mick Inkpen (4)
6 ....Janet & Allan Ahlberg (7)
7 ......John Grisham (11)
8 ....Ian Rankin (9)
9 ....Roald Dahl (10)
10..Bernard Cornwell(14)
[2003–4 results in brackets]

ESSENTIAL BOOKS FOR CHILDREN

In 2006, the Royal Society of Literature asked J.K. Rowling, Philip Pullman, and Andrew Motion to nominate the books they thought all children should have read by the time they leave school. Below are a few of their choices:

J.K. ROWLING
Wuthering Heights · Emily Brontë
Charlie & the Chocolate Factory
Roald Dahl
Robinson Crusoe · Daniel Defoe
David Copperfield · Charles Dickens
Catch 22 · Joseph Heller

PHILIP PULLMAN
Romeo & Juliet · William Shakespeare
The Rime of the Ancient Mariner
Samuel Coleridge
Finn Family Moomintroll · Tove Jansson
The Magic Pudding · Norman Lindsay
Emil and the Detectives · Erich Kästner

ANDREW MOTION, Poet Laureate
The Odyssey · Homer
Don Quixote · Cervantes
Ulysses · James Joyce
Hamlet · William Shakespeare
Paradise Lost · John Milton

BEST-SELLING AUDIO-BOOKS · 2006

Over 7·3m MP3 players have been sold in Britain, a trend that has contributed to a boom in the sale of audio-books, creating a market worth *c.*£38m. In 2006, the 10 best-selling audio-titles according to audio-book specialist audible.co.uk were:

1 .... *Ricky Gervais Show: the Complete First Series*................Ricky Gervais &c.
2 .... *A Short History of Nearly Everything*.................................Bill Bryson
3 .... *The Da Vinci Code*...Dan Brown
4 .... *Jonathan Strange & Mr Norrell*.................................Susanna Clarke
5 .... *Ricky Gervais Show: the Complete Second Series* ....Ricky Gervais &c.
6 .... *Angels and Demons*..Dan Brown
7 .... *Memoirs of a Geisha*.. Arthur Golden
8 .... *The Time Traveller's Wife*..................................... Audrey Niffenegger
9 .... *Freakonomics*...........................Steven D. Levitt & Stephen J. Dubner
10... *The Hobbit* .... J.R.R. Tolkien

THE TURNER PRIZE · 2005

Founded in 1984, the Turner Prize is awarded each year to a British artist under 50, for an outstanding exhibition or other presentation in the twelve months prior to each May. The winner receives £25,000 – and three runners-up receive £5,000.

Simon Starling, 38, won the 2005 Turner prize amidst the usual media uproar. Starling, whose past works include an attempt to create an 'island of weeds' in the middle of Loch Lomond, describes his works as 'the physical manifestation of my thought process'. The centrepiece of his Turner entry, *Shedboatshed* (Mobile Architecture No. 2) is a dilapidated former guard-hut. Having discovered it in the Swiss town of Schweizerhalle, Starling turned it into a boat and paddled it for 7 miles down the Rhine to Basel, where he rebuilt it in its original incarnation. He said of the piece, 'You can start to sort of read the shed and rebuild the boat in your mind.' Another exhibit, *Tabernas Desert Run 2004*, saw him cross the Spanish desert on an improvised hydrogen bicycle, then use the waste water it produced to paint a watercolour cactus. Painting and vehicle are exhibited side by side in

Simon Starling

a glass cabinet. Starling will apparently spend a portion of his Turner winnings placing a replica Henry Moore sculpture in Lake Ontario and growing zebra mussels on its surface. He also has plans to construct a replica of the car built by erotic photographer Carlo Mollino for the Le Mans 24 Hour Race, and drive it around the Turin ring road for an entire day. *Shedboatshed* was hailed by Tate Britain curators as 'poetic ... a buttress against the pressures of modernity, mass production and global capitalism', and the audio guide to the exhibition applauds its 'wonderful, absurd circularity.' Artist Charles Thomson, however, was less charitable: 'The Turner should be renamed the B&Q DIY prize. Starling should get his Craft Badge, 1st class, but not the Turner.' David Lee, editor of *The Jackdaw* magazine, concluded, 'He's got some quaint charm, provided you don't take him too seriously'.

Year	previous winner				
'84	Malcolm Morley	'91	Anish Kapoor	'98	Chris Ofili
'85	Howard Hodgkin	'92	Grenville Davey	'99	Steve McQueen
'86	Gilbert & George	'93	Rachel Whiteread	'00	Wolfgang Tillmans
'87	Richard Deacon	'94	Antony Gormley	'01	Martin Creed
'88	Tony Cragg	'95	Damien Hirst	'02	Keith Tyson
'89	Richard Long	'96	Douglas Gordon	'03	Grayson Perry
		'97	Gillian Wearing	'04	Jeremy Deller

2006 NOMINATIONS

It was announced in May 2006 that the following four artists are shortlisted for the 2006 Turner Prize, the winner of which will be announced on 4 December:

sculptor Rebecca Warren · German-born abstract painter Tomma Abts
photographer & video-artist Phil Collins · installation-artist Mark Titchener

──────────── THE GULBENKIAN PRIZE · 2006 ────────────

The £100,000 Gulbenkian Prize is the UK's largest prize for innovative and challenging museums and galleries. In 2006, the prize went to Brunel's *SS Great Britain* in Bristol. The other finalists were: *The Collection: Art & Archaeology in Lincolnshire;* the *Hunterian Museum* in London; and the *Yorkshire Sculpture Park.*

──────────── TOP EXHIBITIONS · 2005 ────────────

The *Art Newspaper's* annual figures for the most popular art exhibitions in the world illustrate the success of shows in Japan – in 2005, the world's top three exhibitions were held there. Below are the most popular art exhibitions from 2005 around the world, and in London, by the number of daily visitors:

GLOBAL TOP TEN

2005 exhibition	museum	daily attendance
Hokusai	Tokyo National	9,436
Treasures of the Toshodaiji Temple	Tokyo National	8,678
C19th Masterpieces from the Louvre	Yokohama Museum of Art	7,066
Vincent Van Gogh: The Drawings	Metropolitan, NY	6,571
Cézanne and Pissarro 1865–85	Museum of Modern Art, NY	6,387
Turner, Whistler, Monet	Grand Palais, Paris	6,043
C19th Masterpieces from the Louvre	Kyoto City Museum	5,992
Thomas Demand	Museum of Modern Art, NY	5,991
Tutankhamun and the Pharaohs	LACMA, Los Angeles	5,934
Van Gogh in Context	Nat. Museum of Modern Art, Tokyo	5,890

LONDON TOP TEN

Turner, Whistler, Monet	Tate Britain	4,024
Turks, 600–1600AD	Royal Academy of Arts	3,358
Frida Kahlo	Tate Modern	3,002
Caravaggio: the Final Years	National Gallery	2,752
Raphael: From Urbino to Rome	National Gallery	2,682
Art in the Making: Degas	National Gallery	2,357
Matisse: His Art and His Textiles	Royal Academy of Arts	2,356
Triumph of Painting, Part II	Saatchi Gallery	2,239
The Show, Part II	Royal College of Art	2,111
Triumph of Painting, Part I	Saatchi Gallery	1,761

A 2006 survey by *Museum & Galleries Month* revealed that nearly a fifth of the 500 respondents had fallen in love while in a museum or gallery; the V&A was declared the most romantic venue.

──────────── BECK'S FUTURES PRIZE ────────────

Beck's Futures rewards innovation in art. In 2006, Matt Stokes received the £20,000 award for *Long After Tonight,* a 7-minute video of a rave in a church.

—————WHERE TO SEE MAJOR WORKS OF ART—————

Garden of Earthly Delights	Bosch	Prado, Madrid
The Birth of Venus	Botticelli	Galleria degli Uffizi, Florence
Massacre of the Innocents	Bruegel (Elder)	Hampton Court, Middlesex
Venice: Regatta on Grand Canal	Canaletto	National Gallery, London
I and the Village	Chagall	Museum of Modern Art, NY
Persistence of Memory	Dalí	Museum of Modern Art, NY
The Last Supper	da Vinci	Santa Maria delle Grazie, Milan
Mona Lisa	da Vinci	Louvre, Paris
The Dancing Lesson	Degas	Musée National d'Orsay, Paris
My Bed	Emin	Saatchi Gallery, London
The Swing	Fragonard	Wallace Collection, London
Girl With a White Dog	Freud	Tate Britain, London
The Blue Boy	Gainsborough	Huntington Library, CA
Merry-Go-Round	Gertler	Tate Britain, London
Turin Shroud	God	Cathedral of St John the Baptist, Turin
Saturn Devouring His Children	Goya	Prado, Madrid
Single Form	Hepworth	United Nations HQ, NY
Nighthawks	Hopper	The Art Institute of Chicago
Composition VIII	Kandinsky	Guggenheim, NY
Magic Garden	Klee	Guggenheim, NY
The Kiss	Klimt	Belvedere, Vienna
Coming from the Mill	Lowry	Salford Museum and Art Gallery
Le Double Secret	Magritte	Centre Pompidou, Paris
Creation of Adam	Michelangelo	Sistine Chapel, Rome
David	Michelangelo	Accademia, Florence
Broadway Boogie Woogie	Mondrian	Museum of Modern Art, NY
Nympheas	Monet	Orangerie, Paris
Reclining Figure	Moore	UNESCO HQ, Paris
Guernica	Picasso	Reina Sofía Museum, Madrid
Almanac	Rauschenberg	Tate Modern, London
Self-Portrait (1661)	Rembrandt	Kenwood House, London
Luncheon of the Boating Party	Renoir	Phillips Collection, Washington
The Thinker	Rodin	Musée Rodin, Paris
Bacchus	Rubens	Hermitage, St Petersburg
At the Moulin Rouge	Toulouse-Lautrec	Art Institute of Chicago
Ulysses Deriding Polyphemus	Turner	National Gallery, London
Ardabil Carpet	unknown	Victoria & Albert, London
Elgin Marbles	unknown	British Museum, London
Rosetta Stone	unknown	British Museum, London
Tutankhamun's gold mask	unknown	Egyptian Museum, Cairo
The Arnolfini Portrait	Van Eyck	National Gallery, London
Starry Night	Van Gogh	Museum of Modern Art, NY
Girl With a Pearl Earring	Vermeer	Mauritshuis, The Hague
100 Soup Cans	Warhol	Albright-Knox Gallery, Buffalo
Marilyn Monroe print	Warhol	The Warhol Museum, Pittsburgh

Because of sales, restoration, loans, multiple copies, and other factors, the location of some works may vary.

————————A SMASHING TIME————————

In January 2006, an unfortunate visitor to the Fitzwilliam Museum in Cambridge stumbled on his loose shoelace and tumbled into a trio of priceless vases, smashing them to pieces. The 300-year-old Qing vases had been displayed, perhaps recklessly, on a window-sill. Margaret Greeves, the museum's assistant director, said, 'they are in very, very small pieces, but we are determined to put them back together'.

The plot thickened in April 2006 when, after studying CCTV footage of the incident, the police arrested the clumsy culprit, Nick Flynn, on suspicion of causing criminal damage. After consultation between the police and the CPS, all charges were dropped in June 2006. ❦ In March 2006, *The Bay*, an abstract painting by Helen Frankenthaler worth *c*.$1·5m, was damaged when a schoolboy of 12 stuck a gobbet of chewing gum onto the canvas during a school trip to the Detroit Institute of Arts.

——————THE MOST POWERFUL PEOPLE IN ART——————

ArtReview's 4th annual 'Power 100' list of the most powerful people in the art world (in 2005) featured a record number of actual artists. The 10 most powerful were:

1 .. Damien Hirst .... *artist*	6 .. Eli Broad .... *collector*
2 .. Larry Gagosian...... *dealer/gallerist*	7 .. Sam Keller.......... *art fair director*
3 .. François Pinault.. *owner of Christies*	8 .. Iwan Wirth.......... *dealer/gallerist*
4 .. Nicholas Serota ... *museum director*	9 .. Bruce Nauman............... *artist*
5 .. Glenn D. Lowry .. *museum director*	10. David Zwirner .... *dealer/gallerist*

——————FBI TOP TEN ART CRIMES——————

In November 2005, the FBI's Art Theft Program & Art Crime Team released a list of the world's most significant unsolved art heists, in a bid to raise public awareness of unrecovered items. The works of art, and their estimated value, are listed below:

Item(s)	country of theft	date	value ($)
7,000–10,000 Iraqi artefacts	Iraq	2003	'priceless'
12 Isabella Stewart Gardner Museum paintings	USA	1990	300m
Munch · *The Scream* and *The Madonna*†	Norway	2004	102m
Da Vinci · *Madonna with the Yarnwinder*	Scotland	2003	65m
Cellini · *The Salt Cellar*‡	Austria	2003	55m
2 Renoirs and 1 Rembrandt*	Sweden	2000	36m
2 Van Goghs	Netherlands	2002	30m
Caravaggio · *Nativity with San Lorenzo & San Francesco*	Italy	1969	20m
Cézanne · *View of Auvers-sur-Oise*	England	1999	3m
Davidoff-Morini Stradivarius violin	USA	1995	3m

† Norwegian police uncovered Munch's two masterpieces in August 2006, two years after they were stolen from Oslo's Munch Museum. ‡ Cellini's sculpture *The Salt Cellar* was found by Austrian police in January 2006. * These works were recovered in 2001 and 2005 after an art-theft ring was foiled.

TOP TEN ARTISTS BY REVENUE · 2005

Artprice annually publishes a ranking of artists based on the sales generated by their works at auction. In 2005, revenue from the top ten artists reached $576 million.

Rank artist ('04 rank)   2005 sales ($)

1 .... Pablo Picasso (1) ....153·2m
2 .... Andy Warhol (3) ....86·7m
3 .... Claude Monet (2).........61·5m
4 .... Canaletto (239)............55·5m
5 .... Mark Rothko (13).........41·6m

6 .... Marc Chagall (11).........36·6m
7 .... Willem de Kooning (36)..36·6m
8 .... Fernand Léger (23)........35·7m
9 .... Jean Michel Basquiat (16) 35·6m
10... Lucian Freud (81).........33·7m

[www.artprice.com]

2005 ARTIST RANKINGS

The Artist Ranking system, developed by Artfacts.net, employs an algorithm to rank artists according to their international prestige. Each time an artist exhibits, they are awarded points based on the international significance of the gallery that hosts the exhibition. The database includes 60,000 artists, and tracks exhibitions within the last 5 years. The top-ranked artist, living or dead, in 2005 was Pablo Picasso, followed by Andy Warhol. The top 5 living artists in 2005 were as follows:

Rank   Artist   Points

1 ......Bruce Nauman ......54,543·34
2 ......Gerhard Richter.....51,266·89
3 ......Sol LeWitt...........39,619·45

4 ......R. Rauschenberg ....38,077·34
5 ......Cindy Sherman......36,897·97

[The first living UK artist on the list, at 19, was Turner Prize winner Douglas Gordon.]

MOST EXPENSIVE PAINTINGS

In June 2006, Gustav Klimt's 1907 portrait of Adele Bloch-Bauer was sold at auction for a record $135m (£73m), after a court ordered the Austrian government to return the Nazi-looted painting to Bloch-Bauer's descendants. The painting was bought by American billionaire Ronald Lauder, who will display the portrait at his New York Neue Galerie. Below are the world's most expensive paintings to date:

Painting	artist	year of sale	cost ($m)
Adele Bloch-Bauer I	Gustav Klimt	2006	$135
Garçon à la Pipe	Pablo Picasso	2004	$104
Dora Maar au Chat	Pablo Picasso	2006	$95
Portrait du Dr Gachet	Vincent Van Gogh	1990	$82
Au Moulin de la Galette	Pierre-Auguste Renoir	1990	$78
The Massacre of the Innocents	Peter Paul Rubens	2002	$76

[Source: *The Times*] ❧ In February 2006, the Dutch Government agreed to return some 202 paintings to the family of the Jewish art dealer Jacques Goudstikker, whose collection was looted by the Nazis in 1940. The paintings, currently displayed in a number of Dutch museums and galleries, include works by Dutch masters such as Rembrandt, Van Goyen, and Van Dyck.

——— THE CRITICAL YEAR · 2005 ———

{OCT} · Trevor Nunn directed Kevin Spacey in a modern-dress *Richard II* at the Old Vic; Benedict Nightingale in the *Times* thought it 'strong enough for us to feel confident about the future of our most venerable classical theatre', and Kate Bassett in the *Independent* praised Spacey's 'really terrifying temper and great authority'. ❦ The Royal Academy's *Edvard Munch by Himself* revealed an anxious and depressive man; Peter Conrad in the *Guardian* wrote that he 'admitted his fear, but the self-portraits show how boldly he overcame it'. ❦ The English National Ballet's touring production of *Sleeping Beauty* met with a tepid response; the *Telegraph*'s Laura Thompson thought 'the heart of the ballet proves, once again, almost entirely elusive'. The *Independent*'s Zoë Anderson nevertheless felt that the production had 'a well-paced clarity, and the company rise to it'. ❦ *Ducktastic*, directed by Kenneth Branagh at the Albery, opened to exuberant acclaim. The *Guardian*'s Michael Billington extolled its 'palpable and extravagant delight in theatre', and Charles Spencer in the *Telegraph* judged it 'as madcap and deliriously enjoyable a production as I have seen in the West End'. ❦ {NOV} · The Royal Opera's *Un Ballo in Maschera* was widely considered a flop. The *Times*' Richard Morrison had 'seen more compelling murder scenes in infant nativities', and Edward Seckerson wrote in the *Independent* that 'Martone's production doesn't do joined-up thinking'. ❦ Bacharach and David's *Promises, Promises* at Sheffield's Crucible disappointed Sam Marlowe of the *Times*, who wrote that, despite stylish costumes, the show 'promises more

Kenneth Branagh

than it delivers'. ❦ Adrian Searle in the *Guardian* was, in keeping with many others, charmed by the imperfections of *Henri Rousseau: Jungles in Paris* at the Tate Modern: 'what is lost in terms of believability is gained in character and presence ... Rousseau's appeal is to the child in all of us'. ❦ Helen Edmunson adapted Jamila Gavin's *Coram Boy* for the stage. The *Independent*'s Paul Taylor called it 'a powerful mix of the horrifying and the heartening', but, in the *Guardian*, Michael Billington considered that 'you lose some of the dense texture of the original'. ❦ {DEC} · Matthew Bourne's much-anticipated ballet *Edward Scissorhands* produced a mixed response: 'Bourne doesn't have the steps to sustain [the narrative]' wrote Anderson in the *Independent*, but the *Times*' Debra Craine was charmed by Sam Archer's 'gentle vulnerability' in the title role. {JAN} · The *Guardian*'s Erica Jeal was left unmoved by the Royal Opera's 'dusting-down' of Verdi's *La Traviata*, writing that the direction 'never gets around the lack of chemistry between the two leads'. ❦ The *Telegraph*'s Richard Dorment considered the Hayward Gallery's *Dan Flavin: A Retrospective* 'demanding ... but it rewards your engagement with an incomparable aesthetic experience'. {FEB} · Neil Armfield's *Marriage of Figaro* in Cardiff was derided by the *Times*' Richard Morrison as overblown and ribald: 'Mozart played as Benny Hill'. ❦ All-female acting troupe Foursight entertained Brian Wheeler of the BBC with *Thatcher: The Musical*, which led its audience through eight different incarnations of the Iron Lady. Despite some 'cursory' elements of the

—————— THE CRITICAL YEAR · 2005 cont. ——————

performance, he found it on the whole to be 'extremely well-researched'. ❦ {MAR} · Jeremy Irons took to the stage for Christopher Hampton's adaptation of Sandor Marai's *Embers*. Billington found it 'highly civilised' but felt an 'absence of any real dramatic danger'; and Nightingale 'ended up feeling the novel was stranger, richer, more satisfying than the play.' ❦ *Michelangelo Drawings. Closer to the Master* at the British Museum was applauded by Jonathan Jones, who wrote in the *Guardian* that the drawings 'live in your mind afterwards with a blazing truth'. {APR} · The Russell Maliphant Company's *Transmission / Push* at Sadler's Wells prompted the *Guardian*'s Judith Mackrell to call Maliphant 'one of the most fertile choreographic minds working in Britain today'. ❦ The *Guardian*'s Lyn Gardner was unwilling to join the general idolatry of Samuel Beckett; *Play/Catastrophe* prompted her to point out that 'the playwright's lesser plays are, well, lesser.' ❦ Wagner's *Götterdämmerung*, the final installment of Stefanos Lazaridis' 18-month Ring cycle at the ROH, was thought as confusing as its forerunners; the *Guardian*'s Tom Service saw its 'visual incoherence [swamp] the efforts of the cast to create ... believable characters.' ❦ Lyn Gardner was not charmed by *Entertaining Angels* at Chichester Festival Theatre, which she described as a 'cosy boulevard comedy washed down with Pimms,' where 'platitudes about the meaning of life trip off the characters' tongues like ready-mixed concrete'. Ian Shuttleworth of the *FT* also considered it 'archetypally Chichester in its middle-class comfort-

Avenue Q

ableness'. ❦ {MAY} · The *Telegraph*'s Richard Dorment was disgusted by *Inner Worlds Outside* at the Whitechapel Gallery, calling it 'a wicked, pernicious exhibition based on a false premise and proselytising for an evil idea.' ❦ {JUN} · Elena Seymenliyska of the *Telegraph* was let down by Ramón Oller's flamenco *Carmen* at Sadler's Wells: 'Rouet is simply too skinny for a temptress ... this Carmen doesn't come alight'. ❦ Eagerly anticipated Broadway puppet-based musical *Avenue Q* proved a let-down for Benedict Nightingale of the *Times*: 'extract the puppetry and the best of the songs, and the story is awfully ordinary'. ❦ Michael Grandage's revival of *Evita* was generally applauded, with Elena Roger's performance in the title-role lauded: 'She has exactly the star quality the role requires' reported Charles Spencer in the *Telegraph*. {JUL} · *Kandinsky: The Path to Abstraction* at Tate Modern was greeted warmly by the *Sunday Times*' Waldemar Januszczak, who was especially pleased that the exhibition gave most space to Kandinsky's finest years: 'The final room contains a mercilessly small sample of his later works. It's a perfect piece of editing, and a superb conclusion to the best exhibition at Tate Modern since the gallery opened'. ❦ Anna Picard of the *Independent* was impressed with the quality of the singing during *Fidelio* at Glyndebourne 'The vibrato-free opening of "*mir ist so wunderbar*" ... is also quite exquisitely sung by Milne, Kampe, Kennedy and Sherratt, which makes this the second Glyndebourne production in one season to have raised the bar on ensemble singing to a dizzying height'.

PRINCIPAL LONDON THEATRES

ADELPHI · Strand, WC2 · [*Tube station* · Charing Cross] 08704 030 303
ALDWYCH · 49 Aldwych, WC2 · [Covent Garden] 08704 000 805
ALMEIDA · Almeida St, N1 · [Angel]. 020 7359 4404
APOLLO · Shaftesbury Ave, W1 · [Piccadilly Circus] 020 7494 5070
APOLLO VICTORIA · Wilton Rd, SW1 · [Victoria]. 0870 161 1977
ARTS THEATRE · Great Newport St, WC2 · [Leicester Square] 020 7836 3334
BARBICAN CENTRE · Silk St, EC2 · [Barbican]. 020 7638 8891
CAMBRIDGE · Earlham St, WC2 · [Covent Garden] 020 7494 5080
COMEDY · Panton St, SW1 · [Leicester Square] 0870 060 6637
CRITERION · Piccadilly Circus, W1 · [Piccadilly Circus] 0870 060 2313
DOMINION · Tottenham Crt Rd, W1 · [Tottenham Court Rd]. 08705 344 444
DONMAR · Earlham St, WC2 · [Covent Garden] 08700 606 624
DRURY LANE, THTR. ROYAL · Catherine St, WC2 · [Covent Garden]. ..08708 901 109
DUCHESS · Catherine St, WC2 · [Covent Garden] 020 7494 5075
DUKE OF YORK'S · St Martin's Lane, WC2 · [Leicester Square] 08700 606 634
FORTUNE · Russell St, WC2 · [Covent Garden] 08700 606 626
GARRICK · Charing Cross Rd, WC2 · [Tottenham Court Rd] 020 7494 5085
GIELGUD · Shaftesbury Ave, W1 · [Piccadilly Circus] 020 7494 5065
GLOBE · Bankside, SE1 · [London Bridge] 020 7401 9919
HAYMARKET · Haymarket, SW1 · [Piccadilly Circus] 020 7930 8800
HER MAJESTY'S · Haymarket, SW1 · [Piccadilly Circus] 020 7494 5400
LONDON APOLLO HM'SMITH · Queen Caroline St, W6 · [H'smith]. .08706 063 400
LONDON PALLADIUM · Argyll St, W1 · [Oxford Circus]. 020 7494 5020
LYCEUM · Wellington St, WC2 · [Covent Garden] 08702 439 000
LYRIC · Shaftesbury Ave, W1 · [Piccadilly Circus]. 020 7494 5045
NATIONAL THEATRE · South Bank, SE1 · [Waterloo] 020 7452 3000
NEW AMBASSADORS · West St, WC2 · [Leicester Square]. 08700 606 627
NEW LONDON · Drury Lane, WC2 · [Covent Garden] 08708 900 141
NOËL COWARD · St Martin's Lane, WC2 · [Leicester Square]. 020 7812 7445
NOVELLO · Aldwych, WC2 · [Charing Cross] 0870 950 0935
OLD VIC · Waterloo Rd, SE1 · [Waterloo] 08700 606 628
PALACE · Shaftesbury Ave, W1 · [Leicester Square] 08708 955 579
PEACOCK · Portugal St, WC2 · [Holborn] 08707 370 337
PHOENIX · Charing Cross Rd, WC2 · [Tottenham Court Rd]. 08700 606 629
PICCADILLY · Denman St, W1 · [Piccadilly Circus] 08700 606 630
PLAYHOUSE · Northumberland Ave, WC2 · [Charing Cross]. 08700 606 631
PRINCE EDWARD · Old Compton St, W1 · [Leicester Square]. 020 7447 5400
PRINCE OF WALES · Coventry St, W1 · [Piccadilly Circus]. 08708 500 393
QUEEN'S · Shaftesbury Ave, W1 · [Piccadilly Circus] 020 7494 5040
ROYAL COURT · Sloane Sq, SW1 · [Sloane Square] 020 7565 5000
SAVOY · Strand, WC2 · [Charing Cross] 020 7836 8888
SHAFTESBURY · Shaftesbury Ave, WC2 · [Covent Garden] 020 7379 5399
ST MARTIN'S · West St, WC2 · [Leicester Square] 020 7836 1443
VICTORIA PALACE · Victoria St, SW1 · [Victoria] 08708 955 577
WYNDHAM'S · Charing Cross Rd, WC2 · [Tottenham Court Rd] 08700 606 633
YOUNG VIC · The Cut, SE1 · [Waterloo]. 020 7928 6363

—————————— LAURENCE OLIVIER AWARDS · 2006 ——————————

Best actor.....................................Brian Dennehy · *Death of a Salesman*
Best actress...Eve Best · *Hedda Gabler*
Best performance in a supporting role....Noma Dumezweni · *A Raisin in the Sun*
Best new play ....*On The Shore of the Wide World* · Simon Stephens
Best new musical..............*Billy Elliot: The Musical* · Lee Hall & Sir Elton John
Best actor (musical).....James Lomas, George Maguire, Liam Mower · *Billy Elliot*
Best actress (musical) .... Jane Krakowski · *Guys and Dolls*
Best director......................................Sir Richard Eyre · *Hedda Gabler*
Best new opera... *Madam Butterfly* · ENO
Best new dance.......................*Push* · Sylvie Guillem & Russell Maliphant
Outstanding musical production.. *Billy Elliot*

————————————— STAGE DIRECTIONS & LAYOUT —————————————

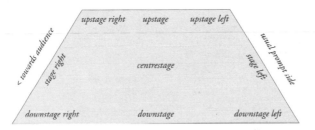

————————————— THEATRE RECIPE BOOK —————————————

A recipe book of luvvies' favourite dishes, first published in 1952, was recently discovered in America. A selection of recipes from *Our Favourite Dish – the Theatre Recipe Book* is now served at Astor's Bar & Grill, in London's theatreland, with £1 from each meal going to the Actors' Charitable Trust. The dishes on offer include:

Chicken Risotto à la Richard Attenborough · Brandy Snaps à la Vivien Leigh
Blanquette de Veau à la Laurence Olivier · Shrimps Romolade à la Sir John Gielgud
Eggs Florentine à la Peter Ustinov · Warsaw Concerto à la Noël Coward

————————————— CRITICS' CIRCLE AWARDS · 2005 —————————————

Best new play ....*Harvest* · Richard Bean
Best musical.. *Billy Elliot*
Best actor...................................Simon Russell Beale · *The Philanthropist*
Best actress...Eve Best · *Hedda Gabler*
Best Shakespearean performance..........................Kevin Spacey · *Richard II*
Best director...................................Michael Grandage · *The Wild Duck*

PRINCIPAL REGIONAL THEATRES

BATH THEATRE ROYAL · Sawclose, BA1................................01225 448 844
BELFAST LYRIC THEATRE · Ridgeway St, BT9.......................02890 381 081
BIRMINGHAM REP · Broad St, B1.....................................01212 364 455
BOLTON OCTAGON THEATRE · Howell Croft South, BL1 ....01204 520 661
BRIGHTON THEATRE ROYAL · New Rd, BN1.......................08700 606 650
BRISTOL OLD VIC · King St, BS1..................................... 01179 877 877
CANTERBURY MARLOWE THEATRE · The Friars, CT1...............01227 787 787
CARDIFF NEW THEATRE · Park Place, CF10.........................02920 878 889
CLWYD THEATRE CYMRU · Civic Centre, Mold, CH7...............01352 756 331
COLCHESTER MERCURY THEATRE · Balkerne Gate, CO1...........01206 573 948
COVENTRY BELGRADE THEATRE · Belgrade Sq, CV1 .... 02476 553 055
EDINBURGH ROYAL LYCEUM THEATRE · Grindlay St, EH3 ....01312 484 848
EDINBURGH TRAVERSE THEATRE · Cambridge St, EH1 ....01312 281 404
GLASGOW KING'S THEATRE · Bath St, G2 ....01412 401 111
LIVERPOOL PLAYHOUSE · Williamson Sq, L1......................01517 094 776
MANCHESTER ROYAL EXCHANGE · St Ann's Sq, M2...............01618 339 833
MILTON KEYNES THEATRE · Marlborough Gate, MK9 ....01908 606 090
NORWICH THEATRE ROYAL · Theatre St, NR2......................01603 630 000
OXFORD PLAYHOUSE · Beaumont St, OX1..........................01865 305 305
PLYMOUTH THEATRE ROYAL · Royal Parade, PL1 ....01752 267 222
ROYAL SHAKESPEARE · Waterside, Stratford-upon-Avon, CV37 .....08706 091 110
SOUTHAMPTON NUFFIELD THEATRE · University Rd, SO17........02380 671 771
YORK THEATRE ROYAL · St Leonard's Place, YO1 ....01904 623 568

WEST END BOX OFFICE FIGURES

In January 2006, the Society of London Theatre reported record-breaking box office figures for 2005. During the year, 12·1m attended a London West End show, generating revenues of £375,163,399. The most popular shows in 2005 were:

Top musicals		Top plays	
Billy Elliot	*The Lion King*	*Mary Stuart*	*Festen*
Mary Poppins	*Mamma Mia*	*Don Carlos*	*The History Boys*
Guys and Dolls		*Journey's End*	

TONY AWARDS · 2006

Best play...*The History Boys*
Best musical...*Jersey Boys*
Best leading actor in a play......................Richard Griffiths · *The History Boys*
Best leading actress in a play...........................Cynthia Nixon · *Rabbit Hole*
Best featured actor in a play...........................Ian McDiarmid · *Faith Healer*
Best featured actress in a play..................Frances de la Tour · *The History Boys*
Best direction of a play.........................Nicholas Hytner · *The History Boys*

IF.COMEDDIES AWARD · 2006

In 2006, Perrier ended its sponsorship of Edinburgh Fringe's comedy awards, and Halifax-offshoot Intelligence Finance was named as its replacement. On 26 August, 2006, the £8,000 award (officially called the IF.comeddies, though inevitably nicknamed the 'Iffies') went to Phil Nichol for *The Naked Racist*. Josie Long was named Best Newcomer, and Mark Watson won the Panel Prize for 'comedy spirit'.

WINNER & NOMINEES 2006		PREVIOUS WINNERS	
PHIL NICHOL	*The Naked Racist*	2005	Laura Solon
David O'Doherty	*is my Name*	2004	Will Adamsdale
Paul Sinha	*Saint or Sinha*	2003	Demetri Martin
Russell Howard	*Wandering*	2002	Daniel Kitson
We Are Klang	*Klangbang*	2001	Garth Merenghi

THE BEST ONE-LINERS

A poll by UKTV Gold, in August 2006, revealed the nation's favourite one-liners:

Garlic bread † – *it's the future. I've tasted it.* – Brian Potter · *Phoenix Nights*

So, what first attracted you to millionaire Paul Daniels? – Mrs Merton to Debbie McGee · *The Mrs Merton Show*

If you were to ask me to name three geniuses, I probably wouldn't say Einstein, Newton ... I'd go Milligan, Cleese, Everett, Sessions. – David Brent · *The Office*

I'm not a Fascist. I'm a priest. Fascists dress up in black and tell people what to do. Whereas priests ... more drink? – Father Ted · *Father Ted*

He's mad! He's mad. He's madder than Mad Jack McMad, the winner of this year's Mr Madman competition. Edmund Blackadder · *Blackadder*

† Garlic bread is one of the many essential items employed to ward off blood-sucking vampires.

BRITISH COMEDY AWARDS · 2005

Best TV comedy actor	Chris Langham · *The Thick of It*
Best TV comedy actress	Ashley Jensen · *Extras*
Best comedy entertainment personality	Paul O'Grady
Best comedy newcomer	Ashley Jensen · *Extras*
Best new TV comedy	*The Thick of It*
Best TV comedy	*Little Britain*
Best TV comedy drama	*Shameless*
Best comedy entertainment programme	*The X Factor*
Best international comedy TV show	*The Simpsons*
The people's choice award	*Ant and Dec's Saturday Night Takeaway*
Ronnie Barker writer of the year	Matt Lucas & David Walliams
Outstanding contribution to comedy	Julie Walters & Victoria Wood

READY-TO-WEAR FASHION WEEKS

NEW YORK
February & September
www.olympusfashionweek.com
Who shows: *Ralph Lauren, Vera Wang,*
Diane Von Furstenberg, Calvin Klein,
Zac Posen, Oscar de la Renta,
Michael Kors, Donna Karan

MILAN
February & September/October
www.cameramoda.it
Who shows: *Gucci, Armani, Prada,*
Dolce & Gabbana, Moschino, Versace,
Roberto Cavalli, Max Mara,
Burberry Prorsum, Fendi

LONDON
February & September
www.londonfashionweek.co.uk
Who shows: *Aquascutum, Ben de Lisi,*
Paul Smith women, Nicole Farhi,
Clements Ribeiro, Betty Jackson,
Margaret Howell, Ghost

PARIS
February/March & October
www.modeaparis.com
Who shows: *Stella McCartney, Chanel,*
Vivienne Westwood, Jean Paul Gaultier,
John Galliano, Issey Miyake,
Christian Dior, Chloé, Lanvin

According to *Vogue*, key trends for Autumn/Winter 2006/07 include: clutch bags, platform shoes, elbow-length gloves, red, chunky knits, black & white, eighties vibe, fur trim, Highland fling, opulence, grey, boyish, short skirts (especially over leggings), voluminous skirts, and ladylike styles.

GRAZIA'S MOST STYLISH BRITISH WOMEN EVER

1 . . . . Kate Moss	8 . . . . . Victoria Beckham	15 . . . . . . Jean Shrimpton
2 . . . . Sienna Miller	9 . . . . Elizabeth Taylor	16 . . . . Joanna Lumley
3 . . . . Keira Knightley	10 . . . . Rachel Weisz	17 . . . . Phoebe Philo
4 . . . . Princess Diana	11 . . . . . . Erin O'Connor	18 . . . . Vivien Leigh
5 . . . . . . Stella McCartney	12 . . . . Peaches Geldof	19. Kristin Scott Thomas
6 . . . . Twiggy	13. Catherine Zeta-Jones	20 . . . . Kate Winslet
7 . . . . Cat Deeley	14 . . . . Lily Cole	[Source: *Grazia* · Feb 2006]

SCENTS OF THE FAMOUS

David Beckham . . . . *Instinct*	Alan Cumming‡ . . . . *Cumming*
Naomi Campbell . . . . *Naomi Campbell*	Sarah Jessica Parker . . . . *Lovely*
Jade Goody . . . . *Shh…* †	Ashanti . . . . *Precious Jewel*
Bo Derek . . . *Bless the Beasts* [a dog perfume]	Shania Twain . . . . *Shania by Stetson*
Sean 'Diddy' Combs . . . . . . *Unforgivable*	Maria Sharapova . . . . . *Maria Sharapova*

† Goody reportedly called her fragrance 'Shh …', because it was what people kept saying to her.
‡ Alan's range also includes: *Cumming Clean* (a body wash); *Cumming Off Buff* (a body scrub); *Cumming All Over* (a body lotion); and *Cumming In A Bar* ('a big hard soap you'll want to drop in the shower!') ❦ In 2006's prestigious 'FiFi Awards' for perfume, *euphoria* by Calvin Klein (a mix of pomegranate, persimmon, and black orchid) won the 'Women's Luxe' award, and *Armani Code* by Giorgio Armani (lemon and bergamot, with hints of orange tree blossom) won 'Men's Luxe'.

THE FACE OF...

Asda .... Colleen McLoughlin
Chanel .... Keira Knightley
Coke Zero .... Cheryl Tweedy
Gap .... Natasha Bedingfield
H&M .... Madonna
Holland & Barrett .... Kim Wilde
Lancôme .... Clive Owen
Louis Vuitton .... Lindsay Lohan
Marks & Spencer .... Twiggy
Matalan .... Gavin Henson
Moschino .... Lily Cole
Nobby's Nuts .... Noddy Holder
Nourkrin . Lee Sharpe & Cheryl Baker
Omega .... Pierce Brosnan
Pepe Jeans .... Sienna Miller
T-Mobile (USA) .. Catherine Zeta-Jones
TAG Heuer .... Tiger Woods
Walkers Crisps .... Charlotte Church

HIGH ST FASHION

Drapers' 10 most influential high-street movers and shakers in 2005:

1 .... Arthur Ryan · *Primark*
2 .... Stuart Rose · *M&S*
3 .... Philip Green · *Arcadia Group*
4 .... Phil Wrigley · *New Look*
5 .... Jane Shepherdson · *Top Shop*
6 .... *The iPod*
7 .... Julia Reynolds · *Tesco*
8 .... Paul Sweetenham · *TK Maxx*
9 .... Peter Simon · *Monsoon*
10 .... Richard Bradbury · *River Island*

According to research by Verdict, *Marks & Spencer* had the largest share of the womenswear market in 2006, with 12%, followed by *Top Shop* with 9%, and *Next* with 7%.

BRITISH FASHION AWARDS · 2005

Designer of the year .... Christopher Bailey for Burberry
Best menswear designer .... Carlo Brandelli
Best accessories designer .... Stephen Jones
Best new designer .... Duro Olowu
Best model .... Karen Elson
Outstanding achievement in fashion .... Suzy Menkes OBE

HOUSE DESIGNERS

Aquascutum .... Michael Hertz
Balenciaga .... Nicolas Ghesquiere
Burberry .... Christopher Bailey
Chanel .... Karl Lagerfeld
Christian Dior .... John Galliano
Fendi .... Karl Lagerfeld
Givenchy .... Riccardo Tisci
Gucci .... Frida Giannini
Lanvin .... Alber Elbaz
Louis Vuitton .... Marc Jacobs
Marni .... Consuelo Castiglioni
Missoni .... Angela Missoni
Prada .... Miuccia Prada
Yves Saint Laurent .... Stefano Pilati

ELLE STYLE AWARDS

Most stylish   *winner*
Actor .... Matt Dillon
Actress .... Rachel Weisz
Male TV star .... James McAvoy
Female TV star .... Mischa Barton
TV show .... The OC
Music star .... Sugababes
Woman of the year ... Charlize Theron
Levi's hot look .... June Sarpong
Style icon .... Elle MacPherson
Model .... Erin O'Connor
British designer .... Luella Bartley
International designer . Roland Mouret
Outstanding contrib. ... Karl Lagerfeld

──────────── A DANCING GENE (?) ────────────

Research published in the September 2005 issue of *Public Library of Science Genetics* suggested that genetics may in part explain why some are more interested in dance than others. Researchers examined three groups: current performing dancers and advanced dancing students, competitive athletes, and those who were neither dancers nor athletes. Researchers found that dancers were much more likely to carry variants of the genes AVPR1a and SLC6A4. Animal studies have shown that AVPR1a may influence social communication and bonding, and SLC6A4 regulates the level of the neurotransmitter serotonin, which has been linked to the experience of spirituality. A further personality questionnaire indicated that dancers tended to be more spiritual, with a greater need for social contact. The researchers concluded that as a 'type', dancers tend to have a 'heightened sense of communication, often of a symbolic and ceremonial nature, and a strong spiritual personality trait'. A fondness for tulle is not thought to be genetically determined.

──── GENÉE INTERNATIONAL BALLET COMPETITION ────

The Genée International Ballet Competition is the Royal Academy of Dance's most prestigious contest for young dancers aged 14–19 years. In 2006, the gold medal and £5,000 were awarded to 18-year-old Italian dancer Valentino Zucchetti.

April 2006 saw the inaugural final of the Fonteyn Nureyev Young Dancers Competition at the Lowry, Salford. The competition aims to reward dancers aged 10–13. The winners of the £1,500 prize were Oliver Taylor (aged 11) for Level 1, and Claire Jobanputra (aged 13) for Level 2.

──────────── NATIONAL DANCE AWARDS · 2005 ────────────

The Critics' Circle National Dance Awards are judged and presented by the critics and journalists involved in reviewing dance productions; they aim to celebrate the diversity of dance in Great Britain. The winners in 2005 included:

Outstanding achievement .... Monica Mason · Director *Royal Ballet*
Best male dancer .... Thomas Lund · *Royal Danish Ballet*
Best female dancer .... Marianela Nuñez · *Royal Ballet*
Audience award ....*Northern Ballet Theatre & Motionhouse Dance Theatre*
Dance UK industry award ....Brendan Keaney
Best choreography: classical .... Christopher Newton · *Ashton's Sylvia*
– modern...Russell Maliphant
– musical theatre...Peter Darling · *Billy Elliot*
Outstanding artist (modern) ....Akram Khan
Outstanding artist (classical) ....Rupert Pennefather · *Royal Ballet*
Company prize for outstanding repertoire (modern) .... *Rambert Dance Company*
Company prize for outstanding repertoire (classical) .... *Royal Ballet*
Best foreign dance company...*Australian Ballet*
Working Title Billy Elliot Award................................Kristopher Spencer

THE STIRLING PRIZE · 2005

In 2005, the 10th Royal Institute of British Architects [RIBA] Stirling Prize was awarded to EMBT/RMJM Ltd for the controversial Scottish Parliament building. The judges said: 'In its context the building manifests itself as an attempt at an organic transition between the city and the drama of the Scottish countryside'.

Client....Scot. Parliament Corp. Body	Concrete used................25,000m³
Structural engineer.........Ove Arup	Exterior Kemnay Granite.....6,000m²
Completion.....................2004	On-site contractors.............. 1,200
Area........................29,321m²	No. of MSP's desks................ 131
Original architect...... Enric Miralles†	Estimated cost of project.......£431m
Number of architects...............40	Budget inflation.................800%

† Miralles died in 2000. ❦ In March 2006, the debating chamber was closed for 2 months after a wooden beam came loose. Further inspections revealed almost 900 other faults in the building.

The other buildings and architects shortlisted for the £20,000 prize were:

BMW Central Building, Leipzig............................Zaha Hadid Architects
Lewis Glucksman Gallery, Cork .... O'Donnell & Tuomey
McLaren Technology Centre, Woking...........................Foster and Partners
Jubilee Library, Brighton....... Bennetts Assocs. with Lomax Cassidy & Edwards
Fawood Children's Centre, Harlesden .... Alsop Design Ltd

FAVOURITE MODERN BUILDINGS

The British public's favourite modern buildings, according to a 2006 YouGov poll:

1 .... Eden Project · Cornwall	6 .... Cardiff Millennium Stadium
2 ....The Gherkin London	7 ....Millennium Bridge · London
3 ......McLaren Tech. Centre · Surrey	8 .....Scottish Parliament · Edinburgh
4 ...Great Court, Brit. Msm · London	9 .... Selfridges · Birmingham
5 ....Gateshead Millennium Bridge	10..............Tate Modern · London

PRITZKER ARCHITECTURE PRIZE

The international Pritzker Architecture Prize honours living architects who have created buildings that contribute to the beauty and functionality of the built environment. In 2006, the prize was awarded to Brazilian Paulo Mendes da Rocha, whose work includes the Brazilian Sculpture Museum, and renovation of the Pinacoteca do Estado. The winner receives a $100,000 prize and a medallion.

Some previous Pritzker Prize winners	1998................ Renzo Piano [ITA]
2004................ Zaha Hadid [UK]	1991............Robert Venturi [USA]
1999......... Sir Norman Foster [UK]	1990.................Aldo Rossi [ITA]

——THE ARCHAEOLOGICAL YEAR 2006 · HIGHLIGHTS——

{JAN} · A large medieval cemetery containing at least 1,300 skeletons was uncovered in Leicester during the building of a new shopping centre. {FEB} · A University of Memphis team found an intact ancient Egyptian tomb (containing a sarcophagus and 5 mummies) in the Valley of the Kings, the first untouched tomb since Tutankhamun's was discovered in 1922. Archaeologists later decided the tomb was in fact an embalming workshop. ❧ Cave paintings were discovered in France which are believed to be 27,000 years old. ❧ A 160m-year-old fossil was uncovered in China; the new species, named *Guanlong wucaii* after the Chinese for 'crowned dragon', is thought to be a forefather of the *Tyrannosaurus rex.* ❧ The largest ever underground tomb in Greece was unearthed near the ancient city of Pella. It is thought the tomb dates back to the power struggles after the death of Alexander the Great. ❧ A *c.*5,000-year-old late-Neolithic circle-henge was uncovered in Cornwall during the building of a dual carriageway at Goss Moor. ❧ Examination of bones from a gladiators' cemetery in Ephesus, Turkey, indicated that the combatants may not have fought to the death. Many of the skulls appeared to show death had been caused by a hammer-blow, suggesting that seriously wounded gladiators were taken from the ring before being killed elsewhere. ❧ An Indonesian village in Sumbawa was discovered perfectly preserved after the eruption of Mount Tambora in 1815; archaeologists described it as a modern Pompeii. {MAR} · An animal recently found in Laos was described as a 'living fossil', after it was discovered to be the sole survivor of a family of mammals thought to have

been extinct for 11m years. ❧ A new dinosaur, *Erketu ellisoni,* discovered in the Gobi, desert was reported to have had the longest neck on record – 24ft. ❧ An ancient skull found in Ethiopia, said to be between 250,000–500,000-years-old, might provide valuable clues on human evolution. {APR} · A fossilised fish was discovered which had wrist joints to allow crawling on land, and a strong rib cage to support breathing outside water. Some have claimed *Tiktaalik roseae* might be the missing link between fish and terrestrial creatures. {MAY} · Figures from a study of early neolithic British skulls showed that those living during the Stone Age had a 1 in 14 chance of being struck on the head, and a 1 in 50 chance of dying from their injuries. ❧ Debate continued to surround the discovery of a hobbit-like skeleton on the Indonesian island of Flores in 2004. Some scientists claimed that the skeleton represented a new dwarf species that had evolved from *Homo erectus*. However, evidence published by Dr Robert Martin in *Science* suggested that the specimen may in fact have been a *Homo sapiens* who was suffering from microcephaly – a congenital disease that stunts brain growth. {JUN} · The first set of well-preserved and intact dodo bones were found on Mauritius, offering the hope of insights into the birds' extinction 300 years ago. {JUL} · Archaeologists working in N. Australia uncovered the fossilised remains of an alarming new species of meat-eating kangaroo. Inevitably, the long-fanged beast was dubbed the 'killer kangaroo'. Also discovered was evidence of a huge carnivorous bird, which they splendidly nicknamed the 'demon duck of doom'. ❧

Sci, Tech, Net

It is, of course, a bit of a drawback that science was invented after I left school.
— LORD CARRINGTON (1919–)

TAMIFLU · OSELTAMIVIR PHOSPHATE

Tamiflu is the proprietary name for *oseltamivir phosphate* – an oral antiviral treatment for influenza, designed to prevent flu viruses from replicating within the body (it is neither a vaccine nor a substitute for one). A neuraminidase inhibitor (NAI), Tamiflu targets neuraminidase – the enzyme found on the surface of flu viruses – and hinders the virus from travelling cell to cell to spread the infection. The drug can be used both for the prevention and treatment of flu, though for full efficacy, Tamiflu should be taken within 48 hours of the onset of flu symptoms. The adult dose is one 75mg capsule taken orally twice a day for 5 days. ❦ Tamiflu is one of two main drugs thought to be effective against avian flu H5N1 [see p.17] – the other drug, *zanamivir,* less conveniently, has to be inhaled. ❦ The drug company Roche acquired the rights to manufacture and distribute Tamiflu from Gilead Sciences in 1996, and the drug's patent expires in 2016[†]. ❦ As the threat of an H5N1 pandemic grew, demand for Tamiflu threatened to outstrip supply. Real and counterfeit supplies of the drug flooded the web (Tamiflu-related spam became rife), and in December 2005 eBay halted a British auction where a 10-capsule course had reached >£100.

Under political pressure from governments worldwide[†] (and market pressure to maximise profits), Roche took steps to increase production. One of the issues affecting Tamiflu's supply is the complexity of its manufacture: the 10-step process takes 6–8 months, and currently starts with the extraction of shikimic acid from star anise pods grown in the Guanxi, Sichuan, Yunnan, and Guizhou mountain provinces of SW China. In March 2006, Roche pledged to manufacture *c.*400m treatments annually by the end of the year, using 15 external contractors in 9 countries. According to Roche, they have fulfilled Tamiflu 'pandemic orders' from >65 countries, with some governments stockpiling treatments for 20–40% of their population. Roche has also donated 5·125m courses of Tamiflu to the WHO for rapid response in flu-hit areas. ❦ While some reports have questioned the effectiveness of oseltamivir for bird flu, Tamiflu remains the drug of choice. As a result, Roche announced a 22% growth in sales during the first 3 months of 2006, to 7·7bn Swiss Francs ($6bn; £3·4bn). [† New drug patents allow the creators a 20-year monopoly of supply. However, international law permits governments to break patents, and 'compulsorily licence' generic versions in the event of severe national health emergencies.]

──────── NOBEL PRIZES IN SCIENCE · 2005 ────────

THE NOBEL PRIZE IN PHYSICS

One half to Roy J. Glauber, *Harvard*

'for his contribution to the quantum theory of optical coherence'

one half jointly to John L. Hall
JILA, University of Colorado & NIST
Theodor W. Hänsch
Max-Planck-Institut & Ludwig-Maximilians-Universität, Munich

'for their contributions to the development of laser-based precision spectroscopy, including the optical frequency comb technique'

THE NOBEL PRIZE IN CHEMISTRY

Yves Chauvin
Institut Français du Pétrole, France
Robert H. Grubbs
Caltech, USA
Richard R. Schrock
Massachusetts Institute of Technology

'for the development of the metathesis method in organic synthesis'

THE NOBEL PRIZE IN PHYSIOLOGY OR MEDICINE

Barry J. Marshall
Australia
J. Robin Warren
Australia

'for the discovery of the bacterium *Helicobacter pylori* and its role in gastritis and peptic ulcer disease'

Glauber's work into how quantum theory relates to the field of optics led him to establish the principles of Quantum Optics. This allowed him to explore the fundamental differences in frequency and phase between sources of light – for example lasers and light-bulbs. Hall and Hänsch built on Glauber's work to develop laser-based precision spectroscopy, encompassing the optical frequency comb technique. This allows the quantum structure of matter to be determined with greater accuracy, facilitating the creation of technologies such as ultra-accurate clocks and improved Global Positioning Systems.

Chauvin, Grubbs, and Schrock each contributed to the development of 'metathesis reactions'. These reactions occur in organic substances and cause the double-bonds between carbon atoms to break, thereby allowing atom groups to change places. Metathesis is now widely used by the chemical industry to make synthesis methods easier, more environmentally friendly, and more efficient.

Marshall and Warren's research challenged the established scientific view that peptic ulcers and gastritis were caused by lifestyle or stress. Through careful observation of ulcer patients, they discovered the bacterium *Helicobacter pylori* was the cause of most types of ulcers. Marshall even went so far as to infect himself with bacteria in order to prove the theory and monitor the curative effects of antibiotics.

──────── AVENTIS PRIZE FOR SCIENCE BOOKS · 2006 ────────

David Bodanis · *Electric Universe – How Electricity Switched on the Modern World.*

—MATHEMATICS · THE ABEL PRIZE & FIELDS MEDAL—

The Abel Prize was created in memory of Norwegian mathematician Niels Henrik Abel (1802–29) who is famous for proving that the general quintic equation is unsolvable algebraically. In 2006, the Abel was awarded to Lennart Carleson for his 'profound and seminal contributions to harmonic analysis and the theory of smooth dynamical systems'. The Fields Medal is awarded every 4 years at the International Congress of Mathematicians, in recognition of past achievements and future promise in maths. In 2006, medals were presented to Andrei Okounkov, Terence Tao, and Wendelin Werner. Notably, the reclusive Russian 'genius' Grigori Perelman was offered a Fields Medal for his proof of the Poincaré Conjecture, but turned down the award, lamenting that he had become disillusioned with mathematics. It was unclear whether Perelman would accept a separate $1m prize for his proof.

—DARWIN AWARDS—

The annual Darwin Awards *'salute the improvement of the human genome by honouring those who accidentally kill themselves in really stupid ways'*. In 2005, the honour went to 'Marko', a 55-year-old Croatian man who wanted to clean his chimney, but lacked a broom long enough for the job. He improvised a makeshift device by attaching a brush to a chain and, requiring a heavy object to weigh it down, selected a hand-grenade, which exploded when he tried to weld it in place.

—IG NOBEL PRIZE—

Ig Nobel prizes are awarded for scientific 'achievements that cannot or should not be reproduced.' In 2005 the esteemed honours were presented to the following:

PHYSICS · John Mainstone and Thomas Parnell (University of Queensland, Australia) *for conducting a very long-term experiment that began in 1927, in which a blob of black tar drips through a funnel, at the rate of approximately one drop every nine years.*

MEDICINE · Gregg A. Miller (Oak Grove, Missouri) *for the invention of 'neuticles' – artificial testicles for dogs who have lost their own.*

CHEMISTRY · Edward Cussler and Brian Gettelfinger (University of Minnesota) *for their tireless investigation into whether people swim faster in syrup or in water.*

BIOLOGY · Benjamin Smith, Michael Tyler, Brian Williams (University of Adelaide &c), Craig Williams (James Cook University), and Yoji Hayasaka (Australian Wine Research Institute) *for their work smelling and compiling the different odours produced by 131 species of frogs while stressed.*

FLUID DYNAMICS · Victor Benno Meyer-Rochow (International University, Bremen) and Jozsef Gal (Loránd Eötvös University, Hungary) *for their seminal paper 'Pressures Produced when Penguins Pooh* [sic] *– Calculations on Avian Defaecation'.*

[Source: www.improb.com/ig/ig-top.html]

——SOME NOTABLE SCIENTIFIC RESEARCH · 2005–06——

{OCT} · Scientists at the University of Tasmania found that eating chillies can help people to sleep better and feel more alert the next day. ❦ A study in the *Lancet* showed that those in their late 40s and early 50s can cut their risk of Alzheimer's by ≤50% by exercising twice a week. {NOV} · Research in the *Lancet* suggested that the 'hip-to-waist ratio' gave a better indication of the risks of heart attack than weight or Body Mass Index – those with a 'beer belly' are most at risk. ❦ The Common Cold Centre in Wales tested the belief that exposure to cold temperatures increases the risk of developing a cold. 90 volunteers immersed their feet in cold water; 90 did not. Over the next few days, >⅓ of those whose feet were chilled developed cold symptoms. ❦ A study in *Neurology* suggested that those with high levels of education or intellectually challenging jobs had an increased risk of developing Parkinson's. {DEC} · Research in the *Proceedings of the National Academy of Science* showed that patients were able to exercise some control over their chronic pain by watching images of their brain's 'pain centres'. {JAN 2006} After years of trial and error, the world's first hydroponically grown rice crop was harvested from a Tokyo bank vault. Hydroponics (growing crops in nutrient solution) could allow four rice crops a year (rather than one), unaffected by adverse weather. ❦ Scientists at the Max Planck Institute for Nuclear Physics shocked climate-change researchers by suggesting that plants contribute to global warming, since they emit *c.*⅓ of the methane entering the atmosphere. ❦ A study in *Science* suggested that humans have an innate sense of geom-

etry. The researchers discovered that the Munduruku Indians (members of a remote Amazonian tribe) had a natural understanding of basic geometrical images they were shown, even though geometry is absent from their culture. {FEB} · Roger Pitman, a psychiatrist at Harvard University, suggested that giving trauma victims the beta-blocker Propranolol for 10 days after an incident, reduced the symptoms of post-traumatic stress disorder. ❦ A British study proposed that forensic scientists might predict a criminal's surname through a DNA sample. Since the Y chromosome is passed down the male line as surnames are, a large enough database of names and DNA could provide police with a possible surname of their suspect. ❦ A study of Romanian orphans found that children who grow up in deprived conditions suffer from impaired growth and lower IQs. {MAR} · A trial began in the Black Mountains of Wales to harvest daffodils grown at high altitude; it was suggested that these plants may contain high levels of galantamine, which has been used in the treatment of dementia. ❦ Paleontologist Dr Neil Clark proposed that sightings of Scotland's mythical Loch Ness Monster were in fact circus elephants bathing in the Loch, leaving only their trunks, the humps of their heads, and their backs on show. ❦ Scientists at MIT and Hong Kong University used nanotechnology to restore the sight of hamsters. The teams cut the optic nerves of the animals, before injecting nanopeptides that formed a bridge of nanofibres to reconnect the severed nerve. ❦ Research presented to the American College of Cardiology indicated that a new statin

—— NOTABLE SCIENTIFIC RESEARCH · 2005 –06 cont. ——

drug, rosuvastatin, might break down the fatty deposits in arteries that cause heart disease. ❦ A study by researchers at the University of Zurich suggested that phobias can be managed by taking the stress hormone, cortisol. ❦ Trials at the University of Edinburgh indicated the success of a new contraceptive pill based on a low-dose of RU486 (a drug used in abortions); it was suggested the pill may also protect against breast cancer. {APR} · The *Lancet* published the results of a successful American trial in which seven patients had new bladders, grown from their own cells, transplanted back into their bodies. ❦ A team of researchers at Massachusetts General Hospital developed a free-electron laser (FEL) that can target and melt fat under the skin. The FEL could provide treatment for arterial heart disease, cellulite, acne, &c. {MAY} · Researchers from Tufts University in Boston studied the 'gender bending' effects of bisphenol A — an oestrogen-mimicking chemical used to make polycarbonate plastics such as bottles and food containers. A mice study by the US Centers for Disease Control and Prevention suggested that bisphenol A 'masculinises' the brains of female mice. ❦ A study showed that Nigerian putty-nosed monkeys were able to put together a number of sounds to construct a primitive sentence, an ability previously thought to be uniquely human. ❦ Research at the University of Toronto suggested that caffeine may cut the time premature babies spend on ventilators, and protect them from lung diseases. ❦ A study at St Andrew's University, Scotland, suggested that girls from broken homes grow up to be less physically attractive. The researchers assessed the bodies and faces of 229 women, and found that those from unhappy homes looked more masculine. {JUN} · Scientists at Guy's and St Thomas' Hospital, London, developed a new technique – pre implantation genetic haplotyping (PGH) – that allows more accurate screening of embryos for genetic diseases. ❦ A team from Ohio State University Medical Centre presented results of a study into alleviating migraines at the American Headache Society. The research showed that patients using an electronic device that emits a magnetic pulse to the brain reported significant improvements in their condition. ❦ Research by Anthony Bogaert at Brock University, Canada, indicated that men with a biological older brother were 30% more likely to be homosexual. {JUL} · The *Journal of Investigative Dermatology* published the results of an Australian trial of a drug that creates an instant tan. The study indicated the drug may protect against skin cancer, but 30 injections were required to achieve a noticeable tan, and some recipients complained of nausea. {AUG} · Researchers at the University of Singapore suggested that brain power in the elderly can be boosted by eating turmeric-rich curries. ❦ A study from the University of Buffalo warned that the drug methamphetamine ('crystal meth') appeared to increase the spread of HIV in those already infected. ❦ Scientists from Japan and Hawaii reported in the *Proceedings of the National Academy of Sciences* that they had produced healthy pups via IVF from the sperm of mice that had died and were frozen 15 years earlier.

WOO SUK HWANG

In January 2006, an investigation by Seoul National University concluded that data used by celebrated S. Korean scientist Dr Woo Suk Hwang in his work on human cloning had been 'intentionally fabricated'. The announcement was deeply embarrassing to the scientific community – tarnishing the integrity of published research and setting back fellow researchers working on cloning. Things started to go wrong for Hwang in November 2005, when he was forced to admit that female researchers from his team had supplied their own eggs for use in his research. Further questions from collaborators about his methods led to a full investigation. ❧ Hwang's ground-breaking work rested on two papers published in the prestigious journal *Science*. The first, published in February 2004, claimed that Hwang's team had created the world's first cloned human embryos. The second, in May 2005, went further, reporting that he had created 11 stem cell lines tailored to individual patients. Such therapeutic cloning could provide new treatments for diseases like Parkinson's and diabetes. Since others had based their research on the techniques described by Hwang, the news that his results were falsified left many scientists with no working blueprint. ❧ Hwang's fall from grace was spectacular: he had been treated like a superstar in S. Korea; granted the title of 'Supreme Scientist' by the government; given large sums of money to fund his research; and gifted as many free first-class flights on Korean Air as he desired. Despite his public disgrace, Hwang claimed that the fabrications were carried out without his knowledge. He nevertheless stated that he could not lift his head for shame and added, 'the use of fake data ... is what I have to take full responsibility for as first author. I acknowledge all of that and apologise once again'. (Hwang's only comfort was the confirmation that his Afghan hound, Snuppy, was indeed the world's first cloned dog.) ❧ In March 2006, Hwang was sacked from his professorship at Seoul National University. At the time of writing Hwang was on trial in S. Korea for fraud and embezzlement.

BREAKTHROUGHS OF THE YEAR · 2005

Science magazine's prestigious list of the major scientific breakthroughs of 2005:

Evolution in Action......... *genome sequencing advanced understanding of evolution*
Planetary Blitz............*a plethora of space explorations shed new light on the galaxy*
Blooming Marvellous... *new discoveries into genes that control the flowering of plants*
Neutron Stars ....*advances in technology gave more information on neutron stars*
Miswiring the Brain .... *research into genes produced links to brain disorders*
Geochemical Turmoil....*isotopes revealed the formation of Earth was not as supposed*
Protein Portrait...... *model of nerve & muscle protein revealed its molecular structure*
Change in Climate.........*further evidence for human influence on global warming*
Systems Biology Signals its Arrival........*new methods for understanding cell signals*
ITER .... *International Thermonuclear Experimental Reactor to be built in France*

———————— ANIMAL EXTREMISTS ————————

The rise in activity by 'extreme' animal rights protesters has been seen in a number of countries – to the extent that the FBI has classified the 'animal rights movement' (ARM) as the greatest US domestic terrorist threat. [ARM is used as an umbrella term for a range of disparate groups.] 2006 data from the Association of the British Pharmaceutical Industry show that, although overall incidence of criminal activities by ARM has decreased since 2004, the ARM's tactics have increased in violence, with 8 car bombs and 6 personal attacks. Below is a summary of illegal incidents against British researchers who use animals in scientific and medical experiments:

Incident	2002	2003	2004	2005
Abusive letters/texts	23	38	108	36
Capitulations†	n/a	n/a	113	103
Criminal damage	60	146	177	85
Demonstrations – advertised	330	298	397	297
Demonstrations – not advertised	500	616	680	908
Average number of protesters	13·9	12·5	10·1	8·9
Total arrests at demos	178	46	124	67
Home visits – director	69	113	90	38
Home visits – employee	66	146	89	12
Incendiary device	2	0	1	8
Personal attack	7	1	0	6

† Capitulation occurs when intimidation, threats, or actual violence by animal rights activists results in third-party companies withdrawing goods or services to animal research scientists. ❦ In February 2006, 16-year-old Laurie Pycroft founded the group Pro-Test and organised a hundred-strong protest march in favour of animal testing at Oxford's biomedical research centre [see also p.88].

———————— DISEASE MONGERING ————————

According to research by David Henry and Ray Moynihan of Newcastle University, Australia, some drug companies may be 'disease mongering' – creating markets for their drugs by inventing or overstating illnesses. The study, published in the *Public Library of Science* in April 2006, argued that some in the drug industry were medicalizing normal aspects of life, such as the menopause; re-branding minor conditions as widespread and serious; and describing what may be risk factors as diseases. Such an inflationary approach, it is suggested, leads the public to believe that some conditions, such as 'sexual dysfunction', are far more prevalent than they really are, and that the solution to these 'problems' can be found in the products produced by drug companies. The study claimed that, 'disease-mongering is the selling of sickness that widens the boundaries of illness and grows the markets for those who sell and deliver treatments ... It is exemplified mostly explicitly by many pharmaceutical industry-funded disease awareness campaigns – more often designed to sell drugs than to illuminate or to inform or educate about the prevention of illness or the maintenance of health'. Henry and Moynihan called for diseases to be defined by independent bodies free from any commercial interests.

———————————————— HABSTARS ————————————————

At the 2006 meeting of the American Association for the Advancement of Science, astronomer Margaret Turnbull of the Carnegie Institution, Washington, DC, proposed a list of 'habstars' stars most likely to have habitable zones). Turnbull analysed a number of criteria, such as the age of the star (it should be over 3bn years old to allow complex life to develop), and the amount of iron in its atmosphere (stars need at least 50% of the iron content of our Sun for planets to form). From over 17,000 habitable stellar systems, Turnbull advised that those seeking radio signals from intelligent life should focus their efforts on the following 5 habstars:

Beta CVn......................*part of constellation Canes Venatici, 26 light-years away*
HD 10307 ....*similar mass, temperature, and iron content to the Sun*
HD 211415.........................*cooler than the sun with 50% of its metal content*
18 Sco ....*part of constellation Scorpio, very similar in form to the Sun*
51 Pegasus......*planet similar to Jupiter orbits the star; terrestrial planets a possibility*

———————————— PLANETARY EVENTS 2007 ————————————

3 January......................Perihelion: Earth is at orbital position closest to Sun
10 February.......................Saturn at opposition (closest approach to Earth)
3 March..total lunar eclipse
19 March...partial solar eclipse
21 March.............Equinox: sun passes northward over equator at 0007 GMT
6 June ....Jupiter at opposition
21 June...............Solstice: Sun directly above Tropic of Cancer at 1806 GMT
7 July......................Aphelion: Earth is at orbital position farthest from Sun
13 August ....Neptune at opposition
28 August ....total lunar eclipse
9 September...Uranus at opposition
11 September ....partial solar eclipse
23 September ....Equinox: Sun passes southward over equator at 0951 GMT
22 December......Solstice: Sun directly above Tropic of Capricorn at 0608 GMT
24 December..Mars at opposition

———————————— NASA'S SPACE SHUTTLES ————————————

Shuttle	operational	years operational	crew carried	no. flights
Atlantis	Y	1985–	167	27
Challenger	N	1983–86	60	10
Columbia	N	1981–2003	160	28
Discovery	Y	1984–	191	31
Endeavour	Y	1992–	130	19

The first commercial space flight in 2004 by SpaceShipOne hinted at the future of space tourism. *Virgin Galactic* is now taking bookings for a planned 2008 space flight, with tickets at $200,000.

KEY SPACE MISSIONS OF 2006

MARS RECONNAISSANCE ORBITER (MRO) · NASA's MRO arrived at Mars on 10 March 2006, and spent the first phase of its mission 'aerobraking' to gain the correct orbit to enable it to collect data. The mission's objective is to investigate the history of water on the planet, and discover if it was present long enough to have sustained life.

STARDUST · On 15 January 2006, after a 7-year mission, the NASA probe Stardust delivered dust samples from the comet Wild-2 to Earth. Scientists hope that the interstellar dust collected from the tail of the comet might provide insights into the formation of the universe which, like Wild 2, is 4·6bn years old. The samples of dust are currently being investigated by *c.*150 scientists across the globe.

VENUS EXPRESS · A European Space Agency (ESA) probe, launched in November 2005, reached Venus in April 2006. Since then, the probe has sent back to Earth ground-breaking images which show a huge 'double-eye' atmospheric vortex over Venus' south pole. It is hoped that further infrared images of the vortex will reveal more about its structure.

CASSINI-HUYGENS · A joint ESA and NASA effort to study Saturn and its moons. In 2006, Cassini sent back radar images which revealed that the areas once thought to be oceans on Saturn's moon Titan were, in fact, large sand dunes. Data from the mission also suggested that Enceladus (another of Saturn's moons) may have a liquid ocean under a layer of ice. Geysers of water were observed erupting from the moon's polar region, implying the moon may be geologically active.

NEW HORIZONS · A NASA mission launched on 19 January 2006, with the aim of being the first to reach Pluto and its moon Charon. The probe (which is roughly the size of a piano) is expected to reach its final destination by 2015.

DISCOVERY · In July 2006, Discovery undertook a 13-day mission during which the crew tested new shuttle safety features and repaired a rail car on the International Space Station. Throughout the flight a number of high-resolution photos of the shuttle were taken, which provided the ground crew with proof that no major damage had occurred during its voyage.

THE PUZZLE OF RED RAIN

In January 2006, Godfrey Louis of Mahatma Gandhi University published a paper in *Astrophysics & Space Science,* which suggested that the mysterious red rain which fell over Kerala, India, for a number of weeks in 2001 may have had an extraterrestrial origin. Louis saw no natural explanation for the 'striking' red rain – samples of which were found to contain cell-like structures with no traces of DNA. Further analysis of the cells was undertaken at Cardiff University by Chandra Wickramasinghe, an expert in 'panspermia' (the theory that life on Earth came from primitive cells carried by comets). Wickramasinghe's research indicated that the red rain cells did in fact contain very simple DNA and might, therefore, be of terrestrial origin. Investigation continues into the origin of the Kerala downpour.

─────── SOME INVENTIONS OF NOTE · 2005–06 ───────

{OCT} · Nicholas Negroponte of MIT designed a cheap laptop (*c.*$100), which he hopes will appeal to the 3rd World. The laptop can be powered by a hand-crank, includes wireless connectivity, and is encased in indestructible rubber. ❦ Stephen Salter, an engineer at Edinburgh University, proposed a system to reduce global warming: a fleet of yachts that spray water droplets into the sky, increasing the whiteness of low-lying clouds that reflect more heat back into space. ❦ Japanese company Denso is developing an in-car system to stop drivers falling asleep at the wheel. The device monitors the blink-rate of drivers and makes a bleeping noise to wake them up should they doze off. {NOV} · Canon of Japan developed a high-resolution ink-jet printer that can print hard copies of images directly from a flat-screen TV. {DEC} · Nissan invented a self-repairing paint for cars. The paint is blended with an elastic resin that, when warmed by the sun, expands to cover small scratches. {JAN 2006} · Elmo-Tech developed an automated home curfew system using voice-recognition. Offenders are phoned at home and prove their identity and whereabouts by repeating a series of vocal tests. ❦ Plastic Logic has developed a 10" flexible screen that, when plugged into a hand-held device, recreates the resolution of a computer monitor. The screen (which can be rolled up) has a number of applications – not least in the future of e-books. {FEB} · Kurita Water Industries of Japan developed a fuel cell that can power a mobile phone for days on a small drop of methanol. {MAR} · Researchers at Boston's MIT Media Lab created a Wi-Fi wine glass

that glows when an absent partner takes a sip, allowing long-distance lovers to share a drink. ❦ A prototype eco-friendly mobile has been unveiled. The phone has a biodegradable cover that contains a sunflower seed; when discarded, the phone will breakdown organically and produce a plant. {APR} · Menssana Research has developed a breath analyser that can identify Volatile Organic Compounds (VOC). The machine is currently used to detect VOCs in the breath of patients whose bodies are rejecting a heart transplant, but in future it may be used to identify the VOCs that indicate breast cancer. ❦ Scientists at the University of Southern California are developing a new wafer-thin material that creates a bright white light when plugged into an electricity supply. The organic light-emitting diode (OLED) is more energy-efficient than standard lightbulbs and gives off a pleasing natural light. {MAY} · US defence researchers have patented a device inspired by circus 'human cannonballs'. The machine uses compressed air to propel firefighters or special forces to the top of a 5-storey building in just 2 seconds. {JUN} · Japanese company Lofty has developed a pillow (the 'Sleep Doctor') that uses sensors to measure body movements and judge the quality of sleep. To aid sleep, the pillow offers helpful suggestions and encouragement, such as: 'You've been sleeping great! Keep it up!' {AUG} · Zenph Studios, NC, have developed software which allows old audio recordings to be programmed into a computerised grand piano, thereby allowing modern audiences to hear 'live' performances from deceased virtuosos like Rachmaninov.

—————————————— DANGEROUS IDEAS ——————————————

Each year since 1998, online magazine *The Edge* has invited notable intellectuals and scientists to answer one probing question – usually with fascinating results. The 2006 question was: '*What is your dangerous idea? An idea you think about (not necessarily one you originated) that is dangerous not because it is assumed to be false, but because it might be true?*' Below is a small selection from the 119 answers offered:

Everything is pointless · Susan Blackmore (psychologist & sceptic)
Retribution as a moral principle is incompatible with a scientific view of human behaviour · Richard Dawkins (evolutionary biologist)
The fight against global warming is lost · Paul Davies (physicist)
There are universes beyond our own · Brian Greene (physicist & mathematician)
The human brain and its products are incapable of understanding the truths about the universe · Karl Sabbagh (writer & TV producer)
Culture is natural · Dan Sperber (social & cognitive scientist)
Modern science is a product of biology · Arnold Trehub (psychologist)
Groups of people may differ genetically in their average talents and temperaments · Steven Pinker (psychologist)
The banality of evil is matched by the banality of heroism
Philip Zimbardo (psychologist)

—————————————————— FLOPS ——————————————————

Flops, short for FLoating point Operations Per Second, are the units used to measure how many calculations per second a computer can make. Standard SI prefixes are employed to show the relative performance level of a given computer:

Megaflops ..... 10^6 flops	Teraflops ...... 10^{12} flops	Exaflops ...... 10^{18} flops
Gigaflops ...... 10^9 flops	Petaflops ...... 10^{15} flops	Zettaflops ..... 10^{21} flops

Home computers generally perform at gigaflops, compared to supercomputers which are capable of teraflops. Supercomputers are used to process calculations with a vast array of variables, such as climate-change models, DNA mapping, and military simulations. To date, only one computer has exceeded 100 teraflops, but new models are improving all the time. The TOP500 project tracks the performance of supercomputers and bi-annually releases a ranking. Its latest top five were:

Computer	manufacturer	country	teraflops
BlueGene/L eServer Blue Gene	IBM	USA	280·60
BGW eServer Blue Gene	IBM	USA	91·29
ASC Purple eServer pSeries p575	IBM	USA	63·39
Columbia, Altix, Infiniband	SGI	USA	51·87
Thunderbird	Dell	USA	38·27

[Incidentally, the 'Fosbury Flop' high-jump approach (a backwards jump arching over the bar) became popular after its pioneer, Richard 'Dick' Douglas Fosbury, won Olympic gold in 1968.]

—————SCI, TECH, NET WORDS OF NOTE—————

RINGXIETY *or* FAUXCELLARM · [1] a false sensation of hearing a mobile phone ring or feeling one vibrate. The phenomenon, akin to 'phantom limbs' felt by amputees, is exacerbated by adverts that use ringtones to jog listeners' attention; [2] when a group of people scramble for their mobiles on hearing a ringtone. *Also* RAINXIETY · the stress of driving in driving rain.

SPIM · instant messaging spam.

BLACKBERRY THUMB · the repetitive strain injury caused by excessive use of a PDA. *Also* GAMEBOY PALM.

VIRAL VIDEO · a video clip that is passed around by email. They feature on websites like *youtube.com* and are said to form part of the CLIP CULTURE.

15 MEGS OF FAME · internet equivalent of Andy Warhol's 15 minutes of fame.

PIGGYBACKING · 'stealing' WiFi access from unsecured wireless networks.

CYBERCHONDRIACS · people who use the internet to self-diagnose illnesses.

MASHUP · websites or web applications that mix content from two or more sources to create new services, such as Gawker's celebrity *gawker.com/stalker*

HTM · internet material that is deemed Harmful to Minors.

PROOF-OF-CONCEPT BUGS · viruses created to demonstrate flaws in an operating system that have not (yet) been released 'into the wild'.

VAMPIRE LOAD · 'always on' features (like TV 'stand-by') that suck energy.

SLIVERCAST *or* NARROWCAST · directing media messages to a specific audience. *Also* SILVERCAST · directing media messages to retired people.

NERD BIRDS · aeroplanes on routes that connect high-tech capitals, such as Silicon Valley (San José, CA) and Silicon Forest (Seattle). Such planes have become networking magnets for executives in high-tech companies.

RING-BACK TONES · where telephone callers hear music, special effects, &c. selected by the party they are calling as the ringing-tone sounds.

REBAY · to sell unloved gifts on eBay.

VIRTUAL VISITATION · long-distance access to a child by a divorced parent using web-cams, VOIP, IM, &c.

DUMB TERMINALS · basic computers that draw down applications and other software from the internet.

MP-SHEs · term to describe women who download music from the net.

CYBER FOOTPRINT · what can be discerned about an individual or entity by its presence online.

GOOGLEJUICE · the ability of a website to appear near the top of Google (or other) search results.

BOOT CAMP · software that allows Mac computers to run Windows software.

VINGLE · video singles that can be mixed by DJs like traditional records.

SPOETRY · poems created (or emerging serendipitously) from spam email.

————— SCI, TECH, NET WORDS OF NOTE cont. —————

BOOK · another word for 'cool', derived from mobile phone predictive text: on many phones, the first word that pops up if you enter the letters c-o-o-l is 'book'. In the same way, 'pint' becomes SHOT, 'Smirnoff' becomes POISONED, 'lips' becomes KISS, 'shag' becomes RICH, 'home' becomes GOOD, &c.

ARTCASTING · when museums, galleries, &c. place their audio tours online to attract more visitors. *Also* GODCASTING · religious podcasting.

THE LONG TAIL · the notion (first popularised by Chris Anderson) that the net allows the sale of a vast array of low-demand items as well as the mainstream hits. Crucially, the Long Tail theory posits that the sum of the former may be as valuable as the latter (e.g. the combined sales of all the niche songs on iTunes generating income is at least as valuable as the Top 10 'hits').

GENERATION M · *myspace.com* users.

FREEMIUM · business model where users sign up to a free service, and are then tempted or persuaded to pay for advanced or premium features.

NOPE · Not On Planet Earth: a global expansion of Not In My Back Yard.

AEROTROPOLI · airports (like Schiphol, Amsterdam) and their surrounds that have such good facilities they are used as mini-cities by local residents.

VICE MAIL · the scam of leaving chatty and supposedly 'accidental' voicemails praising a stock, in the hope that investors will think they have stumbled on inside-information and buy.

NET NEUTRALITY · the increasingly controversial idea that all internet content and applications should be treated equally, and that service providers should not discriminate in favour of their internet content or against the content of another – in the same way that phone companies do not ensure faster connections to numbers within their own networks.

ECOLONOMICS · sustainable living via environmentally friendly (e)business.

GREENWASH · fraudulently to portray something as environmentally sound.

DEAD TREE EDITION · a book.
DEAD TREE PRESS · newspapers.

FOLKSONOMICS · the organisation of digital content in a transparent and community-minded manner.

———————— TECHNO HARASSMENT ————————

The Home Office's 2006 *Fraud and Technology Crimes Survey* provided an insight into the level of 'high-tech' harassment experienced by members of the British public. Shown below are those who have received offensive messages, by media:

Group	received offensive e-mail	offensive texts	offensive voicemail
♂	12·0%	3·7%	3·3%
♀	11·1%	4·8%	4·1%
All Adults	11·6%	4·2%	3·7%

——————————— GOOGLE CHINA ———————————

Google announced in January 2006 that it would allow the Chinese government to censor its services, in return for being granted access to China's fast-growing and potentially vast online market. Google has been available in China for a number of years via a US server, but government blocks and lengthy delays frustrated users. The new service will use a server based in China that self-censors to restrict access to sites the Chinese state deems unacceptable. Yahoo and Microsoft already run censored services in China and, in a bid to appear more transparent, Google promises to inform surfers when pages are removed from search results by order of the government. China is one of the most heavily censored societies in the world, and it is thought that >30,000 online police monitor websites, chatrooms, and blogs for subversion. Groups fighting for press freedom have criticised Google for facilitating China's suppression of information – noting that of the 64 known internet dissidents in prison worldwide, 54 are Chinese. Furthermore, some have questioned whether Google's decision to engage with China in this way is in keeping with the company's goal 'to make all possible information available to everyone who has a computer', or their mission statement: 'Don't be evil'. Google's response to this has been that providing no information at all is more inconsistent with its mission. Below are some searches that had been adapted for the Chinese:

'TIANANMEN SQUARE' · Whereas google.com returned sites about the massacre of student protesters in 1989, Chinese users were directed to positive, tourist sites about the square.

'FALUN GONG' · Information on the spiritual group that has been labelled an 'evil cult' by the Chinese government is heavily censored – returned results that were universally negative.

'TAIWANESE INDEPENDENCE' · A very sensitive subject for the Chinese government. Chinese users were taken to sites that quote Foreign Minister Li Zhaoxing, warning that China could not tolerate such an outcome.

'DONGZHOU' · Any reference to the alleged killing by paramilitary police of protesters in Dongzhou village had been removed.

Western users can compare results for a search of 'Tiananmen Square' on *google.com/images* with those on *google.cn/images*. The former returns pictures of tanks and protesters, the latter does not. ❦ In June 2006, Sergey Brin (one of Google's co-founders) signalled a possible reversal of the Google's decision to censor some Chinese content, saying, 'perhaps now the principled approach makes more sense'.

——————————— GOOGLE PORN SEARCHES ———————————

Web-use tracker 'Google Trends' found that in 2005 searches for the word 'porn' had reached an all-time high. Below are the top global locations for such searches:

1 .... Birmingham†, UK	5 .... Delhi, India	9 ....San Diego, US
2 ....Manchester, UK	6 ....St Louis, US	10............Seattle, US
3 .... Brisbane, Australia	7 ...... Sydney, Australia	† Brummies were the 2nd most
4 ..Melbourne, Australia	8 ....Brentford, UK	likely to search for 'kittens'.

——————— COMPUTER GAME RATINGS ———————

From 2003 computer games sold in the UK have voluntarily displayed the PEGI (Pan European Game Information) age-rating system. The ratings are designed to help parents judge the age-suitability of games. The ratings are as follows:

3+ · May show violence in a comical context.

7+ · May include: nudity in a non-sexual context; pictures or sounds may be frightening to young children; occasional violence to non-realistic fantasy characters.

12+ · May include graphic violence towards fantasy characters; non-graphic violence towards humans or animals; explicit sexual description or images; mild swearing.

16+ · May include: graphic, detailed and sustained violence towards unrealistic humans or animals; graphic and detailed depictions of death or injury to unrealistic humans or animals; sexual intercourse without

displaying genitals; erotic or sexual nudity; sexual expletives or blasphemy; encouragement of use of tobacco or alcohol; use of illegal drugs; glamorisation of crime.

18 · May include: Gross violence (massive blood and gore, dismemberment, torture, sadism &c) towards realistic humans or animals; graphic detailed and sustained violence towards realistic humans or animals; violence towards vulnerable or defenceless humans; sexual activity with visible genital organs; sexual violence or threat (including rape); detailed descriptions of techniques that could be used in criminal offences; glamorisation of the use of illegal drugs; ethnic, religious, nationalistic or other stereotypes likely to encourage hatred.

Under the Video Recordings Act (1984) most computer games are exempt from classification by the British Board of Film Classification (BBFC) [see p.154]. However, the increasing sophistication of computer graphics means that images may be realistic enough to come under the Act. Games that depict very realistic images of humans or animals engaging in gross violence, human sexual activity; human urinary or excretory functions; depict images of genital organs; or techniques that could be used in criminal offences must by law be submitted for classification to the BBFC.

——————— INTERNET USAGE BY AGE ———————

Research by Nielsen/NetRatings in January 2006, revealed the most popular internet brands by age group. Youngsters were most attracted to social 'member communities' like MySpace; those in their twenties favoured the traditional web giants (Amazon, eBay); thirtysomethings visited sites concerning finance; and 40–50-year-olds used a diverse range of services. The top brands by age group were:

Age group	≤20	20s	30s	40s
Top internet brand	*Bebo*	*BSkyB*	*Barclays*	*Premium TV*
% of brand's total audience	69%	18%	30%	45%
Visitors in age group (thousands)	1,042	465	564	626

– CONTINUOUS PARTIAL – ATTENTION

Continuous Partial Attention [CPA] is the trend of stretching our 'attention bandwidth' to cope with the myriad demands on our concentration posed by technology. The term was coined by the writer Linda Stone, formerly of Apple and Microsoft, who describes CPA as 'the behaviour of continuously monitoring as many inputs as possible, paying partial attention to each'. Stone, notes that CPA is a 'post-multitasking behaviour'. If multitasking is 'motivated by a desire to be more productive and more efficient', CPA is 'motivated by a desire to be a live node on the network'. Anxious to connect and desperate not to miss any opportunities, CPA 'contributes to a feeling of overwhelm, over-stimulation, and a sense of being unfulfilled'. Indeed, the 'always on' character of technology (such as emails, PDAs, IM, VOIP) compromises 'normal' social interactions (checking your Blackberry at lunch) and, in Stone's analysis, 'has created an artificial sense of constant crisis'. Like wild animals in a continuous state of alert, an 'adrenalised fight or flight mechanism kicks in'. Of the hundreds of emails received each day, Stone asks, how many are 'tigers', requiring immediate action, and how many are merely 'mice'? (Most, in fact, are likely to be spam.) Faced with this profusion of inputs we increasingly turn to *filters* (Sky+) and *blocks* (iPods) to find a signal amidst the noise. ❦ Stone elegantly, and perhaps presciently, calls committed and undivided attention 'the real aphrodisiac'. And she suggests that 'the world may continue to be noisy, but, our yearning and fulfilment are more likely to come from getting to the bottom of things, from stillness, and from opportunities for meaningful connection'.

—WEBLOG AWARDS—

Now in its 6th year, the Weblogs are independent, unsponsored awards, nominated and voted for by the public. Some of the 2005 winners were:

Best new blog...	*bobgeiger.blogspot.com*
Oz or NZ	*timblair.net*
Asian	*xiaxue.blogspot.com*
Afr./M.East..	*iraqthemodel.blogspot.com*
British/Irish	*normblog.typepad.com*
Europe..	*.medienkritik.typepad.com/blog*
Canadian	*smalldeadanimals.com*
Latin Amer. ..	*blogs.salon.com/0001330*
Journalism	*michaelyon-online.com*
Group	*reason.com/hitandrun*
Blog design	*ljcfyi.com*
Photo	*zombietime.com*
Video	*crooksandliars.com*
Humourous	*patriotboy.blogspot.com*
Weblog of the year	*dailykos.com*

—BLOOKER PRIZE—

The first 'Blooker Prizes' were awarded in April 2006, to books that started life as blogs. The top prize of £1,140 went to:

Julie Powell
Julie and Julia: 365 Days, 524 Recipes, One Tiny Apartment Kitchen.

—INTERNET LEAGUE—

The following ranks countries making the greatest and most constructive use of computers and the net in 2006:

1	US	6	Canada
2	Singapore	7	Taiwan
3	Denmark	8	Sweden
4	Iceland	9	Switzerland
5	Finland	10	UK

[Source: WEF Networked Readiness Index]

——WEBBY AWARDS——

Awarded by the International Academy of Digital Arts and Sciences, the Webby Awards reward excellence in web design, innovation, and functionality. Below is a selection of the winners at the 10th annual awards:

Breakout of the year ...... *myspace.com*
Webby artist of the year ... *gorillaz.com*
Activism .... *youthink.worldbank.org*
Best writing .... *newyorker.com*
Best homepage *remembersegregation.org*
Blog – political...... *huffingtonpost.com*
Celebrity/fan ....*npgmusicclub.com*
Humour...................*theonion.com*
Lifestyle .... *epicurious.com*
Magazine.......................*ngm.com*
Movies...... *festival.sundance.org/2006/*
Music...................*fabchannel.com*
News ....*bbc.co.uk/news*
Newspaper ....*guardian.co.uk*
Politics...................*opensecrets.org*
Sports.........................*espn.com*

At the Webby awards ceremony, all winners are limited to a five-word acceptance speech. In 2005, Al Gore, recipient of a lifetime achievement award, accepted the award with the plea, 'please don't recount this vote!'

——TOP INTERNET USES——

Below are the ten top reasons given by British children for their internet use:

age	8–11	12–15
School work	85%	86
Playing games	75	68
Email	29	57
Instant messaging	16	52
Downloading music	15	42
TV programme websites	20	29
Finding out info	13	24
Sports news	13	17
Auction sites	14	24
Listening to radio	7	15

[Source: Ofcom Media Literacy Audit · 2006]

——— eBAYers ———

In February 2006, eBay revealed the places in the UK that have the highest proportion of its (10 million) users:

Norwich	62%	Nottingh'm	49%
Ilford	55%	Manchester	48%
Cambridge	54%	Preston	46%
Reading	54%	South'pton	46%
Lincoln	52%	Bristol	41%

—— WEB MOMENTS THAT CHANGED THE WORLD——

To celebrate 10 years of the Webby Awards [see above], the International Academy of Digital Arts and Sciences listed their ten web moments that changed the world:

1 ....the dotcom boom and bust, 1995–2001
2 .... Drudge Report, a one-man news site, broke Monica Lewinsky scandal, 1998
3 ....Amazon's Jeff Bezos named *Time*'s Man of the Year, 1999
4 ....worldwide elections – widespread use of internet to garner support, 2004
5 .... 9/11 – people turned to email and internet for immediate news, 2001
6 .... Asian Tsunami, citizen reporters first on scene to document disaster, 2004
7 ....court ruling shut down innovative file-sharing site Napster, 2001
8 ....internet coverage of Live8 concert on AOL, 2005
9 ...... Match.com booms – internet became the place to make connections, 2002
10 ....web played central role in discovery of SARS virus, 2003

————————— SOME WEBSITES OF THE YEAR —————————

mostwanted-uk.org . . . . *Britain's most wanted criminals*
number-10.gov.uk/output/page8849.asp . . . . . . *film of a day in the life of Tony Blair*
stuffonmycat.com . . . . *cats with various objects attached*
deadbodyguy.com . . . . *man stages photos of himself dead to get part in film*
ready.gov/kids/home.html . . . . *US Homeland Security advice for kids*
kittenwar.com . . . . *kitties battle it out to be the cutest*
order-order.com . . . *Guido Fawkes' news-making blog featuring British political gossip*
deathlist.net . . . . *predictions of which celebs will die in the coming year*
danielcraigisnotbond.com . . . . *Bond fans urge a boycott of* Casino Royale
usinfo.state.gov/media/misinformation.html . . . . *response to conspiracy theories*
archibot.com/ratings/index.html . . . . *rate your favourite buildings*
housingmaps.com . . . . *Google's maps with Craigslist's property listings*
milliondollarhomepage.com . . . . *selling pixels to pay for college*
bl.uk/onlinegallery/ttp/ttpbooks.html . . . . *15 great books of the British library*
dontdatehimgirl.com . . . . *girls expose their ex-boyfriends online*
gethuman.com . . . . *tips to bypass automated answering systems*
the-bc.com . . . . *The OC – but with Jesuits!*
realultimatepower.net . . . . *the 'official' Ninja webpage*
sfcompact.blogspot.com . . . . *surviving without shopping*
riverbendblog.blogspot.com . . . . *Iraqi blog nominated for Samuel Johnson prize*
siteinstitute.org . . . . *tracks terrorist sources on the net*
president.ir/eng . . . . *official website of the President of Iran*
youtube.com . . . . *watch and share homemade video*
myspace.com . . . . *create your own homepage and network with other people*
myspacesucks.8m.com . . . . *myspace backlash*
nationalarchives.gov.uk/domesday . . . . *Domesday Book online*
thefatmanwalking.com . . . . *journal of Steve Vaught as he walked across America*
spatial-literacy.org . . . . *track the geographical spread of your surname*
pandora.com . . . . *free radio based on your favourite songs and artists*

————————— GOOGLE ZEITGEIST —————————

Ubiquitous search engine Google regularly publishes its *Zeitgeist* list, detailing the most frequent search requests. Below are the top 5 UK searches for some recent months:

2006	1st	2nd	3rd	4th	5th
Aug					
Jul	*Big Brother*	*Argos*	*BBC news*	*World Cup 2006*	*easyjet*
Jun	*Big Brother*	*BBC*	*World Cup*	*easyjet*	*England flag*
May	*Big Brother*	*BBC news*	*Amazon*	*Autotrader*	*BBC sport*
Apr	*eBay*	*air travel*	*Angelina Jolie*	*BBC*	*Argos*
Mar	*cheap flights*	*C'wealth games*	*Nat. Lottery*	*computer games*	*insurance*
Feb	*National Lottery*	*50 Cent*	*dictionary*	*Wikipedia*	*holidays*

Zeitgeist is a German word for 'spirit of the age' (*Zeit* time + *Geist* spirit). Presumably, these lists have been 'cleaned'.

—————————MMORPGs & REAL LIFE—————————

Massive Multiplayer Online Role-Playing Games (MMORPGs, or simply MMOs)
are simulated online gaming environments to which players anywhere in the world
can log on, usually for a monthly subscription. In most games, players control and
customise characters ('avatars'), guiding them through virtual landscapes. The most
successful MMOs are set in worlds inspired by Dungeons & Dragons role-playing, Tolkien-esque fantasy, and science fiction. Thus, orcs, goblins, ogres, elves,
dragons, druids, shamans, and warlocks abound, as do spells, potions, swords, and
armour. (Inevitably, spaceships and extraterrestrials also feature). In June 2006,
mmogchart.com estimated that there were *c*.12·5m MMO subscriptions, of which
World of Warcraft (WoW) had a 53% share. Below is mmogchart.com's estimate of
MMO and WoW subscriptions since 1998 – with some comparative populations:

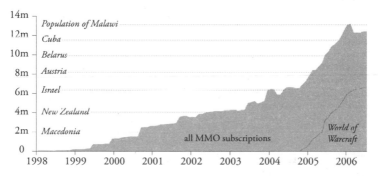

The online gaming economy is impressive. NDP Research estimated that in 2005
MMO subscriptions (in the US alone) generated >$290m. Yet, a novel feature
of MMOs is Real Money Trading (RMT) in virtual goods, where in-game objects
(weapons, spells, gold, &c.) are sold for hard cash (often via eBay). Some players
('gold farmers') 'grind' out repetitive tasks to create objects to sell; others play a
character to a high level before selling it on. In 2005, an *Entropia* player bought a
virtual space station for $100,000; he now makes $12,000 a month rent. And, in
a disturbing parallel to real-life capitalism, workers in Mexico, China, Vietnam,
Eastern Europe, &c., play MMOs for sweatshop wages to create online goods for
affluent players. Despite most games prohibiting RMT, estimates of this grey market
range from $300m–$800m. Keen to cash in, some games now have their own RMT
markets – in *Entropia*, the Project Entropia Dollar (PED) can be exchanged for
real money via ATMs (10 PED=1 US$). While the tax implications of RMT remain
baffling, they may prove simple compared to the ethical and legal dilemmas posed
by MMOs, in which real life (im)morality is mirrored online. Many players now join
together to protect themselves from online 'griefers' (bullies), 'Pkers' (player killers),
cheats, and mercenaries. As 'criminal' acts increase online, real-life risks also grow.
Already, courts are ruling on virtual theft and fraud (and, presumably, soon assault),
and on the legality of online punishments (like account suspension, banishment,
or crucifixion). As MMOs become more complex, popular, and lucrative, it seems
inevitable that the boundary between the virtual and the real will increasingly blur.

──────────────LOVE ONLINE──────────────

Increasingly people are using the internet to find love and manage their love lives. A 2006 study by PEW Internet and American Life Project found that 74% of single web users in America have taken part in at least one online dating activity. Below are the percentages of those who have used the internet for romantic endeavours:

Flirted with someone online...40%
Visited an online dating site..37%
Asked someone on a date online...28%
Searched online for information on someone you dated in the past............18%
Maintained a long-distance relationship online 18%
Searched online for information about someone you are currently dating 17%
Broken up with someone online 9%

────────────── TEENAGE MOBILE PHONE USE ──────────────

The chart bellow illustrates how teenagers (aged 12–15) use their mobile phones:

Text messages	93%		Photo messages	21
Calls	86		Making videos	11
Playing games	43		Internet access	11
Taking photos	41		Video messages	7

[Source: Ofcom Media Literacy Audit, 2006]

────────────── INTERNET USE WORLDWIDE ──────────────

According to research by comScore Networks, 694m people (aged ≥15) worldwide used the internet (in March 2006) – 14% of the population in that age group. And, while the US accounts for a *c.*22% of global users, this represents a decline from a decade ago, when it had two-thirds of users. Below are some online populations:

Online population	*visitors* (m)	*%*			
Worldwide	694·3	100·0	Germany	31·8	4·6
United States	152·1	21·9	United Kingdom	30·2	4·3
China	74·7	10·8	South Korea	24·7	3·5
Japan	52·1	7·5	France	23·9	3·4
			Canada	18·9	2·7

comScore further analysed average monthly hours spent online in various countries:

hours/month online					
World average	31·3	Netherlands	43·5	Portugal	39·8
Israel	57·5	Taiwan	43·2	Canada	38·4
Finland	49·3	Sweden	41·4	(US	29·3)
South Korea	47·2	Brazil	41·2	(UK	29·2)
		Hong Kong	41·2	[March 2006]	

——————ON MOBILE PHONES, TEXTING, &c.——————

Ultra-orthodox Jews are forbidden from using new-generation mobile phones because they offer access to the worldly temptations of film, internet, photos, and text messaging. However, in 2006, Mirs Communication, a subsidiary of Motorola, developed a 'kosher mobile' approved by the Rabbinical Committee for Communications. It is a call-only service, stripped of potential distractions (>10,000 numbers for phone sex and dating services are blocked), and it has a biased tariff structure that encourages members of the network to stick to 'kosher-to-kosher' calls. The service was launched in Israel and is expected to spread to America and beyond. (It has, ironically, already been embraced by conservative Islamic groups who are equally concerned with moral rectitude.) The invention of kosher mobiles is the latest development in 'faith phones' that offer services like: religious ringtones; prayers and sermons by text; digital *muezzin* calls to prayer; and internal compasses to identify the direction of Mecca. ❦ The think-tank Future Laboratory recently reported that the old Australian custom of burying the dead with their favourite status symbol has been revived, with more people requesting to be buried with their mobile. ❦ The mobile phone market has also benefited from the rise in taphephobia – the primal (and perhaps reasonable) fear of being buried alive. In South Africa, taphephobia is compounded by the widespread belief that witches can cause a death-like trance. To counteract this menace, morticians have begun advertising special 'burial' mobiles, with extra-long battery life. ❦ In the Muslim world even marriage customs have been affected by the rise of the mobile phone. Islamic Sharia law allows instant divorce by repeating *talaq* ('I divorce you') three times. Nowadays, an alarming number of (callous or busy) men use three *talaq* text messages to effect a divorce. However, in April 2006, Malaysia's Minister for Women and Family, Shahrizat Abdul Jalil, condemned the practice, calling it 'disrespectful and impolite'. ❦ At a charity event in Doha, Qatar, in May 2006, an anonymous bidder paid a record $2·75m for the mobile number 666 6666 (the number 6 is considered lucky). ❦ Publisher Harlequin Books introduced a daily text message service to send snippets of their romantic novels for fans to read on the go. ❦ Specialised internet and GPS-enabled mobiles in Japan allow tourists to point their handset at historical monuments, restaurants, &c., and receive relevant data about them on their screens. ❦ In August, Sweden became the first country in Europe to introduce a law preventing the use of mobile phones in designated areas of public transport. ❦ Korean mobile phone manufacturer LG Electronics has produced a new phone to prevent drunk dialling. The LP4100 includes a built-in breathalyser which can be linked to certain numbers in the phone book, to prevent embarrassing late-night drunken rants to an ex. ❦ The 'Mosquito' is a device that emits a particularly unpleasant noise at a frequency so high that only those <20 years old can usually hear it; it has been used to prevent youths from congregating and causing trouble in urban areas. Recently, the Mosquito's buzz has been converted into a mobile ringtone that can only be heard by youthful ears – causing some trouble in classrooms.

——————— SI PREFIXES ——————— | —— ° C – ° F ——

Below are the SI prefixes and symbols for the decimal multiples and submultiples of SI Units from 10^{24} to 10^{-24}:

10^{24}	yotta	Y	1 000 000 000 000 000 000 000 000
10^{21}	zetta	Z	1 000 000 000 000 000 000 000
10^{18}	exa	E	1 000 000 000 000 000 000
10^{15}	peta	P	1 000 000 000 000 000
10^{12}	tera	T	1 000 000 000 000
10^{9}	giga	G	1 000 000 000
10^{6}	mega	M	1 000 000
10^{3}	kilo	k	1 000
10^{2}	hecto	h	100
10	deca	da	10
1			1
10^{-1}	deci	d	0.1
10^{-2}	centi	c	0.01
10^{-3}	milli	m	0.001
10^{-6}	micro	µ	0.000 001
10^{-9}	nano	n	0.000 000 001
10^{-12}	pico	p	0.000 000 000 001
10^{-15}	femto	f	0.000 000 000 000 001
10^{-18}	atto	a	0.000 000 000 000 000 001
10^{-21}	zepto	z	0.000 000 000 000 000 000 001
10^{-24}	yocto	y	0.000 000 000 000 000 000 000 001

——————— SOME USEFUL CONVERSIONS ———————

A	A *to* B *multiply by*	B *to* A *multiply by*	B
inches	25·4	0·0397	millimetres
inches	2·54	0·3937	centimetres
feet	0·3048	3·2808	metres
yards	0·9144	1·0936	metres
miles	1·6093	0·6214	kilometres
acres	0·4047	2·471	hectares
square feet	0·0929	10·76	square metres
square miles	2·5899	0·3861	square kilometres
UK pints	0·5682	1·7598	litres
UK gallons	4·546	0·2199	litres
cubic inches	16·39	0·0610	cubic centimetres
ounces	28·35	0·0353	grams
pounds	0·4536	2·2046	kilograms
stones	6·35	0·157	kilograms
miles/gallon	0·3539	2·825	kilometres/litre
miles/US gallon	0·4250	2·353	kilometres/litre
miles/hour	1·609	0·6117	kilometres/hour

ºC	ºF	ºC	ºF
100	212	49	120·2
99	210·2	48	118·4
98	208·4	47	116·6
97	206·6	46	114·8
96	204·8	45	113
95	203	44	111·2
94	201·2	43	109·4
93	199·4	42	107·6
92	197·6	41	105·8
91	195·8	40	104
90	194	39	102·2
89	192·2	38	100·4
88	190·4	37	98·6
87	188·6	36	96·8
86	186·8	35	95
85	185	34	93·2
84	183·2	33	91·4
83	181·4	32	89·6
82	179·6	31	87·8
81	177·8	30	86
80	176	29	84·2
79	174·2	28	82·4
78	172·4	27	80·6
77	170·6	26	78·8
76	168·8	25	77
75	167	24	75·2
74	165·2	23	73·4
73	163·4	22	71·6
72	161·6	21	69·8
71	159·8	20	68
70	158	19	66·2
69	156·2	18	64·4
68	154·4	17	62·6
67	152·6	16	60·8
66	150·8	15	59
65	149	14	57·2
64	147·2	13	55·4
63	145·4	12	53·6
62	143·6	11	51·8
61	141·8	10	50
60	140	9	48·2
59	138·2	8	46·4
58	136·4	7	44·6
57	134·6	6	42·8
56	132·8	5	41
55	131	4	39·2
54	129·2	3	37·4
53	127·4	2	35·6
52	125·6	1	33·8
51	123·8	0	32
50	122	−1	30·2
		−2	28·4

Normal body temp.
= 37ºC (98·6ºF)
range 36·1–37·2ºC
(97·7–98·9ºF)

Travel & Leisure

Like all great travellers, I have seen more than I remember,
and I remember more than I have seen.
— BENJAMIN DISRAELI (1804–81)

CRISP COLOUR CODING

In January 2006, Golden Wonder, the iconic snack company which produced *Nik Naks*, *Wheat Crunchies*, *Ringos*, and a wide range of no-nonsense crisps, went into administration. In 1962, the firm produced the UK's first flavoured crisps (*cheese & onion*), and with them set a precedent for the colouring of crisp packets: *salt & vinegar* was light blue, *cheese & onion* was green, and so on. But, as rivals entered the market, this coding was challenged, and now a baffling array of colours exists:

Flavour	Golden Wonder	Walkers	Hula Hoops	Pringles
Ready salted	dark blue	red	red	red
Cheese & onion	green	blue	green	dark green
Salt & vinegar	light blue	green	blue	blue
Bacon	·	maroon	purple	cherry
Beef	·	brown	black	·
Prawn cocktail	·	hot pink	violet	·
Barbecue	·	black	brown	aubergine
Pickled onion	purple	yellowy green	·	·
Roast chicken	light brown	yellow	orangey yellow	·
Tomato ketchup	red	brick red	·	·

BBC's BLUE PETER BADGE SCANDAL

The BBC awards *c*.800 Blue Peter badges a week for hard work or achievement. Holders >15 gain free entry to around 200 British attractions. Sadly, in 2006 these perks were temporarily withdrawn when badges appeared on eBay for prices as high as £130. By June, the BBC had reinstated the badges with accompanying ID cards – a suggestion made by 11-year-old Helen, from Chester, which won her a silver badge. Different coloured Blue Peter badges are presented for a variety of achievements:

Colour	awarded for
Blue	*interesting letters, stories, poems, pictures; appearance on the programme*
Silver	*blue badge holders who do something additional for the programme*
Green	*entries with a conservation or environmental theme*
Purple	*for 12 children a month who spend a day with the Blue Peter team*
Competition (round with a blue ship)	*winners of Blue Peter competitions*
Gold	*exceptional achievements, such as outstanding bravery*

——EUROPEAN MOTORWAY NETWORK LENGTHS——

Belgium 1,729*km*	France 10,223	Italy........ 6,478	UK......... 3,609
Bulgaria 328	Germany . 12,037	Spain 9,910	[Source: Eurostat '02]

———————————— UK MOTORWAYS ————————————

M1 ....London – Yorkshire	M58 ....Liverpool – Wigan
M2 .... London – Faversham	M60 ....Manchester ring road
M3 ....London – Southampton	M61 ....Manchester – Preston
M4 .... London – South Wales	M62 ....Liverpool – Hull
M5 ....Birmingham – Exeter	M65 ....Calder Valley
M6 .... Catthorpe – Carlisle	M66 ....Bury easterly bypass
M8 .... Edinburgh – nr. Greenock	M67 .....Manchester Hyde – Denton
M9 ....Edinburgh – Dunblane	M69 ....Coventry – Leicester
M10 ....St Albans spur	M73 .... Maryville – Mollinsburn
M11 ....London – Cambridge	M74 ....Glasgow – Gretna
M18 ....Rotherham – Goole	M77 ....Ayr Road route
M20 ....London – Folkestone	M80 ....Stirling – Haggs
M23 ....London – Gatwick	M90 ...... Inverkeithing – Perth
M25 ....London orbital	M180 ....South Humberside
M26 ....M20 – M25 spur	M181 ....Bottesford – Scunthorpe
M27 ....Southampton bypass	M271 ....Upton – Totton
M32 .... M4 – Bristol spur	M275 ....Hilsea – Portsmouth
M40 ....London – Birmingham	M602 .... Eccles – Manchester
M41 ....London – West Cross	M606 .... Cleckheaton – Bradford
M42 .... Birmingham – Measham	M621 .... Leeds southern motorway
M45 .... Dunchurch spur	M876 .... M80 – Kincardine Bridge
M48 .... Severn Bridge	
M49 ...Avonmouth – Severn Crossing	NORTHERN IRELAND
M50 ....Ross spur	M1 ....Belfast – Dungannon
M53 ....Chester – Birkenhead	M2 ....Belfast – Antrim/Ballymena
M54 ....M6 – Telford	M3 ....Belfast Cross – Harbour Bridge
M55 ....Preston – Blackpool	M5 .... M2 – Greencastle
M56 .... Manchester – Chester	M12 ....M1 – Craigavon
M57 .... Liverpool outer ring	M22 ..'........ Antrim – Randalstown

——————————SPEED LIMITS & SPEEDING——————————

Type of vehicle (mph)	*built-up areas*	*single carriageway*	*dual carriageway*	*motor -way*
Car or motorcycle	30	60	70	70
Cars towing caravans	30	50	60	60
Buses and coaches	30	50	60	70
Goods vehicles ≤7·5t	30	50	60	70
Goods vehicles >7·5t	30	40	50	60

——————————— POLLUTANT EXPOSURE ———————————

In January 2006, results were published of an Imperial College London study that measured the public's exposure to pollution by different forms of transport. The data were compiled by examining videos of individuals' daily activity, and recording the concentrations of ultrafine particles around them at any given time:

Mode of Transport	*particles/cm³*	Car	40,000
Taxi	over 100,000	Cycling	8,000
Bus	just under 100,000	Walking	5,000

——————————— GREENHOUSE GAS EMISSIONS ———————————

Below are the quantities of greenhouse gases, in thousand tonnes, emitted by different forms of transport in the UK in recent years. Greenhouse gases include CO_2, methane, hydrofluorocarbons, perfluorocarbon and sulphur hexafluoride:

(Thousand tonnes of gasses)	1990	1997	2000	2004
Road transport	112,300	122,507	123,640	127,639
Water transport	17,032	19,299	16,344	27,060
Air transport	20,367	28,044	37,347	38,971
Total transport emissions	149,699	169,850	177,331	193,670
Total overall emissions[†]	801,460	754,793	722,586	731,915

[Source: ONS · † Includes agriculture, trade, mining, construction, and public services]

——————————— SOME GREEN VEHICLE ACRONYMS ———————————

New 'environmental' transport has produced an array of acronyms, including:

CAFE – Corporate Average Fuel Economy · CAFE Clean Air for Europe
EGR – Exhaust Gas Recirculation · FCV – Fuel Cell Vehicle
GDI – Gasoline Direct Injection · HEV – Hybrid Electric Vehicle
ISAD – Integrated Starter Alternator Device · MtC – Million tonnes of Carbon
NZEV – Near Zero Emissions Vehicle · PEM – Proton Exchange Membrane
RFG – Reformulated Gasoline · SOFC – Solid Oxide Fuel Cell
SULEV – Super Ultra-Low Emissions Vehicle · ZEV – Zero Emissions Vehicle

——————————— BICYCLE USAGE ———————————

DfT figures show the comparative paucity of bicycle journeys made in the UK:

[2002]	*% of journeys made by bike*	Germany	11
Denmark	18	Sweden	10
Switzerland	15	UK	2

—————————————— PETROL PRICES ——————————————

The forecourt price of petrol across the UK continued to rise in 2006. Record oil prices ($78·6 a barrel in mid-July) were catalysed by international concern over security of supply, specifically: the threat of sanctions against Iran, the ongoing conflict in Iraq, the Israel/Hezbollah crisis, insurgency in Nigeria, and damage to BP's largest US refinery. However, in September 2006, oil prices slipped and a 'price war' broke out as the UK's largest supermarket chains passed on savings to their customers.

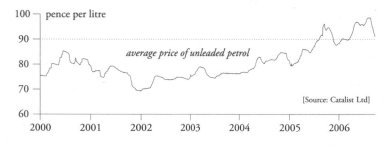

—————————————— DRIVING TEST FAILURE ——————————————

The Driving Standards Authority conducted more than 1·9 million practical tests in 2005/6 [costing £48·50–£58·00]; 113,000 vocational tests [£83·00–£92·83]; and >87,000 motorcycle tests [£58–£68]†. Below are the most common reasons for failing the test:

Fault	number of drivers failed
Failure to act properly at road junctions	149,439
Reversing round a corner incorrectly	119,617
Failure to make proper use of steering	101,318
Problems with parking	94,728
Failure to make proper use of gears	76,945

† Prices are for the driving segment of the test, and do not include theory tests or the instructional components of the Approved Driving Instructor (ADI) tests. [Source: DSA/2Pass.co.uk 2005/6]

—————————————— ELDERLY DRIVERS ——————————————

Cognitive tests were introduced in 2006 for the rising number of elderly drivers in the UK. The Driver & Vehicle Licensing Agency (DVLA) claimed that the present system, where motorists over 70 are trusted to declare any medical conditions, was widely abused. Below is a breakdown of elderly UK driving licence holders:

Age	number of licences		
76–80	844,043	91–95	21,405
81–85	453,773	96–100	1,555
86–90	121,694	≥101	34

[Source: DVLA]

GB PASSENGER DEATH RATES

Mode of transport	1980	1990	2000	2002	2004
Motorcycle	137	110	122	111	105
Walking	78	80	49	44	37
Bicycle	59	49	31	29	35
Car	6·2	4·3	2·7	2·7	2·7
Van	4·4	2·4	0·9	1·0	0·8
Bus or coach	0·5	0·4	0·3	0·4	0·4
Rail	0·7	0·9	0·3	0·4	0·2
Air	2·0	0·03	0·0	0·0	0·0

[Rate per billion passenger kilometres · Source. DfT Transport Trends, 2006]

Research by the AA Motoring Trust found that, in terms of safety, Britain's most improved main road was the A452, which runs from Sutton Coldfield to Brownhills. After the introduction of new speed limits, KSIs (Killed or Serious Injury) were reduced by 73% (or 16 collisions) between 1999–2001 and 2002–04. Britain's most dangerous road was the A682, Jct 13, at M65–A65 Long Preston.

CAR COLOURS

British car buyers are becoming more conservative, according to figures published in 2005 by the Society of Motor Manufacturers & Traders. Cars in sober shades have risen in popularity, but red vehicles, the most popular in 1997, have since suffered a decline of 50%. Disappointingly, there are now only 4,184 pink cars on British roads. The colours of cars leaving showrooms in 2004 are shown below:

Colour	No. sold		
Silver	823,000	Grey	244,000
Blue	585,000	Red	201,000
Black	436,000	Green	117,000

[Source: SMMT]

DEFECTIVE VEHICLES

Below are the percentages of cars that failed their MOT, and the components that were judged inadequate. [Recent years have seen a marked improvement. Source: DfT]

Reason failed (%)	2001–02	2002–03	2003–04	2004–05
Brakes	12·4	12·0	11·1	10·6
Steering	13·9	13·5	12·3	11·4
Lights	16·1	15·8	15·7	14·9
Tyres	8·0	8·2	8·0	7·7
Petrol emission	3·1	2·4	1·8	1·4
Diesel emission	5·5	5·0	4·4	3·8
Other	12·1	11·2	9·9	9·0
TOTAL FAILED	32	31	29	29

―――――――――― DRUG DRIVING ――――――――――

A survey by performance car magazine *Max Power* of its (mainly young male) readers showed a dramatic increase in self-reported 'drug driving' – highlighting a growing national problem where 18% of road deaths (1996–2000) involved drugs.

20% *(of survey respondents)* .... drug drive every day
37% ....have driven after taking cocaine
44% .... regularly drug drive with passengers in the car
46% .... think they are unlikely to get caught drug driving
59% ....have driven after smoking marijuana
67% .... believe drink driving is worse than drug driving

―――――――――― FIELD IMPAIRMENT TESTS ――――――――――

Police officers may ask drivers suspected of being under the influence of drink or drugs to carry out one or more of the following 'field impairment tests'. These are designed to assess the 'observational' and 'psychophysical' capabilities of the driver, and have been adapted in the wake of increased drug driving. The tests include:

ROMBERG 'INTERNAL CLOCK' · head is tilted back with eyes closed for the driver's estimate of 30 seconds (±10 seconds is allowed).

EYE PUPIL SIZE · eyes are examined for the dilation or constriction of the pupils which often denotes drug use. Anything outside the normal range (between 3mm and 6·5mm) is treated with suspicion.

WALK AND TURN · walk heel-to-toe for nine steps along a line, turn, and repeat, counting steps aloud.

ONE-LEGGED STAND · standing on one leg, with the foot raised to 15–20cm counting upward from 1,001.

FINGER ON NOSE · tilt head back and stretch out hands; touch tip of nose with fingers on alternate hands.

―――――――――― DRINK DRIVE LIMITS AND PENALTIES ――――――――――

Country	limit	disqualification (max)	imprisonment (max)
Denmark	50 mg/100ml	24–30 months	nil
Germany	50	6 months–5 years	5 years (if fatal)
France	50	1 month–1 year	2 months–2 years
Ireland	80	1 year	6 months
Italy	80	15 days–1 year	1–6 months
Portugal	50	15 days–1 year	nil
Spain†	50	3 months–5 years	1–6 months
UK	80	>12 months	6 months–10 years (if fatal)

† In January 1999, the limit became 30 mg/100ml for drivers of HGVs & public transport vehicles.
[Source: Royal Society for the Prevention of Accidents · Drinking and Driving Policy Paper, 2005]

USE OF PUBLIC TRANSPORT

2005 DfT figures show how frequently the British use public transport, if at all:

Mode	(%)	every day	≥1/week	≥1/month	≤2/year	never
Bus		12	15	14	15	44
Mainline/Intercity train		1	2	8	17	72
Local/commuter train		2	2	8	10	78
Tram/light railway		–	1	2	4	93
Underground/metro		2	3	8	13	73

SAT(ELLITE) NAV(IGATION) VOICES

In 2006 the Co-operative Bank and *What Car?* magazine asked drivers to name a 'favourite comedy voice' and a 'least favourite voice' to guide them by sat nav[†]:

Favourite comedy sat navigator	%	Least favourite sat navigator	%
Peter Kay	49	Joe Pasquale	35
Homer Simpson	24	Janet Street-Porter	29
Dawn French	12	Cilla Black	16
Jonathan Ross	9	David Beckham	12
Victoria Wood	6	Tony Blair	8

† Satellite navigation operates using signals from Global Positioning System (GPS) satellites. The potential for GPS was first spotted when the Russians launched Sputnik in 1957. Researchers from MIT realised that they could determine the satellite's orbit by noting how the radio signal became stronger as it approached Earth, and weakened as it moved away. This effect, known as the 'Doppler shift', was instrumental in allowing researchers to pinpoint positions on the ground using satellites. The first GPS was launched in 1978, and by 1993 the system was fully operational with 24 satellites. GPS is run by the US military and, for some time, civilian signals were distorted to be accurate only to 100m, compared to the army's 18m; in May 2000, Bill Clinton made public GPS more accurate.

SPEED CAMERA SITES

The number and location of speed camera sites in England and Wales (as at December 2005) were released by Transport Minister Dr Stephen Ladyman, in March 2006:

MOST SPEED CAMERA SITES		FEWEST SPEED CAMERA SITES	
Mid and South Wales	377	Hertfordshire	31
Thames Valley	344	Cumbria	40
London	320	Surrey	42
Lancashire	280	Cheshire	42
West Yorkshire	166	Merseyside	46
Essex	162	Suffolk	48
Greater Manchester	154	Cleveland	56
Avon and Somerset	147	Devon and Cornwall	56

―――――――――― LONDON CONGESTION CHARGE ――――――――――

GENERAL INFORMATION	HOW TO PAY
Current price................£8 per day	Online.............www.cclondon.com
Operating times........ 7am – 6·30pm	Phone.................. 0845 900 1234
Days of operation.......... Mon – Fri	Text message (SMS) 81099

The £8 charge must be paid by 12am on the day of travel; or £10 by 12am the next day. Payment is accepted in shops and petrol stations displaying the CC logo.

―――――――――― LONDON CONGESTION 'TAX' FURORE ――――――――――

An international fracas erupted in 2006, when it came to Mayor of London Ken Livingstone's attention that the US embassy had accrued a large debt for unpaid congestion charges (and the consequent fines) over a 6 month period (Oct '05–Apr '06). The US claimed that the charge was a *tax* and thus did not apply to foreign diplomats who are exempt under the 1961 Vienna Convention. Livingstone considered the payment a *charge* for the service of reduced congestion, from which US diplomats benefited. As the row rumbled on, Livingstone likened one of the ambassadorial team to a 'chiselling little crook'. The table below shows the amount of unpaid congestion charges accrued, over 6 months, by various embassies in London:

Country	*fines over 6 months*		
USA £271,000	Angola........................£127,150
Nigeria £202,150	Sudan..........................£94,250
	Switzerland....................£52,300

―――――――――― ROAD CONGESTION ――――――――――

Figures published by the Department for Transport in February 2006 showed that traffic on all roads increased by 11% from 1997–2005. Below are the roads with the greatest congestion and delays during the morning and evening rush hours:

Morning rush hour

Road	Start Point	End Point	Length (mi)	Delay (min/mi)
A556	M6 Knutsford	M56 Altrincham	4	21·8
M26	M20 Addington	M25 Sevenoaks	10	16·7
A453	Kegworth	Nottingham	10	15·6
M25	J23 Barnet	J16 Uxbridge	22	14·3
M60	J18 Whitefield	J4 Gatley	17	14·1

Evening rush hour

Road	Start Point	End Point	Length (mi)	Delay (min/mi)
A556	M6 Knutsford	M56 Altrincham	4	24·0
A404	M4 Maidenhead	M40 High Wycombe	10	23·8
A556	M56 Altrincham	M6 Knutsford	4	20·7
M60	J4 Gatley	J18 Whitefield	17	14·7
M25	J23 Barnet	J30 Dartford Crossing	32	13·9

——— UK AIRPORTS ———

Airport	passengers (m)	code
Birmingham	9·3	BHX
Bristol	5·2	BRS
Cardiff	1·8	CWL
East Midlands	4·2	EMA
Edinburgh	8·4	EDI
Gatwick	32·7	LGW
Glasgow	8·8	GLA
Heathrow	67·7	LHR
Liverpool	4·4	LPL
London City	2·0	LCY
Luton	9·1	LTN
Manchester	22·1	MAN
Stansted	22·0	STN

[Source: Civil Aviation Authority, 2005]

——— TOP DESTINATIONS ———

Below are the most popular destinations from all UK airports:

	Destination	Flights	% on time
1	Amsterdam	13,624	78·6
2	Edinburgh	13,033	78·1
3	Dublin	11,870	74·5
4	Heathrow	11,078	76·6
5	Paris	10,319	74·2
6	Manchester	9,461	77·3
7	Glasgow	9,412	79·9
8	Frankfurt	7,181	70·7
9	Geneva	6,925	66·5
10	Brussels	5,897	80·4

[Source: CAA, figures from Q1 2006]

——————— CUSTOMS ALLOWANCES ———————

WITHIN THE EU

Passengers may bring back unlimited amounts of EU duty-paid tobacco and alcohol, so long as they can prove it is for their own consumption or a gift for family or friends. They cannot bring back goods for commercial purposes. Bringing back more than the quantities below may cause eyebrows to be raised and questions asked at customs†:

800 .... cigarettes
400 .... cigarillos
200 .... cigars
1kg .... smoking tobacco
110 litres........................... beer
10 litres.......................... spirits
20 litres.............. port and sherry
90 litres............................ wine
20 litres.................. fortified wine

OUTSIDE THE EU

Passengers may bring the following goods into the UK for their personal use without paying UK tax or duty; if the items exceed the allowances then the goods must be declared, and the appropriate tax paid. It is against the law to fail to declare excess goods:

200 .... cigarettes
or 100 .... cigarillos
or 50............................. cigars
or 250g........................ tobacco
no limit................... *eau de toilette*
no limit....................... perfume
16 litres............................ beer
2 litres................. still table-wine
1 litre............ spirits/liqueurs >22%
or 2 litres ...... fortified/sparkling wine
£340 worth‡........... all other goods

† The above are guidelines based on EU regulations; no absolute limits exist. ‡ For items worth >£340: duty must be paid on full value, not just the difference. Car and boat travellers are limited to £150. ❦ <17 cannot bring in tobacco or alcohol. ❦ Gordon Brown's campaign to raise the limit to £1,000 was given greater publicity when Colleen McLoughlin, girlfriend of Wayne Rooney, was fined £3,000 at Manchester airport after returning from a £15,000 shopping spree in New York.

—————————————— PILOT FATIGUE ——————————————

Research into the effects of fatigue on aircrew performance was undertaken on behalf of the Civil Aviation Authority (CAA) in 2005. The deterioration of several important aspects of pilot alertness was examined over a 24-hour period of wakefulness, and measured against the pilot's performance at maximum alertness:

Measure	baseline alertness	after 16h	after 24h
Visual vigilance – response time (sec)	0·43s	0·46s	0·49s
Visual vigilance – % missed	16%	41%	73%
Memory recall – response time (sec)	0·46s	0·53s	0·65s
Memory recall – % missed	5%	8·8%	15·5%
Unstable tracking – RMS error†	329	513	819

† The RMS (Root Mean Square) error is calculated to illustrate a pilot's point-by-point deviation from an intended course. The lower the figure, the fewer tracking errors have been made.

——————————————— AIR PASSENGERS ———————————————

The chart below illustrates the sharp rise in passenger numbers at British airports:

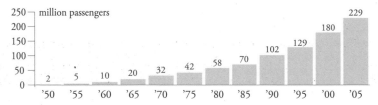

————————————— CABIN BAGGAGE RESTRICTIONS —————————————

On 10 August 2006, new airline cabin baggage restrictions were introduced after the police foiled an alleged terrorist plot to bomb transatlantic flights [see p.28]. Initially, all cabin baggage was banned, except for travel documents and a few small, essential items carried in clear plastic bags. When JTAC reduced the UK threat level from *Critical* to *Severe* on 14 August [see p.22], new cabin baggage restrictions were introduced (that remain in force at the time of writing): each passenger is allowed one item of hand luggage (maximum dimensions: length 56cm, width 45cm, depth 25cm); no liquids are allowed through the security search points, except essential medicines (like diabetic kits) which have been verified as authentic; baby food and milk are allowed on board, but only if tasted by an accompanying passenger. In addition to the standard banned items, the following are also forbidden: all drinks; toiletries like toothpaste, mascara, lip balm, or deodorant; any liquid-based foods, such as yoghurts, jams, or curries; ink cartridges for fountain pens; cigarette lighters and non-safety matches. At the time of going to press these restrictions were under review, and readers were advised to consult baa.com before travelling.

'EU DUBIOUS CARRIERS'

In March 2006, EU countries pooled their respective blacklists of passenger and cargo carriers that failed to meet security and safety requirements, creating a list of 92 'dubious' airlines. Carriers on the list are banned from flying to (or over) all 25 EU countries. European Transport Commissioner Jacques Barrot denounced some of the airlines as 'flying coffins'. The list includes all but one of the 51 carriers operating from the DR Congo, and all airlines from Sierra Leone, Liberia, Swaziland, and Equatorial Guinea. Familiar to many British travellers, Phuket Airlines had all of its aircraft banned from British airspace after an in-flight fuel leak in 2005.

FATAL AIRLINE CRASHES

The number of fatal air crashes (and deaths), according to *Flight International*:

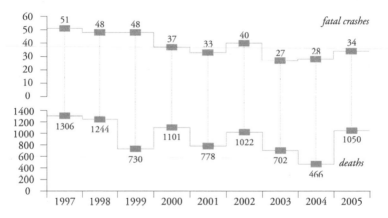

EU AIRLINE COMPENSATION

Air passengers affected by cancellations, overbooking, or delays within Europe can apply to the airline for EU-regulated compensation. The rules apply to all European airlines and to any flight leaving from a European airport. Airlines are exempt if flights are blighted by 'extraordinary circumstances', though what exactly these might be remains unclear. It is feared that the added expense of compensation payments, as tabulated below, may cause the cost of airline tickets to rise:

Length of journey	examples from UK	delay	compensation
up to 1,500km	Paris *or* Amsterdam	≥2 hours	€250
1,500km–3,500km	Lisbon *or* Moscow	≤3 hours	€200
1,500km–3,500km	Tangiers *or* Reykjavik	≥3 hours	€400
>3,500km	New York *or* Tel Aviv	≤4 hours	€300
>3,500km	Doha *or* Hobart	≥4 hours	€600

UNDERGROUND, LIGHT RAIL, & TRAM

Location	type	opened	lines	stations	passengers (m)	volts DC
London	U	1863	12	275	7,606	630
Blackpool	TL	1885	1	124	12	550
Glasgow	U	1896	1	15	43	600
Tyne & Wear	LR	1980	2	58	283	1,500
Docklands	LR	1987	1	34	245	750
Manchester	LR	1992	3	37	204	750
Sheffield	TL	1994	3	48	44	750
West Midlands	TL	1999	1	23	52	750
Croydon	TL	2000	3	38	112	750
Nottingham	TL	2004	1	23	37	750

Underground · Light Rail · Tram Link · [Passenger numbers per passenger km, 2004/05 · DfT]

CRIME & DISORDER ON THE BUSES

Listed below are the incidents witnessed by regular bus users over a period of 12 months, according to the Department for Transport's 2005 statistical bulletin:

Incident	% witnessed
Rubbish/litter	44
Noisy/disruptive passengers	37
Vandalism/graffiti	29
Drunken/rowdy behaviour	27
Smoking in non-smoking areas	23
Fare dodging	14
Begging	12
People being insulted/pestered	9
People being harassed/threatened	6
Drug dealing/drug use	4
Harassment for ethnicity/skin colour	4
Ticket touts	3
People being spat at	3
Physical attacks	1
Muggings/robberies	1
Other	1
None	33

OVERCROWDED TRAINS

Overcrowded train service	company	capacity	passengers
08:02 Cambridge – Liverpool St†	ONE	234	433
16:33 Sutton – Luton	Thameslink	412	618
07:51 Victoria – London Bridge	Southern	635	944
18:15 King's Cross – Cambridge	WAGN	494	713
08:04 Isleworth – Waterloo	South West	792	1,138
18:06 Paddington – Oxford	First Great Western	270	385
06:38 Margate – Cannon St	South Eastern	218	310
06:42 Haslemere – Waterloo	South West	598	845
17:50 Victoria – Rochester	South Eastern	494	681
07:03 Weybridge – Waterloo	South West	792	1,084

† In 2006, the timetable was altered, and the 08:02 now departs at 07:51 · [Source: DfT 2005]

—————————— TRAIN PUNCTUALITY ——————————

Regional	% trains on time	
Arriva Trains Wales	(82·6)	88·4
Central Trains	(74·6)	85·1
First ScotRail	(83·7)	89·5
Gatwick Express	(87·1)	92·6
Island Line	(98·3)	97·8
Merseyrail	(94·7)	93·3
Northern Rail	(87·3)	89·4
TransPennine Express	(78·5)	87·3
Wessex Trains	(86·6)	89·4

Long-distance	% trains on time	
First Great Western	(79·6)	78·6
GNER	(79·2)	88·4
Midland Mainline	(92·9)	96·1
ONE (InterCity)	(83·3)	85·5
Virgin Cross Country	(82·7)	86·4
Virgin West Coast	(74·7)	89·3

London & SE	% trains on time	
c2c	(94·0)	93·1
Chiltern Railways	(93·9)	93·9
First Great West. Link	(84·2)	86·6
ONE	(90·8)	89·8
Silverlink	(89·7)	92·4
South Eastern	(84·5)	90·0
South West Trains	(90·0)	92·2
Southern	(84·8)	90·9
Thameslink	(89·6)	90·5
WAGN	(90·0)	92·7

Figures from Q4 2005/06, figures in brackets are Q4 2004/05. Long-distance trains are deemed 'on time' if they arrive within 10 minutes of timetabled arrival time; London & regional trains are 'on time' if they arrive within 5 mins.

[Source: Office of Rail Regulation 2005–06]

—————————— EUROSTAR JOURNEY TIMES ——————————

From Ashford	destination	from Waterloo
1h 55m	PARIS	2h 35m
1h 40m	BRUSSELS	2h 20m
57m	LILLE	1h 40m
2h	DISNEYLAND PARIS	2h 50m
5h 20m	AVIGNON	6h 10m

In 2007, Eurostar will switch from Waterloo to the St Pancras International terminal. Journey times will then decrease: London–Paris to 2h 15m, London–Brussels 1h 51m, and London–Lille 1h 20m. Since the service began in 1994, 68m people have travelled by Eurostar; 7·45m passengers in 2005. The average punctuality in 2005 was 86·3% of trains arriving and departing on time.

—————————— LONDON STATION DESTINATION GUIDE ——————————

Charing Cross	*serves* South & South-east
Euston	Midlands, North-west of England & Scotland
King's Cross	Midlands, North of England & Scotland
Liverpool Street	East of England & East Anglia · Stansted Express
Marylebone	Chilterns
Paddington	West of England & Wales · Heathrow Express
St Pancras	East Midlands · Eurostar (from 2007)
Victoria	South & South-east · Gatwick Express
Waterloo	South of England · Eurostar (until 2007)

——————————— ITEMS LOST IN HOTELS ———————————

In January 2006, Travelodge drew up an inventory of the items in the lost property offices of their 290 hotels. The objects most often mislaid (or abandoned) were:

1 ....mobile phones and chargers	6.....................electrical gadgets
2................................clothes	7...................cash or credit cards
3..............................toiletries	8..............................jewellery
4.............................false teeth	9.......... hen/stag night 'accessories'
5.............................. laptops	10.................................keys

——————————— UP-AND-COMING DESTINATIONS ———————————

Frommer's travel guides published a list of up-and-coming holiday destinations in December 2005, which (until publication) had escaped full-scale tourist invasion:

1 .... Amador County, California[†]	7.................Margarita, Venezuela
2..........................Belém, Brazil	8.....................Molokai, Hawaii
3.......... Charleston, South Carolina	9................. Ramah, New Mexico
4.................... Glasgow, Scotland	10................. Tasmania, Australia
5.............................Goa, India	† Amador County produced *c.*$200,000,000
6.................. Kenyan Game Parks	(£108,000,000) in gold between 1848–1965.

——————————— CLEAN BEACHES ———————————

A Blue Flag is awarded to beaches across the world that are safe, clean, well maintained, and whose water quality meets European legislation. 120 flags were awarded in England and Wales for 2005/6, an increase of 25 from the previous year. The water quality must meet exacting microbiological standards, with E. coli (faecal coliform) and other bacteria kept within guideline and mandatory limits:

	guideline	*mandatory (must be ≤)*	*compliance(%)*
Total coliform	500 per 100ml	10,000 per 100ml	80
Faecal coliform	100 per 100ml	2,000 per 100ml	80
Faecal streptococci	100 per 100ml	—	80

In 2005, several (mandatory) physical and chemical parameters were also added:

Surface active substances..no lasting foam
Colour .... no abnormal change
Mineral oils..no visible film on the surface
pH..6–9 boundary
Oil pollution.. absence
Phenols .... no specific colour
Tarry residues and floating materials .... absence of floatables and sewage solids
Transparency..........................secchi depth >2m or 'no abnormal decrease'

WONDERS OF THE WATERWAYS

In 1955, Robert Aickman, co-founder of the Inland Waterways Association, named what he considered to be the 'Seven Wonders of the Waterways' in his classic text *Know Your Waterways*. Aickman's selected zeniths points of British canalage were:

Aickman's Wonder	*Waterway*
Pontcysyllte Aqueduct	Llangollen Canal
Standedge Tunnel	Huddersfield Narrow Canal
Devizes Caen Hill Lock Flight	Kennet & Avon Canal
Barton Swing Aqueduct	Bridgewater Canal
Anderton Boat Lift	River Weaver/Trent & Mersey Canal
Bingley Five Rise Locks	Leeds & Liverpool Canal
Burnley Embankment	Leeds & Liverpool Canal

THE LOCK-MILE

The UK has 2,000 miles (3,200km) of inland waterways, most of them developed in the C18th to facilitate trade in materials like coal and pottery. The canals were nationalised in 1947, and are now used principally for leisure purposes. Because the wash from fast-moving narrowboats can wear away the banks of a canal, a strict speed limit of 4mph is imposed; but since the typical craft does not feature a speedometer, and because one must account for the time taken to negotiate locks, progress is measured by a unit known as a 'lock-mile'. Thus the average boat speed, reckoned at four lock-miles per hour, can be divided as shown below:

either:
FOUR MILES *in an hour*
or THREE MILES *and* ONE LOCK
or TWO MILES *and* TWO LOCKS
or ONE MILE *and* THREE LOCKS
or FOUR LOCKS

MARINE ACCIDENTS

Injuries and fatalities recently sustained by crew on marine vessels ≥100 tonnes:

Incident	2000	2001	2002	2003	2004
Death	3	3	5	3	4
Major fractures	11	6	25	26	24
Other fractures	55	62	53	54	45
Strained back	23	28	29	36	45
Other strains, hernias	43	51	48	36	37
Bruising	39	34	33	42	43
Cuts/lacerations	41	40	39	35	40
Other injuries	85	68	70	57	70
Total	300	292	302	289	308

[Source: DfT · Transport Statistics 2005]

——————— UK'S UNESCO WORLD HERITAGE SITES ———————

The United Nations Educational, Scientific, and Cultural Organization (UNESCO) seeks to encourage the worldwide identification, protection, and preservation of cultural and natural heritage considered to be of outstanding value to humanity. To this end, UNESCO has granted World Heritage Status to 812 sites across the globe. The following 23 are the World Heritage Sites in the United Kingdom:

Giant's Causeway and Causeway coast (*added in* 1986)
Durham Castle and Cathedral (1986) · Ironbridge Gorge (1986)
Studley Royal Park inc. the ruins of Fountains Abbey (1986)
Stonehenge, Avebury and associated sites (1986)
Castles and town walls of King Edward in Gwynedd (1986)
St Kilda (1986, 2004) · Blenheim Palace (1987)
Westminster Palace, Westminster Abbey and St Margaret's Church (1987)
City of Bath (1987) · Hadrian's Wall (1987) · Tower of London (1988)
Canterbury Cathedral, St Augustine's Abbey and St Mary's Church (1988)
Old and new towns of Edinburgh (1995) · Maritime Greenwich (1997)
Heart of neolithic Orkney (1999) · Blaenavon industrial landscape (2000)
Saltaire (2001) · Dorset and East Devon coast (2001)
Derwent Valley mills (2001) · New Lanark (2001)
Royal Botanic Gardens, Kew (2003) · Liverpool's maritime mercantile city (2004)
Cornwall and West Devon mining landscape (2006)

——————— NEWLY INSCRIBED HERITAGE SITES · 2006 ———————

Cultural Properties: Aflaj Irrigation System of Oman
Aapravasi Ghat, Mauritius
Agave Landscape and Ancient Industrial Facilities of Tequila, Mexico
Bisotun, Iran · Centennial Hall in Wroclaw, Poland
Chongoni Rock Art Area, Malawi
Cornwall and West Devon mining landscape, UK
Crac des Chevaliers and Qal'at Salah El-Din, Syria
Le Strade Nuove and the system of the Palazzi dei Rolli, Genoa, Italy
Harar Jugol, the Fortified Historic Town, Ethiopia
Kondoa Rock Art Sites, Tanzania
Old town of Regensburg with Stadtamhof, Germany
Sewell Mining Town, Chile
Stone Circles of Senegambia, Gambia/Senegal
Vizcaya Bridge, Spain · Yin Xu, China
Natural Properties: Malpelo Fauna and Flora Sanctuary, Colombia
Sichuan Giant Panda Sanctuaries, China
Extensions approved for: Medieval Monuments in Kosovo, Serbia
Kvarken Archipelago & High Coast, Finland/Sweden

After the 2003 Iraq invasion, American soldiers damaged the World Heritage site of Babylon. Col. John Coleman offered an apology, but claimed that looters would have caused more serious damage.

──────────────── THE COUNTRYSIDE CODE ────────────────

Be safe – plan ahead and follow any signs
Leave gates and property as you find them
Protect plants and animals, and take your litter home
Keep dogs under close control
Consider other people

──────────────── NATIONAL PARKS ────────────────

The Association of National Park Authorities (ANPA) abides by J. Dower's definition of a national park, as noted in his 1945 book, *National Parks in England and Wales*:

An extensive area of beautiful and relatively wild country in which:
The characteristic landscape beauty is strictly preserved
Access and facilities for open-air enjoyment are amply provided
Wildlife and buildings and places of architectural and historic interest are protected
Established farming use is effectively maintained

The fourteen National Parks account for 10% of the UK's rural areas, and are home to nearly 250,000 people. They attract an estimated 150 million visitors each year.

Park	location	designated	area (ha)
Brecon Beacons	Mid-Wales	1957	135,144
Broads	Norfolk/Suffolk	1989	30,292
Cairngorms	Scottish Highlands	2003	380,000
Dartmoor	Devon	1951	95,570
Exmoor	South-west England	1954	69,280
Lake District	North-west England	1951	229,198
Loch Lomond	West Scotland	2002	186,500
New Forest	Hampshire/Wiltshire	2005	57,086
Northumberland	Northeast England	1956	104,947
North York Moors	Northeast England	1952	143,603
Peak District	Derbyshire &c.	1951	143,833
Pembrokeshire Coast	West Wales	1952	62,000
Snowdonia	North-west Wales	1951	214,159
Yorkshire Dales	Yorkshire	1954	176,869

The South Downs attract *c.*32 million visitors per year, more than any existing National Park; since 1999, the Countryside Agency has campaigned for its designation. Below are the estimated visitor numbers for selected National Parks:

National Park	visits per year	National Park	visits per year
Broads	5·4m	Northumberland	1·4m
Dartmoor	3·8m	North York Moors	7·8m
Exmoor	1·4m	Peak District	21·9m
Lake District	13·9m	Yorkshire Dales	8·3m

[Source: ANPA/Countryside Agency 2004/5]

——————————— FOREIGN WEDDINGS ———————————

25% of Britons who wed in the last 2 years married abroad. The top locations were:

South Africa........6%	Las Vegas............4%	Jamaica..............4%
St Lucia..............5%	Antigua..............4%	Greek islands........3%
Mauritius............4%	Rep. Ireland.........4%	Hawaii...............3%

[Source: Direct Line Home Insurance survey, Mar 2006] · The trend for marrying abroad is mirrored by the increase in foreign 'hen' and 'stag' parties. During the last five years, the top destinations, according to Egg Online, were: Spain, 26%; Netherlands, 23%; France, 15%; Ireland, 8%; Czech Republic, 8%; and Greece 7%. ❦ In April 2006 the Public Accounts Committee recommended that consular staff charge revellers for their services if hen or stag parties get into trouble. Consulates are allowed to charge £84·50 an hour for assisting Britons abroad, but rarely invoke this charge at present. In 2005, only 323 people out of *c.*84,000 cases were billed for Consular time and trouble.

——————————— TOP BRITISH ATTRACTIONS ———————————

Free admission	*visits*	*Charged admission*	*visits*
Blackpool Pleasure Beach.........5·9m		London Eye.......................3·2m	
British Museum...................4·5m		Tower of London ....1·9m	
National Gallery ....4·2m		Kew Gardens......................1·5m	
Tate Modern ....3·9m		Edinburgh Castle ....1·1m	
Natural History Museum.........3·0m		Eden Project ....1·1m	
Science Museum..................2·0m		Chester Zoo......................1·0m	
V&A Museum ....1·9m		Canterbury Cathedral ....1·0m	

[Source: Association of Leading Visitor Attractions, 2005]

——————————— STEALTH ROLLER-COASTER ———————————

Thorpe Park opened its Stealth roller-coaster, the fastest ride in operation in Europe, on 15 March 2006. Some of its nauseating specifications, along with those of the other roller-coasters that make up Europe's five fastest, are listed below:

Roller-coaster	*location*	*speed (mph)*	*height (ft)*	*length (ft)*	*G-force*[†]
Stealth	UK	79·5	205	1,312	4·5
Silver Star	Germany	78·9	239	5,315	4
Expedition G-Force	Germany	74·6	173	4,002	4·5
Colossos	Germany	74·6	196	4,409	—
Pepsi Max Big One	UK	74·0	213	5,497	3·5

† G-force is technically a unit of acceleration. To calculate its value, one divides the acceleration of a given object by the acceleration caused by gravity which, at the Earth's surface, is measured at $9·81 m/s^2$ (=$1g$). G-force often manifests itself as a feeling of increased weight; fighter pilots can experience impaired vision or even blackouts if a force of 4–$6g$ is sustained for a few seconds.

——————— HOW TO SURVIVE ... ———————

❦ BEAR ATTACK · If you see a bear and can escape without being spotted, do so! Do not shout. If you cannot escape, show the bear you are human by waving your arms slowly and speaking to the bear, then back away. If attacked, 'shoot to kill' (at the heart), and continue firing until the bear is dead. *Never* try to out-swim a bear [CBC News] ❦ SNAKEBITE · Keep bite below heart level, remove restrictive clothing, and go to a hospital. Do not eat or drink, cut into the bite with a blade, 'use a stun gun', 'freeze or apply extreme cold to the area' [Savannah River Ecology Lab] ❦ CIVIL UNREST · If you are in your hotel when unrest begins, stay there and contact the embassy. If phones are down, 'hire someone to take a note'. 'Do not watch activity from your window', and choose a room 'which provides greater protection from gunfire, rocks, grenades, etc'. If you are caught in the middle of the unrest, 'do not take sides' [US Dept of State] ❦ SHARK ATTACK · 'Punch and kick at the animal's nose and eyes'; shout for help. Raise one arm, but 'do not wave', as others on the beach may simply wave back [Bugbog.com] ❦ HOTEL FIRE · Crawl to the door; if it is cool, 'open the door slowly'. If your exit is clear, crawl to the hallway and walk down stairs. If you meet heavy smoke, do not run through it – go to the roof, find the windward side and wait for help. If exits are blocked and the hall has heavy smoke, stay in your room, 'open a window and turn on the bathroom vent'. 'Hang a sheet out the window' to alert firefighters, 'tie a wet towel over your mouth and nose to help filter out smoke', and 'stuff wet towels into cracks under and around doors' [Dept of State] ❦

❦ SCORPION STING · Try to remain calm as the effects will be exacerbated by anxiety. Clean affected area with soap and water and apply a cold compress, then 'lift the limb to heart-level': chances of death are low [Bugbog.com] ❦ HIJACKING · 'Stay alert, but do not challenge [captors] physically or verbally'; follow their instructions. 'If interrogated, keep answers short and limited to non-political topics'. 'Carry a family photo ... you may be able to appeal to captors' family feeling'. 'Give innocuous reasons for travelling' [Dept of State] ❦ KIDNAPPING · 'If drugs are administered, do not resist; 'if conscious, follow your captors' instructions'. Establish rapport; 'family is a universal subject'. 'Plan on a lengthy stay', and find a way to track the passage of time. 'Devise ways to communicate' with other hostages. 'Take note of the characteristics of your captors and surroundings'. 'Establish exercise and relaxation programmes' (Most governments do not pay ransoms) [Dept of State] ❦ ALLIGATOR ATTACK · If you can, run away in a straight line; otherwise strike the animal repeatedly on its nose; 'poke it in the eyes and scream'. If all else fails, 'play dead' [Bugbog.com] ❦ KILLER BEE ATTACK · 'Run for shelter' in a straight line, covering your face. Remove stingers promptly; victims of swarming may require hospitalization. 'Do not try to hide underwater' [insecta-inspecta.com; *Webster's New World Medical Dictionary*]. ❦ MOOSE ATTACK · Generally when a moose charges it is merely a warning. 'Get behind something solid'; 'it is okay to run'. If a moose knocks you down, do not try to fight back, but 'curl up in a ball and protect your head' [Kenai Fjords National Park] ❦

──────────── THE CHELSEA FLOWER SHOW ────────────

The following gardens were awarded top prizes at the 2006 Chelsea Flower Show:

Best show garden .... *Daily Telegraph*
Best chic garden...:. Kazahana Co. Ltd
Best city garden .... Natural Elements
Best courtyard garden ......Cyrus Design @ Leeds Met. Uni./HBG Properties Ltd
Best junior display ....Devonshi Mody
President's award................................. Bournemouth Borough Council

> 'We can in fact only define a weed, *mutatis mutandis*, in terms of the well known definition
> of dirt – as matter growing out of place. What we call a weed is in fact merely a plant
> growing where we do not want it.' – E.J. Salisbury, *The Living Garden*, 1935

──────────── BRITAIN IN BLOOM ────────────

The Royal Horticultural Society's (RHS) 'Britain in Bloom' competition rewards entrants not only for their horticultural skill, but also for the environmental sustainability of their entry, the regeneration of their local environment, and their community's involvement. The category winners of Britain in Bloom 2005 were:

Category	winner	
Large city	Cardiff	Large village .... Usk
City	Derry/Londonderry	Village .... Heysham
Lrg.town/sml. city (12–35k)	Durham	Small village.......................Bray
– (35–100K)	Newcastle-under-Lyme	Urban regeneration .. St Philip/St Paul
Town	Hexham	Urban community ....Spondon
Small town	Garstang	Coastal resort ....Sidmouth
		Floral award (discretionary)... Nottingham

──────────── GARDEN PESTS ────────────

The Royal Horticultural Society's (RHS) Entomology Department compiled a list of the species of garden pests that provoked the most complaints during 2005:

1 .... slugs and snails	5 .... grey squirrel	9 .... cushion scale
2 .... lily beetle	6 .... leatherjackets	10 ......glasshouse bugs
3 ....vine weevil	7 .... chafer grubs	
4 ....rosemary beetle	8 ....soft scale	[Source: RHS, 2006]

──────────── GARDEN OF THE YEAR ────────────

The 2005 Historic Houses Association – Christie's Garden of the Year Award, was presented to BURTON AGNES HALL in East Yorkshire. The beautiful grounds are set around a delightful walled kitchen garden, inspired by the Elizabethan house.

——————————— BRITISH HOMES ABROAD ———————————

The ONS estimated that, by 2003/4, UK households had invested £23·2bn in second properties overseas. The most popular foreign locations are listed below:

[Source: ONS 2006]	2000–2001	2001–02	2002–03	2003–04
Spain	49,204	55,321	57,802	69,284
France	36,448	40,979	42,816	51,322
Portugal	3,645	4,098	4,282	5,132
Italy	1,822	2,049	2,141	2,566
Other European	27,336	30,734	32,112	38,491
All Europe	118,455	133,181	139,153	166,795
United States	10,934	12,294	12,845	15,397
Other non-European	52,849	59,419	62,084	74,417
All non-European	63,783	71,713	74,929	89,814
All countries	182,238	204,894	214,082	256,609

——————————— OVERSEAS TRAVEL ———————————

The table below shows the number of visits to the UK by foreign tourists, their spending while on holiday, and the equivalent for UK residents while abroad:

	Dec '05	*Jan '06*	*Feb '06*	*Mar '06*	*Apr '06*
Foreign visits to the UK	2·4m	2·7m	2·4m	2·6m	2·8m
Expenditure in the UK	£1·4m	£1·2m	£1·2m	£1·3m	£1·3m
UK residents' visits overseas	5·7m	5·6m	5·6m	5·5m	5·8m
Expenditure overseas	£2·7m	£2·8m	£2·6m	£2·7m	£2 8m

[Source: ONS · period: December 2005–April 2006]

——————————— EUROPEAN CRUISES ———————————

The popularity of sea cruises is increasing across Europe, with Greece in particular experiencing a massive boom. Cruise passenger numbers worldwide are expected to reach 20m by 2011. Below are cruise passenger numbers by European country:

[Source: PSA–IRN CruiseStat, May 2006]	*2004*	*2005*	*change*
France	222,000	233,000	+5%
Germany	583,000	639,000	+10%
Greece	14,000	104,000	+643%
Italy	400,000	514,000	+29%
Spain	300,000	379,000	+26%
Other European	286,000	276,000	–3%
UK	1,029,000	1,071,000	+4%
Europe (excluding UK)	1,805,000	2,145,000	+19%

THE WORLD'S TOP TABLES

Restaurant Magazine's 2006 survey of the world's finest tables listed the following:

El Bulli .... Girona, Spain	*Bras* .... Laguiole, France
The Fat Duck ....Bray, UK	*Le Louis XV* .... Monte Carlo, Monaco
Pierre Gagnaire ....Paris, France	*Per Se* ....New York, US
French Laundry.......... California, US	*Arzak* .... San Sebastián, Spain
Tetsuya's ....Sydney, Australia	*Mugaritz*.......... San Sebastián, Spain

NEW UK MICHELIN STARS · 2006

The *Michelin Guide* was first published in 1900 by the Michelin Tyre Company. A three-star rating system is employed on a deceptively simple set of criteria: [*] 'A very good restaurant in its category'; [**] 'Excellent cooking, worth a detour'; [***] 'Exceptional cuisine, worth a special trip'. In reality, the award of one Michelin star confers instant recognition; two stars confer fame; and three stars are the culinary equivalent of a Nobel prize. The following gained UK stars in 2006:

**	*Andrew Fairlie*	Auchterarder, Perth, Scotland	01764 694 267
*	*Lucknam Park*	Bath	01225 742 777
*	*Le Poussin*.................	Brockenhurst, Hampshire...........	01590 622 354
*	*The Hare*..................	Hungerford, Berkshire	01488 7 13 86
*	*The Hand & Flowers*......	Marlow, Buckinghamshire	01628 482 277
*	*The Moody Goose*	Midsomer Norton, Bath	01225 466 688
*	*St Ervan Manor*	Padstow, Cornwall....................	01841 540 255
*	*The Mason's Arms*.........	South Molton, Devon................	01398 341 231
*	*Waldo's*	Taplow, Berkshire.....................	01628 668 561
*	*Orestone Manor*...........	Torquay, Devon.......................	01803 328 098
*	*The Elephant*...............	Torquay, Devon.......................	01803 200 044
*	*Gilpin Lodge*..............	Windermere, Cumbria	01539 488 818
*	*Winteringham Fields*......	Winteringham, Humberside.........	01724 733 096
*	*Ynyshir Hall*..............	Machynlleth, Powys, Wales	01654 781 249
*	*Rasoi Vineet Bhatia*.......	Lincoln St, London SW3.............	020 7225 1881
*	*The Ledbury*...............	Ledbury Rd, London W11	020 7792 9090
*	*Amaya*	Motcomb St, London SW1..........	020 7823 1166
*	*Maze*......................	Grovesnor Sq, London W1..........	020 7107 0000
*	*Nobu Berkeley*.............	Berkeley St, London W1	020 7290 9222

CHOCOPHILES

An April 2006 survey by Datamonitor showed that the British are the foremost consumers of chocolate in Europe, munching through a quarter of the continent's entire supply, at a cost of £4·3bn. The average Briton spends £72 a year on 10kg of the confectionary – preferring products like Snickers and Mars, designed to be consumed in one go. Dark chocolate sales are predicted to increase by 48%.

BRITAIN'S MOST HATED FOOD

In April 2006, *Olive* magazine asked people to name their most hated British dish:

1 . . . . .tripe†	5 . . . . black pudding	9 . . . . semolina
2 . . . . .jellied eels	6 . . . . tapioca	10. . . beetroot in vinegar
3 . . . deep-fried Mars bar	7 . . . . faggots	[† The fore-stomach of a
4 . . . . brawn	8 . . . . Marmite	ruminant; nice with onions]

HARDEN'S TOP LONDON RESTAURANTS

Harden's London Restaurant Guide is compiled from an extensive survey of 8,000 London diners. The top ten most talked about tables in 2006 were the following:

J. Sheekey · Hakkasan · Gordon Ramsay · Chez Bruce · The Wolseley
Bleeding Heart · The Ivy · Claridges · La Poule au Pot · Andrew Edmunds

MISS GREAT BRITAIN 2006

Danielle Lloyd (22) of Warrington was crowned Miss Great Britain 2006 by Noel Edmonds and Jenni Falconer. The judges included John McCrirrick, Faria Alam, Christine Hamilton, Lord Charlie Brocket, and Jean-Cristophe Novelli, whose votes were combined with those of the public to decide the winner. Danielle, a brunette Sagittarian with hazel eyes, is 5'8" tall, weighs in at 112lbs, and boasts the following 'vital statistics': 30(E)·25·34. As Miss Great Britain, Danielle won:

a speaking part in a Hollywood film · a modelling contract £5,000 in clothes
a personalised number plate · and automatic entry into a Miss World contest

Danielle's website states her admirable goal in life – 'I would like to visit many countries and work towards helping those people less fortunate than others. We have so many children and parents who are living in poverty and have to beg, or work from a very early age just to be able to eat day by day. Surely everyone should be able to eat a meal and drink clean fresh water whenever they want. I know it won't happen overnight, but if we can do something to make a start and put a smile on just one child's face, it would be an achievement'.

TOY OF THE YEAR

The Toy of the Year Award is presented every January by the Toy Industry Association (TIA). The 2006 winner was the educational device FLY PENTOP COMPUTER. Below are some of the winners of other specific categories:

Category	winner		
Infant. . . . . Weebly Wobbly Tree House		Outdoor. . . . . .Air Hogs Dominator	
Girl . . . . .Dora's Talking Kitchen		Activity . . . . .LEGO Star Wars	
		Speciality . . . . .3-D Pool Table/Uglydoll	

CRUFTS BEST IN SHOW · 2006

The 2006 Crufts Best in Show was Australian Shepherd *Caitland Isle Take a Chance*, handled by Larry Fenner. The winning pair were presented with the famous Keddell Memorial trophy, and won £100 and a year's supply of Pedigree Chum (worth £1,500). Confusingly, Australian shepherd dogs are actually an American breed – they were awarded full Breed Status by the Kennel Club in 2000.

PREVIOUS BEST IN SHOW WINNING BREEDS

'05 . . . . *Norfolk terrier*	'02 . . . . *Poodle*	'99 . . . . *Irish setter*
'04 . . . . *Whippet*	'01 . . . . *Basenji*	'98 . . . . *Welsh terrier*
'03 . . . . *Pekingese*	'00 . . . . *Kerry blue terrier*	'97 . . . . . . *Yorkshire terrier*

DESIGNER MIXED-BREED DOGS

The trend for designer mixed-breed dogs continues. Some mixes of note follow:

Basselier . . . . Cavalier King Charles Spaniel & Basset Hound
Boxador . . . . Boxer & Labrador
Bug . . . . Boston Terrier & Pug
Chiweenie . . . . Chihuahua & Dachshund
Cockeranian . . . . Cocker Spaniel & Pomeranian
Doodleman Pinscher . . . . Dobermann & Standard Poodle
Dorgi . . . . Dachshund & Corgi [see p.274]
Labradoodle . . . . Labrador & Poodle
Peek-a-pom . . . . Pekingese & Pomeranian
St Berdoodle . . . . St Bernard & Poodle
Schnoodle . . . . Schnauzer & Poodle
St Weiler . . . . Rottweiler & St Bernard
Taco Terrier . . . . Chihuahua & Toy Fox Terrier

FAVOURITE TV PETS

[1] Lassie · [2] Wellard (*EastEnders*) · [3] Shep (*Blue Peter*) · [4] Petra (*Blue Peter*)
[5] Skippy · [6] Bagpuss · [7] Garfield · [8] Bouncer (*Neighbours*)
[9] Scooby Doo · [10] Goldie (*Blue Peter*) [Source: Pets at Home, 2006]

MOST POPULAR PEDIGREE DOG BREEDS

Breed	*no. registered*		
Labrador retriever	45,779	Staffordshire bull terrier	13,070
Cocker spaniel	17,468	Cavalier King Charles spaniel	11,165
English springer spaniel	15,180	Golden retriever	10,165
German shepherd	13,165	West Highland white terrier	9,775
		[Source: The Kennel Club, 2005]	

Money

Money differs from an automobile, a mistress or cancer in being equally important to those who have it and those who do not.
— JOHN KENNETH GALBRAITH (1908–2006)

MONEY IN CIRCULATION

Note	featured personality	notes issued in 2006	size mm	circulation value 2005
£5	Elizabeth Fry	63m	135x70	£1,054m
£10	Charles Darwin	229m	142x75	£5,670m
£20	Sir Edward Elgar	341m	149x80	£21,649m
£50	Sir John Houblon†	7m	156x85	£6,082m
Others‡	—	—	—	£960m
Total	—	640m	—	£35,416m

† The first Governor of the Bank of England (1694–7); and also Lord Mayor of London (1695).

‡ Includes higher-value notes used for internal transactions. [Source: Bank of England]

Coin	issued in 2005
GOLD · Sovereign	45,542
Half Sovereign	30,299
SILVER · 4p Maundy	1,685
3p Maundy	1,685
2p Maundy	1,685
1p Maundy	1,685
NICKEL BRASS · £2	15,331,500
£1	68,138,000

CUPRO-NICKEL · £5†	101,106,000
50p	30,254,500
20p	81,356,250
10p	66,836,000
5p	210,012,000
BRONZE · 2p	131,133,000
1p	378,752,000

† Includes special editions
[Source: Royal Mint]

DAMAGED NOTES

The Bank of England reported that in 2004 the following claims for damaged or mutilated bank notes, with a value of £28,536,000, were received:

Reason for claim	number	value (£)
Torn/partial note	17,220	1·1m
Chewed/eaten	4,272	86,000
Washed	3,238	89,000
Contaminated	2,869	26·5m
Fire/flood damage	1,579	761,000

DESTROYED NOTES

The life span of bank notes ranges from 1 year for a fiver, to >5 years for a fifty. Between 2004–2005, the Bank of England reported that the following numbers of notes were shredded:

£5	153,531,778
£10	215,355,730
£20	201,526,303
£50	2,135,221
Total	572,549,032

BUDGET 2006 · KEY POINTS

Gordon Brown's 10th budget (22 March 2006) was widely seen as an attempt to set out his agenda for a future leadership bid, with education taking centre stage. Some of his key measures are below (others are detailed elsewhere in this section):

Income tax	rates frozen; allowances raised from £4,895 to £5,035
Stamp duty	threshold raised to £125,000; rates frozen
Inheritance tax	threshold raised from £275,000 to £325,000 by 2009
Housing	£970m for shared-equity schemes to help 35,000 buy property
National off-peak bus travel	to be made free for pensioners & disabled in 2008
Education	over 5 years investment to increase from £5·6bn to £8bn a year
State schools	aim to match £8,000 spending on private school children
Further education	fees waived for under 25's seeking A levels
Science teaching	3,000 science teachers to be recruited and retained
Sport	£200m over next 6 years to fund world-class British athletes
Schools Olympics	to be held annually until 2012
Sports clubs	£2m to fund evening sports clubs for young people
Climate Change Levy	will be indexed in line with inflation from 2007
Car rates	lowest emission cars pay no vehicle excise duty; highest to pay £210
Fuel duty	annual inflation rise delayed until 1st September
Child tax credit	child element to rise by 14% over next 3 years
Child Trust Funds	extra £250 for children when they reach 7
Child care	vouchers for child care increased by £5 a week to £55
R&D tax credit	companies with ≥500 employees can claim higher credit rate
Public sector pay	to rise on average by 2·25%
7/7 London bombings	a memorial to victims to be built
Victims of terrorism	£1m to go to victims of terrorism at home & abroad
International peacekeeping	£200m to go towards peacekeeping
Armed forces	an extra £800m for troops in Iraq and Afghanistan
Contraception	VAT on condoms and 'morning after pill' cut from 17·5% to 5%
Community support officers	£100m to accelerate recruitment
Cultural heritage	VAT to be refunded on renovation of churches & monuments
Assets	government to raise £30bn by selling assets such as the Tote
Research	£1bn of private & public money for energy & environmental research
Biofuel	target to increase proportion of fuel made from biofuel to 5% by 2010
New homes	plans for 100,000 new homes
Medical research	£1bn budget for Medical Research Council and NHS research

BUDGET 2006 BOOZE 'n' FAGS

Typical unit	*budget*		
Pack 20 cigarettes	+9p	175ml glass wine	+1p
Pack 5 cigars	+3p	75cl bottle wine	+4p
25g rolling tobacco	+8p	Sparkling wine	*frozen*
25g pipe tobacco	+5p	Spirits	*frozen*
Pint beer	+1p	Cider	*frozen*
		Sparkling cider	*frozen*

—————————— BUDGET 2006 · REACTION & MISC ——————————

David Cameron *'This Chancellor is mortgaging this country's future'* · Sir Menzies Campbell *'Why does he tinker with the tax system when it is so fundamentally unfair and requires radical reform?'* · Telegraph *'Brown rattles door to No 10'* · Guardian *'Brown taunts the Tories: we invest, you cut taxes* · Sun *'Chancellor of the Sex-chequer'*

Brown's speech lasted 61 minutes; he talked at a rate of 147 words per minute.

Word Count	Inflation 16	Tax cut(s) 6	Africa 3
Tax(es) 45	Growth 16	Pensioner(s) 5	Prudent(-ence) .. 2
Child(ren) 38	Stability 16	Euro 5	Iraq 1
Family(-ies) 23	Young people 9	Public services .. 3	Prime Minister .. 1

COMPUTERISED CONDENSATION

When Brown's speech (8,782 words) is entered into the Auto Summarize feature of *Microsoft Word* and reduced to *c.*1% of the original (5 sentences), the result is:

Since 1997 interest rates have averaged 5 per cent. Net debt is now 47 per cent of national income in France, 47 per cent in America, in Germany 62 per cent, in Japan 83 per cent and in Italy over 100 per cent – but this year in Britain 36·4%. So 3 million of Britain's 7 million families with children have their income tax liability effectively wiped out by this family tax cut. 94 per cent of estates pay no tax. A budget for Britain's future.

—————————— GORDON BROWN'S TIE ——————————

Below is tabulated the colour of Gordon Brown's necktie for each of his budgets:

2006 .... *lavender*	2002 ...... *blue/pink spots*	1998 .... *red*
2005 .... *red*	2001 .... *red*	1997 .... *red*
2004 .... *lilac*	2000 .... *purple spots*	[Brown has sported red
2003 ..... *orange and red*	1999 .... *red*	ties at 50% of his budgets]

—————————— BEER DUTY ——————————

According to the Campaign for Real Ale, although Gordon Brown added just 1p to a pint of beer, prices have risen by 10p. In 2006, the average cost of a pint of ale rose from £2·15 to £2·24. The duty on a pint of beer in other EU states is as follows:

Austria .... 9·4p	France .... 5·1p	Latvia .... 3·4p
Belgium .... 8·1p	Germany .... 3·7p	Netherlands .... 9·9p
Denmark .... 13·4p	Ireland .... 39·1p	Spain .... 3·6p
Finland .... 38·3p	Italy .... 9·3p	UK .... 36·7p

[Source: CAMRA · Duty based on exchange rates as of March 2005]

———————————INCOME TAX · 2006–07———————————

Income tax was first levied in 1799 by Pitt the Younger, as a 'temporary measure' to finance the French Revolutionary War. The initial rate was 2 shillings in the pound. The tax was abolished in 1816, only to be re-imposed in 1842 by Robert Peel (again temporarily) to balance reductions in customs duties. By the end of the C19th, income tax was a permanent feature of the British economy.

Income tax allowances	2005–06	2006–07
Personal allowance	4,895	5,035
Personal allowance (65–74)	7,090	7,280
Personal allowance (>75)	7,220	7,420
Income limit for age-related allowances	19,500	20,100
Married couple's allowance (born before 6·4·1935)	5,905	6,065
Married couple's allowance (aged ≤75)	5,975	6,135
Minimum amount of married couple's allowance	2,280	2,350
Blind person's allowance	1,610	1,660

The rate of relief for the continuing married couple's allowance, maintenance relief for people born before 6 April 1935, and for the children's tax credit, remains at 10%.

Income tax rates	*threshold*	%
Starting rate	£0–2,150	10
Basic rate	£2,151–33,300	22
Higher rate	>£33,300	40

Payment bands 0%	10%	22%	40%
Personal allowance	*from* 0–2,150	*from* 2,151–33,300	*after* 33,300

The 10% starting rate includes SAVINGS income. Where an individual has savings income in excess of the starting rate limit they will be taxed at 20% up to the basic rate limit, and at the higher rate for income above the basic rate limit. The tax rates for dividends are 10% for income up to the basic rate limit, and 32·5% thereafter.

———————————STAMP DUTY———————————

The thresholds below (in £) represent the 'total value of consideration' of the deal. The rate that applies to any given transfer applies to the whole value of that deal.

rate %	*Residential* not *in a disadvantaged area*	*Residential in a disadvantaged area*	*Non-residential*
0	0–125,000	0–150,000	0–150,000
1	125,001–250,000	150,001–250,000	150,001–250,000
3	250,001–500,000	250,001–500,000	250,001–500,000
4	>500,001	>500,001	>500,001

The rate of stamp duty on the transfer of SHARES and SECURITIES is set at 0·5%.

————— NATIONAL INSURANCE · 2006–07 —————

Although National Insurance dates from 1911, modern funding of social security was proposed by Beveridge and established by the National Insurance Act (1946).

Lower earnings limit, primary Class 1	£84/w
Upper earnings limit, primary Class 1	£645/w
Primary threshold	£97/w
Secondary threshold	£97/w
Employees' primary Class 1 rate	11% of £97–£645/w · 1% >£645/w
Employees' contracted-out rebate	1·6%
Married women's reduced rate	4·85% of £97–£645/w · 1% >£645/w
Employers' secondary Class 1 rate	12·8% on earnings above £97/w
Employers' contracted-out rebate, salary-related schemes	3·5%
Employers' contracted-out rebate, money-purchase schemes	1·0%
Class 2 rate	£2·10/w
Class 2 small earnings exception	£4,465/y
Special Class 2 rate for share fishermen	£2·75/w
Special Class 2 rate for volunteer development workers	£4·20/w
Class 3 rate	£7·55/w
Class 4 lower profits limit	£5,035/y
Class 4 upper profits limit	£33,540/y
Class 4 rate	8% of £5,035–£33,540/y · 1% >£33,540/y

————— CAPITAL GAINS TAX —————

Annual exemptions 2006–07   Individuals &c. = £8,800 · Other trustees = £4,400

The amount chargeable to Capital Gains Tax is added onto the top of income liable to income tax for individuals, and is charged to CGT at the following levels:

Below the Starting Rate limit	10%
Between the Starting Rate and Basic Rate limits	20%
Above the Basic Rate limit	40%

Capital gains arising on disposal of a 'principal private residence' remain exempt.

————— CORPORATION TAX ON PROFITS —————

2006–07	*£ per year*
Small companies' rate: 19%	0–300,000
Marginal small companies' relief	300,001–1,500,000
Main rate: 30%	>1,500,001

The 2006 pre-Budget Report announced that the starting rate and non-corporate distribution rate would be replaced with a single banding for small companies set at the existing companies' rate.

—————————— OTHER TAXES OF NOTE ——————————

Value Added Tax (VAT)
Standard rate   17·5%
Reduced rate (e.g. energy saving materials; women's sanitary products)   5%
Zero rate (e.g. young children's clothing and footwear; books and newspapers)   0%
VAT registration threshold (i.e. the level of income at which you must register) ≥£61,000

Religious rules affecting food (like halal or kosher laws) do not affect liability for VAT; however, some sacramental foods (like communion wafers) have been VAT zero-rated.

Inheritance Tax 2006–07
Threshold £285,000 · Rate 40%

Air Passenger Duty 2006–07	*standard*	*reduced*
Specified European Destination	£10	£5
All other destinations	£40	£20

Insurance Premium Tax 2006–07
Standard rate 5% · Higher rate (for travel and some vehicle & domestic) 17·5%

Fuel Duty (effective September 2006)	*per litre*
Sulphur-free petrol/diesel	48·35p
Ultra low sulphur petrol/diesel	48·35p
Biodiesel	28·35p
Bioethanol	28·35p
Rebated gas oil (red diesel)	7·69p
Rebated fuel oil	7·29p
Road fuel gas other than natural gas (e.g. LPG)	12·21p/kg
Natural gas used as road fuel	10·81p/kg

—————————— GRADUATED VEHICLE EXCISE DUTY ——————————

Cars first registered and licensed on or after 1 March 2001 qualify for the new system of charging vehicle excise duty for private cars based on Carbon Dioxide (CO_2) emissions; those registered prior to this will be charged at the old rates, based on engine size. Current bands and charges for a period of twelve months are:

Band	CO2 emissions g/km	diesel car	petrol car	alt. fuel
A	≤100	£0	£0	£0
B	101–120	£50	£40	£30
C	121–150	£110	£100	£90
D	151–165	£135	£125	£115
E	166–185	£160	£150	£140
F	>185	£195	£190	£180
G†	>225	£215	£210	£200

[Source: DVLA · † New band introduced for cars registered on or after 23 March 2006]

—— ADAM SMITH INSTITUTE'S TAX FREEDOM DAY ——

Each year the Adam Smith Institute [adamsmith.org] calculates the 'Tax Freedom Day'. This is the theoretical day in the calendar when the average tax-payer ceases to work 'for the Government' and starts to earn for themselves. In 2006, the Tax Freedom Day moved forward 3 days to 3 June. (According to the Tax Foundation, the US Tax Freedom Day in 2006 was 26 April.) Charted below is how the Adam Smith Institute's Tax Freedom Day has shifted across the year, since 1963:

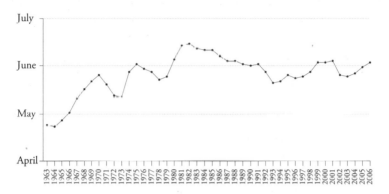

——— WEEKLY HOUSEHOLD EXPENDITURE BY AGE———

Expenditure	age <30	30–49	50–64	65–74	>75	All
Food/non-alcoholic drinks	£8	£10	£11	£13	£16	£10
Alcohol, tobacco & narcotics	3	3	3	3	3	3
Clothing & footwear	6	6	5	4	4	5
Housing	20	16	13	11	13	15
– Mortgage interest/net rent	16	12	6	3	4	9
– Council tax	3	3	4	5	6	4
– Repair & maintenance	1	2	2	3	3	2
Fuel, power & water	3	3	4	5	7	4
Household goods/services	7	7	7	9	8	7
Health	1	1	2	2	3	1
Transport	15	15	15	12	11	15
Communication	3	3	3	2	3	3
Recreation & culture	11	13	15	16	12	14
Education	1	2	1	–	–	1
Restaurants & hotels	9	9	8	7	6	8
Misc. goods & services	8	8	8	8	10	8
Other	4	5	5	6	5	5
Total expenditure/week	408·40	524·80	441·30	289·60	183·30	418·10
Weighted average household size	2·3	3·0	2·2	1·7	1·4	2·4

[Source: Family spending 2003/04, Office for National Statistics]

─── INCOME DISTRIBUTION ───

The distribution bands of real UK/GB disposable household income per week:

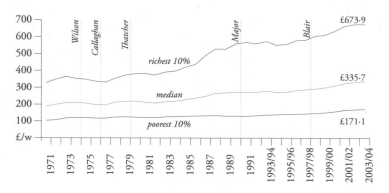

[Adjusted to 2003/04 prices using RPI less local taxes. Equivalised household disposable income before deduction of housing costs. Data from 1993/94 onwards are for financial years. Source of data changed in 1994/95: income definition changed and geographic coverage changed from UK to GB. Source: Social Trends 36 · Crown ©]

─── BRITISH WORK & PAY ───

Median gross pay (Apr 2005)	♂	♀	*difference*	*average*
Per year full-time	£25,087·00	£19,447·00	£5,640·00	£22,901·00
Per week full-time	£471·50	£371·80	£99·70	£431·20
Per week part-time	£120·80	£133·60	–£12·80	£131·10
Per hour full-time	£11·44	£9·86	£1·58	£10·79
Per hour part-time	£6·51	£6·70	–£0·19	£6·67

Of all employees gross annual pay	
10% earn less than.............£5,837	30% earn more than......... £26,450
20% earn less than.............£9,788	20% earn more than......... £31,592
30% earn less than........... £13,084	10% earn more than......... £40,544
	[Ann. Survey of Hours & Earnings 2005]

Most hours worked (Apr 2005)	*average hours per week*
Transport and mobile machine drivers	47·0
Skilled metal and electrical trades	42·9
Skilled construction and building trades	42·8
Average hours worked (all full-time workers)	39·4
Fewest hours worked	*average hours per week*
Teaching and research professionals	33·3
Secretarial and related occupations	37·0
Business and public service professionals	37·2
Administrative occupations	37·4

INCOME TAX PAYABLE · 2005–06

Annual income (£)	No. of taxpayers (m)	Total tax liability (£m)	Average rate of tax (%)	Average amount of tax (£)
4,895–4,999	0·1	1	0·1	5
5,000–7,499	2·9	369	2·0	126
7,500–9,999	3·5	1,580	5·1	445
10,000–14,999	6·1	7,560	9·8	1,220
15,000–19,999	5·1	11,500	13·0	2,260
20,000–29,999	6·4	24,000	15·4	3,760
30,000–49,999	4·3	28,900	17·9	6,690
50,000–99,999	1·5	25,900	25·7	17,000
100,000 and over	0·5	34,200	33·4	71,100
ALL INCOMES	30·5m	£134,000	18·2%	£4,390

[Total annual income of the individual for income tax purposes including earned and investment income. Figures relate to taxpayers only. Based on projections in line with the March 2005 Budget. In this context tax reductions refer to allowances given at a fixed rate, for example the Married Couple's Allowance. Source: HM Revenue and Customs Crown ©]

HIGHEST TAX RATES WORLDWIDE

Country	highest %
Sweden	55·5
Denmark	54·4
Germany	51·2
Australia	48·5
Spain	48·0
Japan	47·2
Canada	46·4
USA	45·2
France	40·0
UK	40·0
Mexico	35·0
Czech Republic	28·0
Poland	26·2

[Source: OECD, 2005]

FORMS OF UK HOUSEHOLD SAVING

Below are the percentages of UK households which have different types of savings:

Type of savings	% of households
Current account	89
Other bank accounts	54
ISAs	33
Premium Bonds	23
Stocks and shares	22
PEPs	8
TESSAs	7
Post office account	6
Unit trusts	5
Company share scheme	4
National Savings Bonds	4
Basic bank account	3
Gilts	1
Save as you earn	1
Guaranteed Equity Bonds	<1

[Source: Family Resources Survey, Department for Work and Pensions, 2003/04]

—————————— DEPRIVATION & HARDSHIP ——————————

Indices of Multiple Deprivation (IMD) are employed by the government to identify areas which are in financial need. The latest index, published in 2004, was calculated by combining a number of measurable factors of deprivation within Super Output Areas (SOAs) – geographic districts with around 1,500 inhabitants, of which England has 32,482. Below are the seven factors used to asses the IMD:

*Income deprivation · employment deprivation · health & disability deprivation
education, skills & training deprivation · barriers to housing & services
the living environment deprivation · crime*

The most deprived 20% of England's SOAs share the following characteristics: just under a third of people are income deprived; one in five women aged 18–59, and men aged 18–64, are employment deprived; just under half of children live in income deprived families; and just over a third of the elderly are income deprived.

The table below lists the regional breakdown of children living in deprivation.

Region	% children in deprivation
East	14·9
East Midlands	18·0
London	28·2
North East	25·9
North West	23·4
South East	13·6
South West	15·5
West Midlands	20·7
Yorkshire & the Humber	21·0

[Source: ODPM, 2004]

The Policy Studies Institute has developed an index of hardship, with 9 indicators:

*Reports >2 problems with accommodation and cannot afford to repair
Lives in overcrowded accommodation · Cannot afford to keep house warm
Worries about money almost all the time, and runs out of money most weeks
Has no bank account and has >2 problem debts
Lacks food items · Lacks clothing items
Lacks consumer durables · Lacks social/leisure activities*

—————————— ADEQUACY OF INCOME ——————————

The British Social Attitudes Survey regularly asks the question, *'which of these phrases would you say is closest to your feelings about your household's income these days?'*

% reporting	1986	1994	2002	2003	2004
Living comfortably	24	29	39	44	40
Coping	50	49	45	43	46
Finding it difficult to manage	18	15	13	10	11
Finding it very difficult to manage	8	6	3	3	3

[Source: British Social Attitudes Survey, National Centre for Social Research]

THE SUNDAY TIMES RICH LIST · 2006

No.	Billionaire (UK)	age	£ billion	activity	last year
1	Lakshmi Mittal	55	14·9	steel	1
2	Roman Abramovich	40	10·8	industry, football	2
3	Duke of Westminster	54	6·6	property	3
4	Hans Rausing & family	80	4·9	packaging	4
5	Philip & Christina Green	54	4·9	retail	5
6	Leonard Blavatnik	48	4·7	industry	25
7	Sri & Gopi Hinduja	70, 66	3·6	industry, finance	13
8	David & Simon Reuben	67, 63	3·3	property	9
9	Sir Richard Branson	56	3·1	various *Virgins*	8
10	John Fredriksen	61	2·9	shipping	16

MINIMUM WAGE

First introduced by Labour on 1 April 1999, the present minimum wage rates are:

Adult rate (aged ≥22)...£5·35/h
Development rate (18–21 inclusive)..£4·45/h
16 and 17 year olds above compulsory school leaving age.................£3·30/h

In many countries the minimum wage is not an hourly rate but an agreed monthly sum. The following is a comparison of some monthly minimum wages across Europe and the US (Ireland, UK, and US have been extrapolated from their hourly rate):

Monthly min. wage £		
France............818	Luxembourg......1,002	UK...................818
Greece.............456	Poland............140	US...................455
Ireland.............808	Romania.............49	[Source: Eurostat, 2005,
	Spain..............409	converted from euros]

FORBES MAGAZINE RICH LIST · 2006

No.	Billionaire (Worldwide)	age	$ billion	activity	last year
1	William Gates III	50	50·0†	Microsoft	1
2	Warren Buffett	75	42·0	investing	2
3	Carlos Slim Helu	66	30·0	telecoms	4
4	Ingvar Kamprad	79	28·0	Ikea	6
5	Lakshmi Mittal	55	23·5	Mittal Steel	3
6	Paul Allen	53	22·0	Microsoft	7
7	Bernard Arnault	57	21·5	LVMH	16
8	Prince Alwaleed	49	20·0	investing	5
9	Kenneth Thomson & family	82	19·6	publishing	14
10	Li Ka-Shing	77	18·8	investing	21

† *To put Bill Gates' fortune in some perspective, it is five times the GDP of Iceland.*

——————————INTEREST RATES & THE MPC——————————

Since 1997, the Monetary Policy Committee (MPC) has been responsible for setting UK interest rates (though in exceptional circumstances the Government can issue instructions to the MPC for a limited period of time). Sitting on the MPC are: the Governor of the Bank of England, the two Deputy Governors, the Bank's Chief Economist, the Executive Director for Market Operations, and four external members appointed by the Chancellor. The MPC meets monthly and decisions are reached by one-member-one-vote with the Governor wielding the casting vote. Below is a chart of the changes in Bank of England interest rates since June 1997:

Date	change	rate						
03·08·06	+0·25	4·75%	04·10·01	−0·25	4·50%	08·04·99	−0·25	5·25%
04·08·05	−0·25	4·50%	18·09·01	−0·25	4·75%	04·02·99	−0·5	5·50%
05·08·04	+0·25	4·75%	02·08·01	−0·25	5·00%	07·01·99	−0·25	6·00%
10·06·04	+0·25	4·50%	10·05·01	−0·25	5·25%	10·12·98	−0·5	6·25%
06·05·04	+0·25	4·25%	05·04·01	−0·25	5·50%	05·11·98	−0·5	6·75%
05·02·04	+0·25	4·00%	08·02·01	−0·25	5·75%	08·10·98	−0·25	7·25%
06·11·03	+0·25	3·75%	10·02·00	+0·25	6·00%	04·06·98	+0·25	7·50%
10·07·03	−0·25	3·50%	13·01·00	+0·25	5·75%	06·11·97	+0·25	7·25%
06·02·03	−0·25	3·75%	04·11·99	+0·25	5·50%	07·08·97	+0·25	7·00%
07·11·01	−0·5	4·00%	08·09·99	+0·25	5·25%	10·07·97	+0·25	6·75%
			10·06·99	−0·25	5·00%	06·06·97		6·50%

——————————MORTGAGES & HOUSING——————————

Below are some UK mortgage indicators, from the Council of Mortgage Lenders:

Indicator	1975	1985	1995	2005
Number of loans	672,200	1,073,100	798,600	1,002,800
Average value of loan (£)	2,948	23,275	38,601	126,829
Median age of borrower	30	31	32	34
Median advance (£)	7,024	20,660	41,550	107,801
Median income (£)	3,640	10,500	19,040	36,950
% advance	69	87	90	78
Income multiple	1·95	1·98	2·29	2·95
Interest as % of income	14·1	19·1	12·3	15·3
Properties repossessed	4,870	19,300	49,410	10,310
– as % of all loans	0·10	0·25	0·47	0·09

Below is the distribution of property values in 2005, for first time buyers and movers:

Value of property	<£125k	£125–250k	>£250k
1st time buyers	53%	42	6
Home movers	21%	55	24

[Source: Council of Mortgage Lenders]

COUNCIL TAX BANDS · 2006–07

ENGLAND	value £	WALES	value £	SCOTLAND	value £
A	≤40,000	A	≤44,000	A	≤27,000
B	40,001–52,000	B	44,001–65,000	B	27,001–35,000
C	52,001–68,000	C	65,001–91,000	C	35,001–45,000
D	68,001–88,000	D	91,001–123,000	D	45,001–58,000
E	88,001–120,000	E	123,001–162,000	E	58,001–80,000
F	120,001–160,000	F	162,001–223,000	F	80,001–106,000
G	160,001–320,000	G	223,001–324,000	G	106,001–212,000
H	>320,001	H	324,001–424,000	H	>212,001
		I	>424,001		

SECOND HOME HOT SPOTS

According to 2006 figures released by the Affordable Rural Housing Commission, the following areas of Britain have the highest proportion of 'second homes':

City of London . 27·2%	North Norfolk ..... 10·0	Westminster......... : 9·1
Isles of Scilly .... 21·5	North Cornwall..... 9·9	Kensington/Chelsea. 8·7
South Hams........ 10·9	Berwick-u-Tweed ... 9·5	Penwith, Cornwall .. 8·6

EXPENSIVE LONDON

London's long-held reputation as an expensive city was confirmed by a November 2005 report, published by the investment bank Dresdner Kleinwort Wasserstein. The table below illustrates the prices of various goods across five European cities:

(Prices in £)	*London*	*Frankfurt*	*Paris*	*Rome*	*Madrid*
Bottled water	0·73	0·78	0·39	0·38	0·37
Bonne Maman jam	1·44	1·02	1·20	1·05	1·43
Pringles	1·36	1·29	1·24	1·29	1·14
Toothpaste	2·58	2·10	2·32	2·69	2·12
Lager	1·44	0·65	0·76	0·74	0·56
An iron	54·26	43·74	45·38	39·81	34·73
A kettle	32·74	30·72	28·06	25·79	29·39
A pair of tights	4·20	2·48	4·08	3·20	2·73
Basket total	98·75	82·78	83·43	74·95	72·47

PROPERTY TRANSACTION FAILURES

According to a March 2006 study by Scottish Widows, 1 in 3 house buyers have had a property transaction fail. The most common causes were:

Gazumped.........................	37%
Property taken off market	29%
Changed mind after survey.......	19%
Problems with financing	5%

COLLAR COLOUR

BLUE-COLLAR workers are manual labourers who, traditionally, wore blue uniforms. In American pre-war slang, blue shirts were '1,000-mile shirts' because of their ability to hide dirt for so long. ❦ WHITE-COLLAR workers are non-manual (usually clerical) workers after whom, as early as 1932, so-called 'victimless', non-violent, and usually financial crime was named[†]. ❦ GREY-COLLAR is used for mechanics, caretakers, and cleaners, or those in semi-skilled technical work. ❦ PINK-COLLAR is for women working in 'traditional' female jobs like teaching, retail, or administration. ❦ GREEN-COLLAR is for environmental workers and BROWN-COLLAR is for those working in recycling. ❦ GOLD-COLLAR is for CEOs and those considered vital to a company. ❦ SCARLET-COLLAR is for women working in prostitution or the porn industry. ❦ BLACK-COLLAR is for those in 'creative' industries and the media, or those in industrial jobs like mining. ❦ SILVER-COLLAR is for robots, or workers of retirement age. ❦ OPEN-COLLAR is for those working from home. ❦ And, inevitably, DOG-COLLAR is for priests and the clergy.

[†] 'Black-collar crime' has been used to describe both sexual abuse within the Church, and judicial corruption.

MONEY & SEX

A 2006 survey by insurance agency AXA indicated that 20% of those with financial problems reported that the worry had adversely affected their sex lives. Of those who had experienced money-related relationship problems, 37% said they spent less 'quality time' with their partners, and 50% said they had more arguments as a result.

TOP SHOPS

In January 2006, Verdict Research published its annual survey of British consumer satisfaction. Retailers were rated by 6,000 customers on ambience, service, layout, price, range, convenience, facilities, and quality. The top shops were (2005 placing in brackets):

1 . John Lewis (2)	6 ... Amazon (14)
2 ...Waitrose (20)	7 ..... Savers (39)
3 ...TK Maxx (4)	8 ......Schuh (31)
4 ... Matalan (10)	9 . Wilkinson (23)
5 ....Ikea (1)	10 ...... B&Q (7)

COST PER USE

Price comparison website pricerunner. co.uk investigated which household items had the highest cost per use. Ice cream makers were so rarely used that each outing cost *c*.£20. Below is a list of items with their associated usage costs:

Item	cost per use (£)
Ice cream maker	19·48
Fondue set	5·52
Exercise bike	4·56
Rowing machine	3·66
TV	2·99
Laptop computer	2·92
DVD player	1·84

BEST BRANDS

A survey by *Marketing* magazine, in May 2006, revealed the most loved and loathed brands in Britain:

Loved	%	Loathed	%
Google	32	Pot Noodle	21
Tesco	29	QVC	19
Nokia	22	Novon	15
eBay	19	McDonald's	15
Persil	18	Tiny	15

—— 2007 ISSUE COINS ——

The Queen graciously gave approval to the Chancellor of the Exchequer's recommendations that the following special coins be issued during 2007:

· A Crown piece to celebrate the diamond wedding anniversary of Queen Elizabeth II and Prince Philip
· £2 coin to mark 200 years of the abolition of the slave trade by the British Empire · 50p coin to mark the 100th anniversary of the Scouts

NEW COINS ——

A survey by Coinstar, in April 2006, revealed that a majority of people thought a £5 coin and a 25p piece would be the most valuable additions to British coinage; the 2p coin was Britain's least favourite. Curiously, in the unlikely event that the Queen's head was removed from the coins, most people wanted her profile to be replaced by a joint portrait of Wallace & Gromit.

—— FOOTBALL BRANDS ——

BBDO annually produces a list of the most valuable football player 'brands', based on the commercial value of a player to their club. The 2006 leaders:

Player (club)	value (€m)
Ronaldinho (Barcelona)	47·0
David Beckham (Real Madrid)	44·9
Wayne Rooney (Man. Utd.)	43·7
Samuel Eto'o (Barcelona)	30·7
Lionel Messi (Barcelona)	30·4
Zlatan Ibrahimovic (Juventus)	30·1
Ronaldo (Real Madrid)	29·4
Frank Lampard (Chelsea)	28·8
Thierry Henry (Arsenal)	28·7
Michael Ballack (Bayern Mun.)	28·6

—— US DOLLARS ABROAD ——

Around the world, the US dollar is adopted as a currency of first resort in times of war, crisis, or uncertainty. The dollar has near universal recognition, and is considered a safe and reliable alternative when domestic currencies falter or fail. In 2003, the US Treasury estimated that *c.*60% of all Federal Reserve notes in circulation were held abroad (*c.*$370bn) of which:

Former Soviet Union &c. *held*	40%
Latin America	25%
Africa & Middle East	20%
Asia	15%

Surveys by the US Treasury indicate that, in addition to the recently dollarized Ecuador and El Salvador, a number of countries are heavily reliant on the dollar. Russia is thought to hold *c.*10% of its GDP in dollars; Argentina, *c.*17·5%; and Cambodia *c.*25·2%. The value of the dollars circulating in Cuba, Africa, Afghanistan, and Iraq is not known, but has been estimated to be significant. While failed states, war zones, and hyper-inflationary economies are obvious locations for informal dollar use, even stable and developed economies see dollars used in 'grey' and 'black' markets, in cross-border deals, and in the funding of crime and the drugs trade. Curiously, the US Treasury states that areas which experience significant dollarization in times of crisis (e.g. Taiwan in 1996), tend to retain their dollars even after the crisis has passed. The introduction of the euro [see p.270] is likely to impact on use of the dollar in Eastern Europe, the former Soviet Union, and even the Middle East. However, global confidence and familiarity mean that the Greenback is likely to remain the most trusted currency in times of trouble.

———— FINANCIAL SNAP-SCHOTT · 2006 ————

Item	09·2005	09·2006
Church of England · marriage service (excluding certificate)	198·00	218·00
– funeral service (excluding burial and certificate)	84·00	87·00
Season ticket · Arsenal FC (2006/7; centre, E & W upper tiers)	1,825·00	1,825·00
– Grimsby Football Club (2006/7; Upper Smith)	325·00	323·00
Annual membership · MCC (full London member)	334·00	344·00
– Stringfellows, London	600·00	600·00
– Groucho Club, London (+35; London member)	550·00	500·00
– Trimdon Colliery & Deaf Hill Workmen's Club	3·00	3·50
– The Conservative Party (>22)	15·00	15·00
– The Labour Party (those in work)	24·00	39·00
– The Liberal Democrats (minimum required)	5·00	6·00
– UK Independence Party	20·00	20·00
– Royal Society for the Protection of Birds (adult)	30·00	31·00
Annual television licence[†] · colour	121·00	131·50
– black & white	40·50	44·00
Subscription, annual · *Private Eye*	21·00	24·00
– *Vogue*	28·50	28·50
– *Saga Magazine*	22·80	19·95
New British Telecom line installation	74·99	124·99
Entrance fee · Thorpe Park (12+ 'thrill seeker' purchased on the day)	30·00	28·50
– Buckingham Palace State Rooms (adult)	13·50	14·00
– Eden Project, Cornwall (adult, day)	12·50	13·80
'Pint of best bitter' · Railway Inn, Yelverton, Devon	1·90	2·20
– Railway Inn, Juniper Green, Edinburgh	2·35	2·45
– Railway Inn, Trafford, Manchester	1·65	1·90
– Railway Inn, Coleshill, Birmingham	2·25	2·40
– Railway Tavern, Liverpool St, London	2·55	2·90
Fishing licence · Salmon and Sea Trout (full season)	63·75	65·00
List price of the cheapest new Ford (Ford Ka 1·3i 'on the road')	7,095·00	7,090·00
British Naturalisation (includes ceremony fee)	268·00	268·00
Manchester United Home Shirt (2006/7 season)	39·99	39·99
Tea at the Ritz, London (afternoon, per person)	34·00	35·00
Kissing the Blarney Stone (admission to Blarney Castle) [€8]	4·78	5·40
Hampton Court Maze (adult)	3·50	3·50
Ordinary London adult single bus ticket (cash)	1·20	1·50
Mersey Ferry (adult return)	2·10	2·15
Passport · new, renewal, or amendment (3 week postal service)	42·00	51·00
Driving test (practical + theory; cars, weekday)	66·50	70·00
Driving licence (first · car, motorcycle, moped)	38·00	38·00
NHS dental examination (standard)	5·84	15·50
NHS prescription charge (per item)	6·50	6·65
Moss Bros three-piece morning suit hire (weekend, basic 'Lombard')	45·00	49·00
FedEx Envelope (≤0·5kg) UK–USA	27·00	44·41

† The blind concession is 50%. Those ≥75 may apply for a free licence.

--------------------- THE COST OF LIVING ---------------------

The 'cost of living' is measured by tracking the Retail Price Index (RPI), and the Consumer Price Index (CPI). The RPI measures a 'basket' of goods and services (modified annually to reflect changing spending patterns) bought by most households [see below]. The CPI is similar to the RPI with a few differences, such as the exclusion of mortgage repayments, house depreciation and insurance, council tax, and the like. The table below shows historic changes in the RPI and CPI since 1971:

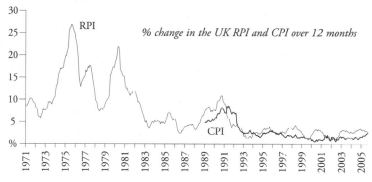

% change in the UK RPI and CPI over 12 months

[Data prior to 1997 are estimates. Source: Social Trends 36 · Crown ©]

--- RPI 'BASKET' CHANGES ---

Some 2006 changes to the RPI basket:

items removed · muesli; home-killed minced lamb; coleslaw; imported sparkling wine; baseball caps; adult's slippers; dishcloths; grass/edge strimmers; contact lens solution; flea drops; personal CD player; child's car seat; frozen cake/gateau; child's sandals; sliced salami, &c

items added · frozen chicken breasts; chicken Kiev; bottle of champagne; wine box, 3 litres; mentholated cigarettes; men's ¾ length casual coat; bottle of lager in nightclub; girl's trousers; wood screws; home office desk; nanny fees; cold/flu drink powder; money transfer fees; personal MP3 player; flat panel television; music downloads, &c

--- RECENT CPI/RPI DATA ---

CPI & RPI % change over 12 months:

Year	month	CPI	RPI
2006	Aug	2·5	3·4
	Jul	2·4	3·3
	Jun	2·5	3·3
	May	2·2	3·0
	Apr	2·0	2·6
	Mar	1·8	2·4
	Feb	2·0	2·4
	Jan	1·9	2·4
2005	Dec	1·9	2·2
	Nov	2·1	2·4
	Oct	2·3	2·5
	Sep	2·5	2·7
	Aug	2·4	2·8
	Jul	2·3	2·9
	Jun	2·0	2·9
	May	1·9	2·9
	Apr	1·9	3·2
	Mar	1·9	3·2

POSTAL PRICING IN PROPORTION

On 21 August 2006, the Royal Mail replaced the traditional weight tariff for postage with the new 'Pricing in Proportion' – a method that takes into account the size of the item to be sent as well as its weight. The three size categories and costs are:

Category	size (mm)	thickness (mm)	weight (g)	1st	2nd
Letter	≤240x165	≤5	0–100	32p	23p
Large Letter	≤353x250	≤25	0–100	44p	37p
			101–250	65p	55p
			251–500	90p	75p
			501–750	131p	109p
Packet	>353 long or >250 wide	or >25	0–100	100p	84p
			101–250	127p	109p
			251–500	170p	139p
			501–750	220p	177p
			751–1kg	270p	212p
			1,001–1,250	474p	—

Items >1,250g will cost an extra 85p for each additional 250g or part thereof.

AIRMAIL RATES

AIRMAIL	Letters Europe	Zone 1	Zone 2				
Postcards	0·44	0·50	0·50	*To find a postcode call*			
≤10g	0·44	0·50	0·50	08456 039 038			
≤20	0·44	0·72	0·72	*For further information see*			
≤40	0·64	1·12	1·19	www.royalmail.com			
≤60	0·83	1·51	1·66	*Small packets*		*Printed papers*	
≤80	1·02	1·91	2·14	*Europe*	*Z 1/2*	*Europe*	*Z 1/2*
≤100	1·21	2·31	2·61	1·10	1·46	0·95	1·44
≤120	1·41	2·70	3·08	1·21	1·66	1·04	1·65
≤140	1·60	3·10	3·55	1·33	1·87	1·14	1·87

Recorded Signed For = postage + 68p · Special Delivery (9am) = £8·85 for up to 100g
A universal stamp can be used to send letters up to 40g to Europe (60p), or worldwide (£1·12)

ROYAL MAIL STAMPS OF 2006

10 Jan .... Animal Tales
7 Feb .... England
23 Feb ..... Isambard Kingdom Brunel
21 Mar .... Ice Age Animals
18 Apr .... Her Majesty The Queen's 80th Birthday
6 Jun.............. World Cup Winners
20 Jun .... Modern Architecture
18 Jul .... National Portrait Gallery
21 Sept .... Victoria Cross
3 Oct .... Sounds of Britain
7 Nov.................. Christmas 2006

―――――――――――― US POSTAL SERVICE · 'GOING POSTAL' ――――――――――

At c.9·15pm on 30 January 2006, a female ex-postal worker shot dead 6 colleagues at a mail processing plant in Santa Barbara, CA, before killing herself. This tragedy was the latest in a series of attacks by US Postal Service workers on their colleagues, the most notorious of which was in 1986, when postman Patrick Henry Sherrill shot dead 14 and wounded 6 postal employees in Edmond, OK, before killing himself. Over time, 'going postal' entered the language to describe random shooting sprees (of co-workers) and, more generally, excessive and irrational anger. The 1995 film *Clueless* has been credited with popularising 'going postal', and the American Dialect Society nominated the phrase as one of its words of 1995. Quite reasonably, the USPS objects to the term as unrepresentative of its c.700,000 staff. In August 2000, the National Center on Addiction and Substance Abuse published a 250-page report on the safety of the USPS. It concluded that postal employees are actually a third less likely as those in the national US workforce to be victims of homicide at work, concluding: '"Going postal" is a myth, a bad rap'. However, now that 'going postal' has entered the vernacular (and, in 2002, the *Oxford English Dictionary*), this statistically unjust stereotyping of US postal workers looks set to continue.

――――――――――――― RETIREMENT AND PENSIONS ――――――――――――

The following chart illustrates the age at which British workers expect to retire:

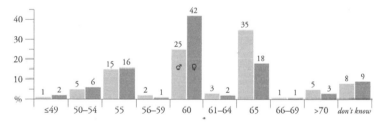

Below is what people consider to be an adequate weekly income after retirement:

<£100 *per week* 5%	£200–249 18	£350–399 3
£100–149 13	£250–299 10	£400–499 5
£150–199 16	£300–349 11	>£500 9

How should government finance the ageing populations?	*Who should bear the financial burden of supporting retired people?*
Reduce pensions 7%	Individuals themselves 43%
Increase taxes 13%	Children/family 20%
Increase retirement age 24%	Employer/previous employer 5%
Enforce additional savings 37%	Local or national government 30%

[Source: HSBC Future of Retirement Research 2006; Dept Work & Pensions]

THE TIPPING POINT

In March 2006, Amanda Newkirk, a 7-month pregnant, 19-year-old waitress in Roanoke, VA, was left $1,000 to cover a $26·35 bill, with a note that said, 'Keep the change! Have a great day'. The $973·65 tip (a cool 3,695%) was left by a self-confessed shopaholic, Erin Dogan, who said of leaving the tip (rather than spending the money herself), 'it made me feel phenomenal ... it has changed my life'. ❦ How, when, who, and what to tip are subjects of considerable confusion – exacerbated by local custom, personal mores, and poor mental arithmetic. In certain countries (e.g. Japan) tipping is eschewed altogether. Where tipping is common, seemingly arbitrary conventions govern the jobs deemed worthy of gratuities. (It is no accident that most travel guides have a section on tipping.) ❦ Perhaps the most commonly tipped group of workers are waiters, for whom tips can range from a welcome bonus to their entire salary. The expected tip for US waiters is 15–20%; much of Europe and the rest of the world expects 10–15%. When *New York Times* restaurant critic Frank Bruni worked as a waiter, in 2006, he highlighted the vital importance of tips and exposed the 'verbal tippers', who 'offer extravagant praise in lieu of 20%'. ❦ A 2003 review of research on restaurant tipping by Michael Lynn of Cornell's Center for Hospitality Research offers some hard facts: credit card payers leave better tips than cash payers; large dining parties leave lower percentage tips than small parties; and, inev-

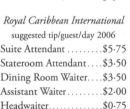

itably, alcohol, sunny weather, good food, and attractive servers increase tips. Lynn also notes that waiters can increase their tips by writing messages or drawing 'smiley' faces on the back of checks, and by squatting down next to the table when interacting with customers. ❦ The verb 'to tip', in its economic sense, derives from thieves' slang of the C17th–18th, when it described the act of passing, giving, or touching. Elisha Cole's 1676 *Dictionary* contains the entry, '*Tip the cole to Adam Tiler*: give the (stolen) money to your (running) Comrade'. Slightly later, 'tipping' described the passing of a private signal ('tip him the wink'), and the bestowing of a gratuity, either to servants and tradesmen, or to schoolchildren. [There is no evidence to suggest 'tip' derives from 'To Insure Promptness']. ❦ Today, certain social scenes (golf clubs, weddings, hunting parties, and country houses) have their own tipping norms. Indeed, tipping aboard cruise ships is so complex that some lines publish lists of expected gratuities. ❦ Emily Post noted in 1922 that 'tipping is undoubtedly a bad system, but it happens to be in force ... one piece of advice: You will not get good service unless you tip generously'. English dandy Wilfred Gowers-Round declared – 'If it moves, tip it!'. And, Groucho Marx famously had the following exchange with a steward in *A Night at the Opera* (1935): 'Do they allow tipping on the boat?' 'Yes, sir.' 'Have you got two fives?' 'Oh, yes, sir.' 'Then you won't need the ten cents I was going to give you.'

Royal Caribbean International
suggested tip/guest/day 2006

Suite Attendant	$5·75
Stateroom Attendant	$3·50
Dining Room Waiter	$3·50
Assistant Waiter	$2·00
Headwaiter	$0·75

ECONOMIC INDICATORS OF NOTE

Indicator	2005	2004	2003	2002	2001	2000	1999	1998	1997	1996	1995	(...) 1986
FTSE all share	5,619	4,814	4,477	3,940	5,217	6,222	6,930	5,883	5,136	4,119	3,689	1,679
Dow Jones Industrial Average	10,547	10,317	8,592	9,226	10,189	10,734	10,464	8,625	7,441	5,742	4,493	—
CBI business optimism survey	-16.5	6.5	-5.5	-3.2	-27.0	-3.0	-7.0	-33.8	0.0	1.8	4.0	—
RPI inflation (% year-on-year)	2.8	3.0	2.9	1.7	1.8	2.9	1.5	3.4	3.1	2.4	3.5	3.4
Real GDP (% year-on-year)	1.8	3.1	2.5	2.0	2.2	4.0	3.0	3.2	3.2	2.7	2.9	3.9
Average mortgage rate (%)	5.21	4.96	4.71	5.03	6.05	6.79	6.47	7.76	7.08	6.73	7.84	12.3
Average gross savers' rate (%)	4.1	4.3	3.4	3.6	3.8	5.5	5.0	6.0	6.1	4.5	5.2	10.9
Number of taxpayers (million)	29.5	29.5	23.5	28.6	29.3	27.0	26.9	26.2	25.7	25.8	25.3	23.7
Highest rate of income tax (%)	40	40	40	40	40	40	40	40	40	40	40	60
Higher-rate taxpayers (% of all taxpayers)	11	11	11	11	10	10	9	9	8	8	8	4
Unemployed (millions)	0.9	0.9	0.9	0.9	1.0	1.1	1.2	1.3	1.6	2.1	2.3	3.1
Unemployment rate (%)	2.8	2.7	3.0	3.1	3.2	3.6	4.1	4.5	5.3	7.0	7.6	10.5
Growth in consumer credit (% year-on-year)	12.2	13.8	14.4	15.3	12.5	13.8	15.3	16.7	16.4	15.1	12.6	—
Total consumer credit (net lending £bn)	17.1	23.0	20.2	21.1	17.7	14.2	14.8	14.4	12.0	11.2	8.1	4.4
Credit cards in issue (millions)	71.5	71.8	66.5	60.4	53.9	49.7	43.5	40.1	36.6	32.5	27.5	N/A
Housing transactions (thousands)	1,531	1,753	1,345	1,588	1,458	1,431	1,470	1,347	1,440	1,243	1,137	1,795
Halifax house price % change year on year	5.5	18.6	22.4	17.4	8.5	9.8	7.2	5.4	6.3	4.5	-1.7	11.0
Change in average earnings (%)	4.1	4.3	3.4	3.5	4.5	4.5	4.8	5.2	4.3	3.5	3.2	8.1
Lending secured on houses (£bn)	288.0	291.2	277.3	220.7	160.1	119.8	114.7	89.4	77.2	71.7	57.3	N/A
Properties repossessed (%)	0.09	0.05	0.07	0.11	0.16	0.20	0.27	0.31	0.31	0.40	0.47	0.30
Outstanding credit (% household income)	24.1	23.7	22.4	22.2	20.6	19.8	19.0	17.6	15.7	14.7	13.7	10.0
US Dollar/GB Pound ($/£)	1.82	1.83	1.63	1.50	1.44	1.52	1.62	1.66	1.64	1.56	1.58	1.47
Euro/GB Pound (€/£) [pre-1999 estimated]	1.46	1.47	1.45	1.59	1.61	1.64	1.52	(1.49)	(1.45)	(1.21)	(1.19)	(1.48)
US Dollar/GB Pound ($/£)	1.82	1.83	1.63	1.50	1.44	1.51	1.62	1.66	1.64	1.56	1.58	—
Oil US Dollar/barrel (Brent spot price)	54.4	38.3	28.9	25.0	24.5	28.4	17.9	12.8	19.1	20.6	17.0	14.5

[Sources: Bank of England; ONS; Halifax Building Society; Council of Mortgage Lenders; HM Treasury; British Bankers' association · Many figures have been rounded]

Parliament & Politics

Die Politik ist die Lehre von Moglichen.
[politics is the art of the possible]
—— OTTO VON BISMARCK (1815–98)

———— THE HOUSE OF COMMONS ————

House of Commons, London, SW1A 0AA
Switchboard: 020 7219 3000 · www.parliament.uk

STATE OF THE PARTIES · as at 18 September 2006

Labour	353	Independent	2
Conservative	196	Ulster Unionist	1
Liberal Democrat	63	Respect	1
Scottish National Party	6	Speaker (Michael Martin)‡	1
Plaid Cymru	3	Deputy Speakers‡	3
Democratic Unionist	9	TOTAL	646
Sinn Féin [seats not taken]	5	GOVERNMENT MAJORITY	69
Social Democratic & Labour	3	(‡ By tradition, these do not normally vote.)	

Oldest MP .... Piara Khabra [Lab; Ealing Southall] *b*.20·11·24
Youngest MP.................... Jo Swinson [Lib Dem; East Dunbartonshire] *b*.05·02·80
Largest majority.........19,519; Thomas Clarke [Lab; Coatbridge, Chryston & Bellshill]
Smallest majority.....................................37; Laura Moffatt [Lab; Crawley]

———— PETITIONING THE COMMONS ————

Despite reforms in 1993 and 2004, a plethora of (often arcane) rules still govern the form of petitions to the House of Commons. ❦ Petitions must be specifically and respectfully addressed to the House, with a clear request the House can grant, and must be decorous and temperate in tone. ❦ Although petitions no longer need to be handwritten, they must contain no erasures, deletions, or interlineations, and must be in English (unless a certified translation is appended). ❦ Every name on a petition must be signed (or marked) and carry an address. ❦ After disorder in the C17th, the presentation of a petition remains limited to just ten people. ❦ Only MPs may formally present petitions to the House, and then only between set hours (petitions may be informally presented at any time by being slipped into a green bag hung off the Speaker's chair). ❦ Although nowadays the number of signatories to a petition is estimated, prior to 1974 signatures were counted by clerks who were paid 12½ pence per 1,000 names. ❦ It is reckoned that the Ambulance Dispute Petition in 1989 had the most signatories (*c*.4½ million), though petitions with one name are still valid (and are not uncommon). [Source: House of Commons Information Office]

————— POLITICAL BESTIARY —————

Animal symbolism is a key element of art, literature, myth, and belief in every culture. Different animals have been ascribed a range of characteristics and associations, which translate into symbolic shorthand: the cunning fox, the wise owl, &c. In the West, the linking of animals with politics was formalised by heraldry's complex menagerie of real and fabled animals. Below are some notes on recent political animal symbolism. ❦ British politicians are familiar with STALKING HORSES. In the C17th, these were specially trained horses used to conceal hunters as close to their timid quarry as possible. In modern politics, a stalking horse is a 'no hope' candidate who challenges an incumbent to gauge their popularity, while providing cover for stronger candidates. A good modern example of a stalking horse is Sir Anthony Meyer, whose doomed challenge to Margaret Thatcher in 1989 exposed her weakness and precipitated her eventual defeat (the press dubbed Meyer a 'stalking donkey'). ❦ Amongst a number of symbols adopted by Gandhi was the COW – a beast sacrificed by Muslims but held sacred by Hindus. The cow was a paradoxical (and unsuccessful) attempt to bridge this divide and create a symbol of national Indian unity, religious tolerance, and respect for all life. ❦ The DOVE has long been associated with goodness, but of three different types: the dove of Noah symbolises *rest*; the dove of David, *peace*; and the dove of Christ, *salvation*. In contrast, from the earliest days of falconry, the HAWK has symbolised war. ❦ The SCAPEGOAT, so often discussed in politics, dates back to Jewish ritual [Lev. XVI] and the Day of Atonement, when one of two goats was chosen by lot to be sent into the wilderness (the sins of the people having been symbolically laid upon it), while the other was sacrificed. ❦ In America, the Democrat DONKEY and the Republican ELEPHANT probably date back to the Congressional elections of 1874, and the work of German-born artist Thomas Nast – the 'father' of US caricature and cartoon. It seems that in 1874 the *New York Herald* ran a hoax story about animals escaping from the Central Park Zoo and scavenging for food. In a cartoon for *Harper's Weekly*, Nast combined the *Herald*'s joke with Ulysses S. Grant's bid for re-election, depicting the *Herald* as a donkey disguised as a lion, trying to scare away a Republican elephant. Depending on your partisan persuasion, the donkey (an C18th euphemism for 'ass') represents either stubbornness and braying stupidity or cleverness, courage, and likeability. (In Biblical times, donkeys were thought suitable mounts for royalty in peacetime.) The elephant symbolises either sturdiness, toughness, and a preternatural memory, or blundering clumsiness, and pachydermal insensitivity. ❦ Two recent additions to the political menagerie are the RINO (*Republican in Name Only*) and the DINO (*Democrat in Name Only*), to represent politicians whose beliefs do not always match their party's line. Michael Bloomberg and Arnold Schwarzenegger have both been called RINOs, and Joe Lieberman a DINO. ❦ LAME DUCK was originally a London stock market term for one who defaulted on a debt. It now describes a seriously discredited politician or a President in (roughly) the second half of their second term.

BRITISH PRIME MINISTERS

1997............................ Tony Blair L	1858............. Viscount Palmerston Li
1990.............................John Major C	1858.................... Edward Stanley C
1979................ Margaret Thatcher C	1855............. Viscount Palmerston Li
1976.................. James Callaghan L	1852............G. Hamilton-Gordon C
1974.................... Harold Wilson L	1852.................... Edward Stanley C
1970...................Edward Heath C	1846.......................John Russell W
1964.................... Harold Wilson L	1841.................... Sir Robert Peel T
1963.............Alec Douglas-Home C	1835...................William Lamb W
1957................ Harold Macmillan C	1834.................... Sir Robert Peel T
1955.................Sir Anthony Eden C	1834...................Arthur Wellesley T
1951.................Winston Churchill C	1834..................William Lamb W
1945....................Clement Attlee L	1830.......................Charles Grey W
1940.................Winston Churchill N/C	1828...................Arthur Wellesley T
1937...........Neville Chamberlain N/C	1827............. Frederick Robinson T
1935.............Stanley Baldwin N/C	1827.................George Canning T
1931.............Ramsay MacDonald N	1812....................Robert Jenkinson T
1929............. Ramsay MacDonald L	1809................. Spencer Perceval T
1924.................Stanley Baldwin C	1807.................William Bentinck T
1924.............. Ramsay MacDonald L	1806.................William Grenville W
1923...................Stanley Baldwin C	1804........ William Pitt [The Younger] T
1922...............Andrew Bonar Law C	1801.................. Henry Addington T
1916.............David Lloyd George Co	1783........ William Pitt [The Younger] T
1908............. Herbert Asquith Li & Co	1783..................William Bentinck T
1905.......H. Campbell-Bannerman Li	1782............William FitzMaurice W
1902.....................Arthur Balfour C	1782.......... C. Watson-Wentworth W
1895............Marquess of Salisbury C	1770............. Frederick Lord North T
1894....................Earl of Rosebery Li	1767.................Augustus Fitzroy W
1892.............. William Gladstone Li	1766..........William Pitt [The Elder] W
1886...........Marquess of Salisbury C	1765.......... C. Watson-Wentworth W
1886............... William Gladstone Li	1763.................George Grenville W
1885...........Marquess of Salisbury C	1762.......................John Stuart T
1880............... William Gladstone Li	1757................. T. Pelham-Holles W
1874.................Benjamin Disraeli C	1756...............William Cavendish W
1868............... William Gladstone Li	1754................. T. Pelham-Holles W
1868.................Benjamin Disraeli C	1743.....................Henry Pelham W
1866.................... Edward Stanley C	1742.................Spencer Compton W
1865.......................John Russell Li	1721................Sir Robert Walpole W

Whig · Liberal · Tory · Labour · Conservative · National · Coalition · The term *Prime Minister* was initially one of abuse; the position was formally referred to as *First Lord of the Treasury.*

SEXIEST POLITICIAN

In a February 2006 poll of the 100 sexiest men by *New Woman* magazine, David Cameron came in at 92, just ahead of singer James Blunt and actor Russell Crowe.

──────── THE CABINET ────────

Damaged by a succession of political setbacks and personal embarrassments, and chastened by heavy losses in the local elections [see p.256], on 5 May 2006 Tony Blair announced what was widely expected to be his last major Cabinet reshuffle:

Old	CABINET POST	New
John Prescott	*Deputy Prime Minister*	John Prescott
Gordon Brown	*Chancellor of the Exchequer*	Gordon Brown
Jack Straw	*Foreign Secretary*	Margaret Beckett
John Hutton	*Work & Pensions*	John Hutton
Margaret Beckett	*Environment, Food, & Rural Affairs*	David Miliband
Alistair Darling	*Transport & Scotland*	Douglas Alexander
John Reid	*Defence*	Des Browne
Geoff Hoon	*Leader of the Commons*	Jack Straw
Patricia Hewitt	*Health*	Patricia Hewitt
Tessa Jowell	*Culture, Media, & Sport*	Tessa Jowell
Hilary Armstrong	*Chief Whip*	Jacqui Smith
Charles Clarke	*Home Secretary*	John Reid
Peter Hain	*Northern Ireland & Wales*	Peter Hain
Ian McCartney	*Min. w/o Portfolio & Labour Party Chair*	Hazel Blears
Baroness Amos	*Leader of the Lords*	Baroness Amos
Lord Falconer	*Constitutional Affairs & Lord Chancellor*	Lord Falconer
Hilary Benn	*International Development*	Hilary Benn
Alan Johnson	*Trade & Industry*	Alistair Darling
Ruth Kelly	*Education & Skills*	Alan Johnson
—	*Min. Cabinet Office & Social Exclusion*	Hilary Armstrong
Des Browne	*Chief Secretary to the Treasury*	Stephen Timms
David Miliband	*Communities, Local Gov. (& Women)*	Ruth Kelly
Lord Goldsmith	*Attorney General*	Lord Goldsmith
Lord Grocott	*Lords' Chief Whip*	Lord Grocott
Douglas Alexander	*Minister of State for Europe*	Geoff Hoon
	Minister of State for Trade	Ian McCartney

After his extra-marital affair with an aide was revealed in the press, John Prescott was relieved of most of his ministerial responsibilities, yet he kept the post, salary, and perks of Deputy Prime Minister – possibly to spare Blair a divisive election for the post. Some days later Prescott was forced to relinquish one of his grace-and-favour homes, Dorneywood, after he was photographed playing croquet there in his shirt-sleeves during 'office hours'. ❦ Notwithstanding Blair's earlier support, Clarke was sacked from the Home Office in an attempt to stem the damage caused by the release of foreign prisoners. Clarke declined the offer of other posts and returned to the backbenches after, unusually, questioning Blair's judgement. Clarke was replaced by Reid, who had previously held Cabinet positions for health, transport, Northern Ireland, Scotland, and defence. ❦ Hewitt remained at Health despite being heckled by health workers over NHS deficits and job cuts. ❦ Inevitably, the reshuffle was analysed by politicians and pundits alike for clues on the state of the Blair-Brown relationship, and hints as to when Blair might resign.

──── DAVID CAMERON & THE TORY LEADERSHIP ────

On 6 May 2005, the day after the General Election, Michael Howard announced that he would resign as Tory leader once the party had had the opportunity to change the rules for electing his successor. Howard cited his age (63), and declared: 'I've said that if people don't deliver then they go. And for me delivering meant winning the election'. ❦ The early months of the contest focused on Howard's attempt to change the electoral rules that gave party members, not MPs, the final vote on leader. This system was blamed for electing Iain Duncan Smith whose tenure was characterised by Parliamentary infighting. However, despite 71% of MPs favouring a system that would return to them the final choice of leader, the party's 'electoral college' rejected any change. ❦ The chance to succeed Howard catalysed a flurry of manoeuvring. A number of MPs mooted their intention to stand – including Theresa May, Tim Yeo, and David Willetts – and the party creaked along its familiar fault-lines of state, tax, and modernisation. Curiously, as during the General Election, Europe did not feature prominently – perhaps because the leading Europhile candidate, Ken Clarke, had ruled out any swift Euro entry. Instead, much of the campaign was mired in rumours that David Cameron had taken drugs while at Oxford University. ❦ The Blackpool Party conference in October saw a beauty-parade of speeches from Malcolm Rifkind, Liam Fox, Ken Clarke, David Cameron, and David Davis. Davis arrived in Blackpool as favourite, with the declared support of 66 MPs. However, his lacklustre conference speech was outclassed by a slick performance from Cameron, that ended with him patting the stomach of his pregnant wife. Rifkind bowed out soon after Conference. The first vote of MPs took place on 18 October:

Ken Clarke [eliminated]	38
Liam Fox	45
David Cameron	56
David Davis	62

Clarke's defeat (his third in a leadership contest since 1997) marked the end of his Prime Ministerial ambitions. The second vote took place on 20 October:

Liam Fox [eliminated]	51
David Davis	57
David Cameron	90

During six weeks of terse debates and interviews, both Davids mocked each other for aping Blair while presenting themselves as the leader most able to perform his electoral magic. ❦ On 6 December a postal vote of Conservative party members was declared:

David Davis	64,398
David Cameron	134,446

The next day, Cameron became the fifth Tory leader to face Blair at the dispatch box for Prime Minister's Questions. ❦ David Cameron, born in 1966 the son of a stockbroker, was educated at Eton and Brasenose, Oxford. After working first as a political special advisor and then in the media, he was elected MP for Witney in 2001. Since his election to Party Leader, Cameron has fought assiduously to position himself and his party as a viable version of Blair and a safer alternative to Brown. Despite a softer approach to 'Punch and Judy politics' and a greener policy agenda, he has largely managed to keep his party unified (or at least silent) behind him.

──────────── LIBERAL DEMOCRAT LEADERSHIP ────────────

Despite leading the Lib Dems to their best general election since the 1920s (62 MPs in 2005), Charles Kennedy finally succumbed to a long whispering campaign against his weak leadership and 'bon viveur' lifestyle. On 5 January 2006, Kennedy confirmed Whitehall's common knowledge by admitting that 'over the past 18 months I've been coming to terms with and seeking to cope with a drink problem'. Two days later, under pressure from colleagues, Kennedy abandoned a bid to seek re-election and resigned. Sir Menzies 'Ming' Campbell, who became acting leader, was the first to declare his candidacy, and received backing from former leader Lord Ashdown. Mark Oaten announced he would challenge Campbell for the leadership, only to pull out of the contest a week later after it emerged that he had the support of only one other MP. (A few days later, Oaten was forced to resign as the Lib Dem home affairs spokesman after the *News of the World* revealed his affair with a 23-year-old male prostitute.) The final names on the ballots sent to 73,000 Lib Dem members on 6 February were: Menzies Campbell (acting leader and foreign affairs spokesman), Chris Huhne (economic spokesman), and Simon Hughes (party president). Notwithstanding an unexpected coup in the Dunfermline and Fife West by-election (the Lib Dems overturned an 11,562 Labour majority in the constituency where Gordon Brown lives), the election veered between the scandalous and the lacklustre. (The fallout of Mark Oaten's affair was exacerbated by a forced admission from Simon Hughes that, despite previous denials, he had enjoyed homosexual relations in his past.) The ballot closed on March 1, with a 72% turnout. The voting was:

1st round: Hughes, 12,081 · Huhne, 16,691 · Campbell, 23,264
2nd round: (*after Hughes' 2nd preferences were re-distributed*)
Huhne, 21,628 · CAMPBELL, 29,697

The election of Sir Menzies Campbell (a 64-year-old Scottish barrister and former Olympic sprinter) was interpreted by some as a bid for stability and by others as a sign of timidity – a contradiction Campbell himself tried to square: 'Safe pair of hands yes, but ready to take risks, ready to challenge orthodoxy and ready to challenge the party too'. However, faced with a rejuvenating Tory party, Campbell found it hard to make a firm first impression – and a series of poor performances at Prime Minister's Questions led some to question how long the Ming dynasty would last.

──────────── 'NUMBER ONE, MR SPEAKER' ────────────

By a tradition that dates back to Harold Macmillan in 1961, the first question at Prime Minister's Questions [PMQ] asks the PM to list his official engagements for the day. The formulaic response is '*This morning I had meetings with ministerial colleagues and others. In addition to my duties in the House, I will have further such meetings later today*'. This catch-all question (Number One on the Order Paper) is designed to circumvent the fact that the PM is technically only responsible for a narrow range of issues (such as national security). Once the PM has introduced the broader range of his governmental responsibilities, MPs are free to ask supplementary questions (of which the PM usually has no foreknowledge) on almost any subject they like.

THE SCOTTISH PARLIAMENT

The current state of parties (as at 18 September 2006)

Number of MSPs	Constituency	Regional	Total
Scottish Labour	46	4	50
Scottish National Party	8	17	25
Scottish Conservative & Unionist	3	14	17
Scottish Liberal Democrat	13	4	17
Scottish Green Party	0	7	7
Scottish Socialist Party	0	6	6
Scottish Senior Citizens' Unity Party	0	1	1
Independent MSPs/No affiliation	2	3	5
Presiding Officer (George Reid)	1	0	1

THE NATIONAL ASSEMBLY FOR WALES

The current state of parties (as at 18 September 2006)

Number of AMs	Constituency	Regional	Total
Labour	29	0	29
Plaid Cymru	5	7	12
Conservative	1	10	11
Liberal Democrat	2	3	5
Others/Independents	2	0	2
Presiding Officer (Lord Dafydd Elis-Thomas)	1	0	1

THE NORTHERN IRELAND ASSEMBLY

The current state of parties (as at 16 June 2006)

DUP..............32[†]	SDLP..............18	UKUP..............1
Sinn Féin............24	Alliance..............6	Independent..........2
Ulster Unionists......24	PUP..................1	† Includes 2 Ulster U. defectors

The Assembly is currently suspended; however, pending restoration of the devolved government, the Northern Ireland Act (2006) allows members to meet in an 'assembly', to which the Secretary of State may refer to for discussion on matters relating to devolved government.

THE LONDON ASSEMBLY

The current state of parties (as at 18 September 2006)

Conservative 9	Liberal Democrat 5	One London Group ..2
Labour................7	Green.................2	(June 2004 turnout, 36·6%)

—————————— THE HOUSE OF LORDS ——————————

State of the parties (as at 2 July 2006)
Conservative 210
Labour............................. 213
Liberal Democrat 79
Crossbench........................ 196

Bishops.............................26
Other..............................17
Total............................. 741

12 Peers on leave of absence are excluded.

Archbishops and Bishops...26 [0]
Life Peers under the Appellate Jurisdiction Act 1876.........................26 [1]
Life Peers under the Life Peerages Act 1958............................609 [138]
Peers under House of Lords Act 1999.......................................92 [3]

[Numbers within brackets indicate the number of women included in the figure.]

In July 2006, Baroness Hayman was elected as the first Speaker of the House of Lords. She will serve a five-year term, and will receive a £101,000 salary as well as a grace-and-favour apartment.

—————————— WORKING OR SHIRKING? ——————————

A report entitled *Working or Shirking? A Closer Look at MPs' Expenses and Parliamentary Attendance* was released in January 2006, by Professor Timothy Besley and Dr Valentino Larcinese of the London School of Economics and Political Science. They used data from 2001–04 to perform a statistical analysis of MPs' expenses, revealing that: those whose constituencies are far from Westminster tend to spend more; older, more experienced MPs spend less; Lib Dems spend most on staff, while Labour MPs spend more on postage and computers, and the Conservatives generally spend less on equipment. The average cost of an individual vote in Parliament was £556, with the 'cheapest' MP costing £257 and the most 'expensive' £3,360. The most 'expensive' votes in Parliament (2001–04) were:

Tony Blair [Lab] .... *per vote* £3,360
Gordon Brown [Lab] £3,114
Jack Straw [Lab]..................£2,043
Brian Wilson [Lab] £1,596
George Galloway [Lab/Res] £1,491

Clare Short [Lab] £1,260
Jane Kennedy [Lab]..............£1,243
Gwyneth Dunwoody [Lab]......£1,187
Michael Mates [Con] £1,070
Alex Salmond [SNP].............£1,043

—————————— GOVERNMENT WASTE ——————————

The Bumper Book of Government Waste was published in February 2006. The book's authors Matthew Elliott and Lee Rotherham used independent reports, press coverage and official statistics to create a dossier of government waste. Their findings for 2005 included: 20 out of 24 government departments overspent their budgets, with total overspend reaching £7·1bn; each European Member of Parliament costs £2·4m per annum in salary, administration, and perks; 459 books were lent by Luxembourg's EU library last year, costing £2,138 per book; and an RAF female aircraft mechanic was given a grant of £2,500 to re-train as a stripper.

ENGLISH LOCAL ELECTIONS 2006

The 4 May 2006 local elections were contested against a backdrop of political turmoil and personal embarrassment for New Labour: John Prescott's affair with his secretary; Patricia Hewitt's slow handclap reception at the Royal College of Nursing; and Charles Clarke's admission that >1,000 foreign criminals had been released by mistake. It was not surprising, then, that Labour lost 319 councillors and 17 councils – one of the worst local election defeats in its history – and received its lowest share of the vote since the early 1980s. If the results had been projected nationally, the Tories would have won 40%, the Lib Dems 27%, and Labour 26%.

Party	Councils		Councillors	
	±	*total*	±	*total*
Conservative	+11	68	+316	1,830
Labour	–17	30	–319	1,439
Liberal Democrat	+1	13	+2	909
Residents' Association	0	0	–13	35
British National Party	0	0	+27	32
Green	0	0	+20	29
Respect-Unity Coalition	0	0	+13	16
Others	0	0	–49	128
No Overall Control	+6	66	N/A	N/A

The Conservatives enjoyed their best local election results since 1992, taking 316 councillors and 11 councils. And, while they failed to make inroads in many northern cities, their showing was easily strong enough to secure and even strengthen the new leadership of David Cameron. The Lib Dems struggled to make any real headway, despite the election of Sir Menzies Campbell only two months earlier. Dogged by recent scandal [see p.253] and squeezed by a revivified Conservative party, the Lib Dems could only manage 2 additional councillors and 1 council. The Greens gained 20 seats, and the British National Party (perhaps aided by dire warnings about it from Margaret Hodge) gained 27 – including 11 in Barking (Hodge's own constituency). BNP leader Nick Griffin declared 'this is a revolt against

I think this shows the Conservative Party is broadening its appeal, that it's attracting new voters, and I think we see a Labour Party that is in some sort of serious meltdown.

– DAVID CAMERON

the entire liberal political elite by the hardworking people of Britain who resent being taxed to have our country transformed.' Many senior Labour figures rejected Cameron's allegations of a 'meltdown', but Gordon Brown admitted 'it's been a very disappointing night ... looking back at the headlines over the last couple of weeks I think we can probably all understand why that has happened'. The election results, and the difficult events that preceded them, increased the pressure on Tony Blair to name the date of his departure. As former Labour Health Secretary, Frank Dobson, said 'we've got to get the party under new management. It ought to happen fairly soon'. And, in an attempt to regain the political initiative, Blair brought forward by two days a controversial reshuffle of his Cabinet [see p.251].

——————— PARTISAN POLITICS & THE BRAIN ———————

Research published in January 2006 by psychologists at Emory University, Atlanta, suggests that both liberals and conservatives may be equally irrational when discussing politics. The study utilised functional MRI brain scanning to examine which parts of the brain appeared active during political discourse. In 2004, 30 adult men were recruited: half committed supporters of George W. Bush; the other half, supporters of John Kerry. Each man was asked to consider a series of doctored statements that portrayed both Bush and Kerry as dishonest. The study's authors concluded that partisan supporters denied obvious contradictions made by their own candidate, but spotted contradictions when they were made by the 'opposition'. Interestingly, the MRI scans seemed to indicate that

> *It appears as if partisans twirl the cognitive kaleidoscope until they get the conclusions they want ... then they get massively reinforced for it, with the elimination of negative emotional states and activation of positive ones*
> — Drew Westen

participants activated *emotional* rather than *analytical* centres of their brains. Drew Westen, Emory Director of Clinical Psychology, stated 'we did not see any increased activation of the parts of the brain normally engaged during reasoning ... what we saw instead was a network of emotion circuits lighting up'. Westen suggested that once partisans had formed utterly biased conclusions (ignoring information that did not fit their preconceptions), circuits that mediate negative emotions (sadness and disgust) 'turned off', and subjects 'activated' circuits involved in reward and pleasure. The research team hypothesised that this kind of emotional reasoning reinforces itself (since it produces feelings of pleasure), which in turns leads to the hardening of defensive, partisan beliefs.

——————— TONY BLAIR'S CONGRESSIONAL GOLD MEDAL ———————

Tony Blair was awarded the Congressional Gold Medal[†] in 2003, for his support of the US after 9/11. The rules of Congress require that the recipient of the award 'shall have performed an achievement that has an impact on American history and culture that is likely to be recognised as a major achievement in the recipient's field long after the achievement'. It was unanimously agreed that Blair had met this test. However, elements of the press cast doubt on Blair's good faith when it transpired in 2006 that he had still not collected the award. The *Times* dismissed reports that the medal was still being designed more than three years after its award (Nelson Mandela collected his medal in under 2 months), and it suggested that Blair was deliberately delaying his approval. The *Guardian* mooted that 'the last thing [Blair] needs is a ceremony celebrating his steadfastness as an American ally'.

† Originally presented to military leaders (the first recipient was Washington in 1776), the medal is now the highest civilian award and the greatest honour Congress can bestow. From time to time, Congress selects individuals who have made a significant contribution in their field, and passes legislation that must be signed by the President. The US Mint strikes bespoke designs for each award. Notable recipients include Frank Sinatra (1997); Rosa Parks (1999); and Charles M. Schulz (2000).

PARLIAMENTARY SALARY & ALLOWANCES

Members of Parliament
Members' Parliamentary Salary . . . . £59,686 (from 1·4·2006) £60,277 (from 1·11·2006)
Staffing Allowance (maximum) £87,276
Incidental Expenses Provision (IEP) £20,440
IT equipment (centrally provided). . . . . worth *c.*£3,000
London Supplement (for inner London seats) £2,712
Additional Costs Allowance (for those with seats outside London) £22,110
Winding up Allowance (maximum) £35,905
Car Mileage, first 10,000 miles . . . . .40p per mile
— thereafter. . . . . .25p per mile
Motorcycle allowance. . . . . .24p per mile
Bicycle allowance . . . . .20p per mile

The House of Commons decided that the annual pay award for MPs and Ministers should be staggered, with 1% increases on 1 April 2006, and 1 November 2006:

Position	1·4·06	1·11·06
Prime Minister†	£126,085	£127,334
Cabinet Minister†	£75,651	£76,400
Cabinet Minister (Lords)	£102,685	£103,701
Minister of State†	£39,243	£39,631
Minister of State (Lords)	£80,176	£80,970
Parliamentary Under Secretary†	£29,786	£30,081
Parliamentary Under Secretary (Lords)	£69,829	£70,521
Government Chief Whip†	£75,651	£76,400
Government Deputy Chief Whip†	£39,243	£39,631
Government Whip†	£25,255	£25,505
Leader of the Opposition†	£69,349	£70,035
Leader of the Opposition (Lords)	£69,829	£70,521
Opposition Chief Whip†	£39,243	£39,631
Speaker†	£75,651	£76,400
Attorney General	£107,422	£108,485
Lord Chancellor	elects to receive the salary of Lords Cabinet Ministers	

† Ministers in the Commons additionally receive their salaries as MPs (as above).

Backbench Peers
Subsistence. . . . . Day £75 · Overnight £150
Office secretarial allowance. . . . .£65 per sitting day and <40 additional days
Travel. . . . . .as for MPs
Spouses/children's expenses. . . . . 6 return journeys per year
Lords' Ministers and paid office holders
Ministers' Night Subsistence Allowance . . .£33,000 for those with a second home in London
London Supplement. . . . .£1,667 except those with official residence &c.
Secretarial allowance. £4,884
Spouses/children's expenses. . . . . 15 return journeys per year

——— SALARIES FOR DEVOLVED LEGISLATURES &c. ———

Scottish Parliament 2006–07	*1·4·2006*	*1·11·2006*
Member of the Scottish Parliament (MSP)	£52,226	£52,743
First Minister†	£75,653	£76,402
Scottish Minister†	£39,246	£39,635
Junior Scottish Minister†	£24,582	£24,825
Presiding Officer†	£39,246	£39,635

† additionally receive their salaries as MSPs (as above).

National Assembly for Wales 2006–07	*additional salary*	*total salary*
Assembly Member (AM)	—	£46,191
Assembly First Minister	£76,491	£120,135
Assembly Minister	£39,677	£84,085
Presiding Officer	£39,677	£84,085
Leader of the largest non-cabinet party	£39,677	£84,085
AMs who are also MPs or MEPs		£15,397

Northern Ireland Assembly	*total salary*
Members of the Legislative Assembly (MLA)	£31,817
Presiding Officer	£48,850

The Assembly has been suspended since 14 October 2002. In December 2003, these salaries were introduced (at a lower rate than if the Assembly were sitting) to pay MLAs for constituency work.

European Parliament 2006–07	*total salary*
UK Members of the European Parliament	as MPs

Members of Parliament who are also members of a devolved legislature receive the full parliamentary salary (see above) and one third of the salary due to them for their other role. Since 2004, Westminster MPs are ineligible to serve additionally as MEPs. The devolved legislatures control their own expenses and allowances.

London Assembly 2006–07	*total salary*
Member of the London Assembly (MLA)	£49,266
Mayor of London	£133,997
Deputy Mayor	£88,586

Since 1997, Tony Blair has spent £1·2m on RAF aircraft to fly him around the world. ❦ Between 2003–06 it cost >£1·4m to maintain Nos. 10, 11, & 12 Downing Street. ❦ During the 2005 election, Cherie Blair spent £7,700 having her hair coiffed by a personal hairdresser. ❦ In the run-up to the 2005 election, the Labour party paid Mark Penn, an advisor to Hilary Clinton based in Washington, £530,372 for his consultation services; the Tories paid Australian consultant Lynton Crosby £441,146, and spent £308,143 on tracker polls and £43,475 on focus groups. ❦ The Conservatives spent £1·5m on targeting voters with leaflets about immigration. ❦ £3,638 was spent on Michael Howard's make-up during the 2005 election; Charles Kennedy spent £4,800 on five suits from a tailor in Dewsbury, West Yorkshire; while Labour spent £299·63 on 6 Mr Spock-style costumes, to be worn by lackeys tormenting Conservative MP John Redwood (a.k.a the Vulcan).

─────────── TIMELINE OF ELECTORAL LAW ───────────

1832............ *property qualifications to vote introduced; 'rotten boroughs' abolished*
1872..*secret ballot introduced*
1885... *distribution of seats reorganised*
1911..............................*five-year Parliamentary terms introduced*
1918....................*all men ≥21 entitled to vote; women ≥30 entitled to vote*
1928.. *all women ≥21 entitled to vote*
1949....................................*'university vote' and 'business vote' abolished*
1969.. *voting aged dropped to 18 for all*
1985.............. *British citizens overseas eligible to vote for ≤5 years after they leave*
1989...............*qualifying period for overseas electors extended from 5 to 20 years*
1994........*EU residents in UK entitled to vote and stand in UK European elections*
1995....*EU residents in UK obliged to register and entitled to stand in local elections*
1998.......................... *registration of political parties and symbols introduced*
2000.......*registration rules changed; postal voting extended; disabled voters assisted;*
 funding and spending of parties controlled; Electoral Commission established
2002.................... *all-women shortlists for Parliamentary candidates permitted*

─────────── THE GOVERNMENT ART COLLECTION ───────────

The Government Art Collection (GAC), within the Department for Culture, Media and Sport, has responsibility for displaying works of art from its collection in government buildings around the world. Since its creation in 1898, the GAC has collected *c.*12,500 works of British art in every media – from paintings and sculpture to textiles and video. The works date from the mid-C16th to the modern day. Some of the many works of art currently on display in 10 Downing St include:

Title	artist	location
William Pitt	William Hoare (1707–92)	Entrance Hall
Benjamin Disraeli	John Adams Acton (1833–1910)	lobby
Horatio Nelson	Lemuel Francis Abbott (*c.*1760–1803)	Terracotta Room
Jane Anne Inglis	John Constable (1776–1837)	Terracotta Room
Mary Gainsborough	Thomas Gainsborough (1727–88)	Terracotta Room
Florence Nightingale	Arthur George Walker (1861–1939)	White Room
Queen Elizabeth I	Anon (*c.*1570–80)	Pillared Drawing Room

─────── SPECTATOR PARLIAMENTARIAN AWARDS '05 ───────

Newcomer of the year .... Sadiq Khan [Lab]
Minister to watch...John Reid [Lab]
Speech of the year..Barbara Follett [Lab]
Inquisitor of the year .... John Denham [Lab]
Peer of the year....................................Baroness Scotland of Asthal [Lab]
Politician of the year..David Cameron [Con]
Parliamentarian of the year..................................Dominic Grieve [Con]

PARLIAMENTARY PERIODS

Parliament...................period from *election* to *dissolution* (maximum 5 years)
Session......................................runs from *State Opening* to *Prorogation*
Recess.............................a break within a *session* – e.g. Christmas, Easter
State Opening†...............................heralds new *session* or new *parliament*
Prorogation..heralds the end of a *session*
Dissolution........................the end of a *parliament* – heralds new elections
Week ....a long time in politics, according to Harold Wilson

† The State Opening of Parliament takes place when Parliament reconvenes after a General Election, and then when each new session begins (normally in November). At the State Opening, members of the Commons are summoned to the Lords by Black Rod to hear the Queen's Speech. The speech, which outlines the government's proposed legislation for the session ahead, is read by the Sovereign but written by her Government. If the Monarch is unable to attend the State Opening (as the Queen was in 1959 and 1963), Parliament is opened by the Lords Commissioners (the Lord Chancellor, the Lord President of the Council, the Lord Privy Seal, the Lord Steward, and the Lord Chamberlain). The Lord Chancellor then delivers the Monarch's speech in the third person. (Before each State Opening, the cellars of the Palace of Westminster are searched by the Yeomen of the Guard to prevent a recurrence of Guy Fawkes' treasonous Gunpowder Plot that took place on 5th November 1605, as if one could forget.)

CHANNEL 4 POLITICAL AWARDS · 2006

Rising star..Michael Gove [Con]
The politician's politician...........Hilary Benn (SoS International Development) [Lab]
Opposition politician of the year ....Dominic Grieve [Con]
Hansard award for opening-up politics   *This Week* · BBC1
Political humorist of the year...*Private Eye*
Campaigning politician... Chris Grayling [Con]
Peer of the year................................Baroness Ashton of Upholland [Lab]
Political book of the year..................................*Rosebery* · Leo McKinstry
Most inspiring political figure.....Jamie Oliver · *campaign for better school dinners*

GOVERNMENT OFFICIAL CARS

Figures from the Government's official car service showed that in 2004–5 the government spent £5·16m providing 85 cars to Ministers and officials – an average of £60,748 per car. Cabinet Ministers are provided with a Vauxhall Omega Elite or a Rover 75 Connoisseur. Ex-Prime Ministers continue to have the privilege of an official car because of a deal Harold Wilson struck shortly before he left office. Under Wilson's arrangement, Margaret Thatcher and John Major still have use of official cars and, by some unexplained anomaly, former Deputy PM Lord Howe is still provided with a £60,000-a-year car and driver, 15 years after leaving office.

———GENERAL ELECTION BREAKDOWN 1979–2005———

Date	3·5·79	9·6·83	11·6·87	9·4·92	1·5·97	7·6·01	5·5·05
Winning party	Con	Con	Con	Con	Lab	Lab	Lab
Seat majority	43	144	102	21	179	167	67
PM	Thatcher	Thatcher	Thatcher	Major	Blair	Blair	Blair
Leader of Op.	Callaghan	Foot	Kinnock	Kinnock	Major	Hague	Howard
Lib (Dem) leader	Steel	Steel	Steel	Ashdown	Ashdown	Kennedy	Kennedy

Conservative

Seats	339	397	375	336	165	166	198
Votes (m)	13·70	13·01	13·74	14·09	9·60	8·36	8·78
Share of votes (%)	43·9	42·4	42·2	41·9	30·7	31·7	32·4
% of seats	53·4	61·1	57·8	51·6	25·0	25·2	30·5

Labour

Seats	268	209	229	271	418	412	355
Votes (m)	11·51	8·46	10·03	11·56	13·52	10·72	9·55
Share of votes (%)	36·9	27·6	30·8	34·4	43·2	40·7	35·2
% of seats	42·4	32·2	35·2	41·6	63·6	62·7	55·2

Liberal Democrat (&c.)

Seats	11	23	22	20	46	52	62
Votes (m)	4·31	7·78	7·34	6·00	5·24	4·81	5·99
Share of votes (%)	13·8	25·4	22·6	17·8	16·8	18·3	22·0
% of seats	1·7	3·5	3·4	3·1	7·0	7·9	9·6

Monster Raving Loony

Candidates	–	11	5	22	24	15	19
Average vote (%)	–	0·7	0·7	0·6	0·7	1·0	–
Lost deposits	–	11	5	22	24	15	19

Women MPs	19	23	41	60	120	118	127
– as %	3·0	3·5	6·3	9·2	18·2	17·9	19·7

Turnout (%)	76·0	72·7	75·3	77·7	71·4	59·4	61·4
– England (%)	75·9	72·5	75·4	78·0	71·4	59·2	61·3
– Wales (%)	79·4	76·1	78·9	79·7	73·5	61·6	62·6
– Scotland (%)	76·8	72·7	75·1	75·5	71·3	58·2	60·8
– N. Ireland (%)	67·7	72·9	67·0	69·8	67·1	68·0	62·9

Postal vote (%)	2·2	2·0	2·4	2·0	2·3	5·2	14·6
Spoilt ballots (%)	0·38	0·17	0·11	0·12	0·30	0·38	0·7
– av. / constituency	186	79	57	61	142	152	291
Deposit to stand	£150	£150	£500	£500	£500	£500	£500
– threshold (%)	12½	12½	5	5	5	5	5

Some figures (e.g. that of the winning party's majority) are disputed. Source: House of Commons.

——CLASSES OF SECRET——

Sensitive government documents are classed into four categories of secrecy:

TOP SECRET

Material likely to: threaten directly the internal stability of the UK or friendly countries; lead to widespread loss of life; cause exceptionally grave damage to the effectiveness or security of UK or allied forces or to the effectiveness of extremely valuable security operations; cause exceptionally grave damage to relations with friendly governments; cause severe long-term damage to the UK economy.

SECRET

Material likely to: raise international tension; damage seriously relations with friendly governments; threaten life directly, or seriously prejudice public order, or individual security or liberty; cause serious damage to the operational effectiveness or security of UK or allied forces or the continuing effectiveness of highly valuable security or intelligence operations; cause substantial material damage to national finances or economic and commercial interests.

CONFIDENTIAL

Material likely to: materially damage diplomatic relations (i.e. cause formal protest or other sanction); prejudice individual security or liberty; cause damage to the operational effectiveness or security of UK or allied forces or the effectiveness of valuable security or intelligence operations; work substantially against national finances or economic and commercial interests; substantially undermine the financial viability of major organisations; impede the investigation or facilitate the commission of serious crime; impede seriously the development or operation of major government policies; shut down or otherwise substantially disrupt significant national operations.

RESTRICTED

Material likely to: affect diplomatic relations adversely; cause substantial distress to individuals; make it more difficult to maintain the operational effectiveness or security of UK or allied forces; cause financial loss or facilitate improper gain or advantage; prejudice the investigation or aid the commission of crime; breach proper undertakings to maintain the confidence of information provided by third parties; impede the effective statutory restrictions on disclosure of information; disadvantage government in commercial or policy negotiations with others; undermine the proper management of the public sector.

A range of 'descriptors' can also be added, for example:

BUDGET..........*pre-announcement Budget measures*
HONOURS ....*actual or potential award of an honour*
INVESTIGATION.............*into discipline or crime*
VISITS.........*by royalty, ministers or very senior staff*
MEDICAL...........*confidential reports and material*
CONTRACTS......*tenders and terms being considered*

——MINISTERS' CONDUCT——

from THE MINISTERIAL CODE
*a Code of Conduct and Guidance
on Procedures for Ministers*

SELFLESSNESS · *Holders of public office should act solely in terms of the public interest. They should not do so in order to gain financial or other material benefits for themselves, their family, or their friends.*

INTEGRITY · *Holders of public office should not place themselves under any financial or other obligation to outside individuals or organisations that might seek to influence them in the performance of their official duties.*

OBJECTIVITY · *In carrying out public business, including making public appointments, awarding contracts, or recommending individuals for rewards and benefits, holders of public office should make choices on merit.*

ACCOUNTABILITY · *Holders of public office are accountable for their decisions and actions to the public and must submit themselves to whatever scrutiny is appropriate to their office.*

OPENNESS · *Holders of public office should be as open as possible about all the decisions and actions that they take. They should give reasons for their decisions and restrict information only when the wider public interest clearly demands.*

HONESTY · *Holders of public office have a duty to declare any private interests relating to their public duties and to take steps to resolve any conflicts arising in a way that protects the public interest.*

LEADERSHIP · *Holders of public office should promote and support these principles by leadership and example.*

—————————— WORLD ORGANISATIONS ——————————

United Nations [UN]
(est. 1945 · 191 member states)
Initially created in a bid to maintain peace and security after WWII, the UN now works across a broad range of areas, spanning international law and economic development. To manage its ever-growing remit, the UN administers a number of agencies with more specific focusses, such as the Security Council, whose prime responsibility is international peace. Nearly every recognised state in the world is a UN member (save the Vatican, Palestine, Taiwan, Niue and the Cook Islands).

North Atlantic Treaty Organisation [NATO] · (est. 1949 · 26 members)
A military alliance of Western countries, originally established to counter a perceived threat from the Soviet Union. NATO now promotes mutual defence and co-operation. In 1995, NATO undertook its first aggressive action – bombing Serbian positions around Sarajevo. NATO has held a peacekeeping role in Afghanistan since 2003.

World Bank (or *International Bank for Reconstruction & Development*)
(est. 1944 · 184 members)
An agency of the UN providing low-interest loans, policy advice, and technical assistance to low and middle income countries to reduce poverty and aid economic development.

World Trade Organisation [WTO]
(est. 1995 · 149 members)
International organisation that aims to facilitate business links. The WTO negotiates rules of trade between nation states and arbitrates international trade disputes.

The Paris Club
(est. 1956 · 19 members)
Informal group of creditor countries that works to ease the burden of debtor countries by renegotiating and rescheduling their debts.

Organisation for Economic Co-operation and Development [OECD]
(est. 1961 · 30 members)
Group of industrialised countries co-operating on social and economic policy and development.

International Monetary Fund [IMF] · (est. 1945 · 184 members)
Works to promote world monetary stability, economic development, and high levels of employment.

Organisation of Petroleum Exporting Countries [OPEC]
(est. 1960 · 11 members)
Encourages co-operation amongst petroleum-producing countries and works to achieve 'stable and fair' prices for oil producers, and a consistent supply of fuel.

Group of Eight [G8] · (est. 1975)
A group of the most powerful (and wealthy) nations – USA, Japan, Germany, Britain, France, Canada, Italy, and Russia – that meets annually to discuss economic and political co-operation.

United Nations Education, Scientific And Cultural Organisation [UNESCO]
(est. 1945 · 191 member states, and 6 associate members)
Fosters collaboration between member states in areas of science, arts, heritage, and culture. Most notably, UNESCO works to preserve the World Heritage sites [see p.218].

—————————— WORLD ORGANISATIONS cont. ——————————

World Health Organisation [WHO]
(est. 1948 · 192 members)
UN agency that aims to attain the
highest possible levels of health across
the globe, and raise awareness of
important health-related issues.

International Atomic Energy Agency
[IAEA] · (est. 1957 · 139 members)
An intergovernmental organisation
that reports to the UN, the IAEA aims
to promote positive uses for nuclear
energy and ensure it is not used for
military purposes [see p.62].

*International Committee of
the Red Cross* [ICRC]
(est. 1863 · 25 individual members,
all Swiss nationals)
Formed to provide humanitarian
aid during wartime, it now also lends
help to refugees and responds to
natural disasters [see p.292].

Association of South East Asian Nations
[ASEAN] · (est. 1967 · 10 members)
Aims to further economic growth,
assist social and cultural development,
and create regional stability amongst
south east Asian countries.

The Commonwealth
(est. 1926 · 53 member states)
A voluntary group of states which
were formerly part of (or associated
with) the British Empire. The
Commonwealth fosters co-operation,
development, and trade between
member states [see p.266].

Commonwealth of Independent States
[CIS] · (est. 1991 · 12 states)
Established to provide co-ordination
of defence, foreign, and economic
policies for states that were formerly
part of the USSR [see p.66].

Council of Europe
(est. 1949 · 46 member countries)
Works to encourage unity between
member states, to safeguard European
heritage, and to promote human
rights and European laws.

*European Bank for Reconstruction
and Development* [ERBD]
(est. 1991 · 62 members)
The ERBD aims to foster market
economies and democracies in 27
countries in central and eastern
Europe, and central Asia.

League of Arab States or *Arab League*
(est. 1945 · 22 members)
Supports economic, social, political,
and military unity amongst Arab states.

Organisation of the Islamic Conference
[OIC] · (est. 1969 · 57 states)
Promotes unity and co-operation
between Muslim countries, works to
safeguard Holy places, and aims to
eliminate racial discrimination.

*Unrepresented Nations and Peoples
Organisation* [UNPO]
(est. 1991 · 63 members)
Works to empower occupied nations,
indigenous people, and national
minorities who lack representation
elsewhere.

African Union [AU]
(est. 1999 · 53 nations)
Aims to encourage solidarity amongst
African nations, and to foster peace,
socio-economic co-operation,
and integration.

The Quartet · (est. 2002)
Informal grouping of the parties (EU,
UN, Russia and the US) concerned
with securing Middle East peace.

BRITISH OVERSEAS TERRITORIES

The fourteen British Overseas Territories [with estimated populations (2003)] are:

Anguilla [12,200] · British Antarctic Territory [0] · Bermuda [64,500]
British Indian Ocean Territory [4,000] · British Virgin Islands [21,300]
Cayman Islands [42,000] · Falkland Islands [2,379, at 2001]
Gibraltar [28,231, at 2001]· Montserrat [4,483]
St Helena [4000] & dependencies (Ascension Is. [1000] & Tristan da Cunha [275])
Turks and Caicos Islands [20,014, at 2001] · Pitcairn Island [47]
South Georgia & South Sandwich Islands [0] · Sovereign Cyprus Base Areas [n/a]

BRITISH PASSPORT WORDING

Her Britannic Majesty's Secretary of State Requests and requires in the Name of Her Majesty all those whom it may concern to allow the bearer to pass freely without let or hindrance, and to afford the bearer such assistance and protection as may be necessary.

Since British passports are issued in the name of Her Majesty, the Queen does not possess one, although all other members of the Royal Family do – including the Duke of Edinburgh. In other States where the Queen is Sovereign, similar wording is used, except that the request is made in the name of the Queen's representative in that realm – such as the Governor-General, or the Minister of Foreign Affairs.

THE COMMONWEALTH

The Commonwealth of Nations is a voluntary association of 53 sovereign states – all of which, excepting Mozambique, have experienced direct or indirect British rule. Although the Commonwealth has no formal constitution or charter, its common goals are declared to be the promotion of 'democracy and good governance, respect for human rights and gender equality, the rule of law, and sustainable economic and social development'. The Commonwealth members are:

Antigua & Barbuda* · Australia* · Bahamas* · Bangladesh · Barbados*
Belize* · Botswana · Brunei Darussalam · Cameroon · Canada* · Cyprus
Dominica · Fiji Islands · The Gambia · Ghana · Grenada* · Guyana
India · Jamaica* · Kenya · Kiribati · Lesotho · Malawi · Malaysia
Maldives · Malta · Mauritius · Mozambique · Namibia · Nauru
New Zealand* · Nigeria · Pakistan · Papua New Guinea*
St Kitts & Nevis* · St Lucia* · St Vincent* · Samoa · Seychelles
Sierra Leone · Singapore · Solomon Islands* · South Africa
Sri Lanka · Swaziland · Tanzania · Tonga · Trinidad & Tobaga
Tuvalu* · Uganda · United Kingdom · Vanuatu · Zambia

In December 2003, Zimbabwe withdrew its membership after its suspension was not lifted.
* The Queen is not only Queen of the UK and its overseas territories, but also of these realms.

——————————BEST & WORST US PRESIDENTS——————————

A Quinnipiac University poll in May 2006 asked registered American voters which US Presidents since World War II they considered to be the best and the worst:

Best post-War President	%	Worst post-War President	%
Ronald Reagan	28	George W. Bush	34
Bill Clinton	25	Richard Nixon	17
John Kennedy	18	Bill Clinton	16
Harry Truman	7	Jimmy Carter	13
Jimmy Carter	5	Lyndon Johnson	4
Dwight Eisenhower	5	George Bush Senior	3
George W. Bush	3	Ronald Reagan	3
George Bush Senior	2	Gerald Ford	2
Gerald Ford	1	John Kennedy	1
Lyndon Johnson	1	Harry Truman	1
Richard Nixon	1	Dwight Eisenhower	–
No opinion	4	No opinion	5

[Additional polling indicates the potentially perilous historical position of George W. Bush. According to a *Newsweek* poll in May 2006, 50% said that he would be viewed as a 'below average President' (32% said 'Average', 16% 'Above Average', and 2% were 'Unsure'). A Diageo/Hotline poll in December 2005, found that 34% thought history would judge Dubya as having done a 'good' or 'excellent' job.]

——————————————— RED & BLUE ———————————————

Since the US Presidential election of 2000, Republican and Democrat states have been represented on TV and in the press by RED and BLUE respectively. (The Federal Election Committee's 2004 report uses the same coding.) Yet, prior to this, most used the opposite colours. In 1976, NBC depicted Ford's states in blue and Carter's in red. Similarly, in 1984 Reagan's 'lake' turned blue. The reason for the switch in colours is unclear. *The Washington Post* ascribed the change to NBC's graphics department, and to a joke by David Letterman who suggested a compromise to 'make George W. Bush president of the red states and Al Gore head of the blue ones'. ❦ One curiosity of associating red with the political right and blue with the left is that it bucks historical political precedent. Red has long been the colour of revolution, Socialism and Communism (red Russia, red China), yet, red is also regal and was the uniform of British soldiers in the Revolutionary war. In heraldry, red signifies magnanimity and fortitude; in folklore, red is linked to magic. Blue is associated with the aristocracy (blue-blood), the sea, the sky, and constancy (true-blue). Yet it is also the colour of depression, and was worn by the lower classes: servants, paupers, charity-school boys, and licensed beggars. Blue was worn by the Union army and is the colour of police uniforms worldwide. In military planning, domestic and allied troops are blue, while enemy troops are red (thus 'friendly fire' is called 'blue on blue'). In Britain, of course, the right-wing Tories are blue, and left-wing Labour is red – although recently, in a scramble for the middle-ground, both parties have toyed with purple and, increasingly, green.

——————————— THE EUROPEAN UNION ———————————

The European Union (EU) has its roots in the European Coal & Steel Community (ECSC), formed in 1951 between Belgium, France, Germany, Italy, Luxembourg, and the Netherlands, who united to co-operate over production of coal and steel: the two key components of war. Since then, through a series of treaties, Europe as an economic and political entity has developed in size, harmonisation, and power. For some, the expansion in EU membership [see below] and the introduction of the euro (in 2002) are welcome developments in securing co-operation and peace; for others, the growth of the EU is a threat to the sovereignty of member nations.

MAJOR EU INSTITUTIONS

European Parliament · the democratic voice of the people of Europe, the EP approves the EU budget; oversees the other EU institutions; assents to key treaties and agreements on accession; and, alongside the Council of Ministers, examines and approves EU legislation. The EP sits in Strasbourg and Brussels, and its members are directly elected every 5 years.

Council of the EU · the pre-eminent decision-making body, the Council is made up of ministers from each national government. The Council meets regularly in Brussels to decide EU policy and approve laws, and every three months Presidents and PMs meet at European Councils to make major policy decisions.

European Commission · proposes new laws for the Council and Parliament to consider, and undertakes much of the EU's day-to-day work, such as overseeing the implementation of EU rules. Commissioners are nominated by each member state, and the President of the Commission is chosen by the national governments. It is based in Brussels.

European Court · ensures EU law is observed and applied fairly, and settles any disputes arising. Each state sends a judge to the Court in Luxembourg.

EU MEMBERSHIP

Since the founding of the European Economic Community [EEC] by the Treaty of Rome in 1957, the (now) EU membership has developed as follows:

Country	entry	members
Belgium		
France		
Germany	1958	6
Italy		
Luxembourg		
Netherlands		
Denmark		
Ireland	1973	9
UK		
Greece	1981	10
Portugal	1986	12
Spain		
Austria		
Finland	1995	15
Sweden		
Cyprus		
Czech Rep.		
Estonia		
Hungary		
Latvia		
Lithuania	2004	25
Malta		
Poland		
Slovakia		
Slovenia		
Bulgaria		
Romania	*on track for 2007*	
Turkey		
Croatia	*negotiating*	

EUROZONE ENTRY REQUIREMENTS

In January 2007, Slovenia will become the 13th European nation to adopt the euro as its official currency. The European Commission revealed in May 2006 that Slovenia had met all the requirements set out in the Maastricht Treaty, but Lithuania narrowly missed out due to their too high level of inflation. The table below shows the countries vying for entry into the Eurozone, and their progress:

	budget deficit <3% GDP	national debt <60% GDP	inflation in check[†]	long-term int. rates[‡]	can join?
Cyprus	✗	✗	✓	✓	✗
Czech Rep.	✓	✓	✓	✓	✓*
Estonia	✓	✓	✗	✓	✗
Hungary	✗	✓	✗	✗	✗
Latvia	✓	✓	✗	✓	✗
Lithuania	✓	✓	✗	✓	✗
Malta	✗	✗	✓	✓	✗
Poland	✗	✓	✓	✓	✗
Slovakia	✗	✓	✗	✓	✗
Slovenia	✓	✓	✓	✓	✓

[Source: *The Times*] · † Inflation in the year before entry must not be more than 1·5% points above the 3 best-performing existing EU members. ‡ Long-term bond market must not be more than 2 points above the 3 best-performing EU members. * Not ready to join yet.

THE FIVE ECONOMIC TESTS

Government policy on Economic and Monetary Union (EMU) was set out by the Chancellor Gordon Brown in a statement to Parliament on 27 October 1997. The Government asserts that a successful single currency within a single European market would in principle be of benefit to Europe and the UK. The Government states that the constitutional issues are 'factors' to be taken into consideration – but they are not overriding so long as: membership is in the national interest; the case is clear and unambiguous; and there is popular consent. The current basis for deciding whether or not there is a clear and unambiguous economic case for membership, and whether the question be put to a national referendum, are Gordon Brown's 'five economic tests':

Are business cycles and economic structures compatible, so that we and others could live comfortably with euro interest rates on a permanent basis?

If problems emerge is there sufficient flexibility to deal with them?

Would joining EMU create better conditions for firms making long-term decisions to invest in Britain?

What impact would entry into EMU have on the competitive position of the UK's financial services industry, particularly the City's wholesale markets?

In summary, will joining EMU promote higher growth, stability and a lasting increase in jobs?

THE EURO

NOTES & COINS IN CIRCULATION

Coin	number	total value €	Note	number	total value €
€2	3,337m	6,675m	€500	388m	194,117m
€1	5,003m	5,003m	€200	148m	29,534m
50¢	4,295m	2,148m	€100	1,020m	102,044m
20¢	6,950m	1,390m	€50	3,591m	179,524m
10¢	8,628m	863m	€20	2,102m	42,046m
5¢	10,482m	524m	€10	1,725m	17,246m
2¢	12,053m	241m	€5	1,265m	6,326m
1¢	14,534m	145m	TOTAL	10,239m	570,837m
TOTAL	65,282m	16,989m			

[Source: European Central Bank, 2006]

Officially, *euro* and *cent* are written lowercase and, in English, the spelling does not change when plural (e.g. 100 euro; 100 cent). Oddly, the plural *euros* and *cents* are permitted with languages like French and Spanish. Euro coins share common faces – there are three different versions, all of which were designed by Luc Luycx of the Royal Belgian Mint. All three designs show maps of Europe and apparently 'symbolise the unity of the EU'. The reverse faces of the coins are country-specific and designed by each country – although all are surrounded by the constellation of 12 stars from the European Union flag. The common side designs are as follows:

Denomination	common side design
€2, €1	EU map before enlargement of 2004
50¢, 20¢, 10¢	individual EU countries before enlargement of 2004
5¢, 2¢, 1¢	Europe in relation to Africa and Asia

Euro notes were designed by Robert Kalina, from Austria's national bank, on the theme of 'ages and styles of Europe'. Each denomination has a single design that is common to all euro area countries, depicting one of seven architectural periods. Windows and gateways adorn the front of each note; bridges are on the reverse:

Note	colour	size (mm)	architecture	Note	colour	size (mm)	architecture
€5	grey	120x62	Classical	€50	orange	140x77	Renaissance
€10	red	127x67	Romanesque	€100	green	147x82	Baroque/Rococo
€20	blue	133x72	Gothic	€200	yellow	153x82	C19th iron/glass
				€500	purple	160x82	C20th modern

CURRENT CIRCULATION OF THE EURO

OFFICIAL CURRENCY
Belgium, Germany, Greece, Spain, France, Ireland, Italy, Luxembourg, the Netherlands, Austria, Portugal, Finland, Slovenia [see p.269]

DE FACTO CURRENCY
without formal agreement
Andorra, Kosovo, Montenegro

SPECIAL ARRANGEMENTS
Monaco, the Vatican City, San Marino

OVERSEAS TERRITORIES
Guadeloupe, French Guiana, Martinique, Mayotte, Réunion, Saint Pierre and Miquelon, French Southern & Antarctic Territories

——————————— EU OPINION BAROMETER ———————————

The May 2006 Eurobarometer Survey gives a snapshot of opinion in the 25 EU states in the wake of France's and Denmark's 2005 rejection of the Constitution.

	% in favour of EU membership	% think EU is going in right direction	% think EU is democratic	% think EU is inefficient	% in favour of EU enlargement	% interested in EU affairs	% happy living in their own country	% consider globalisation a threat
UK	33	34	53	55	49	41	91	38
EU25 average	49	39	67	43	55	47	90	47
Austria	31	24	49	53	40	55	91	52
Belgium	60	44	71	46	64	44	93	64
Cyprus	43	47	81	38	71	41	92	65
Czech Rep	44	52	74	43	64	48	85	45
Denmark	61	50	64	59	60	65	98	16
Estonia	43	53	73	30	65	46	94	22
Finland	36	38	48	60	45	73	98	57
France	44	29	59	41	42	43	94	72
Germany	52	38	69	53	52	54	84	59
Greece	50	41	70	44	59	75	95	72
Hungary	40	37	73	38	59	50	59	49
Ireland	68	56	74	32	62	55	93	35
Italy	49	33	79	33	59	38	90	40
Latvia	29	58	65	33	59	40	87	47
Lithuania	52	60	75	25	69	41	86	22·
Luxembourg	71	37	64	36	48	60	96	59
Malta	42	40	68	25	62	53	91	40
Netherlands	71	42	63	61	61	56	92	38
Poland	52	58	79	27	73	71	87	31
Portugal	47	41	65	31	52	26	87	47
Slovakia	54	42	77	32	68	55	83	34
Slovenia	44	56	77	35	76	53	95	53
Spain	62	39	72	30	55	25	96	33
Sweden	42	40	54	67	66	42	98	37

As can be seen, opinions differ significantly across the EU in many areas – for example, while 71% of Netherlanders are in favour of EU membership, roughly the same percentage of Austrians oppose it. When asked what changes to the European Union would be helpful for the future of Europe, the average EU25 responses were:

Comparable living standards 51%		A common language.............. 22%	
The euro in all EU countries 26%		Well-defined external borders 19%	
A common constitution 25%		A common army..................... 9%	

Establishment & Faith

There will soon be only five kings left:
the Kings of England, Diamonds, Hearts, Spades and Clubs.
— FAROUK I (1920–65), the last king of Egypt

THE SOVEREIGN

ELIZABETH II
by the Grace of God, of the United Kingdom of Great Britain
and Northern Ireland and of her other Realms and Territories Queen,
Head of the Commonwealth, Defender of the Faith

Born at 17 Bruton Street, London W1, on 21 April 1926, at *c.*2·40am
Ascended the throne, 6 February 1952 · Crowned, 2 June 1953

To celebrate the Queen's 80th birthday, Buckingham Palace released 80 facts about Her Majesty, including: since 1952, HM has conferred over 387,700 honours and awards. ❦ During her reign HM has received over 3 million items of correspondence. ❦ HM has given regular Tuesday evening audiences to ten British Prime Ministers. ❦ HM is patron of over 620 charities and organisations. ❦ HM has been on 256 official overseas visits, to 129 different countries. ❦ HM has been to Australia 15 times, Canada 23 times, Jamaica 6 times, and New Zealand 10 times. ❦ HM has been given many unusual gifts during her reign, including: sloths from Brazil, a box of snail shells, two black beavers from Canada, a grove of maple trees, and 7kg of prawns. ❦ HM has sent over 100,000 telegrams to centenarians, and 280,000 to those celebrating their diamond wedding anniversary. ❦ HM has opened 15 bridges in the UK. ❦ HM has hosted 91 State banquets. ❦ HM has launched 23 ships. ❦ HM has 30 godchildren. ❦ HM was the first member of the Royal family to collect a gold disc after selling over 100,000 copies of the CD 'Party at the Palace'. ❦ In 2005 HM claimed ownership of 88 cygnets on the Thames. ❦

ORDER OF SUCCESSION

The Prince of Wales · Prince William of Wales · Prince Henry of Wales
The Duke of York · Princess Beatrice of York · Princess Eugenie of York
The Earl of Wessex · The Lady Louise Windsor · The Princess Royal
Mr Peter Phillips · Miss Zara Phillips · Viscount Linley [&c...]

The eldest son of the monarch is heir to the throne followed by his heirs. After whom come any other sons of the monarch and their heirs, followed by any daughters of the monarch and their heirs. Roman Catholics are barred from succession under the Act of Settlement (1701).

ENGLISH MONARCHS

The monarchy is the oldest profession in the world.
— CHARLES, PRINCE OF WALES (1948–)

Danish Line

Svein Forkbeard	1014
Canute the Great	1016–35
Harald Harefoot	1035–40
Hardicanute	1040–42
Edward the Confessor	1042–66
Harold II	1066

Norman Line

William the Conqueror	1066–87
William II Rufus	1087–1100
Henry I Beauclerc	1100–35
Stephen	1135–54
Henry II Curtmantle	1154–89
Richard I Coeur de Lion	1189–99
John (Lackland)	1199–1216
Henry III	1216–72
Edward I	1272–1307
Edward II	1307–27
Edward III	1327–77
Richard II	1377–99

Plantagenet, Lancastrian Line

Henry IV	1399–1413
Henry V	1413–22
Henry VI	1422–61, 1470–71

Plantagenet, Yorkist Line

Edward IV	1461–70, 1471–83
Edward V	1483
Richard III Crookback	1483–85

House of Tudor

Henry VII Tudor	1485–1509
Henry VIII	1509–47
Edward VI	1547–53
Lady Jane Grey	[9 days] 1553
Mary I Tudor	1553–8
Elizabeth I	1558–1603

House of Stuart

James I	1603–25
Charles I	1625–49

Commonwealth & Protectorate

Oliver Cromwell	1649–58
Richard Cromwell	1658–59

House of Stuart, Restored

Charles II	1660–85
James II	1685–88

House of Orange and Stuart

William III, Mary II	1689–1702

House of Stuart

Anne	1702–14

House of Brunswick, Hanover

George I	1714–27
George II	1727–60
George III	1760–1820
George IV	1820–30
William IV	1830–37
Victoria	1837–1901

House of Saxe-Coburg-Gotha

Edward VII	1901–10

House of Windsor

George V	1910–36
Edward VIII	1936
George VI	1936–52
Elizabeth II	1952– *Whom God Preserve*

MONARCH MNEMONIC

Willy, Willy, Harry, Stee, Harry, Dick, John, Harry III. I, II, III Neds, Richard II, Harrys IV, V, VI... then who? Edwards IV, V, Dick the bad, Harrys (twain) & Ned the Lad, Mary, Bessie, James the vain, Charlie, Charlie, James again ... William & Mary, Anne Gloria, 4 Georges, William & Victoria; Edward VII next & then George V in 1910; Edward VIII soon abdicated: George the VI was coronated; After which Elizabeth who is our Queen until her death.

──────────── THE QUEEN'S CORGIS ────────────

The Queen received her first Pembroke Welsh corgi (Susan) for her 18th birthday, kindling a lifelong love for the breed. Since then, she has owned more than thirty corgis, most of whom descended from Susan – who died at the age of 15 and was buried at Sandringham. In 2003, Dotty (Princess Anne's English bull terrier) attacked Pharos, one of the Queen's oldest and most beloved dogs, savaging him so badly that he had to be put down. At present, the Queen owns five corgis – Emma, Linnet, Monty, Willow, and Holly. ❦ The royal corgis are pampered pooches. They have little rubber bootees to protect their paws from the Buckingham Palace gravel, wicker beds raised a few inches off the ground to protect them from draughts, and individual Christmas stockings each year. ❦ The Queen is also a keen dog breeder, producing four 'dorgis' (a corgi-dachshund cross [see p.226]): Cider, Berry, Candy, and Vulcan. She also keeps five cocker spaniels: Bisto, Oxo, Flash, Spick, and Span.

──────────── ROYAL FINANCES ────────────

The Queen receives income from public funds to meet expenditure that relates to her duties as Head of State and the Commonwealth. This derives from 4 sources:

Source (year ending 31 March)	2005	2006
The Queen's Civil List	£10·6m	£11·2m
Parliamentary Annuities	£0·4m	£0·4m
Grants-in-Aid	£19·4m	£20·3m
Expenditure met directly by Government Departments and the Crown Estate	£5·5m	£5·5m
TOTAL	£35·9m	£37·4m

The Queen's Civil List is provided by Parliament on a 10-year cycle to meet the central staff costs and expenses of HM's household. The Parliamentary Annuity is paid to the Duke of Edinburgh to meet official expenses; annuities paid to other members of the Royal Family are reimbursed by The Queen. Grants-in-Aid are paid by the Departments of Transport, & Culture, Media, and Sport.

──────────── CHARLES III? ────────────

In December 2005, newspapers speculated that Prince Charles would assume the title George VII rather than Charles III (George is one of the Prince's many middle names). Previous Charleses had set a somewhat unfortunate precedent – Charles I was beheaded for treason, Charles II was a playboy, and Bonnie Prince Charlie ended his life a drunk. However, Clarence House denied any such discussion had occurred. The Prince had already indicated his openness to change by suggesting that, in order to reflect the multi-faith character of modern Britain, his official title be *Defender of faiths*, rather than the traditional *Defender of the faith*. The title *Fidei Defensor* was first conferred on Henry VIII by Pope Leo X, in recognition of his rejection of Martin Luther, and has been used by every monarch since then.

—————————— ROYAL FAMILY ENGAGEMENTS ——————————

Mr Tim O'Donovan compiled a list of official engagements undertaken by the Royal Family during 2005 – as reported in the pages of the Court Circular:

	Official visits, openings, &c	Receptions, lunches, dinners, &c	Other, e.g. investitures, meetings	Total official engagements UK	Total official engagements abroad
The Queen	109	60	209	378	48
Duke of Edinburgh	143	161	48	352	54
Prince of Wales	153	95	137	385	94
Duchess of Cornwall	84	46	3	133	21
Duke of York	158	89	44	291	244
Earl of Wessex	123	62	37	222	127
Countess of Wessex	105	39	27	171	34
Princess Royal	293	95	96	484	156
Duke of Gloucester	137	50	26	213	30
Duchess of Gloucester	108	27	14	149	30
Duke of Kent	140	36	13	189	28
Princess Alexandra	62	17	13	92	—

———————————— THE UNION FLAG ————————————

Government buildings are obliged to fly the Union Flag on these days:

BD Countess of Wessex......... 20 Jan
Queen's Accession............... 6 Feb
BD of the Duke of York   19 Feb
St David's Day (Wales*)...........1 Mar
Commonwealth Day .... 13 Mar
BD Earl of Wessex.............. 10 Mar
BD The Queen ....21 Apr
St George's Day (England*) ......23 Apr

Europe Day† .... 9 May
Coronation Day ....2 Jun
BD Duke of Edinburgh........ 10 Jun
Official BD The Queen .... 11 Jun
BD Duchess of Cornwall ....17 Jul
BD The Princess Royal..........15 Aug
Remembrance Day .... 11 Nov
BD Prince of Wales............. 14 Nov
Queen's Wedding Day......... 20 Nov
St Andrew's Day (Scotland*) .... 30 Nov
Also, the Opening & Prorogation of Parliament‡

The Union flag must be flown with the wider diagonal white stripe above the red diagonal strip in the half nearest to the flag pole. (To fly the flag upside-down is a signal of distress.) On the above days, flags should be flown 8am–sunset. * If a building has more than one flagstaff, the appropriate national flag may be flown with the Union Flag but not in a superior position. † The Union Flag should fly alongside the European flag, though always taking precedence. ‡ In London only, whether the Queen performs the ceremony or not. ❦ In 2006, the Union Flag celebrated its 400th birthday. When devised in 1606 (after the union of the crowns of England and Scotland), the flag combined the crosses of St George and St Andrew. On the union with Ireland in 1801, the cross of St Patrick was added. Originally, the term 'Union Jack' was only used when the flag was flown at sea, but since an Admiralty circular of 1902 (despite some protestations) the terms 'Union Jack' and 'Union Flag' may be used interchangeably.

──────────── THE GREAT BRITISH MENU ────────────

In May 2006, fourteen of Britain's top chefs took part in a cookery contest, on BBC2, to create a *Great British Menu* to be eaten at a royal banquet to celebrate the Queen's 80th birthday. The recipes were intended to reflect the diversity of modern British food and the best local ingredients. The competition comprised heats during which chefs battled it out to represent seven regions; the finalists then had their 4-course menus put to the public vote. The winning dishes and chefs were as follows:

Course	chef	region	dish
Starter	Richard Corrigan	N. Ireland	*smoked salmon with Irish soda bread*
Fish	Bryn Williams	Wales	*turbot with cockles & oxtail*
Main	Nick Nairn	Scotland	*roe venison with rosti & game gravy*
Dessert	Marcus Wareing	North	*custard tart with Garibaldi biscuits*

──────────── ROYAL CONGRATULATIONS ────────────

The tradition of sending messages of royal congratulations to subjects on certain auspicious days was inaugurated in 1917 by George V, who sent telegrams to those celebrating their 60th wedding anniversary or 100th birthday. Nowadays, on request, the Queen sends congratulatory cards, via the Royal Mail, to citizens of Her Realms or UK Overseas Territories, on the following celebratory occasions:

WEDDING ANNIVERSARIES	BIRTHDAYS
60th, 65th, & 70th anniversaries	100th & 105th birthdays
and then every year thereafter	and then every year thereafter

Contact: Private Sec.'s Office, Buckingham Palace, London SW1A 1AA, 020 7930 4832.

──────── WHALES, STURGEONS & ROYAL PREROGATIVE ────────

The statute *Prerogativa Regis* ('Of the King's Prerogative'), probably dating back to the reign of Edward II (1307–27), states that 'the King shall have throughout the realm, whales and great sturgeons taken in the sea or elsewhere within the realm'. This right still stands, and consequently no whales or sturgeons washed up on British shores may be disposed of without the consent of the Monarch. However, when in January 2006 a whale died in the Thames, the Crown waived this ancient prerogative and the carcass was donated to London's Natural History Museum.

❦ The crown has asserted its prerogative over mute swans since the C12th, viewing them as a valuable (and tasty) foodstuff for Royal banquets. Traditionally, every 3rd week in July the Queen's Swan Marker and the Swan Uppers of the Vintners' and Dyers' Companies take part in the Swan Upping ceremony, an annual census of the swan population on the Thames [see p.272]. The swans are captured, examined, ringed with individual identification numbers, and then set free – they are no longer eaten, since consumption of swans is prohibited by the *Wildlife and Countryside Act* (1981).

—— THE QUEEN'S CHRISTMAS BROADCAST 2005 ——

'The day after my last Christmas message was broadcast, the world experienced one of the worst natural disasters ever recorded. The devastating tsunami struck countries around the Indian Ocean causing death and destruction on an unprecedented scale. This was followed by a number of vicious hurricanes across the Caribbean and the inundation of the city of New Orleans. Then in the autumn came the massive earthquake in Pakistan and India. This series of dreadful events has brought loss and suffering to so many people – and their families and friends – not only in the countries directly affected, but here in Britain and throughout the Commonwealth. As if these disasters were not bad enough, I have sometimes thought that humanity seemed to have turned on itself – with wars, civil disturbances and acts of brutal terrorism. In this country many people's lives were totally changed by the London bombings in July. ... These natural and human tragedies provided the headline news; they also provoked a quite remarkable humanitarian response. ... There may be an instinct in all of us to help those in distress, but in many cases I believe this has been inspired by religious faith. Christianity is not the only religion to teach its followers to help others and to treat your neighbour as you would want to be treated yourself. It has been clear that in the course of this year relief workers and financial support have come from members of every faith and from every corner of the world. ... Certainly the need for selflessness and generosity in the face of hardship is nothing new. The veterans of the Second World War whom we honoured last summer can tell us how so often ... those around them seemed able to draw on some inner strength to find courage and compassion. We see this today in the way that young men and women are calmly serving our country around the world often in great danger. This last year has reminded us that this world is not always an easy or a safe place to live in, but it is the only place we have. I believe also that it has shown us all how our faith – whatever our religion – can inspire us to work together in friendship and peace for the sake of our own and future generations. For Christians this festival of Christmas is the time to remember the birth of the one we call 'the Prince of Peace' and our source of 'light and life' in both good times and bad. It is not always easy to accept his teaching, but I have no doubt that the New Year will be all the better if we do but try. I hope you will all have a very happy Christmas ... '

> *... I have sometimes thought that humanity seemed to have turned on itself – with wars, civil disturbances and acts of brutal terrorism ...*

When the Queen's Christmas broadcast is entered into Microsoft Word's 'Auto Summarize' feature and is condensed down to two sentences, the result is:

The day after my last Christmas message was broadcast, the world experienced one of the worst natural disasters ever recorded. People of compassion all over the world responded with immediate practical and financial help.

WHO'S NEW IN WHO'S WHO

Published annually since 1849, *Who's Who* is one of the most respected biographical reference books in the world. When, during WWII, paper rationing threatened its publication, Churchill personally intervened to ensure the book continued to be printed. Below are some of those who were added to the 2006 edition (those who have died during the year enter the companion *Who Was Who*):

Mark Austin. . . . . *presenter ITV news*	John Inverdale . . . . *sports presenter*
Sylvia Auton . . . . *Chief Exec. IPC Media*	Aled Jones . . . . *singer, presenter*
Duncan Bannatyne . . . . *entrepreneur*	John Kampfner . . . . *Ed. New Statesman*
Linda Bennett . . . . *founder L.K. Bennett*	Sarah Lancashire . . . . *actress*
Karan Bilimoria . . . *founder, Cobra beer*	Prof Colin Lawson . . . . *Dir. RCM*
Heston Blumenthal . . . . *chef*	Kathryn (Kathy) Lette . . . . *writer*
Kathy Burke. . . . . *actress*	Andrea Levy. . . . . *novelist*
John Burnside. . . . . *writer*	Roger Lewis . . . . *journalist, author*
Darren Campbell . . . . *athlete*	Richard Madeley. . . . . *TV presenter*
Michael Clark. . . . . *choreographer*	Simon Mayo . . . . *radio presenter*
Natalie Clein. . . . . *solo cellist*	George Michael. . . . . *singer*
David Collier . . . . *Chief Exec. ECB*	Phil Mickelson. . . . . *golfer*
David Cracknell . . . . *political editor*	Keith Mills . . . . *Pres. London 2012*
James Cracknell. . . . . *rower*	Simon Nye . . . . *writer*
Ian Dejardin *Dir. Dulwich Pic. Gallery*	Julian Opie. . . . . *artist*
Trevor Eve. . . . . *actor*	Roxanna Panufnik . . . . *composer*
Judy Finnigan . . . . *TV presenter*	David Pyatt . . . . . . *Principal Horn, LSO*
Adrian Fisher. . . . . *maze designer, author*	Shirley Robertson. . . . . *sailor*
Caroline Flanagan . *Pres. Law Soc, Scot*	Bryan Robson. . . . . *football manager*
Bruce Fogle. . . . . . *vet, writer, broadcaster*	Poul Ruders . . . . *composer*
Angus Fraser . . . *former cricketer, writer*	Greg Rusedski. . . . . *tennis player*
Juliet Gardiner . . . . *writer, historian*	Ziauddin Sardar. . . . . *writer, critic*
Michael George. . . . *bass-baritone singer*	Nicolas Sarkozy . . . . *French politician*
Patrick Harverson.	David Selbourne . . . . *writer*
Communications Sec. to Prince of Wales	Frank Skinner. . . . . *comedian*
Prof. Christine Hawley . . . . *Dean, UCL*	Graeme Souness. . . . . . . *football manager*
Nigel Hess. . . . . *composer, conductor*	Kevin Spacey. . . . . *actor, director*
Anthony Hobman . . . *pensions regulator*	Amanda Thompson. . . . . *MD Blackpool*
Dame Kelly Holmes . . . . *athlete*	*Pleasure Beach*
Jeremy Hughes. . . . . *Chief Exec.*	Ian Thorpe . . . . *swimmer*
Breakthrough Breast Cancer	Simon Woodroffe. . . . *founder Yo! Sushi*
Celia Imrie . . . . *actress*	Nicholas Wright . . . . *playwright*

A few recreations – SIR JOHN BOURNE 'bad tennis, UK's largest collection of inkwells' · PROF. COLIN DIVALL 'failing to build Wimborne Station at 1/76th scale' · GEOFFREY EDEN 'cutting down trees' · BRUCE FOGLE 'stalking painted Gustavian furniture in rural Sweden, acting as putty in my dog's paws' · SIMON MAYO 'etymology, astronomy, the school run, walking in bad weather, thinking up quizzes' · ANDREW REID 'trying to enjoy life between moderation and excess as appropriate' · JOHN SAVILLE 'fishing, pulling sofas from the River Wandle'.

SOME HONOURS OF NOTE · 2006

New Year's Honours

GCMG
Lord Paddy Ashdown

KBE
Lord Sebastian Coe

KNIGHT BACHELOR
John Dankworth............ musician
Tom Jones........................singer
Keith Mills.............. London 2012
John Ritblat................British Land
Arnold Wesker..............playwright

DBE
Liz Forgan...................BBC radio
Julie Mellor......... Equal Opp. Cmsn
Vivienne Westwood...........designer

CBE
Bruce Forsyth ....entertainer
Jonathan Ives..................designer
Alan Mills........ Wimbledon referee
Tim O'Toole..Lon. Underground MD
Peter Snow .... broadcaster

OBE
Sanjeev Bhaskar................... actor
Heston Blumenthal............... chef
Peter Clarke.... Scot. Yard Anti-Terror
Robbie Coltrane .... actor
Clare Connor ... Cpt. women's cricket
Duncan Fletcher... Eng. cricket coach
David Graveney.... Eng. cricket select.
Gordon Ramsay...................chef
Imelda Staunton .... actor
Michael Vaughan .... cricketer
Jeanette Winterson.............. writer

MBE
Roy Barraclough .... actor
Babette Beverley ....singer/sister
Joy Beverley................singer/sister
Teddie Beverley ....singer/sister
David Boyce.... Russell Sq. Tube Spvsr

Queen's Birthday Honours

KNIGHT BACHELOR
Michael Aaronson ..Save the Children
Philip Green .... tycoon
Stelios Haji-Ioannou........easyperson
David Richards ....FA Premier League
Charles Wheeler .... journalist

DBE
Carole Jordan .... physicist
Janet Nelson...................historian
Ruth Silver   Lewisham College

CBE
Darcey Bussell.................. dancer
Lynn Davies.............. UK Athletics
Rolf Harris.........entertainer/painter
Andy Hayman . Met. Police Asst. Cmr
Peter Lord........Aardman Animation
Esther Rantzen............. broadcaster
David Sproxton..Aardman Animation
Deborah Warner.......theatre director

OBE
Gurinder Chadha.........film director
Bernard Cornwell.............. novelist
Charles Dance .... actor
James Goodfellow........PIN inventor
Lulu Guinness ....designer
Julien Macdonald.............designer
Gary Rhodes .... chef
Alastair Stewart .... broadcaster
Rudolph Walker .... actor

MBE
Craig Cowley ....UK Deaf Sport
Jill Edwards .... golfer
Barry Ferguson............... footballer
Katherine Grainger .... rower
Gerardine Hemingway ....designer
Wayne Hemingway...........designer
Robert Jack.......... services to bowls
Beverley Knight.................. singer
Niall McShea................rally driver
Graham Thorpe............... cricketer

——————— ON VISITING CARDS ———————

The celebrated royal and society printer Smythson of Bond Street (London & NY) offers visiting cards in the following traditional sizes, each for a different clientele:

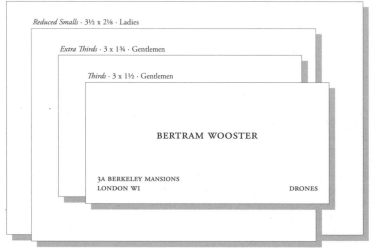

Smalls · 3⅝ x 2⅜ · Ladies & Couples

Reduced Smalls · 3½ x 2⅛ · Ladies

Extra Thirds · 3 x 1¾ · Gentlemen

Thirds · 3 x 1½ · Gentlemen

BERTRAM WOOSTER

3A BERKELEY MANSIONS
LONDON W1

DRONES

[For reasons of space, the above cards are shown at 85% of their actual size · Dimensions in inches]

Since the cards carried by ladies were significantly larger than those carried by gentlemen, in C19th Britain, ladies of dubious repute would have their visiting cards made up in male *Thirds* or *Extra Thirds*. This meant that if one of their married 'friends' chanced to take out his wallet in front of his wife, all of his cards would resemble those of gentlemen – thus averting wifely suspicion and unwanted interrogation. ❦ Much flummery surrounded the text on traditional visiting cards: initials were avoided, as were qualifications; the text was usually elegantly plain black on white unglazed card; and while women and couples would have their address in the lower right-hand corner, many gentlemen (especially bachelors) would just give their club(s). (Bret Easton Ellis' American Psycho had business cards the colour of 'bone'.)

❦ Nowadays, visiting cards have been superseded by business cards cluttered with logos and details of every conceivable form of communication. Different cultures have different attitudes towards cards. Of note are the Japanese, for whom cards are just part of a complex etiquette. In Japan, they are exchanged by all participants at the start of a business meeting. You should stand, face your counterpart and bow slightly, while offering your card with the right or both hands. (If you have your details printed in Japanese on the reverse of your card, offer this side facing upwards.) The same procedure should be applied when receiving business cards. It is considered polite to study carefully any cards you receive, and to keep them in front of you during meetings. Never fold cards, write on them, or slip them into your back pocket.

—————————— ON INTRODUCTIONS ——————————

With the exception of reigning Sovereigns (including the Pope), Presidents, and Cardinals, introductions made between strangers should follow the following rules:

Youth is introduced to age – "Teddy Sheringham, may I present Theo Walcott?'

Men are introduced to women – 'Dame Edna, this is Count Victor Grezhinski.'

Lower ranks are introduced to higher – 'Captain Mainwaring, this is Private Pike.'

—————————— DRESS CODES OF NOTE ——————————

BLACK TIE (or Tuxedo; Smoking Jacket; Dinner Jacket; DJ; *Cravate Noire*) consists of a single or double-breasted black (or midnight blue) dinner jacket worn with matching trousers with a single row of braid down the leg, a soft white dress shirt and a black bow tie. (Wing collars, cummerbunds, white jackets, and showy bow ties are to be avoided.) WHITE TIE consists of a black tail-coat worn with matching trousers with a double row of braid down the leg, a white stiff-fronted wing collar shirt, a white waistcoat, and a white bow tie. MORNING DRESS consists of a morning coat, waistcoat, striped grey trousers, and (often) a top hat. Below are some of the more unusual dress codes to be found on formal invitations:

Bush shirt .... long- or short-sleeved (embroidered) shirt worn outside trousers
Evening dress... white tie
Informal..................... business suit or jacket with or without tie (not jeans)
Island casual....................Hawaiian shirt and casual (usually khaki) trousers
Lounge suit... business suit and tie
National dress.......... self-explanatory; if one has no national dress, a lounge suit
Planters........................long-sleeved white shirt with a tie and dark trousers
Red Sea Rig; or Gulf Rig .... black tie (or lounge suit) without the jacket
Tenue de Ville............................. business suit (sometimes national dress)
Tenue Decontractée; Tenue de Détente.................................. smart-casual
Tenue de Gala ....black tie
Tenue de Sport/Voyage .... sporting/travelling attire
Tenue de Cérémonie .... white tie
Windsor Uniform.. see below

A degree of debate and dispute exists between different sources, and different rules apply in military, academic, and ecclesiastical settings. The above listing follows the tradition of most formal invitations in giving only the requirements for male attire, on the understanding that women have an intuitive understanding of these things. ❦ Windsor Uniform consists of a dark blue evening tail coat with scarlet at the collar and cuffs, worn with a white single-breasted waistcoat and plain black evening trousers. The buttons are gilt and feature a Garter star within a Garter, surmounted by the imperial crown. Introduced by George III in 1779, the Uniform was discontinued by William IV, and revived by Queen Victoria. According to Buckingham Palace, the Uniform is worn by male members of the Royal Family and those holding certain appointments in the Royal Household – when approved by The Queen.

AN ELEMENTARY GUIDE TO FORMS OF ADDRESS

Personage	envelope	start of letter	verbal address
The Queen	The Queen's Most Excellent Majesty†	Madam/May it please your Majesty	Your Majesty/Ma'am
The Duke of Edinburgh	HRH The Duke of Edinburgh†	Sir	Your Royal Highness/Sir
The Queen Mother	Her Majesty Queen —— The Queen Mother†	Madam	Your Majesty/Ma'am
Royal Prince	HRH The Prince ——, (The Prince of ——)†	Sir	Your Royal Highness/Sir
Royal Princess	HRH The Princess (of) ——†	Your Royal Highness	Your Royal Highness/Madam
Royal Duke	HRH The Duke of ——†	Your Royal Highness	Your Royal Highness/Sir
Royal Duchess	HRH The Duchess of ——†	Your Royal Highness	Your Royal Highness/Madam
Duke	His Grace the Duke of ——	My Lord Duke/Dear Duke	Your Grace/Duke
Duchess	Her Grace the Duchess of ——	Dear Madam/Dear Duchess	Your Grace/Duchess
Marquess	The Most Honourable The Marquess of ——	My Lord/Dear Lord	My Lord/Lord
Marchioness	The Most Honourable The Marchioness of ——	Madam/Dear Lady	Madam/Lady
Earl	The Rt Hon The Earl of ——	My Lord/Dear Lord	My Lord/Lord
Earl's wife	The Rt Hon The Countess of ——	Madam/Dear Lady	Madam/Lady
Countess	The Rt Hon The Countess of ——	Madam/Dear Lady	Madam/Lady
Viscount	The Rt Hon The Viscount ——	My Lord/Dear Lord	Lord
Viscount's wife	The Rt Hon The Viscountess ——	Madam/Dear Lady	Lady
Baron	The Rt Hon Lord ——	My Lord/Dear Lord	Lord
Baron's wife	The Rt Hon Lady ——	My Lady/Dear Lady	Lady
Baroness	The Rt Hon The Lady —— (*or* The Baroness) ——	My Lady/Dear Lady	Madam/Lady
Baronet	Sir Bertie Wooster Bt (*or* Bart)	Dear Sir Bertie	Sir Bertie
Baronet's wife	Lady ——	Dear Madam/Dear Lady ——	Lady ——
Knight of an Order	Sir Bertie Wooster (*and order*)	Dear Sir Bertie	Sir Bertie
Knight Bachelor	Sir Bertie Wooster	Dear Sir Bertie	Sir Bertie
Knight's wife	Lady ——	Dear Madam/Dear Lady ——	Lady ——
Dame	Dame ——	Dear Madam/Dear Dame	Dame ——

—— AN ELEMENTARY GUIDE TO FORMS OF ADDRESS ——

Personage	envelope	start of letter	verbal address
Life Peer	The Rt Hon Lord —— (of ——).	My Lord/Dear Lord ——	......Lord ——
Life Peeress	The Rt Hon The Lady (or Baroness) —— (of ——)	My Lady/Dear Lady ——	......Lady ——
Archbishop	The Most Rev & Rt Hon the Lord Archbishop of ——	Dear Archbishop	Your Grace/Archbishop
Bishop	((The Rt Rev) (and Right Hon)) The Bishop of ——	Dear Bishop	......Bishop
Lord Chancellor	The Rt Hon The Lord Chancellor	......by rank	......by rank
Prime Minister	The Rt Hon The Prime Minister PC MP	Dear Prime Minister	Prime Minister/Sir
Deputy PM	The Rt Hon The Deputy Prime Minister PC MP	Dear Deputy Prime Minister	Deputy Prime Minister/Sir
Chancellor of the Exchequer	The Rt Hon The Chancellor of the Exchequer PC MP	Dear Chancellor	Chancellor/Sir
Foreign Secretary	The Rt Hon The SoS for Foreign & Comwlth Affairs	Dear Foreign Secretary	Foreign Secretary/by rank
Home Secretary	The Rt Hon The SoS for the Home Department	Dear Home Secretary	Home Secretary/by rank
Secretary of State	The Rt Hon The SoS for ——	Dear Secretary of State	Secretary of State/by rank
Minister	(The Rt Hon) Bertie Wooster Esq (PC) MP	Dear Minister	Minister/by rank
MP‡	Bertie Wooster Esq. MP	Dear Mr Wooster	......Mr Wooster
MP Privy Councillor	The Rt Hon Bertie Wooster PC MP	Dear Mr Wooster	......Mr Wooster
Privy Councillor	The Rt Hon Bertie Wooster PC	Dear Mr Wooster	......Mr Wooster
High Court Judge	The Hon Mr Justice ——	Dear Sir ——/Dear Judge	Sir/My Lord/Your Lordship
Ambassador (British)	His Excellency —— HM Ambassador to ——	......by rank	......Your Excellency
Lord Mayor	The Rt Hon the Lord Mayor of ——	My (Dear) Lord Mayor	......Lord Mayor
Mayor	The Worshipful Mayor of ——	(Dear) Mr Mayor	......Mr Mayor

It is hard to overstate the complexity of 'correct' form which (especially in the legal and clerical fields, as well as Chivalry) can become extremely rococo, and is the subject of considerable dispute between sources. Consequently, the above tabulation can only hope to provide a very elementary guide. ● Readers interested in the correct formal styling of the wives of younger sons of Earls, for example, are advised to consult specialist texts on the subject. † It is usual to address correspondence to members of the Royal Family in the first instance to their Private Secretary. ‡ A similar styling is used for Members of the European Parliament [MEP]; Scottish Parliament [MSP]; National Assembly for Wales [AM]; and Northern Ireland Assembly [MLA]. From the moment Parliament is dissolved there are no Members of Parliament, and consequently the letters MP should not be used. By convention medical doctors are styled Dr——, whereas surgeons use the title Mr——; many gynaecologists, although surgeons, are styled Dr.

THE LEGAL YEAR & LAW TERMS

The legal year starts in October when judges process two miles (nowadays by car) from Temple Bar to Westminster Abbey for a service conducted by the Dean of Westminster, at which the Lord Chancellor reads the lesson. This is followed by a 'breakfast' in Westminster Hall. The legal year is divided into these four terms:

HILARY† .... 11 Jan – 4 Apr	TRINITY .... 5 Jun – 31 Jul
EASTER .... 17 Apr – 25 May	MICHAELMAS .... 1 Oct – 21 Dec

The origin of these terms is thought to derive from a prohibition by the church of swearing any form of oath between these three periods: Advent and Epiphany; Septuagesima and fourteen days after Easter; and Ascension and Corpus Christi.

† This term is so named after St Hilary, whose feast is celebrated on 13 January.

AVERAGE LENGTH OF SENTENCE

The average lengths of custodial sentences handed down at the Crown Courts:

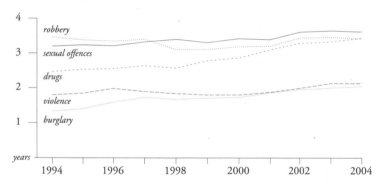

[Excludes life sentences · England & Wales · Source: Social Trends 2006]

THE JUDICIARY & WIGS

The judiciary began wearing wigs *c.*1680, when they were the fashion of the day. Initially, wigs were made from human hair sold to wig-makers by the poor or taken from the dead, a morally dubious practice halted when horse hair found favour. In the C17th, wigs were made from black horse hair and required a great deal of upkeep – curling, powdering, and general titivation. However, in 1822 the celebrated wig maker Humphrey Ravenscroft invented a new form of wig, known as the 'forensic' wig, made from white horse hair that came ready-curled and did not require as much maintenance. Until *c.*1770, judges wore long full-bottomed wigs, but these were later superseded by the more practical short bobbed wig, still sported today.

COURT STRUCTURE IN ENGLAND & WALES

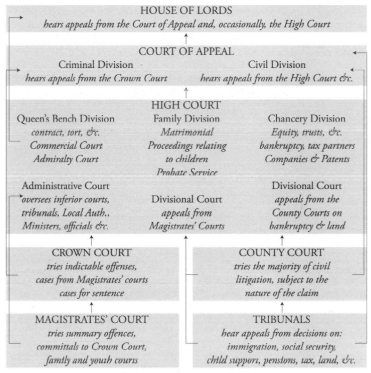

HOUSE OF LORDS
hears appeals from the Court of Appeal and, occasionally, the High Court

COURT OF APPEAL

Criminal Division	Civil Division
hears appeals from the Crown Court	*hears appeals from the High Court &c.*

HIGH COURT

Queen's Bench Division	Family Division	Chancery Division
contract, tort, &c.	*Matrimonial*	*Equity, trusts, &c.*
Commercial Court	*Proceedings relating*	*bankruptcy, tax partners*
Admiralty Court	*to children*	*Companies & Patents*
	Probate Service	

Administrative Court		Divisional Court
oversees inferior courts,	Divisional Court	*appeals from the*
tribunals, Local Auth.,	*appeals from*	*County Courts on*
Ministers, officials &c.	*Magistrates' Courts*	*bankruptcy & land*

CROWN COURT	COUNTY COURT
tries indictable offenses,	*tries the majority of civil*
cases from Magistrates' courts	*litigation, subject to the*
cases for sentence	*nature of the claim*

MAGISTRATES' COURT	TRIBUNALS
tries summary offences,	*hear appeals from decisions on:*
committals to Crown Court,	*immigration, social security,*
family and youth courts	*child support, pensions, tax, land, &c.*

[Source: The Court Service · Crown ©]

JURY SERVICE

Since the 2003 Criminal Justice Act, anyone on the electoral register is liable to random selection to serve on a jury. The grounds for eligibility or ineligibility are:

To be ELIGIBLE for jury service you must be older than 18 and younger than 70 on the day your service is to start; a registered parliamentary or local government elector; and you must have lived in the UK, Channel Islands or the Isle of Man for any period of at least 5 years since you were 13 years old.

INELIGIBLE individuals include: those on bail or involved in criminal proceedings; those sentenced to life imprisonment; those who have in the previous 10 years served any part of a sentence of imprisonment or had passed on them a suspended sentence of imprisonment; and those with mental disorders.

Individuals may request deferral of service to another date within 12 months (if, for example, the date clashes with an exam), or excusal from the summons (if, for example, they do not speak English).

————————ARMED FORCES & DEFICIT————————

The graph below illustrates the strength of UK Regular Armed forces since 1974.

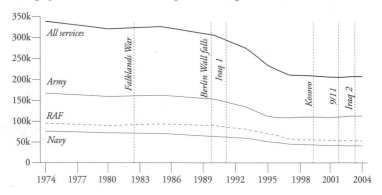

[Figures are for trained and untrained personnel; they exclude Gurkhas, mobilised reservists, and others not counted as the UK Regular Forces. Source: Defence Analytical Services Agency]

The Ministry of Defence admitted in February 2006 that the Iraq conflict and allegations of bullying within the army were damaging recruitment. The data below show the respective forces' personnel requirements in 2006 – and the shortfall:

[Source: DASA]	Navy	RAF	Army	Total
Requirement	37,110	48,760	101,800	187,660
Total strength	35,660	47,630	101,140	184,430
Deficit	–1,440	–1,130	–660	–3,230

————FORCES SUICIDE————   ————CHAPLAINS————

A report published by the Defence Analytical Services Agency (DASA) into suicides in the armed forces, from 1984–2005, showed that the male suicide rate in the British armed forces was statistically significantly lower than that in the general UK population – with the exception of army males aged under 20, who had a increased risk of *c.*50%. ❦ From 1984–2005 there were 638 suicides among army personnel, 624 of whom were male, and 14 female; of the male suicides 96 served in the Navy, 389 in the army, and 139 in the Royal Air Force.

The MoD appointed its first Buddhist (Dr Sunil Kariyakarawana), Hindu (Krishan Attri), Muslim (Imam Asim Hafiz), and Sikh (Mandeep Kaur) chaplains in 2005. Unlike the 300 regular commissioned Christian chaplains (who serve the 183,000 Christians in the forces), these new chaplains will serve as civilians with cross-service responsibility. The number of serving Hindus (230), Sikhs (90), Buddhists (220), and Muslims (305) was deemed insufficient to justify regular commissioned chaplains. As of 1 July 2005, there were 65 Jews in the forces, with one honorary officiating chaplain.

UK SERVICE RANKS

service	ROYAL NAVY	ROYAL MARINES†	ARMY	ROYAL AIR FORCE	NATO
OFFICERS					
	Admiral of the Fleet	—	Field Marshal	Marshal of the RAF	OF-10
	Admiral	General	General	Air Chief Marshal	OF-9
	Vice-Admiral	Lieutenant General	Lieutenant General	Air Marshal	OF-8
	Rear Admiral	Major General	Major General	Air Vice-Marshal	OF-7
	Commodore	Brigadier	Brigadier	Air Commodore	OF-6
	Captain	Colonel	Colonel	Group Captain	OF-5
	Commander	Lieutenant Colonel	Lieutenant Colonel	Wing Commander	OF-4
	Lieutenant Commander	Major	Major	Squadron Leader	OF-3
	Lieutenant	Captain	Captain	Flight Lieutenant	OF-2
	Sub-Lieutenant	Lieutenant/2nd Lieutenant	Lieutenant/2nd Lieutenant	Flying Officer/Pilot Officer	OF-1
	Midshipman	—	Officer Cadet	Officer Designate	OF-(D)
OTHER RANKS					
	Warrant Officer Class 1	Warrant Officer Class 1	Warrant Officer Class 1	Warrant Officer	OR-9
	Warrant Officer Class 2	Warrant Officer Class 2	Warrant Officer Class 2		OR-8
	Chief Petty Officer	Colour Sergeant	Staff Sergeant	Flight Sergeant/Chief Technician	OR-7
	Petty Officer	Sergeant	Sergeant	Sergeant	OR-6
	Leading Rate	Corporal	Corporal	Corporal	OR-4
		—	Lance Corporal		OR-3
	Able Rating	Marine	Private (Class 1–3)	Junior Technician /	OR-2
				Leading & Senior Aircraftman	
	—	—	Private (Class 4)/Junior	Aircraftman	OR-1

[Source: DASA] The Naval rank of Warrant Officer Class 2 was introduced in 2004. † The Royal Marines were established in 1664 as a corps of sea soldiers to be raised and disbanded as required. In 1755, they became a permanent part of the Navy, trained as soldiers and seamen to fight and to maintain discipline on ships. The Royal Marines gained their tough fighting reputation during the capture of Gibraltar in 1704, and have since played a decisive role in military deployments across the world.

─────── MAIN ETHNIC GROUP BY RELIGION · GB───────

Ethnicity (%)	Christian	Buddhist	Hindu	Jewish	Muslim	Sikh	Any other	No religion	Not stated
White British	75·7	0·1	–	0·5	0·1	–	0·2	15·7	7·7
White Irish	85·7	0·2	–	0·2	0·1	–	0·3	6·2	7·4
Mixed	52·3	0·7	0·9	0·5	9·7	0·4	0·6	23·3	11·6
Indian	5·0	0·2	44·8	0·1	12·6	29·2	1·7	1·8	4·7
Pakistani	1·1	–	0·1	0·1	91·9	0·1	0·1	0·6	6·2
Bangladeshi	0·5	0·1	0·6	–	92·4	–	–	0·5	5·8
Black Caribbean	73·7	0·2	0·3	0·1	0·8	–	0·6	11·3	13·0
Black African	68·8	0·1	0·2	0·1	20·0	0·1	0·2	2·4	8·2
Chinese	21·1	15·1	0·1	0·1	0·3	–	0·5	53·0	9·8

[Source: Census 2001 · Crown ©]

─────── RELIGIOUS COMPOSITION OF THE UK───────

Religion	thousands	%	Religion	thousands	%
Christian	42,079	71·6	No religion	9,104	15·5
Muslim	1,591	2·7	Not stated	4,289	7·3
Hindu	559	1·0	(All religions	45,163	76·8)
Sikh	336	0·6	(All No or Not	13,626	23·2)
Jewish	267	0·5	TOTAL	58,789	100
Buddhist	152	0·3			

[Source: Census 2001 · Crown ©]

─────── RELIGIOUS PERCEPTIONS ───────

The following shows the percentage of favourable/unfavourable views of religions:

		CHRISTIANS		JEWS		MUSLIMS	
Country	%	fav	unfav	fav	unfav	fav	unfav
China		26	47	28	49	20	50
France		84	15	82	16	64	34
Germany		83	13	67	21	40	47
India		61	19	28	17	46	43
Indonesia		58	38	13	76	99	1
Jordan		58	41	0	100	99	1
Pakistan		22	58	5	74	94	2
Russia		92	3	63	26	55	36
Turkey		21	63	18	60	83	11
UK		85	6	78	6	72	14
USA		87	6	77	7	57	22

[Source: Pew Global Attitudes Project, 2005]

──────── ATTENDANCE AT RELIGIOUS SERVICES ────────

The following data from the European Social Survey (2002) show the percentage of respondents across Europe who replied 'at least once a month' to the question 'how often do you attend religious services apart from special occasions?':

Country	Percentage
Poland	75.5%
Ireland	67.2
Greece	54.6
Portugal	46.9
Italy	44.1
Austria	35.3
Slovenia	30.0
Spain	28.9
Netherlands	20.9
Germany	20.1
Belgium	18.9
UK	18.6
Hungary	18.2
France	14.2
Denmark	9.3

──────────── TEMPLETON PRIZE ────────────

The winner of the 2006 *Templeton Prize For Progress Toward Research or Discoveries About Spiritual Realities* was Cambridge University mathematical sciences professor John D. Barrow. Barrow (b.1952) is best known for his work on the anthropic principle, the notion that the Earth is in its present form in order to allow life capable of observing it to evolve. (In other words, the universe exists as it does because, if it were different, we would not exist to observe it.) Barrow received his prize on 3 May during a ceremony at Buckingham Palace. Finding himself somewhat surprised to have won, he remarked 'I thought this particular prize usually went to people who were rather older.' ❦ Philanthropist Sir John Templeton founded his eponymous prize in 1972 'to encourage and honour the advancement of knowledge in spiritual matters'. The prize (currently $1·4m) is said to be the largest annual monetary prize of any kind presented to an individual. Templeton stipulated its value should always be greater than the Nobel Prize, to 'underscore that research and advances in spiritual discoveries can be quantifiably more significant than disciplines recognized' by the Nobel committees. Previous Templeton winners have included: Mother Teresa (1973), Billy Graham (1982), and Alexander Solzhenitsyn (1983). ❦ Born in Winchester, Tennessee, John Templeton once dreamed of a career in religious service. After graduating from Yale University (with a stint at Oxford), he amassed great wealth through success in international investment funds. He was Knighted in 1987 for his philanthropy, including his endowment of Templeton College, Oxford, and now lives as a 'full-time philanthropist' in the Bahamas.

——————————— THE HAJJ ———————————

The Hajj is the pilgrimage to Mecca, Saudi Arabia, that all Muslims who have the means and ability are obliged to make at least once in their lifetime. It is the fifth and most significant of the five 'Arkan' (or 'Pillars') of Islam. Pilgrims must be sane, healthy, adult Muslims, free from debt, who have provided for their family. ❦ In January 2006, *c.*362 pilgrims were trampled to death at the Jamarat Bridge in Mina. This was not the first time tragedy had struck the Hajj. Prompted by Islam's global growth and facilitated by cheap air travel, participation in the Hajj has risen from *c.*250,000 in 1930 to *c.*2·5 million in 2006. The sheer force of people (measured in 'pilgrims per minute') has caused numerous fatal incidents. In 1990, 1,426 were killed in a tunnel leading to the holy sites; in 1994, 270 died in stampedes; in 1997, 343 pilgrims died in fires; in 1998, >118 were trampled to death; and since 2000, >650 have been crushed, including, in 2004, 251 pilgrims at the Jamarat bridge. ❦ It is hard to overstate the complexity of the various forms of Hajj, which runs from 9th to 13th of *Dhu al-Hijjah* – the 12th Islamic month. Pilgrims arrive in Mecca, where they ablute and exchange their clothes for two simple, white, unstitched pieces of cloth (*Ihram*). Through prayers, pilgrims enter a state of *Ihram* in which they may not have sex, harm another living thing, or cut their hair. During the following five days, pilgrims journey many miles back and forth between Mecca, Mina, Arafat, and Muzdalifah, offering prayers to Allah and performing a series of rituals based upon the lives of Abraham and Muhammad. For example, on arriving in Mecca, pilgrims

Labbayka Allahumma Labbayk
(Here I am at Your service,
O God, Here I am)

perform their first *Tawaf*, 7 counter-clockwise journeys round the *Ka'ba* – a cube-shaped building in the sacred mosque *Masjid al Haram* that was built by Adam, rebuilt by Abraham, and rededicated to Allah by Muhammad. The pilgrims drink water from the Zam Zam well and make 7 journeys between the hills of Safra and Marwa. This commemorates God's benevolence in bringing forth water, after Abraham had been commanded to abandon his wife Hagar and son Ishmael in the desert. On the 2nd day of the Hajj, pilgrims walk to the Plain of Arafat (where Muhammad delivered his last sermon) to perform *Waqoof* – standing in the open, meditating, praising Allah, and praying for forgiveness. The 3rd day celebrates the willingness of Abraham to defy Satan and obey God's demand to sacrifice his son. Pilgrims stone three pillars (*Jamarat*) where Satan appeared, and sacrifice an animal as Abraham did. ❦ While most of the Hajj's many rituals have not changed in 1,400 years, much of the infrastructure has had to adapt. Prompted by tragedies such as those at the Jamarat Bridge (as well as the annual death toll from exhaustion, disease, and dehydration), the Saudi royal family has invested heavily in Mecca. A factory produces some 50m bags of cool water and ice; fire-proof and air-conditioned tents in Mina can house 1·5m; a vast abattoir handles animal sacrifices; and Mecca's morgue can hold >900. It is likely, however, that infrastructural advances will not be enough. In 2006, a number of Saudi newspapers called for Islamic scholars to rethink the ceremonies of the Hajj to protect the lives of 'God's guests'.

THE VATICAN SWISS GUARD

In January 2006, the Vatican Swiss Guard celebrated 500 years of service to the Catholic Church. The corps officially assumed Papal defence duties in 1506, when Julius II asked 150 Helvetian mercenaries to march from their native land to the Vatican, to act as his personal guard and protect the Apostolic Palace. To commemorate their call to arms, 80 veterans journeyed on foot from Switzerland to Rome in 2006. ❦ Recruits must be unmarried, celibate, Roman Catholic males, aged 19–30, at least 5' 8" (1·73m), who have completed military training in the Swiss armed forces. Once enlisted, recruits are taught tactics, security, and counter-terrorism, and learn to handle not only modern firearms but also the unwieldy swords and elaborate halberds of their Renaissance predecessors.

The Guards are instantly recognisable by their splendid apparel – full armour, helmets plumed with ostrich feathers, and striped tunics and breeches in the red, yellow, and blue livery of the Medici family. Competition to join one of the world's smallest armies is fierce, and each guard must recite and abide by an historic oath: *I swear I will faithfully, loyally and honourably serve the Supreme Pontiff – and his legitimate successors and also dedicate myself to them with all my strength, sacrificing if necessary my life to defend them. I assume this same commitment with regard to the Sacred College of Cardinals whenever the See is vacant. Furthermore, I promise to the commanding captain and my other superiors, respect, fidelity and obedience. This I swear! May God and our holy patrons assist me!*

SOUTH PARK AND SCIENTOLOGY

South Park became the focus of media gossip after a November 2005 episode parodying Scientology allegedly upset Isaac Hayes and Tom Cruise – both of whom are followers. In the controversial episode, the character Stan was declared the reincarnation of Scientology founder L. Ron Hubbard after taking a Scientology test and scoring unprecedented 'Thetan levels'. On hearing the news, a cartoon Tom Cruise hid in Stan's bedroom hoping for a meeting with his new hero. After Stan insulted his acting, Cruise shut himself in Stan's wardrobe and refused to come out, despite many characters exhorting him to 'come out of the closet'. ❦ The episode was due to repeat in March 2006, but was abruptly withdrawn after Hayes (who voices the character Chef) announced his resignation, citing the show's 'inappropriate ridicule' of religion. Some media outlets speculated that Cruise may have influenced the decision not to re-broadcast the episode. In response to the furore, the *South Park* creators Matt Stone and Trey Parker issued this statement:

> *'So, Scientology, you may have won THIS battle, but the million-year war for Earth has just begun! Temporarily anozinizing our episode will NOT stop us from keeping Thetans forever trapped in your pitiful man-bodies!'*

After Hayes left, the show spoofed the controversy by depicting Chef as a member of the Super Adventure Club, a group of brain-washing paedophiles. Chef was saved by the children of South Park, but then perished after being set on fire, impaled, shot, and attacked by a mountain lion and a bear.

──────── RED CROSS, CRESCENT, & CRYSTAL ────────

On 22 June 2006, the 29th International Conference of the Red Cross and Red Crescent (ICRC) amended its statutes to incorporate the 'Red Crystal' and afford it the same status as the Red Cross and Red Crescent. The significance of this decision went well beyond graphic design, since it allowed Israel to join the Red Cross movement (despite objections from some Muslim countries). Israel's equivalent to the Red Cross (the Magen David Adom) had previously had only 'observer status', since its logo, a red Star of David, was not accepted under the Geneva Conventions.

The Red Cross, a reversal of the Swiss Flag, was designed in 1864, and given official international status of battlefield neutrality by the Geneva Convention.	*The Red Crescent was adopted c.1877 as a rejection of the Red Cross which had associations with the Christian Crusades. It is currently used by 32 countries.*	*The religiously neutral Red Crystal was adopted in 2006, and can be used alone, or in combination with the Cross, Crescent, or other symbols such as the Star of David.*

At the same conference, Palestinian humanitarian societies were included (they had previously been excluded for not representing an internationally recognised state).

──── USA · UNDERSTANDING & PERCEPTIONS OF ISLAM ────

For a number of reasons, from 9/11 and Iraq to the Muhammad cartoon controversy [see p.19], Islam has featured heavily in recent American media coverage. In March 2006, an ABC News/*Washington Post* poll indicated that 59% of US adults did *not* have a 'good basic understanding of the teachings and beliefs of Islam'. Notwithstanding this ignorance, 46% had a 'generally unfavourable opinion of Islam'; 45% thought Islam did not 'teach respect for the beliefs of non-Muslims'; 33% thought mainstream Islam 'encourages violence against non-Muslims'; and 58% thought there were 'more violent extremists within Islam' compared to other religions. (A CNN/*USA Today* poll in February 2006 found that 61% of Americans thought the cartoon controversy was due to 'Muslim intolerance of different points of view', compared to 21% who cited 'Western lack of respect'.) A report in March 2006, by the Pew Forum on Religion and Public Life, showed that 55% of Americans had a favourable overall opinion of Muslim-Americans, but only 41% had a generally favourable opinion of Islam. Interestingly, those who knew Muslims personally were 24% more likely to think favourably of Muslim-Americans than those who knew none. ❦ In June 2006, a *Times*/Populus poll of British Muslims found that 79% felt that their community had experienced increased hostility since the 7/7 bombs, and 74% said that Muslims were viewed by others with suspicion.

EVOLUTION

Over a third of the British population do not accept the theory of evolution. 2,000 people were asked by BBC's *Horizon* what best described their view of the origin and development of life:

Evolution theory 48%
Creationism 22%
Intelligent design 17%
Don't know 13%

[Source: MORI/*Horizon*, 2006]

GOSPEL OF JUDAS

A Coptic manuscript found in the El Minya desert, Egypt, in 1978, was unveiled by the National Geographic Society in 2006 as the long-lost gospel of Judas Iscariot. After years of diligent scrutiny, some biblical scholars considered its content to absolve the 13th apostle of the sins which had earned him his reputation for treachery. In support they cited the following passages, reported as Jesus' words to Judas:

Step away from the others and I shall tell you the mysteries of the kingdom. It is possible for you to reach it, but you will grieve a great deal ... you will be cursed by the other generations, and you will come to rule over them ... you will exceed all of them. For you will sacrifice the man that saves me.

Many debated the validity of the gospel, claiming that the style and date of its composition (*c.*AD300) fell well outside Judas' lifetime, and pointed to its gnostic origin. The Archbishop of Canterbury Rowan Williams denounced it, along with *The Da Vinci Code*, as part of a general culture of conspiracy where truth is considered to be hidden by those in power.

COSMIC ORDERING

2006 saw a resurgence in the television career of Noel Edmonds, who had not graced TV screens since his BBC contract expired in 2000. Edmonds scored a hit with the daytime game show *Deal or No Deal*, which earned him a Bafta nomination. He attributed this success to a book by German 'positive thinking' journalist Barbel Mohr – *The Cosmic Ordering Service: A Guide to Realising Your Dreams.* The New Age philosophy claims that by writing wishes on a piece of paper or the palm of the hand, one places an order in the cosmos for those wishes to come true. Edmonds' apparent adherence to the system angered some of the more traditional clergy, who derided the concept of a 'heavenly shopping trolley'. Edmonds declined to reveal his cosmic orders that had yet to be delivered. ❦ Edmonds has written a book about his cosmic beliefs, titled *Positively Happy*, for which he was reportedly paid £500,000.

NATIONAL DAY

A survey by BBC *History Magazine*, in May 2006, tested which significant anniversaries the British public most wanted to see marked by a proposed British National Day. The ten most popular anniversaries were:

15 Jun 1215 .... *Magna Carta signed*
8 May 1945 .... *VE Day*
6 Jun 1944 .... *D Day*
11 Nov 1918 .... *Remembrance Day*
21 Oct 1805 .... *Nelson & Trafalgar*
25 Mar 1807 ... *Abolition of slave trade*
18 Jun 1815 ...... *Napoleon & Waterloo*
30 Nov 1874 .... *Churchill born*
19 May 1649 .... *Cromwellian Commonwealth established*
7 Jun 1832 .... *Reform Act passed*

Sport

I'm sorry for the fans, who have been fantastic, that we couldn't give them a final.
— SVEN-GÖRAN ERIKSSON

I feel the time is right to pass on the armband as we enter a new era.
— DAVID BECKHAM

FIFA WORLD CUP 2006 · ENGLAND & MISC

England had high expectations for World Cup 2006, fielding what was arguably their strongest team for decades – although the press did question Sven-Göran Eriksson's squad selection: particularly his decision to bring just four strikers, one of whom was injured (Wayne Rooney), and another untested (17-year-old Theo Walcott). ✤ Despite these concerns, England progressed through the competition, achieving the required results while never quite reaching their potential. Rooney's early recovery from a metatarsal fracture boosted the team, but an injury to Michael Owen in the opening minutes of the game against Sweden appeared to justify concerns about the lack of viable strikers. England's run ended in a quarter-final against Portugal, during which Rooney scuffled with Ronaldo and was sent off for stamping on Carvalho. Ironically, with 10 men England finally started to produce the form the fans had expected. Sadly, it proved insufficient to avoid the (inevitable) penalty shoot-out, where Ricardo saved 3 English shots and only Hargreaves scored. Mournful dissection followed England's defeat, with failure blamed on everything from the heat to the presence of the all-shopping and all-tanning WAGs [see p.12].

✤ England took to their Baden-Baden training camp: 24 boxes of Frosties, 108 packets of Jaffa Cakes, 12 packets of Bird's instant custard, and 120 bottles of Ribena. ✤ An epidemic of play-acting and diving brought an uneven standard of refereeing under scrutiny. The tournament's only English referee, Graham Poll, did not excel, showing Croatian Josip Simunic 3 yellow cards in one match. In contrast, Russian ref Valentin Ivanov made World Cup history during Portugal *vs* Holland: he booked 16 players and sent off 4. ✤ Of the 3m tickets available for the World Cup, 1m were reserved for the sponsors. ✤ Germany made the most tackles (220 completed); Portugal had the most bookings (24 yellow, 2 red); Germany scored the most goals (13); and

Italian Gianluigi Buffon was the best goalkeeper (27 saves). ✤ English club Chelsea had the most players competing (16). ✤ The World Cup's mascot, a lion named 'Goleo', did not amuse the fans (many noted his shocking lack of shorts), and Nici, the company producing the toy, went bust. ✤ McDonald's produced a special World Cup 'Bigger Mac' (which had 11·06g more fat than a Big Mac). ✤ Economists estimated that the World Cup generated £900m for the British economy through sales of barbecue food, snacks, and beer.

Golden Ball	Zinedine Zidane
Golden Boot	Miroslav Klose (5 goals)
Best Goalkeeper	Gianluigi Buffon
Best young player	Lukas Podolski
Most 'entertaining' team	Portugal

—— FIFA · WORLD CUP · GERMANY 2006 ——

Group A

Germany [1]	4–2	Costa Rica
Poland	0–2	Ecuador
Germany	1–0	Poland
Ecuador [2]	3–0	Costa Rica
Ecuador	0–3	Germany
Costa Rica	1–2	Poland

Group B

England [1]	1–0	Paraguay
Trin & Tob	0–0	Sweden
England	2–0	Trin & Tob
Sweden	1–0	Paraguay
Sweden [2]	2–2	England
Paraguay	2–0	Trin & Tob

Group C

Argentina [1]	2–1	Ivory Coast
Serbia & Mon	0–1	Holland
Argentina	6–0	Serbia & Mon
Holland [2]	2–1	Ivory Coast
Holland	0–0	Argentina
Ivory Coast	3–2	Serbia & Mon

Group D

Mexico [2]	3–1	Iran
Angola	0–1	Portugal
Mexico	0–0	Angola
Portugal [1]	2–0	Iran
Portugal	2–1	Mexico
Iran	1–1	Angola

Group E

Italy [1]	2–0	Ghana
USA	0–3	Czech Rep
Italy	1–1	USA
Czech Rep	0–2	Ghana
Czech Rep	0–2	Italy
Ghana [2]	2–1	USA

Group F

Brazil [1]	1–0	Croatia
Australia [2]	3–1	Japan
Brazil	2–0	Australia
Japan	0–0	Croatia
Japan	1–4	Brazil
Croatia	2–2	Australia

Group G

France [2]	0–0	Switzerland
Korea	2–1	Togo
France	1–1	S Korea
Togo	0–2	Switzerland
Togo	0–2	France
Switzerland [1]	2–0	S Korea

Group H

Spain [1]	4–0	Ukraine
Tunisia	2–2	Saudi Arabia
Spain	3–1	Tunisia
Saudi Arabia	0–4	Ukraine
Saudi Arabia	0–1	Spain
Ukraine [2]	1–0	Tunisia

2nd Round

Germany	2		England	1
Sweden	0		Ecuador	0
Argentina	2		Portugal	1
Mexico	1		Holland	0
Italy	1		Brazil	3
Australia	0		Ghana	0
Switzerland	0 (0)		Spain	1
Ukraine	0 (3)		France	3

QUARTER-FINAL

Germany	1 (4)		England	(1) 0
Argentina	1 (2)		Portugal	(3) 0
30 June · Berlin			*1 July · Gelsenkirchen*	
Italy	3		Brazil	0
Ukraine	0		France	1
30 June · Hamburg			*1 July · Frankfurt*	

SEMI-FINAL

Germany	0		Portugal	0
Italy	2		France	1
4 July · Dortmund			*5 July · Munich*	

· FINAL ·

9 July 2006
Berlin 20:00

Italy
bt
France
5–3
on penalties
[1–1 AET]

8 July · *Stuttgart* · Germany *bt* Portugal 3–1 for 3rd place

——————— WINTER OLYMPICS · TORINO 2006 ———————

Preparations for the 2006 Winter Olympics were beset by financial difficulties and organisational strife. The Italian government stepped in to rescue the Games from bankruptcy, and international concerns over venues, transport, and security were compounded by disappointing attendance figures. However, the Games saw a number of exhilarating contests and unpredictable outcomes, with shock wins in the men's downhill and women's figure skating. Germany dominated the medal table [below], taking every Gold in the women's luge, and 11 medals in the biathlon; Austria also managed a clean sweep in the men's slalom. The USA's many achievements were overshadowed by the showboating and underperformance of 'sport celebs' Bode Miller and Lindsey Jacobellis. Despite high hopes for curling, the sole GB medal came in the skeleton bob, where Shelley Rudman took Silver.

Country	G	S	B	All					
Germany	11	12	6	29	China	2	4	5	11
United States	9	9	7	25	Czech Rep.	1	2	1	4
Austria	9	7	7	23	Croatia	1	2	0	3
Russian Fed.	8	6	8	22	Australia	1	0	1	2
Canada	7	10	7	24	Japan	1	0	0	1
Sweden	7	2	5	14	Finland	0	6	3	9
S. Korea	6	3	2	11	Poland	0	1	1	2
Switzerland	5	4	5	14	Belarus	0	1	0	1
Italy	5	0	6	11	Bulgaria	0	1	0	1
France	3	2	4	9	Great Britain	0	1	0	1
Netherlands	3	2	4	9	Slovakia	0	1	0	1
Estonia	3	0	0	3	Ukraine	0	0	2	2
Norway	2	8	9	19	Latvia	0	0	1	1

[61 countries won no medals]

Results of note	*winner*	*medal*
♀ Alpine skiing · downhill, super-G	Michaela Dorfmeister [AUT]	G
♂ Alpine skiing · downhill	Antoine Deneriaz [FRA]	G
♂ Alpine skiing · super-G	Hermann Maier[1] [AUT]	S
♀ Alpine skiing · combined	Janica Kostelic[2] [CRO]	G
♂ Alpine skiing · combined	Ivica Kostelic[2] [CRO]	S
♂ Biathlon · 15km mass, 20km ind.	Michael Greis [GER]	G
♂ Bobsleigh · two-man	Andre Lange/Kevin Kuske [GER]	G
♀♂ Figure skating · pairs	Zhang Dan/Zhang Hao[3] [CHI]	S
♂ Figure skating · single	Evgeni Plushenko [RUS]	G
♂ Ski jumping · NH individual	Lars Bystoel [NOR]	G
♂ Snowboard · half-pipe	Shaun White [USA]	G
♂ Speed skating · 1,500m	Enrico Fabris [ITA]	G
♀ Speed skating · 1,500m	Cindy Klassen [CAN]	G

[1] Hermann 'Hermanator' Maier had recovered from horrific injuries sustained in a motorcycle accident. [2] Extreme poverty and Ivica's repeated knee injuries proved major obstacles for these medal-winning siblings. [3] Zhang Dan and Zhang Hao resumed their programme after a nasty fall on the ice, re-igniting the Salt Lake City 'Skategate' debate over stoppages during performances.

——————THE TOUR DE FRANCE · 2006——————

The 2006 (93rd) Tour de France thoroughly earned its 'Tour de Farce' nickname, living down to the 1998 'Tour of Shame'. Before the race had even started, 13 riders (including favourites Jan Ullrich and Ivan Basso) were withdrawn amidst controversy surrounding a Spanish doping probe. American Floyd Landis won the 3-week, 2,267-mile race in 89h 39' 30", despite riding while in need of a hip replacement. However, his jubilation was cut short when his 'A' and 'B' drug test samples indicated excessive levels of testosterone. Landis denied any wrongdoing, and insisted that these high levels were a 'natural occurrence'. At the time of writing, Landis' lawyers are formally challenging the test results, and he has pledged to clear his name.

——————LONDON MARATHON · 2006——————

On Sunday 23 April 2006, *c*.35,000 took part in the 26th London Marathon.

♂ *race results*		♂ *wheelchair race results*	
F. Limo [KEN]	2h 6m 39s	D. Weir [GBR]	01·29·48
M. Lel [KEN]	02·06·41	S. Mendoza [MEX]	01·37·52
H. Ramaala [RSA]	02·06·55	A. Fuss [FRA]	01·39·37

♀ *race results*		♀ *wheelchair race results*	
D. Kastor [USA]	02·19·36	F. Porcellato [ITA]	01·59·57
L. Petrova [RUS]	02·21·29	S. Woods [GBR]	02·04·37
S. Chepkemei [KEN]	02·21·46	D. Brennan [GBR]	02·21·02

Celebrity Jade Goody ran in to trouble after 18½ miles when, turning blue, she called to paramedics, 'I'm dying!'. Goody prepared for the race on a diet of curry, and she raised £355 for the NSPCC.

– OTHER MARATHONS OF NOTE · 2005/06 –

BERLIN	*first run* 1974	NEW YORK	*first run* 1970
2005 · Sep 24–25	sunny, warm	2005 · Nov 6	warm, humid
♂	P. Manyim [KEN] · 2:07:41	♂	P. Tergat [KEN] · 2:09:30
♀	M. Noguchi [JAP] · 2:19:22	♀	J. Prokopcuka [LAT] · 2:24:41
Purse	*c*.$50,848	Purse	$>600,000

CHICAGO	*first run* 1977	BOSTON	*first run* 1897
2005 · Oct 9	overcast, then sunny	2006 · April 17	cloudy, cool
♂	F. Limo [KEN] · 2:07:02	♂	R. Cheruiyot [KEN] · 2:07:14
♀	D. Kastor [USA] · 2:21:25	♀	R. Jeptoo [KEN] · 2:23:38
Purse	$650,000	Purse	$575,000

In 2006, the 'big five' marathons (all those listed above) joined to create the body 'World Marathon Majors'. The World Marathon Majors Series was then announced; a competition including all the Majors as well as the IAAF World Marathon Championships and the Olympic marathon. The inaugural series began with Boston's 2006 run, and will end in New York in autumn 2007.

─────── COMMONWEALTH GAMES · 2006 ───────

At the 18th Commonwealth Games in Melbourne, Australia, in 2006, *c.*4,500 athletes from 71 nations participated in 24 disciplines, resulting in the award of *c.*750 medals. The host nation was notably dominant, but England put in strong performances in swimming, cycling, and boxing to come second in the medals. (Disappointingly, England's male sprinters failed to translate promise into success.) Scotland enjoyed its best ever Games, collecting 29 medals. The full table is below:

Country	G	S	B	total	Country	G	S	B	total
Australia	84	69	68	221	Namibia	1	0	1	2
England	36	40	34	110	Tanzania	1	0	1	2
Canada	26	29	31	86	Sri Lanka	1	0	0	1
India	22	17	11	50	Mauritius	0	3	0	3
South Africa	12	13	13	38	Bahamas	0	2	0	2
Scotland	11	7	11	29	N. Ireland	0	2	0	2
Jamaica	10	4	8	22	Cameroon	0	1	2	3
Malaysia	7	12	10	29	Botswana	0	1	1	2
New Zealand	6	12	13	31	Malta	0	1	1	2
Kenya	6	5	7	18	Nauru	0	1	1	2
Singapore	5	6	7	18	Bangladesh	0	1	0	1
Nigeria	4	6	7	17	Grenada	0	1	0	1
Wales	3	5	11	19	Lesotho	0	1	0	1
Cyprus	3	1	2	6	Trin. & Tob.	0	0	3	3
Ghana	2	0	1	3	Seychelles	0	0	2	2
Uganda	2	0	1	3	Barbados	0	0	1	1
Pakistan	1	3	1	5	Fiji	0	0	1	1
Papua N. G.	1	1	0	2	Mozambique	0	0	1	1
Isle of Man	1	0	1	2	Samoa	0	0	1	1
					Swaziland	0	0	1	1

SOME GOLD MEDALS OF NOTE

	Event	winner	record	result
♂	Athletics · decathlon	Dean Macey [ENG]		8,143 pts
♀	Athletics · heptathlon	Kelly Sotherton [ENG]		6,396 pts
♀	Athletics · 400m	Christine Ohuruogu [ENG]		50·28s
♂	Athletics · 100m	Asafa Powell [JAM]		10·03s
♀	Athletics · 100m	Sheri-Ann Brooks [JAM]		11·19s
♀♂	Badminton · mixed doubles	Robertson/Emms [ENG]		2–0
♂	Boxing · light heavyweight 81kg	Kenneth Anderson [SCO]		23–19 pts
♂	Cycling · individual pursuit	Paul Manning [ENG]		4:23·799
♂	Cycling · 20km scratch	Mark Cavendish [IOM]		N/A
♀	Cycling · 200m sprint	Victoria Pendleton [ENG]		2–1
♂	Shooting · 50m rifle prone	David Phelps [WAL]		698·3 pts
♀	Swimming · 200m freestyle	Caitlin McClatchey [SCO]	CR	1:57·25
♀	Swimming · 100m breast-stroke	Leisel Jones [AUS]	WR	1:05·09
♀	Weightlifting · 63kg	Michaela Breeze [WAL]		220kg

Key: CR – Championship Record · WR – World Record

SPORTING INTRIGUE

{SEP} · After 17 months of injury, Jonathan Woodgate made a disastrous debut for Real Madrid; he scored an own goal before being sent off. {OCT} · Annoyed by the news that women might be able to qualify for the 2006 British Open, French golfer Jean Van de Velde threatened to enter the Women's British Open wearing a kilt. {NOV} · Manchester United TV was forced to shelve an interview with Roy Keane after he allegedly launched an outspoken critique of fellow players; he later quit the club. {DEC} · Paul Gascoigne was sacked as manager of non-league Kettering town after just 39 days; Chairman Imraan Ladak accused Gazza of turning up drunk. ❦ Sprinter Tim Montgomery received a 2-year ban for doping offences, although the ban did not result from positive doping tests but from the testimony of a former team-mate; his world record was annulled and his winnings from that period were demanded back. {FEB} · Drugs scandals hit Torino 2006; biathlete Olga Pyleva was stripped of her silver after testing positive for carphedon, and the Brazilian bobsleigher Armando dos Santos tested positive for nandrolone. The Austrian biathlon team came under scrutiny after it was discovered that they had been visited by coach Walter Mayer, who was banned by the IOC for blood doping in Salt Lake City 2002. Mayer later fled the scene and crashed into a road-block in an apparent suicide attempt. {MAR} · Oxford boat captain Barney Williams was arrested and fined for drunk and disorderly behaviour and criminal

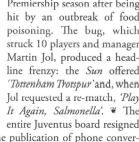

Zinedine Zidane

It is now my goal to clear my name and restore what I worked so hard to achieve. – FLOYD LANDIS [see p.297]

damage 3 days after his team's victory in the Boat Race. ❦ {APR} · The *Sunday Mirror* alleged that Wayne Rooney had accrued £700,000 in gambling debts. The debt was later reported to have been settled. ❦ {MAY} · Tottenham lost their final game of the Premiership season after being hit by an outbreak of food poisoning. The bug, which struck 10 players and manager Martin Jol, produced a headline frenzy: the *Sun* offered *'Tottenham Throtspur'* and, when Jol requested a re-match, *'Play It Again, Salmonella'.* ❦ The entire Juventus board resigned after the publication of phone conversations, in which the club appeared to have colluded in the appointment of referees for its games. {JUNE} · It was alleged that All Black Chris Masoe cried after team-mate Tana Umaga hit him in a bar with a woman's handbag. The bag's owner auctioned the trophy on the internet for NZ$22,800 (£7,546). {JUL} · In a defining moment of the 2006 World Cup final, Zidane headbutted Materazzi [see p.26]. ❦ After a protracted match-fixing investigation, the Italian Football Federation issued the following punishments: Juventus were stripped of their last 2 Serie A titles, relegated to Serie B, and had 17 points deducted; Fiorentina, Lazio, and AC Milan were allowed to stay in Serie A but had 19, 11, and 8 points deducted respectively. {AUG} · The IAAF announced that Olympic champion sprinter Justin Gatlin must serve at least a 4-year ban for testing positive for testosterone. After a second drug's test, sprinter Marion Jones was cleared of any doping offences.

THE LAUREUS AWARDS · 2006

The Laureus World Sporting Academy encourages the 'positive and worthwhile in sport', presenting awards to athletes in all disciplines. Some 2006 winners were:

World sportsman of the year .... Roger Federer (tennis)
World sportswoman of the year .... Janica Kostelic (skiing)
Comeback of the year .... Martina Hingis (tennis)
Sportsperson with a disability .... Ernst Van Dyk (wheelchair racing)
Alternative sportsperson of the year..................... Angelo d'Arrigo[†] (aviation)

† In 2003, hang-glider Angelo 'The Human Condor' d'Arrigo escorted a flock of endangered Siberian cranes 3,400 miles across the Arctic Circle, teaching them the traditional migratory route. Two years later he adopted two Andean condors and taught them to fly. d'Arrigo's Laureus Award was given posthumously – the ornithologist, who had broken his own altitude record for hang-gliding in January 2006, died in March after the light aircraft in which he was a passenger crashed.

BDO WORLD DARTS CHAMPIONSHIP · 2006

In January 2006, the Lakeside World Championship was finally wrested from the four-year grasp of Dutchman Raymond 'Barney' Van Barneveld, by compatriot Jelle 'The Matador' Klaasen. Aged just 21, Klaasen began the tournament as a 100–1 outsider, but took the final match 7–5, ruthlessly capitalising on Barneveld's crucial missed doubles to claim the £60,000 cash prize. Klaasen's trim physique and chiselled jaw also gained him pin-up status, drawing comparisons with former 'dart-throb' Eric 'The Crafty Cockney' Bristow. After Klassen won a pedestrian first-round victory, several female spectators donated their underwear to his cause.

SPORTSPEOPLE & THEIR SPONSORS · 2006

David Beckham................. *Adidas*	Andy Murray................ *Fred Perry*
Justin Gatlin .... *Nike*	Asafa Powell................... *Nutrilite*
Thierry Henry................... *Reebok*	Wayne Rooney..................... *Nike*
Justine Henin-Hardenne .... *Adidas*	Maria Sharapova.................. *Nike*
Gavin Henson .... *Nike*	Michelle Wie...................... *Nike*

THE WORLD SERIES OF POKER

The appropriately named Jamie Gold from California won the $12m grand prize at the close of the 37th World Series of Poker. A record 8,773 hopefuls entered the 12-day contest at the Rio Hotel and Casino in Las Vegas. Nine players reached the final, just four of whom were poker professionals. After 13 hours of play, only 36-year-old (TV producer) Jamie Gold and 25-year-old (bartender) Paul Wasicka remained at the table. Eventually, Wasicka fell for a bluff by Gold and went all in with a pair of tens, only to come up against Gold's paired queens.

——BBC SPORTS PERSONALITY OF THE YEAR · 2005——

*Being involved in the Ashes was something special, a great thing. It was
a real team effort. As for Vaughany leading us, [he] was outstanding.
Thank you to everyone who voted for me.*
— ANDREW 'FREDDIE' FLINTOFF

Sports personality of the year .... Andrew Flintoff
Team of the year .... England's Ashes cricket team
Overseas personality .... Shane Warne
Coach of the year .... José Mourinho
Lifetime achievement .... Pelé
Young personality .... Harry Aikines-Aryeetey (sprinter)
Unsung hero .... Trevor Collins (West Wight Swimming Club)
Helen Rollason award 'for courage and achievement in the face of adversity' .... Geoff Thomas
Special Award .... Lord Coe (for London's 2012 Olympic bid)

————MOST COMPETITIVE SPORT————

Researchers at Los Alamos National Laboratory assessed the competitiveness of five
sports (American hockey, football, baseball, basketball, and English Premiership
soccer) by measuring 'upset frequency' – or how often a superior team is beaten
by lesser opponents. After reviewing 300,000 C20th matches, the researchers
concluded that soccer had the greatest 'upset frequency', and consequently was the
most competitive. To the delight of soccer fans, press reviews of this study noted
that the most competitive sports tended to be the most exciting and, therefore, the
'best'. (When reviewing games from only the previous 10 years, baseball triumphed over soccer.)

——ROLEX/IGFA OFFSHORE ANGLING TOURNAMENT——

The Rolex/IGFA (International Game Fish Association) Championship held in
Cabo San Lucas, Mexico, in May 2006 attracted 64 teams from 33 countries, the
most international teams ever to compete in a fishing contest. The 2005 Rolex/
IGFA team[†] successfully defended their title – a single day record of 10 marlin
saw the team easily out-fish their nearest rivals. Besides 3 species of marlin (blue,
black, striped), teams may catch swordfish, sailfish, and spearfish. They also
receive 'weight points' for tuna, wahoo, and dorado. The heaviest catches were:

Fish	angler	team	weight (lb)
Wahoo	Jamie Paul	3rd Annual Salmon Masters	50·6
Dorado	Edward Day	TAA Ixtapa Sailfish Tournament	36·2
Tuna	Ustar Marjan	7th Big Game Comp. Croatia	117·0

† To qualify for the tournament, a team must have won at least one IGFA-sanctioned competition,
and, having done so, they may take the name of that competition as their team name. This
explains the confusing similarity between the tournament name and that of the returning winners.

THE PREMIERSHIP · 2005/06

Team	won	drew	lost	goals for	goals against	prize money†	points
Chelsea	29	4	5	72	22	£47·5m	91
Manchester Utd	25	8	5	72	34	£39·8m	83
Liverpool	25	7	6	57	25	£43·2m	82
Arsenal	20	7	11	68	31	£52·7m	67
↑ CHAMPION'S LEAGUE ↑							
Tottenham	18	11	9	53	38	£26·2m	65
Blackburn	19	6	13	51	42	£23·6m	63
Newcastle	17	7	14	47	42	£24·0m	58
↑ UEFA CUP ↑							
Bolton	15	11	12	49	41	£23·7m	56
West Ham	16	7	15	52	55	£24·4m	55
Wigan	15	6	17	45	52	£22·9m	51
Everton	14	8	16	34	49	£22·4m	50
Fulham	14	6	18	48	58	£20·3m	48
Charlton	13	8	17	41	55	£21·0m	47
Middlesbrough	12	9	17	48	58	£24·3m	45
Manchester City	13	4	21	43	48	£20·6m	43
Aston Villa	10	12	16	42	55	£19·6m	42
Portsmouth	10	8	20	37	62	£18·0m	38
↓ RELEGATION ↓							
Birmingham	8	10	20	28	50	£19·4m	34
West Bromwich	7	9	22	31	58	£16·9m	30
Sunderland	3	6	29	26	69	£16·1m	15

Top scorer.......................................Thierry Henry (Arsenal): 27 goals
Most red cards ....Birmingham; Everton; Newcastle: 7
Most yellow cards..Blackburn Rovers: 76

† These figures represent a combination of TV income and prize money, and exclude gates and merchandise. Arsenal out-earned Chelsea after greater success in the Champions League.

OTHER DIVISIONS – UP & DOWN

Up	2005/06	Down
Reading, Sheffield Utd Watford	*Championship*	Crewe, Millwall Brighton
Southend, Colchester, Barnsley	*League One*	Hartlepool, MK Dons Swindon, Walsall
Carlisle, Northampton Leyton Orient, Cheltenham	*League Two*	Oxford Rushden & Diamonds
Accrington Stanley, Hereford	*Conference*	Canvey Island, Scarborough

——— FA CUP FINAL ———

13 May 2006 · Millennium Stadium,
Wales · Attendance: 74,000
LIVERPOOL 3–3 WEST HAM (AET)
LIVERPOOL WON 3–1 ON PENALTIES
1st ½: Carragher 21' *og*; Ashton 28'
Cissé 32' · 2nd ½: Gerrard 54';
Konchesky 64'; Gerrard 90'
Referee: Alan Wiley

PENALTY SHOOT-OUT

1–0	Hamann scores
1–0	Reina saves Zamora low shot
1–0	Hislop denies Hyypia
1–1	Sheringham lashes home
2–1	Gerrard scores
2–1	Reina collects Konchesky's effort
3–1	Riise wrong-foots Hislop
3–1	Reina saves Ferdinand's shot

——— CH. LEAGUE FINAL ———

17 May 2006 · Stade de France, Paris
Attendance: 79,500
BARCELONA 2–1 ARSENAL
Referee: Terje Hauge

THE KEY MOMENTS

3'	Henry shot saved by Valdes
8'	shot by Giuly caught by Lehman
18'	Lehmann off for foul on Eto'o
22'	Ebouc booked
37'	Campbell scores for Arsenal
45'	Eto'o hits the post
51'	Henry booked
66'	Ljunberg shot saved by Valdes
69'	Oleguer booked
76'	Eto'o scores for Barcelona
80'	Belletti scores for Barcelona
90'	Larsson booked

——— SOME FOOTBALL AWARDS OF NOTE · 2005/06 ———

FIFA world player of the year . . . . Ronaldinho [Barcelona]
European footballer of the year . . . . Ronaldinho [Barcelona]
Prof. Footballers' Assoc. player of the year . . . . Steven Gerrard [Liverpool]
PFA young player award . . . . Wayne Rooney [Man. Utd.]
PFA special merit award . . . . . George Best[†] [see p.56]
Football Writers' Assoc. player of the year . . . . Thierry Henry [Arsenal]
FA women's football awards: best international player . . . . Rachel Unitt [Everton]
FA women's football awards: players' player of the year . . . . Kelly Smith [Arsenal]

† The first time the special merit award was given posthumously; Best died in November 2005.

——— LITERARY GAFFERS ———

In 2006, the National Football Museum in Preston conducted a survey in which
football managers were asked to name their favourite book. Below is a selection:

José Mourinho (Chelsea) . . . . *The Bible*
Sir Alex Ferguson (Man. Utd) . . . . *Treasure Island* · Robert Louis Stevenson
Martin Jol (Tottenham) . . . . *Old Man and the Sea* · Ernest Hemingway
David O'Leary (Aston Villa) . . . . *Kane and Abel* · Jeffrey Archer
Sam Allardyce (Bolton Wanderers) . . . . *The Soul of a Butterfly* · Muhammad Ali
Paul Jewell (Wigan) . . . . *Bravo Two Zero* · Andy McNab
David Moyes (Everton) . . . . *Animal Farm* · George Orwell

——HOME NATIONS' FOOTBALL RECORD · 2005/06——

Date		result		type	venue
08·10·05	England	1–0	Austria	WCQ	Old Trafford, Manchester
08·10·05	Scotland	0–1	Belarus	WCQ	Hampden Park, Glasgow
08·10·05	N. Ireland	2–3	Wales	WCQ	Windsor Park, Belfast
12·10·05	England	2–1	Poland	WCQ	Old Trafford, Manchester
12·10·05	Slovenia	0–3	Scotland	WCQ	Petrol Arena Stad., Slovenia
12·10·05	Wales	2–0	Azerbaijan	WCQ	Millennium Stad., Cardiff
12·10·05	Austria	2–0	N. Ireland	WCQ	Ernst Happel Stad., Vienna
12·11·05	England	3–2	Argentina	F	Stade de Genève, Switzerland
12·11·05	Scotland	1–1	USA	F	Hampden Park, Glasgow
15·11·05	N. Ireland	1–1	Portugal	F	Windsor Park, Belfast
16·11·05	Cyprus	1–0	Wales	F	Tsirion Stadium, Cyprus
01·03·06	England	2–1	Uruguay	F	Anfield, Liverpool
01·03·06	N. Ireland	1–0	Estonia	F	Windsor Park, Belfast
01·03·06	Wales	0–0	Paraguay	F	Millennium Stadium, Cardiff
01·03·06	Scotland	1–3	Switzerland	F	Hampden Park, Glasgow
21·05·06	Uruguay	1–0	N. Ireland	F	Giants Stad., New York
26·05·06	Romania	2–0	N. Ireland	F	Soldier Field, Chicago
30·05·06	England	3–1	Hungary	F	Old Trafford, Manchester
03·06·06	England	6–0	Jamaica	F	Old Trafford, Manchester
15·08·06	Wales	0–0	Bulgaria	F	Liberty Stadium, Swansea
16·08·06	Finland	1–2	N. Ireland	F	Helsinki's Olympic Stadium
16·08·06	England	4–0	Greece	F	Old Trafford, Manchester
02·09·06	Scotland	6–0	Faroe Is.	ECQ	Celtic Park, Glasgow
02·09·06	N. Ireland	0–3	Iceland	ECQ	Windsor Park, Belfast
02·09·06	England	5–0	Andorra	ECQ	Old Trafford, Manchester
02·09·06	Czech Rep.	2–1	Wales	ECQ	Na Stinadlech Stad., Teplice
05·09·06	Wales	0–2	Brazil	F	White Hart Lane, London
06·09·06	N. Ireland	3–2	Spain	ECQ	Windsor Park, Belfast
06·09·06	Lithuania	1–2	Scotland	ECQ	Dariaus Ir Gireno, Kaunas
06·09·06	FYR Mac.	0–1	England	ECQ	Gradski Stadium, Skopje

KEY: F – Friendly · WCQ – World Cup Qualifier · ECQ – European Champ. Qualifier. · In May 2006, Scotland won their first trophy in 20 years: the Kirin Cup is an annual contest in which Japan plays 2 other national teams. Scotland beat Bulgaria 5–1, then drew 0–0 with Japan to secure the win.

——————TEAM OF THE SEASON——————

The Professional Footballers' Association annually nominates a Premiership 'team' of the season. In 2005/06, the following players were selected:

Shay Given [NEW] · Pascal Chimbonda [WIG] · John Terry [CHE]
Jamie Carragher [LIV] · William Gallas [CHE] · Cristiano Ronaldo [MAN U]
Steven Gerrard [LIV] · Frank Lampard [CHE] · Joe Cole [CHE]
Thierry Henry [ARS] · Wayne Rooney [MAN U]

---------------GOLF MAJORS · 2006---------------

♂	course	winner	score
MASTERS	Augusta, Georgia [see below]	Phil Mickelson [USA]	−7
US OPEN	Winged Foot, New York	Geoff Ogilvy [AUS]	+5
THE OPEN	Royal Liverpool, Hoylake	Tiger Woods [USA]	−18
USPGA	Medinah Country Club, Illinois	Tiger Woods [USA]	−18
♀			
KRAFT NABISCO	Rancho Mirage, California	Karrie Webb [AUS]	−9
LPGA	Havre de Grace, Maryland	Se Ri Pak [KOR]	−8
US OPEN	Newport CC, Rhode Island	Annika Sorenstam [SWE]	Par
WOMEN'S OPEN	Royal Lytham & St Annes	Sherri Steinhauer [USA]	−7

In 2006, the Chinese claimed to have invented golf, citing as evidence four C13th paintings. Professor Cui Lequan also asserted that the rules for the Chinese sport of 'Hitball', written in 1282, differed little from those drawn up at St Andrews in 1754. The Scots remained utterly unconvinced.

---------------THE RYDER CUP · 2006---------------

Europe won a record Ryder Cup hat-trick after comprehensively demolishing the USA, 18½–9½, at the K Club, outside Dublin. Even the likes of Tiger Wood (albeit not playing at his best) could do little to halt the Europeans' roll. Perhaps the stand-out performance, not least for the Irish fans, came from N. Ireland's Darren Clarke, who was one of Captain Ian Woosnam's controversial wildcard picks. Clarke's wife Heather had died from cancer just weeks before the tournament, and his emotion at playing and winning was matched only by the vociferous support of the crowd. ❦ America's captain, Tom Lehman, was generous in defeat, saying, 'I just don't think there's ever been a European team which has played better'.

---------------AUGUSTA · CHANGES TO THE 'BIG GREEN'---------------

The Augusta National golf course, among the most famous in the sport, was designed in 1934 by golfer and engineer Bobby Jones (1902–71), but has been subject to numerous remodellings. Some of the most controversial changes to the 'Big Green' were made before the 2006 Masters tournament, and overseen by Hootie Johnson, Augusta chairman, and Tom Fazio, course architect. The changes were:

Hole	par	alteration
1st	4	was 398m, now 416m · trees added · bunker expanded
4th	3	was 187m, now 219m
7th	4	was 376m, now 411m · trees added both sides of fairway
11th	4	was 447m, now 461m · trees added · extra wooded area
15th	5	was 457m, now 484m · tee moved 20m to left
17th	4	was 389m, now 402m

Some players criticised these alterations, claiming that they favoured big hitters like Tiger Woods.

WISDEN CRICKETER OF THE YEAR

Presented since 1889 by the cricketing bible *Wisden*, the Cricketer of the Year has been awarded to such luminaries as W.G. Grace, Don Bradman, and Ian 'Beefy' Botham. No player can win the award twice. In part to circumvent this rule, but equally to honour an outstanding Ashes performance, in 2006 the 'Leading Cricketer of the Year' award was created and presented to Andrew 'Freddie' Flintoff. Five other Ashes heroes were named as 2006's Cricketers of the Year: Simon Jones, Kevin Pietersen, Brett Lee, Ricky Ponting, and Matthew Hoggard.

LG ICC BATTING RANKINGS

LG ICC Test rankings have been backdated historically to include all Tests. The ranking system awards points based on the number of runs scored, and takes into account the strength of the opposition. The 8 best-ever batsmen are listed below:

D. Bradman . 961 (points) *vs* India,1948 | G. Sobers . . . . 938 *vs* India, 1967
L. Hutton . . . . . 945 *vs* W. Indies, 1954 | C. Walcott . . . . . . 938 *vs* Australia, 1956
J. Hobbs . . . . .942 *vs* S. Africa, 1913 | V. Richards . . . . . .938 *vs* England, 1981
P. May . . . . 941 *vs* Australia, 1956 | R. Ponting . . . . . . .937 *vs* S. Africa, 2006

TWENTY20 CUP FINAL DAY · 2006

Leicestershire's Darren Maddy became the first player to score 1,000 runs in Twenty20, when his team beat Notts by 4 runs to claim their second Twenty20 Cup Final. The umpires admitted missing a crucial no-ball, which had it been awarded, would have given Notts a chance to score the 3 runs they required to win.

Semi-final 1	Leicestershire (173–4) *bt* Essex (150–9) by 23 runs
Semi-final 2	Nottinghamshire (176–6) *bt* Surrey (139) by 37 runs
Cup Final	Leicestershire (177–2) *bt* Nottinghamshire (173–8) by 4 runs

ICC TEST & ODI WORLD RANKINGS

Test matches [21·8·06]	*rating*	*rank*	*rating*	*ODI* [20·9·06]
Australia	130	1	128	Australia
England	119	2	124	South Africa
Pakistan	112	3	112	India
India	111	4	111	Pakistan
Sri Lanka	103	5	111	New Zealand
South Africa	94	6	107	Sri Lanka
New Zealand	92	7	105	West Indies
West Indies	72	8	99	England
Zimbabwe	28	9	33	Zimbabwe
Bangladesh	2	10	33	Bangladesh

——— TEST MATCH SERIES · ENGLAND vs SRI LANKA ———

Spectacular bowling by Muttiah Muralitharan in the 3rd Test (8 for 70), gave Sri Lanka their second Test victory in England (the first was in 1998). Yet a draw in the 1st Test, and England's victory in the 2nd, resulted in the series being drawn 1–1.

1st Test · Lord's 11–15 May 2006 *England won the toss*		2nd Test · Edgbaston 25–28 May 2006 *Sri Lanka won the toss*		3rd Test · Trent Bridge 2–5 June 2006 *Sri Lanka won the toss*	
ENG	551 for 6 dec	SRI	141 all out	SRI	231 all out
SRI	192 all out	ENG	295 all out	ENG	229 all out
SRI	537 for 9	SRI	231 all out	SRI	322 all out
		ENG	81 for 4	ENG	190 all out
Match drawn		*Eng. won by 6 wickets*		*SL won by 134 runs*	

——— TEST MATCH SERIES · ENGLAND vs PAKISTAN ———

Andrew Strauss captained England to a 3–0 victory over Pakistan, after injury forced out Vaughan and Flintoff. Taking 17 wickets during the series, Monty Panesar was hailed as England's hero. The 4th Test ended in controversy when, after 56 overs of England's 2nd innings, the umpires judged that the condition of the ball had been artificially altered to gain an advantage. They replaced the ball and awarded England 5 penalty runs. In protest, the Pakistani team refused to take the field after tea; following some confusion, the umpires declared the game forfeited. This was the first time in Test history that a match had been conceded by forfeit.

1st Test · Lord's 13–17 July 2006 *Eng. won the toss*		2nd · Old Trafford 27–31 July 2006 *Pak. won the toss*		3rd · Headingley 4–8 August 2006 *Eng. won the toss*		4th · The Oval 17–21 Aug. 2006 *Pak. won the toss*	
ENG	528 for 9	PAK	119 all out	ENG	515 all out	ENG	173 all out
PAK	445 all out	ENG	461 for 9	PAK	538 all out	PAK	504 all out
ENG	296 for 8	PAK	222 all out	ENG	345 all out	ENG	298 for 4
PAK	214 for 4			PAK	155 all out		
Match drawn		*England won by an innings & 120 runs*		*England won by 167 runs*		*Pakistan forfeited the match*	

So-called 'ball tampering' is addressed in the 42nd Law of Cricket (Fair and unfair play), section 3 of which concerns 'The match ball · changing its condition'. Section 3 begins: a) Any fielder may (i) polish the ball provided that no artificial substance is used and that such polishing wastes no time. (ii) remove mud from the ball under the supervision of the umpire.

(iii) dry a wet ball on a towel. (b) It is unfair for anyone to rub the ball on the ground for any reason, interfere with any of the seams or the surface of the ball, use any implement, or take any other action whatsoever which is likely to alter the condition of the ball, except as permitted in (a) above. (c) The umpires shall make frequent and irregular inspections of the ball.

————— RUGBY UNION SIX NATIONS · 2005 —————

Date		result		venue
04·02·06	England	47–13	Wales	Twickenham
04·02·06	Ireland	26–16	Italy	Lansdowne Road
05·02·06	Scotland	20–16	France	Murrayfield
11·02·06	Italy	16–31	England	Stadio Flaminio
11·02·06	France	43–31	Ireland	Stade de France
12·02·06	Wales	28–18	Scotland	Millennium Stadium
25·02·06	France	37–12	Italy	Stade de France
25·02·06	Scotland	18–12	England	Murrayfield
26·02·06	Ireland	31–5	Wales	Lansdowne Road
11·03·06	Ireland	15–9	Scotland	Lansdowne Road
11·03·06	Wales	18–18	Italy	Millennium
12·03·06	France	31–6	England	Stade de France
18·03·06	Wales	16–21	France	Millennium Stadium
18·03·06	England	24–28	Ireland	Twickenham
18·03·06	Italy	10–13	Scotland	Stadio Flaminio

FINAL TABLE 2006						TOTAL EVER HONOURS		
points	w	d	l	pd	country	triple crowns	grand slams	titles
8	4	0	1	63	France	n/a	8	15
8	4	0	1	34	Ireland	8	1	10
6	3	0	2	–3	Scotland	10	3	14
4	2	0	3	24	England	23	12	25
3	1	1	3	–55	Wales	18	9	23
1	0	1	4	–53	Italy	n/a	0	0

——— INTERNATIONAL RUGBY BOARD AWARDS · 2005 ———

International player of the year ....Daniel Carter [NZL]
International team of the year...New Zealand
International coach of the year...............................Graham Henry [NZL]
International sevens team of the year..Fiji
International sevens player of the year............................Orene Ai'i [NZL]
Spirit of rugby award..Jean-Pierre Rives [FRA]
International women's personality of the year..................Farah Palmer [NZL]

——————GUINNESS PREMIERSHIP · 2005/06——————

Champions	Sale
Heineken Cup qualifiers	Wasps, Gloucester, Sale, Ospreys, Leicester, London Irish
European Challenge Cup qualifiers	Bristol, Saracens, Newcastle, Bath, Harlequins, Worcester
Relegated	Leeds

—————————— MAN OF STEEL · 2005 ——————————

In 2005, St Helens' Jamie Lyon was presented with the Man of Steel prize, awarded by sports journalists to the most outstanding player in Rugby League's Super League. The Australian is only the fourth overseas player to win the coveted prize.

————— RUGBY LEAGUE CHALLENGE CUP · 2006 —————

ST HELENS 42–12 HUDDERSFIELD
26·08·06 · TWICKENHAM

St Helens – *tries*: Talau, Long, Wilkin (2), Fa'asavalu, Lyon, Cayless
conversions: Lyon (7)
Huddersfield – *tries*: Aspinwall, Paul · *conversions*: De Vere (2)

Favourites St Helens took their fifth Challenge Cup trophy in 11 years, beating Huddersfield Giants by an impressive 30 points. The Lance Todd trophy, which is chosen by members of the Rugby League Writer's Association and awarded to the man of the match, was presented to St Helens' Sean Long, for a record third time.

———— EUROPEAN SWIMMING CHAMPIONSHIPS · 2006 ————

At the European Championships in Budapest in July–August 2006, Great Britain amassed a record 13 medals. Russia topped the medal table with 7 golds, but the outstanding performance of the championship was from Laure Manaudou of France, who won 4 golds and broke the 400m freestyle world record. Great Britain capped a strong performance by winning the team trophy, which is awarded to the country that fills the most places in finals. Below are some selected results:

Country	G	S	B	total	TEAM TROPHY
1 Russia	7	1	2	10	*for the team which filled*
2 Germany	6	4	2	12	*the most places in finals*
3 Italy	5	6	4	15	[1] Great Britain · [2] France
(7 Great Britain	2	5	6	13)	[3] Italy · [4] Russia · [5] Germany

	Event	winner	record	result
♂	100m backstroke	Arkady Vyatchanin [RUS]	CR	53·50
♂	50m butterfly	Sergiy Breus [UKR]	CR	23·41
♀	100m freestyle	Britta Steffen [GER]	WR	53·30
♀	4x100m freestyle	Germany	WR	3:35·22
♂	200m butterfly	Pawel Korzeniowski [POL]	CR	1:55·04
♀	200m breaststroke	Kirsty Balfour [GBR]		2:25·66
♀	4x100m medley	Great Britain	BR	4:02·24
♀	400m freestyle	Laure Manaudou [FRA]	WR	4:02·13
♂	200m individual medley	Laszlo Cseh [HUN]	CR	1:58·17

Key: CR – Championship Record · WR – World Record · BR – British Record

─────SOME ATHLETICS WORLD RECORDS OF NOTE─────

Event		set by	when	record
♂	100m	Asafa Powell [JAM]	2005, 2004	9·77s
♀	100m	Florence Griffith-Joyner [USA]	1988	10·49s
♂	110m hurdles	Xiang Liu [CHN]	2006	12·88s
♀	100m hurdles	Yordanka Donkova [BUL]	1988	12·21s
♂	200m	Michael Johnson [USA]	1996	19·32s
♀	200m	Florence Griffith-Joyner [USA]	1988	21·34s
♂	400m	Michael Johnson [USA]	1999	43·18s
♀	400m	Marita Koch [GER]	1985	47·60s
♂	400m hurdles	Kevin Young [USA]	1992	46·78s
♀	400m hurdles	Yuliya Nosova [RUS]	2003	52·34s
♂	800m	Wilson Kipketer [DEN]	1997	1:41·11
♀	800m	Jarmila Kratochvílová [TCH]	1983	1:53·28
♂	1,500m	Hicham El Guerrouj [MAR]	1998	3:26·00
♀	1,500m	Yunxia Qu [CHN]	1993	3:50·46
♂	Mile	Hicham El Guerrouj [MAR]	1999	3:43·13
♀	Mile	Svetlana Masterkova [RUS]	1996	4:12·56
♂	5,000m	Kenenisa Bekele [ETH]	2004	12:37·35
♀	5,000m	Meseret Defar [ETH]	2006	14:24·53
♂	10,000m	Kenenisa Bekele [ETH]	2005	26:17·53
♀	10,000m	Junxia Wang [CHN]	1993	29:31·78
♂	Marathon	Paul Tergat [KEN]	2003	2:04·55
♀	Marathon	Paula Radcliffe [GBR]	2003	2:15·25
♂	High jump	Javier Sotomayor [CUB]	1993	2·45m
♀	High jump	Stefka Kostadinova [BUL]	1987	2·09m
♂	Long jump	Mike Powell [USA]	1991	8·95m
♀	Long jump	Galina Christiakova [URS]	1988	7·52m
♂	Triple jump	Jonathan Edwards [GBR]	1995	18·29m
♀	Triple jump	Inessa Kravets [UKR]	1995	15·50m
♂	Pole vault	Sergey Bubka [UKR]	1994	6·14m
♀	Pole vault	Yelena Isinbayeva [RUS]	2005	5·01m
♂	Shot put	Randy Barnes [USA]	1990	23·12m
♀	Shot put	Natalya Lisovskaya [URS]	1987	22·63m
♂	Discus	Jürgen Schult [GER]	1986	74·08m
♀	Discus	Gabriele Reinsch [GER]	1988	76·80m
♂	Hammer	Yuriy Sedykh [URS]	1986	86·74m
♀	Hammer	Tatyana Lysenko [RUS]	2006	77·80m†
♂	Javelin	Jan Zelezny [CZE]	1996	98·48m
♀	Javelin	Osleidys Menéndez [CUB]	2005	71·70m
♂	Decathlon	Roman Sebrle [CZE]	2001	9,026pts
♀	Heptathlon	Jackie Joyner-Kersee [USA]	1988	7,291pts
♂	4x100m relay	USA	1992	37·40s
♀	4x100m relay	Germany	1985	41·37s
♂	4x400m relay	USA	1998	2:54·20
♀	4x400m relay	USSR	1988	3:15·17

[Records correct as of 21·09·06 · †=awaiting ratification]

———EUROPEAN ATHLETICS CHAMPIONSHIPS · 2006———

The 2006 European Athletics Championships were held in Gothenburg, Sweden. The British team gave its worst performance since 1978, claiming just 11 medals. Its only gold came from the men's 4x100m relay†. Below are some notable wins:

Men	*event*	*Women*
F. Obikwelu [POR] 9·99s CR	100m	K. Gevaert [BEL] 11·06s
S. Olijar [LAT] 13·24s	110/100m hurdles	S. Kallur [SWE] 12·59s
F. Obikwelu [POR] 20·01s NR	200m	K. Gevaert [BEL] 22·68s
M. Raquil [FRA] 45·02s	400m	V. Stambolova [BUL] 49·85s
B. Som [NED] 1:46·56s	800m	O. Kotlyarova [RUS] 1:57·38s
M. Baala [FRA] 3:39·02s	1,500m	T. Tomashova [RUS] 3:56·91s CR
J. España [ESP] 13:44·70s	5,000m	M. Dominguez [ESP] 14:56·18 CR
A. Silnov [RUS] 2·36m CR	high jump	T. Hellebaut [BEL] 2·03m NR/CR
A. Howe [ITA] 8·20m	long jump	L. Kolchanova [RUS] 6·93m
R. Bartels [GER] 21·13m	shot put	N. Khoroneko [BLR] 19·43m
C. Olsson [SWE] 17·67m	triple jump	T. Lebedeva [RUS] 15·15m CR
A. Averbukh [ISR] 5·70m	pole vault	Y. Isinbayeva [RUS] 4·80m CR
R. Sebrle [CZE] 8,526pts	dec-/heptathlon	C. Klüft [SWE] 6,740pts CR

† Darren Campbell declined to join his team's lap of honour. He later said 'I felt that the fact that I have lost two medals because of what occurred with Dwain [Chambers], it wasn't appropriate'.

———THE EUROPEAN ATHLETICS CUP · 2006———

In June 2006, France's men and Russia's women won the European Athletics Cup. The cup is contested annually by national teams – each fielding one representative per event, who accumulates points for their team (8 points for 1st to 1 point for 8th). At the close of competition, the lowest-scoring 2 teams are relegated. In 2006 the event was held in Málaga, where the stadium has 9 lanes (instead of the usual 8). This anomaly allowed Britain's men to remain in the elite group, despite being relegated last year. GB's women were promoted in 2005. Below are the results:

♂ *country*	*points*	♀ *country*	*points*
1 ... France	118	1 ... Russia	155
2 ... Russia	116	2 ... Poland	111·5
3 ... Great Britain & NI	109	3 ... Ukraine	99
4 ... Poland	107	4 ... France	98
5 ... Ukraine	103	5 ... Germany	93
6 ... Spain†	99·5	6 ... Spain	90
7 ... Italy†	93	7 ... Great Britain & NI†	85
8 ... Germany*	86·5	8 ... Sweden†	81
9 ... Finland†	65	9 ... Romania†	76·5

† These teams will be relegated into the lower leagues for the 2007 European Cup. * As Germany are hosting the 2007 Cup in Munich, they were protected from the horrors of relegation.

WIMBLEDON WINNERS · 2006

MEN'S SINGLES
Roger Federer [SUI]
bt Rafael Nadal [ESP]
6–0, 7–6 (7–5), 6–7 (2–7), 6–3

LADIES' SINGLES
Amelie Mauresmo [FRA]
bt Justine Henin-Hardenne [BEL]
2–6, 6–3, 6–4

*'I definitely wanted this win today and
I don't want anybody to talk about my
nerves anymore. This trophy is so special
in the world of tennis and it feels great.'*
AMELIE MAURESMO
reacting to her first Wimbledon title

MEN'S DOUBLES
Bob Bryan [USA]
& Mike Bryan [USA]
bt Fabrice Santoro [FRA]
& Nenad Zimonjic [SCG]
6–3, 4–6, 6–4, 6–2

LADIES' DOUBLES
Zi Yan [CHN]
& Jie Zheng [CHN]
bt Virginia Ruano Pascual [ESP]
& Paola Suarez [ARG]
6–3, 3–6, 6–2

MIXED DOUBLES
Andy Ram [ISR]
& Vera Zvonareva [RUS]
bt Bob Bryan [USA]
& Venus Williams [USA]
6–3, 6–2

BOYS' SINGLES
Thiemo De Bakker [NED]
bt Marcin Gawron [POL]
6–2, 7–6 (7–4)

GIRLS' SINGLES
Caroline Wozniacki [DEN]
bt Magdalena Rybarikova [SVK]
3–6, 6–1, 6–3

BOYS' DOUBLES
Kellen Damico [USA]
& Nathaniel Schnugg [USA]
bt Martin Klizan [SVK]
& Andrei Martin [SVK]
7–6 (9–7), 6–2

GIRLS' DOUBLES
Alisa Kleybanova [RUS]
& Anastasia Pavlyuchenkova [RUS]
bt Kristina Antoniychuk [UKR]
& Alexandra Dulgheru [ROM]
6–1, 6–2

WIMBLEDON 2006 PRIZE MONEY & MISC.

Round (No. prizes)	♂ singles	♀ singles
Winner (1)	£655,000	625,000
Runner-up (1)	£327,500	312,500
Semi-final (2)	£163,750	151,500
Quarter-final (4)	£85,150	76,650
4th round (8)	£45,850	38,970
3rd round (16)	£26,520	21,210
2nd round (32)	£16,050	12,840
1st round (64)	£9,830	7,860

[winnings for doubles are different]

No. GB men in 1st round [2005] [9] 10
No. GB men in 2nd round .... [4] 5
No. GB women in 1st round ...... [6] 5
No. GB women 2nd round .... [1] 2
Tennis balls used 52,000
Tim Henman out in R2

Best performing Brit .... A. Murray, R4
Fastest serve ♂ ..... A. Roddick 143mph
Fastest serve ♀ .... V. Williams 121mph
Most aces ♂ . R. Stepanek (90 in 5 matches)
Most aces ♀ ...... A. Mauresmo (35 in 7)
Total attendance 447,126

THE DAVIS CUP

The Davis Cup began in 1900 and now involves 134 countries, of which only 16 qualify to play in the World Group. The rest fight it out in continental leagues in an effort to gain promotion into the elite World Group. Great Britain currently plays in the Europe–Africa Zone Group 1. Below are Britain's results for 2006:

21–23 July · Europe–Africa Zone Group 1, 1st round play-off
International Lawn Tennis Centre, Eastbourne (surface: grass)
Israel *bt* Great Britain 3–2

Noam Okun [ISR] *bt* Alex Bogdanovic [GBR] 6–4, 7–5, 6–2
Andy Murray [GBR] *bt* Andy Ram [ISR] 2–6, 4–6, 7–5, 6–2, 6–3
Jonathan Erlich & Andy Ram [ISR]
bt Jamie Delgado & Andy Murray [GBR] 3–6, 6–3, 5–7, 6–3, 6–4
Noam Okun [ISR] *bt* Jamie Delgado [GBR] 6–3, 6–4, 6–7 (5–7), 2–6, 6–3
Alan Mackin [GBR] *bt* Dekel Valtzer [ISR] 6–2, 6–1

22–24 September · Europe–Africa Zone Group 1, 2nd round play-off
Lawn Tennis Club, Odessa, Ukraine (surface: grass)
Great Britain 3–2 Ukraine

Greg Rusedski [GBR] *bt* Sergiy Stakhovsky [UKR] 1–6, 6–3, 5–7, 6–4, 9–7
Andy Murray [GBR] *bt* Aleksandr Dolgopolov [UKR] 6–3, 6–4, 6–2
Sergiy Stakhovsky & Orest Tereshchuk [UKR]
bt Jamie Delgado & Andy Murray [GBR] 6–3, 6–3, 6–3
Andy Murray [GBR] *bt* Sergiy Stakhovsky [UKR] 6–3, 6–2, 7–5
Sergei Bubka [UKR] *bt* Jamie Baker [GBR] 6–3, 7–6 (8–6)

GB remain in Europe–Africa Group 1. Russia & Argentina will contest the final in December 2006.

TENNIS GRAND SLAM TOURNAMENTS · 2006

Event	*month*	*surface*	♂	*winner*	♀
Australian Open	Jan	Rebound Ace	Roger Federer	Amelie Mauresmo	
French Open	May/Jun	clay	Rafael Nadal	J. Henin-Hardenne	
Wimbledon	Jun/Jul	grass	Roger Federer	Amelie Mauresmo	
US Open	Aug/Sep	cement	Roger Federer	Maria Sharapova	

Andre Agassi's defeat by Benjamin Becker in the 3rd-round of the US Open ended his glittering 20-year career, after 60 ATP titles, 8 'Grand Slam' titles, and thousands of column inches. On court, a tearful Agassi paid tribute to the crowd: 'over the last 20 years I have found loyalty, you have pulled me through on court and also in life'. ❦ In 2006, Martina Navratilova also ended an impressive career, after winning an astounding 59th career 'Grand Slam' title at Flushing Meadow. Navratilova and Bob Bryan won the mixed doubles, adding to her 18 'Grand Slam' singles titles, and 40 doubles titles.

FORMULA ONE TEAMS & DRIVERS · 2006

Renault . . . . Fernando Alonso [ESP] & Giancarlo Fisichella [ITA]
McLaren Mercedes . . . . Kimi Räikkönen [FIN] & Juan Pablo Montoya [COL]
Ferrari . . . . Michael Schumacher [GER] & Felipe Massa [BRA]
Toyota . . . . Jarno Trulli [ITA] & Ralf Schumacher [GER]
Williams . . . . Mark Webber [AUS] & Nico Rosberg [GER]
Honda . . . . Rubens Barrichello [BRA] & Jenson Button [GBR]
Red Bull . . . . David Coulthard [GBR] & Christian Klien [AUT]
BMW Sauber . . . . Robert Kubica [POL] & Nick Heidfeld [GER]
Midland F1 . . . . Tiago Monteiro [POR] & Christijan Albers [NED]
Toro Rosso . . . . Vitantonio Liuzzi [ITA] & Scott Speed [USA]
Super Aguri . . . . Takuma Sato [JAP] & Sakon Yamamoto [JAP]

FORMULA ONE WORLD CHAMPIONSHIP · 2006

Date	Grand Prix	track	winning driver	car
12·03·06	Bahrain	Sakhir	Fernando Alonso	Renault
19·03·06	Malaysia	Kuala Lumpur	Giancarlo Fisichella	Renault
02·04·06	Australia	Melbourne	Fernando Alonso	Renault
23·04·06	San Marino	Imola	Michael Schumacher	Ferrari
07·05·06	Europe	Nürburgring	Michael Schumacher	Ferrari
14·05·06	Spain	Barcelona	Fernando Alonso	Renault
28·05·06	Monaco	Monte Carlo	Fernando Alonso	Renault
11·06·06	Britain	Silverstone	Fernando Alonso	Renault
25·06·06	Canada	Montreal	Fernando Alonso	Renault
02·07·06	America	Indianapolis	Michael Schumacher	Ferrari
16·07·06	France	Magny-Cours	Michael Schumacher	Ferrari
30·07·06	Germany	Hockenheim	Michael Schumacher	Ferrari
06·08·06	Hungary	Hungaroring	Jenson Button	Honda
27·08·06	Turkey	Istanbul Otodrom	Felipe Massa	Ferrari
10·09·06	Italy	Monza	Michael Schumacher	Ferrari
01·10·06	China	Shanghai		
08·10·06	Japan	Suzuka		
22·10·06	Brazil	São Paulo		

[Michael Schumacher announced his retirement from the sport at the end of the 2006 season.]

SUPERBIKES, RALLY & MOTORSPORT

Isle of Man TT (senior) [2006] . . . . John McGuinness (HM Plant)
Isle of Man TT (Supersport junior) [2006] . . . . John McGuinness (HM Plant)
Moto GP [2005] . . . . Valentino Rossi (Yamaha)
British Superbikes [2005] . . . . Gregorio Lavilla (Ducati)
World Superbikes [2005] . . . . Troy Corser (Suzuki)
World Rally [2005] . . . . Sébastian Loeb (Citroën)
Le Mans [2006] . . . . Emanuele Pirro, Frank Biela, Marco Werner (Audi)

F1 REGULATIONS

Formula One has undergone significant rule changes every season since 2002, and 2006 was no exception. The modifications were proposed by the FIA (International Automobile Federation) in a bid to reinvigorate the sport. The key new rules were:

QUALIFYING · cars compete in a knockout format, split into 3 blocks lasting 15 mins, 15 mins, and 20 mins. All cars start, but the slowest 6 are dropped after the first 15 min session (taking places 17–22 on the grid), with 6 more dropped after the next session (grid places 11–16). The remaining 10 drivers then use the final 20 mins to race for pole position.

TYRES · in contrast to 2005, when tyres could not be changed between qualifying and the race, in 2006 teams may change sets of tyres up to 7 times per car over the race weekend.

ENGINES[†] · the 3-litre V10 engine was replaced by a new generation 2·4-litre V8. This reduces power by 20%, and places less stress on tyres.

† For the 2006–07 season the Toro Rosso team was allowed to use a rev-limited V10 under special dispensation, despite the protestations of Super Aguri and Midland who claimed unfair advantage.

888.COM WORLD SNOOKER CHAMPIONSHIP · 2006

The longest final in Crucible history saw Graeme Dott defeat 2002 World Champion Peter Ebdon in a match that persisted for 13 hours, 39 minutes, and 40 seconds. The 27th frame was the longest in Championship history: Ebdon won in 74 mins, 8 secs (by comparison, Ronnie O'Sullivan's 147 clearance in 1997 took just 5 mins, 20 secs). Despite a valiant final-day rally from Ebdon, the match was perceived as plodding and dull ('*A Yawn Winner*' was the *Sun*'s headline). Dott's highest break was just 68, and the final ended at 1am to a half-deserted theatre.

THE FINAL · FRAME-BY-FRAME
Peter Ebdon [ENG] 14 18 Graeme Dott [SCO]

DAY ONE					DAY TWO				
Frame	*tally*	20–53	2–6		*Frame*	*tally*	66–51 (51)	9–15	
		20–53	2–7				67–29 (55)	10–15	
79–12 (63)	1–0	16–63	2–8		0–75 (56)	5–12	70–38 (66)	11–15	
53–62 (53 Eb.)	1–1	66–25	3–8		100–0 (78)	6–12	66–59	12–15	
1–91(56)	1–2	124–6 (89)	4–8		67–44	7–12	84–0 (84)	13–15	
48–70	1–3	47–72	4–9		41–75 (62)	7–13	16–78 (66)	13–16	
9–71 (66)	1–4	65–51	5–9		31–90 (65)	7–14	99–17	14–16	
67–32 (62)	2–4	5–61	5–10		49–70	7–15	61–69 (51-68)	14–17	
6–78	2–5	16–92	5–11		117–22 (117)	8–15	31–70	14–18	

Online gaming company 888.com replaced Embassy as the title sponsor of snooker's World Championship, signing a 5-year contract in January 2006. Embassy cigarettes had enjoyed a 30-year association with the sport of snooker, and were granted a special dispensation to continue sponsorship into 2005, after restrictions on tobacco advertising at sporting events came into force.

—NIKOLAY VALUEV—

In December 2005, Russian pugilist Nikolay Valuev became the tallest and heaviest champion in boxing history, when he took the World Boxing Association (WBA) heavyweight title from John Ruiz. The giant, perhaps unsurprisingly, drew a record number of uppercuts from his opponent (a diminutive 6' 3") before claiming the points victory, which also made him the first Russian ever to take the title. Valuev is something of a national hero: he has starred in a popular TV show as a bungling decorator, and President Putin personally commended him for a heroic display. Despite his astonishing dimensions, Valuev is known as a sensitive and cultured man; he is an avid reader of Tolstoy and Jack London, and regularly composes poetry for his wife. Below are some particulars of the mighty 'Beast from the East':

Date of Birth	21·08·73	Stance	orthodox
Height	7' 2"	Trainer	Manuel Gabrielian
Weight	c.152kg	Manager	Wilfried Sauerland
Reach	85"	Fights	45; won 44; 32 K.O.s

One adversary, Larry Donald, referred to Valuev as a 'Neanderthal man, like something from the Dark Ages'. Another, Clifford Etienne, was so intimidated at the weigh-in by Valuev's mammoth stature that he reportedly returned to his hotel, began drinking, and later attempted to flee the city.

—WORLD BOXING CHAMPIONS · AT 21·9·2006—

Weight	WBC	WBA	IBF	WBO
Heavy	Maskaev [USA]	Valuev [RUS]	Klitschko [UKR]	Lyakhovich [BLR]
Cruiser	Bell [JAM]	Bell [JAM]	*vacant*	Nelson [GBR]
Light heavy	Adamek [POL]	Tiozzo [FRA]	Woods [GBR]	Erdei [HUN]
Super middle	Beyer [GER]	Kessler [DEN]	Calzaghe [GBR]	Calzaghe [GBR]
Middle	Taylor [USA]	Castillejo [ESP]	Abraham [GER]	Taylor [USA]
Light middle	De la Hoya [USA]	Rivera [USA]	Spinks [USA]	Dzindziruk [UKR]
Welter	Baldomir [ARG]	*vacant*	*vacant*	Margarito [MEX]
Light welter	Witter [GBR]	M'Baye [FRE]	Urango [COL]	Cotto [PUR]
Light	Corrales [USA]	Diaz [USA]	Chavez [MEX]	Freitas [BRA]
Super feather	Barrera [MEX]	Valero [VEN]	St Clair [GUY]	Guzman [DOM]
Feather	Lopez [MEX]	John [INA]	Aiken [USA]	Harrison [GBR]
Super bantam	Vazquez [MEX]	Sithchatchawal [THA]	*vacant*	De Leon [MEX]
Bantam	Hasegawa [JAP]	Sidorenko [UKR]	Marquez [MEX]	Gonzalez [MEX]
Super fly	Tokuyama [JAP]	Castillo [MEX]	Perez [NCA]	Montiel [MEX]
Fly	Wonjongkam [THA]	Parra [USA]	Darchinyan [AUS]	Narvaez [ARG]
Light fly	Romero [MEX]	Kameda [JAP]	Solis [MEX]	Cazares [MEX]
Straw	Kyowa [THA]	Niida [JAP]	Rachman [INA]	Calderon [PUR]

Category	lb	Super fly	115	Spr feather	130	Lgt middle	154	Cruiser	200
Straw	105	Bantam	118	Light	135	Middle	160	Heavy	>200
Light fly	108	Spr bantam	122	Light welter	140	Spr middle	168		
Fly	112	Feather	126	Welter	147	Light heavy	175	*US names differ*	

SUDOKU WORLD CHAMPIONSHIP

The first ever Sudoku World Championship was held in Lucca, Tuscany, during March 2006. 85 competitors puzzled over a total of 45 fiendish grids, ranging from the classic 9x9 Sudoku to mechanical, irregular, toroidal, odd/even, combined, diagonal, and sum variations. The competition was dominated by two Americans – Thomas Snyder (a 26-year-old Harvard chemistry student) and Wei-Hwa Huang (a 30-year-old Google software engineer). And, for a while, Huang thought he had clinched victory in the

			7	5				
	3			4	8		2	
1								6
	4							8
7	9						3	1
2						7		
5								7
	8		3	2			4	
				6	9			

final. However, Huang had mistakenly placed two of the same number in a single row – and while he prematurely celebrated and posed for photographs, Jana Tylova, a 31-year-old female Czech economist, quietly completed the final puzzle [above] to take the title. Snyder came second, Huang third, and fourth place went to Japan's Tetsuya Nishio, who sets the *Times'* 'Killer Sudoku'. In a ceremony at the Ducal Palace in Lucca, Tylova was presented with a Perspex trophy, a bunch of roses, a bottle of Prosecco, a wooden Sudoku box, and a week-long holiday in Lucca, by Wayne Gould, the man who reintroduced Sudoku to Europe. ❦ In 2006, the *Independent* reported a 700% increase in pencil sales, possibly attributable to the Sudoku craze, and British Airways sent a memo to its cabin crews, forbidding them from working on Sudoku puzzles.

CHEER-LEADING & INJURY

Though cheer-leaders are known for their flashy outfits, athletic routines, and toned, nubile bodies, less attention has been paid to their injuries. A January 2006 *Pediatrics* study showed that 208,800 US youths (5–18) were seen in 'ER's for 'cheer-leading-related injuries' between 1990–2002, and the number of injuries increased 110% during the period. In response, a US database is in development to track such injuries and determine the most dangerous stunts. Thus far, it seems probable that the 'human pyramid' and 'basket toss' are most likely to imperil participants.

Type of cheer-leading injury	%	Body part injured	%
Strains & sprains	52.4	Lower extremity	37.2
Soft tissue	18.4	Upper extremity	26.4
Fractures & dislocations	16.4	Head/neck	18.8
Lacerations & avulsions	3.8	Trunk	16.8
Concussions/closed head injuries	3.5	Other	0.8
Other (dental, crushing)	5.5	[Source: *Pediatrics*, Jan 2006]	

─────READY RECKONER OF OTHER RESULTS · 2006─────

AMERICAN FOOTBALL · Superbowl　　　Pittsburgh Steelers *bt* Seattle Seahawks 21–10
ANGLING · National Coarse Ch. Div.1　　　　　　　　Drennan North West 23·15kg
BADMINTON · World Ch.　　　　　　　　　　　G. Emms & N. Robertson [ENG] *bt*
　　　　　　　　　　　　　　　　　　　A. Clark & D. Kellogg [ENG] 21–15, 21–12
　　　　　English National Ch.　　　　Nick Kidd *bt* Aamir Ghaffar 13–15, 15–3, 15–2
BASEBALL · World Series [2005]　　　　　Chicago White Sox *bt* Houston Astros 4–0
BASKETBALL · BBL Trophy final　　　　　Newcastle Eagles 71–50 Leicester Riders
　　NBA finals　　　　　　　　　　　　　　Miami Heat 4–2 Dallas Mavericks
THE BOAT RACE　　　　　　Oxford *bt* Cambridge [by five lengths, in 18min 26s]
BOG SNORKELLING · World Championships　　　　　Haydn Pitchforth 1min 41s
CHEESE ROLLING · Cooper's Hill　　♂ Jason Crowther [WAL] ♀ Dione Carter [NZL]
CHESS · British Championship　　　　　　　　　　Jonathan Rowson 8·5pts
COMPETITIVE EATING · Int. Hot Dog Eating　　Takeru Kobayashi 53¾ hot dogs
CRICKET · Test series – Pakistan *vs* England [2006/7]　　　　　　　won 2–0
　　Test series – India *vs* England [2006/7]　　　　　　　　　　　drew 1–1
　　NatWest Series　　　　　　　　　　　　　Sri Lanka *bt* England 5–0
　　NatWest Series　　　　　　　　　　　　　Pakistan *drew* England 2–2
　　NatWest Women's series　　　　　　　　　　　England *bt* India 4–0
　　C&G Trophy final　　　　　　　　　Sussex *bt* Lancashire by 15 runs
　　County Championship　　　　　　　　　　　　　　　　Sussex
CYCLING · Tour de France　　　　　　　　　　Floyd Landis [see p.297]
　　Tour of Britain　　　　　　　　　　　　　Martin Pedersen [DEN]
DARTS · Ladbrokes W. Ch. [PDC]　　Phil 'The Power' Taylor *bt* Peter Manley
　　Lakeside World Championship [BDO]　Jelle Klaasen *bt* Raymond Van Barneveld
ELEPHANT POLO · World Championships　Scotland *bt* National Parks of Nepal 7–6
ENDURANCE RACES · Marathon des Sables　　　Lahcen Ahansal [MAR] 17:14·01
　　　　　　　　　　　　　　　　　　Geraldine Courdesses [FRA] 26:33·23
　　Devil o' the Highlands　　　　　　*cancelled due to unforeseen circumstances*
EQUESTRIANISM · Badminton　　Moonfleet *ridden by* Andrew Hoy [AUS] 36·5pen
　　World Equestrian Games · 3-day Ev.　Toytown *ridden by* Zara Phillips [ENG] 46.70pts
FOOTBALL · FA Cup　　　Liverpool 3–3 West Ham (Liverpool win 3–1 on penalties)
　　FA Cup · Womens'　　　　　　　　　　　　　Arsenal 5–0 Leeds
　　Champions League　　　　　　　　　　　　Arsenal 1–2 Barcelona
　　UEFA Cup　　　　　　　　　　　　　Sevilla 4–0 Middlesbrough
　　Community Shield　　　　　　　　　　　　Chelsea 1–2 Liverpool
　　Carling Cup　　　　　　　　　　　　Manchester Utd 4–0 Wigan
　　LDV Vans Trophy　　　　　　　　　　　　Carlisle 1–2 Swansea
　　Premiership [2005/06]　　　　　　　　　　　　　　　Chelsea
　　Championship　　　　　　　　　　　　　　　　　Reading
　　League 1　　　　　　　　　　　　　　　　　　Southend
　　League 2　　　　　　　　　　　　　　　　　　Carlisle
　　Scottish Premiership　　　　　　　　　　　　　　Celtic
　　Scottish Cup　　　　　　Hearts 1–1 Gretna (4–2 on penalties)
FORMULA ONE · World Drivers' Champion [2005]　　Fernando Alonso · Renault
GOLF · Women's World Cup of Golf　　　　　　　　　Sweden (–7)
　　World Match Play Championship　　　　　　　　Paul Casey [ENG]

—— READY RECKONER OF OTHER RESULTS · 2006 cont. ——

GREYHOUND RACING · William Hill Greyhound Derby   Westmead Hawk
GYMNASTICS · World Acrobatic Gymnastics Championships
     Mixed pairs   Revaz Gurgenidze/Anna Katchalova [RUS] 29·252
     Women's Group   Elena Moiseeva/Elena Kirilova/Tatiana Alexeeva [RUS] 28·800
     Men's Group   Adam Smith/Adam Dobbs/Adam Denny/Andrew Price [GBR] 28·450
HORSE RACING
     Grand National   Numbersixvalverde *trained by* M.Brassil *ridden by* N.Madden
     Vodafone Epsom Derby   Sir Percy *trained by* M.Tregoning *ridden by* M.Dwyer
     Cheltenham Gold Cup   War of Attrition *trained by* Mouse Morris *ridden by* Conor O'Dwyer
     1,000 Guineas   Speciosa *trained by* Pamela Sly *ridden by* Michael Fenton
     2,000 Guineas   George Washington *trained by* Aidan O'Brien *ridden by* Kieren Fallon
     The Oaks   Alexandrova *trained by* Aidan O'Brien *ridden by* Kieren Fallon
     St Leger   Sixties Icon *trained by* Jeremy Noseda *ridden by* Frankie Dettori
ICE HOCKEY · Stanley Cup   Carolina Hurricanes *bt* Edmonton Oilers, 4–3
PARACHUTING · World Championships 8-way   France
POKER · World Strip Poker Tournament   John Young
RUGBY LEAGUE · Super League [2005]   Leeds
     Challenge Cup   St Helens
     League Leaders Shield   St Helens
     World Club Challenge   Bradford Bulls 30–10 Wests Tigers
     Tri-Nations   New Zealand
RUGBY UNION · Guinness Premiership   Sale Sharks
     Guinness Premiership Championship   Sale Sharks 45–20 Leicester Tigers
     Powergen Cup   Wasps 26–10 Llanelli
     Celtic Cup   Ospreys 17–19 Ulster
     Heineken Cup   Munster 23–19 Biarritz
     European Challenge Cup   Gloucester 36–34 London Irish
     Varsity Match [2005]   Cambridge 31–16 Oxford
     Celtic League   Ulster
RUNNING · Great North Run [2005]   ♂ Zersenay Tadesse [ERI] 00:59 05
     ♀ Deratu Tulu [ETH] 1:07·03
SAILING · Star European Ch.   Mark Mendelblatt & Mark Strube
     Volvo Ocean Race   Abn Amro One 96pts
SNOOKER · Saga Insurance Masters   John Higgins 10–9 Ronnie O'Sullivan
SQUASH · Super Series   A. Ricketts [AUS] *bt* L.Beachill [GBR] 11–7, 6–11, 11–4, 12–10
SUMMER X GAMES · Skateboarding Big Air   Danny Way 95
     Skateboard street   ♂ Chris Cole ♀ Elissa Steamer
     Moto X freestyle   Travis Pastrana 94·20
     BMX freestyle dirt   Corey Bohan 91·66
     BMX Big Air   Kevin Robinson 95
TENNIS · Oz. Op.   Roger Federer [SUI] *bt* Marcos Baghdatis [CYP] 5–7, 7–5, 6–0, 6–2
     Amélie Mauresmo [FRA] *bt* Justine Henin-Hardenne [BEL] (ret.) 6–1, 2–0
French Open   Rafael Nadal [ESP] *bt* Roger Federer [SUI] 1–6, 6–1, 6–4, 7–6
     Justine Henin-Hardenne [BEL] *bt* Svetlana Kuznetsova [RUS] 6–4, 6–4
US Open   Roger Federer [SUI] *bt* Andy Roddick [USA] 6–2, 4–6, 7–5, 6–1
     Maria Sharapova [RUS] *bt* Justine Henin-Hardenne [BEL] 6–4, 6–4

Ephemerides

God sees their sins ... and in his Ephemerides
his Journals, he writes them downe.
— JOHN DONNE (1572–1631)

2007

Roman numerals.............. MMVII		Indian (Saka) year...... 1929 (Mar 22)	
Regnal year[1] ....55th (6 Feb)		Sikh year ... 539 Nanakshahi Era (Mar 14)	
Dominical Letter[2].................. G		Jewish year ....5768 (Sep 13)	
Epact[3] XI		Roman year [AUC][5] .....2760 (Apr 21)	
Golden Number (Lunar Cycle)[4] ..XIII		Masonic year................6007 AL[6]	
Chinese New Year.. Pig 4705 (Feb 18)		Knights Templar year........ 889 AO[7]	
Hindu New Year.......2063 (Mar 19)		Baha'i Year...............164 (21 Mar)	
Islamic year.............1428 (Jan 20)		Queen bee colour.............. yellow	

[1] The number of years from the accession of a monarch; traditionally, legislation was dated by the Regnal year of the reigning monarch. [2] A way of categorising years to facilitate the calculation of Easter. If 1 January is a Sunday, the Dominical letter for the year will be A, if 2 January is a Sunday it will be B, and so on. [3] The number of days by which the solar year exceeds the lunar year. [4] The number of the year (1–19) in the 19-year Metonic cycle; it is used in the calculation of Easter, and is found by adding 1 to the remainder left after dividing the number of the year by 19. [5] see p.341. [6] Anno Lucis, the 'Year of Light' when the world was formed. [7] Anno Ordinis , the 'Year of the Order'.

SUNDIAL MOTTOES

Perhaps the most famous modern sundial motto is 'Two Worlds, One Sun' which was inscribed on the sundial created for NASA's Mars Surveyor in 2001. There is a long tradition of mottoes on sundials, often in Latin, some of which include:

DISCE TUOS NUMERARE DIES Learn to number thy days	NESCITIS HORAM Ye know not the hour
FESTINA LENTE Hasten slowly	LEX DEI LUX DIEI The law of God is the light of day
HORA QUASI UMBRA Time is but a shadow	ICH DIEN I serve
TEMPUS EDAX RERUM Time devours all things	NON REDIBIS Thou shall not come again

RED-LETTER DAYS

Red-letter days are those days of ecclesiastical or civil significance – so named because they were marked out in red ink on early religious calendars. (The Romans marked unlucky days with black chalk, and auspicious days with white.) When these days fall within law sittings, the judges of the Queen's Bench Division sit wearing elegant scarlet robes. The Red-letter days in Great Britain are tabulated below:

Conversion of St Paul	25 Jan	St Barnabas	11 Jun
Purification	2 Feb	Official BD HM the Queen[†]	16 Jun
Accession of HM the Queen	6 Feb	St John the Baptist	24 Jun
Ash Wednesday	1 Mar	St Peter	29 Jun
St David's Day	1 Mar	St Thomas	3 Jul
Annunciation	25 Mar	St James	25 Jul
BD HM the Queen	21 Apr	St Luke	18 Oct
St Mark	25 Apr	SS Simon & Jude	28 Oct
SS Philip & James	1 May	All Saints	1 Nov
St Matthias	14 May	Lord Mayor's Day[†]	—
Ascension	25 May	BD HRH the Prince of Wales	14 Nov
Coronation of HM the Queen	2 Jun	St Andrew's Day	30 Nov
BD HRH Duke of Edinburgh	10 Jun	(† *indicates the date varies by year*)	

THIRTY DAYS...

30 days hath September,
April, June and November,
February hath 28 alone,
And all the rest have 31.

or

30 days hath September,
April, June and November,
Of 28 there is but one
And the rest 30 and 1

Dirty days hath September,
April, June, and November,
From January up to May
The rain it raineth every day.
February hath twenty-eight alone,
And all the rest have thirty-one.
If any of them had two and thirty
They'd be just as wet and dirty.

— THOMAS HOOD (1799–1845)

KEY TO SYMBOLS USED OVERLEAF

[★ BH]	UK Bank Holiday	[§ *patronage*]	Saint's Day
[◑]	Clocks change (UK)	[WA 1900]	Wedding Anniversary
[☞]	Hunting season (traditional)	[AD 1900]	Admission Day [US States]
[ND]	National Day	●	Full Moon
[NH]	National Holiday	[✦]	Annual meteor shower
[ID 1900]	Independence Day	[UN]	United Nations Day
[BD 1900]	Birthday	[◉]	Eclipse
[†1900]	Anniversary of death	[£]	Union Flag to be flown (UK)

Certain dates are subject to change, estimated, or tentative at the time of printing.

JANUARY

 Capricorn [♑]　　*Birthstone* · GARNET　　*Aquarius* [♒]
(Dec 22–Jan 20)　　*Flower* · CARNATION　　(Jan 21–Feb 19)

1★.................New Year's Day [★BH] · Solemnity of Mary.................M
2.....[★BH Scotland] · Switzerland – Berchtold's Day [NH] · Georgia [AD1788]....Tu
3..............Josiah Wedgwood [†1795] · J.R.R. Tolkien [BD1892]..............W
4...................Albert Camus [†1960] · Quadrantids [☄]...................Th
5.................Twelfth Night · Sir Ernest Shackleton [†1922].................F
6.....................Epiphany · St Joan of Arc [BD1412].......................Sa
7........................Catherine of Aragon [†1536]..........................Su
8................Galileo Galilei [†1642] · David Bowie [BD1947]................M
9.......................Gracie Fields [BD1898]...........................Tu
10.............Grigori Rasputin [BD1871] · Rod Stewart [BD1945].............W
11.......................Nepal – National Unity Day [NH]......................Th
12............Hermann Goering [BD1893] · Michael Aspel [BD1933].............F
13.............................James Joyce [†1941].............................Sa
14........Richard Briers [BD1934] · Anthony Eden [†1977]................Su
15...........Martin Luther King Jr Day, USA · Ivor Novello [BD1893]..........M
16..........................Kate Moss [BD1974].............................Tu
17.............St Anthony of Egypt [§ *basket makers*].......................W
18.............David Bellamy [BD1933] · Rudyard Kipling [†1936].............Th
19..........Edgar Allan Poe [BD1809] · Paul Cézanne [BD1839]..............F
20.......Presidential Inauguration Day, USA · Islamic New Year (AH 1428).......Sa
21........................Benny Hill [BD1925]............................Su
22.............Francis Bacon [BD1561] · Claire Rayner [BD1931]..............M
23.........................St John the Almsgiver...........................Tu
24.............Caligula [†AD41 *murdered*] · Winston Churchill [†1965].............W
25...............Scotland – Burns' Night · Conversion of St Paul...............Th
26..............Australia – Australia Day [NH] · Michigan [AD1837]..............F
27...............Lewis Carroll [BD1832] · Thomas Crapper [†1910]..............Sa
28..........................King Henry VIII [†1547].........................Su
29.................St Julian the Hospitaller [§ *innkeepers and boatmen*].................M
30..........................Charles I [†1649 *beheaded*]..........................Tu
31...........Tallulah Bankhead [BD1903] · Justin Timberlake [BD1981]..........W

French Rev. calendar...... *Pluvôse* (rain)	Dutch month ...... *Lauwmaand* (chilly)
Angelic governor................*Gabriel*	Saxon month....... *Wulf-monath* (wolf)
Epicurean calendar..... *Marronglaçaire*	Talismanic stone .... *Jasper*

❦ The Latin month *Ianuarius* derives from *ianua* ('door'), since it was the opening of the year. It was also associated with *Janus*, the two-faced Roman god of doors and openings, who guarded the gates of heaven. Janus could simultaneously face the year just past and the year to come. ❦ *If January Calends be summerly gay, 'Twill be winterly weather till the calends of May.* ❦ *Janiveer – Freeze the pot upon the fier.* ❦ *He that will live another year, Must eat a hen in Januvere.* ❦ On the stock market, the *January Effect* is the trend of stocks performing especially well that month. ❦

FEBRUARY

Aquarius [♒]　*Birthstone* · AMETHYST　*Pisces* [♓]
(Jan 21–Feb 19)　*Flower* · PRIMROSE　(Feb 20–Mar 20)

1 . . . . . . .National Freedom Day, USA · Partridge shooting season ends [♥] . . . . . .Th
2 . . . . Candlemas · Groundhog Day, USA. . . . . F
3 . . . . .Buddy Holly [†1959] . . . . Sa
4 . . . . Karen Carpenter [†1983] · Liberace [†1987]. . . . . .Su
5 . . . . .Sir Robert Peel [BD1788] · Captain W. E. Johns [BD1893] . . . . M
6 . . . . New Zealand – Waitangi Day [NH]. . . . . .Tu
7 . . . . .Grenada [ID 1974] · Eddie Izzard [BD1962] . . . . W
8 . . . . .St Jerome Emiliani [§ *abandoned children and orphans*] . . . . .Th
9 . . . . St Apollonia [§ *dentists*] · Mia Farrow [BD1945]. . . . . F
10. . . . . Bertolt Brecht [BD1898] . . . . Sa
11. . . . . .Scottish salmon fishing season opens [♥] . . . . .Su
12. . . . . Lady Jane Grey [†1554 *beheaded*] · Abraham Lincoln [BD1809]. . . . . M
13. . . . . St Modomnoc [§ *bee keepers*] · Oliver Reed [BD1938] . . . . .Tu
14. . . . . St Valentine [§ *lovers*] · P.G. Wodehouse [†1975] . . . . W
15. . . . . Susan B. Anthony Day, USA · Nat King Cole [†1965] . . . . .Th
16. . . . . .Lithuania [ID 1918] . . . . F
17. . . . . .Ruth Rendell [BD1930] · Paris Hilton [BD1981]. . . . . Sa
18. . . . . 'Bloody' Mary I [BD1516] · Martin Luther [†1546]. . . . . Su
19. . . . . Prince Andrew [BD1960] [£] · USA – President's Day [NH] . . . . M
20. . . . . Shrove Tuesday · Jimmy Greaves [BD1940]. . . . . .Tu
21. . . . . .Ash Wednesday · International Mother Language Day [UN] . . . . W
22. . . . . .Feast of Chair of St Peter · St Lucia [ID 1979]. . . . . .Th
23. . . . . .John Keats [†1821] · Stan Laurel [†1965] . . . . F
24. . . . . .George Harrison [BD1943] . . . . Sa
25. . . . . Pierre Auguste Renoir [BD1841] · Tennessee Williams [†1983]. . . . . Su
26 . . . . .Johnny Cash [BD1932]. . . . . M
27. . . . . Dominican Republic [ID 1844] · Chelsea Clinton [BD1980] . . . . .Tu
28. . . . . .Hind stalking season closes [♥] · Henry James [†1916]. . . . . W

French Rev. calendar. . . . . *Ventôse* (wind)	Dutch month *Sprokelmaand* (vegetation)
Angelic governor. . . . . *Barchiel*	Saxon month. . . . .*Sol monath* (Sun)
Epicurean calendar. . . . *Harrengsauridor*	Talismanic stone . . . . *Ruby*

♥ Much mythology and folklore consider February to have the bitterest weather: *February is seldom warm.* ♥ *February, if ye be fair, The sheep will mend, and nothing mair; February, if ye be foul, The sheep will die in every pool.* ♥ *As the day lengthens, the cold strengthens.* ♥ That said, a foul February is often said to presage a fine year: *All the moneths in the year curse a fair Februeer.* ♥ The word February derives from *februa* – which means cleansing or purification, and reflects the rituals undertaken before Spring. ♥ Having only 28 days in non-leap years [see p.344], February was known in Welsh as '*y mis bach*' – the little month. ♥ February is traditionally personified in pictures, either by an old man warming himself by the fireside, or as 'a sturdy maiden, with a tinge of the red hard winter apple on her hardy cheek'. ♥

——————————————— MARCH ———————————————

Pisces [♓]   *Birthstone* · BLOODSTONE   *Aries* [♈]
(Feb 20–Mar 20)   *Flower* · JONQUIL   (Mar 21–Apr 20)

1 .... St David [§ *Wales*] · Trout fishing season begins [❦]................ Th
2 ....D. H. Lawrence [†1930] · John Irving [BD1942] .... F
3 .... Doll's Festival, Japan · Bulgaria [ID 1878].................... Sa
4 ....Vermont [AD1791] · Ronald Reagan & Nancy Davis [WA 1952] .... Su
5 .... St Piran [§ *tin miners*] · Elaine Paige [BD1951] .... M
6 ....Gabriel García Márquez [BD1928] .... Tu
7 ....Aristotle [†322BC] · Sir Ranulph Fiennes [BD1944]............... W
8 ....Women's Rights & International Peace day [UN]............... Th
9 ....Yuri Gagarin [BD1934]............................ F
10 ....Sharon Stone [BD1958] · Prince Edward [BD1964] [£].............. Sa
11 ....Sir Henry Tate [BD1819] · Harold Wilson [BD1916] .... Su
12 ....Paul McCartney & Linda Eastman [WA 1969] .... M
13 .... Earl Grey [BD1764] · Baroness Amos [BD1954] ....Tu
14 .... St Matilda [§ *parents with many children*] · Michael Caine [BD1933] .... W
15 .... Elizabeth Taylor & Richard Burton [WA 1964] .... Th
16 .... St Urho [§ *Finnish immigrants in America*] .... F
17 ....St Patrick's Day [§ *Ireland*] · World Maritime Day [UN] .... Sa
18 ....Mothering Sunday · Fra Angelico [†1455] .... Su
19 .... [★ BH N. Ireland] · Wyatt Earp [BD1848] · Janis Joplin [BD1943] .... M
20 ....Spike Lee [BD1957] · John Lennon & Yoko Ono [WA 1969] ....Tu
21 .....International Day for the Elimination of Racial Discrimination [UN] .... W
22 .... World Day for Water [UN] · Andrew Lloyd Webber [BD1948].........Th
23 ....World Meteorological Day [UN] · Chaka Khan [BD1953] .... F
24 ....Sir Alan Sugar [BD1947] · E.H. Shepard [†1976] .... Sa
25 .... [◑ 01:00] · Annunciation Day · Elton John [BD1947].............. Su
26 ....Ludwig Van Beethoven [†1827] · Diana Ross [BD1944].............. M
27 ....Yuri Gagarin [†1968] · Dudley Moore [†2002] ....Tu
28 .... Dwight D. Eisenhower [†1969] .... W
29 ....Eric Idle [BD1943] · John Major [BD1943]................Th
30 ....Vincent Van Gogh [BD1853] .... F
31 ....Christopher Walken [BD1943].................... Sa

French Rev. cal. ..... *Germinal* (budding)	Dutch month .... *Lentmaand* (spring)
Angelic governor............ *Machidiel*	Saxon month..... *Hrèth-monath* (rough)
Epicurean calendar.... *Oeufalacoquidor*	Talismanic stone .... *Topaz*

❦ The first month of the Roman year, March is named after Mars, the god of war (and also an agricultural deity). ❦ The unpredictability of March weather leads to some confusion (*March has many weathers*), though it is generally agreed that March *comes in like a lion, and goes out like a lamb*. Yet, because March is often too wet for crops to flourish, many considered *a bushel of Marche dust* [a dry March] *is worth a ransom of gold*. ❦ March hares are 'mad' with nothing more than lust, since it is their mating season. ❦ The *Mars* bar is named after its creator, Frank Mars. ❦

APRIL

Aries [♈]
(Mar 21–Apr 20)

Birthstone · DIAMOND
Flower · SWEET PEA

Taurus [♉]
(Apr 21–May 21)

1 . . . . April Fool's Day [except in Scotland] · Roebuck season opens [❦] . . . . Su
2 . . . . First Seder night · Charlemagne [BD AD742] · Linford Christie [BD1960] . . . M
3 . . . . First day of Passover · Jesse James [†1882] · Tony Benn [BD1925] . . . . . . Tu
4 . . . . Sir Charles Siemens [BD1823] . . . . W
5 . . . . Howard Hughes [†1976] · Kurt Cobain [†1994 *suicide*] . . . . Th
6★ . . . . Good Friday [★BH] · Raphael [†1520] · John Betjeman [BD1906] . . . . F
7 . . . . World Health Day [UN] · St John Baptist de la Salle [§ *teachers*] . . . . Sa
8 . . . . Easter Sunday · Kofi Annan [BD1938] · Pablo Picasso [†1973] . . . . Su
9★ . . . . . Easter Monday [★BH] · Traditionally, slugs and snails start to appear . . . . . M
10 . . . . Dante Gabriel Rossetti [†1882] · Evelyn Waugh [†1966] . . . . Tu
11 . . . . St Stanislaus of Krakow [§ *Poland*] . . . . W
12 . . . . St Zeno [§ *Verona*] · David Letterman [BD1947] . . . . Th
13 . . . . Samuel Beckett [BD1906] · Alan Clark [BD1928] . . . . F
14 . . . . Christiaan Huygens [BD1629] · John Gielgud [BD1904] . . . . Sa
15 . . . . Leonardo da Vinci [BD1452] · Jean-Paul Sartre [†1980] . . . . Su
16 . . . . Charlie Chaplin [BD1889] · Peter Ustinov [BD1921] . . . . M
17 . . . . Benjamin Franklin [†1790] . . . . Tu
18 . . . . Zimbabwe [ID 1980] · James Woods [BD1947] . . . . W
19 . . . . Dickie Bird [BD1933] · Sue Barker [BD1956] . . . . Th
20 . . . . Canaletto [†1768] · Bram Stoker [†1912] . . . . F
21 . . . . . . Queen Elizabeth II [BD1926] [£] · St Beuno [§ *sick animals*] · Lyrids [☄] . . . . . . Sa
22 . . . . Richard Nixon [†1994] . . . . Su
23 . . . . St George [§ *England*] · World Book & Copyright Day [UN] . . . . M
24 . . . . William I of Orange [BD1533] . . . . Tu
25 . . . . Australia & New Zealand – Anzac Day · Eric Bristow [BD1957] . . . . W
26 . . . . Marcus Aurelius [BDAD121] · Lucille Ball [†1989] . . . . Th
27 . . . . St Zita [§ *bakers*] · Michael Fish [BD1944] . . . . F
28 . . . . Francis Bacon [†1992] . . . . Sa
29 . . . . Adolf Hitler & Eva Braun [WA 1945] · Andre Agassi [BD1970] . . . . Su
30 . . . . Louisiana [AD1812] · Stag stalking season closes [❦] . . . . M

French Rev. calendar. . . *Floréal* (blossom)	Dutch month . . . . *Grasmaand* (grass)
Angelic governor . . . . *Asmodel*	Saxon month . . . . *Easter-monath*
Epicurean calendar . . . . *Petitpoisidor*	Talismanic stone . . . . *Garnet*

❦ April, T.S. Eliot's 'cruellest month', heralds the start of spring and is associated with new growth and sudden bursts of rain. ❦ Its etymology might derive from the Latin *aperire* ('to open') – although in Old English it was known simply as the *Eastre-monath*. ❦ *April with his hack and his bill, Plants a flower on every hill*. ❦ The custom of performing pranks and hoaxes on April Fool's Day (or *poisson d'avril* as it is known in France) is long established, although its origins are much disputed. ❦ According to weather folklore, *If it thunders on All Fools' day, it brings good crops of corn and hay*. Usually, cuckoos will first appear in *The Times* around 8 April. ❦

—————————————— MAY ——————————————

🐂 *Taurus* [♉]   *Birthstone* · EMERALD   *Gemini* [♊] 🚸
   (Apr 21–May 21)   *Flower* · LILY OF THE VALLEY   (May 22–Jun 22)

1 ....May Day · Calamity Jane [BD1852]......................Tu
2 ....Engelbert Humperdinck [BD1936] · David Beckham [BD1975] ....W
3 ....World Press Freedom Day [UN] · St James the Lesser [§ *hatmakers*].......Th
4 ....Audrey Hepburn [BD1929] · Diana Dors [†1984]................ F
5 ....Japan – Children's Day · Eta Aquarids [☄]...................Sa
6 ....Orson Welles [BD1915] ....Su
7 ★ ....[★BH] · Johannes Brahms [BD1833] · Eva Perón [BD1919]............M
8 ....VE Day · Sir David Attenborough [BD1926].................Tu
9 ....Liberation Day – Channel Islands · Billy Joel [BD1949] ....W
10 ....Jonathan Edwards [BD1966] · Joan Crawford [†1977].............Th
11 ....Salvador Dalí [BD1904] · Bob Marley [†1981] .... F
12 ....Katharine Hepburn [BD1907]..........................Sa
13 ....Garland Day – Dorset · Harvey Keitel [BD1939]................Su
14 ....Paraguay [ND] · Frank Sinatra [†1998]........................ M
15 ....International Day of Families [UN] · St Isidore [§ *rural life*] ....Tu
16 ....Pierce Brosnan [BD1953] · Sammy Davis Jnr [†1990]..............W
17 ....Ascension · Sandro Botticelli [†1510] ....Th
18 ....International Museum day...........................F
19 ....St Yves [§ *lawyers & Brittany*] · Ho Chi Minh [BD1890] ....Sa
20 ....St Bernardino of Siena [§ *advertisers*]......................Su
21 ...Lauren Bacall & Humphrey Bogart [WA 1945] · Barbara Cartland [†2000] ..M
22 ....International Day for Biological Diversity [UN] ....Tu
23 ....Feast of Weeks (Shavuot) · Heinrich Himmler [†1945 *suicide*].........W
24 ....Nicolaus Copernicus [†1543] ....Th
25 ....The Venerable Bede [†AD735] · Ian McKellen [BD1939] ....F
26 ....Georgia [ID 1991] · Michael Portillo [BD1953].................Sa
27 ....Pentecost · Isadora Duncan [BD1878].....................Su
28 ★ ....[★BH] · Ethiopia [ND] · Anne Brontë [†1849] ....M
29 ....International Day of United Nations Peacekeepers [UN]...........Tu
30 ....St Hubert [§ *dogs and hunters*] · Mel Blanc [BD1908].................W
31 ....The Visitation of the Blessed Virgin Mary...................Th

French Rev. cal. ....*Prairial* (meadow)	Dutch month ...... *Blowmaand* (flower)
Angelic governor...............*Ambriel*	Saxon month...... *Trimilchi* [see below]
Epicurean calendar...........*Aspergial*	Talismanic stone ....*Emerald*

❦ Named after *Maia*, the goddess of growth, May is considered a joyous month, as Milton wrote: 'Hail bounteous May that dost inspire Mirth and youth, and warm desire.' ❦ However, May has long been thought a bad month in which to marry: *who weds in May throws it all away.* ❦ Anglo-Saxons called May *thrimilce*, since in May cows could be milked three times a day. ❦ May was thought a time of danger for the sick; so to have *climbed May hill* was to have survived the month. ❦ Kittens born in May were thought weak, and were often drowned. ❦

—————————————— JUNE ——————————————

 *Gemini* [♊]　　*Birthstone* · PEARL　　*Cancer* [♋]
(May 22–Jun 22)　　*Flower* · ROSE　　(Jun 23–Jul 23)

1 .... Tennessee [AD1796] · Morgan Freeman [BD1937] .... F
2 .... Coronation of Elizabeth II [1953] [£] · Marquis de Sade [BD1740] ...... Sa
3 .... Tony Curtis [BD1925] · Ayatollah Khomeini [†1989] .... Su
4 .... Socrates [BD469BC] · Casanova [†1798] .... M
5 .... World Environment Day [UN] · Ronald Reagan [†2004] .... Tu
6 .... D Day · Robert Kennedy [†1968 *assassinated*] .... W
7 .... Malta [ND] · Alan Turing [†1954 *suicide*] .... Th
8 .... Bonnie Tyler [BD1953] · Mick Hucknall [BD1960] .... F
9 .. HM The Queen's Official Birthday (provisional) · Charles Saatchi [BD1943] . Sa
10 .... HRH Prince Philip [BD1921] [£] · Portugal [ND] .... Su
11 .... Gene Wilder [BD1935] · John Wayne [†1979] .... M
12 .... Russia [ID 1990] · Anne Frank [BD1929] .... Tu
13 ..... St Anthony of Padua [§ *finder of lost articles*] · Charles the Bald [BDAD823] ..... W
14 .... Flag Day, USA · John Logie Baird [†1946] .... Th
15 .... Noddy Holder [BD1946] .... F
16 .... Freshwater fishing season opens [♥] · Bloomsday (*Ulysses*) .... Sa
17 .... Father's Day · Iceland [ID 1945] · Barry Manilow [BD1946] .... Su
18 .... Seychelles [ND] · Roald Amundsen [†1928 *lost in the Arctic*] .... M
19 .... Prince Edward & Sophie Rhys-Jones [WA 1999] .... Tu
20 .... World Refugee Day [UN] · West Virginia [AD1863] .... W
21 .... St Aloysius Gonzaga [§ *youth*] · Niccolo Machiavelli [†1527] .... Th
22 .... Judy Garland [†1969] · Fred Astaire [†1987] .... F
23 .... Midsummer's Eve · Zinedine Zidane [BD1972] .... Sa
24 .... Midsummer's Day · Juan Manuel Fangio [BD1911] .... Su
25 .... Slovenia [ID 1991] · Virginia [AD1788] .... M
26 .... United Nations Charter Day [UN] · Madagascar [ID 1960] .... Tu
27 .... Jack Lemmon [†2001] · John Entwistle [†2002] .... W
28 .... Peter Paul Rubens [BD1577] .... Th
29 .... Elizabeth Barrett Browning [†1861] · Paul Klee [†1940] .... F
30 .... Stanley Spencer [BD1891] .... Sa

French Rev. cal. .... *Messidor* (harvest)	Dutch month ... *Zomermaand* (Summer)
Angelic governor .... *Muriel*	Saxon month .... *Sere-monath* (dry)
Epicurean calendar .... *Concombrial*	Talismanic stone .... *Sapphire*

❦ June is probably derived from *iuvenis* ('young'), but it is also linked to the goddess *Juno*, who personifies young women. In Scots Gaelic the month is known as *Ian t-òg-mbìos*, the 'young month', and in Welsh as *Mehefin*, the 'middle'. ❦ According to weather lore, *Calm weather in June, Sets corn in tune*. ❦ To 'june' a herd of animals is to drive them in a brisk or lively manner. ❦ Wilfred Gowers-Round asserts that 'June is the reality of the Poetic's claims for May'. ❦ In parts of South Africa the verb 'to june-july' is slang for shaking or shivering with fear – because these months, while summer in the north, are midwinter in the south. ❦

—————————————— JULY ——————————————

🦀 *Cancer* [♋]   *Birthstone* · RUBY   *Leo* [♌] 🦁
   (Jun 23–Jul 23)   *Flower* · LARKSPUR   (Jul 24–Aug 23)

1 ....Canada – Canada Day [NH] · Pamela Anderson [BD1967] ....Su
2 .... Nostradamus [†1566] · Ken Clarke [BD1940] .... M
3 .... Idaho [AD1890] · Franz Kafka [BD1883]......................Tu
4 ....USA – Independence Day [NH] · Barry White [†2003]............. W
5 ....Algeria [ID 1962]..................................Th
6 .... Frida Kahlo [BD1907] · Louis Armstrong [†1971]................ F
7 .... Ringo Starr [BD1940] · Michael Howard [BD1941] .... Sa
8 ....Vivien Leigh [†1967].............................Su
9 ....Argentina [ID 1816] · Donald Rumsfeld [BD1932]................ M
10.................. Hadrian [†AD138] · George Stubbs [†1806]...................Tu
11...........World Population Day [UN] · Robert the Bruce [BD1274]........... W
12.........[★BH N. Ireland] · Kiribati [ID 1979] · Julius Caesar [BD100BC].........Th
13...................Frida Kahlo [†1954] · Ian Hislop [BD1960] .... F
14................ France – Bastille Day · Anton Chekhov [†1904] .... Sa
15................St Swithin's Day · Iris Murdoch [BD1919]....................Su
16......................Feast of Our Lady of Mount Carmel...................... M
17.............James Cagney [BD1899] · David Hasselhoff [BD1952].............Tu
18........William Makepeace Thackeray [BD1811] · Jane Austen [†1817] .... W
19...................... Samuel Colt [BD1814].............................Th
20........... Diana Rigg [BD1938] · Bruce Lee [†1973]..................... F
21...................... Ernest Hemingway [BD1899] .... Sa
22...............St Mary Magdalene [§ *hairdressers & repentant women*] .... Su
23................ Prince Andrew & Sarah Ferguson [WA 1986].................. M
24............... Simón Bolívar Day – Venezuela & Ecuador..................Tu
25.................. St James [§ *labourers*] · Matt Le Blanc [BD1967] .... W
26............... Aldous Huxley [BD1894] · Helen Mirren [BD1945]...............Th
27.................Hilaire Belloc [BD1870] · Bob Hope [†2003] .... F
28...................Peru [ND] · Delta Aquarids (South) [☄] .... Sa
29.............St Martha [§ *cooks*] · Vincent Van Gogh [†1890 *suicide*] .... Su
30...............Kate Bush [BD1958] · Daley Thompson [BD1958]................ M
31...................Franz Liszt [†1886] · Primo Levi [BD1919]...................Tu

French Rev. Cal. ....*Thermidor* (heat)	Dutch month ....*Hooymaand* (hay)
Angelic governor............... *Verchiel*	Saxon month....*Mæd-monath* (meadow)
Epicurean calendar...........*Melonial*	Talismanic stone .... *Diamond*

❦ July was originally called *Quintilis* (from *Quintus* – meaning 'fifth'), but it was renamed by Mark Antony to honour the murdered Julius Caesar, who was born on 12 July. ❦ *A swarm of bees in May is worth a load of Hay; A swarm of bees in June is worth a silver spoon; But a swarm of bees in July is not worth a fly.* ❦ *If the first of July be rainy weather, 'Twill rain mair or less for forty days together.* ❦ *Bow-wow, dandy fly – Brew no beer in July.* ❦ July used to be known as the thunder month, and some churches rang their bells in the hope of driving away thunder and lightning. ❦

―――――――――――――― AUGUST ――――――――――――――

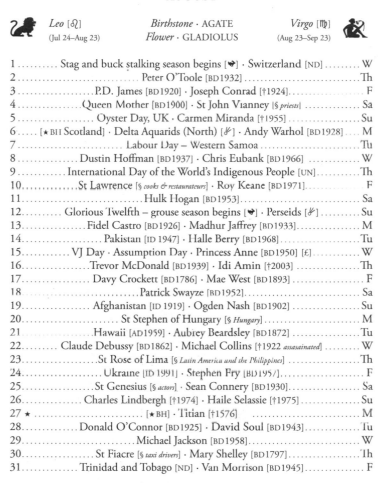

Leo [♌]   *Birthstone* · AGATE   *Virgo* [♍]
(Jul 24–Aug 23)   *Flower* · GLADIOLUS   (Aug 23–Sep 23)

1 .... Stag and buck stalking season begins [♥] · Switzerland [ND] .... W
2 .... Peter O'Toole [BD1932] .... Th
3 .... P.D. James [BD1920] · Joseph Conrad [†1924]................. F
4 .... Queen Mother [BD1900] · St John Vianney [§ *priests*] .... Sa
5 .... Oyster Day, UK · Carmen Miranda [†1955] .... Su
6 ..... [★ BH Scotland] · Delta Aquarids (North) [☞] · Andy Warhol [BD1928] .... M
7 .... Labour Day – Western Samoa .... Tu
8 .... Dustin Hoffman [BD1937] · Chris Eubank [BD1966] .... W
9 .... International Day of the World's Indigenous People [UN] .... Th
10 .... St Lawrence [§ *cooks & restaurateurs*] · Roy Keane [BD1971]........... F
11 .... Hulk Hogan [BD1953]............................ Sa
12 .... Glorious Twelfth – grouse season begins [♥] · Perseids [☞] .... Su
13 .... Fidel Castro [BD1926] · Madhur Jaffrey [BD1933]............... M
14 .... Pakistan [ID 1947] · Halle Berry [BD1968].................. Tu
15 .... VJ Day · Assumption Day · Princess Anne [BD1950] [£].......... W
16 .... Trevor McDonald [BD1939] · Idi Amin [†2003] .... Th
17 .... Davy Crockett [BD1786] · Mae West [BD1893] .... F
18 .... Patrick Swayze [BD1952]........................... Sa
19 .... Afghanistan [ID 1919] · Ogden Nash [BD1902] .... Su
20 .... St Stephen of Hungary [§ *Hungary*] .... M
21 .... Hawaii [AD1959] · Aubrey Beardsley [BD1872] .... Tu
22 .... Claude Debussy [BD1862] · Michael Collins [†1922 *assassinated*] .... W
23 .... St Rose of Lima [§ *Latin America and the Philippines*] .... Th
24 .... Ukraine [ID 1991] · Stephen Fry [BD1957]............... F
25 .... St Genesius [§ *actors*] · Sean Connery [BD1930]................. Sa
26 .... Charles Lindbergh [†1974] · Haile Selassie [†1975]............... Su
27 ★ .... [★ BH] · Titian [†1576] .... M
28 .... Donald O'Connor [BD1925] · David Soul [BD1943]............. Tu
29 .... Michael Jackson [BD1958]........................... W
30 .... St Fiacre [§ *taxi drivers*] · Mary Shelley [BD1797]................. Th
31 .... Trinidad and Tobago [ND] · Van Morrison [BD1945].............. F

French Rev. cal. .... *Fructidor* (fruits)	Dutch month ...... *Oostmaand* (harvest)
Angelic governor .... *Hamaliel*	Saxon month ...... *Weod-monath* (weed)
Epicurean calendar .... *Raisinose*	Talismanic stone .... *Zircon*

❦ Previously called *Sextilis* (as the sixth month of the old calendar), August was renamed in 8BC, in honour of the first Roman Emperor, Augustus, who claimed this month to be lucky as it was the month in which he began his consulship, conquered Egypt, and had many triumphs. ❦ *Greengrocers rise at dawn of sun, August the fifth – come haste away, To Billingsgate the thousands run, Tis Oyster Day! Tis Oyster Day!* ❦ *Dry August and warme, Dothe harvest no harme.* ❦ *Take heed of sudden cold after heat.* ❦ *Gather not garden seeds near the full moon.* ❦ *Sow herbs.* ❦

—— SEPTEMBER ——

Virgo [♍]   *Birthstone* · SAPPHIRE   *Libra* [♎]
(Aug 23–Sep 23)   *Flower* · ASTER   (Sep 24–Oct 23)

1 ....Partridge shooting season opens [❥] · Uzbekistan [ND] ....Sa
2 ....Jimmy Connors [BD1952] · Keanu Reeves [BD1964] ....Su
3 ....USA – Labor Day [NH] · e.e. cummings [†1962] ....M
4 ....Edvard Grieg [†1907] · Beyoncé Knowles [BD1981]...............Tu
5 ....Freddie Mercury [BD1946] · Mother Teresa [†1997]...............W
6 ....Greg Rusedski [BD1973] · Tim Henman [BD1974] ....Th
7 ....Brazil [ID 1822] · Keith Moon [†1978].......................F
8 ...... International Literacy Day [UN] · Nativity of Blessed Virgin Mary......Sa
9 ....Japan – Chrysanthemum Day · William the Conqueror [†1087] ....Su
10.......................Karl Lagerfeld [BD1938].............................M
11............New Year – Ethiopia · Nikita Khrushchev [†1971]...............Tu
12............Elizabeth Barrett & Robert Browning [WA 1846]...............W
13...... Jewish New Year [AM 5768] · First day of Ramadan · Titus [†AD81]......Th
14...........Exaltation of the Holy Cross · Isadora Duncan [†1927]........... F
15....................Battle of Britain Day · Nicaragua [ND]....................Sa
16.......International Day for the Preservation of the Ozone Layer [UN] ....Su
17.................Tessa Jowell [BD1947] · Spiro Agnew [†1996] ....M
18......................Chile [ND] · Jimi Hendrix [†1970].....................Tu
19...............William Golding [BD1911] · Kate Adie [BD1945]...............W
20.............Jakob Grimm [†1863] · Sophia Loren [BD1934].................Th
21................ International Day of Peace [UN] · Belize [ND].................F
22............ Day of Atonement (Yom Kippur) · Shaka Zulu [†1828] ....Sa
23............ Wilkie Collins [†1889] · Mickey Rooney [BD1920] ....Su
24......................Howard Hughes [BD1905]...........................M
25.............. Mark Rothko [BD1903] · Mark Hamill [BD1951]...............Tu
26. St Cosmas & St Damian [§ *pharmacists & doctors*] · Olivia Newton-John [BD1948]. W
27............. Feast of Tabernacles (Succoth) · Edgar Degas [†1917] ....Th
28...........................Louis Pasteur [†1895] ....F
29................ Michaelmas Day · Horatio Nelson [BD1758].................Sa
30..............Trout fishing season ends [❥] · James Dean [†1955]..............Su

French Rev. cal. ... *Vendémiaire* (vintage)	Dutch month .... *Herstmaand* (Autumn)
Angelic governor.................. *Uriel*	Saxon month...... *Gerst-monath* (barley)
Epicurean calendar............ *Huitrose*	Talismanic stone .... *Agate*

❦ September is so named as it was the seventh month in the Roman calendar. ❦ *September blows soft, Till the fruit's in the loft. Forgotten, month past, Doe now at the last.* ❦ *Eat and drink less, And buy a knife at Michaelmas.* ❦ To be 'Septembered' is to be multihued in autumnal colours; as Blackmore wrote: 'His honest face was Septembered with many a vintage.' ❦ *Poor Robin's Almanac* (1666) stated, 'now *Libra* weighs the days and night in an equal balance, so that there is not an hair's breadth difference betwixt them in length; this moneth having an R in it, Oysters come again in season.' ❦ The Irish name *Meán Fómhair* means 'mid-Autumn'. ❦

—— OCTOBER ——

 Libra [♎]   *Birthstone* · OPAL   *Scorpio* [♏]
(Sep 24–Oct 23)   *Flower* · CALENDULA   (Oct 24–Nov 22)

1 ......Int. Day of Older Persons [UN] · Pheasant shooting season opens [❦] .... M
2 .... Graham Greene [BD1904] · Trevor Brooking [BD1948] .... Tu
3 .... Germany [ND] · James Herriot [BD1916] .... W
4 .... Buster Keaton [BD1895] · Charlton Heston [BD1924]............. Th
5 ...... International Teachers' Day [UN] · Louis Jean Lumière [BD1864] ...... F
6 .... Children's Day [UN] · Alfred Lord Tennyson [†1892] .... Sa
7 .... James Whitcomb Riley [BD1849] · Heinrich Himmler [BD1900]........ Su
8 .... USA – Columbus Day Holiday [NH] · Clement Attlee [†1967]......... M
9 ....Uganda [ND] · John Lennon [BD1940] .... Tu
10 .... Nicholas Parsons [BD1928] · Edith Piaf [†1963]................ W
11 .... Henry John Heinz [BD1844]   .... Th
12 .... Spain [ND] · Luciano Pavarotti [BD1935] .... F
13 .... End of Ramadan (Eid al-Fitr) · Paul Simon [BD1941] .... Sa
14 .... King Harold [†1066] · Roger Moore [BD1927] .... Su
15 .... Chris de Burgh [BD1948] .... M
16 .... World Food Day [UN] · Oscar Wilde [BD1854] .... Tu
17 .... International Day for the Eradication of Poverty [UN]............. W
18 .... Alaska Day, USA · Jean-Claude Van Damme [BD1960]............. Th
19 .... John Le Carré [BD1931] .... F
20 .... Sir Christopher Wren [BD1632] · Ian Rush [BD1961]............. Sa
21 .... St Hilarion [§ *hermits*] · Orionids [☄]..................... Su
22 .... Derek Jacobi [BD1938] · Franz Liszt [BD1811]................ M
23 .... St John of Capistrano [§ *jurors*] · Al Jolson [†1950]............... Tu
24 .... United Nations Day [UN] · Wayne Rooney [BD1985]............. W
25 .... Kazakhstan [ND] · Imran Khan [BD1952]................... Th
26 .... Joseph Hansom [BD1803]............................ F
27 .... Turkmenistan [ND] · Desiderius Erasmus [BD1466].............. Sa
28 .... [● 01:00] · David Dimbleby [BD1938] · Bill Gates [BD1955].......... Su
29 .... Turkey [ND] · Joseph Pulitzer [†1911]..................... M
30 .... John Chubb [†1872] · Diego Maradona [BD1960] .... Tu
31 .... Halloween · Harry Houdini [†1926] .... W

French Rev. cal. .... *Brumaire* (fog; mist)	Dutch month .... *Wynmaand* (wine)
Angelic governor .... *Barbiel*	Saxon month .... *Win-monath* (wine)
Epicurean calendar .... *Bécassinose*	Talismanic stone .... *Amethyst*

❦ October was originally the eighth month of the calendar. ❦ *Dry your barley land in October, Or you'll always be sober.* ❦ October was a time for brewing, and the month gave its name to a 'heady and ripe' ale: 'five Quarters of Malt to three Hogsheads, and twenty-four Pounds of Hops'. Consequently, *often drunk and seldom sober falls like the leaves in October.* ❦ In American politics, an *October surprise* is an event thought to have been engineered to garner political support just before an election (like the release of US hostages in Tehran in October 1980). ❦

— NOVEMBER —

 Scorpio [♏]
(Oct 24–Nov 22)

Birthstone · TOPAZ
Flower · CHRSYANTHEMUM

Sagittarius [♐]
(Nov 23–Dec 21)

1 ....All Saints' Day · Hind and doe stalking season opens [❦]...........Th
2 ....All Souls' Day · Marie Antoinette [BD1755]...................F
3 ....Henri Matisse [†1954] · Dolph Lundgren [BD1959]...............Sa
4 .....St Charles Borromeo [§ *learning and the arts*] · Yitzhak Rabin [†1995 *assassinated*] ...Su
5 .... Guy Fawkes Night · Taurids [☄].........................M
6 .... Colley Cibber [BD1671] · Adolphe Sax [BD1814]................Tu
7 .... Marie Curie [BD1867] · Steve McQueen [†1980] ....W
8 .... Edmond Halley [BD1656] · John Milton [†1674]...............Th
9 ....First day of Diwali ....F
10 .... William Hogarth [BD1697] · Tim Rice [BD1944] ....Sa
11 ....Remembrance Day · USA – Veterans' Day..................Su
12 .... François Auguste Rodin [BD1840] · Roland Barthes [BD1915] ....M
13 ....St Homobonus [§ *cloth workers*] · Camille Pissarro [†1903].............Tu
14 ....Prince Charles [BD1948] [£] · Boutros Boutros-Ghali [BD1922].......W
15 .... St Albert the Great [§ *scientists*] · J.G. Ballard [BD1930]..............Th
16 .... International Day for Tolerance [UN] · Oklahoma [AD1907]..........F
17 ....Leonids [☄] · Danny DeVito [BD1944] ....Sa
18 .... Margaret Atwood [BD1939] · Kim Wilde [BD1960]...............Su
19 ....Monaco [ND] ....M
20 ....Queen Elizabeth II & Prince Philip [WA 1947] [£] · Leo Tolstoy [†1910] ...Tu
21 ....Presentation of the Blessed Virgin Mary in the Temple..........W
22 ...... USA – Thanksgiving [NH] · St Cecilia [§ *music*] · Lebanon [ID 1941].......Th
23 ....Billy the Kid [BD1859] · Roald Dahl [†1990] ....F
24 ....Henri de Toulouse-Lautrec [BD1864] · Scott Joplin [BD1868] ....Sa
25 ....Joe DiMaggio [BD1914] · Charles Kennedy [BD1959]...........Su
26 ....William George Armstrong [BD1810].....................M
27 ....Anders Celsius [BD1701] · Ross McWhirter [†1975 *assassinated*]..........Tu
28 ....East Timor [ND] · Nancy Mitford [BD1904]..................W
29 .... Jacques Chirac [BD1932] · Cary Grant [†1986] ....Th
30 ....St Andrew [§ *Scotland & Russia*] · Jonathan Swift [BD1667] ....F

French Rev. calendar.... *Frimaire* (frost)	Dutch month ....*Slagtmaand* [see below]
Angelic governor............. *Advachiel*	Saxon month...... *Wind-monath* (wind)
Epicurean calendar.......*Pommedetaire*	Talismanic stone .... *Beryl*

❦ Originally the ninth (*novem*) month, November has long been associated with slaughter, hence the Dutch *Slaghtmaand* ('slaughter month'). The Anglo-Saxon was *Blotmonath* ('blood' or 'sacrifice month'). ❦ A dismal month, November has been the subject of many writers' ire; as J.B. Burges wrote: 'November leads her wintry train, And stretches o'er the firmament her veil Charg'd with foul vapours, fogs and drizzly rain.' ❦ Famously, Thomas Hood's poem *No!* contains the lines 'No warmth, no cheerfulness, no healthful ease ... No shade, no shine, no butterflies, no bees, No fruits, no flowers, no leaves, no birds, —— November!' ❦

DECEMBER

 Sagittarius [♐]   *Birthstone* · TURQUOISE   *Capricorn* [♑]
(Nov 23–Dec 21)   *Flower* · NARCISSUS   (Dec 22–Jan 20)

```
1 ................. World AIDS Day [UN] · Woody Allen [BD1935]................ Sa
2 ........... Advent Sunday · Kyrgyzstan [ND] · Britney Spears [BD1981]......... Su
3 ......... International Day of Disabled Persons [UN] · Illinois [AD1818]....... M
4 ............. Wassily Kandinsky [BD1866] · Benjamin Britten [†1976]........... Tu
5 ...... First day of Chanukah · Henry Tate [†1899] · Walt Disney [BD1901] ..... W
6 ......................... St Nicholas [§ bakers & pawnbrokers] ....................... Th
7 ............. Pearl Harbor Day, USA · Ivory Coast Republic [ID 1960]........... F
8 ........ The Immaculate Conception · Mary Queen of Scots [BD1542] ...... Sa
9 ............................. John Milton [BD1608]............................ Su
10 ............... Nobel Prizes awarded · Human Rights Day [UN] ............... M
11 ............... St Damasus [§ archaeologists] · Burkina Faso [NH]................ Tu
12 ............... Frank Sinatra [BD1915] · Lionel Blair [BD1931]................ W
13 ..... Japan – Soot Sweeping Day · M. Roberts & D. Thatcher [WA 1951] ..... Th
14 ................ Geminids [☄] · George Washington [†1799] ................ F
15 ........ National Bill of Rights Day, USA · John Paul Getty [BD1892]........ Sa
16 ......... Ludwig Van Beethoven [BD1770] · Arthur C. Clarke [BD1917]........ Su
17 .................... Bhutan [ND] · Simón Bolívar [†1830].................... M
18 ........... International Migrants Day [UN] · New Jersey [AD1787] .......... Tu
19 ....................... William Edward Parry [BD1790] ....................... W
20 ......... Yvonne Arnaud [BD1890] · John Steinbeck [†1968]............... Th
21 ............... Thomas à Becket [BD1118] · Joseph Stalin [BD1879] .............. F
22 ............... First Day of Winter · Noel Edmonds [BD1948]................. Sa
23 ............... Ursids [☄] · Samuel Smiles [BD1812] ..................... Su
24 ............... Christmas Eve · Ava Gardner [BD1922].................... M
25 ............... Christmas Day [NH] · Humphrey Bogart [BD1899]............... Tu
26 ★ ........ [★BH] Boxing Day [NH] · St Stephen [§ stonemasons & horses]........... W
27 ................ St John [§ Asia Minor] · Marlene Dietrich [BD1901]............... Th
28 ................ Childermass · Denzel Washington [BD1954] ................. F
29 ........... Percy Bysshe Shelley & Mary Wollstonecraft [WA 1816] .......... Sa
30 .............. Rudyard Kipling [BD1865] · L.P. Hartley [BD1895]............... Su
31 ................... New Year's Eve · Scotland – Hogmanay ................... M
```

French Rev. calendar...... *Nivôse* (snow)	Dutch month ... *Wiutermaand* (Winter)
Angelic governor................ *Hanael*	Saxon month...... *Mid-Winter-monath*
Epicurean calendar.......... *Boudinaire*	Talismanic stone .... *Onyx*

❦ *If the ice will bear a goose before Christmas, it will not bear a duck afterwards.* ❦ Originally the tenth month, December now closes the year. ❦ *If Christmas Day be bright and clear there'll be two winters in the year.* ❦ The writer Saunders warned in 1679, 'In December, Melancholy and Phlegm much increase, which are heavy, dull, and close, and therefore it behoves all that will consider their healths, to keep their heads and bodies very well from cold'. ❦ Robert Burns splendidly wrote in 1795 – 'As I am in a complete Decemberish humour, gloomy, sullen, stupid'. ❦

—————————— ANNIVERSARIES OF 2007 ——————————

25th Anniversary (1982)
Argentina invaded the Falklands ❦
Grace Kelly was killed in a car crash

50th Anniversary (1957)
Russians launched the first unmanned
satellite, Sputnik 1, into space ❦ *West
Side Story*, premiered on Broadway ❦
On the Road by Jack Kerouac
was published

75th Anniversary (1932)
Sydney Harbour Bridge was opened
❦ Amelia Earhart became the first
woman to fly solo over the Atlantic
❦ The Kingdoms of Hejaz and Nejd
were renamed the Kingdom of Saudi
Arabia ❦ John Douglas Cockcroft and
Ernest Walton split the atom

100th Anniversary (1907)
Robert Baden-Powell founded the Boy
Scouts ❦ The Northern Line opened ❦
The oldest printed book, the
Diamond Sutra, was acquired
by the British Library

150th Anniversary (1857)
Queen Victoria made Ottawa the
capital of Canada ❦ The first public
passenger lift was installed in a New
York skyscraper by Elisha Otis ❦
Madame Bovary by Gustave Flaubert
was published

200th Anniversary (1807)
Parliament abolished the slave trade ❦
Pall Mall became the first street in the
world to be illuminated by gas lamps

250th Anniversary (1757)
William Blake was born ❦
Britain captured Calcutta, India

500th Anniversary (1507)
A world map published by Martin
Waldseemüller was the first to
use the name America

700th Anniversary (1307)
The Knights Templar were suppressed
in France ❦ Dante began his
Divina Commedia

————————————— FOOL'S ERRANDS —————————————

Elbow Grease · Tartan Paint · Bodge Tape · Universal Solvent
Box of Pixels · Bottled Vacuum · Dehydrated Water · Bag of Sparks
Sky-hooks · Portable Holes · Long Stand · Long Weight
Left Handed Hammer · Prop Wash · Rainbow Ink · Glass Nails
Golden Rivets · Bag of Steam · Electric Anvil · Blinker Fluid · 10ft of Shoreline
Threadless Screws™ · Keyboard Fluid · Population Tool · Medicinal Compound
Metric Spanner · Grid Squares · Error Bars · Plinth Ladder · Pigeon Milk
Strap Oil · Powdered Water · Iced Steam · Blackboard Sharpener
Curve Straightener · Rust Polish · Inch Creeper · Ethernet Tape

————————————— BRITISH SUMMER TIME —————————————

BST starts and ends at 1am on these Sundays (*'spring forward – fall back'*):
2007 . . . . clocks forward 1 hour, 25 March · clocks back 1 hour, 28 October
2008 . . . . clocks forward 1 hour, 30 March · clocks back 1 hour, 26 October

─── A TIMEPIECE OF ADVICE ───

Below is an C18th 'timepiece of advice' to guide a gentleman's courtship. Curiously, in giving tips for every hour of the day and night, it leaves no time for sleep.

─── SUPERSTITIOUS ADVICE FOR THE YEAR ───

January	Kindness, like grain, increase by sowing
February	Make your model before you build
March	It is a great journey to life's end
April	More than enough is too much
May	In every fault there is a folly
June	Learn not and know not
July	He is not dead whose fame survives
August	We readily believe what we wish
September	In the end, things may mend
October	By doing nothing we learn to do ill
November	Small things increase by union
December	Caution is the best keeper of the castle

— *Shenton's Almanack*, 1882

CARDINAL DAYS & THE SEASONS

The adjective *cardinal* derives from the Latin for 'hinge', and tends to be employed for those concepts upon which other things depend. For example, the cardinal points of the compass (N, S, E, W); the cardinal humours of the body (blood, phlegm, yellow bile, and black bile); the cardinal virtues and sins; and so on. In astronomy, the Cardinal Days are the two solstices and the two equinoxes.

SOLSTICES occur when the Sun is at its furthest point from the equator. In the northern hemisphere the Sun's northernmost position occurs at the Summer Solstice (*c.*21 June) – the 'longest day'; and its southernmost position occurs at the Winter Solstice (*c.*22 December) – the 'shortest day'. EQUINOXES occur when the Sun is directly overhead at the equator, and the hours of daylight and darkness are of equal length at all latitudes. This occurs twice yearly: the Spring or Vernal Equinox (*c.*21 March); and the Autumn Equinox (*c.*23 September).

QUARTER DAYS

Quarter Days are those days traditionally employed to divide the year for legal, financial, or contractual purposes such as tenancies, interests, rents, &c. They are:

QUARTER DAYS – *England & Wales*
25 March (Lady Day) · 24 June (Midsummer Day)
29 September (Michaelmas) · 25 December (Christmas Day)

QUARTER DAYS – *Scotland*
2 February (Candlemas Day) · 15 May (Whitsuntide)
1 August (Lammas) · 11 November (Martinmas)

DAYS OF THE WEEK

In AD321, Constantine introduced a seven-day week, the first day of which was decreed a day of rest. Initially the days were referred to by number, but over time they became associated with the seven celestial bodies. In Teutonic languages Roman names were replaced with equivalent local Gods.

Day	Old English	Roman
Sunday	Sun	Sol
Monday	Moon	Luna
Tuesday	Tiu	Mars
Wednesday	Woden	Mercury
Thursday	Thunor	Jupiter
Friday	Frigg	Venus
Saturday	Saeternes	Saturn

NOTABLE CHRISTIAN DATES · 2007

Epiphany · *manifestation of the Christ to the Magi*..................................... 6 Jan
Presentation of Christ in the Temple.. 2 Feb
Ash Wednesday · *1st day of Lent*... 21 Feb
The Annunciation · *when Gabriel told Mary she would bear Christ* .... 20 Mar
Good Friday · *Friday before Easter; commemorating the Crucifixion* .... 6 Apr
Easter Day (Western churches) · *commemorating the Resurrection*...................... 8 Apr
Easter Day (Eastern Orthodox) · *commemorating the Resurrection* .... 8 Apr
Rogation Sunday · *the Sunday before Ascension Day*............................. 13 May
Ascension Day · *commemorating the ascent of Christ to heaven* .... 17 May
Pentecost (Whit Sunday) · *commemorating the descent of the Holy Spirit* .... 27 May
Trinity Sunday · *observed in honour of the Trinity* .... 3 Jun
Corpus Christi · *commemorating the institution of the Holy Eucharist* .... 10 Jun
All Saints' Day · *commemorating all the Church's saints collectively* ....1 Nov
Advent Sunday · *marking the start of Advent* .... 2 Dec
Christmas Day · *celebrating the birth of Christ*................................... 25 Dec

A few other terms from the Christian Calendar:

Bible Sunday.................. 2nd in Advent	Palm Sunday................... before Easter
Black/Easter Monday ..... the day after Easter	Passion Sunday................. 5th in Lent
Collop/Egg Monday......... first before Lent	Plough Monday.............. after Epiphany
Egg Saturday..... day prior to Quinquagesima	Quadragesima............ 1st Sunday in Lent
Fig/Yew Sunday .... Palm Sunday	Quinquagesima .... Sunday before Lent
Holy Saturday.................. before Easter	Refreshment .... 4th Sunday in Lent
Holy Week .... before Easter	Septuagesima .... 3rd Sunday before Lent
Low Sunday .... Sunday after Easter	Sexagesima ....2nd Sunday before Lent
Maundy Thursday .... day before Good Friday	Shrove Tuesday ('pancake day').... before Lent
Mothering Sunday.............. 4th in Lent	Shrovetide.............period preceding Lent
	St Martin's Lent ,.................... Advent
	Tenebrae .... last 3 days of Holy Week

CHRISTIAN CALENDAR MOVEABLE FEASTS

Year	Ash Wednesday	Easter Day	Ascension	Pentecost	Advent Sunday
2008	6 Feb	23 Mar	1 May	11 May	30 Nov
2009	25 Feb	12 Apr	21 May	31 May	29 Nov
2010	17 Feb	4 Apr	13 May	23 May	28 Nov
2011	9 Mar	24 Apr	2 Jun	12 Jun	27 Nov
2012	22 Feb	8 Apr	17 May	27 May	2 Dec
2013	13 Feb	31 Mar	9 May	19 May	1 Dec
2014	5 Mar	20 Apr	29 May	8 Jun	30 Nov
2015	18 Feb	5 Apr	14 May	24 May	29 Nov
2016	10 Feb	27 Mar	5 May	15 May	27 Nov
2017	1 Mar	16 Apr	25 May	4 Jun	3 Dec
2018	14 Feb	1 Apr	10 May	20 May	2 Dec
2019	6 Mar	21 Apr	30 May	9 Jun	1 Dec

————— NOTABLE RELIGIOUS DATES FOR 2007 —————

HINDU

Makar Sankrant · *Winter festival* .... 14 Jan
Vasant Panchami · *dedicated to Saraswati and learning* .... 23 Jan
Maha Shivaratri · *dedicated to Shiva* .... 16 Feb
Holi · *spring festival of colours dedicated to Krishna* .... 3/4 Mar
Varsha Pratipada (Chaitra) · *Spring New Year* .... 4 Mar
Hindu New Year & Ramayana Week .... 19 Mar
Rama Navami · *birthday of Lord Rama* .... 27 Mar
Hanuman Jayanti · *birthday of Hanuman, the Monkey God.* .... 2 Apr
Raksha Bandhan · *festival of brotherhood and love.* .... 28 Aug
Janmashtami · *birthday of Lord Rama* .... 4 Sep
Ganesh Chaturthi · *birthday of Lord Ganesh.* .... 15 Sep
Navarati & Durga-puja · *celebrating triumph of good over evil.* .... *starts* 12 Oct
Saraswati-puja · *dedicated to Saraswati and learning* .... *starts* 18 Oct
Dassera (Vijay Dashami) · *celebrating triumph of good over evil* .... 21 Oct
Diwali (Deepvali) · *New Year festival of lights* .... 9 Nov
New Year .... 10 Nov

JEWISH

Purim (Feast of Lots) · *commemorating defeat of Haman.* .... 4 Mar
Pesach (Passover) · *commemorating exodus from Egypt.* .... 3 Apr
Shavuot (Pentecost) · *commemorating revelation of the Torah* .... 23 May
Tisha B'Av · *day of mourning* .... 24 Jul
Rosh Hashanah (New Year) .... 13 Sep
Yom Kippur (Day of Atonement) · *fasting and prayer for forgiveness* .... 22 Sep
Sukkoth (Feast of Tabernacles) · *marking the time in wilderness.* .... 27 Sep
Simchat Torah · *9th day of Sukkoth* .... 5 Oct
Hanukkah · *commemorating re-dedication of Jerusalem Temple.* .... 5 Dec

ISLAMIC

Eid al-Adha · *celebrating the faith of Abraham.* .... 20 Dec
Al Hijra (New Year) .... 20 Jan
Ashura · *celebrating Noah leaving the Ark, and the saving of Moses* .... 30 Jan
Milad Al-Nabi · *birthday of Muhammad* .... 31 Mar
Ramadan · *the month in which the Koran was revealed.* .... *starts* 13 Sep
Eid al-Fitr · *marks end of Ramadan* .... 13 Oct

SIKH

Birthday of Guru Gobind Singh · *founder of the Khalsa.* .... 5 Jan
Sikh New Year (Nanakshahi calendar) .... 14 Mar
Hola Mahalla · *festival of martial arts* .... 14/15 Mar
Vaisakhi (Baisakhi) · *founding of the Khalsa* .... 13/14 Apr
Birthday of Guru Nanak (founder of Sikhism) .... 14 Apr
Martyrdom of Guru Arjan .... 16 Jun
Martyrdom of Guru Tegh Bahadur .... 24 Nov
Divali · *festival of light* .... 21 Oct

—————— NOTABLE RELIGIOUS DATES FOR 2007 cont. ——————

BAHA'I

Nawruz (New Year) . . . . 21 Mar	Day of the Covenant . . . . 26 Nov
Ridvan . . . . Apr 21–2 May	Ascension of Abdu'l-Baha . . . . . 28 Nov
Declaration of the Báb . . . . 23 May	*World Religion day* . . . . 15 Jan
Ascension of Baha'u'llah . . . . . . 29 May	*Race Unity Day* . . . . 11 Jun
Martyrdom of the Báb . . . . 9 July	*World Peace Day* . . . . 21 Nov
Birth of the Báb . . . . 20 Oct	*In addition, the eve of each of the*
Birth of Baha'u'llah . . . . 12 Nov	*nineteen Baha'i months is celebrated.*

JAIN

Mahavira Jayanti · *celebrates the day of Mahavira's birth* . . . . .31 Mar

Paryushan · *time of reflection and repentance* . . . . 20–26 Aug

Divali · *celebrated when Mahavira gave his last teachings and attained ultimate liberation*   9 Nov

New Year . . . . .22 Oct

Kartak Purnima · *time of pilgrimage* . . . . .Oct/Nov

BUDDHIST

Parinivana Day · *marks the death of the Buddha* . . . . 8 Feb

Losar · *Tibetan New Year* . . . . 18 Feb

Wesak (Vesak) · *marks the birth, death & enlightenment of the Buddha* . . . . .2 May

Dharma Day · *marks the start of the Buddha's teaching* . . . . 30 Jun

Sangha Day (Magha Puja Day) · *celebration of Buddhist community* . . . . .5 Nov

RASTAFARIAN

Ethiopian Christmas . . . . .7 Jan	Birthday of Marcus Garvey . . . . .17 Aug
Ethiopian Constitution . . . . 16 Jul	Ethiopian New Year's Day . . . . . . 11 Sep
Haile Selassie birthday . . . . 23 Jul	Crowning of Haile Selassie . . . . . .2 Nov

PAGAN

Imbolc · *fire festival anticipating the new farming season* . . . . 1/2 Feb

Spring Equinox · *celebrating the renewal of life* . . . . .21 Mar

Beltane · *fire festival celebrating Summer and fertility* . . . . 30 Apr/1 May

Summer Solstice (Midsummer; Litha) · *celebrating the sun's power* . . . . 21 Jun

Lughnasadh · *harvest festival* . . . . 2–4 Aug

Autumn Equinox (Harvest Home; Mabon) · *reflection on the past season* . . . . 21 Sep

Samhain (Halloween; All Hallows Eve) · *Pagan New Year* . . . . 31 Oct/1 Nov

Winter Solstice (Yule) · *celebrating Winter* . . . . 20/21 Dec

CHINESE LUNAR NEW YEAR · 18 Feb

[Every effort has been taken to validate these dates. However, readers should be aware that there is a surprising degree of debate and dispute. This is caused by the interplay of: regional variations; differing interpretations between religious authorities; seemingly arbitrary changes in dates when holidays conflict; avoidance of days considered for one or other reason inauspicious; as well as the inherent unpredictability of the lunar cycle. Many festivals, especially Jewish holidays, start at sundown on the preceding day.]

——————————— PUBLIC & BANK HOLIDAYS ———————————

England, Wales, & N. Ireland	2007	2008	2009
New Year's Day	1 Jan	1 Jan	1 Jan
[NI *only*] St Patrick's Day	19 Mar	17 Mar	17 Mar
Good Friday	6 Apr	21 Mar	10 Apr
Easter Monday	9 Apr	24 Mar	13 Apr
Early May Bank Holiday	7 May	5 May	4 May
Spring Bank Holiday	28 May	26 May	25 May
[NI *only*] Battle of the Boyne	12 July	14 July	13 Jul
Summer Bank Holiday	27 Aug	25 Aug	31 Aug
Christmas Day	25 Dec	25 Dec	25 Dec
Boxing Day	26 Dec	26 Dec	28 Dec

Scotland	2007	2008	2009
New Year's Day	1 Jan	1 Jan	1 Jan
2nd January	2 Jan	2 Jan	2 Jan
Good Friday	6 Apr	21 Mar	10 Apr
Early May Bank Holiday	7 May	5 May	4 May
Spring Bank Holiday	28 May	26 May	25 May
Summer Bank Holiday	6 Aug	4 Aug	3 Aug
Christmas Day	25 Dec	25 Dec	25 Dec
Boxing Day	26 Dec	26 Dec	28 Dec

These are the expected dates of holidays; some are subject to proclamation by the Queen.

——————————— THE DIVISION OF MAN'S AGES ———————————

The Ape, the Lion, the Fox, the Ass, Thus sets forth man as in a glass.
APE — Like apes we be toying, till twenty-and-one;
LION — Then hasty as lions, till forty be gone;
FOX — Then wily as foxes, till threescore-and-three;
ASS — Then after for asses accounted we be.

—— TRADITIONAL WEDDING ANNIVERSARY SYMBOLS ——

1st . . . . Cotton	10th . . . . Tin	35th . . . . Coral
2nd . . . . Paper	11th . . . . Steel	40th . . . . Ruby
3rd . . . . Leather	12th . . . . Silk, Linen	45th . . . . Sapphire
4th . . . . Fruit, Flowers	13th . . . . Lace	50th . . . . Gold
5th . . . . Wood	14th . . . . Ivory	55th . . . . Emerald
6th . . . . Sugar	15th . . . . Crystal	60th . . . . Diamond
7th . . . . Wool, Copper	20th . . . . China	70th . . . . Platinum
8th . . . . Pottery	25th . . . . Silver	75th . . . . Diamond
9th . . . . Willow	30th . . . . Pearl	*American symbols differ.*

PHASES OF THE MOON · 2007

NEW MOON				FIRST QUARTER				FULL MOON				LAST QUARTER		
d	*h*	*m*		*d*	*h*	*m*		*d*	*h*	*m*		*d*	*h*	*m*
Jan.... 19.... 4 ...01				Jan .... 25... 23 ..01				Jan.....3 ... 13 ..57				Jan.... 11... 12 ..45		
Feb.... 17... 16 ..14				Feb.... 24....7 ...56				Feb....2 ....5 ...45				Feb.... 10....9 ...51		
Mar... 19... 2 ...43				Mar... 25... 18 ..16				Mar...3 ... 23 ..17				Mar... 12....3 ...54		
Apr 17 11 36				Apr ... 24....6 ...36				Apr ...2 ... 17 ..15				Apr ... 10... 18 ..04		
May.. 16... 19 ..27				May... 23... 21 ..03				May...2 ... 10 ..09				May... 10....4 ...27		
Jun.... 15... 3 ...13				Jun... 22... 13 ..15				Jun....1 ....1 ...04				Jun.....8 ... 11 ..43		
Jul 14 12 04				Jul.... 22....6 ...29				Jun.... 30... 13 ..49				Jul 7 16 ..54		
Aug ... 12... 23 ..03				Aug... 20... 23 ..54				Jul.... 30... 0 48				Aug ....5 ... 21 ..20		
Sep.... 11... 12 ..44				Sep... 19... 16 ..48				Aug... 28... 10 ..35				Sep.....4 ....2 ...32		
Oct ... 11....5 ...01				Oct ... 19....8 ..33				Sep.... 26... 19 ..45				Oct ....3 ... 10 ..06		
Nov ..9 ... 23 ..03				Nov... 17... 22 ..33				Oct ...26....4 ..52				Nov....1 ... 21 ..18		
Dec ....9 ... 17 ..40				Dec... 17... 10 18				Nov... 24... 14 ..30				Dec ....1 ... 12 44		
								Dec... 24....1 ...16				Dec... 31....7 ...51		

[Key: *days, hours*, and *minutes* of Universal Time]

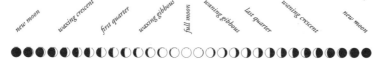

new moon   waxing crescent   first quarter   waxing gibbous   full moon   waning gibbous   last quarter   waning crescent   new moon

FULL MOON NICKNAMES

Month	nickname of full moon		
January	Moon after Yule	August	Grain Moon
February	Wolf Moon	September	Fruit Moon
March	Lent(en) Moon	October	Harvest Moon
April	Egg Moon	November	Hunter's Moon
May	Milk Moon	December	Moon before Yule
June	Flower Moon		
July	Hay Moon		

A 'Blue Moon' is usually defined as the second of two full moons that happens to appear in the same month.

EPOCHS & ERAS

An EPOCH is a fixed point in time (e.g. the birth of Christ), and the succession of events in the period following is an ERA. Some common epoch abbreviations are:

AD................ Anno Domini (*in the year of our Lord*) · after the birth of Christ

AH ....Anno Hegirae (*in the year of the Hegira*) · the Muslim era is dated from the day of Muhammad's flight from Mecca (July 16, 622AD)

AUC........ Ab Urbe Condita (*since the founding of the city* [Rome]) · after 753BC

BC....................................... Before Christ · before the birth of Christ

BCE ....Before the Christian/Common Era · before the birth of Christ

CE...............................Christian/Common Era · after the birth of Christ

—ANONYMOUS ALPHABET OF FORM & ADVICE · c.1832—

A*bove* all rules observe this – *honesty is the best policy.*

B*e* just to others, that you may be just to yourself.

C*ut* your coat according to your cloth.

D*esperate* cuts must have desperate cures.

E*nough* is as good as a feast.

F*air* and softly go sure and far.

G*entility* without ability is worse than beggary.

H*alf* a loaf is better than no bread.

I*dle* folks take the most pains.

J*okes* are as bad coin to all but the jocular.

K*eep* your business and conscience well, and they will keep you well.

L*ive* and let live; that is, do as you would be done by.

M*isunderstandings* are best prevented by pen and ink.

N*ever* take credit; as much as possible, avoid giving it.

O*ut* of debt, out of danger.

P*assion* will master you, if you do not master your passion.

Q*uick* at meat, quick at work.

R*evenge* a wrong by forgiving it.

S*hort* reckonings make long friends.

T*he* early bird catcheth the worm.

U*nmannerliness* is not so impolite as overpoliteness.

V*enture* not all you have at once.

W*ade* not into unknown waters.

X*amine* your accounts and your conduct every night.

Y*ou* may find your worst enemy, or best friend, in yourself.

Z*ealously* keep down little expenses, and you will not incur large ones.

—ITCHING SIGNIFICANCE—

Body part	itching signifies
Ears	longing to hear news or gossip
Palm	the imminent receipt of money
Thumb	the approach of danger or evil[†]
Right eye	imminent laughter or jollity; arrival of a loved one
Left eye	imminent sadness or grief
Lips	imminent prospect of kissing
Nose	imminent arrival of a stranger; the risk of a fire; fighting

† 'By the pricking of my thumbs, Something wicked this way comes.' *Macbeth*, IV i

————— CHARACTERISTICS OF STAR SIGNS —————

ARIES · Produces a dry rather lean body; dark bushy eyebrows; neck long & scraggy; swarthy complexion; rough hair & wiry, usually brown; whiskers reddish; disposition angry & violent.

TAURUS · A short, well-set person; thick neck & lips; shining face; given to eating; unfeeling, melancholy, slow to anger, but when provoked, furious.

GEMINI · Tall, upright straight body, long arms, but hands & feet generally short & fleshy; eyes hazel with a sharp, quick, active look, & rather wanton gaze.

CANCER · Moderate stature, larger from the middle upwards than below. Sad brown hair; constitution seldom strong: if a female, prolific, dull, & timid.

LEO · A large fair stature, full & fleshy; bushy, curling hair, usually very light; in disposition bold & courageous; aspect austere, & when angry, terrible.

VIRGO · Middle stature, rather slender. Dark, ruddy complexion, well favoured, but not handsome; voice weak & unmusical; very ingenious, but fickle-minded.

LIBRA · Tall & elegantly formed, graceful, rather slender; hair brown, smooth, & glossy, yet, sometimes jet-black; face round & lovely, having generally a great beauty. Mind well principled.

SCORPIO · Middle size; strong & robust; complexion dark or dusky; neck thick; legs coarse & hairy, ill-made feet or bow-legged; mind active yet reserved & thoughtful, generally deceitful.

SAGITTARIUS · A well-formed person, rather tall; hair chestnut or bright brown, growing off the temples, soon bald; mind active; a strong, bold, intrepid person, very fond of horses & hunting.

CAPRICORN · A short slender person, & ill formed; a long thin face, generally plain; thin beard; black, lanky hair; weak knees; manner active & skippish, nodding like a goat; subtle & witty, but capricious.

AQUARIUS · Middle stature, stout, well set, robust & strong; distorted teeth if Saturn be rising; hazel eyes; the mind well disposed, gentle, & benevolent; taking great delight on the water.

PISCES · Short stature, thick-made, round-shouldered, & stooping gait; arms & legs short & fin-like; ill-made feet; the disposition indolent & dull; given to drinking; effeminate & sickly in general.

The hand-book of astrology;
by which every question of the future on
which the mind is anxious
may be truly answered.

— ZADKIEL TAO SZE, 1861

————— THE BESTIARY OF A GOOD HOST —————

The Good Host must have the forehead of an OX; the ears of an ASS;
the back of a NAG; the belly of a SWINE; the subtlety of a FOX;
skip up and down like a FROG; and fawn and lie like a DOG.

NAIL CUTTING SUPERSTITIONS

Cut your nails on a MONDAY, cut them for news.
Cut your nails on a TUESDAY, a new pair of shoes.
Cut your nails on a WEDNESDAY, cut them for health.
Cut your nails on a THURSDAY, cut them for wealth.
Cut your nails on a FRIDAY, cut them for woe.
Cut your nails on a SATURDAY, a journey to go.
Cut your nails on a SUNDAY, you cut them for evil
For all the next week you'll be ruled by the DEVIL.

LEAP YEARS

In the Gregorian calendar, leap years have 366 days, with the addition of an extra day: 29 February. Any year whose date is a number exactly divisible by four is a leap year, except years ending in '00', which must be divisible by 400. The extra day is added every four years to allow for the difference between a year of 365 days and the actual time it takes the Earth to circle the Sun. The table below shows the recent leap years, as well as the day of the week upon which each 29 February falls:

Monday	1932	1960	1988	2016	2044
Saturday	1936	1964	1992	2020	2048
Thursday	1940	1968	1996	2024	2052
Tuesday	1944	1972	2000	2028	2056
Sunday	1948	1976	2004	2032	2060
Friday	1952	1980	2008	2036	2064
Wednesday	1956	1984	2012	2040	2068

Tradition dictates that the normal conventions of gallantry are suspended on 29 February, and a woman may ask for a man's hand in marriage. By custom, if the man declines this request he is then bound by honour to buy the woman a silk gown by way of recompense. Of course, those born on 29 February (including Pope Paul III and Rossini) celebrate only one birthday in four – which, as Frederic discovered in *The Pirates of Penzance,* can lead to all sorts of elaborate difficulties.

BORN & DIED ON THE SAME DAY

Etienne Dolet, French printer .... 3 August 1509–1546
William Shakespeare[†], playwright .... 23 April 1564–1616
Sir Thomas Browne, author .... 19 October 1605–1682
Levi Morton, US Vice-President .... 16 May 1824–1920
Bidhan Chandra Roy, Indian politician .... 1 July 1882–1962
Ingrid Bergman, actress .... 29 August 1915–1982
Betty Friedan, feminist writer .... 2 April 1921–2006

† Shakespeare's birthday is not officially recorded.

Index

Should not the Society of Indexers be known as Indexers, Society of, The?
— KEITH WATERHOUSE

————————BLAIR, TONY - CRITICAL YEAR————————

——————— GAZA, ISRAEL, &c. – MAN BOOKER PRIZE ———————

─────── MARATHONS – POPULATION, AGEING ───────

——POPULATION, LARGEST – STATION DESTINATIONS——

─────────STIRLING PRIZE – YOUNG, KIRSTY─────────

——————————— ERRATA, CORRIGENDA, &c. ———————————

In keeping with many newspapers and journals, *Schott's Almanac* will publish in this section any significant corrections from the previous year. Below are some errata from *Schott's Almanac 2006* – many of which were kindly supplied by readers.

[p.8 *of the 2006 edition*] A greengrocer's apostrophe snuck into 'Cotswolds'. [p.69] The date of the highest UK temperature should have been 2003, as corrected on p.76. [pp.76–7] The British currency code is GBP, as corrected on pp.84–5. [p.84] The immunisation schedule has been updated, and an omission rectified on p.93. [p.119] Inevitably, dispute surrounds the *Doctor Who* entry. [p.135] T in the Park festival is held in Balado airfield, near Kinross. [p.136] Natalie Clein won the Classical Brit for Best Young British Classical Performer, not composer as stated. [p.136] Winner of ensemble/ orchestral album should read Harry Christophers and the Sixteen. [p.142] The correct spelling is *Shaun of the Dead*. [p.166] The *Fast Show* catch-phrase appears to be 'Suit you!', not 'Suits you!'. [p.174] Quarks build protons and neutrons, not electrons. [p.183] Due to a typographical error, Fermat's Last Theorem was misprinted, it is: $x^n + y^n = z^n$. [p.186] The spelling is zettabyte, which is 10^{21}. [p.196] The list of motorways was not intended to be exhaustive, but some additions can be found on p.204. [p.203] It is Stansted, not Stanstead. [p.207] Confusion over the regions served by Euston has been clarified on p.215. [p.211] The Pennine Way was accidentally omitted from the list of 15 National Trails. [p.221] The spelling of morning suit has been corrected on p.242. [p.239] In addition to those listed, stamps celebrating England's Ashes victory were released in October 2005. [p.258] The last UK general election held in December was in 1923, not 1918 as stated. [p.275] Brian Turner, not Tuner. [p.278] When addressing the Queen, 'Ma'am' should be pronounced as 'ham'. [p.285] The spelling of marshal has been corrected on p.287. [p.291] The singular is 'candelabrum'. [p.301] Shaun Murphy beat Matthew Stevens. [pp.320–31] Debate surrounds the spellings of the Dutch months, but they have tentatively been left as they were. [p.340] A typographical error omitted Wednesday from the week, and confused the other days. This has been rectified on p.336.

——————————— ACKNOWLEDGMENTS ———————————

The author would like to thank:

Jonathan, Judith, & Geoffrey Schott · Benjamin Adams, Richard Album,
Joanna Begent, Martin Birchall, Andrew Cock-Starkey, James Coleman,
Gordon Corera, Aster Crawshaw, Jody & Liz Davies, George Derbyshire,
Colin Dickerman, Will Douglas, Miles Doyle, Charlotte Druckman,
Stephanie Duncan, Jennifer Epworth, Sabrina Farber, Kathleen Farrar, Josh Fine,
Minna Fry, Alona Fryman, Panio Gianopoulos, Yelena Gitlin, Catherine Gough,
Allison Hatfield, Charlotte Hawes, Mark & Sharon Hubbard, Max Jones,
Amy King, Robert Klaber, Maureen Klier, Alison Lang, Jim Ledbetter,
Suzie Lee, Annik LeFarge, John Lloyd, Ruth Logan, Josh Lovejoy, Chris Lyon,
Sam MacAuslan, Jess Manson, Michael Manson, Sarah Marcus, Blake Martin,
Lauren Mechling, Sara Mercurio, Susannah McFarlane, Colin Midson,
David Miller, Peter Miller, Polly Napper, Nigel Newton, Sarah Norton,
Elizabeth Peters, Cally Poplak, Dave Powell, Alexandra Pringle, Karen Rinaldi,
Pavia Rosati, Jared Van Snellenberg, Bill Swainson, Caroline Turner,
Greg Villepique, David Ward, Alexander Weber, & Michael Winawer.